SHADOW & LIGHT

Literature and

the Life of Faith

THIRD EDITION

Shadow
&Light

Literature and the Life of Faith

DARRYL TIPPENS · JEANNE MURRAY WALKER · STEPHEN WEATHERS
Pepperdine University   *University of Delaware*   *Abilene Christian University*

Third Edition
REVIEW COPY

 Abilene Christian University Press

SHADOW AND LIGHT:
Literature and the Life of Faith

Third Edition

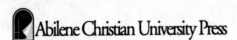 Abilene Christian University Press

1626 Campus Court
Abilene, TX 79601
www.abilenechristianuniversitypress.com

Cover design: Nicole Weaver, Zeal Design Studio
Book design & typesetting · William Rankin & Sandra Armstrong

ISBN 978-0-89112-070-4
LCCN 2013005156
LIBRARY OF CONGRESS CATALOGING-IN-PUBLICATION DATA
Shadow & light : literature and the life of faith / [compiled by] Darryl Tip-
pens, Pepperdine University, Jeanne Murray Walker, University of Deleware,
Stephen Weathers, Abilene Christian University. -- Third edition.
    pages cm
  ISBN 978-0-89112-070-4
  1. Faith--Literary collections. I. Tippens, Darryl L. II. Walker, Jeanne
Murray. III. Weathers, Stephen. IV. Title: Shadow and light.
  PN6071.F17S43 2013
  808.8'0382--dc23
                                            2013005156

Contents

FICTION

POETRY

Preface to the Third Edition

A s we send the third edition of *Shadow and Light* to press, we are mindful of the increasing speed and fragmentation of our lives. Americans are hooked on technology – on smart phones, iPads, Kindles, and other electronic devices. We blog and email, stream movies and watch YouTube. We text and tweet and chat on Facebook. Many of us, particularly younger Americans, multi-task, simultaneously streaming a TV show, chatting on Facebook, texting, and carrying on a conversation with someone in the room.

In reading lies the possibility of gaining a little perspective on our speed-driven, technologically complex, fragmented, shopping-mad, postmodern lives. The kind of reading we do when we're on the web has taught us all to scan quickly, and it's tempting to do that all the time. The truth is, many of us have lost the art of reading slowly and deeply. But to sit still with great works of visionary literature, to dwell in their lines with slow and careful attention, is to open the window to mystery. It is to ask childlike questions again and either to piece the fragments of our lives into some kind of sensible mosaic, or else to discover that they don't go together. Even to know that is valuable.

The works in this volume offer many different approaches to spiritual questing, but they all involve reading. To re-imagine ourselves and to grasp our relationship to the Creator, the Scripture counsels stillness and quiet. Not in the whirlwind, but in stillness, Elijah heard the voice of God. The most famous of the Psalms says, "He leadeth me beside the still waters." At one time these passages seemed to advocate desirable but optional alternatives. As we become more distracted and speed-driven, they seem to describe a fundamental and inescapable human need. Arthur Miller wrote, "people need news of the inner world and if they go too long without it, they go mad with the chaos of their lives." The poet William Carlos Williams said, "It is difficult to get the news from poems, yet men die miserably every day for lack of what is found there."

We have put together a third edition of *Shadow & Light* because we believe that now, more than ever, we need to find a deep place to retreat to, to meditate and to reflect on the meaning of what we are doing. We need to be reminded that what we can see and touch is not all that exists. We need to use our imaginations – our ability to think with images. We need to conceive of our own spiritual questing as significant and our choices as important. The stakes are higher than ever.

In this edition we respond to the suggestions of many faithful readers of the previous editions. We have omitted the plays found in the second edition, on the grounds that excellent, stand-alone editions of plays are easily available; and we have increased the number of nonfiction essays, short stories, and poems. This edition contains a greater number of contemporary voices, providing a more diverse and lively conversation about culture, nature, and faith. Many of the new writers are women; several are minorities. We have strengthened the anthology further by adding selections by Robert Browning, and by increasing the number of selections from Shakespeare and Gerard Manley Hopkins. In our time, there is a growing interest in the human responsibility to care for creation, and so a noteworthy feature of this edition is greater attention to nature and the environment, with ample selections by Henry David Thoreau and John Muir.

The editors are profoundly grateful to those who have made contributions to this edition through their editorial assistance, including Marilyn McEntyre, Julie L. Moore, Eric Potter, John Struloeff, and Paul J. Willis. We also wish to express our special thanks to Leonard Allen, Director of ACU Press, and Tammy Anderson, ACU Press, whose faithful support, patience, and indefatigable efforts have made this edition possible. Finally, we express our unending gratitude to all those who have taught from the anthology and who have found insight, provocation, and inspiration in these pages.

Darryl Tippens
Jeanne Murray Walker
December 2012

Introduction

And we must extinguish the candle, put out the light and
    relight it;
Forever must quench, forever relight the flame.
Therefore we thank Thee for our little light, that is dappled
    with shadow

+ + +

And we thank Thee that darkness reminds us of light.
O Light Invisible, we give Thee thanks for Thy great glory!

T. S. Eliot, "The Rock"

THE FRENCH NOVELIST Albert Camus once observed that
the hallmark trait of his age was its wholesale rejection of the
spiritual dimension. "We live in an unsacrosanct moment in history," the writer contends; "whole societies have wanted to discard
the sacred." For many, Camus's statement has been borne out by
experience. With the passing of each decade, the perception deepened that writers had less to say about faith or the possibility of the
transcendent. A parallel development took place in educational
institutions. The eclipse of mystery and the sacred occurred in
many North American classrooms as students encountered fewer
and fewer works concerned with the spiritual quest. As a result,
a whole generation of readers has been dispossessed. Now, when
an assigned literary text engages religious concerns, teachers are
often reluctant to make explicit the spiritual themes of writers
who, whatever their faith or philosophy, devoted much of their
lives to exploring such subjects in their work.

Some scholars and critics still claim that literature can only
be about our lives as material creatures. Literature about "the
above and beyond," the transcendent, or the God of Scripture

1

is still sometimes seen as peculiar and anachronistic. The view goes something like this: Religion used to be an important element of our culture, but the writing of religious literature ended somewhere around the Renaissance (possibly with Donne or Milton); there were a few holdouts into the nineteenth century, but it's all over now. God is dead as far as significant literature is concerned.

This anthology argues otherwise. It is an attempt to restore what has been missing for fifty years in anthologies of literature. It is an attempt to right the balance and to supply to students, faculty, and general readers the tradition which began disappearing over fifty years ago

As many readers are realizing, literature about the life of faith is, in fact, richly diverse and of high quality; and, against all odds, it continues to be produced at a remarkable rate. No matter if we are living in a secular, "post-Christendom" age – stars are best seen in a dark sky. This anthology is a reminder that just as Western literature began with the quest to know the *Logos* (in Greek terms) or *Yahweh* (in biblical terms), so today a number of writers continue to seek to know God and his creation. Václav Havel, the great Czech playwright and statesman, articulated the challenge and opportunity for the person who seeks faith in our largely pessimistic age:

> There are times when we must sink to the bottom of our
> misery to understand truth, just as we must descend to
> the bottom of a well to see the stars in broad daylight.

Deep in the shadows of a secular society, we are strategically positioned to rediscover the light of the sacred. In T. S. Eliot's terms, "darkness reminds us of light."

WHAT IS THE LITERATURE OF SHADOW AND LIGHT?

FOR THE MOST PART, the readings which follow are not "spiritual classics" in the usual sense of the term. They are significant, artistically mature poems, stories, essays, and plays by recognized writers, some Jewish, some Christian, some of an uncertain or undeclared stance. What they hold in common is an attitude: they honor the spiritual quest. Whether these texts mention God directly or not – and many profoundly religious works, like the Book of Esther, do not – these works strive to present human dilemmas in their full roundness, including a significant element of mystery. Almost relentlessly, they are concerned with the search for truth, not as an exercise in futility, but as a purposeful activity of the highest order. At the same time, these authors are not afraid to ask the tough questions which people on a quest must have the courage to face. We might say these are works by writers who have gazed into the heavens for themselves. Having seen the celestial designs that others have discarded or missed, they report their findings through story, poem, meditation, and essay.

HOW SHOULD YOU APPROACH THESE READINGS?

FIRST, WELCOME THE CHALLENGES inherent in these selections. Unfortunately, many people avoid "religious" literature on the grounds that it is predictable, closed, or even propagandistic. This complaint may hold for many popular religious publications, but nothing could be further from the truth when it comes to the best works in the tradition. Mature religious art invites us to ask questions and then to move about within the space such questions open up for us. The German poet Rainer Maria Rilke's advice to a young poet seems appropriate for readers of *Shadow and Light*:

> Have patience with everything unresolved in your heart and try to love the questions themselves as if they were locked rooms or books written in a very foreign language.... And the point is, to live everything. Live the questions now.

But asking questions isn't all we are required to do. Often great works stir our moral and religious imaginations. A literary text may ultimately break its æsthetic bounds in order to interrogate the reader and demand a personal response.

Reading Tolstoy and Dickinson, Dillard and Malamud, Levertov and Singer is intellectually challenging, but it can also be potentially life-changing. "Although literature is one thing and morality a quite different one," Jean-Paul Sartre once observed, "at the heart of the æsthetic imperative we discern the moral imperative." Some narratives, like the carefully crafted parables of Jesus, demand more than æsthetic appreciation; they demand deep thought and a changed life. Stories like Dostoyevsky's "The Grand Inquisitor" and Tolstoy's "How Much Land Does a Man Need?" in the final analysis, are not about others, but about you and me. When writers aim their words at the heart, the encounter will not leave the reader indifferent or merely "entertained." Action will be the harvest of a good reading.

WHY SO MANY DOUBTS?

THE LITERATURE OF FAITH is by its very nature dialectical. Belief and doubt are as often as not near neighbors both in the Bible and in the classics. One need only think of Jeremiah, Job, or Shakespeare's King Lear to see that faith can be on speaking terms with confusion and ambiguity. In the earthly realm inhabited by such richly drawn characters, life is not a single thread, but a tapestry, as Denise Levertov describes in her poem "Web":

> Intricate and untraceable
> weaving and interweaving,
> dark strand with light...

Should we be so surprised that the literature of faith is honest about the shadows of doubt that flicker in our hearts?

Flannery O'Connor once singled out the prayer of the desperate father of an epileptic boy who cries – "I believe; help my unbelief!" (Mark 9:24) – calling it "the most natural and most human and most agonizing prayer in all the gospels, and...the foundation prayer of faith." The literature of belief, in the same way, if it is any good at all, owns up to its doubts, even when the cracks run all the way to the bedrock of belief: Why does tragedy befall the innocent? Why do my prayers appear to go unanswered? What is justice? Who is my neighbor? Where did I come from? Where am I going?

This kind of literature also asks other questions that skeptics seldom consider: How does one account for so much beauty and goodness in the world? Why, in an age that exalts the "individual," do some people still sacrifice themselves for others? Why am I the recipient of gifts I did not earn and do not deserve? Are there blessings from beyond, or are even the most beneficial wonders of life mere accident?

Sometimes, the literature of faith asks daring questions, even to the point of laying charges at the feet of God: "Why does the way of the guilty prosper?" Jeremiah the prophet demands. "Why do all who are treacherous thrive?" To the primly pious, questions such as Jeremiah's are disturbing, even blasphemous. But being free to argue with God may be the only way back to faith. Dwelling in the House of the Lord may require a walk through the Valley of the Shadow of Death.

Elie Wiesel's works are among the best contemporary examples of the proximity of faith and doubt. Wiesel sets his masterful play, *The Trial of God*, in a Ukrainian village, the site of a terrible *pogrom* which almost completely wipes out the Jewish population in 1649. One character, Mendel, keeps protesting, "And [where is] God in all this?" Questioning God's absence or injustice can be a form of pure prayer. In *The Town Beyond the Wall*, Wiesel presents Pedro, a man who suffers unspeakable affliction. Pedro cries out:

> I want to blaspheme and I can't quite manage it. I go up against Him, I shake my fist, I froth with rage, but it's still a way of telling Him that He's there, that He exists, that He's never the same twice, that denial itself is an offering to His grandeur. The shout becomes a prayer in spite of me.

A shout of protest fading into prayer – this is the essence of shadow and light. This is the dialectic of faith.

WHY DON'T WE SEE BETTER?

HENRY JAMES'S ADVICE to writers is much quoted: "Try to be one of those on whom nothing is lost." The novelist's admonition is equally applicable to readers. To handle the literature of faith with success, one must read with extraordinary attention. "Do you have eyes, and fail to see? Do you have ears, and fail to hear?" Jesus asked those who gathered about him. These are not idle, rhetorical questions but solemn warnings that echo down to our day. Most of us "see" rather poorly. We not only fail to notice the night sky, we don't even see the important details in a story or a poem, facets of a glittering jewel just inches from us, that might change our understanding of the world. "The secret of seeing is, then, the pearl of great price," writes Annie Dillard.

Why don't we see better? We do not, in part, because frameworks of bias obscure our vision. Our formulaic assumptions may keep us from recognizing the good, the true, or the beautiful. Tennyson recognizes that our universe and its Maker are much bigger and more wondrous than our conceptual frameworks allow us to see:

> Our little systems have their day;
> They have their day and cease to be;
> They are but broken lights of thee,
> And thou, O Lord, art more than they.

Similarly, as O'Connor reminds a young man studying to become a poet, "You can't fit the Almighty into your intellectual categories." One needs a "sense of the immense sweep of creation, ... of how incomprehensible God must necessarily be to be the God of heaven and earth." Effective reading, then, requires open-mindedness. Ernst Bloch's aphorism—"Seek and ye shall wonder"—is both a rule of life and a guide for effective reading.

Of course, all readers are products of a particular age, culture, and upbringing, factors as inescapable as our genetic inheritance. Who we are and where we are in time necessarily affect the experience of literature. Still, this ought not to leave us unthinking slaves to the present age. With a spirit of adventure, imagination, and generosity, the motivated reader can enter the wonderful kingdom of literary experience, making familiar what is strange and new. C. S. Lewis says:

> To enjoy our full humanity we ought, so far as is possible, to contain within us potentially at all times, and on occasion actualize, all the modes of feeling and thinking through which [humans have] passed. You must, so far as in you lies, become an Achæan chief while reading Homer, a medieval knight while reading Malory, and an eighteenth century Londoner while reading Johnson. Only thus will you be able to judge the work "in the same spirit that its author writ"....

Because there is much in this foreign realm of literature that you might fail to understand, the challenge is to learn the idioms, the ways, "the elements" of this literary world as best you can. It is not easy to train your eyes and your heart to see deeply. Denis

Diderot declares: "Learning to see is not like learning a new language. It's like learning language for the first time." Some advice, then. Keep pen and paper handy; annotate your text; record your responses in a journal or notebook. Engage your classmates and friends in discussions of what you read. Above all, expect surprise, mystery, and wonder like a child learning to put together the first words that will be hers for a lifetime.

ARE WE HAVING FUN YET?

A FINAL TIP ON READING these works: enjoy the trip. Although literature often deals with serious and enduring questions, it was never meant to be an exercise in boredom or obscurity. Literature is a form of play, sometimes serious, sometimes amusing, often both. "Blessed are they that play, for theirs is the kingdom of heaven," exclaims Dickinson, and for good reason. In the guise of a word game we may catch a spell-binding glimpse of our lives. If this happens, literature becomes more than recreation; it becomes re-creation, touching our hearts, reshaping our moral imagination, and – sometimes – moving us to decisive action.

Unfortunately, many people assume that since religion and ethics are "serious" matters, literature concerned with faith or moral conduct must be ever earnest, ever stern. Yet the gospel by definition is always "glad tidings," and God's original intent for humanity has always been profound delight. "What is all this juice and all this joy?" Hopkins asks in his sonnet "Spring." It is, he replies, "A strain of the earth's sweet being in the beginning / In Eden garden." If these selections do not bring some pleasure, then they will have been misread.

SO WHAT HAVE WE LOST?

M OST OF US HAVE GROWN UP in the glare of the city. We are accustomed to pulsing neon, well-lit sidewalks, and cross-town freeways bathed in mercury-vapor lamps. Yet we pay dearly for these privileges. Humanity's lights obliterate the shining evidence of a vast cosmos. Beneath our artificial halo few of us have opportunity to see the marvelous constellations of Leo, Andromeda, or Pegasus. Though we may have spent years staring into a luminous electronic tube, we know far less about the heavens than did Plato, Chaucer, or Columbus.

So what have we lost? Not knowing the coordinates of Cassiopeia or Orion is perhaps no tragedy, but what if the modern environment we have constructed for ourselves, both physical and intellectual, has caused us to lose sight of other elements of our universe, of which the night sky is only one example? What happens if we lose sight of whole worlds of understanding that are basic to our humanity? What if we forget our origin and our destination? What if we forget about mystery and the experience of the sacred? Poets, writers, and artists are among those people who care deeply about such questions. Emily Dickinson once said that "mystery" is the greatest need of the human soul, yet we forget to thank God for it.

Our society is in crisis today, not because it lacks technical knowledge, tools, or skills, but because its citizens have lost touch with their origin and destination. Without a past, a future, or an "above," they do not remember where they are. Shadow and Light is an invitation to find ourselves, reorient ourselves, and to be thankful for "our little light, that is dappled with shadow." This anthology is an invitation not only to remember what it means to be human in this shadowy world, but also to imagine what creation once was and what it can be, by the grace of God. Too much has been eclipsed by the secular world. It is time for a bigger, fuller vision. As Hopkins and Vaughan knew, gazing into that deep, dazzling darkness of the Welsh night sky, there is much to behold:

> Look at the stars! look, look up at the skies!
> O look at all the fire-folk sitting in the air.
> The bright boroughs, the circle-citadels there!

✦ ✦ ✦

> I saw eternity the other night
> Like a great ring of pure and endless light,
> All calm as it was bright...

Nonfiction

John Donne

⊰ 1 5 7 2 – 1 6 3 1 ⊱

Donne, the most celebrated English clergyman of the 17th century, became seriously ill in the winter of 1623. Through a richly textured sentence structure, replete with vivid and memorable metaphors, Donne recorded his own private experience of suffering in a set of meditations entitled Devotions Upon Emergent Occasions *(1624). Louis Martz defines the central motif of the meditation as "an interior drama in which a man projects a self upon a mental stage, and there comes to understand that self in the light of the divine presence." In "Meditation 17" Donne views his illness as a form of treasure that can be used to bring the Christian soul nearer to its destination – heaven. The writer is somewhat traditional in saying that suffering is educational, teaching us that we are not self-secure, for God "is our only security." However, his colorful, dramatic figures of speech make "Meditation 17" one of the most original – and memorable – interpretations of human affliction in the English language.*

MEDITATION 17

Nunc lento sonitu dicunt, Morieris•

1 PERCHANCE HE FOR WHOM THIS BELL• tolls may be so ill, as that he knows not it tolls for him; and perchance I may think myself so much better than I am, as that they who are about me, and see my state, may have caused it to toll for me, and I know not that. The church is catholic, universal, so are all her actions; all that she does belongs to all. When she baptizes a child, that action concerns me; for that child is thereby connected to that head which is my head too, and ingrafted into that body• whereof I am a member. And when she buries a man, that action concerns me. All mankind is of one author, and is

Nunc ... Morieris • literally, "Now, with slow sounding, they say 'you [singular] shall die'" (Latin)

this bell • passing bell, sounded for the dying

body • the church

11

one volume; when one man dies, one chapter is not torn out 1
of the book, but translated into a better language; and every
chapter must be so translated; God employs several translators;
some pieces are translated by age, some by sickness, some by
war, some by justice; but God's hand is in every translation,
and his hand shall bind up all our scattered leaves again, for
that library where every book shall lie open to one another.
As therefore the bell that rings to a sermon calls not upon the
preacher only, but upon the congregation to come, so this bell
calls us all; but how much more me, who am brought so near
the door by this sickness.

suit · a dispute taken to court
estimation · self-esteem

There was a contention as far as a suit* (in which piety and 2
dignity, religion and estimation,* were mingled) which of the
religious orders should ring to prayers first in the morning; and
it was determined, that they should ring first that rose earliest.
If we understand aright the dignity of this bell that tolls for our
evening prayer, we would be glad to make it ours by rising early,
in that application, that it might be ours as well as his, whose
indeed it is. The bell doth toll for him that thinks it doth; and

intermit · to cease temporarily or periodically

though it intermit* again, yet from that minute that that occasion
wrought upon him, he is united to God. Who casts not up his eye
to the sun when it rises? But who takes off his eye from a comet
when that breaks out? Who bends not his ear to any bell which
upon any occasion rings? But who can remove it from that bell
which is passing a piece of himself out of this world?

main · main part of the continent, mainland

No man is an island, entire of itself; every man is a piece of 3
the continent, a part of the main.* If a clod be washed away by
the sea, Europe is the less, as well as if a promontory were, as
well as if a manor of thy friend's or of thine own were: any man's
death diminishes me, because I am involved in mankind, and
therefore never send to know for whom the bell tolls; it tolls for
thee. Neither can we call this a begging of misery, or a borrowing
of misery, as though we were not miserable enough of ourselves,
but must fetch in more from the next house, in taking upon us
the misery of our neighbors.

Truly it were an excusable covetousness if we did, for afflic- 4
tion is a treasure, and scarce any man hath enough of it. No man
hath affliction enough that is not matured and ripened by it, and
made fit for God by that affliction.

5   If a man carry treasure in bullion,* or in a wedge of gold, and have none coined into current monies, his treasure will not defray* him as he travels. Tribulation is treasure in the nature of it, but it is not current money* in the use of it, except we get nearer and nearer our home, heaven, by it. Another man may be sick too, and sick to death, and this affliction may lie in his bowels, as gold in a mine, and be of no use to him; but this bell, that tells me of his affliction, digs out and applies that gold to me, if by this consideration of another's danger I take mine own into contemplation, and so secure myself, by making my course to my God, who is our only security.

bullion · gold or silver in bulk, before it is turned into coin

defray · to pay for expenses

current money · currency, coins

John Bunyan

⟨ 1 6 2 8 - 1 6 8 8 ⟩

*Born near Bedford, England, John Bunyan acquired a basic educa-
tion while also learning his father's trade as a brazier. At age 16 he
was drafted into the Puritan cause in a civil war against Charles I.
Bunyan saw no actual combat. But after leaving the army at age
18, he quickly found himself in a more serious battle regarding the
state of his salvation. Before the civil war, he had been a conforming
member of the national Church of England; but after the war and
his marriage, his sensibilities had become more Puritan. Attending
the Nonconformist church in Bedford, Bunyan faced questions that
led to a direct confrontation with the Word of God, an engagement
compellingly described in* Grace Abounding to the Chief of Sinners
(1666). *Later in* The Pilgrim's Progress (1678), *he would present the
warfare of the universal Christian soldier in a thicker, more involved
allegorical style. But in this spiritual autobiography Bunyan provides
an unadorned though powerful account of his own personal conversion. In the preface he writes, "I could... have stepped into a style much
higher than this... and could have adorned all things more than here
I have seemed to do, but I dare not. God did not play in convincing
of me, the devil did not play in tempting of me, neither did I play
when I sunk as into a bottomless pit...; wherefore I may not play in
my relating of these experiences, but be plain and simple, and lay
down the thing as it was." He did not consider spiritual warfare to
be an intellectual pastime but a matter of life and death. It is not
surprising, then, that he wrote* Grace Abounding *from jail while
serving a twelve-year term for preaching the Word without a license.*

from GRACE ABOUNDING TO THE CHIEF OF SINNERS

[126] 1 IT WOULD BE TOO LONG for me here to stay, to tell you in
particular how God did set me down in all the things of Christ,

Bunyan's original
paragraph numbers
appear in brackets

15

and how he did, that he might so do, lead me into his words, 1 [126]
yea and also how he did open them unto me, make them shine
before me, and cause them to dwell with me, talk with me, and
comfort me over and over, both of his own being, and the being
of his Son, and Spirit, and Word, and Gospel.

Only this, as I said before, I will say unto you again, that in 2 [127]
general he was pleased to take this course with me, first to suffer
me to be afflicted with temptation concerning them, and then
reveal them to me; as sometimes I should lie under great guilt
for sin, even crushed to the ground therewith, and then the
Lord would show me the death of Christ, yea and so sprinkle my
conscience with his blood, that I should find, and that before I
was aware, that in that conscience, where but just now did reign
and rage the law, even there would rest and abide the peace and
love of God through Christ.

Now had I an evidence, as I thought, of my salvation from 3 [128]
Heaven, with many golden seals thereon, all hanging in my sight;
now could I remember this manifestation, and the other discovery of grace with comfort; and should often long and desire that
the last day were come, that I might for ever be inflamed with the
sight, and joy, and communion of him, whose head was crowned
with thorns, whose face was spit on, and body broken, and soul
made an offering for my sins: for whereas before I lay continually
trembling at the mouth of hell; now methought I was got so far
therefrom, that I could not, when I looked back, scarce discern
it; and O thought I, that I were fourscore years old now, that I
might die quickly, that my soul might be gone to rest.

But before I had got thus far out of these my temptations, 4 [129]
I did greatly long to see some ancient godly man's experience,
who had writ some hundred of years before I was born; for, for
those who had writ in our days, I thought (but I desire them now
to pardon me) that they had writ only that which others felt, or

Martin Luther ·
German priest
(1483–1546) who
became one of the
primary voices of the
Protestant Reformation

a book . . . Galatians ·
an English translation
of Luther's commentary
on Galatians was
published in 1575

else had, through the strength of their wits and parts, studied to
answer such objections as they perceived others were perplexed
with, without going down themselves into the deep. Well, after
many such longings in my mind, the God in whose hands are
all our days and ways, did cast into my hand, one day, a book
of Martin Luther,· his comment on the Galatians,· so old that it
was ready to fall piece from piece, if I did but turn it over. Now

[129] 4   I was pleased much that such an old book had fallen into my hand; the which, when I had but a little way perused, I found my condition in his experience, so largely and profoundly handled, as if his book had been written out of my heart; this made me marvel: for thus thought I, this man could not know anything of the state of Christians now, but must needs write and speak of the experience of former days.

[130] 5   Besides, he doth most gravely also, in that book debate of the rise of these temptations, namely, blasphemy, desperation, and the like, shewing that the law of Moses,˙ as well as the devil, death, and hell, hath a very great hand therein; the which at first was very strange to me, but considering and watching, I found it so indeed. But of particulars here I intend nothing, only this methinks I must let fall before all men, I do prefer this book of Mr. Luther upon the Galatians, (excepting the Holy Bible) before all the books that ever I have seen, as most fit for a wounded conscience.

law of Moses ˙ the law of the Old Testament, seen by Luther as emphasizing works over grace

[131] 6   And now I found, as I thought, that I loved Christ dearly. O methought my soul cleaved unto him, my affections cleaved unto him. I felt love to him as hot as fire, and now, as Job˙ said, I thought I should die in my nest; but I did quickly find, that my great love was but little, and that I, who had, as I thought, such burning love to Jesus Christ, could let him go again for a very trifle. God can tell how to abase us; and can hide pride from man. Quickly after this my love was tried to purpose.

Job ˙ Job 29:18

[132] 7   For after the Lord had in this manner thus graciously delivered me from this great and sore temptation, and had set me down so sweetly in the faith of his holy gospel, and had given me such strong consolation and blessed evidence from heaven touching my interest in his love through Christ; the tempter came upon me again, and that with a more grievous and dreadful temptation than before.

[133] 8   And that was to sell and part with this most blessed Christ, to exchange him for the things of this life; for any thing: the temptation lay upon me for the space of a year, and did follow me so continually, that I was not rid of it one day in a month, no not sometimes one hour in many days together, unless I was asleep.

[134] 9   And though, in my judgment, I was persuaded, that those who were once effectually in Christ (as I hoped, through his grace, I had seen myself) could never lose him for ever, "for the land shall not

be sold for ever, for the land is mine," saith God (Leviticus 25:23), 9 [134]
yet it was a continual vexation to me, to think that I should have
so much as one such thought within me against a Christ, a Jesus,
that had done for me as he had done; and yet then I had almost
none others, but such blasphemous ones.

But it was neither my dislike of the thought, nor yet any desire 10 [135]
and endeavour to resist it, that in the least did shake or abate the
continuation or force and strength thereof; for it did always in
almost whatever I thought, intermix itself therewith, in such sort
that I could neither eat my food, stoop for a pin, chop a stick, or
cast mine eye to look on this or that, but still the temptation would
come, *Sell Christ for this, or sell Christ for that; sell him, sell him.*

Sometimes it would run in my thoughts not so little as a hun- 11 [136]
dred times together, sell him, sell him, sell him; against which,
I may say, for whole hours together I have been forced to stand
as continually leaning and forcing my spirit against it, lest haply
before I were aware, some wicked thought might arise in my
heart that might consent thereto; and sometimes also the tempter
would make me believe I had consented to it, then should I be
as tortured on a rack* for whole days together.

This temptation did put me to such scares lest I should at 12 [137]
sometimes, I say, consent thereto, and be overcome therewith,
that by the very force of my mind in labouring to gainsay* and
resist this wickedness, my very body also would be put into
action or motion, by way of pushing or thrusting with my hands
or elbows; still answering, as fast as the destroyer said, *Sell him,*
I will not, I will not, I will not, I will not, no not for thousands,
thousands, thousands of worlds; thus reckoning lest I should in
the midst of these assaults, set too low a value of him, even until
I scarce well knew where I was, or how to be composed again.

At these seasons he would not let me eat my food at quiet, 13 [138]
but forsooth,* when I was set at the table at my meat, I must go
hence to pray, I must leave my food now, just now, so counterfeit*
holy would this devil be. When I was thus tempted, I should say
in myself, *Now I am at my meat, let me make an end. No,* said he,
you must do it now, or you will displease God, and despise Christ.
Wherefore I was much afflicted with these things; and because
of the sinfulness of my nature, (imagining that these things were
impulses from God) I should deny to do it as if I denied God; and

rack · a device on
which prisoners were
tied and stretched

gainsay · to speak
against, contradict,
or deny

forsooth · in truth,
indeed

counterfeit ·
fraudulently

[138] 13   then should I be as guilty because I did not obey a temptation of the devil, as if I had broken the law of God indeed.

[139]   But to be brief, one morning as I did lie in my bed, I was, as at
14   other times, most fiercely assaulted with this temptation, *to sell and part with Christ;* the wicked suggestion still running in my mind, *sell him, sell him, sell him,* as fast as a man could speak; against which also in my mind, as at other times I answered, no, no, not for thousands, thousands, thousands, at least twenty times together; but at last, after much striving, even until I was almost out of breath, I felt this thought pass through my heart, *Let him go if he will!* and I thought also that I felt my heart freely consent thereto. O, the diligence of Satan! O, the desperateness of man's heart!

    Now was the battle won, and down fell I, as a bird that is shot
[140] 15   from the top of a tree, into great guilt and fearful despair; thus getting out of my bed, I went moping into the field, but God knows with as heavy a heart as mortal man, I think, could bear; where for the space of two hours, I was like a man bereft of life, and as now past all recovery, and bound over to eternal punishment.

    And withal, that scripture did seize upon my soul, "Or profane person, as Esau, who for one morsel of meat sold his birthright;
[141] 16   for you know how that afterwards when he would have inherited the blessing, he was rejected, for he found no place of repentance, though he sought it carefully with tears" (Hebrews 12:16–17).

    Now was I as one bound, I felt myself shut up unto the judgment to come; nothing now for two years together would abide with me,
[142] 17   but damnation, and an expectation of damnation: I say, nothing now would abide with me but this, save some few moments for relief, as in the sequel you will see.

    These words were to my soul like fetters of brass to my legs, in the continual sound of which I went for several months together.
[143]   But about ten or eleven o'clock one day, as I was walking under a
18   hedge, full of sorrow and guilt God knows, and bemoaning myself for this hard hap,· that such a thought should arise within me, suddenly this sentence bolted in upon me, The blood of Christ remits all guilt; at this I made a stand in my spirit: with that, this word took hold upon me, "The blood of Jesus Christ his Son cleanseth us from all sin" (1 John 1:7).

hap · chance, accident

Now I began to conceive peace in my soul, and methought I 19 [144]
saw as if the tempter did lear* and steal away from me, as being
ashamed of what he had done. At the same time also I had my
sin and the blood of Christ thus represented to me, that my sin
when compared to the blood of Christ, was no more to it, than
this little clot* or stone before me, is to this vast and wide field
that here I see: this gave me good encouragement for the space of
two or three hours, in which time also methought I saw by faith
the Son of God as suffering for my sins. But because it tarried
not, I therefore sunk in my spirit under exceeding guilt again.

But chiefly by the aforementioned scripture, concerning Esau's 20 [145]
selling of his birthright; for that scripture would lie all day long,
all the week long; yea, all the year long in my mind, and hold
me down, so that I could by no means lift up myself; for when
I would strive to turn me to this scripture, or that for relief, still
that sentence would be sounding in me, "For ye know, how that
afterward, when he would have inherited the blessing he found
no place of repentance, though he sought it carefully with tears."

Sometimes, indeed, I should have a touch from that in Luke 21 [146]
22:31, "I have prayed for thee, that thy faith fail not; but it would
not abide upon me:" neither could I indeed, when I considered
my state, find ground to conceive in the least, that there should
be the root of that grace within me, having sinned as I had done.
Now was I tore and rent in heavy case, for many days together.

Then began I with sad and careful heart, to consider of the 22 [147]
nature and largeness of my sin, and to search in the Word of God,
if I could in any place espy a word of promise, or any encouraging sentence by which I might take relief. Wherefore I began to
consider that third of Mark, "All manner of sins and blasphemies
shall be forgiven unto the sons of men, wherewith soever they
shall blaspheme:"* which place, methought, at a blush, did contain
a large and glorious promise for the pardon of high offences; but
considering the place more fully, I thought it was rather to be
understood, as relating more chiefly to those who had, while in a
natural estate,* committed such things as there are mentioned, but
not to me, who had not only received light and mercy, but that had
both after and also contrary to that, so slighted Christ as I had done.

I feared therefore that this wicked sin of mine might be that 23 [148]
sin unpardonable, of which he there thus speaketh, "But he that

lear · slink

dot · clod

"All … blaspheme" ·
Mark 3:28

natural estate ·
ignorant of the gospel
and, thus, not born again

[148] 23 shall blaspheme against the Holy Ghost, hath never forgiveness, but is in danger of eternal damnation" (Mark 3:29): and I did the rather give credit to this, because of that sentence in the Hebrews, "For you know how that afterwards, when he would have inherited the blessing he was rejected; for he found no place of repentance, though he sought it carefully with tears."* For this stuck always with me.

"For you know ... with tears" · see Hebrews 12:17

[149]
24 And now was I both a burden and a terror to myself, nor did I ever so know, as now, what it was to be weary of my life, and yet afraid to die. O, how gladly now would I have been anybody but myself. Any thing but a man! And in any condition but mine now! For it was impossible for me to be forgiven my transgression, and to be saved from wrath to come.

And now began I to labour to call again time that was past, wishing a thousand times twice told, that the day was yet to come, when I should be tempted to such a sin; concluding with great indignation, both against my heart and all assaults, how I would rather have been torn in pieces, than found a consenter thereto: but alas! these thoughts and wishings, and resolvings, were now too late to help me; the thought had passed my heart, God hath let me go, and I am fallen: "O," thought I, "that it was with me as in months past, as in the days when God preserved me!" (Job 29:2).

[150] 25

[151] 26 Then again, being loath and unwilling to perish, I began to compare my sin with others, to see if I could find that any of those that are saved had done as I had done. So I considered David's adultery and murder,* and found them most heinous crimes, and those too committed after light and grace received: but yet by considering, I perceived that his transgressions were only such as were against the law of Moses, from which the Lord Christ could with the consent of his Word deliver him: but mine was against the gospel, yea, against the Mediator thereof; I had sold my Saviour.

David's ... murder · 2 Samuel 11

[152] 27 Now again should I be as if racked upon the wheel;* when I considered, that, besides the guilt that possessed me, I should be *so* void of grace, *so* bewitched: what, thought I, must it be no sin but this? must it needs be the *great transgression* (Psalm 19:13)? must *that* wicked one touch my soul (1 John 5:18)? O what stings did I find in all these sentences!

wheel · a device upon which prisoners were tortured

[153] 28 What? thought I, is there but one sin that is unpardonable? but one sin that layeth the soul without the reach of God's mercy,

and must I be guilty of that? must it needs be that? is there but 28 [153] one sin among so many millions of sins, for which there is no forgiveness, and must I commit this? O! unhappy sin! O unhappy man! These things would so break and confound my spirit, that I could not tell what to do, I thought at times they would have broke my wits, and still to aggravate my misery, that would run in my mind, *You know how that afterwards when he would have inherited the blessing, he was rejected.* O! none knows the terrors of those days but myself.

Peter's sin · see Matthew 26:69–75; Mark 14:66–72; Luke 22:54–62; John 18:25–27

After this, I came to consider of Peter's sin* which he com- 29 [154] mitted in denying his master; and indeed this came nighest to mine, of any that I could find; for he had denied his Saviour as I, and that after light and mercy received; yea, and that too, after warning given him: I also considered that he did it both once and twice, and that after time to consider betwixt. But though I put all these circumstances together, that if possible I might find help, yet I considered again, that his was but a denial of his master, but mine was a selling of my Saviour. Wherefore I thought with myself, that I came nearer to Judas, than either to David or Peter.

Here again, my torment would flame out, and afflict me; yea, 30 [155] it would grind me as it were to powder, to discern the preservation of God towards others, while I fell into the snare: for in my thus considering of other men's sins, and comparing of them with my own, I could evidently see how God preserved them notwithstanding their wickedness, and would not let them, as he had let me, to become a son of perdition.

But O, how did my soul at this time prize the preservation that 31 [156] God did set about his people! Ah how safely did I see them walk, whom God had hedged in! They were within his care, protection, and special providence: though they were full as bad as I by nature, yet because he loved them, he would not suffer them to fall without the range of mercy: but as for me, I was gone, I had done it, he would not preserve me, nor keep me, but suffered me, because I was a reprobate, to fall as I had done. Now did those

God's ... people · see, for example, Ezekiel 11:20 and Deuteronomy 28:9

blessed places, that spake of *God's keeping his people,** shine like the sun before me, though not to comfort me, but to show me the blessed state and heritage of those whom the Lord had blessed.

Now I saw, that as God had his hand in all providences and 32 [157] dispensations that overtook his elect, so he had his hand in all the

[157] 32   temptations that they had to sin against him, not to animate them unto wickedness, but to choose their temptations and troubles for them; and also to leave them, for a time, to such sins only as might not destroy, but humble them; as might not put them beyond, but lay them in the way of the renewing of his mercy. But O, what love, what care, what kindness and mercy did I now see, mixing itself with the most severe and dreadful of all God's ways to his people! He would let David, Hezekiah, Solomon, Peter, and others fall, but he would not let them fall into sin unpardonable, nor into hell for sin. O! thought I, these be the men that God hath loved; these be the men that God, though he chastised them, keeps them in safety by him, and them whom he makes to abide under the shadow of the Almighty.* But all these thoughts added sorrow, grief, and horror to me, as whatever I now thought on, it was killing to me. If I thought how God kept his own, that was killing to me; if I thought of how I was falling myself, that was killing to me. As all things wrought together for the best, and to do good to them that were the called, according to his purpose;* so I thought that all things wrought for my damage, and for my eternal overthrow.

abide ... Almighty · see Psalm 91:1

all things ... purpose · see Romans 8:28

[158] 33   Then again, I began to compare my sin with the sin of Judas, that if possible I might find that mine differed from that which in truth is unpardonable; and, O thought I, if it should differ from it, though but the breadth of an hair, what a happy condition is my soul in! And by considering, I found that Judas did his intentionally, but mine was against my prayer and strivings; besides, his was committed with much deliberation, but mine in a fearful hurry, on a sudden; all this while I was tossed to and fro, like the locusts,* and driven from trouble to sorrow; hearing always the sound of Esau's fall in mine ears, and of the dreadful consequences thereof.

tossed ... locusts · see Psalm 109:23

[159] 34   Yet this consideration about Judas his sin, was for a while some little relief unto me: for I saw I had not, as to the circumstances, transgressed so foully as he: but this was quickly gone again, for I thought with myself there might be more ways than one to commit the unpardonable sin; and that too, there might be degrees of that, as well as of other transgressions: wherefore, for ought I yet could perceive, this iniquity of mine might be such as might never be passed by.

I was often now ashamed, that I should be like such an ugly 35 [160]
man as Judas: I thought also how loathsome I should be unto
all the saints at the day of judgment, insomuch that now I could
scarce see a good man, that I believed had a good conscience, but
I should feel my heart tremble at him, while I was in his presence.
O! now I saw a glory in walking with God, and what a mercy it
was to have a good conscience before him.

I was much about this time tempted to content myself, by 36 [161]
receiving some false opinion; as that there should be no such thing
as a day of judgment, that we should not rise again, and that sin
was no such grievous thing. The tempter suggesting thus, *For if
these things should indeed be true, yet to believe otherwise would
yield you ease for the present. If you must perish, never torment
yourself so much beforehand, drive the thoughts of damning out
of your mind, by possessing your mind with some such conclusions
that Atheists and Ranters* use to help themselves withal.*

But O! when such thoughts have passed through my heart, 37 [162]
how as it were within a step hath death and judgment been in
my view! Methought the judge stood at the door, I was as if 'twas
come already: so that such things could have no entertainment;
but methinks I see by this, that Satan will use any means to keep
the soul from Christ. He loveth not an awakened frame of spirit;
security, blindness, darkness, and error is the very kingdom and
habitation of the wicked one.

Ranters · flourishing in
the 1600s, the Ranters
were *antinomi-
ans* – they believed that
moral law is not binding
upon Christians, who are
forgiven and filled with
the Holy Spirit

Samuel Johnson

Johnson, born into poverty and poor for most of his adulthood, became the pre-eminent literary figure in England, such that the last half of the 18th century is sometimes called The Age of Johnson. His varied output is astonishing: poetry, moralistic essays, a landmark English dictionary, a scholarly edition of Shakespeare's plays, the fable Rasselas (1759), travel commentary, and literary criticism. His poverty was relieved when the government granted him a pension in 1762. Johnson's personal complexity elicited disdain from some and reverence from others. Prone to depression, he feared insanity. His marriage to a widow twenty years his senior seemed strange to nearly everyone. A large, hulking man with eccentric and often unpleasant habits, he was nevertheless a model of the will to succeed despite handicaps. Laziness and procrastination gave him much trouble in his professional life, and many works were written hurriedly because he had delayed too long. This habit was offset by his prodigious memory, which allowed him to compose in his head, and by his vast reading. One acquaintance said of him, "Johnson knew more books than any man alive." His Christian faith and a keen sense of his own failings kept him humble in outlook. "The Vanity of Human Wishes" (1749), Johnson's poetic meditation on human existence, ends with the idea that mankind can find peace only through religion. James Boswell struck the same note in The Life of Samuel Johnson *(1791), saying that piety was the "ruling principle" in this writer's life.*

from PRAYERS AND MEDITATIONS

APRIL 25, 1752

1 O LORD, OUR HEAVENLY FATHER, almighty and most merciful God, in whose hands are life and death, who givest and takest away, castest down and raisest up, look with mercy on the

25

affliction of thy unworthy servant, turn away thine anger from me, [1]
and speak peace to my troubled soul. Grant me the assistance and
comfort of thy Holy Spirit, that I may remember with thankfulness

departed wife ·
Elizabeth "Tetty" Johnson
died March 28, 1752

the blessings so long enjoyed by me in the society of my departed
wife*; make me so to think on her precepts and example, that I
may imitate whatever was in her life acceptable in thy sight, and
avoid all by which she offended Thee. Forgive me, O merciful Lord,
all my sins, and enable me to begin and perfect that reformation
I promised her, and to persevere in that resolution, which she
implored Thee to continue, in the purposes which I recorded in
thy sight, when she lay dead before me, in obedience to thy laws,
and faith in thy word. And now, O Lord, release me from my
sorrow, fill me with just hopes, true faith, and holy consolations,
and enable me to do my duty in that state of life to which Thou
hast been pleased to call me, without disturbance from fruitless
grief, or tumultuous imaginations; that in all my thoughts, words,
and actions, I may glorify thy Holy Name, and finally obtain, what
I hope Thou hast granted to thy departed servant, everlasting joy
and felicity, through our Lord Jesus Christ. Amen.

EASTER EVE, 1761

S INCE THE COMMUNION of last Easter, I have led a life so dis- [2]
sipated and useless, and my terrors and perplexities have so
much increased, that I am under great depression and discour-
agement; yet I purpose to present myself before God tomorrow,

break ... reed · see
Isaiah 42:3

with humble hope that he will not break the bruised reed.*

Come ... travail ·
Matthew 11:28

Come unto me all ye that travail.* [2a]

I have resolved, I hope not presumptuously, till I am afraid to
resolve again. Yet hoping in God, I steadfastly purpose to lead a
new life. O God, enable me, for Jesus Christ's sake.

WEDNESDAY, MARCH 28, 1770

T HIS IS THE DAY ON WHICH, in 1752, I was deprived of poor [3]
dear Tetty. Having left off the practice of thinking on her with
some particular combinations, I have recalled her to my mind
of late less frequently; but when I recollect the time in which
we lived together, my grief for her departure is not abated; and I
have less pleasure in any good that befalls me, because she does

3 not partake it. On many occasions, I think what she would have said or done. When I saw the sea at Brighthelmstone, I wished for her to have seen it with me. But with respect to her, no rational wish is now left, but that we may meet at last where the mercy of God shall make us happy, and perhaps make us instrumental to the happiness of each other. It is now eighteen years.

AUGUST 12, 1784

4 O LORD, MY MAKER AND PROTECTOR, who hast graciously sent me into this world to work out my salvation,* enable me to drive from me all such unquiet and perplexing thoughts as may mislead or hinder me in the practice of those duties which Thou hast required. When I behold the works of thy hands, and consider the course of thy providence, give me grace always to remember that thy thoughts are not my thoughts, nor thy ways my ways.* And while it shall please Thee to continue me in this world, where much is to be done, and little is to be known, teach me, by thy Holy Spirit, to withdraw my mind from unprofitable and dangerous enquiries, from difficulties vainly curious, and doubts impossible to be solved. Let me rejoice in the light which Thou hast imparted, let me serve Thee with active zeal and humble confidence, and wait with patient expectation for the time in which the soul which Thou receivest shall be satisfied with knowledge. Grant this, O Lord, for Jesus Christ's sake. Amen.

work ... salvation · see Philippians 2:12

thy thoughts ... ways · see Isaiah 55:8

John Henry Newman

⟨ 1 8 0 1 – 1 8 9 0 ⟩

The tension between the gift of intellect and its potential dangers is an important theme in Newman's writing. While the development of one's God-given intellectual faculties is a natural good – a conviction evidenced by his 1854–1858 term as rector of the newly established Catholic University of Dublin – Newman also warns that an atheistic inclination is the natural bent of the fallen, sin-influenced mind. The latter conviction led him in 1845 to leave the Anglican priesthood, as well as a position at Oxford University, and to enter the Roman Catholic church – the only bulwark, Newman felt, that would ultimately stand against the flood of unbelief washing over western Europe. During a brief youthful infatuation with religious liberalism, the writer had witnessed the power of the critical faculty ("the all-corroding, all-dissolving skepticism of the intellect") to undermine Christian doctrine. Consequently, as he explains in Apologia Pro Vita Sua *(1864–1865), his spiritual autobiography, he was led in maturity to accept "the Church's infallibility, as a provision, adapted by the mercy of the Creator, to preserve religion in the world, and to restrain that freedom of thought, which of course in itself is one of the greatest of our natural gifts, and to rescue it from its own suicidal excesses." Despite his caution, Newman was an avid champion of liberal education, producing a series of lectures on the purpose of the college experience, later collected and entitled* The Idea of a University *(1852). Here Newman argues, against those who would view the university as a vocational training school, that true education transcends narrow utilitarian ends.*

from THE IDEA OF A UNIVERSITY

KNOWLEDGE VIEWED IN RELATION TO PROFESSIONAL SKILL

1 TODAY I HAVE CONFINED MYSELF to saying that that training of the intellect, which is best for the individual himself, best

enables him to discharge his duties to society. The Philosopher, 1
indeed, and the man of the world differ in their very notion, but
the methods, by which they are respectively formed, are pretty
much the same. The Philosopher has the same command of
matters of thought, which the true citizen and gentleman has of
matters of business and conduct. If then a practical end must be
assigned to a University course, I say it is that of training good
members of society. Its art is the art of social life, and its end is
fitness for the world. It neither confines its views to particular
professions on the one hand, nor creates heroes or inspires
genius on the other. Works indeed of genius fall under no art;
heroic minds come under no rule; a University is not a birthplace
of poets or of immortal authors, of founders of schools, leaders
of colonies, or conquerors of nations. It does not promise a generation of Aristotles or Newtons, of Napoleons or Washingtons,
of Raphaels or Shakespeares, though such miracles of nature it
has before now contained within its precincts. Nor is it content
on the other hand with forming the critic or the experimentalist,
the economist or the engineer, though such too it includes within
its scope. But a University training is the great ordinary means
to a great but ordinary end; it aims at raising the intellectual
tone of society, at cultivating the public mind, at purifying the
national taste, at supplying true principles to popular enthusiasm and fixed aims to popular aspiration, at giving enlargement
and sobriety to the ideas of the age, at facilitating the exercise
of political power, and refining the intercourse of private life. It
is the education which gives a man a clear conscious view of
his own opinions and judgments, a truth in developing them,
an eloquence in expressing them, and a force in urging them.
It teaches him to see things as they are, to go right to the point,

skein · a loose coil

sophistical · associated
with sophistry, which is
characterized by the use
of overly subtle and often
misleading arguments

to disentangle a skein* of thought, to detect what is sophistical,*
and to discard what is irrelevant. It prepares him to fill any post
with credit, and to master any subject with facility. It shows him
how to accommodate himself to others, how to throw himself
into their state of mind, how to bring before them his own,
how to influence them, how to come to an understanding with
them, how to bear with them. He is at home in any society, he
has common ground with every class; he knows when to speak
and when to be silent; he is able to converse, he is able to listen;

1 he can ask a question pertinently, and gain a lesson seasonably, when he has nothing to impart himself; he is ever ready, yet never in the way; he is a pleasant companion, and a comrade you can depend upon; he knows when to be serious and when to trifle, and he has a sure tact which enables him to trifle with gracefulness and to be serious with effect. He has the repose of a mind which lives in itself, while it lives in the world, and which has resources for its happiness at home when it cannot go abroad. He has a gift which serves him in public, and supports him in retirement, without which good fortune is but vulgar,* and with which failure and disappointment have a charm. The art which tends to make a man all this, is in the object which it pursues as useful as the art of wealth or the art of health, though it is less susceptible of method, and less tangible, less certain, less complete in its result.

vulgar · unrefined, deficient in taste

from KNOWLEDGE VIEWED IN RELATION TO RELIGION

2 Now, on opening the subject, we see at once a momentous benefit which the philosopher is likely to confer on the pastors of the Church. It is obvious that the first step which they have to effect in the conversion of man and the renovation of his nature, is his rescue from that fearful subjection to sense* which is his ordinary state. To be able to break through the meshes of that thraldom,* and to disentangle and to disengage its ten thousand holds upon the heart, is to bring it, I might almost say, halfway to Heaven. Here, even divine grace, to speak of things according to their appearances, is ordinarily baffled, and retires, without expedient or resource, before this giant fascination. Religion seems too high and unearthly to be able to exert a continued influence upon us: its effort to rouse the soul, and the soul's effort to cooperate, are too violent to last. It is like holding out the arm at full length, or supporting some great weight, which we manage to do for a time, but soon are exhausted and succumb. Nothing can act beyond its own nature; when then we are called to what is supernatural, though those extraordinary aids from Heaven are given us, with which obedience becomes possible, yet even with them it is of transcendent difficulty. We are drawn down to earth every moment with the ease and certainty of a natural gravitation, and it is only by sudden impulses and, as it were, forc-

sense · sensuality

thraldom · slavery, bondage

ible plunges that we attempt to mount upwards. Religion indeed 2
enlightens, terrifies, subdues; it gives faith, it inflicts remorse,
it inspires resolutions, it draws tears, it inflames devotion, but
only for the occasion. I repeat, it imparts an inward power which
ought to effect more than this; I am not forgetting either the real
sufficiency of its aids, nor the responsibility of those in whom
they fail. I am not discussing theological questions at all, I am
looking at phenomena as they lie before me, and I say that, in
matter of fact, the sinful spirit repents, and protests it will never
sin again, and for a while is protected by disgust and abhorrence
from the malice of its foe. But that foe knows too well that such
seasons of repentance are wont to have their end: he patiently
waits, till nature faints with the effort of resistance, and lies passive and hopeless under the next access of temptation. What
we need then is some expedient or instrument, which at least
will obstruct and stave off the approach of our spiritual enemy,
and which is sufficiently congenial and level with our nature to
maintain as firm a hold upon us as the inducements of sensual
gratification. It will be our wisdom to employ nature against itself.
Thus sorrow, sickness, and care are providential antagonists to
our inward disorders; they come upon us as years pass on, and
generally produce their natural effects upon us, in proportion as
we are subjected to their influence. These, however, are God's
instruments, not ours; we need a similar remedy, which we can
make our own, the object of some legitimate faculty, or the aim
of some natural affection, which is capable of resting on the mind,
and taking up its familiar lodging with it, and engrossing it, and
which thus becomes a match for the besetting power of sensuality,
homeopathic and a sort of homeopathic medicine* for the disease. Here then I
medicine · medical think is the important aid which intellectual cultivation furnishes
treatment using minute to us in rescuing the victims of passion and self-will. It does not
quantities of substances supply religious motives; it is not the cause or proper antecedent
that in massive doses of any thing supernatural; it is not meritorious of heavenly aid or
produce effects similar reward; but it does a work, at least *materially* good (as theologians
to those of the disease speak), whatever be its real and formal character. It expels the
being treated excitements of sense by the introduction of those of the intellect.

prima facie · "at first This then is the *prima facie** advantage of the pursuit of 3
sight" (Latin), before Knowledge; it is the drawing the mind off from things which will
thorough analysis harm it to subjects which are worthy a rational being; and, though

3   it does not raise it above nature, nor has any tendency to make us
pleasing to our Maker, yet is it nothing to substitute what is in itself
harmless for what is, to say the least, inexpressibly dangerous? is it
a little thing to exchange a circle of ideas which are certainly sinful,
for others which are certainly not so? You will say, perhaps, in the
words of the Apostle, "Knowledge puffeth up:"* and doubtless this
mental cultivation, even when it is successful for the purpose for
which I am applying it, may be from the first nothing more than
the substitution of pride for sensuality. I grant it, I think I shall have
something to say on this point presently; but this is not a necessary
result, it is but an incidental evil, a danger which may be realized
or may be averted, whereas we may in most cases predicate guilt,
and guilt of a heinous kind, where the mind is suffered to run wild
and indulge its thoughts without training or law of any kind; and
surely to turn away a soul from mortal sin is a good and a gain so
far, whatever comes of it. And therefore, if a friend in need is twice
a friend, I conceive that intellectual employments, though they
do no more than occupy the mind with objects naturally noble or
innocent, have a special claim upon our consideration and gratitude.

"Knowledge puffeth up" · 1 Corinthians 8:1

Henry David Thoreau

❂{ 1 8 1 7 – 1 8 6 2 }❂

Thoreau's Walden, *or* Life in the Woods *(1854) has fueled generations of American efforts to preserve wilderness, resist destructive industrial practices, and retrieve a way of simplicity and good stewardship in the midst of spreading consumerism. It is Thoreau's record of an experiment in simple living, taken from journals he kept during nearly two years of living in a small cabin with a beanfield, two books, and a variety of wild "neighbors" about a mile from his home village of Concord, Massachusetts. But it is far more than a record: it is also a literary experiment, analogous to contemporary "mixed media" experiments in the way he plays with genres. His long sentences are rich with historical allusion, word play, biblical echoes, and poetic devices. He combines the meticulous observation and accuracy of a natural historian with a keen understanding of how parable draws spiritual teaching from the facts of everyday life. He appropriates devices from Aesop's fables and writes about his fellow New Englanders in the satirical tradition of Swift and Voltaire. His deep reading of the Bible, especially the Gospels, is evident in direct imitations of some of the prophets' and Jesus' admonitions. But his impatience with the church and the New England Protestants of his generation is equally evident. His challenge of superficial piety, materialism, and self-serving reading of Scripture are as pertinent in our day as in 1854. Moreover, as a writer, he gave close and sustained attention to the pliability, history, and vitality of language itself: he often uses words in ways that call attention to obsolete dimensions of meaning, and plays with ambiguities of words. The passages selected here articulate his complex intentions in a direct address to his readers, situating his own story on a broad canvas that includes both Asian cultures and the ancient world as comparative frames of reference. Like his younger contemporary, Melville, he took a keen interest in world religions and the lifestyles of tribal peoples who, he believed, might offer important reminders to "advanced" industrial nations about how to live rightly and well on the earth we share.*

WALDEN, OR LIFE IN THE WOODS

from CHAPTER 1: ECONOMY

When I wrote the following pages, or rather the bulk of them, 1 I lived alone, in the woods, a mile from any neighbor, in a house which I had built myself, on the shore of Walden Pond, in Concord, Massachusetts, and earned my living by the labor of my hands only. I lived there two years and two months. At present I am a sojourner in civilized life again.

I should not obtrude my affairs so much on the notice of my 2 readers if very particular inquiries had not been made by my townsmen concerning my mode of life, which some would call impertinent, though they do not appear to me at all impertinent, but, considering the circumstances, very natural and pertinent. Some have asked what I got to eat; if I did not feel lonesome; if I was not afraid; and the like. Others have been curious to learn what portion of my income I devoted to charitable purposes; and some, who have large families, how many poor children I maintained. I will therefore ask those of my readers who feel no particular interest in me to pardon me if I undertake to answer some of these questions in this book. In most books, the I, or first person, is omitted; in this it will be retained; that, in respect to egotism, is the main difference. We commonly do not remember that it is, after all, always the first person that is speaking. I should not talk so much about myself if there were anybody else whom I knew as well. Unfortunately, I am confined to this theme by the narrowness of my experience. Moreover, I, on my side, require of every writer, first or last, a simple and sincere account of his own life, and not merely what he has heard of other men's lives; some such account as he would send to his kindred from a distant land; for if he has lived sincerely, it must have been in a distant land to me. Perhaps these pages are more particularly addressed to poor students. As for the rest of my readers, they will accept such portions as apply to them. I trust that none will

2   stretch the seams in putting on the coat, for it may do good service to him whom it fits.

3   I would fain say something, not so much concerning the Chinese and Sandwich Islanders* as you who read these pages, who are said to live in New England; something about your condition, especially your outward condition or circumstances in this world, in this town, what it is, whether it is necessary that it be as bad as it is, whether it cannot be improved as well as not. I have travelled a good deal in Concord; and everywhere, in shops, and offices, and fields, the inhabitants have appeared to me to be doing penance in a thousand remarkable ways. What I have heard of Bramins* sitting exposed to four fires and looking in the face of the sun; or hanging suspended, with their heads downward, over flames; or looking at the heavens over their shoulders "until it becomes impossible for them to resume their natural position, while from the twist of the neck nothing but liquids can pass into the stomach"; or dwelling, chained for life, at the foot of a tree; or measuring with their bodies, like caterpillars, the breadth of vast empires; or standing on one leg on the tops of pillars – even these forms of conscious penance are hardly more incredible and astonishing than the scenes which I daily witness. The twelve labors of Hercules* were trifling in comparison with those which my neighbors have undertaken; for they were only twelve, and had an end; but I could never see that these men slew or captured any monster or finished any labor. They have no friend Iolaus* to burn with a hot iron the root of the hydra's head,* but as soon as one head is crushed, two spring up.

4   I see young men, my townsmen, whose misfortune it is to have inherited farms, houses, barns, cattle, and farming tools; for these are more easily acquired than got rid of. Better if they had been born in the open pasture and suckled by a wolf, that they might have seen with clearer eyes what field they were called to labor in. Who made them serfs of the soil? Why should they eat their sixty acres, when man is condemned to eat only his peck* of dirt? Why should they begin digging their graves as soon as they are born? They have got to live a man's life, pushing all these things before them, and get on as well as they can. How many a poor immortal soul have I met well-nigh crushed and smothered under its load, creeping down the road of life, push-

Sandwich Islanders · Name given to the Hawaiian islands by the explorer Captain James Cook in the 1770s

Brahmins · members of Hindu priestly class in India

twelve labors of Hercules · A series of episodes about labors assigned to the Greek hero as penance; as a reward for completing the twelve dangerous tasks he was forgiven, given a bride, and granted the gift of immortality by Zeus, his father

Iolaus · Companion and help to Hercules on some of his assigned tasks

hydra's head · A serpent with nine heads that grew two more when one was cut off

peck · A unit measure of dry volume, equivalent to two gallons. Four pecks make a bushel

Augean stables · Stables of a Greek mythological king who owned more cattle than anyone else in the kingdom; they were never cleaned until the time of Hercules

ing before it a barn seventy-five feet by forty, its Augean stables* 4 never cleansed, and one hundred acres of land, tillage, mowing, pasture, and woodlot! The portionless, who struggle with no such unnecessary inherited encumbrances, find it labor enough to subdue and cultivate a few cubic feet of flesh.

book · Bible (Matthew 6:19-20)

But men labor under a mistake. The better part of the man is 5 soon plowed into the soil for compost. By a seeming fate, commonly called necessity, they are employed, as it says in an old book* laying up treasures which moth and rust will corrupt and thieves break through and steal. It is a fool's life, as they will find when they get to the end of it, if not before. . . .

Most men, even in this comparatively free country, through 6 mere ignorance and mistake, are so occupied with the factitious cares and superfluously coarse labors of life that its finer fruits cannot be plucked by them. Their fingers, from excessive toil, are too clumsy and tremble too much for that. Actually, the laboring man has not leisure for a true integrity day by day; he cannot afford to sustain the manliest relations to men; his labor would be depreciated in the market. He has no time to be anything but a machine. How can he remember well his ignorance – which his growth requires – who has so often to use his knowledge? We should feed and clothe him gratuitously sometimes, and recruit

cordials · Refers both to medicinal beverages and to sweet alcoholic drinks

him with our cordials,* before we judge of him. The finest qualities of our nature, like the bloom on fruits, can be preserved only by the most delicate handling. Yet we do not treat ourselves nor one another thus tenderly.

Some of you, we all know, are poor, find it hard to live, are 7 sometimes, as it were, gasping for breath. I have no doubt that some of you who read this book are unable to pay for all the dinners which you have actually eaten, or for the coats and shoes which are fast wearing or are already worn out, and have come to this page to spend borrowed or stolen time, robbing your creditors of an hour. It is very evident what mean and sneaking lives many of you live, for my sight has been whetted by experience; always on the limits, trying to get into business and trying to get out of debt, a very ancient slough, called by the Latins aes alienum, another's brass, for some of their coins were made of brass; still living, and dying, and buried by this other's brass; always promising to pay, promising to pay, tomorrow, and dying

7   today, insolvent; seeking to curry favor, to get custom, by how many modes, only not state-prison offenses; lying, flattering, voting, contracting yourselves into a nutshell of civility or dilating into an atmosphere of thin and vaporous generosity, that you may persuade your neighbor to let you make his shoes, or his hat, or his coat, or his carriage, or import his groceries for him; making yourselves sick, that you may lay up something against a sick day, something to be tucked away in an old chest, or in a stocking behind the plastering, or, more safely, in the brick bank; no matter where, no matter how much or how little.

8   I sometimes wonder that we can be so frivolous, I may almost say, as to attend to the gross but somewhat foreign form of servitude called Negro Slavery, there are so many keen and subtle masters that enslave both North and South. It is hard to have a Southern overseer; it is worse to have a Northern one; but worst of all when you are the slave-driver of yourself. Talk of a divinity in man! Look at the teamster on the highway, wending to market by day or night; does any divinity stir within him? His highest duty to fodder and water his horses! What is his destiny to him compared with the shipping interests? Does not he drive for Squire Make-a-stir? How godlike, how immortal, is he? See how he cowers and sneaks, how vaguely all the day he fears, not being immortal nor divine, but the slave and prisoner of his own opinion of himself, a fame won by his own deeds. Public opinion is a weak tyrant compared with our own private opinion. What a man thinks of himself, that it is which determines, or rather indicates, his fate. Self-emancipation even in the West Indian provinces of the fancy and imagination – what Wilberforce is there to bring that about? Think, also, of the ladies of the land weaving toilet cushions against the last day, not to betray too green an interest in their fates! As if you could kill time without injuring eternity. The mass of men lead lives of quiet desperation. What is called resignation is confirmed desperation. From the desperate city you go into the desperate country, and have to console yourself with the bravery of minks and muskrats. A stereotyped but unconscious despair is concealed even under what are called the games and amusements of mankind. There is no play in them, for this comes after work. But it is a characteristic of wisdom not to do desperate things. When we consider what, to use the words

Wilberforce · William Wilberforce (1759-1833) British evangelical politican who led the movement to abolish the slave trade; largely through his influence the Slave Trade Act was passed in 1807

of the catechism, is the chief end of man, and what are the true 8
necessaries and means of life, it appears as if men had deliberately
chosen the common mode of living because they preferred it to
any other. Yet they honestly think there is no choice left. But alert
and healthy natures remember that the sun rose clear. It is never
too late to give up our prejudices. No way of thinking or doing,
however ancient, can be trusted without proof. What everybody
echoes or in silence passes by as true today may turn out to be
falsehood tomorrow, mere smoke of opinion, which some had
trusted for a cloud that would sprinkle fertilizing rain on their
fields. What old people say you cannot do, you try and find that
you can. Old deeds for old people, and new deeds for new. Old
people did not know enough once, perchance, to fetch fresh fuel
to keep the fire a-going; new people put a little dry wood under a
pot, and are whirled round the globe with the speed of birds, in
a way to kill old people, as the phrase is. Age is no better, hardly
so well, qualified for an instructor as youth, for it has not profited
so much as it has lost. One may almost doubt if the wisest man
has learned anything of absolute value by living. Practically, the
old have no very important advice to give the young, their own
experience has been so partial, and their lives have been such
miserable failures, for private reasons, as they must believe; and
it may be that they have some faith left which belies that experience, and they are only less young than they were. I have lived
some thirty years on this planet, and I have yet to hear the first
syllable of valuable or even earnest advice from my seniors. They
have told me nothing, and probably cannot tell me anything to
the purpose. Here is life, an experiment to a great extent untried
by me; but it does not avail me that they have tried it. If I have
any experience which I think valuable, I am sure to reflect that
this my Mentors said nothing about.

One farmer says to me, "You cannot live on vegetable food 9
solely, for it furnishes nothing to make bones with"; and so he
religiously devotes a part of his day to supplying his system with
the raw material of bones; walking all the while he talks behind
his oxen, which, with vegetable-made bones, jerk him and his
lumbering plow along in spite of every obstacle. Some things are
really necessaries of life in some circles, the most helpless and

9   diseased, which in others are luxuries merely, and in others still
are entirely unknown. . . .

10   I think that we may safely trust a good deal more than we
do. We may waive just so much care of ourselves as we honestly
bestow elsewhere. Nature is as well adapted to our weakness as
to our strength. The incessant anxiety and strain of some is a
well-nigh incurable form of disease. We are made to exaggerate
the importance of what work we do; and yet how much is not
done by us! or, what if we had been taken sick? How vigilant we
are! determined not to live by faith if we can avoid it; all the day
long on the alert, at night we unwillingly say our prayers and
commit ourselves to uncertainties. So thoroughly and sincerely
are we compelled to live, reverencing our life, and denying the
possibility of change. This is the only way, we say; but there are
as many ways as there can be drawn radii from one centre. . . .

11   Most of the luxuries, and many of the so-called comforts of
life, are not only not indispensable, but positive hindrances to
the elevation of mankind. With respect to luxuries and comforts,
the wisest have ever lived a more simple and meagre life than
the poor. The ancient philosophers, Chinese, Hindoo, Persian,
and Greek, were a class than which none has been poorer in
outward riches, none so rich in inward. We know not much about
them. It is remarkable that we know so much of them as we do.
The same is true of the more modern reformers and benefac-
tors of their race. None can be an impartial or wise observer of
human life but from the vantage ground of what we should call
voluntary poverty. Of a life of luxury the fruit is luxury, whether
in agriculture, or commerce, or literature, or art. There are
nowadays professors of philosophy, but not philosophers. Yet it
is admirable to profess because it was once admirable to live. To
be a philosopher is not merely to have subtle thoughts, nor even
to found a school, but so to love wisdom as to live according to
its dictates, a life of simplicity, independence, magnanimity, and
trust. It is to solve some of the problems of life, not only theoreti-
cally, but practically. . . .

12   In any weather, at any hour of the day or night, I have been
anxious to improve the nick of time, and notch it on my stick too;
to stand on the meeting of two eternities, the past and future,
which is precisely the present moment; to toe that line. You will

pardon some obscurities, for there are more secrets in my trade 12
than in most men's, and yet not voluntarily kept, but inseparable
from its very nature. I would gladly tell all that I know about it,
and never paint "No Admittance" on my gate. . . .

To anticipate, not the sunrise and the dawn merely, but, if pos- 13
sible, Nature herself! How many mornings, summer and winter,
before yet any neighbor was stirring about his business, have I
been about mine! No doubt, many of my townsmen have met
me returning from this enterprise, farmers starting for Boston
in the twilight, or woodchoppers going to their work. It is true,
I never assisted the sun materially in his rising, but, doubt not,
it was of the last importance only to be present at it.

So many autumn, ay, and winter days, spent outside the town, 14
trying to hear what was in the wind, to hear and carry it express!
I well-nigh sunk all my capital in it, and lost my own breath into
the bargain, running in the face of it. If it had concerned either of
the political parties, depend upon it, it would have appeared in
the Gazette with the earliest intelligence. At other times watching
from the observatory of some cliff or tree, to telegraph any new
arrival; or waiting at evening on the hill-tops for the sky to fall,
that I might catch something, though I never caught much, and
that, manna-wise, would dissolve again in the sun. . . .

For many years I was self-appointed inspector of snow-storms 15
and rain-storms, and did my duty faithfully; surveyor, if not of
highways, then of forest paths and all across-lot routes, keeping
them open, and ravines bridged and passable at all seasons, where
the public heel had testified to their utility.

I have looked after the wild stock of the town, which give a 16
faithful herdsman a good deal of trouble by leaping fences; and
I have had an eye to the unfrequented nooks and corners of the
farm; though I did not always know whether Jonas or Solomon
worked in a particular field today; that was none of my business.
I have watered the red huckleberry, the sand cherry and the
nettle-tree, the red pine and the black ash, the white grape and
the yellow violet, which might have withered else in dry seasons.

In short, I went on thus for a long time (I may say it without 17
boasting), faithfully minding my business, till it became more
and more evident that my townsmen would not after all admit
me into the list of town officers, nor make my place a sinecure

17 with a moderate allowance. My accounts, which I can swear to have kept faithfully, I have, indeed, never got audited, still less accepted, still less paid and settled. However, I have not set my heart on that. . . .

from **CHAPTER 2:**
WHERE I LIVED AND WHAT I LIVED FOR

18 The real attractions of the Hollowell farm, to me, were: its complete retirement, being, about two miles from the village, half a mile from the nearest neighbor, and separated from the highway by a broad field; its bounding on the river, which the owner said protected it by its fogs from frosts in the spring, though that was nothing to me; the gray color and ruinous state of the house and barn, and the dilapidated fences, which put such an interval between me and the last occupant; the hollow and lichen-covered apple trees, nawed by rabbits, showing what kind of neighbors I should have; but above all, the recollection I had of it from my earliest voyages up the river, when the house was concealed behind a dense grove of red maples, through which I heard the house-dog bark. I was in haste to buy it, before the proprietor finished getting out some rocks, cutting down the hollow apple trees, and grubbing up some young birches which had sprung up in the pasture, or, in short, had made any more of his improvements. To enjoy these advantages I was ready to carry it on; like Atlas,⁕ to take the world on my shoulders – I never heard what compensation he received for that – and do all those things which had no other motive or excuse but that I might pay for it and be unmolested in my possession of it; for I knew all the while that it would yield the most abundant crop of the kind I wanted, if I could only afford to let it alone. But it turned out as I have said.

Atlas · A Greek mythological character who was punished by Zeus and made to bear the weight of the heavens

19 All that I could say, then, with respect to farming on a large scale – I have always cultivated a garden – was, that I had had my seeds ready. Many think that seeds improve with age. I have no doubt that time discriminates between the good and the bad; and when at last I shall plant, I shall be less likely to be disappointed. But I would say to my fellows, once for all, As long as possible live free and uncommitted. It makes but little difference whether you are committed to a farm or the county jail.

Old Cato, whose "De Re Rustica" is my "Cultivator," says – and   20
the only translation I have seen makes sheer nonsense of the
passage – "When you think of getting a farm turn it thus in your
mind, not to buy greedily; nor spare your pains to look at it, and
do not think it enough to go round it once. The oftener you go
there the more it will please you, if it is good." I think I shall not
buy greedily, but go round and round it as long as I live, and be
buried in it first, that it may please me the more at last.

The present was my next experiment of this kind, which I   21
purpose to describe more at length, for convenience putting the
experience of two years into one. As I have said, I do not propose
to write an ode to dejection, but to brag as lustily as chanticleer in
the morning, standing on his roost, if only to wake my neighbors up.

When first I took up my abode in the woods, that is, began   22
to spend my nights as well as days there, which, by accident,
was on Independence Day, or the Fourth of July, 1845, my house
was not finished for winter, but was merely a defence against the
rain, without plastering or chimney, the walls being of rough,
weather-stained boards, with wide chinks, which made it cool
at night. The upright white hewn studs and freshly planed door
and window casings gave it a clean and airy look, especially in
the morning, when its timbers were saturated with dew, so that
I fancied that by noon some sweet gum would exude from them.
To my imagination it retained throughout the day more or less
of this auroral character, reminding me of a certain house on a
mountain which I had visited a year before. This was an airy and
unplastered cabin, fit to entertain a travelling god, and where a
goddess might trail her garments. The winds which passed over
my dwelling were such as sweep over the ridges of mountains,
bearing the broken strains, or celestial parts only, of terrestrial
music. The morning wind forever blows, the poem of creation

Olympus · Mt. is uninterrupted; but few are the ears that hear it. Olympus* is
Olympus in northern but the outside of the earth everywhere.
Greece, home of the
twelve gods of Olympus The only house I had been the owner of before, if I except a   23
in Greek mythology boat, was a tent, which I used occasionally when making excur-
sions in the summer, and this is still rolled up in my garret; but the
boat, after passing from hand to hand, has gone down the stream
of time. With this more substantial shelter about me, I had made
some progress toward settling in the world. This frame, so slightly

23   clad, was a sort of crystallization around me, and reacted on the builder. It was suggestive somewhat as a picture in outlines. I did not need to go outdoors to take the air, for the atmosphere within had lost none of its freshness. It was not so much within doors as behind a door where I sat, even in the rainiest weather. The Harivansa* says, "An abode without birds is like a meat without seasoning." Such was not my abode, for I found myself suddenly neighbor to the birds; not by having imprisoned one, but having caged myself near them. I was not only nearer to some of those which commonly frequent the garden and the orchard, but to those smaller and more thrilling songsters of the forest which never, or rarely, serenade a villager – the wood thrush, the veery, the scarlet tanager, the field sparrow, the whip-poor-will, and many others.

Harivansa · An ancient Sanskrit text of Hindu mythology, containing creation stories and a history of the Hindus

24   I was seated by the shore of a small pond, about a mile and a half south of the village of Concord and somewhat higher than it, in the midst of an extensive wood between that town and Lincoln, and about two miles south of that our only field known to fame, Concord Battle Ground; but I was so low in the woods that the opposite shore, half a mile off, like the rest, covered with wood, was my most distant horizon. For the first week, whenever I looked out on the pond it impressed me like a tarn high up on the side of a mountain, its bottom far above the surface of other lakes, and, as the sun arose, I saw it throwing off its nightly clothing of mist, and here and there, by degrees, its soft ripples or its smooth reflecting surface was revealed, while the mists, like ghosts, were stealthily withdrawing in every direction into the woods, as at the breaking up of some nocturnal conventicle.* The very dew seemed to hang upon the trees later into the day than usual, as on the sides of mountains.

conventicle · A small, unofficial and unsupervised meeting of laypeople to discuss religious issues

25   This small lake was of most value as a neighbor in the intervals of a gentle rain-storm in August, when, both air and water being perfectly still, but the sky overcast, mid-afternoon had all the serenity of evening, and the wood thrush sang around, and was heard from shore to shore. A lake like this is never smoother than at such a time; and the clear portion of the air above it being, shallow and darkened by clouds, the water, full of light and reflections, becomes a lower heaven itself so much the more important. From a hill-top near by, where the wood had been recently cut off,

there was a pleasing vista southward across the pond, through a wide indentation in the hills which form the shore there, where their opposite sides sloping toward each other suggested a stream flowing out in that direction through a wooded valley, but stream there was none. That way I looked between and over the near green hills to some distant and higher ones in the horizon, tinged with blue. Indeed, by standing on tiptoe I could catch a glimpse of some of the peaks of the still bluer and more distant mountain ranges in the northwest, those true-blue coins from heaven's own mint, and also of some portion of the village. But in other directions, even from this point, I could not see over or beyond the woods which surrounded me. It is well to have some water in your neighborhood, to give buoyancy to and float the earth. One value even of the smallest well is, that when you look into it you see that earth is not continent but insular. This is as important as that it keeps butter cool. When I looked across the pond from this peak toward the Sudbury meadows, which in time of flood I distinguished elevated perhaps by a mirage in their seething valley, like a coin in a basin, all the earth beyond the pond appeared like a thin crust insulated and floated even by this small sheet of interverting water, and I was reminded that this on which I dwelt was but dry land.

Though the view from my door was still more contracted, I 26 did not feel crowded or confined in the least. There was pasture enough for my imagination. The low shrub oak plateau to which the opposite shore arose stretched away toward the prairies of the West and the steppes of Tartary,* affording ample room for all the roving families of men. "There are none happy in the world but beings who enjoy freely a vast horizon" – said Damodara,* when his herds required new and larger pastures.

Both place and time were changed, and I dwelt nearer to 27 those parts of the universe and to those eras in history which had most attracted me. Where I lived was as far off as many a region viewed nightly by astronomers. . . .

Every morning was a cheerful invitation to make my life of 28 equal simplicity, and I may say innocence, with Nature herself. I have been as sincere a worshipper of Aurora* as the Greeks. I got up early and bathed in the pond; that was a religious exercise, and one of the best things which I did. They say that characters

steppes of Tartary · Tartary, the name used through the 19th century for a large portion of northern and central Asia from the Caspian Sea and Ural Mountains to the Pacific Ocean, inhabited by peoples of the Mongol Empire

Damodar · another name for Vishnu, the Hindu god

Aurora · Goddess of dawn in Roman mythology

28 were engraven on the bathing tub of King Tchingthang* to this effect: "Renew thyself completely each day; do it again, and again, and forever again." I can understand that. Morning brings back the heroic ages. I was as much affected by the faint hum of a mosquito making its invisible and unimaginable tour through my apartment at earliest dawn, when I was sitting with door and windows open, as I could be by any trumpet that ever sang of fame. It was Homer's requiem; itself an Iliad and Odyssey in the air, singing its own wrath and wanderings. There was something cosmical about it; a standing advertisement, till forbidden, of the everlasting vigor and fertility of the world. The morning, which is the most memorable season of the day, is the awakening hour. Then there is least somnolence in us; and for an hour, at least, some part of us awakes which slumbers all the rest of the day and night. Little is to be expected of that day, if it can be called a day, to which we are not awakened by our Genius, but by the mechanical nudgings of some servitor, are not awakened by our own newly acquired force and aspirations from within, accompanied by the undulations of celestial music, instead of factory bells, and a fragrance filling the air – to a higher life than we fell asleep from; and thus the darkness bear its fruit, and prove itself to be good, no less than the light. That man who does not believe that each day contains an earlier, more sacred, and auroral hour than he has yet profaned, has despaired of life, and is pursuing a descending and darkening way. After a partial cessation of his sensuous life, the soul of man, or its organs rather, are reinvigorated each day, and his Genius tries again what noble life it can make. All memorable events, I should say, transpire in morning time and in a morning atmosphere. The Vedas* say, "All intelligences awake with the morning." Poetry and art, and the fairest and most memorable of the actions of men, date from such an hour. All poets and heroes, like Memnon,* are the children of Aurora, and emit their music at sunrise. To him whose elastic and vigorous thought keeps pace with the sun, the day is a perpetual morning. It matters not what the clocks say or the attitudes and labors of men. Morning is when I am awake and there is a dawn in me. Moral reform is the effort to throw off sleep. Why is it that men give so poor an account of their day if they have not been slumbering? They are not such poor calculators. If they

King Tchingthang · Chinese king to whom this saying is attributed

Vedas · A body of sacred Hindu texts originating in ancient India

Memnon · Ethiopian king and warrior in Greek mythology who defended Troy and was killed by Achilles

had not been overcome with drowsiness, they would have per- 28
formed something. The millions are awake enough for physical
labor; but only one in a million is awake enough for effective
intellectual exertion, only one in a hundred millions to a poetic
or divine life. To be awake is to be alive. I have never yet met a
man who was quite awake. How could I have looked him in the
face? We must learn to reawaken and keep ourselves awake, not
by mechanical aids, but by an infinite expectation of the dawn,
which does not forsake us in our soundest sleep. I know of no
more encouraging fact than the unquestionable ability of man
to elevate his life by a conscious endeavor. It is something to be
able to paint a particular picture, or to carve a statue, and so to
make a few objects beautiful; but it is far more glorious to carve
and paint the very atmosphere and medium through which
we look, which morally we can do. To affect the quality of the
day, that is the highest of arts. Every man is tasked to make his
life, even in its details, worthy of the contemplation of his most
elevated and critical hour. If we refused, or rather used up, such
paltry information as we get, the oracles would distinctly inform
us how this might be done.

I went to the woods because I wished to live deliberately, to 29
front only the essential facts of life, and see if I could not learn
what it had to teach, and not, when I came to die, discover that
I had not lived. I did not wish to live what was not life, living is
so dear; nor did I wish to practise resignation, unless it was quite
necessary. I wanted to live deep and suck out all the marrow of
life, to live so sturdily and Spartan-like as to put to rout all that
was not life, to cut a broad swath and shave close, to drive life
into a corner, and reduce it to its lowest terms, and, if it proved
to be mean, why then to get the whole and genuine meanness of
it, and publish its meanness to the world; or if it were sublime,
to know it by experience, and be able to give a true account of it
in my next excursion. For most men, it appears to me, are in a
strange uncertainty about it, whether it is of the devil or of God,
and have somewhat hastily concluded that it is the chief end of
man here to "glorify God and enjoy him forever."

Still we live meanly, like ants; though the fable tells us that 30
we were long ago changed into men; like pygmies we fight with
cranes; it is error upon error, and clout upon clout, and our best

30 virtue has for its occasion a superfluous and evitable wretched-
ness. Our life is frittered away by detail. An honest man has
hardly need to count more than his ten fingers, or in extreme
cases he may add his ten toes, and lump the rest. Simplicity,
simplicity, simplicity! I say, let your affairs be as two or three,
and not a hundred or a thousand; instead of a million count half
a dozen, and keep your accounts on your thumb-nail. In the
midst of this chopping sea of civilized life, such are the clouds
and storms and quicksands and thousand-and-one items to be
allowed for, that a man has to live, if he would not founder and
go to the bottom and not make his port at all, by dead reckoning,
and he must be a great calculator indeed who succeeds. Simplify,
simplify. Instead of three meals a day, if it be necessary eat but
one; instead of a hundred dishes, five; and reduce other things in
proportion. Our life is like a German Confederacy, made up of
petty states, with its boundary forever fluctuating, so that even
a German cannot tell you how it is bounded at any moment.
The nation itself, with all its so-called internal improvements,
which, by the way are all external and superficial, is just such an
unwieldy and overgrown establishment, cluttered with furniture
and tripped up by its own traps, ruined by luxury and heedless
expense, by want of calculation and a worthy aim, as the million
households in the land; and the only cure for it, as for them, is
in a rigid economy, a stern and more than Spartan simplicity of
life and elevation of purpose. It lives too fast. Men think that it
is essential that the Nation have commerce, and export ice, and
talk through a telegraph, and ride thirty miles an hour, without
a doubt, whether they do or not; but whether we should live
like baboons or like men, is a little uncertain. If we do not get
out sleepers,* and forge rails, and devote days and nights to the   **sleepers ·** Railroad ties
work, but go to tinkering upon our lives to improve them, who
will build railroads? And if railroads are not built, how shall we
get to heaven in season? But if we stay at home and mind our
business, who will want railroads? We do not ride on the railroad;
it rides upon us. Did you ever think what those sleepers are that
underlie the railroad? Each one is a man, an Irishman, or a Yankee
man. The rails are laid on them, and they are covered with sand,
and the cars run smoothly over them. They are sound sleepers,
I assure you. And every few years a new lot is laid down and run

over; so that, if some have the pleasure of riding on a rail, others 30
have the misfortune to be ridden upon. And when they run over
a man that is walking in his sleep, a supernumerary sleeper in the
wrong position, and wake him up, they suddenly stop the cars,
and make a hue and cry about it, as if this were an exception. I
am glad to know that it takes a gang of men for every five miles
to keep the sleepers down and level in their beds as it is, for this
is a sign that they may sometime get up again.

Why should we live with such hurry and waste of life? We are 31
determined to be starved before we are hungry. Men say that a
stitch in time saves nine, and so they take a thousand stitches
today to save nine tomorrow. As for work, we haven't any of
any consequence. We have the Saint Vitus' dance,* and cannot

Saint Vitus' dance ·
A disease characterized
by rapid, jerking
movements

possibly keep our heads still. If I should only give a few pulls at
the parish bell-rope, as for a fire, that is, without setting the bell,
there is hardly a man on his farm in the outskirts of Concord,
notwithstanding that press of engagements which was his excuse
so many times this morning, nor a boy, nor a woman, I might
almost say, but would forsake all and follow that sound, not
mainly to save property from the flames, but, if we will confess
the truth, much more to see it burn, since burn it must, and we,
be it known, did not set it on fire – or to see it put out, and have
a hand in it, if that is done as handsomely; yes, even if it were
the parish church itself. Hardly a man takes a half-hour's nap
after dinner, but when he wakes he holds up his head and asks,
"What's the news?" as if the rest of mankind had stood his senti-
nels. Some give directions to be waked every half-hour, doubtless
for no other purpose; and then, to pay for it, they tell what they
have dreamed. After a night's sleep the news is as indispensable
as the breakfast. "Pray tell me anything new that has happened
to a man anywhere on this globe" – and he reads it over his coffee
and rolls, that a man has had his eyes gouged out this morning
on the Wachito River; never dreaming the while that he lives in
the dark unfathomed mammoth cave of this world, and has but
the rudiment of an eye himself.

For my part, I could easily do without the post-office. I think 32
that there are very few important communications made through
it. To speak critically, I never received more than one or two letters in my life – I wrote this some years ago – that were worth the

32 postage. The penny-post is, commonly, an institution through which you seriously offer a man that penny for his thoughts which is so often safely offered in jest. And I am sure that I never read any memorable news in a newspaper. If we read of one man robbed, or murdered, or killed by accident, or one house burned, or one vessel wrecked, or one steamboat blown up, or one cow run over on the Western Railroad, or one mad dog killed, or one lot of grasshoppers in the winter – we never need read of another. One is enough. If you are acquainted with the principle, what do you care for a myriad instances and applications? To a philosopher all news, as it is called, is gossip, and they who edit and read it are old women over their tea. Yet not a few are greedy after this gossip. There was such a rush, as I hear, the other day at one of the offices to learn the foreign news by the last arrival, that several large squares of plate glass belonging to the estab-lishment were broken by the pressure – news which I seriously think a ready wit might write a twelve-month, or twelve years, beforehand with sufficient accuracy. . . .

33 Shams and delusions are esteemed for soundest truths, while reality is fabulous. If men would steadily observe realities only, and not allow themselves to be deluded, life, to compare it with such things as we know, would be like a fairy tale and the Arabian Nights' Entertainments. If we respected only what is inevitable and has a right to be, music and poetry would resound along the streets. When we are unhurried and wise, we perceive that only great and worthy things have any permanent and absolute existence, that petty fears and petty pleasures are but the shadow of the reality. This is always exhilarating and sublime. By closing the eyes and slumbering, and consenting to be deceived by shows, men establish and confirm their daily life of routine and habit everywhere, which still is built on purely illusory foundations. Children, who play life, discern its true law and relations more clearly than men, who fail to live it worthily, but who think that they are wiser by experience, that is, by failure. I have read in a Hindoo book, that "there was a king's son, who, being expelled in infancy from his native city, was brought up by a forester, and, growing up to maturity in that state, imagined himself to belong to the barbarous race with which he lived. One of his father's ministers having discovered him, revealed to him what he was, and the misconception of his character was

removed, and he knew himself to be a prince. So soul," continues 33
the Hindoo philosopher, "from the circumstances in which it is
placed, mistakes its own character, until the truth is revealed to
it by some holy teacher, and then it knows itself to be Brahme." I
perceive that we inhabitants of New England live this mean life
that we do because our vision does not penetrate the surface of
things. We think that that is which appears to be. If a man should
walk through this town and see only the reality, where, think you,
would the "Mill-dam" go to? If he should give us an account of the
realities he beheld there, we should not recognize the place in his
description. Look at a meeting-house, or a court-house, or a jail,
or a shop, or a dwelling-house, and say what that thing really is
before a true gaze, and they would all go to pieces in your account
of them. Men esteem truth remote, in the outskirts of the system,
behind the farthest star, before Adam and after the last man. In
eternity there is indeed something true and sublime. But all these
times and places and occasions are now and here. God himself
culminates in the present moment, and will never be more divine
in the lapse of all the ages. And we are enabled to apprehend at
all what is sublime and noble only by the perpetual instilling and
drenching of the reality that surrounds us. The universe constantly
and obediently answers to our conceptions; whether we travel fast
or slow, the track is laid for us. Let us spend our lives in conceiving
then. The poet or the artist never yet had so fair and noble a design
but some of his posterity at least could accomplish it.

Let us spend one day as deliberately as Nature, and not be 34
thrown off the track by every nutshell and mosquito's wing that
falls on the rails. Let us rise early and fast, or break fast, gently and
without perturbation; let company come and let company go, let
the bells ring and the children cry – determined to make a day of
it. Why should we knock under and go with the stream? Let us not
be upset and overwhelmed in that terrible rapid and whirlpool
called a dinner, situated in the meridian shallows. Weather this
danger and you are safe, for the rest of the way is down hill. With
unrelaxed nerves, with morning vigor, sail by it, looking another
way, tied to the mast like Ulysses.* If the engine whistles, let it
whistle till it is hoarse for its pains. If the bell rings, why should
we run? We will consider what kind of music they are like. Let us
settle ourselves, and work and wedge our feet downward through

Ulysses · Latin name for Odysseus, who had himself tied to the mast of his ship to avoid being fatally tempted by the sirens' song

the mud and slush of opinion, and prejudice, and tradition, and delusion, and appearance, that alluvion* which covers the globe, through Paris and London, through New York and Boston and Concord, through Church and State, through poetry and philosophy and religion, till we come to a hard bottom and rocks in place, which we can call reality, and say, This is, and no mistake; and then begin, having a point d'appui,* below freshet and frost and fire, a place where you might found a wall or a state, or set a lamp-post safely, or perhaps a gauge, not a Nilometer,* but a Realometer, that future ages might know how deep a freshet of shams and appearances had gathered from time to time. If you stand right fronting and face to face to a fact, you will see the sun glimmer on both its surfaces, as if it were a cimeter,* and feel its sweet edge dividing you through the heart and marrow, and so you will happily conclude your mortal career. Be it life or death, we crave only reality. If we are really dying, let us hear the rattle in our throats and feel cold in the extremities; if we are alive, let us go about our business.

35   Time is but the stream I go a-fishing in. I drink at it; but while I drink I see the sandy bottom and detect how shallow it is. Its thin current slides away, but eternity remains. I would drink deeper; fish in the sky, whose bottom is pebbly with stars. I cannot count one. I know not the first letter of the alphabet. I have always been regretting that I was not as wise as the day I was born. The intellect is a cleaver; it discerns and rifts its way into the secret of things. I do not wish to be any more busy with my hands than is necessary. My head is hands and feet. I feel all my best faculties concentrated in it. My instinct tells me that my head is an organ for burrowing, as some creatures use their snout and fore paws, and with it I would mine and burrow my way through these hills. I think that the richest vein is somewhere hereabouts; so by the divining-rod and thin rising vapors I judge; and here I will begin to mine.

from CONCLUSION

36   I left the woods for as good a reason as I went there. Perhaps it seemed to me that I had several more lives to live, and could not spare any more time for that one. It is remarkable how easily and insensibly we fall into a particular route, and make a beaten

alluvion · Increase in the area of land due to sediment deposited by a river

point d'appui · Location where troops are assembled prior to a battle

Nilometer · An instrument for measuring water level of the Nile during flood season

A large curved cooking knife

track for ourselves. I had not lived there a week before my feet 36
wore a path from my door to the pond-side; and though it is
five or six years since I trod it, it is still quite distinct. It is true,
I fear, that others may have fallen into it, and so helped to keep
it open. The surface of the earth is soft and impressible by the
feet of men; and so with the paths which the mind travels. How
worn and dusty, then, must be the highways of the world, how
deep the ruts of tradition and conformity! I did not wish to take
a cabin passage, but rather to go before the mast and on the deck
of the world, for there I could best see the moonlight amid the
mountains. I do not wish to go below now.

I learned this, at least, by my experiment: that if one advances 37
confidently in the direction of his dreams, and endeavors to
live the life which he has imagined, he will meet with a success
unexpected in common hours. He will put some things behind,
will pass an invisible boundary; new, universal, and more liberal
laws will begin to establish themselves around and within him;
or the old laws be expanded, and interpreted in his favor in a
more liberal sense, and he will live with the license of a higher
order of beings. In proportion as he simplifies his life, the laws
of the universe will appear less complex, and solitude will not
be solitude, nor poverty poverty, nor weakness weakness. If you
have built castles in the air, your work need not be lost; that is
where they should be. Now put the foundations under them.

It is a ridiculous demand which England and America make, 38
that you shall speak so that they can understand you. Neither
men nor toadstools grow so. As if that were important, and
there were not enough to understand you without them. As if
Nature could support but one order of understandings, could
not sustain birds as well as quadrupeds, flying as well as creeping
things, and hush and whoa, which Bright can understand, were
the best English. As if there were safety in stupidity alone. I fear
chiefly lest my expression may not be extravagant enough, may
not wander far enough beyond the narrow limits of my daily
experience, so as to be adequate to the truth of which I have been
convinced. Extravagance! it depends on how you are yarded. The
migrating buffalo, which seeks new pastures in another latitude,
is not extravagant like the cow which kicks over the pail, leaps the
cowyard fence, and runs after her calf, in milking time. I desire

38   to speak somewhere without bounds; like a man in a waking moment, to men in their waking moments; for I am convinced that I cannot exaggerate enough even to lay the foundation of a true expression. Who that has heard a strain of music feared then lest he should speak extravagantly any more forever? In view of the future or possible, we should live quite laxly and undefined in front, our outlines dim and misty on that side; as our shadows reveal an insensible perspiration toward the sun. The volatile truth of our words should continually betray the inadequacy of the residual statement. Their truth is instantly translated; its literal monument alone remains. The words which express our faith and piety are not definite; yet they are significant and fragrant like frankincense to superior natures.

39   Why level downward to our dullest perception always, and praise that as common sense? The commonest sense is the sense of men asleep, which they express by snoring. Sometimes we are inclined to class those who are once-and-a-half-witted with the half-witted, because we appreciate only a third part of their wit. Some would find fault with the morning red, if they ever got up early enough. "They pretend," as I hear, "that the verses of Kabir* 'have four different senses; illusion, spirit, intellect, and the exoteric doctrine of the Vedas"; but in this part of the world it is considered a ground for complaint if a man's writings admit of more than one interpretation. While England endeavors to cure the potato-rot, will not any endeavor to cure the brain-rot, which prevails so much more widely and fatally?

Kabir · Hindu mystic poet

40   I do not suppose that I have attained to obscurity, but I should be proud if no more fatal fault were found with my pages on this score than was found with the Walden ice. Southern customers objected to its blue color, which is the evidence of its purity, as if it were muddy, and preferred the Cambridge ice, which is white, but tastes of weeds. The purity men love is like the mists which envelop the earth, and not like the azure ether beyond.

41   Some are dinning in our ears that we Americans, and moderns generally, are intellectual dwarfs compared with the ancients, or even the Elizabethan men. But what is that to the purpose? A living dog is better than a dead lion. Shall a man go and hang himself because he belongs to the race of pygmies, and not be the

biggest pygmy that he can? Let every one mind his own business, 41
and endeavor to be what he was made.

Why should we be in such desperate haste to succeed and in 42
such desperate enterprises? If a man does not keep pace with his
companions, perhaps it is because he hears a different drummer.
Let him step to the music which he hears, however measured or
far away. It is not important that he should mature as soon as an
apple tree or an oak. Shall he turn his spring into summer? If the
condition of things which we were made for is not yet, what were
any reality which we can substitute? We will not be shipwrecked
on a vain reality. Shall we with pains erect a heaven of blue glass
over ourselves, though when it is done we shall be sure to gaze still
at the true ethereal heaven far above, as if the former were not? . . .

No face which we can give to a matter will stead us so well 43
at last as the truth. This alone wears well. For the most part, we
are not where we are, but in a false position. Through an infinity
of our natures, we suppose a case, and put ourselves into it, and
hence are in two cases at the same time, and it is doubly difficult
to get out. In sane moments we regard only the facts, the case
that is. Say what you have to say, not what you ought. Any truth
is better than make-believe. Tom Hyde, the tinker, standing on
the gallows, was asked if he had anything to say. "Tell the tailors,"
said he, "to remember to make a knot in their thread before they
take the first stitch." His companion's prayer is forgotten.

However mean your life is, meet it and live it; do not shun it 44
and call it hard names. It is not so bad as you are. It looks poorest when you are richest. The fault-finder will find faults even
in paradise. Love your life, poor as it is. You may perhaps have
some pleasant, thrilling, glorious hours, even in a poorhouse.
The setting sun is reflected from the windows of the almshouse
as brightly as from the rich man's abode; the snow melts before
its door as early in the spring. I do not see but a quiet mind may
live as contentedly there, and have as cheering thoughts, as in
a palace. The town's poor seem to me often to live the most
independent lives of any. Maybe they are simply great enough to
receive without misgiving. Most think that they are above being
supported by the town; but it oftener happens that they are not
above supporting themselves by dishonest means, which should
be more disreputable. Cultivate poverty like a garden herb, like

44 sage. Do not trouble yourself much to get new things, whether clothes or friends. Turn the old; return to them. Things do not change; we change. Sell your clothes and keep your thoughts. God will see that you do not want society. If I were confined to a corner of a garret all my days, like a spider, the world would be just as large to me while I had my thoughts about me. The philosopher said: "From an army of three divisions one can take away its general, and put it in disorder; from the man the most abject and vulgar one cannot take away his thought." Do not seek so anxiously to be developed, to subject yourself to many influences to be played on; it is all dissipation. Humility like darkness reveals the heavenly lights. The shadows of poverty and meanness gather around us, "and lo! creation widens to our view." We are often reminded that if there were bestowed on us the wealth of Croesus,· our aims must still be the same, and our means essentially the same. Moreover, if you are restricted in your range by poverty, if you cannot buy books and newspapers, for instance, you are but confined to the most significant and vital experiences; you are compelled to deal with the material which yields the most sugar and the most starch. It is life near the bone where it is sweetest. You are defended from being a trifler. No man loses ever on a lower level by magnanimity on a higher. Superfluous wealth can buy superfluities only. Money is not required to buy one necessary of the soul.

wealth of Croesus · King of Lydia in 6th century BCE, renowned for his wealth

45 I live in the angle of a leaden wall, into whose composition was poured a little alloy of bell-metal. Often, in the repose of my mid-day, there reaches my ears a confused tintinnabulum from without. It is the noise of my contemporaries. My neighbors tell me of their adventures with famous gentlemen and ladies, what notabilities they met at the dinner-table; but I am no more interested in such things than in the contents of the Daily Times. The interest and the conversation are about costume and manners chiefly; but a goose is a goose still, dress it as you will. They tell me of California and Texas, of England and the Indies, of the Hon. Mr. – of Georgia or of Massachusetts, all transient and fleeting phenomena, till I am ready to leap from their court-yard like the Mameluke bey.· I delight to come to my bearings – not walk in procession with pomp and parade, in a conspicuous place, but to walk even with the Builder of the

Mameluke bey · Member of a military cast that ruled Egypt 1250–1517

universe, if I may – not to live in this restless, nervous, bustling, 45
trivial Nineteenth Century, but stand or sit thoughtfully while it
goes by. What are men celebrating? They are all on a committee
of arrangements, and hourly expect a speech from somebody.
God is only the president of the day, and Webster is his orator.
I love to weigh, to settle, to gravitate toward that which most
strongly and rightfully attracts me – not hang by the beam of
the scale and try to weigh less – not suppose a case, but take the
case that is; to travel the only path I can, and that on which no
power can resist me. It affords me no satisfaction to commerce
to spring an arch before I have got a solid foundation. Let us not
play at kittly-benders.* There is a solid bottom everywhere. We
read that the traveller asked the boy if the swamp before him
had a hard bottom. The boy replied that it had. But presently the
traveller's horse sank in up to the girths, and he observed to the
boy, "I thought you said that this bog had a hard bottom." "So
it has," answered the latter, "but you have not got half way to it
yet." So it is with the bogs and quicksands of society; but he is
an old boy that knows it. Only what is thought, said, or done at
a certain rare coincidence is good. I would not be one of those
who will foolishly drive a nail into mere lath and plastering; such
a deed would keep me awake nights. Give me a hammer, and
let me feel for the furring. Do not depend on the putty. Drive a
nail home and clinch it so faithfully that you can wake up in the
night and think of your work with satisfaction – a work at which
you would not be ashamed to invoke the Muse.* So will help you
God, and so only. Every nail driven should be as another rivet in
the machine of the universe, you carrying on the work.

Rather than love, than money, than fame, give me truth. I 46
sat at a table where were rich food and wine in abundance, and
obsequious attendance, but sincerity and truth were not; and I
went away hungry from the inhospitable board. The hospitality
was as cold as the ices. I thought that there was no need of ice
to freeze them. They talked to me of the age of the wine and the
fame of the vintage; but I thought of an older, a newer, and purer
wine, of a more glorious vintage, which they had not got, and
could not buy. The style, the house and grounds and "entertainment" pass for nothing with me. I called on the king, but he made
me wait in his hall, and conducted like a man incapacitated for

kittly-benders · A game in which children would dare each other to skate on thin ice

Muse · Goddesses or spirits in Greek mythology who inspire creation of literature and the arts

hospitality. There was a man in my neighborhood who lived in a hollow tree. His manners were truly regal. I should have done better had I called on him.

47 How long shall we sit in our porticoes practising idle and musty virtues, which any work would make impertinent? As if one were to begin the day with long-suffering, and hire a man to hoe his potatoes; and in the afternoon go forth to practise Christian meekness and charity with goodness aforethought! Consider the China pride and stagnant self-complacency of mankind. This generation inclines a little to congratulate itself on being the last of an illustrious line; and in Boston and London and Paris and Rome, thinking of its long descent, it speaks of its progress in art and science and literature with satisfaction. There are the Records of the Philosophical Societies, and the public Eulogies of Great Men! It is the good Adam contemplating his own virtue. "Yes, we have done great deeds, and sung divine songs, which shall never die" – that is, as long as we can remember them. The learned societies and great men of Assyria – where are they? What youthful philosophers and experimentalists we are! There is not one of my readers who has yet lived a whole human life. These may be but the spring months in the life of the race. If we have had the seven-years' itch, we have not seen the seventeen-year locust yet in Concord. We are acquainted with a mere pellicle of the globe on which we live. Most have not delved six feet beneath the surface, nor leaped as many above it. We know not where we are. Beside, we are sound asleep nearly half our time. Yet we esteem ourselves wise, and have an established order on the surface. Truly, we are deep thinkers, we are ambitious spirits! As I stand over the insect crawling amid the pine needles on the forest floor, and endeavoring to conceal itself from my sight, and ask myself why it will cherish those humble thoughts, and bide its head from me who might, perhaps, be its benefactor, and impart to its race some cheering information, I am reminded of the greater Benefactor and Intelligence that stands over me the human insect.

48 There is an incessant influx of novelty into the world, and yet we tolerate incredible dulness. I need only suggest what kind of sermons are still listened to in the most enlightened countries. There are such words as joy and sorrow, but they are only the

burden of a psalm, sung with a nasal twang, while we believe 48 in the ordinary and mean. We think that we can change our clothes only. It is said that the British Empire is very large and respectable, and that the United States are a first-rate power. We do not believe that a tide rises and falls behind every man which can float the British Empire like a chip, if he should ever harbor it in his mind. Who knows what sort of seventeen-year locust will next come out of the ground? The government of the world I live in was not framed, like that of Britain, in after-dinner conversations over the wine.

The life in us is like the water in the river. It may rise this 49 year higher than man has ever known it, and flood the parched uplands; even this may be the eventful year, which will drown out all our muskrats. It was not always dry land where we dwell. I see far inland the banks which the stream anciently washed, before science began to record its freshets. Every one has heard the story which has gone the rounds of New England, of a strong and beautiful bug which came out of the dry leaf of an old table of apple-tree wood, which had stood in a farmer's kitchen for sixty years, first in Connecticut, and afterward in Massachusetts – from an egg deposited in the living tree many years earlier still, as appeared by counting the annual layers beyond it; which was heard gnawing out for several weeks, hatched perchance by the heat of an urn. Who does not feel his faith in a resurrection and immortality strengthened by hearing of this? Who knows what beautiful and winged life, whose egg has been buried for ages under many concentric layers of woodenness **alburnum** · sapwood in the dead dry life of society, deposited at first in the alburnum* of the green and living tree, which has been gradually converted into the semblance of its well-seasoned tomb – heard perchance gnawing out now for years by the astonished family of man, as they sat round the festive board – may unexpectedly come forth from amidst society's most trivial and handselled furniture, to enjoy its perfect summer life at last! I do not say that John or Jonathan will realize all this; but such is the character of that morrow which mere lapse of time can never make to dawn. The light which puts out our eyes is darkness to us. Only that day dawns to which we are awake. There is more day to dawn. The sun is but a morning star.

Frederick Douglass

◀{ 1 8 1 8 − 1 8 9 5 }▶

Frederick Augustus Washington Bailey (later Douglass) was born in Maryland. His mother was a slave and his father an unknown white slaveholder. After several heartrending attempts for freedom, he was finally victorious on September 3, 1838, when he escaped to New York. While there, Douglass married Anna Murray, a free black woman, and the one who was instrumental in helping him escape. They journeyed to New Bedford, Massachusetts, where Douglass began a career that would dramatically change his life. While attending a convention of the Massachusetts Anti-Slavery Society in Nantucket, Douglass was overheard sharing his experiences as a slave with some of his friends. A leading abolitionist was drawn to his story, and he persuaded the reluctant Douglass to share it at the convention. He was so nervous that he made several blunders during the address. He thought his speech was a disaster, but the assembly thought otherwise. Those present loved his sincere passion and his captivating voice. They were so impressed with his story that they immediately employed him as a traveling lecturer and a social activist for their cause. After the publication of his narrative, he fled to Great Britain to avoid persecution and capture. In 1847, he returned to the United States, buying his own freedom and establishing a newspaper for the black race, the North Star. During the Civil War, he was invited several times by President Lincoln to discuss matters concerning black soldiers in the Union Army. In 1877, he was appointed United States Marshal for the District of Columbia and in 1881, Recorder of Deeds. In 1884, Douglass married again. His second wife, Helen Pitts, was a white woman, and this marriage brought criticism and controversy. Douglass was an activist to the very end of his life. On February 20, 1895, after delivering a passionate speech at a woman-suffrage convention, he died of a heart attack.

from THE LIFE OF FREDERICK DOUGLASS

I HAVE HAD TWO MASTERS. My first master's name was Anthony. I do not remember his first name. He was generally called Captain Anthony – a title which, I presume, he acquired by sailing a craft on the Chesapeake Bay. He was not considered a rich slaveholder. He owned two or three farms, and about thirty slaves. His farms and slaves were under the care of an overseer. The overseer's name was Plummer. Mr. Plummer was a miserable drunkard, a profane swearer, and a savage monster. He always went armed with a cowskin* and a heavy cudgel.* I have known him to cut and slash the women's heads so horribly, that even master would be enraged at his cruelty, and would threaten to whip him if he did not mind himself. Master, however, was not a humane slaveholder. It required extraordinary barbarity on the part of an overseer to affect him. He was a cruel man, hardened by a long life of slaveholding. He would at times seem to take great pleasure in whipping a slave. I have often been awakened at the dawn of day by the most heart-rending shrieks of an old aunt of mine, whom he used to tie up to a joist, and whip upon her naked back till she was literally covered with blood. No words, no tears, no prayers, from his gory victim, seemed to move his iron heart from its bloody purpose. The louder she screamed, the harder he whipped; and where the blood ran fastest, there he whipped longest. He would whip her to make her scream, and whip her to make her hush; and not until overcome by fatigue, would he cease to swing the blood-clotted cowskin. I remember the first time I ever witnessed this horrible exhibition. I was quite a child, but I well remember it. I never shall forget it whilst I remember any thing. It was the first of a long series of such outrages, of which I was doomed to be a witness and a participant. It struck me with awful force. It was the blood-stained gate, the entrance to the hell of slavery, through which I was about to pass. It was a most terrible spectacle. I wish I could commit to paper the feelings with which I beheld it.

This occurrence took place very soon after I went to live with my old master, and under the following circumstances. Aunt Hester went out one night, – where or for what I do not know – and happened to be absent when my master desired

cowskin · a leather whip

cudgel · a short, heavy club

1

2

2 her presence. He had ordered her not to go out evenings and warned her that she must never let him catch her in company with a young man, who was paying attention to her, belonging to Colonel Lloyd. The young man's name was Ned Roberts, generally called Lloyd's Ned. Why master was so careful of her, may be safely left to conjecture. She was a woman of noble form, and of graceful proportions, having very few equals, and fewer superiors, in personal appearance, among the colored or white women of our neighborhood.

3 Aunt Hester had not only disobeyed his orders in going out, but had been found in company with Lloyd's Ned; which circumstance, I found, from what he said while whipping her, was the chief offence. Had he been a man of pure morals himself, he might have been thought interested in protecting the innocence of my aunt; but those who knew him will not suspect him of any such virtue. Before he commenced whipping Aunt Hester, he took her into the kitchen, and stripped her from neck to waist, leaving her neck, shoulders, and back, entirely naked. He then told her to cross her hands, calling her at the same time a d – d b – h. After crossing her hands, he tied them with a strong rope, and led her to a stool under a large hook in the joist, put in for the purpose. He made her get upon the stool, and tied her hands to the hook. She now stood fair for his infernal purpose. Her arms were stretched up at their full length, so that she stood upon the ends of her toes. He then said to her, "Now, you d – d b – h, I'll learn you how to disobey my orders!" and after rolling up his sleeves, he commenced to lay on the heavy cowskin, and soon the warm, red blood (amid heartrending shrieks from her, and horrid oaths from him) came dripping to the floor. I was so terrified and horror-stricken at the sight, that I hid myself in a closet, and dared not venture out till long after the bloody transaction was over. I expected it would be my turn next. It was all new to me. I had never seen any thing like it before. I had always lived with my grandmother on the outskirts of the plantation, where she was put to raise the children of the younger women. I had therefore been, until now, out of the way of the bloody scenes that often occurred on the plantation.

4 I lived with Mr. Covey one year. During the first six months, of that year, scarce a week passed without his whipping me. I was

seldom free from a sore back. My awkwardness was almost always 4
his excuse for whipping me. We were worked fully up to the point
of endurance. Long before day we were up, our horses fed, and
by the first approach of day we were off to the field with our hoes
and ploughing teams. Mr. Covey gave us enough to eat, but scarce
time to eat it. We were often less than five minutes taking our
meals. We were often in the field from the first approach of day
till its last lingering ray had left us; and at saving-fodder time,·
midnight often caught us in the field binding blades.

saving-fodder time · the late fall, after initial harvest, when corn stalks are gathered to be mixed with hay to make animal feed for the winter

Covey would be out with us. The way he used to stand it, was 5
this. He would spend the most of his afternoons in bed. He would
then come out fresh in the evening, ready to urge us on with his
words, example, and frequently with the whip. Mr. Covey was one
of the few slaveholders who could and did work with his hands.
He was a hard-working man. He knew by himself just what a man
or a boy could do. There was no deceiving him. His work went on
in his absence almost as well as in his presence; and he had the
faculty of making us feel that he was ever present with us. This he
did by surprising us. He seldom approached the spot where we
were at work openly, if he could do it secretly. He always aimed
at taking us by surprise. Such was his cunning, that we used to
call him, among ourselves, "the snake." When we were at work in
the cornfield, he would sometimes crawl on his hands and knees
to avoid detection, and all at once he would rise nearly in our
midst, and scream out, "Ha, ha! Come, come! Dash on, dash on!"
This being his mode of attack, it was never safe to stop a single
minute. His comings were like a thief in the night.· He appeared
to us as being ever at hand. He was under every tree, behind every
stump, in every bush, and at every window, on the plantation. He
would sometimes mount his horse, as if bound to St. Michael's, a
distance of seven miles, and in half an hour afterwards you would
see him coiled up in the corner of the wood-fence, watching every
motion of the slaves. He would, for this purpose, leave his horse
tied up in the woods. Again, he would sometimes walk up to us,
and give us orders as though he was upon the point of starting
on a long journey, turn his back upon us, and make as though he
was going to the house to get ready; and, before he would get half
way thither, he would turn short and crawl into a fence-corner, or
behind some tree, and there watch us till the going down of the sun.

His comings … night · see 1 Thessalonians 5:20, 2 Peter 3:10

6   Mr. Covey's *forté* consisted in his power to deceive. His life was devoted to planning and perpetrating the grossest deceptions. Every thing he possessed in the shape of learning or religion, he made conform to his disposition to deceive. He seemed to think himself equal to deceiving the Almighty. He would make a short prayer in the morning, and a long prayer at night; and, strange as it may seem, few men would at times appear more devotional than he. The exercises of his family devotions were always commenced with singing; and, as he was a very poor singer himself, the duty of raising the hymn generally came upon me. He would read his hymn, and nod at me to commence. I would at times do so; at others, I would not. My non-compliance would almost always produce much confusion. To show himself independent of me, he would start and stagger through with his hymn in the most discordant manner. In this state of mind, he prayed with more than ordinary spirit. Poor man! such was his disposition, and success at deceiving, I do verily believe that he sometimes deceived himself into the solemn belief, that he was a sincere worshipper of the most high God; and this, too, at a time when he may be said to have been guilty of compelling his woman slave to commit the sin of adultery. The facts in the case are these: Mr. Covey was a poor man; he was just commencing in life; he was only able to buy one slave; and, shocking as is the fact, he bought her, as he said, for a *breeder.* This woman was named Caroline. Mr. Covey bought her from Mr. Thomas Lowe, about six miles from St. Michael's. She was a large, able-bodied woman, about twenty years old. She had already given birth to one child, which proved her to be just what he wanted. After buying her, he hired a married man of Mr. Samuel Harrison, to live with him one year; and him he used to fasten up with her every night! The result was, that, at the end of the year, the miserable woman gave birth to twins. At this result Mr. Covey seemed to be highly pleased, both with the man and the wretched woman. Such was his joy, and that of his wife, that nothing they could do for Caroline during her confinement* was too good, or too hard, to be done. The children were regarded as being quite an addition to his wealth.

confinement · a euphemism referring to the time of pregnancy

7   If at any one time of my life more than another, I was made to drink the bitterest dregs of slavery, that time was during the

first six months of my stay with Mr. Covey. We were worked in 7
all weathers. It was never too hot or too cold; it could never rain,
blow, hail, or snow too hard for us to work in the field. Work,
work, work, was scarcely more the order of the day than of the
night. The longest days were too short for him, and the shortest
nights too long for him. I was somewhat unmanageable when I
first went there, but a few months of this discipline tamed me. Mr.
Covey succeeded in breaking me. I was broken in body, soul, and
spirit. My natural elasticity was crushed, my intellect languished,
the disposition to read departed, the cheerful spark that lingered
about my eye died; the dark night of slavery closed in upon me;
and behold a man transformed into a brute!

Sunday was my only leisure time. I spent this in a sort of 8
beast-like stupor, between sleep and wake, under some large
tree. At times I would rise up, a flash of energetic freedom would
dart through my soul, accompanied with a faint beam of hope,
that flickered for a moment, and then vanished. I sank down
again, mourning over my wretched condition. I was sometimes
prompted to take my life, and that of Covey, but was prevented by
a combination of hope and fear. My sufferings on this plantation
seem now like a dream rather than a stern reality.

a few rods · a rod is a
unit of measure equal
to 5.5 yards (16.5 feet)

Our house stood within a few rods* of the Chesapeake Bay, 9
whose broad bosom was ever white with sails from every quarter
of the habitable globe. Those beautiful vessels, robed in purest
white, so delightful to the eye of freemen, were to me so many
shrouded ghosts, to terrify and torment me with thoughts of
my wretched condition. I have often, in the deep stillness of a
summer's Sabbath, stood all alone upon the lofty banks of that
noble bay, and traced, with saddened heart and tearful eye, the
countless number of sails moving off to the mighty ocean. The
sight of these always affected me powerfully. My thoughts would
compel utterance; and there, with no audience but the Almighty,
I would pour out my soul's complaint, in my rude* way, with an
apostrophe* to the moving multitude of ships: –

rude · uncouth, with-
out formal training

apostrophe · a digres-
sion, often addressed to
an absent or imagined
other

"You are loosed from your moorings, and are free; I am fast in 10
my chains, and am a slave! You move merrily before the gentle
gale, and I sadly before the bloody whip! You are freedom's
swift-winged angels, that fly round the world; I am confined in
bands of iron! O that I were free! O, that I were on one of your

10 gallant decks, and under your protecting wing! Alas! betwixt me and you, the turbid waters roll. Go on, go on. O that I could also go! Could I but swim! If I could fly! O, why was I born a man, of whom to make a brute! The glad ship is gone; she hides in the dim distance. I am left in the hottest hell of unending slavery. O God, save me! God, deliver me! Let me be free! Is there any God? Why am I a slave? I will run away. I will not stand it. Get caught, or get clear, I'll try it. I had as well die with ague as the fever. I have only one life to lose. I had as well be killed running as die standing. Only think of it; one hundred miles straight north, and I am free! Try it? Yes! God helping me, I will. It cannot be that I shall live and die a slave. I will take to the water. This very bay shall bear me into freedom. The steamboats steered in a north-east course from North Point. I will do the same; and when I get to the head of the bay, I will turn my canoe adrift, and walk straight through Delaware into Pennsylvania. When I get there, I shall not be required to have a pass; I can travel without being disturbed. Let but the first opportunity offer, and, come what will, I am off. Meanwhile, I will try to bear up under the yoke. I am not the only slave in the world. Why should I fret? I can bear as much as any of them. Besides, I am but a boy, and all boys are bound to some one. It may be that my misery in slavery will only increase my happiness when I get free. There is a better day coming."

11 Thus I used to think, and thus I used to speak to myself; goaded almost to madness at one moment, and at the next reconciling myself to my wretched lot.

APPENDIX

12 I FIND, SINCE READING OVER the foregoing Narrative that I have, in several instances, spoken in such a tone and manner, respecting religion, as may possibly lead those unacquainted with my religious views to suppose me an opponent of all religion. To remove the liability of such misapprehension, I deem it proper to append the following brief explanation. What I have said respecting and against religion, I mean strictly to apply to the *slaveholding religion* of this land, and with no possible reference to Christianity proper; for, between the Christianity of this land, and the Christianity of Christ, I recognize the

widest possible difference – so wide, that to receive the one as 12
good, pure, and holy, is of necessity to reject the other as bad,
corrupt, and wicked. To be the friend of the one, is of necessity
to be the enemy of the other. I love the pure, peaceable, and
impartial Christianity of Christ: I therefore hate the corrupt,
slaveholding, women-whipping, cradle-plundering, partial and
hypocritical Christianity of this land. Indeed, I can see no reason,
but the most deceitful one, for calling the religion of this land
Christianity. I look upon it as the climax of all misnomers, the
boldest of all frauds, and the grossest of all libels. Never was
there a clearer case of "stealing the livery* of the court of heaven
to serve the devil in." I am filled with unutterable loathing when
I contemplate the religious pomp and show, together with the
horrible inconsistencies, which everywhere surround me. We
have men-stealers for ministers, women worshippers for missionaries, and cradle-plunderers for church members. The man
who wields the blood-clotted cowskin during the week fills the
pulpit on Sunday, and claims to be a minister of the meek and
lowly Jesus. The man who robs me of my earnings at the end
of each week meets me as a class-leader on Sunday morning,
to show me the way of life, and the path of salvation. He who
sells my sister, for purposes of prostitution, stands forth as the
pious advocate of purity. He who proclaims it a religious duty to
read the Bible denies me the right of learning to read the name
of the God who made me. He who is the religious advocate of
marriage robs whole millions of its sacred influence, and leaves
them to the ravages of wholesale pollution. The warm defender
of the sacredness of the family relation is the same that scatters
whole families, – sundering husbands and wives, parents and
children, sisters and brothers, – leaving the hut vacant, and the
hearth desolate. We see the thief preaching against theft, and the
adulterer against adultery. We have men sold to build churches,
women sold to support the gospel, and babes sold to purchase
Bibles for the *poor heathen! all for the glory of God and the good
of souls!* The slave auctioneer's bell and the church-going bell
chime in with each other, and the bitter cries of the heart-broken
slave are drowned in the religious shouts of his pious master.
Revivals of religion and revivals in the slave-trade go hand in
hand together. The slave prison and the church stand near each

livery · the uniform or distinctive dress worn by the servants of a lord or master. The quotation is taken from *The Course of Time* by popular Scottish religious poet Robert Pollok (1798–1827)

12   other. The clanking of fetters and the rattling of chains in the prison, and the pious psalm and solemn prayer in the church, may be heard at the same time. The dealers in the bodies and souls of men erect their stand in the presence of the pulpit, and they mutually help each other. The dealer gives his blood-stained gold to support the pulpit, and the pulpit, in return, covers his infernal business with the garb of Christianity. Here we have religion and robbery the allies of each other – devils dressed in angels' robes, and hell presenting the semblance of paradise.

12a   Just God! and these are they,
       Who minister at thine altar, God of right!
       Men who their hands, with prayer and blessing, lay
       On Israel's ark of light.

12b   What! preach, and kidnap men?
       Give thanks, and rob thy own afflicted poor?
       Talk of thy glorious liberty, and then
       Bolt hard the captive's door?

12c   What! servants of thy own
       Merciful son, who came to seek and save
       The homeless and the outcast, fettering down
       The tasked and plundered slave!

12d   Pilate* and Herod* friends!
       Chief priests and rulers, as of old, combine!
       Just God and holy! is that church which lends
       Strength to the spoiler thine?

13   The Christianity of America is a Christianity, of whose votaries* it may be as truly said, as it was of the ancient scribes and Pharisees,* "They bind heavy burdens, and grievous to be borne, and lay them on men's shoulders, but they themselves will not move them with one of their fingers. All their works they do for to be seen of men. – They love the uppermost rooms at feasts, and the chief seats in the synagogues, ... and to be called by men, Rabbi, Rabbi. – But woe unto you, scribes and Pharisees, hypocrites! for ye shut up the kingdom of heaven against men; for ye neither go in yourselves, neither suffer ye them that are entering to go in. Ye devour widows' houses, and for a pretence

Pilate · Pontius Pilate (d 36), Roman prefect of Judea under the emperor Tiberius; he presided at the trial of Jesus and gave the order for his crucifixion

Herod · Herod Antipas (21 BC–39), tetrarch of Galilee who ruled throughout Jesus' life. When Pilate sent Jesus to Herod for condemnation, Herod was unwilling to pass judgment

votaries · those bound to live a life of religious service, those who have affiliated themselves formally with a particular religious movement

scribes and Pharisees · members of the religious elite whom Jesus routinely condemned for their hypocrisy and evil ways

"They bind ... iniq-
uity" · this lengthy
passage is taken from
Matthew 23:4–29

make long prayers; therefore ye shall receive the greater damna- 13
tion. Ye compass sea and land to make one proselyte, and when
he is made, ye make him twofold more the child of hell than
yourselves. – Woe unto you, scribes and Pharisees, hypocrites!
for ye pay tithe of mint, and anise, and cumin, and have omitted
the weightier matters of the law, judgment, mercy, and faith;
these ought ye to have done, and not to leave the other undone.
Ye blind guides! which strain at a gnat, and swallow a camel. Woe
unto you, scribes and Pharisees, hypocrites! for ye make clean
the outside of the cup and of the platter; but within, they are full
of extortion and excess. Woe unto you, scribes and Pharisees,
hypocrites! for ye are like unto whited sepulchres, which indeed
appear beautiful outward, but are within full of dead men's bones,
and of all uncleanness. Even so ye also outwardly appear righteous unto men, but within ye are full of hypocrisy and iniquity."*

Dark and terrible as is this picture, I hold it to be strictly true
of the overwhelming mass of professed Christians in America. 14
They strain at a gnat, and swallow a camel. Could any thing be
more true of our churches? They would be shocked at the proposition of fellowshipping a sheep-stealer; and at the same time
they hug to their communion a man-stealer, and brand me with
being an infidel, if I find fault with them for it. They attend with
Pharisaical strictness to the outward forms of religion, and at the
same time neglect the weightier matters of the law, judgment,
mercy, and faith. They are always ready to sacrifice, but seldom
to show mercy. They are they who are represented as profess-
ing to love God whom they have not seen, whilst they hate their
brother whom they have seen. They love the heathen on the other
side of the globe. They can pray for him, pay money to have the
Bible put into his hand, and missionaries to instruct him; while
they despise and totally neglect the heathen at their own doors.

Such is, very briefly, my view of the religion of this land; and
to avoid any misunderstanding, growing out of the use of general 15
terms, I mean, by the religion of this land, that which is revealed
in the words, deeds, and actions, of those bodies, north and south,
calling themselves Christian churches, and yet in union with
slaveholders. It is against religion, as presented by these bodies,
that I have felt it my duty to testify.

John Muir

◀(1838-1914)▶

When John Muir was ten years old, his father enthusiastically joined the Stone-Campbell movement, a religious group that gave rise to the present-day denominations of the Disciples of Christ, Christian Churches, and Churches of Christ. With other follow-ers of this movement, the family quickly emigrated from Scotland to Wisconsin, where John Muir worked long hours clearing their homestead while his father traveled as a lay preacher. Made to memorize the entire New Testament and much of the Old, Muir developed a sense of resentment toward his father's faith along-side a growing interest in both mechanical invention and natural history. At age twenty-nine, he was temporarily blinded in a fac-tory accident and put aside a conventional career. "I might have become a millionaire," he later said. "Instead I chose to become a tramp." After walking a thousand miles to the Gulf of Mexico, he boarded a boat to California and more or less remained there for the rest of his peripatetic life. In the summer of 1869 he accompanied a herd of sheep into the Sierra Nevada in what is now Yosemite National Park. Ecstatic with what he found there, he wrote about the Sierra in a biblically resonant language that did much to inspire support for preservation of wild areas in the United States. In 1892 he helped to found the Sierra Club and served as its first president. The following excerpts are taken from My First Summer in the Sierra *(1911), a revision of the journal he kept in 1869.*

from MY FIRST SUMMER IN THE SIERRA

THROUGH THE FOOTHILLS

1 JUNE 6. WE ARE NOW ON WHAT may be called the second bench or plateau of the Range, after making many small ups

and downs over belts of hill-waves, with, of course, correspond- 1
ing changes in the vegetation. In open spots many of the lowland

compositae ·
composite flowers

compositae* are still to be found, and some of the Mariposa
tulips and other conspicuous members of the lily family; but
the characteristic blue oak of the foothills is left below, and its

***Quercus californica* ·**
California black oak

place is taken by a fine large species (*Quercus californica*)* with
deeply lobed deciduous leaves, picturesquely divided trunk,
and broad, massy, finely lobed and modeled head. Here also at
a height of about twenty-five hundred feet we come to the edge

yellow pine ·
ponderosa pine

of the great coniferous forest, made up mostly of yellow pine*
with just a few sugar pines. We are now in the mountains and
they are in us, kindling enthusiasm, making every nerve quiver,
filling every pore and cell of us. Our flesh-and-bone tabernacle
seems transparent as glass to the beauty about us, as if truly an
inseparable part of it, thrilling with the air and trees, streams
and rocks, in the waves of the sun, – a part of all nature, neither
old nor young, sick nor well, but immortal. Just now I can hardly
conceive of any bodily condition dependent on food or breath
any more than the ground or the sky. How glorious a conversion,
so complete and wholesome it is, scarce memory enough of old
bondage days left as a standpoint to view it from! In this newness
of life we seem to have been so always.

Through a meadow opening in the pine woods I see snowy 2

Yosemite · Yosemite
Valley

peaks about the headwaters of the Merced above Yosemite.*
How near they seem and how clear their outlines on the blue
air, or rather *in* the blue air; for they seem to be saturated with
it. How consuming strong the invitation they extend! Shall I be
allowed to go to them? Night and day I'll pray that I may, but
it seems too good to be true. Some one worthy will go, able for
the Godful work, yet as far as I can I must drift about these
love-monument mountains, glad to be a servant of servants in
so holy a wilderness.

✦ ✦ ✦

THE YOSEMITE

*J*ULY 15. FOLLOWED THE MONO TRAIL up the eastern rim of 3
the basin nearly to its summit, then turned off southward to
a small shallow valley that extends to the edge of the Yosemite,
which we reached about noon, and encamped. After luncheon I

3   made haste to high ground, and from the top of the ridge on the
west side of Indian Cañon gained the noblest view of the summit
peaks I have ever yet enjoyed. Nearly all the upper basin of the
Merced was displayed, with its sublime domes and cañons, dark
upsweeping forests, and glorious array of white peaks deep in
the sky, every feature glowing, radiating beauty that pours into
our flesh and bones like heat rays from fire. Sunshine over all;
no breath of wind to stir the brooding calm. Never before had I
seen so glorious a landscape, so boundless an affluence of sublime
mountain beauty. The most extravagant description I might give
of this view to anyone who has not seen similar landscapes with
his own eyes would not so much as hint its grandeur and the
spiritual glow that covered it. I shouted and gesticulated in a wild
burst of ecstasy, much to the astonishment of St. Bernard Carlo,
who came running up to me, manifesting in his intelligent eyes
a puzzled concern that was very ludicrous, which had the effect
of bringing me to my senses. A brown bear, too, it would seem,
had been a spectator of the show I had made of myself, for I had
gone but a few yards when I started one from a thicket of brush.
He evidently considered me dangerous, for he ran away very
fast, tumbling over the tops of the tangled manzanita bushes in
his haste. Carlo drew back, with his ears depressed as if afraid,
and kept looking me in the face, as if expecting me to pursue and
shoot, for he had seen many a bear battle in his day.

4   Following the ridge, which made a gradual descent to the
south, I came at length to the brow of that massive cliff that
stands between Indian Cañon and Yosemite Falls, and here the
far-famed valley came suddenly into view throughout almost its
whole extent. The noble walls – sculptured into endless variety of
domes and gables, spires and battlements and plain mural preci-
pices – all a-tremble with the thunder tones of the falling water.
The level bottom seemed to be dressed like a garden – sunny
meadows here and there, and groves of pine and oak; the river
of Mercy sweeping in majesty through the midst of them and
flashing back the sunbeams. The great Tissiack, or Half-Dome,
rising at the upper end of the valley to a height of nearly a mile,
is nobly proportioned and life-like, the most impressive of all
the rocks, holding the eye in devout admiration, calling it back
again and again from falls or meadows, or even the mountains

beyond, – marvelous cliffs, marvelous in sheer dizzy depth and 4
sculpture, types of endurance. Thousands of years have they
stood in the sky exposed to rain, snow, frost, earthquake and
avalanche, yet they still wear the bloom of youth.

I rambled along the valley rim to the westward; most of it is 5
rounded off on the very brink, so that it is not easy to find places
where one may look clear down the face of the wall to the bottom.
When such places were found, and I had cautiously set my feet
and drawn my body erect, I could not help fearing a little that the
rock might split off and let me down, and what a down! – more
than three thousand feet. Still, my limbs did not tremble, nor
did I feel the least uncertainty as to the reliance to be placed
on them. My only fear was that a flake of the granite, which in
some places showed joints more or less open and running parallel with the face of the cliff, might give way. After withdrawing
from such places, excited with the view I had got, I would say to
myself, "Now don't go out on the verge again." But in the face of
Yosemite scenery cautious remonstrance is vain; under its spell
one's body seems to go where it likes with a will over which we
seem to have scarce any control.

After a mile or so of this memorable cliff work I approached 6
Yosemite Creek, admiring its easy, graceful, confident gestures
as it comes bravely forward in its narrow channel, singing the
last of its mountain songs on its way to its fate – a few rods more
over the shining granite, then down half a mile in showy foam to
another world, to be lost in the Merced, where climate, vegetation, inhabitants, all are different. Emerging from its last gorge,
it glides in wide lace-like rapids down a smooth incline into a
pool where it seems to rest and compose its gray, agitated waters
before taking the grand plunge, then slowly slipping over the lip
of the pool basin, it descends another glossy slope with rapidly
accelerated speed to the brink of the tremendous cliff, and with
sublime, fateful confidence springs out free in the air.

I took off my shoes and stockings and worked my way cau- 7
tiously down alongside the rushing flood, keeping my feet and
hands pressed firmly on the polished rock. The booming, roaring
water, rushing past close to my head, was very exciting. I had
expected that the sloping apron would terminate with the per-
pendicular wall of the valley, and that from the foot of it, where

7 it is less steeply inclined, I should be able to lean far enough out to see the forms and behavior of the fall all the way down to the bottom. But I found that there was yet another small brow over which I could not see, and which appeared to be too steep for mortal feet. Scanning it keenly, I discovered a narrow shelf about three inches wide on the very brink, just wide enough for a rest for one's heels. But there seemed to be no way of reaching it over so steep a brow. At length, after careful scrutiny of the surface, I found an irregular edge of a flake of the rock some distance back from the margin of the torrent. If I was to get down to the brink at all that rough edge, which might offer slight finger-holds, was the only way. But the slope beside it looked dangerously smooth and steep, and the swift roaring flood beneath, overhead, and beside me was very nerve-trying. I therefore concluded not to venture farther, but did nevertheless. Tufts of artemisia* were **artemisia ·** sagebrush growing in clefts of the rock nearby, and I filled my mouth with the bitter leaves, hoping they might help to prevent giddiness. Then, with a caution not known in ordinary circumstances, I crept down safely to the little ledge, got my heels well planted on it, then shuffled in a horizontal direction twenty or thirty feet until close to the outplunging current, which, by the time it had descended thus far, was already white. Here I obtained a perfectly free view down into the heart of the snowy, chanting throng of comet-like streamers, into which the body of the fall soon separates.

8   While perched on that narrow niche I was not distinctly conscious of danger. The tremendous grandeur of the fall in form and sound and motion, acting at close range, smothered the sense of fear, and in such places one's body takes keen care for safety on its own account. How long I remained down there, or how I returned, I can hardly tell. Anyhow I had a glorious time, and got back to camp about dark, enjoying triumphant exhilaration soon followed by dull weariness. Hereafter I'll try to keep from such extravagant, nerve-straining places. Yet such a day is well worth venturing for. My first view of the High Sierra, first view looking down into Yosemite, the death song of Yosemite Creek, and its flight over the vast cliff, each one of these is of itself enough for a great life-long landscape fortune – a most memorable day of days – enjoyment enough to kill if that were possible.

✛ ✛ ✛

MOUNT HOFFMAN AND LAKE TENAYA

*J*ULY 26. RAMBLE TO THE summit of Mount Hoffman, eleven   9
thousand feet high, the highest point in life's journey my feet
have yet touched. And what glorious landscapes are about me,
new plants, new animals, new crystals, and multitudes of new
mountains far higher than Hoffman, towering in glorious array
along the axis of the range, serene, majestic, snow-laden, sun-
drenched, vast domes and ridges shining below them, forests,
lakes, and meadows in the hollows, the pure blue bell-flower sky
brooding them all, – a glory day of admission into a new realm
of wonders as if Nature had wooingly whispered, "Come higher."
What questions I asked, and how little I know of all the vast show,
and how eagerly, tremulously hopeful of some day knowing more,
learning the meaning of these divine symbols crowded together
on this wondrous page.

Mount Hoffman is the highest part of a ridge or spur about   10
fourteen miles from the axis of the main range, perhaps a remnant brought into relief and isolated by unequal denudation.
The southern slopes shed their waters into Yosemite Valley by
Tenaya and Dome Creeks, the northern in part into the Tuolumne
River, but mostly into the Merced by Yosemite Creek. The rock
is mostly granite, with some small piles and crests rising here
and there in picturesque pillared and castellated remnants of
red metamorphic slates. Both the granite and slates are divided
by joints, making them separable into blocks like the stones of
artificial masonry, suggesting the Scripture* "He hath builded
the mountains." Great banks of snow and ice are piled in hollows
on the cool precipitous north side forming the highest perennial
sources of Yosemite Creek. The southern slopes are much more
gradual and accessible. Narrow slot-like gorges extend across the
summit at right angles, which look like lanes, formed evidently by
the erosion of less resisting beds. They are usually called "devil's
slides," though they lie far above the region usually haunted by
the devil;for though we read that he once climbed * an exceeding high mountain,he cannot be much of a mountaineer, for his
tracks are seldom seen above the timber-line.

Scripture · Paraphrase
of William Cowper's
hymn "Ere God had
built the mountains"
(*Olney Hymns*,1779);
see also Psalm 90:2
and 104:8

**the devil . . . once
climbed** · Matthew 4:8

11   The broad gray summit is barren and desolate-looking in general views, wasted by ages of gnawing storms; but looking at the surface in detail, one finds it covered by thousands and millions of charming plants with leaves and flowers so small they form no mass of color visible at a distance of a few hundred yards. Beds of azure daisies smile confidingly in moist hollows, and along the banks of small rills, with several species of eriogonum, silky-leaved ivesia, pentstemon, orthocarpus, and patches of *Primula* suffruticosa,* a beautiful shrubby species. Here also I found bryanthus, a charming heathwort covered with purple flowers and dark green foliage like heather, and three trees new to me – a hemlock and two pines. The hemlock (*Tsuga mertensiana*)* is the most beautiful conifer I have ever seen; the branches and also the main axis droop in a singularly graceful way, and the dense foliage covers the delicate, sensitive, swaying branchlets all around. It is now in full bloom, and the flowers, together with thousands of last season's cones still clinging to the drooping sprays, display wonderful wealth of color, brown and purple and blue. Gladly I climbed the first tree I found to revel in the midst of it. How the touch of the flowers makes one's flesh tingle! The pistillate are dark, rich purple, and almost translucent, the staminate blue, – a vivid, pure tone of blue like the mountain sky, – the most uncommonly beautiful of all the Sierra tree flowers I have seen. How wonderful that, with all its delicate feminine grace and beauty of form and dress and behavior, this lovely tree up here, exposed to the wildest blasts, has already endured the storms of centuries of winters!

Primula suffruticosa · Sierra primrose

Tsuga mertensiana · mountain hemlock

12   The two pines also are brave storm-enduring trees, the mountain pine (*Pinus monticola*)* and the dwarf pine (*Pinus albicaulis*). The mountain pine is closely related to the sugar pine, though the cones are only about four to six inches long. The largest trees are from five to six feet in diameter at four feet above the ground, the bark rich brown. Only a few storm-beaten adventurers approach the summit of the mountain. The dwarf or white-bark pine is the species that forms the timberline, where it is so completely dwarfed that one may walk over the top of a bed of it as over snow-pressed chaparral.

Pinus monticola · western white pine

13   How boundless the day seems as we revel in these storm-beaten sky gardens amid so vast a congregation of onlooking

mountains! Strange and admirable it is that the more savage and 13
chilly and storm-chafed the mountains, the finer the glow on their
faces and the finer the plants they bear. The myriads of flowers
tingeing the mountain-top do not seem to have grown out of
the dry, rough gravel of disintegration, but rather they appear as
visitors, a cloud of witnesses to Nature's love in what we in our
timid ignorance and unbelief call howling desert. The surface of
the ground, so dull and forbidding at first sight, besides being rich
in plants, shines and sparkles with crystals: mica, hornblende,
feldspar, quartz, tourmaline. The radiance in some places is so
great as to be fairly dazzling, keen lance rays of every color flashing, sparkling in glorious abundance, joining the plants in their
fine, brave beauty-work – every crystal, every flower a window
opening into heaven, a mirror reflecting the Creator.

From garden to garden, ridge to ridge, I drifted enchanted, 14
now on my knees gazing into the face of a daisy, now climbing
again and again among the purple and azure flowers of the hem-
locks, now down into the treasuries of the snow, or gazing afar
over domes and peaks, lakes and woods, and the billowy glaciated
fields of the upper Tuolumne, and trying to sketch them. In the
midst of such beauty, pierced with its rays, one's body is all one
tingling palate. Who wouldn't be a mountaineer! Up here all the
world's prizes seem nothing.

The largest of the many glacier lakes in sight, and the one 15
with the finest shore scenery, is Tenaya, about a mile long, with
an imposing mountain dipping its feet into it on the south side,
Cathedral Peak a few miles above its head, many smooth swelling rock-waves and domes on the north, and in the distance
southward a multitude of snowy peaks, the fountain-heads of
rivers. Lake Hoffman lies shimmering beneath my feet, mountain
pines around its shining rim. To the northward the picturesque
basin of Yosemite Creek glitters with lakelets and pools; but the
eye is soon drawn away from these bright mirror wells, however
attractive, to revel in the glorious congregation of peaks on the
axis of the range in their robes of snow and light. Carlo caught an
unfortunate woodchuck when it was running from a grassy spot
to its boulder-pile home – one of the hardiest of the mountain
animals. I tried hard to save him, but in vain. After telling Carlo
that he must be careful not to kill anything, I caught sight, for

15 the first time, of the curious pika, or little chief hare, that cuts large quantities of lupines and other plants and lays them out to dry in the sun for hay, which it stores in underground barns to last through the long, snowy winter. Coming upon these plants freshly cut and lying in handfuls here and there on the rocks has a startling effect of busy life on the lonely mountain-top. These little haymakers, endowed with brain stuff something like our own, – God up here looking after them, – what lessons they teach, how they widen our sympathy!

16 An eagle soaring above a sheer cliff, where I suppose its nest is, makes another striking show of life, and helps to bring to mind the other people of the so-called solitude – deer in the forest caring for their young; the strong, well-clad, well-fed bears; the lively throng of squirrels; the blessed birds, great and small, stirring and sweetening the groves; and the clouds of happy insects filling the sky with joyous hum as part and parcel of the down-pouring sunshine. All these come to mind, as well as the plant people, and the glad streams singing their way to the sea. But most impressive of all is the vast glowing countenance of the wilderness in awful, infinite repose.

17 Toward sunset, enjoyed a fine run to camp, down the long south slopes, across ridges and ravines, gardens and avalanche gaps, through the firs and chaparral, enjoying wild excitement and excess of strength, and so ends a day that will never end.

Langston Hughes

◄{ 1 9 0 2 - 1 9 6 7 }►

Multiple childhood influences shaped Hughes's writing. The Christian faith of his grandmother, with whom he spent his early years in Lawrence, Kansas, had a profound impact on his artistic sensibilities and linguistic development. His urban experience living with his mother and stepfather, moreover, would provide him with the material he eventually used to present the emergent "New Negro" to readers. His father's expatriation to Mexico to escape racial prejudice – Hughes spent a year with him there – further affected his worldview, helping to free him from American provincialism. After a period of international travel as a merchant seaman, Hughes entered and graduated from Lincoln University, in Pennsylvania. Unlike many African American writers of the 1920s, Hughes focused less on rural Southern blacks, preferring instead to treat the lives of black city dwellers. As an adult, Hughes was drawn to Communism, visiting Russia for a year (1932–1933). He applauded Marxism's ostensible respect for the working class and disdain for racial boundaries. During the "red scare" of the McCarthy era, therefore, Hughes was considered a security risk and was restricted by the government of the United States from traveling abroad. The ban was lifted in the 1960s, and the writer resumed his travels, reading and lecturing to international audiences. Though Hughes is perhaps best remembered for poetry, his literary output was varied and included the collecting and editing of black folklore. Perhaps more than any other artist of the Harlem Renaissance, the cultural movement of which he was part, Langston Hughes presented and embodied a portrait of the African American in ideological transition.

SALVATION

1   I WAS SAVED FROM SIN when I was going on thirteen. But not really saved. It happened like this. There was a big revival at my

Auntie Reed's church. Every night for weeks there had been much preaching, singing, praying, and shouting, and some very hardened sinners had been brought to Christ, and the membership of the church had grown by leaps and bounds. Then just before the revival ended, they held a special meeting for children, "to bring the young lambs to the fold." My aunt spoke of it for days ahead. That night I was escorted to the front row and placed on the mourners' bench* with all the other young sinners, who had not yet been brought to Jesus.

My aunt told me that when you were saved you saw a light, and something happened to you inside! And Jesus came into your life! And God was with you from then on! She said you could see and hear and feel Jesus in your soul. I believed her. I had heard a great many old people say the same thing and it seemed to me they ought to know. So I sat there calmly in the hot, crowded church, waiting for Jesus to come to me.

The preacher preached a wonderful rhythmical sermon, all moans and shouts and lonely cries and dire pictures of hell, and then he sang a song about the ninety and nine safe in the fold, but one little lamb was left out in the cold.* Then he said: "Won't you come? Won't you come to Jesus? Young lambs, won't you come?" And he held out his arms to all us young sinners there on the mourners' bench. And the little girls cried. And some of them jumped up and went to Jesus right away. But most of us just sat there.

A great many old people came and knelt around us and prayed, old women with jet-black faces and braided hair, old men with work-gnarled hands. And the church sang a song about the lower lights are burning, some poor sinners to be saved.* And the whole building rocked with prayer and song.

Still I kept waiting to *see* Jesus.

Finally all the young people had gone to the altar and were saved, but one boy and me. He was a rounder's son named Westley. Westley and I were surrounded by sisters and deacons praying. It was very hot in the church, and getting late now. Finally Westley said to me in a whisper:

"God damn! I'm tired o' sitting here. Let's get up and be saved." So he got up and was saved.

Then I was left all alone on the mourners' bench. My aunt came and knelt at my knees and cried, while prayers and songs

mourners' bench · a special seat on the front row of a church reserved for those asking for prayers or responding to a call for repentance

the ninety and nine ... cold · the hymn "The Ninety and Nine" (words E. C. Clephane, music I. D. Sankey, 1874) is based on Christ's parable of the lost sheep (Luke 15:3–7)

lower lights are burning ... be saved · "Let the Lower Lights Be Burning" (words and music P. P. Bliss, 1871) uses the metaphor of a lighthouse to encourage Christian witness and evangelism

8   swirled all around me in the little church. The whole congregation prayed for me alone, in a mighty wail of moans and voices. And I kept waiting serenely for Jesus, waiting, waiting – but he didn't come. I wanted to see him, but nothing happened to me. Nothing! I wanted something to happen to me, but nothing happened.

9   I heard the songs and the minister saying: "Why don't you come? My dear child, why don't you come to Jesus? Jesus is waiting for you. He wants you. Why don't you come? Sister Reed, what is this child's name?"

10   "Langston," my aunt sobbed.

11   "Langston, why don't you come? Why don't you come and be saved? Oh, Lamb of God! Why don't you come?"

12   Now it was really getting late. I began to be ashamed of myself, holding everything up so long. I began to wonder what God thought about Westley, who certainly hadn't seen Jesus either, but who was now sitting proudly on the platform, swinging his knickerbockered* legs and grinning down at me, surrounded by deacons and old women on their knees praying. God had not struck Westley dead for taking his name in vain or for lying in the temple. So I decided that maybe to save further trouble, I'd better lie, too, and say that Jesus had come, and get up and be saved.

> knickerbockered · knickerbockers are short pants gathered just below the knee, commonly worn at that time by young boys

13   So I got up.

14   Suddenly the whole room broke into a sea of shouting, as they saw me rise. Waves of rejoicing swept the place. Women leaped in the air. My aunt threw her arms around me. The minister took me by the hand and led me to the platform.

15   When things quieted down, in a hushed silence, punctuated by a few ecstatic "Amens," all the new young lambs were blessed in the name of God. Then joyous singing filled the room.

16   That night, for the last time in my life but one – for I was a big boy twelve years old – I cried. I cried, in bed alone, and couldn't stop. I buried my head under the quilts, but my aunt heard me. She woke up and told my uncle I was crying because the Holy Ghost had come into my life, and because I had seen Jesus. But I was really crying because I couldn't bear to tell her that I had lied, that I had deceived everybody in the church, that I hadn't seen Jesus, and that now I didn't believe there was a Jesus any more, since he didn't come to help me.

Thomas Merton

{ 1 9 1 5 - 1 9 6 8 }

Born in France, orphaned at sixteen, and educated at Clare College, Cambridge, Merton emigrated to the United States in 1934. Merton attended Columbia University, where he became a Catholic. In 1941 he entered the Cistercians of the Strict Observance (Trappist). He spent the rest of his life writing works of poetry, spirituality, and theology. His best-selling autobiography, The Seven Storey Mountain *(1948), helped make him a public figure. Merton succeeded in introducing large numbers of readers to the value of the spiritual life and the disciplines of meditation and prayer without their having to enter the monastic life (themes reiterated and extended by Henri Nouwen). Merton emphasized the deep connection between the spiritual life and service to humanity: "Go into the desert not to escape other men but in order to find them in God," he writes in* New Seeds of Contemplation *(1961). "There is no true solitude except interior solitude. And interior solitude is not possible for anyone who does not accept his true place in relation to other men." Merton died in an accident in Bangkok, Thailand, in December 1968.*

PRAY FOR YOUR OWN DISCOVERY

1 THERE EXISTS SOME POINT at which I can meet God in a real and experimental* contact with His infinite actuality. This is the "place" of God, His sanctuary – it is the point where my contingent being depends upon His love. Within myself is a metaphorical apex of existence at which I am held in being by my Creator.

experimental · experiential

2 God utters me like a word containing a partial thought of Himself.

3 A word will never be able to comprehend the voice that utters it.

4 But if I am true to the concept that God utters in me, if I am true to the thought of Him I was meant to embody, I shall be

full of His actuality and find Him everywhere in myself, and find 4
myself nowhere. I shall be lost in Him: that is, I shall find myself.
I shall be "saved."

It is a pity that the beautiful Christian metaphor "salvation" 5
has come to be so hackneyed and therefore so despised. It has
been turned into a vapid synonym for "piety"– not even a truly
ethical concept. "Salvation" is something far beyond ethical
propriety. The word connotes a deep respect for the fundamental metaphysical reality of man. It reflects God's own infinite
concern for man, God's love and care for man's inmost being,
God's love for all that is His own in man, His son. It is not only
human nature that is "saved" by the divine mercy, but above
all the human person. The object of salvation is that which is
unique, irreplaceable, incommunicable – that which is myself
alone. This true inner self must be drawn up like a jewel from the
bottom of the sea, rescued from confusion, from indistinction,
from immersion in the common, the nondescript, the trivial, the
sordid, the evanescent.˙

evanescent · vanishing
or fleeting

We must be saved from immersion in the sea of lies and pas- 6
sions which is called "the world." And we must be saved above
all from that abyss of confusion and absurdity which is our own
worldly self. The person must be rescued from the individual.
The free son of God must be saved from the conformist slave of
fantasy, passion and convention. The creative and mysterious
inner self must be delivered from the wasteful, hedonistic˙ and
destructive ego that seeks only to cover itself with disguises.

hedonistic · hedonism
holds pleasure to be the
greatest good

To be "lost" is to be left to the arbitrariness and pretenses of 7
the contingent ego, the smoke-self that must inevitably vanish.
To be "saved" is to return to one's inviolate and eternal reality
and to live in God.

✦ ✦ ✦

WHAT ONE OF YOU CAN ENTER into himself and find the 8
God Who utters him?

"Finding God" means much more than just abandoning all things 9
that are not God, and emptying oneself of images and desires.

If you succeed in emptying your mind of every thought and 10
every desire, you may indeed withdraw into the center of yourself
and concentrate everything within you upon the imaginary point

10   where your life springs out of God: yet you will not really find God. No natural exercise can bring you into vital contact with Him. Unless He utters Himself in you, speaks His own name in the center of your soul, you will no more know Him than a stone knows the ground upon which it rests in its inertia.

✦ ✦ ✦

11   OUR DISCOVERY OF GOD IS, in a way, God's discovery of us. We cannot go to heaven to find Him because we have no way of knowing where heaven is or what it is. He comes down from heaven and finds us.

12   He looks at us from the depths of His own infinite actuality, which is everywhere, and His seeing us gives us a new being and a new mind in which we also discover Him. We only know Him in so far as we are known by Him, and our contemplation of Him is a participation in His contemplation of Himself.

13   We become contemplatives when God discovers* Himself in us.

discovers · reveals

14   At that moment the point of our contact with Him opens out and we pass through the center of our own nothingness and enter into infinite reality, where we awaken as our true self.

15   It is true that God knows Himself in all the things that exist. He sees them, and it is because He sees them that they exist. It is because He loves them that they are good. His love in them is their intrinsic goodness. The value He sees in them is their value. Insofar as He sees and loves them, all things reflect Him.

16   But although God is present in all things by His knowledge and His love and His power and His care of them, He is not necessarily realized and known by them. He is only known and loved by those to whom He has freely given a share in His own knowledge and love of Himself.

17   In order to know and love God as He is, we must have God dwelling in us in a new way, not only in His creative power but in His mercy, not only in His greatness but in His littleness, by which He empties Himself* and comes down to us to be empty in our emptiness, and so fill us in His fullness. God bridges the infinite distances between Himself and the spirits created to love Him, by supernatural missions of His own life. The Father, dwelling in the depths of all things and in my own depths, communicates to me His Word and His Spirit. Receiving them I am

He empties Himself · the New Testament doctrine of *kenosis*, Christ's voluntary surrender of divine prerogatives. See Philippians 2:5–11

drawn into His own life and know God in His own Love, being [17] one with Him in His own Son.

My discovery of my identity begins and is perfected in these [18] missions, because it is in them that God Himself, bearing in Himself the secret of who I am, begins to live in me not only as my Creator but as my other and true self. *Vivo, iam non ego, vivit vero in me Christus* ("I live, now not I, but Christ lives in me").*

"I live ... me" · Galatians 2:20

✦ ✦ ✦

THESE MISSIONS BEGIN at Baptism. But they do not take on [19] any practical meaning in the life of our spirit until we become capable of conscious acts of love. From then on God's special presence in us corresponds to our own free decisions. From then on our life becomes a series of choices between the fiction of our false self, whom we feed with the illusions of passion and selfish appetite, and our loving consent to the purely gratuitous mercy of God.

When I consent to the will and the mercy of God as it "comes" [20] to me in events of life, appealing to my inner self and awakening my faith, I break through the superficial exterior appearances that form my routine vision of the world and of my own self, and I find myself in the presence of hidden majesty. It may appear to me that this majesty and presence is something objective, "outside myself." Indeed, the primitive* saints and prophets saw this divine presence in vision as a light or an angel or a man or a burning fire, or a blazing glory upheld by cherubim.* Only thus could their minds do justice to the supreme reality of what they experienced. Yet this is a majesty we do not see with our eyes and it is all within ourselves. It is the mission of the Word and the Spirit, from the Father, in the depths of our own being. It is a majesty communicated to us, shared with us, so that our whole being is filled with the gift of glory and responds with adoration.

primitive · original or early

cherubim · see Exodus 25:18–22

This is the "mercy of God" revealed to us by the secret mis- [21] sions in which He gives Himself to us, and awakens our identity as sons and heirs of His Kingdom. This is the Kingdom of God within us,* and for the coming of this Kingdom we pray each time we say the "Our Father."* In the revelation of mercy and majesty we come to an obscure intuition of our own personal secret, our true identity. Our inner self awakens, with a momentary flash, in the instant of recognition when we say "Yes!" to

Kingdom ... within us · "the kingdom of God is within you" (Luke 17:21)

"Our Father" · The Lord's Prayer (Matthew 6:9–13)

21   the indwelling Divine Persons. We are only really ourselves when we completely consent to "receive" the glory of God into ourselves. Our true self is, then, the self that receives freely and gladly the missions that are God's supreme gift to His sons. Any other "self" is only an illusion.

22   As long as I am on earth my mind and will remain more or less impervious to the missions of God's Word and His Spirit. I do not easily receive His light.

23   Every movement of my own natural appetite, even though my nature is good in itself, tends in one way or another to keep alive in me the illusion that is opposed to God's reality living within me.

     Even though my natural acts are good they have a tendency,
24 when they are only natural, to concentrate my faculties on the man that I am not, the one I cannot be, the false self in me, the character that God does not know. This is because I am born in selfishness. I am born self-centered. And this is original sin.*

     Even when I try to please God, I tend to please my own ambi-
25 tion, His enemy. There can be imperfection even in the ardent love of great perfection, even in the desire of virtue, of sanctity. Even the desire of contemplation can be impure, when we forget that true contemplation means the complete destruction of all selfishness – the most pure poverty and cleanness of heart.

original sin · doctrine developed by Augustine of Hippo (354–430) that all humans are born sinful, carrying the taint of Adam's primal disobedience

❖ ❖ ❖

26   Aʟᴛʜᴏᴜɢʜ Gᴏᴅ ʟɪᴠᴇs in the souls of men who are unconscious of Him, how can I say that I have found Him and found myself in Him if I never know Him or think of Him, never take any interest in Him or seek Him or desire His presence in my soul? What good does it do to say a few formal prayers to Him and then turn away and give all my mind and all my will to created things, desiring only ends that fall far short of Him? Even though my soul may be justified, yet if my mind does not belong to Him then I do not belong to Him either. If my love does not reach out toward Him but scatters itself in His creation, it is because I have reduced His life in me to the level of a formality, forbidding it to move me with a truly vital influence.

     Justify my soul, O God, but also from Your fountains fill my
27 will with fire. Shine in my mind, although perhaps this means "be darkness to my experience," but occupy my heart with Your

tremendous Life. Let my eyes see nothing in the world but Your 27
glory, and let my hands touch nothing that is not for Your service.
Let my tongue taste no bread that does not strengthen me to
praise Your great mercy. I will hear Your voice and I will hear all
harmonies You have created, singing Your hymns. Sheep's wool
and cotton from the field shall warm me enough that I may live
in Your service; I will give the rest to Your poor. Let me use all
things for one sole reason: to find my joy in giving You glory.

Therefore keep me, above all things, from sin. Keep me from
the death of deadly sin which puts hell in my soul. Keep me 28
from the murder of lust that blinds and poisons my heart. Keep
me from the sins that eat a man's flesh with irresistible fire until
he is devoured. Keep me from loving money in which is hatred,
from avarice and ambition that suffocate my life. Keep me from
the dead works of vanity and the thankless labor in which artists
destroy themselves for pride and money and reputation, and
saints are smothered under the avalanche of their own importunate* zeal. Stanch in me the rank wound of covetousness and
the hungers that exhaust my nature with their bleeding. Stamp
out the serpent envy that stings love with poison and kills all joy.

importunate · stub-
bornly or unreasonably
persistent

Untie my hands and deliver my heart from sloth. Set me free
from the laziness that goes about disguised as activity when 29
activity is not required of me, and from the cowardice that does
what is not demanded, in order to escape sacrifice.

But give me the strength that waits upon You in silence and
peace. Give me humility in which alone is rest, and deliver me 30
from pride which is the heaviest of burdens. And possess my
whole heart and soul with the simplicity of love. Occupy my
whole life with the one thought and the one desire of love, that
I may love not for the sake of merit, not for the sake of perfection, not for the sake of virtue, not for the sake of sanctity, but
for You alone.

For there is only one thing that can satisfy love and reward
it, and that is You alone. 31

This then is what it means to seek God perfectly: to withdraw
from illusion and pleasure, from worldly anxieties and desires, 32
from the works that God does not want, from a glory that is
only human display; to keep my mind free from confusion in
order that my liberty may be always at the disposal of His will;

32   to entertain silence in my heart and listen for the voice of God; to cultivate an intellectual freedom from the images of created things in order to receive the secret contact of God in obscure love; to love all men as myself; to rest in humility and to find peace in withdrawal from conflict and competition with other men; to turn aside from controversy and put away heavy loads of judgment and censorship and criticism and the whole burden of opinions that I have no obligation to carry; to have a will that is always ready to fold back within itself and draw all the powers of the soul down from its deepest center to rest in silent expectancy for the coming of God, poised in tranquil and effortless concentration upon the point of my dependence on Him; to gather all that I am, and have all that I can possibly suffer or do or be, and abandon them all to God in the resignation of a perfect love and blind faith and pure trust in God, to do His will.

And then to wait in peace and emptiness and oblivion of
33   all things.

Bonum est præstolari cum silentio salutare Dei ("It is good to
34   wait in silence for the salvation of God").·   **"It is ... God"**·
                                                      Lamentations 3:26

Flannery O'Connor

◄(1 9 2 5 - 1 9 6 4)►

O'Connor was under no illusions as to how odd her overt Christian emphases might appear to non-religious readers. Her subject in writing, she once remarked, "is the action of grace in territory held largely by the devil. I have also found that what I write is read by an audience which puts little stock either in grace or the devil." However, the author was neither defensive nor abrasive in her approach to those who did not share her beliefs. In her fiction, essays, and letters, in fact, O'Connor was deeply compassionate about the crisis of faith in a religionless age: "Nihilism is the gas we breathe," she once observed. "I think there is no suffering greater than what is caused by the doubts of those who want to believe. I know what torment this is, but I can only see it, in myself anyway, as the process by which faith is deepened. What people don't realize is how much religion costs. They think it is a big electric blanket, when of course it is the cross." O'Connor frequently lectured on university campuses, often addressing the tension between intellect and religious convictions. The following letter, published posthumously in a collection of letters under the title The Habit of Being *(1979), is O'Connor's response to an Emory University student who had written to her concerning his doubts about the truth of Christianity.*

A LETTER TO ALFRED CORN

30 MAY 1962

1   I THINK THAT THIS EXPERIENCE you are having of losing your faith, or as you think, of having lost it, is an experience that in the long run belongs to faith; or at least it can belong to faith if it is still valuable to you, and it must be or you would not have written me about this.

2   I don't know how the kind of faith required of a Christian living in the 20th century can be at all if it is not grounded on

93

this experience that you are having right now of unbelief. This may be the case always and not just in the 20th century. Peter said, "Lord, I believe. Help my unbelief."* It is the most natural and most human and most agonizing prayer in the gospels, and I think it is the foundation prayer of faith. 2

As a freshman in college you are bombarded with new ideas, or rather pieces of ideas, new frames of reference, an activation of the intellectual life which is only beginning, but which is already running ahead of your lived experience. After a year of this, you think you cannot believe. You are just beginning to realize how difficult it is to have faith and the measure of a commitment to it, but you are too young to decide you don't have faith just because you feel you can't believe. About the only way we know whether we believe or not is by what we do, and I think from your letter that you will not take the path of least resistance in this matter and simply decide that you have lost your faith and that there is nothing you can do about it. 3

One result of the stimulation of your intellectual life that takes place in college is usually a shrinking of the imaginative life. This sounds like a paradox, but I have often found it to be true. Students get so bound up with difficulties such as reconciling the clashing of so many different faiths such as Buddhism, Mohammedanism,* etc., that they cease to look for God in other ways. Bridges* once wrote Gerard Manley Hopkins and asked him to tell him how he, Bridges, could believe. He must have expected from Hopkins a long philosophical answer. Hopkins wrote back, "Give alms." He was trying to say to Bridges that God is to be experienced in Charity (in the sense of love for the divine image in human beings). Don't get so entangled with intellectual difficulties that you fail to look for God in this way. 4

The intellectual difficulties have to be met, however, and you will be meeting them for the rest of your life. When you get a reasonable hold on one, another will come to take its place. At one time, the clash of the different world religions was a difficulty for me. Where you have absolute solutions, however, you have no need of faith. Faith is what you have in the absence of knowledge. The reason this clash doesn't bother me any longer is because I have got, over the years, a sense of the immense sweep of creation, of the evolutionary process in everything, of how incomprehensible God must necessarily be to be the God of heaven and earth. You can't fit the Almighty into your 5

5   intellectual categories. I might suggest that you look into some of the works of Pierre Teilhard de Chardin* (*The Phenomenon of Man* et al.). He was a paleontologist – helped to discover Peking man – and also a man of God. I don't suggest you go to him for answers but for different questions, for that stretching of the imagination that you need to make you a skeptic in the face of much that you are learning, much of what is new and shocking but which when boiled down becomes less so and takes its place in the general scheme of things. What kept me a skeptic in college was precisely my Christian faith. It always said: wait, don't bite on this, get a wider picture, continue to read.

Pierre Teilhard de Chardin · Jesuit French philosopher and paleontologist (1881–1955)

6   If you want your faith, you have to work for it. It is a gift, but for very few is it a gift given without any demand for equal time devoted to its cultivation. For every book you read that is anti-Christian, make it your business to read one that presents the other side of the picture; if one isn't satisfactory read others. Don't think that you have to abandon reason to be a Christian. A book that might help you is *The Unity of Philosophical Experience* by Étienne Gilson.* Another is Newman's *The Grammar of Assent.* To find out about faith, you have to go to the people who have it and you have to go to the most intelligent ones if you are going to stand up intellectually to agnostics and the general run of pagans that you are going to find in the majority of people around you. Much of the criticism of belief that you find today comes from people who are judging it from the standpoint of another and narrower discipline. The Biblical criticism of the 19th century, for instance, was the product of historical disciplines. It has been entirely revamped in the 20th century by applying broader criteria to it, and those people who lost their faith in the 19th century because of it, could better have hung on in blind trust.

Étienne Gilson · French professor of medieval philosophy (1884–1978)

Newman's *The Grammar of Assent* · John Henry Newman (1801–1890), English theologian and philosopher. See Newman's *The Idea of a University* on pages 31–35

7   Even in the life of a Christian, faith rises and falls like the tides of an invisible sea. It's there, even when he can't see it or feel it, if he wants it to be there. You realize, I think, that it is more valuable, more mysterious, altogether more immense than anything you can learn or decide upon in college. Learn what you can, but cultivate Christian skepticism. It will keep you free – not to do anything you please, but free to be formed by something larger than your own intellect or the intellects of those around you.

8   I don't know if this is the kind of answer that can help you, but any time you care to write me, I can try to do better.

Frederick Buechner

◄{ 1 9 2 6 - }►

Buechner is a rarity on the literary scene, being both an ordained minister ("the most quoted living writer among Christians of influence," according to one critic) and a respected novelist, author of The Book of Bebb *(1979),* Godric *(1980), and* Brendan *(1987). He was reared in a secular home in New York and the Bahamas, then attended Princeton University and Union Theological Seminary. Buechner believes that the signs of God's presence may be seen and heard everywhere, especially in our ordinary lives: "There is no place or time so lowly and earthbound but that holiness can be there too," Buechner writes. "Listen to your life. See it for the fathomless mystery that it is... because in the last analysis all moments are key moments, and life itself is grace." In this respect, Buechner continues a longstanding Christian tradition of spiritual self-examination. The "inner frontier" of the soul, "where doubt is pitted against faith, hope against despair, grief against joy," is the domain that most fascinates Buechner both as fiction writer and theologian. The excerpt which follows is the opening chapter of Buechner's third autobiographical work,* Telling Secrets *(1991).*

THE DWARVES IN THE STABLE

1 ONE NOVEMBER MORNING IN 1936 when I was ten years old, my father got up early, put on a pair of gray slacks and a maroon sweater, opened the door to look in briefly on my younger brother and me, who were playing a game in our room, and then went down into the garage where he turned on the engine of the family Chevy and sat down on the running board to wait for the exhaust to kill him. Except for a memorial service for his Princeton class the next spring, by which time we had moved away to another part of the world altogether, there was no

funeral because on both my mother's side and my father's there 1
was no church connection of any kind and funerals were simply
not part of the tradition. He was cremated, his ashes buried in
a cemetery in Brooklyn, and I have no idea who if anybody was
present. I know only that my mother, brother, and I were not.

There was no funeral to mark his death and put a period at 2
the end of the sentence that had been his life, and as far as I can
remember, once he had died my mother, brother, and I rarely
talked about him much ever again, either to each other or to
anybody else. It made my mother too sad to talk about him, and
since there was already more than enough sadness to go round,
my brother and I avoided the subject with her as she avoided
it for her own reasons also with us. Once in a while she would
bring it up but only in very oblique ways. I remember her saying
things like "You're going to have to be big boys now," and "Now
things are going to be different for all of us," and to me, "You're
the man of the family now," with that one little three-letter adverb
freighted with more grief and anger and guilt and God knows
what all else than it could possibly bear.

We didn't talk about my father with each other, and we didn't 3
talk about him outside the family either partly at least because
suicide was looked on as something a little shabby and shameful
in those days. Nice people weren't supposed to get mixed up with
it. My father had tried to keep it a secret himself by leaving his
note to my mother in a place where only she would be likely to
find it and by saying a number of times the last few weeks of his
life that there was something wrong with the Chevy's exhaust
system, which he was going to see if he could fix. He did this partly
in hopes that his life insurance wouldn't be invalidated, which of
course it was, and partly too, I guess, in hopes that his friends
wouldn't find out how he had died, which of course they did.
His suicide was a secret we nonetheless tried to keep as best we
could, and after a while my father himself became such a secret.
There were times when he almost seemed a secret we were trying
to keep from each other. I suppose there were occasions when
one of us said, "Remember the time he did this," or, "Remember
the time he said that," but if so, I've long since forgotten them.
And because words are so much a part of what we keep the past
alive by, if only words to ourselves, by not speaking of what we

3   remembered about him we soon simply stopped remembering at all, or at least I did.

4   Within a couple of months of his death we moved away from New Jersey, where he had died, to the island of Bermuda of all places – another house, another country even – and from that point on I can't even remember remembering him. Within a year of his death I seem to have forgotten what he looked like except for certain photographs of him, to have forgotten what his voice sounded like and what it had been like to be with him. Because none of the three of us ever talked about how we had felt about him when he was alive or how we felt about him now that he wasn't, those feelings soon disappeared too and went underground along with the memories. As nearly as I can find out from people who knew him, he was a charming, good-looking, gentle man who was down on his luck and drank too much and had a great number of people who loved him and felt sorry for him. Among those people, however inadequately they may have showed it, I can only suppose were his wife and two sons; but in almost no time at all, it was as if, at least for me, he had never existed.

5   "Don't talk, don't trust, don't feel" is supposed to be the unwritten law of families that for one reason or another have gone out of whack, and certainly it was our law. We never talked about what had happened. We didn't trust the world with our secret, hardly even trusted each other with it. And as far as my ten-year-old self was concerned anyway, the only feeling I can remember from that distant time was the blessed relief of coming out of the dark and unmentionable sadness of my father's life and death into fragrance and greenness and light.

6   Don't talk, trust, feel was the law we lived by, and woe to the one who broke it. Twenty-two years later in a novel called *The Return of Ansel Gibbs* I told a very brief and fictionalized version of my father's death, and the most accurate word I can find to describe my mother's reaction to it is fury. For days she could hardly bring herself to speak to me, and when she did, it was with words of great bitterness. As she saw it, I had betrayed a sacred trust, and though I might have defended myself by saying that the story was after all as much mine as his son to tell as it was hers as his widow to keep hidden, I not only didn't say any such things

but never even considered such things. I felt as much of a traitor 6
as she charged me with being, and at the age of thirty-two was as
horrified at what I had done as if I had been a child of ten. I was
full of guilt and remorse and sure that in who-knows-what grim
and lasting way I would be made to suffer for what I had done.

I was in my fifties and my mother in her eighties before I dared
write on the forbidden subject again. It was in an autobiographical 7
book called *The Sacred Journey* that I did so, and this time I told
the story straight except that out of deference to her, or perhaps
out of fear of her, I made no reference to her part in it. Otherwise
I set it down as fully and accurately as I could, and the only reason
I was able to do so was that I suspected that from *Ansel Gibbs* on
my mother had never really read any other book I had written
for fear of what she might find there. I was sure that she wouldn't
read this one either. And I turned out to be right. She never read
the book or the second autobiographical one that followed it even
though, or precisely because, it was the story of her son's life and
in that sense a part of her own story too. She was a strong and
brave woman in many ways, but she was not brave and strong
enough for that. We all have to survive as best we can.

She survived to within eleven days of her ninety-second birthday and died in her own bed in the room that for the last year or 8
so of her life when her arthritic knees made it virtually impossible
for her to walk became the only world that really interested her.
She kept track more or less of the world outside. She had a rough
idea what her children and grandchildren were up to. She read
the papers and watched the evening news. But such things as that
were dim and far away compared to the news that was breaking
around her every day. Yvonne, who came days, had been trying
to tell her something but God only knew what, her accent was
so thick. Marge, who came nights, was an hour late because of
delays on the subway, or so she said. My mother's cane had fallen
behind the radiator, and the super was going to have to come do
something about it. Where was her fan? Where was the gold purse
she kept her extra hearing aids in? Where was the little peach-
colored pillow, which of all the pillows she had was the only one
that kept her tray level when they brought in her meals? In the
world where she lived, these were the things that made headlines.

9   "If I didn't have something to look for, I would be lost," she said once. It was one of her most shimmering utterances. She hunted for her lost pills, lost handkerchief, lost silver comb, the little copy of Les Malheurs de Sophie* she had lost, because with luck she might even find them. There was a better chance of it anyway than of finding her lost beauty or the friends who had mostly died or the life that had somehow gotten mislaid in the debris of her nonlife, all the aches and pains and indignities of having outlived almost everything including herself. But almost to the end she could laugh till the tears ran down and till our tears ran down. She loved telling how her father in the confusion of catching a train handed the red-cap* his wallet once, or how one of her beaux had stepped through somebody's straw hat in the hall closet and was afraid to come out. Her laughter came from deep down in herself and deep down in the past, which in one way was lost and gone and in other ways was still as much within her reach as the can of root beer with a straw sticking in it which she always had on her bedside table because she said it was the only thing that helped her dry throat. The sad times she kept locked away never to be named, but the funny, happy times, the glamorous, romantic, young times, continued to be no less a part of her life than the furniture.

10   She excoriated the ravages of old age but never accepted them as the inevitable consequence of getting old. "I don't know what's wrong with me today," she must have said a thousand days as she tried once, then again, then a third time, to pull herself out of her chair into her walker. It never seemed to occur to her that what was wrong with her was that she was on her way to pushing a hundred. Maybe that was why some part of her remained unravaged. Some surviving lightness of touch let her stand back from the wreckage and see that among other things it was absurdly funny. When I told her the last time she was mobile enough to visit us in Vermont that the man who had just passed her window was the gardener, she said, "Tell him to come in and take a look at the last rose of summer."

11   She liked to paste gold stars on things or to antique things with gold paint – it was what she did with the past too of course – and lampshades, chairs, picture frames, tables, gleamed like treasure in the crazy little museum of her bedroom. The *chaise longue**

Les Malheurs de Sophie · "Sophie's Misfortunes" (French), written by the Comtesse de Ségur (1799–1874) and published in 1864, featured a naughty 4-year-old girl

red-cap · a railroad porter

chaise longue · "long chair" (French), a lounge for reclining

was heaped with pillows, a fake leopard-skin throw, a velvet quilt, **11**
fashion magazines, movie magazines, catalogues stacked on a
table beside it, stories by Dorothy Parker[*] and Noël Coward,[*]
Kahlil Gibran's *The Prophet.*[*] Victorian beadwork pincushions
hung from the peach-colored walls along with pictures of happier times, greener places. The closet was a cotillion[*] of pretty
clothes she hadn't been able to wear for years, and her bureau
overflowed with more of them – blouses, belts, costume jewelry,
old evening purses, chiffon scarves, gloves. On top of the bureau
stood perfume bottles, pill bottles, jars, tubes, boxes of patent
medicine, a bowl of M & MS, which she said were good for her.
She had a theory that when you have a craving for something,
including M & MS, it means that your system needs it.

The living heart and command center of that room was the **12**
dressing table. When she was past getting out of her bed to sit
at it any longer, what she needed from it was brought to her on
a tray as soon as she woke up every morning, before breakfast
even – the magnifying mirror, the lipsticks, eyebrow pencils,
tweezers, face powder, hair brush, combs, cold cream, mascara.
Before she did anything else, she did that and did it with such
artistry that even within weeks of her end she managed a not
implausible version of the face that since girlhood had been her
principal fame and fairest fortune.

Over that dressing table there hung for years a mirror that **13**
I can remember from childhood. It was a mirror with an olive
green wooden frame which she had once painted in oils with a
little garland of flowers and medallions bearing the French words:
Il faut souffrir pour être belle. It was the motto of her life: You
have to suffer in order to be beautiful. What she meant, of course,
was all the pains she took in front of the mirror: the plucking and
primping and powdering, the brushing and painting – that kind of
suffering. But it seems clear that there was another kind too. To
be born as blonde and blue-eyed and beautiful as she was can be
as much of a handicap in its way as to be born with a cleft palate
because if you are beautiful enough you don't really have to be
anything much else to make people love you and want to be near
you. You don't have to be particularly kind or unselfish or generous
or compassionate because people will flock around you anyway
simply for the sake of your *beaux yeux.*[*] My mother could be all

Dorothy Parker ·
American writer and
wit (1893–1967)

Noël Coward · English
comic playwright
(1899–1973)

Kahlil Gibran's *The*
Prophet · Kahlil Gibran
(1883–1931) Lebanese-
American essayist and
poet. *The Prophet* was
first published in 1923

cotillion · a formal
ballroom dance

beaux yeux · "beauti-
ful eyes" (French)

13 of those good things when she took a notion to, but she never made a habit of it. She never developed the giving, loving side of what she might have been as a human being, and, needless to say, that was where the real suffering came – the two failed marriages after the death of my father, the fact that among all the friends she had over the course of her life, she never as far as I know had one whom she would in any sense have sacrificed herself for and by doing so might perhaps have begun to find her best and truest self. W. B. Yeats* in his poem "A Prayer for My Daughter" writes, "Hearts are not had as a gift but hearts are earned/By those that are not entirely beautiful." My almost entirely beautiful mother was by no means heartless, but I think hers was a heart that, who knows why, was rarely if ever touched in its deepest place. To let it be touched there was a risk that for reasons known only to her she was apparently not prepared to take.

W. B. Yeats · Irish poet and playwright (1865–1939)

14 For the twenty years or so she lived in New York she made no new friends because she chose to make none and lost all contact with the few old ones who were still alive. She believed in God, I think. With her eyes shut she would ask me what I thought about the afterlife from time to time, though when I tried to tell her she of course couldn't hear because it is hard to shout anything very much about the afterlife. But she never went to church. It always made her cry, she said. She wouldn't have been caught dead joining a club or group of any kind. "I know I'm queer," she often said. "I'm a very private person." And it was true. Even with the people closest to her she rarely spoke of what was going on inside her skin or asked that question of them. For the last fifteen years or so it reached the point where she saw virtually nobody except her immediate family and most of them not often. But by a miracle it didn't destroy her.

15 She had a cruel and terrible tongue when she was angry. When she struck, she struck to kill, and such killings must have been part of what she closed her eyes to, together with the other failures and mistakes of her life and the guilt they caused her, the shame she felt. But she never became bitter. She turned away from the world but never turned in upon herself. It was a kind of miracle, really. If she was lonely, I never heard her complain about it. Instead it was her looks she complained about: My hair looks like straw. When I wake up in the morning I have

this awful red spot on my cheek. These God-awful teeth don't [15] fit. I don't know what's wrong with me today. From somewhere she was nourished, in other words, and richly nourished, God only knows how, God only knows. That was the other part of the miracle. Something deep within her stayed young, stayed beautiful even, was never lost. And till the end of her life she was as successful at not facing the reality of being a very old woman as for almost a century she was successful at not facing her dark times as a young one.

Being beautiful was her business, her art, her delight, and it [16] took her a long way and earned her many dividends, but when, as she saw it, she lost her beauty – you stand a better chance of finding your cane behind the radiator than ever finding blue eyes and golden hair again – she was like a millionaire who runs out of money. She took her name out of the phone book and got an unlisted number. She eventually became so deaf that it became almost impossible to speak to her except about things simple enough to shout – her health, the weather, when you would be seeing her next. It was as if deafness was a technique she mastered for not hearing anything that might threaten her peace. She developed the habit of closing her eyes when she spoke to you as if you were a dream she was dreaming. It was as if she chose not to see in your face what you might be thinking behind the simple words you were shouting, or as if, ostrich-like, closing her eyes was a way of keeping you from seeing her. With her looks gone she felt she had nothing left to offer the world, to propitiate the world. So what she did was simply to check out of

Greta Garbo · a movie star of the 1920s and 1930s, Garbo (1905–1990) lived in seclusion in New York for almost 50 years

Marlene Dietrich · a movie star, Dietrich (1901–1992) was active from the 1920s through the 1950s, but became increasingly reclusive in later life

the world – that old, last rose of summer – the way Greta Garbo* and Marlene Dietrich* checked out of it, holing themselves up somewhere and never venturing forth except in disguise. My mother holed herself up in her apartment on 79th Street, then in just one room of that apartment, then in just one chair in that room, and finally in the bed where one morning a few summers ago, perhaps in her sleep, she died at last.

It is so easy to sum up other people's lives like this, and nec- [17] essary too, of course, especially our parents' lives. It is a way of reducing their giant figures to a size we can manage, I suppose, a way of getting even maybe, of getting on, of saying goodbye. The day will come when somebody tries to sum you up the same

17 way and also me. Tell me about old Buechner then. What was
he really like? What made him tick? How did his story go? Well,
you see, this happened and then that happened, and then that,
and that is why he became thus and so, and why when all is said
and done it is not so hard to understand why things turned out
for him as they finally did. Is there any truth at all in the patterns
we think we see, the explanations and insights that fall so readily
from our tongues? Who knows. The main thing that leads me to
believe that what I've said about my mother has at least a kind
of partial truth is that I know at first hand that it is true of the
mother who lives on in me and will always be part of who I am.

18   In the mid 1970s, as a father of three teenage children and a
husband of some twenty years standing by then, I would have
said that my hearing was pretty good, that I could hear not only
what my wife and children were saying but lots of things they
weren't saying too. I would have said that I saw fairly well what
was going on inside our house and what was going on inside me.
I would also have said if anybody had asked me that our family
was a close and happy one – that we had our troubles like everybody else but that we loved each other and respected each other
and understood each other better than most. And in a hundred
ways, praise God, I believe I was right. I believe that is the way
it was. But in certain other ways, I came to learn, I was as deaf
as my mother was with her little gold purse full of hearing aids
none of which really ever worked very well, and though I did
not shut my eyes when I talked to people the way she did, I shut
them without knowing it to a whole dimension of the life that
my wife and I and our children were living together on a green
hillside in Vermont during those years.

19   There are two pieces of stained glass that sit propped up in
one of the windows in the room where I write – a room paneled
in old barn siding gone silvery gray with maybe as much as two
centuries of weathering and full of a great many books, many of
them considerably older than that which I've collected over the
years and try to keep oiled and repaired because books are my
passion, not only writing them and every once in a while even
reading them but just having them and moving them around and
feeling the comfort of their serene presence. One of those pieces
of stained glass, which I think I asked somebody to give me one

Christmas, shows the Cowardly Lion from *The Wizard of Oz* with   19
his feet bound with rope and his face streaming with tears as a
few of the Winged Monkeys who have bound him hover around
in the background. The other is a diptych* that somebody gave me
once and that always causes me a twinge of embarrassment when
I notice it because it seems a little too complacently religious.
On one of its panels are written the words "May the blessing of
God crown this house" and on the other "Fortunate is he whose
work is blessed and whose household is prospered by the Lord."

diptych · a painting
made on 2 hinged panels

I have never given either the lion or the diptych much thought   20
as they've sat there year after year gathering dust, but I happened
to notice them as I was preparing these pages and decided they
might well serve as a kind of epigraph for this part of the story
I'm telling. The Cowardly Lion is me, of course – crying, tied up,
afraid. I am crying because at the time I'm speaking of, some fifteen years ago, a lot of sad and scary things were going on in our
house that I felt helpless either to understand or to do anything
about. Yet despite its rather self-satisfied religiosity, I believe the
diptych is telling a truth about that time too.

I believe the blessing of God was indeed crowning our house   21
in the sense that the sad and scary things themselves were, as it
turned out, a fearsome blessing. And all the time those things
were happening, the very fact that I was able to save my sanity
by continuing to write among other things a novel called *Godric*
made my work blessed and a means of grace at least for me.
Nothing I've ever written came out of a darker time or brought
me more light and comfort. It also – far more than I realized at
the time I wrote it – brought me a sharper glimpse than I had
ever had before of the crucial role my father has always played
in my life and continues to play in my life even though in so
many ways I have long since lost all but a handful of conscious
memories of him.

I did not realize until after I wrote it how much of this there   22
is in the book. When Godric is about to leave home to make his
way in the world and his father Ædlward raises his hand to him
in farewell, Godric says, "I believe my way went from that hand
as a path goes from a door, and though many a mile that way has
led me since, with many a turn and crossroad in between, if ever
I should trace it back, it's to my father's hand that it would lead."

22 And later, when he learns of his father's death, he says, "The sadness was I'd lost a father I had never fully found. It's like a tune that ends before you've heard it out. Your whole life through you search to catch the strain, and seek the face you've lost in strangers' faces." In writing passages like that, I was writing more than I had known I knew with the result that the book was not only a word *from* me – my words painstakingly chosen and arranged into sentences by me alone – but also a word out of such a deep and secret part of who I am that it seemed also a word *to* me.

23 If writers write not just with paper and ink or a word processor but with their own life's blood, then I think something like this is perhaps always the case. A book you write out of the depths of who you are, like a dream you dream out of those same depths, is entirely your own creation. All the words your characters speak are words that you alone have put into their mouths, just as every situation they become involved in is one that you alone have concocted for them. But it seems to me nonetheless that a book you write, like a dream you dream, can have more healing and truth and wisdom in it at least for yourself than you feel in any way responsible for.

24 A large part of the truth that *Godric* had for me was the truth that although death ended my father, it has never ended my relationship with my father – a secret that I had never so clearly understood before. So forty-four years after the last time I saw him, it was to my father that I dedicated the book – *In memoriam patris mei.** I wrote the dedication in Latin solely because at the time it seemed appropriate to the medieval nature of the tale, but I have come to suspect since that Latin was also my unconscious way of remaining obedient to the ancient family law that the secret of my father must be at all costs kept secret.

In memoriam patris mei · "in memory of my father" (Latin)

25 The other half of the diptych's message –"whose household is prospered by the Lord"– was full of irony. Whether because of the Lord or good luck or the state of the stock market, we were a prosperous family in more ways than just economic, but for all the good our prosperity did us when the chips were down, we might as well have been paupers.

26 What happened was that one of our daughters began to stop eating. There was nothing scary about it at first. It was just the sort of thing any girl who thought she'd be prettier if she lost a

few pounds might do – nothing for breakfast, maybe a carrot or 26
a Diet Coke for lunch, for supper perhaps a little salad with low
calorie dressing. But then, as months went by, it did become scary.
Anorexia nervosa is the name of the sickness she was suffering
from, needless to say, and the best understanding of it that I have
been able to arrive at goes something like this. Young people crave
to be free and independent. They crave also to be taken care of
and safe. The dark magic of *anorexia* is that it satisfies both of
these cravings at once. By not eating, you take your stand against
the world that is telling you what to do and who to be. And by not
eating you also make your body so much smaller, lighter, weaker
that in effect it becomes a child's body again and the world flocks
to your rescue. This double victory is so great that apparently not
even self-destruction seems too high a price to pay.

Be that as it may, she got more and more thin, of course, till she 27
began to have the skull-like face and fleshless arms and legs of a
victim of Buchenwald,˙ and at the same time the Cowardly Lion
got more and more afraid and sad, felt more and more helpless.
No rational argument, no dire medical warning, no pleading or
cajolery or bribery would make this young woman he loved eat
normally again but only seemed to strengthen her determina-
tion not to, this young woman on whose life his own in so many
ways depended. He could not solve her problem because he was
of course himself part of her problem. She remained very much
the same person she had always been – creative, loving, funny,
bright as a star – but she was more afraid of gaining weight than
she was afraid of death itself because that was what it came to
finally. Three years were about as long as the sickness lasted in its
most intense form with some moments when it looked as though
things were getting better and some moments when it was hard
to imagine they could get any worse. Then finally, when she had
to be hospitalized, a doctor called one morning to say that unless
they started feeding her against her will, she would die. It was
as clear-cut as that. Tears ran down the Cowardly Lion's face as
he stood with the telephone at his ear. His paws were tied. The
bat-winged monkeys hovered.

I will not try to tell my daughter's story for two reasons. One 28
is that it is not mine to tell but hers. The other is that of course I
do not know her story, not the real story, the inside story, of what

Buchenwald · one of
the first and largest of
the Nazi concentration
camps

28 it was like for her. For the same reasons I will not try to tell what
    it was like for my wife or our other two children, each of whom
    in her own way was involved in that story. I can tell only my part
    in it, what happened to me, and even there I can't be sure I have
    it right because in many ways it is happening still. The fearsome
    blessing of that hard time continues to work itself out in my life
    in the same way we're told the universe is still hurtling through
    outer space under the impact of the great cosmic explosion that
    brought it into being in the first place. I think grace sometimes
    explodes into our lives like that – sending our pain, terror, aston-
    ishment hurtling through inner space until by grace they become
    Orion, Cassiopeia, Polaris to give us our bearings, to bring us
    into something like full being at last.

29   My anorectic daughter was in danger of starving to death,
    and without knowing it, so was I. I wasn't living my own life any
    more because I was so caught up in hers. If in refusing to eat
    she was mad as a hatter, I was if anything madder still because
    whereas in some sense she knew what she was doing to herself,
    I knew nothing at all about what I was doing to myself. She had
    given up food. I had virtually given up doing anything in the
    way of feeding myself humanly. To be at peace is to have peace
    inside yourself more or less in spite of what is going on outside
    yourself. In that sense I had no peace at all. If on one particular
    day she took it into her head to have a slice of toast, say, with her
    dietetic supper, I was in seventh heaven. If on some other day
    she decided to have no supper at all, I was in hell.

30   I choose the term *hell* with some care. Hell is where there is
    no light but only darkness, and I was so caught up in my fear for
    her life, which had become in a way my life too, that none of the
    usual sources of light worked any more, and light was what I was
    starving for. I had the companionship of my wife and two other
    children. I read books. I played tennis and walked in the woods. I
    saw friends and went to the movies. But even in the midst of such
    times as that I remained so locked inside myself that I was not
    really present in them at all. Toward the end of C. S. Lewis's *The
    Last Battle** there is a scene where a group of dwarves sit huddled
    together in a tight little knot thinking that they are in a pitch black,
    malodorous stable when the truth of it is that they are out in the
    midst of an endless grassy countryside as green as Vermont with

**C. S. Lewis's *The Last
Battle*** · part of the
"Chronicles of Narnia"
series written by Lewis
(1898–1963), English
writer and popular
theologian.

Aslan · In Lewis's "Narnia" series, Aslan is the Christ figure

the sun shining and blue sky overhead. The huge golden lion, 30
Aslan* himself, stands nearby with all the other dwarves "kneeling
in a circle around his forepaws" as Lewis writes, "and burying
their hands and faces in his mane as he stooped his great head
to touch them with his tongue." When Aslan offers the dwarves
food, they think it is offal.* When he offers them wine, they take
it for ditch water. "Perfect love casteth out fear," John writes
(1 John 4:18), and the other side of that is that fear like mine
casteth out love, even God's love. The love I had for my daughter
was lost in the anxiety I had for my daughter.

offal · trimmings of a slaughtered animal; rotting material or rubbish unfit for food

The only way I knew to be a father was to take care of her, as 31
my father had been unable to take care of me, to move heaven and
earth if necessary to make her well, and of course I couldn't do
that. I didn't have either the wisdom or the power to make her well.
None of us has the power to change other human beings like that,
and it would be a terrible power if we did, the power to violate the
humanity of others even for their own good. The psychiatrists we
consulted told me I couldn't cure her. The best thing I could do
for her was to stop trying to do anything. I think in heart I knew
they were right, but it didn't stop the madness of my desperate
meddling, it didn't stop the madness of my trying. Everything I
could think to do or say only stiffened her resolve to be free from,
among other things, me. Her not eating was a symbolic way of
striking out for that freedom. The only way she would ever be well
again was if and when she freely chose to be. The best I could do
as her father was to stand back and give her that freedom even at
the risk of her using it to choose for death instead of life.

Love ... yourself · see Leviticus 19:18, Matthew 22:37–39

Love your neighbor as yourself* is part of the great command- 32
ment. The other way to say it is, Love yourself as your neighbor.
Love yourself not in some egocentric, self-serving sense but
love yourself the way you would love your friend in the sense of
taking care of yourself, nourishing yourself, trying to understand,
comfort, strengthen yourself. Ministers in particular, people in
the caring professions in general, are famous for neglecting their
selves with the result that they are apt to become in their own
way as helpless and crippled as the people they are trying to care
for and thus no longer selves who can be of much use to anybody.
If your daughter is struggling for life in a raging torrent, you do
not save her by jumping into the torrent with her, which leads

32 only to your both drowning together. Instead you keep your feet on the dry bank – you maintain as best you can your own inner peace, the best and strongest of who you are – and from that solid ground reach out a rescuing hand. "Mind your own business" means butt out of other people's lives because in the long run they must live their lives for themselves, but it also means pay mind to your own life, your own health and wholeness, both for your own sake and ultimately for the sake of those you love too. Take care of yourself so you can take care of them. A bleeding heart is of no help to anybody if it bleeds to death.

33 How easy it is to write such words and how impossible it was to live them. What saved the day for my daughter was that when she finally had to be hospitalized in order to keep her alive, it happened about three thousand miles away from me. I was not there to protect her, to make her decisions, to manipulate events on her behalf, and the result was that she had to face those events on her own. There was no one to shield her from those events and their consequences in all their inexorability. In the form of doctors, nurses, social workers, the judge who determined that she was a danger to her own life and thus could be legally hospitalized against her will, society stepped in. Those men and women were not haggard, dithering, lovesick as I was. They were realistic, tough, conscientious, and in those ways, though they would never have put it in such terms themselves, loved her in a sense that I believe is closer to what Jesus meant by love than what I had been doing.

34 God loves in something like their way, I think. The power that created the universe and spun the dragonfly's wing and is beyond all other powers holds back, in love, from overpowering us. I have never felt God's presence more strongly than when my wife and I visited that distant hospital where our daughter was. Walking down the corridor to the room that had her name taped to the door, I felt that presence surrounding me like air – God in his very stillness, holding his breath, loving her, loving us all, the only way he can without destroying us. One night we went to compline* in an Episcopal cathedral, and in the coolness and near emptiness of that great vaulted place, in the remoteness of the choir's voices chanting plainsong, in the grayness of the stone, I felt it again – the passionate restraint and hush of God.

Little by little the young woman I loved began to get well, 35
emerging out of the shadows finally as strong and sane and wise
as anybody I know, and little by little as I watched her healing
happen, I began to see how much I was in need of healing and
getting well myself. Like Lewis's dwarves, for a long time I had
sat huddled in the dark of a stable of my own making. It was
only now that I started to suspect the presence of the green
countryside, the golden lion in whose image and likeness even
cowardly lions are made.

This is all part of the story about what it has been like for the 36
last ten years or so to be me, and before anybody else has the
chance to ask it, I will ask it myself: Who cares? What in the world
could be less important than who I am and who my father and
mother were, the mistakes I have made together with the occasional discoveries, the bad times and good times, the moments
of grace. If I were a public figure and my story had had some
impact on the world at large, that might be some justification for
telling it, but I am a very private figure indeed, living very much
out of the mainstream of things in the hills of Vermont, and my
life has had very little impact on anybody much except for the
people closest to me and the comparative few who have read
books I've written and been one way or another touched by them.

But I talk about my life anyway because if, on the one hand, 37
hardly anything could be less important, on the other hand,
hardly anything could be more important. My story is important
not because it is mine, God knows, but because if I tell it anything
like right, the chances are you will recognize that in many ways
it is also yours. Maybe nothing is more important than that we
keep track, you and I, of these stories of who we are and where
we have come from and the people we have met along the way
because it is precisely through these stories in all their particularity, as I have long believed and often said, that God makes himself
known to each of us most powerfully and personally. If this is
true, it means that to lose track of our stories is to be profoundly
impoverished not only humanly but also spiritually.

The God of biblical faith is a God who started history going 38
in the first place. He is also a God who moment by moment, day
by day continues to act in history always, which means both the
history that gets written down in the *New York Times* and the *San*

38 *Francisco Chronicle* and at the same time my history and your history, which for the most part don't get written down anywhere except in the few lines that may be allotted to us some day on the obituary page. The Exodus, the Covenant, the entry into the Promised Land•–such mighty acts of God as these appear in Scripture, but no less mighty are the acts of God as they appear in our own lives. I think of my father's death as in its way his exodus, his escape from bondage, and of the covenant that my mother made with my brother and me never to talk about him, and of the promised land of pre-World War II Bermuda that we reached through the wilderness and bewilderness of our first shock and grief at losing him.

Exodus ... Promised Land · see Exodus 12:31–14:31, Exodus 20:1–40:33, and Joshua 3–4, respectively

39 As I understand it, to say that God is mightily present even in such private events as these does not mean that he makes events happen to us which move us in certain directions like chessmen. Instead, events happen under their own steam as random as rain, which means that God is present in them not as their cause but as the one who even in the hardest and most hair-raising of them offers us the possibility of that new life and healing which I believe is what salvation is. For instance I cannot believe that a God of love and mercy in any sense willed my father's suicide; it was only father himself who willed it as the only way out available to him from a life that for various reasons he had come to find unbearable. God did not will what happened that early November morning in Essex Falls, New Jersey, but I believe that God was present in what happened. I cannot guess how he was present with my father–I can guess much better how utterly abandoned by God my father must have felt if he thought about God at all – but my faith as well as my prayer is that he was and continues to be present with him in ways beyond my guessing. I can speak with some assurance only of how God was present in that dark time for me in the sense that I was not destroyed by it but came out of it with scars that I bear to this day, to be sure, but also somehow the wiser and the stronger for it. Who knows how I might have turned out if my father had lived, but through the loss of him all those long years ago I think that I learned something about how even tragedy can be a means of grace that I might never have come to any other way. As I see it, in other words, God acts in history and in your and my brief

histories not as the puppeteer who sets the scene and works the 39
strings but rather as the great director who no matter what role
fate casts us in conveys to us somehow from the wings,* if we
have our eyes, ears, hearts open and sometimes even if we don't,
how we can play those roles in a way to enrich and ennoble and
hallow the whole vast drama of things including our own small
but crucial parts in it.

wings · the areas at either side of a stage, backstage and out of sight

In fact I am inclined to believe that God's chief purpose in 40
giving us memory is to enable us to go back in time so that if
we didn't play those roles right the first time round, we can still
have another go at it now. We cannot undo our old mistakes or
their consequences any more than we can erase old wounds that
we have both suffered and inflicted, but through the power that
memory gives us of thinking, feeling, imagining our way back
through time we can at long last finally finish with the past in
the sense of removing its power to hurt us and other people and
to stunt our growth as human beings.

The sad things that happened long ago will always remain part 41
of who we are just as the glad and gracious things will too, but
instead of being a burden of guilt, recrimination, and regret that
make us constantly stumble as we go, even the saddest things
can become, once we have made peace with them, a source of
wisdom and strength for the journey that still lies ahead. It is
through memory that we are able to reclaim much of our lives
that we have long since written off by finding that in everything
that has happened to us over the years God was offering us
possibilities of new life and healing which, though we may have
missed them at the time, we can still choose and be brought to
life by and healed by all these years later.

Another way of saying it, perhaps, is that memory makes it 42
possible for us both to bless the past, even those parts of it that
we have always felt cursed by, and also to be blessed by it. If
this kind of remembering sounds like what psychotherapy is all
about, it is because of course it is, but I think it is also what the
forgiveness of sins is all about – the interplay of God's forgiveness of us and our forgiveness of God and each other. To see
how God's mercy was for me buried deep even in my father's
death was not just to be able to forgive my father for dying and
God for letting him die so young and without hope and all the

42 people like my mother who were involved in his death but also to be able to forgive myself for all the years I had failed to air my crippling secret so that then, however slowly and uncertainly, I could start to find healing. It is in the experience of such healing that I believe we experience also God's loving forgiveness of us, and insofar as memory is the doorway to both experiences, it becomes not just therapeutic but sacred.

43 In a book called *The Wizard's Tide* I wrote the story of my father's death the way I would tell it to a child, in other words the way I need to tell it to the child who lives on inside me as the children we were live on inside all of us. By telling it as a story, I told it not from the outside as an observer, the way I have told it in these pages, but from the inside as a participant. By telling it in language a child could understand, I told it as the child who I both was in 1936 and still am in 1990. I relived it for that child and as that child with the difference that this time I was able to live it right.

44 The father in the story dies in much the way my father did, and the mother and the children in the story hushed it up in much the way my mother and her two children did, but there comes the difference. At the end of the story, on Christmas eve, the boy Teddy, who is me, comes to a momentous conclusion.

44a   He thought about how terrible it was that nobody talked
      about [his father] any more so that it was almost as if there
      had never been any such person. He decided that from
      now on he wanted to talk about him a lot. He wanted to
      remember everything about him that he could remember
      so someday he could tell about him to other people who
      had never seen him.

44 And then, just before turning off the lights, Teddy actually does this. For the first time since his father's death, Teddy brings the subject up to his younger sister, Bean. He doesn't say anything about his father, he just mentions his name, but as I wrote the story, I knew that was enough. It was enough to start a healing process for the children in the story that for me didn't start till I was well into my fifties. Stranger still, it was enough also to start healing the child in me the way he might have been healed in 1936 if his real story had only turned out like the make-believe story in the book. By a kind of miracle, the make-believe story

became the real story or vice versa. The unalterable past was in   44
some extraordinary way altered. Maybe the most sacred func-
tion of memory is just that: to render the distinction between
past, present, and future ultimately meaningless; to enable us at
some level of our being to inhabit that same eternity which it is
said that God himself inhabits.

We believe in God – such as it is, we have faith – because cer-   45
tain things happened to us once and go on happening. We work
and goof off, we love and dream, we have wonderful times and
awful times, are cruelly hurt and hurt others cruelly, get mad and
bored and scared stiff and ache with desire, do all such human
things as these, and if our faith is not mainly just window dressing
or a rabbit's foot or fire insurance, it is because it grows out of
precisely this kind of rich human compost. The God of biblical
faith is the God who meets us at those moments in which for
better or worse we are being most human, most ourselves, and if
we lose touch with those moments, if we don't stop from time to
time to notice what is happening to us and around us and inside
us, we run the tragic risk of losing touch with God too.

Sad to say, the people who seem to lose touch with themselves   46
and with God most conspicuously are of all things ministers. As
a minister myself I am peculiarly aware of this. I don't say they do
it more than other people but they do it more publicly. It could
hardly be more ironic. First of all, ministers give preeminence
to of all books the Bible whose absolutely central and unifying
thesis is that God makes himself known in historical experience.
Secondly, they call their congregations to examine their own
experience as human beings in that most intimate and searching
of all ways which is known as prayer. Thirdly, in their sermons,
if they do it right, they proclaim above all else the staggeringly
good news that God so loves the world that he is continually at
work in our lives in the world in order to draw us, in love, closer
and closer to himself and to each other. In other words, a major
part of their ministry is to remind us that there is nothing more
important than to pay attention to what is happening to us, yet
again and again they show little sign of doing so themselves.
There is precious little in most of their preaching to suggest that
they have rejoiced and suffered with the rest of mankind. If they
draw on their own experience at all, it is usually for some little

46 anecdote to illustrate a point or help make the pill go down but rarely if ever for an authentic, first-hand, flesh-and-blood account of what it is like to love Christ, say, or to feel spiritually bankrupt, or to get fed up with the whole religious enterprise.

47 Along with much of the rest of mankind, ministers have had such moments, we can only assume, but more often than not they don't seem to trust them, don't draw on them, don't talk about them. Instead they keep setting them aside for some reason – maybe because they seem too private to share or too trivial or too ambiguous or not religious enough; maybe because what God seems to be saying to them through their flesh-and-blood experience has a depth and mystery and power to it which make all their homiletical pronouncements about God sound empty by comparison. The temptation then is to stick to the homiletical* pronouncements. Comparatively empty as they may be, they are at least familiar. They add up. Congregations have come to expect homiletical pronouncements and to take comfort from them, and the preachers who pronounce them can move them around in various thought-provoking and edifying ways which nobody will feel unsettled or intimidated by because they have heard them so often.

homiletical · relating to a sermon

48 Ministers run the awful risk, in other words, of ceasing to be witnesses to the presence in their own lives – let alone in the lives of the people they are trying to minister to – of a living God who transcends everything they think they know and can say about him and is full of extraordinary surprises. Instead they tend to become professionals who have mastered all the techniques of institutional religion and who speak on religious matters with what often seems a maximum of authority and a minimum of vital personal involvement. Their sermons often sound as bland as they sound bloodless. The faith they proclaim appears to be no longer rooted in or nourished by or challenged by their own lives but instead free-floating, secondhand, passionless. They sound, in other words, burnt out.

49 Obviously ministers are not called to be in that sense professionals. God forbid. I believe that they are called instead, together with all other Christians and would-be Christians, to consider the lilies of the field, to consider the least of these my brethren, to consider the dead sparrow by the roadside.* Maybe prerequisite

consider ... roadside · see Luke 12:6–28, Luke 9:48

to all those, they are called upon to consider themselves – what 49 they love and what they fear, what they are ashamed of, what makes them sick to their stomachs, what rejoices their hearts. I believe that ministers and everyone are called also to consider Jesus of Nazareth in whom God himself showed how crucial human life is by actually living one and hallowed human death by actually dying one and who lives and dies still with us and for us and in spite of us. I believe that we are called to see that the day-by-day lives of all of us – the things that happened long ago, the things that happened only this morning – are also hallowed and crucial and part of a great drama in which souls are lost and souls are saved including our own.

That is why to keep track of these lives we live is not just a 50 means of enriching our understanding and possibly improving our sermons but a truly sacred work. In these pages I tell secrets about my parents, my children, myself because that is one way of keeping track and because I believe that it is not only more honest but also vastly more interesting than to pretend that I have no such secrets to tell. I not only have my secrets, I am my secrets. And you are your secrets. Our secrets are human secrets, and our trusting each other enough to share them with each other has much to do with the secret of what it is to be human.

Henri Nouwen

◄(1 9 3 2 - 1 9 9 6)►

Nouwen was a Dutch theologian, priest, and professor of psychology who spent much of his adult life in North America, where he preached and wrote about the virtues of service to the poor and the weak and the practice of the spiritual disciplines. Although he taught at Notre Dame, Yale, and Harvard, he found his greatest fulfillment living and working at Daybreak – a community for the severely handicapped near Toronto. Nouwen was a prolific writer on the spiritual life. In such books as Life of the Beloved, In the Name of Jesus, The Road to Daybreak, Way of the Heart, *and* Return of the Prodigal Son, *he emphasizes the paradoxes of the Christian faith – that the Divine Presence is evident in the "downward way" taught by Jesus. Nouwen tries to counter the forces of secularism with the story of a loving God who waits patiently for the return of his rebellious creatures. The writer died of a heart attack while visiting in the Netherlands in the fall of 1996.*

ADAM'S PEACE

1   IN THE MIDDLE OF THIS DECADE I moved from Harvard to Daybreak – from an institution for very bright people to a community for mentally handicapped ones.

2   Daybreak, situated near Toronto, is part of an international federation of communities called *l'Arche* – the Ark – where mentally handicapped men and women and their assistants try to live together in the spirit of the beatitudes* of Jesus.

beatitudes · see Matthew 5:3-12

3   I live in a house with six handicapped people and four assistants. We live together as a family. None of the assistants is specially trained to work with people with a mental handicap, but we receive all the help we need from nearby professionals.

4   When there are no special crises we live just as a family, gradually forgetting who is handicapped and who is not. All have their

gifts, all have their struggles. We eat together, play together, pray 4
together and go out together. We all have our own preferences in
terms of work, food and movies, and we all have our problems
getting along with someone in the house, whether handicapped
or not. We laugh a lot. We cry a lot too. Sometimes both at the
same time. That is *l'Arche*, that is Daybreak, that is the family of
ten I live with day in and day out.

When asked to return to Harvard to speak about peace, I 5
suddenly realized that speaking about peace from this tiny
family is not like speaking about peace as a professor. I need a
new perspective and a new sensibility, a new language. It is not
easy. It is even quite painful. I feel so vulnerable and so naked.
But I will tell you the story of Adam, one of the ten people in
our home, and let him become the silent witness for the peace
that is not of this world.

Adam is the weakest person in our family. He is a 25-year-old 6
man who cannot speak, cannot dress or undress himself, cannot
walk alone, cannot eat without much help. He does not cry or
laugh. Only occasionally does he make eye contact. His back is
distorted. His arm and leg movements are twisted. He suffers
from severe epilepsy and, despite heavy medication, sees few days
without grand-mal seizures. Sometimes, as he grows suddenly
rigid, he utters a howling groan. On a few occasions I've seen
one big tear roll down his cheek.

It takes me about an hour and a half to wake Adam up, give 7
him his medication, carry him into his bath, wash him, shave him,
clean his teeth, dress him, walk him to the kitchen, give him his
breakfast, put him in his wheelchair and bring him to the place
where he spends most of the day with therapeutic exercises.

I tell you this not to give you a nursing report, but to share 8
with you something quite intimate. After a month of working
this way with Adam, something happened to me. This deeply
handicapped young man, who is considered by many outsid-
ers a vegetable, a distortion of humanity, a useless animal-like
creature who shouldn't have been born, started to become my
dearest companion.

As my fears gradually lessened, a love emerged in me so full 9
of tender affection that most of my other tasks seemed boring
and superficial compared with the hours spent with Adam. Out

9 of his broken body and broken mind emerged a most beautiful human being offering me a greater gift than I would ever offer him: Somehow Adam revealed to me who he is, and who I am, and how we can love each other.

10 When I carried him into his bath, made big waves to let the water run fast around his chest and neck, rubbed noses with him and told him all sorts of stories about him and me, I knew that two friends were communicating far beyond the realm of thought or emotion. Deep speaks to deep, spirit speaks to spirit, heart speaks to heart. I started to realize that ours was a mutual love based not on shared knowledge or shared feelings, but on shared humanity. The longer I stayed with Adam the more clearly I saw him as my gentle teacher, teaching me what no book, school or professor could ever teach me.

11 The gift of peace hidden in Adam's utter weakness is a gift not of this world, but certainly for this world. For this gift to become known, someone has to lift it up and pass it on. That may be the deepest meaning of being an assistant to handicapped people: helping them to share their gifts.

12 Adam's peace is first of all a peace rooted in being. Being is more important than doing. How simple a truth, but how hard to live.

13 Adam can do nothing. He is completely dependent on others. His gift is purely being with us. Every evening when I run home to take care of Adam – to help him with his supper and put him to bed – I realize that the best thing I can do for him is to be with him. And indeed, that is the great joy: paying total attention to his breathing, his eating, his careful steps; noticing how he tries to lift a spoon to his mouth or offers his left arm a little to make it easier for me to take off his shirt.

14 Most of my life has been built around the idea that my value depends on what I do. I made it through school. I earned my degrees and awards and I made my career. Yes, with many others, I fought my way up to a little success, a little popularity and a little power. But as I sit beside the slow and heavy-breathing Adam, I start to see how violent that journey was. So marked by rivalry and competition, so pervaded with compulsion and obsession, so spotted with moments of suspicion, jealousy, resentment and revenge.

15 Oh sure, most of what I did was called ministry, the ministry of justice and peace, the ministry of forgiveness and reconcilia-

tion, the ministry of healing and wholeness. But when those who   15
want peace are as interested in success, popularity and power
as those who want war, what then is the real difference between
war and peace? When the peace is as much of this world as the
war is, the choice is between a war which we euphemistically call
pacification and a peace in which the peacemakers violate each
other's deepest values.

Adam says to me: Peace is first of all the art of being. I know   16
he is right because, after four months of being a little with Adam,
I am discovering in myself the beginning of an inner at-homeness
that I didn't know before.

When I cover him with his sheets and blankets, turn out the   17
lights and pray with Adam, he is always very quiet. It's as if he
knows my praying voice from my speaking voice. I whisper in his
ear: "May all the angels protect you," and often he looks up to me
from his pillow and seems to know what I am saying.

Ever since I've been praying with Adam I've known better   18
than before that praying is being with Jesus, simply "wasting
time" with him. Adam keeps teaching me that.

Adam's peace is not only a peace rooted in being, but also a   19
peace rooted in the heart. Somehow through the centuries we
have come to believe that what makes us human is our mind.
Many people define a human being as a rational animal. But
Adam keeps telling me over and over again that what makes us
human is not our mind but our heart, not our ability to think but
our ability to love. Whoever speaks about Adam as a vegetable or
an animal-like creature misses the sacred mystery that Adam is
fully capable of receiving and giving love. He is not half human,
not nearly human, but fully, completely human because he is
all heart and it is the heart that is made in the likeness of God.

Let me quickly add that by "heart" I do not mean the seat of   20
human emotions, in contrast to the mind as the seat of human
thought. No, by "heart" I mean the center of our being, where
God has hidden the divine gifts of trust, hope and love. Whereas
the mind tries to understand, grasp problems, discern different
aspects of reality and probe mysteries, the heart allows us to
become sons and daughters of God and brothers and sisters of
each other. Long before the mind is able to exercise its power,
the heart is already able to develop a trusting human relationship.

21   When I say that I believe deeply that Adam can give and receive love and that there is a true mutuality between us, I make no naïve psychological statement overlooking his severe handicaps; I speak of a love between us that transcends all thoughts and feelings, precisely because it is rooted in God's first love, a love that precedes all human loves. The mystery of Adam is that in his deep mental and emotional brokenness he has become so empty of all human pride that he has become the preferable mediator of that first love. Maybe this will help you see why Adam is giving me a whole new understanding of God's love for the poor and the oppressed.

22   The peace that flows from Adam's broken heart is not of this world. It is not the result of political analysis, roundtable debates, discernment of the signs of the times or well advised strategies. All these activities of the mind have their role in peacemaking. But they are all easily perverted to a new way of warmaking if they are not in the service of the divine peace that flows from the broken heart of those who are called the poor in spirit.* Adam's peace, while rooted more in being than in doing, and more in the heart than in the mind, is a peace that calls forth community. At *l'Arche* the people hold us together as a family; in fact, the most handicapped people are the true center of gravity. Adam in his total vulnerability calls us together as a family.

> **poor in spirit ·** see
> Matthew 5:3

23   The weakest members are not the handicapped residents but the assistants. Our commitments are ambiguous at best. Some stay longer than others, but most move on after one or two years. Closer to the center are Raymond, Bill, John, and Trevor, each of whom is relatively independent, but still in need of much help and attention. They are permanent family members; they are with us for life; they keep us honest. Because of them, conflicts never last very long, tensions are talked out, disagreements are resolved. But in the heart of our community are Rose and Adam, both deeply handicapped, and the weaker of the two is Adam. Adam, the most broken of us all, is without any doubt the strongest bond among us.

24   Because of Adam there is always someone home. Because of Adam there is a quiet rhythm in the house. Because of Adam there are words of affection, gentleness and tenderness. Because of Adam there is always space for mutual forgiveness and healing. Adam, the weakest among us, is our true peacemaker. How mysterious are God's ways!

Most of my adult life I have tried to show the world that I could do it on my own, that I needed others only to get me back on my lonely road as a strong, independent, creative man. And most of my fellow intellectuals joined me in that desire. But all of us highly trained individuals today are facing a world on the brink of total destruction. Now we wonder how we might join forces to make peace! 25

What kind of peace can this possibly be? Who can paint a group portrait of people who all want the center seat? When all want the honor of being the final peacemaker, there will be no peace. 26

Adam needs many people, none of whom can boast of any success. Adam will never be better. Medically, he will only grow worse. Each person who works with him does only a little bit. My part in his life is very small. Some cook for him, some do his laundry, some give him massages, some let him listen to music or take him for a walk or a swim or a ride. Others look after his blood pressure, regulate his medicine, look after his teeth. Even with all this assistance Adam often slips into total exhaustion. Yet a community of peace has emerged around him, a peace community not just for Adam, but for all who belong to Adam's race. It's a community that proclaims that God has chosen to reveal his glory in complete weakness and vulnerability. 27

I've told you about Adam and about his peace. But you're not part of *l'Arche*, you don't live at Daybreak, you're not a member of Adam's family. Like me, however, you search for peace in your heart, in your family and in your world. 28

I've told you about Adam and his peace to offer you a quiet guide with a gentle heart, a little light for walking through this dark world. In Adam's name, therefore, I say to you: Do not give up working for peace. But remember that the peace you seek is not of this world. Don't be distracted by the great noises of war, the dramatic descriptions of misery, the sensational exploitation of cruelty. Newspapers, movies and war novels may numb you, but they do not create a true desire for peace. They mostly create feelings of shame, guilt and powerlessness – the worst motives for peace work. 29

refuses ... temporal power · see Matthew 4:1–11, Luke 4:1–12

Keep your eyes on the one who refuses to turn stones into bread, jump from great heights or rule with great temporal power.* Keep your eyes on the one who says, 30

30a   Blessed are the poor, the gentle, those who mourn and those who hunger and thirst for righteousness; blessed are the merciful, the pure of heart, the peacemakers and those who are persecuted in the cause of uprightness.*

Blessed ... upright-ness · Matthew 5:3–10

31   Keep your eyes on the one who touches the lame and the blind, the one who speaks forgiveness and encouragement, the one who dies alone. Keep your eyes on the one who is poor with the poor, weak with the weak and rejected with the rejected. That one is the source of all peace.

32   As long as we think and live as if there is no peace and that it all depends on ourselves to make it come about, we are on the road to self-destruction. But when we trust that the God of love has already given the peace we are searching for, we will see this peace poking through the broken soil of our human condition and we will be able to let it grow fast, even to heal the economic and political maladies of our time.

33   An old Hassidic* tale summarizes much of what I have tried to say.

Hassidic · The Hassidim are followers of a strict sect of orthodox Judaism

34   The Rabbi asks his students, "How can we determine the hour of dawn, when the night ends and the day begins?"

35   One student suggests, "When, from a distance, you can distinguish between a dog and a sheep?"

36   "No," the Rabbi answers.

37   "Is it when you can distinguish between a fig tree and a grapevine?" asks a second student.

38   "No," the Rabbi says.

39   "Please tell us the answer, then," say the students .

40   "It is," says the wise teacher, "when you have enough light to look human beings in the face and recognize them as your brothers and sisters. Until then the darkness is still with us."

41   Let us pray for that light. It is the peace that the world cannot give.

Wendell Berry

⟨ 1 9 3 4 - ⟩

*Berry is a farmer, a teacher, an essayist, a novelist, and a poet, in
addition to being a respected environmental activist. Born in rural
Kentucky, he has denounced the "industrial vandalism" his home
state has suffered at the hands of coal companies. For Berry, as he
has argued in* A Continuous Harmony *(1972), there are two irreconcilable philosophies of land management. One philosophy, that of
Christian stewardship, begins with a commitment that the earth is
the Lord's. The current stewards, according to this viewpoint, hold
natural resources in trust, using them with restraint in the knowledge that as-yet-unborn generations must also depend upon those
same resources for survival. The other philosophy, one Berry terms
"exploitation," begins with a commitment to immediate profit: whatever is profitable is good. This approach to nature, of course, Berry
opposes vehemently. Perhaps because his environmental ethic is
based upon his Christian beliefs, Berry has also opposed views like
those expounded by entomologist E. O. Wilson in* Consilience *(1998),
views which tend to reduce humanity's religious instinct to a mere
biological survival trait and a useful product of natural evolution.
In his response to Wilson, Berry insists upon the limited validity of
scientific explanations. "Science cannot replace art or religion," Berry
writes in* Life is a Miracle *(2001), "for the same reason that you cannot
loosen a nut with a saw or cut a board in two with a wrench."*

GOD AND COUNTRY

1 THE SUBJECT OF CHRISTIANITY and ecology is endlessly, perhaps infinitely, fascinating. It is fascinating theologically and
artistically because of our never-to-be-satisfied curiosity about
the relation between a made thing and its maker. It is fascinating
practically because we are unrelentingly required to honor in all

127

things the relation between the world and its Maker, and because 1
that requirement implies another, equally unrelenting, that we
ourselves, as makers, should always honor that greater making;
we are required, that is, to study the ways of working well, and
those ways are endlessly fascinating. The subject of Christianity
and ecology also is politically fascinating, to those of us who are
devoted both to biblical tradition and to the defense of the earth,
because we are always hankering for the support of the churches,
which seems to us to belong, properly and logically, to our cause.

This latter fascination, though not the most difficult and fear- 2
ful, is certainly the most frustrating, for the fact simply is that
the churches, which claim to honor God as the "maker of heaven
and earth,"* have lately shown little inclination to honor the earth
or to protect it from those who would dishonor it.

"maker ... earth" · a
quotation from the
Apostles' Creed

Organized Christianity seems, in general, to have made peace 3
with "the economy" by divorcing itself from economic issues,
and this, I think, has proved to be a disaster, both religious and
economic. The reason for this, on the side of religion, is suggested by the adjective "organized." It is clearly possible that, in
the condition of the world as the world now is, organization can
force upon an institution a character that is alien or even anti-
thetical to it. The organized church comes immediately under a
compulsion to think of itself, and identify itself to the world, not
as an institution synonymous with its truth and its membership,
but as a hodgepodge of funds, properties, projects, and offices,
all urgently requiring economic support. The organized church
makes peace with a destructive economy and divorces itself from
economic issues because it is economically compelled to do so.
Like any other public institution so organized, the organized
church is dependent on "the economy"; it cannot survive apart
from those economic practices that its truth forbids and that
its vocation is to correct. If it comes to a choice between the

fowls ... field · see
Matthew 5:25–34, Luke
12:24–31

extermination of the fowls of the air and the lilies of the field*
and the extermination of a building fund, the organized church
will elect – indeed, has already elected – to save the building fund.
The irony is compounded and made harder to bear by the fact
that the building fund can be preserved by crude applications
of money, but the fowls of the air and the lilies of the field can
be preserved only by true religion, by the practice of a proper

3   love and respect for them as the creatures of God. No wonder so many sermons are devoted exclusively to "spiritual" subjects. If one is living by the tithes* of history's most destructive economy, then the disembodiment of the soul becomes the chief of worldly conveniences.

tithes · a tenth of one's income which is contributed for religious purposes

4   There are many manifestations of this tacit* alliance between the organized churches and "the economy," but I need to speak only of two in order to make my point. The first is the phrase "full-time Christian service," which the churches of my experience have used exclusively to refer to the ministry, thereby at once making of the devoted life a religious specialty or career and removing the possibility of devotion from other callings. Thus the $50,000-a-year preacher is a "full-time Christian servant," whereas a $20,000 or a $10,000-a-year farmer, or a farmer going broke, so far as the religious specialists are concerned, must serve "the economy" in his work or in his failure and serve God in his spare time. The professional class is likewise free to serve itself in its work and to serve God by giving the church its ten percent. The churches in this way excerpt sanctity from the human economy and its work just as Cartesian* science has excerpted it from the material creation. And it is easy to see the interdependence of these two desecrations: the desecration of nature would have been impossible without the desecration of work, and vice versa.

tacit · unspoken, silent

Cartesian · named for French philosopher, mathematician and scientist René Descartes (1596–1650)

5   The second manifestation I want to speak of is the practice, again common in the churches of my experience, of using the rural ministry as a training ground for young ministers and as a means of subsidizing their education. No church official, apparently, sees any logical, much less any spiritual, problem in sending young people to minister to country churches before they have, according to their institutional superiors, become eligible to be ministers. These student ministers invariably leave the rural congregations that have sponsored or endured their educations as soon as possible once they have their diplomas in hand. The denominational hierarchies, then, evidently regard country places in exactly the same way as "the economy" does: as sources of economic power to be exploited for the advantage of "better" places. The country people will be used to educate ministers for the benefit of city people (in wealthier churches) who, obviously,

are thought more deserving of educated ministers. This, I am 5
well aware, is mainly the fault of the church organizations; it is
not a charge that can be made to stick to any young minister in
particular: not all ministers should be country ministers, just
as not all people should be country people. And yet it is a fact
that in the more than fifty years that I have known my own rural
community, many student ministers have been "called" to serve
in its churches, but not one has ever been "called" to stay. The
message that country people get from their churches, then, is
the same message that they get from "the economy": that, as
country people, they do not matter much and do not deserve
much consideration. And this inescapably imposes an economic
valuation on spiritual things. According to the modern church, as
one of my Christian friends said to me, "The soul of the plowboy
ain't worth as much as the soul of the delivery boy."

If the churches are mostly indifferent to the work and the 6
people by which the link between economy and ecosystem must
be enacted, it is no wonder that they are mostly indifferent to the
fate of the ecosystems themselves. One must ask, then: is this
state of affairs caused by Christian truth or by the failures and
errors of Christian practice? My answer is that it is caused by
the failures and errors of Christian practice. The evident ability
of most church leaders to be "born again in Christ" without in
the least discomforting their faith in the industrial economy's
bill of goods, however convenient and understandable it may
be, is not scriptural.

Anyone making such a statement must deal immediately with 7
the belief of many non-Christian environmentalists as well as at
least some Christians that Genesis 1:28, in which God instructs
Adam and Eve to "be fruitful and multiply and replenish the earth,
and subdue it," gives unconditional permission to humankind
to use the world as it pleases. Such a reading of Genesis 1:28 is
contradicted by virtually all the rest of the Bible, as many people
by now have pointed out. The ecological teaching of the Bible
is simply inescapable: God made the world because He wanted
it made. He thinks the world is good, and He loves it. It is His
world; He has never relinquished title to it. And He has never
revoked the conditions, bearing on His gift to us of the use of it,
that oblige us to take excellent care of it. If God loves the world,

7 then how might any person of faith be excused for not loving it or justified in destroying it?

8 But of course, those who see in Genesis 1:28 the source of all our abuse of the natural world (most of them apparently having read no more of the Bible than that verse) are guilty of an extremely unintelligent misreading of Genesis 1:28 itself. How, for example, would one arrange to "replenish the earth" if "subdue" means, as alleged, "conquer" or "defeat" or "destroy"?

9 We have in fact in the biblical tradition, rooted in the Bible but amplified in agrarian, literary, and other cultural traditions stemming from the Bible, the idea of stewardship as conditioned by the idea of *usufruct*. George Perkins Marsh[*] was invoking biblical tradition when he wrote, in 1864, that "man has too long forgotten that the earth was given to him for *usufruct* alone, not for consumption, still less for profligate waste." The Mormon essayist Hugh Nibley[*] invoked it explicitly when he wrote that "man's dominion is a call to service, not a license to exterminate."

George Perkins Marsh · American conservationist and scholar (1801–1882)

Hugh Nibley · American historian and Mormon apologist (1910–)

10 That service, stewardship, is the responsible care of property belonging to another. And by this the Bible does not mean an absentee landlord, but one living on the property, profoundly and intimately involved in its being and its health, as Elihu says to Job: "if he gather unto himself his spirit and his breath; All flesh shall perish together."[*] All creatures live by God's spirit, portioned out to them, and breathe His breath. To "lay up ... treasures in heaven,"[*] then, cannot mean to be spiritual at the earth's expense, or to despise or condemn the earth for the sake of heaven. It means exactly the opposite: do not desecrate or depreciate these gifts, which take part with us in the being of God, by turning them into worldly "treasure"; do not reduce life to money or to any other mere quantity.

"if he ... together" · Job 34:14–15

"lay up ... heaven" · Matthew 6:20

11 The idea of *usufruct* gives this point to the idea of stewardship, and makes it practical and economic. *Usufruct*, the *Oxford English Dictionary* says, is "the right of temporary possession, use, or enjoyment of the advantages of property belonging to another, so far as may be had without causing damage or prejudice to this." It is hardly a "free-market economy" that the Bible prescribes. Large accumulations of land were, and are, forbidden because the dispossession and privation of some cannot be an acceptable or normal result of the economic activity of others, for that destroys

a people as a people; it destroys the community. Usury* was, and 11
is, forbidden because the dispossession and privation of some
should not be regarded by others as an economic opportunity,
for that is contrary to neighborliness; it destroys the community.
And the greed that destroys the community also destroys the
land. What the Bible proposes is a moral economy, the standard
of which is the health of properties belonging to God.

Usury · the practice of charging interest for lending money. See Exodus 22:25, Leviticus 25:36–37

But we have considered so far only those things of the Creation 12
that can be included within the human economy – the usable
properties, so to speak. What about the things that are outside
the human economy? What about the things that from the point
of view of human need are useless or only partly usable? What
about the places that, as is increasingly evident, we should not
use at all? Obviously we must go further, and the Bible can take
us further. Many passages take us beyond a merely economic
stewardship, but the one that has come to seem most valuable to
me is Revelation 4:11, because I think it proposes an indispensable
standard for the stewardship both of things in use and of useless
things and things set aside from use: "Thou art worthy, O Lord,
to receive glory and honour and power: for thou hast created all
things, and for thy pleasure they are and were created."

The implications of this verse are relentlessly practical. The 13
ideas that we are permitted to use things that are pleasing to God,
that we have nothing at all to use that is not pleasing to Him, and
that necessarily implicated in the power to use is the power to
misuse and destroy are troubling, and indeed frightening, ideas.
But they are consoling, too, precisely insofar as we have the ability
to use well and the goodness or the character required to limit
use or to forbear to use.

Our responsibility, then, as stewards, the responsibility that 14
inescapably goes with our dominion over the other creatures,
according to Revelation 4:11, is to safeguard God's pleasure in
His work. And we can do that, I think (I don't know how else
we could do it), by safeguarding our pleasure in His work, and
our pleasure in our own work. Or, if we no longer can trust ourselves to be more than economic machines, then we must do it
by safeguarding the pleasure of children in God's work and in
ours. It is impossible, admittedly, to give an accurate economic
value to the goodness of good work, much less to the goodness

14 of an unspoiled forest or prairie or desert, or to the goodness of pure sunlight or water or air. And yet we are required to make an economy that honors such goods and is conversant with them. An economy that ignores them, as our present one does, "builds a Hell in Heaven's despite."•

15   As a measure of how far we have "progressed" in our industrial economy, let me quote a part of a sentence from the prayer "For Every Man in His Work" from the 1928 *Book of Common Prayer:*• "Deliver us, we beseech thee, in our several callings, from the service of mammon,• that we may do the work which thou givest us to do, in truth, in beauty, and in righteousness, with singleness of heart as thy servants, and to the benefit of our fellow men." What is astonishing about that prayer is that it is a relic. Throughout the history of the industrial revolution, it has become steadily less prayable. The industrial nations are now divided, almost entirely, into a professional or executive class that has not the least intention of working in truth, beauty, and righteousness, as God's servants, or to the benefit of their fellow men, and an underclass that has no choice in the matter. Truth, beauty, and righteousness now have, and can have, nothing to do with the economic life of most people. This alone, I think, is sufficient to account for the orientation of most churches to religious feeling, increasingly feckless, as opposed to religious thought or religious behavior.

16   I acknowledge that I feel deeply estranged from most of the manifestations of organized religion, partly for reasons that I have mentioned. Yet I am far from thinking that one can somehow become righteous by carrying Protestantism to the logical conclusion of a one-person church. We all belong, at least, to the problem. "There is…a price to be paid," Philip Sherrard says, "for fabricating around us a society which is as artificial and as mechanized as our own, and this is that we can exist in it only on condition that we adapt ourselves to it. This is our punishment."•

17   We all, obviously, are to some extent guilty of this damnable adaptation. We all are undergoing this punishment. But as Philip Sherrard well knows, it is a punishment that we can set our hearts against, an adaptation that we can try with all our might to undo. We can ally ourselves with those things that are worthy: light, air, water, earth; plants and animals; human families and commu-

"builds … despite"• the quotation comes from "The Clod and the Pebble" by English Romantic poet William Blake (1757–1827)

Book of Common Prayer • a book of prayers and liturgy used by Anglican and Episcopal churches

mammon • material goods, worldly wealth

"There is … punishment" • Philip Sherrard (1922–1995) religious thinker and Christian apologist. The quotation is from Sherrard's *The Rape of Man and Nature* (1987)

nities; the traditions of decent life, good work, and responsible 17
thought; the religious traditions; the essential stories and songs.

It is presumptuous, personally and historically, to assume that
one is a part of a "saving remnant."• One had better doubt that one
deserves such a distinction, and had better understand that there 18
may, after all, be nothing left to save. Even so, if one wishes to save
anything not protected by the present economy – topsoil, groves
of old trees, the possibility of the goodness or health of anything,
even the economic relevance of the biblical tradition – one is a
part of a remnant, and a dwindling remnant too, though not
without hope, and not without the necessary instructions, the
most pertinent of which, perhaps, is this, also from Revelation:
"Be watchful, and strengthen the things which remain, that are
ready to die."•

"saving remnant" ·
see Romans 9:27

"Be watchful ... die" ·
Revelation 3:2

Annie Dillard

◀ 1 9 4 5 - ▶

Dillard was born in Pittsburgh and educated at Hollins College, Virginia. Her collection of meditative essays on nature, Pilgrim at Tinker Creek, *earned her the Pulitzer Prize in 1974. One of America's leading prose stylists, Dillard composes essays noted for their vivid metaphors and singular lyricism. She characteristically explores the inherent mystery of the natural world, her vision imbued with the intuition that what she sees there is a hieroglyph of sorts. Extending and enlarging the naturalist tradition of Emerson and Thoreau, Dillard resensitizes readers to the numinous quality of their embodied existence. If the natural world cloaks horror, as every diligent observer must concede, it also veils an intense glory – overwhelming evidence, in other words, that mystery is at the heart of the cosmos. Dillard has written a book on her craft,* The Writing Life *(1989), and an autobiography of her early years,* An American Childhood *(1987), from which the following selection is taken. She currently serves as writer-in-residence at Wesleyan University (Connecticut).*

from AN AMERICAN CHILDHOOD

1   THAT MORNING IN CHURCH after our first subscription dance,* we reconvened on the balcony of the Shadyside Presbyterian Church. I sat in the first balcony row, and resisted the impulse to stretch my Charleston-stiff legs on the balcony's carved walnut rail. The blond boy I'd met at the dance was on my mind, and I intended to spend the church hour recalling his every word and gesture, but I couldn't concentrate. Beside me sat my friend Linda. Last night at the dance she had been a laughing, dimpled girl with an advanced sense of the absurd. Now in church she was grave, and didn't acknowledge my remarks.

> subscription dance · a dance held to raise money, often for a charitable organization

135

Near us in the balcony's first row, and behind us, were the   2
boys – the same boys with whom we had traveled on a bus to and
from the Sewickley Country Club dance. Below us spread the
main pews, filling with adults. Almost everyone in the church
was long familiar to me. But this particular Sunday in church
bore home to me with force a new notion: that I did not really
know any of these people at all. I thought I did – but, being now a
teenager, I thought I knew almost everything. Only the strongest
evidence could penetrate this illusion, which distorted everything I saw. I knew I approved almost nothing. That is, I liked,
I adored, I longed for, everyone on earth, especially India and
Africa, and particularly everyone on the streets of Pittsburgh – all
those friendly, democratic, openhearted, sensible people – and

Forbes Field · home
stadium of the Pittsburgh
Pirates baseball team
from 1909 until 1970

at Forbes Field,* and in all the office buildings, parks, streetcars,
churches, and stores, excepting only the people I knew, none of
whom was up to snuff.

The church building, where the old Scotch-Irish families assem-   3

Romanesque · an
artistic and architectural
style that flourished in
medieval Europe

bled weekly, was a Romanesque* chunk of rough, carved stone and
panes of dark slate. Covered in creeper, long since encrusted into
its quietly splendid site, it looked like a Scottish rock in the rain.

Everywhere outside and inside the church and parish hall,   4
sharp carved things rose from the many dim tons of stone. There
were grainy crossed keys, pelicans, anchors, a phoenix, ivy vines,
sheaves of wheat, queer and leering mammal heads like gargoyles,
thistles for Scotland, lizards, scrolls, lions, and shells. It looked
as if someone had once in Pittsburgh enjoyed a flight or two of
fancy. If your bare hand or arm brushed against one of the stone
walls carelessly, the stone would draw blood.

My wool coat sat empty behind me; its satin lining felt cool   5
on the backs of my arms. I hated being here. It looked as if the
boys did, too. Their mouths were all open, and their eyelids half
down. We were all trapped. At home before church, I had been
too rushed to fight about it.

I imagined the holy war each boy had fought with his family   6
this morning, and lost, resulting in his sullen and suited presence

ruddy · red

in church. I thought of Dan there, ruddy* cheeked, and of wild,
sweet Jamie beside him, each flinging his silk tie at his hypocrite
father after breakfast, and making a desperate stand in some
dark dining room lighted upward by snowlight from the lawns

6   outside – struggling foredoomed to raise the stone and walnut weight of this dead society's dead institutions, battling for liberty, freedom of conscience, and so forth.

7   The boys, at any rate, slumped. Possibly they were hung over.

8   While the nave* filled we examined, or glared at, the one thing before our eyes: the apse's* enormous gold mosaic of Christ. It loomed over the chancel;* every pew in the nave and on the balcony looked up at it. It was hard to imagine what long-ago board of trustees had voted for this Romish* looking mosaic, so glittering, with which we had been familiarizing ourselves in a lonely way since infancy, when our eyes could first focus on distance.

9   Christ stood barefoot, alone and helpless-looking, his palms outcurved at his sides. He was wearing his robes. He wasn't standing on anything, but instead floated loose and upright inside a curved, tiled dome. The balcony's perspective foreshortened the dome's curve, so Christ appeared to drift flattened and clumsy, shriveled but glorious. Barefoot as he was, and with the suggestion of sandstone scarps* behind him, he looked rural. Below me along the carpeted marble aisles crept the church's families; the women wore mink and sable stoles. Hushed, they sat and tilted their hatted heads and looked at the rural man. His skies of shattered gold widened over the sanctuary and almost met the square lantern tower, gold-decorated, over the nave.

10   The mosaic caught the few church lights – lights like tapers* in a castle – and spread them dimly, a dusting of gold like pollen, throughout the vast and solemn space. There was nothing you could see well in this rich, Rembrandt* darkness – nothing save the minister's shining face and Christ's gold vault – and yet there was no corner, no scratchy lily work, you couldn't see at all.

11   It was a velvet cord, maroon, with brass fittings, that reserved our ninth-grade balcony section for us. We sat on velvet cushions. Below us, filling the yellow pews with dark furs, were the rest of the families of the church, who seemed to have been planted here in dignity – by a God who could see how hard they worked and how few pleasures they took for themselves – just after the Flood* went down. There were Linda's parents and grandparents and one of her great-grandparents. Always, the same old Pittsburgh families ran this church. The men, for whose forefathers streets

---

nave · the chief part of a Christian church, extending from the entrance (the narthex) to the area just before the altar

apse · the area behind the altar

chancel · also known as the choir, the chancel is the area just before the altar

Romish · Roman Catholic

scarps · cliffs

tapers · long, slender candles

Rembrandt · Rembrandt van Rijn (1606–1669), Dutch painter

the Flood · see Genesis 6:13–9:17

all over town were named, served as deacons, trustees, and elders. 11
The women served in many ways, and ran the Christmas bazaar.

I knew these men; they were friends and neighbors. I knew 12
what they lived for, I thought. The men wanted to do the right
thing, at work and in the community. They wore narrow, tight
neckties. Close-mouthed, they met, in volunteer boardrooms
and in club locker rooms, the same few comfortable others they
had known since kindergarten. Their wives and children, in those
days, lived around them on their visits home. Some men found
their families bewildering, probably; a man might wonder, wak-
ened by reports of the outstanding misdeeds of this son or that
son, how everyone had so failed to understand what he expected.
Some of these men held their shoulders and knuckles tight; their
laughter was high and embarrassed; they seemed to be looking
around for the entrance to some other life. Only some of the
doctors, it seemed to me, were conspicuously interested and
glad. During conversations, they looked at people calmly, even
at their friends' little daughters; their laughter was deep, long,
and joyful; they asked questions; and they knew lots of words.

I knew the women better. The women were wise and strong. 13
Even among themselves, they prized gaiety and irony, gaiety and
irony come what may. They coped. They sighed, they permitted
themselves a remark or two, they lived essentially alone. They
reared their children with their own two hands, and did all their
own cooking and driving. They had no taste for waste or idleness.
They volunteered their considerable energies, wisdom, and ideas
at the church or the hospital or the service organization or charity.

Life among these families partook of all the genuine seriousness of life in time. A child's birth was his sole entrée, just as it
is to life itself. His birthright was a regiment of families and a
phalanx · a tightly   phalanx* of institutions which would accompany him, solidly but
packed mass   at a distance, through this vale of tears.*

this vale of tears ·   Families whose members have been acquainted with each 14
the world as a place of   other for as long as anyone remembers grow not close, but
sorrow and loss   respectful. They accumulate dignity by being seen at church
every Sunday for the duration of life, despite their troubles and
sorrows. They accumulate dignity at club luncheons, dinners,
and dances, by gracefully and persistently, with tidy hair and
fitted clothes, occupying their slots.

15   In this world, some grown women went carefully wild from
time to time. They appeared at parties in outlandish clothes,
hair sticking out, faces painted in freckles. They shrieked, sang,
danced, and parodied anything – that is, anything at all outside
the tribe – so that nothing, almost, was sacred. These clowns were
the best-loved women, and rightly so, for their own sufferings
had taught them what dignity was worth, and every few years
they reminded the others, and made them laugh till they cried.

16   My parents didn't go to church. I practically admired them
for it. Father would drive by at noon and scoop up Amy and me,
saying, "Hop in quick!" so no one would see his weekend khaki
pants and loafers.

17   Now, in unison with the adults in the dimness below, we read
responsively, answering the minister. Our voices blended low,
so their joined sound rose muffled and roaring, rhythmic, like
distant seas, and soaked into the rough stone vaults and plush
fittings, and vanished, and rose again:

17a   The heavens declare the glory of God:
    and the firmament showeth his handywork.
Day unto day uttereth speech,
    and night unto night showeth knowledge.
There is no speech nor language, where their voice is
not heard.*

The heavens … not heard · see Psalm 19:1–3

18   The minister was a florid, dramatic man who commanded
a batch of British vowels, for which I blamed him absolutely,
not knowing he came from a Canadian farm. His famous radio
ministry attracted letters and even contributions from Alaskan
lumberjacks and fishermen. The poor saps. What if one of them,
a lumberjack, showed up in Pittsburgh wearing a lumberjack
shirt and actually tried to enter the church building? Maybe the
ushers were really bouncers.

19   I had got religion at summer camp, and had prayed nightly
there and in my bed at home, to God, asking for a grateful heart,
and receiving one insofar as I requested it. Inasmuch as I despised
everything and everyone about me, of course, it was taken away,
and I was left with the blackened heart I had chosen instead. As the
years wore on, the intervals between Julys at camp stretched, and
filled with country-club evenings, filled with the slang of us girls, our

gossip, and our intricately shifting friendships, filled with the sight 19 of the boys whose names themselves were a litany,* and with the absorbing study of their nonchalance and gruff ease. All of which I professed, from time to time, when things went poorly, to disdain.

litany · a repetitive chant or prayer

Nothing so inevitably blackened my heart as an obligatory 20 Sunday at the Shadyside Presbyterian Church: the sight of orphan-girl Liz's "Jesus" tricked out in gilt; the minister's Britishy accent; the putative hypocrisy of my parents, who forced me to go, though they did not; the putative hypocrisy of the expensive men and women who did go. I knew enough of the Bible to damn these people to hell, citing chapter and verse. My house shall be called the house of prayer; but ye have made it a den of thieves.* Every week I had been getting madder; now I was going to plain quit. One of these days, when I figured out how.

My house ... thieves · see Matthew 21:13, Mark 11:17, Luke 19:46

After the responsive reading there was a pause, an expectant 21 hush. It was the first Sunday of the month, I remembered, shocked. Today was Communion. I would have to sit through Communion, with its two species,* embarrassment and tedium – and I would be late getting out and Father would have to drive around the block a hundred times. I had successfully avoided Communion for years.

two species · the two eucharistic elements, bread and wine, are sometimes termed "species"

From their pews below rose the ushers and elders – every- 22 body's father and grandfather, from Mellon Bank & Trust *et cetera* – in tailcoats. They worked the crowd smoothly, as always. When they collected money, I noted, they were especially serene. Collecting money was, after all, what they did during the week; they were used to it. Down each pew an usher thrust a long-handled velvet butterfly net, into the invisible interior of which we each inserted a bare hand to release a crushed, warm dollar bill we'd stored in a white glove's palm.

Now with dignity the ushers and elders hoisted the round ster- 23 ling silver trays which bore Communion. A loaded juice tray must have weighed ten pounds. From a cunning array of holes in its top layer hung wee, tapered, lead-crystal glasses. Each held one-half ounce of Welch's grape juice.

The seated people would pass the grape-juice trays down the pews. 24 After the grape juice came bread: flat silver salvers* bore heaps of soft bread cubes, as if for stuffing a turkey. The elders and ushers spread swiftly and silently over the marble aisles in discreet pairs, some for bread cubes, some for grape juice, communicating by eyebrow only.

salvers · large serving trays

24 An unseen organist, behind stone screens, played a muted series of single notes, a restless, breathy strain in a minor key, to kill time.

25 Soon the ushers reached the balcony where we sat. There our prayers had reached their intensest pitch, so fervent were we in our hopes not to drop the grape-juice tray.

26 I passed up the Welch's grape juice, I passed up the cubed bread, and sat back against my coat. Was all this not absurd? I glanced at Linda beside me. Apparently it was not. Her hands lay folded in her lap. Both her father and her uncle were elders.

27 It was not surprising, really, that I alone in this church knew what the barefoot Christ, if there had been such a person, would think about things – grape juice, tailcoats, British vowels, sable stoles. It was not surprising because it was becoming quite usual. After all, I was the intelligentsia around these parts, single-handedly. The intelligentsium. I knew why these people were in church: to display to each other their clothes. These were sophisticated men and women, such as we children were becoming. In church they made business connections; they saw and were seen. The boys, who, like me, were starting to come out for freedom and truth, must be having fits, now that the charade of Communion was in full swing.

28 I stole a glance at the boys, then looked at them outright, for I had been wrong. The boys, if mine eyes did not deceive me, were praying. Why? The intelligentsia, of course, described itself these days as "agnostic" – a most useful word. Around me, in seeming earnest, the boys prayed their unthinkable private prayers. To whom? It was wrong to watch, but I watched.

29 On the balcony's first row, to my right, big Dan had pressed his ruddy cheeks into his palms. Beside him, Jamie bent over his knees. Over one eye he had jammed a fist; his other eye was crinkled shut. Another boy, blond Robert, lay stretched over his arms, which clasped the balcony rail. His shoulders were tight; the back of his jacket rose and fell heavily with his breathing. It had been a long time since I'd been to Communion. When had this praying developed?

30 Dan lowered his hands and leaned back slowly. He opened his eyes, unfocused to the high, empty air before him. Wild Jamie moved his arm; he picked up a fistful of hair from his forehead and held it. His eyes fretted tightly shut; his jaws worked. Robert's head still lay low on his outstretched sleeves; it moved once from side to side and back again. So they struggled on. I finally looked away.

Below the balcony, in the crowded nave, men and women 31
were also concentrating, it seemed. Were they perhaps pretending to pray? All heads were bent; no one moved. I began to doubt
my own omniscience. If I bowed my head, too, and shut my eyes,
would this be apostasy?* No, I'd keep watching the people, in case
I'd missed some clue that they were actually doing something
else – bidding bridge hands.

apostasy · the abandonment of Christian faith

For I knew these people, didn't I? I knew their world, which 32
was, in some sense, my world, too, since I could not, outside of
books, name another. I knew what they loved: their families, their
houses, their country clubs, hard work, the people they knew best,
and summer parties with old friends full of laughter. I knew what
they hated: labor unions, laziness, spending, wildness, loudness.
They didn't buy God. They didn't buy anything if they could help
it. And they didn't work on spec.*

on spec · on specula- tion, without a contract or formal agreement

Nevertheless, a young father below me propped his bowed 33
head on two fists stacked on a raised knee. The ushers and
their trays had vanished. The people had taken Communion.
No one moved. The organist hushed. All the men's heads were
bent – black, white, red, yellow, and brown. The men sat absolutely still. Almost all the women's heads were bent down, too,
and some few tilted back. Some hats wagged faintly from side
to side. All the people seemed scarcely to breathe.

I was alert enough now to feel, despite myself, some faint, 34
thin stream of spirit braiding forward from the pews. Its flawed
and fragile rivulets pooled far beyond me at the altar. I felt, or
saw, its frail strands rise to the wide tower ceiling, and mass in
the gold mosaic's dome.

tesseræ · the fragments composing a mosaic

The gold tesseræ* scattered some spirit like light back over the 35
cavernous room, and held some of it, like light, in its deep curve.
Christ drifted among floating sandstone ledges and deep, absor-
bent skies. There was no speech nor language. The people had
been praying, praying to God, just as they seemed to be praying.
That was the fact. I didn't know what to make of it.

Who is my neighbor? · see Luke 10:25–37

I left Pittsburgh before I had a grain of sense. Who is my 36
neighbor?* I never learned what the strangers around me had
known and felt in their lives – those lithe, sarcastic boys in the
balcony, those expensive men and women in the pews below – but
it was more than I knew, after all.

Robert A. Fink

⫷ 1 9 4 6 - ⫸

A native Texan, Robert Fink is an award-winning poet and veteran of the Vietnam War. His experience as a first lieutenant in the United States Marine Corps often figures in his poetry and essays. Fink's three books of poetry, Azimuth Points *(1981),* The Ghostly Hitchhiker *(1989), and* The Tongues of Men and of Angels *(1995), often describe passionate wrestlings with moral and spiritual questions. His works cover a wide range of topics – family, marriage, baseball, war, religion – and often reveal a happy blend of humor and spiritual insight. Fink is the Bond Professor of English and director of the Creative Writing Workshops at Hardin-Simmons University.*

HOW I FOUND RELIGION AT A BASEBALL GAME

1   I ALWAYS SIT FOUR ROWS UP, directly behind home plate. It's important to be in position to see the whole picture. I discovered this spot several years ago when I recognized the invisible line connecting home plate to the pitching rubber, to second base, to the middle of the twenty-foot green monster wall in dead center. This is the line dividing the playing field into halves resembling angels' wings. The line originates at my fourth-row position.

2   The poet Theodore Rœthke* is supposed to have said he never realized he could think until he turned forty. There's something to this. The view from forty is similar to my fourth-row vantage point. It's more of an introspective look at what's happening around me, and I'm not as important to the picture as I used to think, and this doesn't bother me as much as I expected. My past begins to look like design, not mine. It's more like religion. Not a bad place to be on a sunny, March afternoon in West Texas, the temperature in the high 70s, the flags at ease above the center

*Theodore Rœthke · American poet (1908–1963)

143

field wall. This is the kind of day you would select if you knew 2
something extraordinary was about to happen.

I recognized the mood because I had felt it seven months earlier. 3
My wife, two teenage sons, and I had spent the summer at Phillips
Academy, Andover, Massachusetts, where my sons took course-
work, and I taught a couple of classes. It was the evening before
we were to start back to Texas early the next morning. We were
rushing around packing the car and cleaning up the house we had
stayed in for the summer. Just outside our back door was the school's
baseball field. This was not your ordinary ballpark. First of all, it
really was a field. When we arrived in June, the outfield grass was
higher than our ankles and so thick that until you took off after a
fly ball in the gap between right and center, you wouldn't notice the
ground had never been leveled but rose and fell like the undulations
of waves twelve miles out in the ocean. There were no fences, the
outfield rising toward the distant tennis courts. Five hundred feet
out in center, a solitary grandfather oak had been left for æsthetics
or possibly as a reminder that the focal point of this picture had
always been nature. Instead of dugouts for each team, two green
benches had been placed along the first-base and the third-base foul
lines. There were no bleachers for the fans. I watched most of the
American Legion games played on the field that summer, and the
moms and dads, the girlfriends and younger brothers of the ball-
players brought folding lawn chairs or stretched out on the grassy
slope running the length of the right field foul line. I preferred to lie
back and shut my eyes, taking in the sounds of the game, especially
the players' chatter, soothing as surf rolling into shore.

Wednesday afternoons, a couple of my friends and I would 4
meet on the field and throw the ball around. We had grown up
playing baseball, and the poet-in-residence had even spent several
years in the Phillies' minor-league system. When the word got
around, other middle-aged faculty started showing up with gloves
no one would believe existed, much less still had some magic in
the pocket. We took turns lobbing batting practice fast balls to
each other, and every now and then someone would slip in what
he announced was a curve. The rest of us would fan out across the
outfield, often gathering in clusters of two and three to visit but
can of corn · an easily-   always with an eye on the batter, always ready to call out "Mine"
caught fly-ball   or "I got it" and amble off after a can of corn,* working hard to

4   make the catch look routine, then rainbow the ball back toward the pitcher's mound. When we took our turn at bat, every hit was a rope,* every fly outta here or at least deep enough to have easily scored a runner tagging at third.

a rope · a hard, line-drive hit

5   A light rain was falling our last afternoon at Andover. The car was pretty much packed, and my wife and my sons were checking the house for any items we had overlooked. It was about 7:00 PM, and as I squeezed my glove into a corner of our Honda Civic's trunk, I decided to walk down to the baseball field. Fog had started to settle around the tennis courts, and the oak in center seemed diaphanous as a vision. I sat down on the Visitor's bench, leaned back and pulled the bill of my shapeless Washington Senators cap lower across my eyes; the rain had become a steady drizzle. I couldn't say how long I sat there staring at the field, at all that green. I don't remember thinking or feeling anything. I couldn't move, didn't want to. It was almost like 1973 on a Santa Monica beach when I lay back in the sand and for a moment couldn't recall what day it was or what I had to do tomorrow. The Andover field was a holy place. Had I been able, I would have removed my shoes. When I could rise from the bench, I had to rediscover my limbs, slowly recognize that I was walking back to the house, my family asking where I had been; why I was soaked to the skin.

6   On that occasion I didn't feel particularly wise, just peaceful; but on a March afternoon, fourth-row up behind home plate, the president of our university sitting beside me, I recalled Herman Melville's statement* that we can't know greatness until we've failed. I had just finished grading a set of Freshman poetry explications of Sylvia Plath's "Metaphors."* The essays had been much better than I expected, and several of the interpretations had bordered on brilliant. One twenty-six-year-old mother of a couple of pre-schoolers had even argued that the poem's last line – "Boarded the train there's no getting off" – didn't mean the speaker of the poem, a pregnant woman, was depressed about becoming a mother. On this day I needed to believe her and didn't write in the margin of the essay – "Then how do you explain Plath's love affair with Death, her later suicide?" I needed the wife in the poem to affirm the life within her, growing larger day by day. I left my third-floor office and walked over to the baseball stadium to take in the first game of a double header.

Herman Melville's statement · Herman Melville (1819–1891), American novelist

Sylvia Plath's "Metaphors" · Sylvia Plath (1932–1963), American poet

Bottom of the second inning, our university president came up 7 the steps leading to the bleachers. He started down the walkway in front of the first row of seats. From the corner of my eye, I watched him wave to the three or four students on the third-base side; then he shook hands with one of the ballplayer's parents. Not many fans show up for Wednesday afternoon games. Our record was 3 and 17, but we weren't that bad; we started the season against the University of Texas, Texas A&M, Baylor, and Oklahoma. After each loss, the coach and the sportswriters emphasized our lack of pitching.

I could tell the president was looking for someone, and that 8 person had failed to show, so I waved and asked if he would like to join me. He sat down, inquired about the score and made a comment about the poor officiating we'd been having. He seemed eager to yell at "Blue" about his lack of good judgment. I grinned and pointed out the similarity between umpires and university presidents – how we needed to loudly shout their sins, a catharsis for fans and faculty members. He smiled and took off his coat, said he'd have to be going soon. He loosened his tie and yelled a word of encouragement to the batter quickly behind in the count, o and 2. The president had announced he would be stepping down from office at the end of the school year. After fourteen years, he wanted to concentrate on writing, maybe teach a class or two. When he arrived on campus he had a head of thick, black hair and often ran with students in 5K races. Now what hair still ringed his crown was gray, and he had back problems. I was hired the same year he was, both of us just starting out.

I was thinking about this connection when our catcher 9 launched a light-stanchion-clearing shot down the left field line. The ball almost disappeared into the western sun but stayed fair by at least ten feet. Everyone but the umpire could see it was a home run. The pitcher knew it. He slammed his fist into his glove and stomped off the mound. Our on-deck batter leaped high and jabbed at the air; the rest of our players burst from the dugout as if a trumpet had sounded calling the dead from their graves. The batter was halfway to first base, easing into his victory trot, when the home plate umpire threw both arms to his left and shouted, "Foul Ball!"

Our coach slammed his cap into the dirt and ran toward the 10 umpire. Each time the ump turned his back, the coach would

10 scoot around to keep his nose and his index finger about an inch in front of the umpire's face. The president jumped up and shouted "Blue!" as if this were the vilest of epithets. Our second baseman, the team captain, stepped in front of the coach and threw his glove against the umpire's shins. He said the call was "Tragic!" Having no comeback for such a word, the umpire aimed his arm at the bench and tossed our second baseman. The coach took up his cause. The president shouted "Blue! Blue!"

11 We ended up losing the game by one run. Now we were 3 and 18, but everyone seemed more exhilarated by this loss than by the three wins. We had been robbed. We could glory in our defeat. We had a cause to champion over coffee in the faculty lounge. Our sports reporter would have a two-column diatribe for the school paper. The president could finally rage with us on an issue; he had found a higher official to sacrifice on the altar of righteous indignation.

12 What really amazed me was that while everyone was shouting and leaping and throwing equipment, I wasn't. I did not feel superior to the participants in this dance; nor did I feel like the only one without a partner. I was thinking of a scene from the movie *Meatballs* where the summer-camp olympics team of klutzes is about to face the champion team from a rival camp. Bill Murray, one of the klutz team's camp counselors, fires up his enervated players by pulling them to their feet and leading a hand-clapping, tent-revival rally. By the end of the scene, all twenty-odd team members are snake dancing around the camp lodge, chanting with Murray, "It just doesn't matter! It just doesn't matter!" Unable to lift myself from my spot in the bleachers, I believed everything mattered. I believed nothing mattered. I was invigorated and exhausted. I somehow knew God had forgiven me for always demanding that things turn out right, that winning bring salvation.

13 In seventh grade, my best friend and I spent hours perfecting our pitches on the narrow strip of lawn, west side of my house. Or we'd take the football and play kick over in the street in front of his house. Sometimes his dad would quarterback pass patterns with us. Sometimes we'd pitch a tent in his backyard and camp out overnight laughing at everything; if we got lucky and uncovered one of his older sister's dirty novels, we'd sneak it from her

room to read the sex scenes, one of us turning the pages while the other held the flashlight. We were not as close in high school, and in college we only dropped each other a line once or twice a year. We sent invitations to our weddings, announcements when our first child was born. [13]

I never believed my friend would die, not from bone cancer, not at twenty-seven, his dad staying at his side the last weeks in the hospital, twice a day lifting his son from the bed and hugging him close, stumbling around the room in a pantomime of exercise. My friend wrote he was running down-and-out pass patterns, juking* the plastic hospital chairs. He swore he was getting better; I didn't need to leave my graduate studies, my wife and my new-born twins, and fly to see him. I was relieved. I mailed him a funny greeting card every day. His wife called to talk after the funeral. She said he had looked forward to the cards. [14]

juking · avoiding defending football players

The year I was in Vietnam, the Marines were packing to leave. Nobody was supposed to die; our operations were designed to show discretion, not valor. Everybody died. The first was one of the guys from my Officer Candidate School platoon. He casually opened the door of a village hut. I remembered his having to stand in front of our OCS platoon of recent college graduates and sing, "I'm a little teapot, short and stout. Here is my handle. Here is my spout." Our platoon sergeant was displeased with him for failing to shine the coffee urn in the officers' lounge. Now he was dead, like the lance corporal who just happened to walk into the Military Police office at the same instant one of his buddies forgot to eject the ammo clip from his .45 automatic, chambering a round instead of clearing the pistol. When the slide shot home, the gun discharged its bullet into the forehead of the lance corporal. [15]

Recon · short for reconnaissance, a unit sent to gain preliminary information on enemy territory and movements

Viet Cong · the communist guerrilla force that aided the North Vietnamese Army in fighting against South Vietnam

Da Nang · chief port of the central lowlands of Vietnam

During a two-week period, five helicopters from Marine Air Group 16 disappeared for no good reason – four exploding in mid-air, one vanishing over the China Sea. A sixth had a steel cable snap extracting a Recon* unit out of triple-canopy jungle north of Da Nang. Four of the team were safe in the chopper when the cable broke and the lieutenant, who was almost close enough for the door gunner to touch, fell a hundred feet back into the canopy, the cable trailing from his waist like an umbilical cord. [16]

The night the Viet Cong* finally got lucky and hit the fuel dump at the Da Nang* Air Base, one of their rockets fell short [17]

17 and exploded in MAG-11.* I had the duty at First Marine Air Wing. I waited at our helicopter Landing Zone for the evacuation chopper called in to rush the seriously wounded to the battalion hospital. When the first ambulance from MAG-11 arrived, the young Marine tucked under the clean sheet didn't look injured at all. I had been expecting blood and gaping wounds; all I saw was a teenager with the whitest face I had seen in my six months in 'Nam. The corpsmen didn't speak. One of them handed me an IV bottle, then each grabbed an end of the stretcher and rushed toward the chopper. I held the bottle high and jogged along beside the stretcher. Keeping my head ducked to try and avoid the helicopter's rotor wash, I looked directly into the boy's eyes. He was scared, so I shouted that he would be all right. I believed it. No blood. He was dead before the chopper reached the hospital. The corpsmen told me the boy was scheduled to rotate back to the states that morning. Things like that didn't happen. Things like that always happened.

MAG-11 · Marine Aircraft Group 11

18 Like my poetry-writing student who told me she had asthma, trained for marathons, and taught ærobic dance at the Y* three times a week. She was always bringing cookies to class to share with the writing workshop members. Her face looked like a skull, her arms and legs little more than bones. Everyone but me knew she was anorexic. Everyone but me knew not to push her to stop writing about birds and flowers, knew not to insist she revise the three-page, incoherent poem about the high school cheerleader who found her father's body in his Cadillac idling in the closed garage. Everyone but me understood she wasn't taking the course to improve her writing.

the Y · The YMCA and YWCA (Young Men's and Young Women's Christian Associations, respectively) sponsor athletic and personal-development activities

19 I always believed in winning. A good loser was still a loser. All you'd learn from losing was why you didn't win. I was wrong. Nobody needs to learn from winning. Failure tempers us for tomorrow; this must be why Jesus warned his followers to concern themselves only with the sufficient evil of each day* and offered forgiveness for yesterday's failures.

sufficient evil of each day · see Matthew 6:34

20 No theologian understands this better than baseball people; that's why coaches schedule as many games as possible each week, sometimes even slipping in a double header. Should you go 0 for 3 at the plate and make two run-scoring errors in the field, you can turn your shame around in the next game. Coaches are fond

of saying that if you screw up in the field, make up for it with 20
your bat; if you couldn't hit a beach ball floated to the plate, then
look flashy at third. Baseball is religion because it admonishes
its converts to accept a second chance, taking comfort in the
knowledge that everyone expects you to fail at least seven out of
ten times at bat. You can always rely on drawing the farsighted
umpire, on getting the bad hop, on having to play the sun field.
Gravity is always pulling at your bones.

On that sunny, March afternoon in the bleachers, I under- 21
Adam … apple · see   stood. God expected Adam and Eve to eat the apple.•
Genesis 3:1–6

John Philip Santos

◄(1 9 5 7 -)►

A native of San Antonio, Texas, Santos has written widely on Latino culture, publishing articles in, among other venues, the Los Angeles Times *and the* New York Times. *Television documentaries written and produced by Santos have appeared on* CBS *and* PBS. *In addition to his other honors, Santos holds the distinction of being the first Mexican American to be appointed a Rhodes scholar. In* Places Left Unfinished At the Time of Creation *(1999), a journalistic memoir, Santos investigates his grandfather's 1939 suicide. Tracing the clues surrounding his ancestor's death, the author is led to an exploration of the Mexican people's dual heritage, of their ties both to Spain and the pre-Columbian culture of the American continents. Mexican mythology, European colonial history, and the Texas present here meld, much as Santos's ancestors melded with the contradictory cultural influences in which they lived.*

from PLACES LEFT UNFINISHED AT THE TIME OF CREATION

1   I WENT BACK TO SAN ANTONIO, having received a letter from the city's fire department helping me locate Mr. A.G. Pompa, one of the two now long-retired firemen who had tried to revive my *abuelo** Juan José on that January morning in 1939. Their names, Rathke and Pompa, had appeared in all of the press accounts of his death, and Mr. Pompa was one of the figures in the photograph in the *San Antonio Light,* crouching alongside my grandfather's body by the bank of the San Antonio River. Along with my father and Uncle Chale, Pompa was the last living witness of the circumstances of that day. The other fireman, a Mr. A. L. Rathke, had died in the early '70s.

abuelo · "grandfather" (Spanish)

When I arrived in San Antonio, the front pages of the news- 2
papers were announcing in banner headlines the report of a
visitation of the Virgin Mary in the city, where she had appeared
to a young witness in the illumination of a porchlight, reflected
off the polished chrome fender of a 1975 Chevrolet Impala. It
happened in an old *barrio** sub-development on the far south
side of the city, off the Pleasanton Road, which had once been
a stagecoach route but was now a long, faceless asphalt trail of
strip malls, feed stores, and massage parlors. The houses there
are flat and weathered from the tea-colored sandstorms that blow
through that part of the San Antonio River plain in the summers.

barrio · "neighborhood"
(Spanish), the Spanish-
speaking area of a city
or town

The "Chevrolet Madonna" was first seen by a Chicano boy on his 3
sixteenth birthday, after taking out the trash around ten that night.
For some weeks, he had been having nightmares that he would be
shot in a drive-by killing on his birthday. In his dream, he would be
taking out the trash, walking across the dry, straw-colored carpet
grass of the front yard, when he would notice a gray Ford Pinto
coming around the corner toward his house. As he saw someone
leaning out of the back window with a pistol in hand, he would try
to run for his front door, but found he was suddenly paralyzed by
a mysterious force. He turned toward the house, but the air was
as dense as deep water. And each night, the dream would end just
after he heard the explosion of the gun firing from behind him.

When he went out to empty the garbage the night of the 4
vision, he said he saw a bright white light descend swiftly onto a
neighbor's lawn across the street, He watched as it moved down
the street, zig-zagging between ash trees and pickup trucks like a
spinning top, veering sharply in the middle of the street in front
of his house and coming directly for him. Before he could move
away, he screamed as he felt what he called "the icy light" pass
directly through him and float farther on the night air, finally
coming to rest against the clapboard wall of the neighbor's house.

When his mother and sister found him kneeling in the yard
just minutes later, his hands were clasped in prayer and his gaze 5
was fixed on the house next door. As he looked at the large, jagged
splash of light before him, he recognized in it a clearly defined
shape where the light was brighter.

"It's our Holy Lady, kneeling, reading the Bible," he told them. 6

7   They looked at the wall and saw the same shape there, and they were awestruck. There was a pool of light that might be a bowed head, one edge that could be a large book held open, a wavy glimmer toward the ground that could seem to some to be a kneeling torso. But you had to look deep into the light, deliberately unfocusing your eyes, to see any of this. After holding hands and saying prayers together, the family went inside and built an altar to receive the blessings the Divine Mother was bestowing on them.

8   Along with the cataclysms, natural and man-made, this has been a century of miracles and visions. The epic of magic remains incomplete. *Promesas** are still being fulfilled. Before an apocalyptic vortex of killing and recrimination descended on Bosnia-Herzegovina,* there were daily visions of Mary taking place in the mountain village of Medjugorje. Three youths, two girls and a boy, carried on a years-long conversation with their vision, whom they described as the Virgin Mary, Mother of God. After the attending crowd for the punctual afternoon apparitions grew too large, the venue was moved by begrudging church authorities to the local church rectory, where only a few witnesses were allowed. Appearing so routinely, the Virgin was able to address herself to such otherwise quotidian matters as the inefficiency of public waterworks in the village and the penurious local property tax rates. An uncle went on a pilgrimage there and claimed, along with other followers, to have looked straight at the sun at midday without harming his eyes. Instead, he saw a rapid dance of many-colored light, as if filtered through a prism in the sky. The visions at Medjugorje ended without fanfare when one of the visionaries went off to join the Bosnian army. Another developed brain cancer. Then the war arrived, and it became too dangerous to even gather at the rectory for daily prayers.

Promesas · "promises" or "pledges" (Spanish)

Bosnia-Herzegovina · a region of the former Yugoslavia where civil war broke out between people of different faiths and ethnicities and where "ethnic cleansing" was practiced from 1992–1995

9   The San Antonio papers reported that after the Chevrolet apparition, the family began a marathon of Rosaries devoted to the Virgin Mary. The son fainted and began speaking in a high-pitched voice, while his family held a minicorder to his mouth, recording his every utterance. When he declared the tapwater in the house was blessed, they placed roses in a vase filled with the water, and the entire house was filled with an intoxicating scent of the flowers.

10   As word spread through the neighborhood and the news media started to report the story, hundreds of people arrived

every evening to see the light for themselves. It didn't take the 10
skeptics long to discern that the light of this apparition was
nothing more than the reflection of the family's porch light off
the front bumper of a maroon Impala, parked in the driveway.
On the second night of the apparition, a couple of *pachuco*•
homeboys who had been sniffing glue all afternoon, started
rocking the car and howling with laughter as the apparition
bobbed up and down against the beige house siding, startling
the devoted onlookers.

pachuco · a young
tough or thug

Nonetheless, on crutches, in wheelchairs, and in large groups, 11
the hopeful, the devout, the sick, and the curious kept coming. A
man with acute colitis was rumored to have rid himself of crippling abdominal pain by touching the wall. Many swooned while
just standing along the chain-link fence of the neighbor's backyard.

Then, another neighbor caught a pilgrim urinating on his lawn. 12
Another found a couple, *in flagrante delicto*,• in their own parked
car as they had come to attempt to conceive a child in the apparition's glow, unable to do so before without divine intervention.

in flagrante delicto ·
"in passionate delight"
(Latin), to be caught
in the very act; to be
caught red-handed: a
euphemism for sexual
activity

A local Bishop said the church was "cautiously skeptical" about 13
the matter. "I see the Blessed Mother every day," he told the
newspaper. "But I don't necessarily invite the whole community.
If it isn't from God, it will die a natural death."

❖ ❖ ❖

AFTER UNCOVERING HIS NAME in the microfilm archives of 14
the newspapers, I had tried to find Mr. Pompa. It seemed he
had left the city. For years the fire department had been unable
to locate him, until they received a notification of a change of
address through his insurance company. After several days'
more of inquiries with the San Antonio Fireman's Benevolent
Association, I learned he was living in Kerrville, Texas, about an
hour and a half north of San Antonio, in the Texas hill country.
Mr. Pompa was a patient at the State Hospital in Kerrville, the
end-of-the-line facility in the Texas State mental health system.
Identifying myself on the phone only as a friend of the family, the
nurse I spoke to there would not discuss his condition with me,
but said I was welcome to visit, with an appointment.

"You can come on up," she said. "He has good days and bad 15
days, but he don't talk much with nobody."

16   I dreaded that hospital from one summer during college when I had a job there doing art therapy with the patients, many of whom are elderly, long-term internees of the state mental health system. The hospital grounds are nestled in the hills outside of Kerrville, and the campus is laid out like a little village unto itself, with its own streets, named after heroes of Texas Independence, and imitation shops meant to give the patients the reassuring feeling of being at home in a real place. After only two weeks of work there, I was haunted by the sounds and scenes from the hospital. While watching a movie, I'd hear the jagged laughter of one of the patients I had been with during the day. I recoiled when I saw the downy translucent flesh hanging from the underarms of patients who had taken prescriptions for decades that had that eerie side effect. I had quit shortly thereafter, and the doctor overseeing the arts program scolded me for leaving, telling me, "It's not so easy to escape these things. You can't quit *them*."

17   When I was shown to the patio in the ward where Mr. Pompa was waiting, I remembered walking through that solarium* years before, encountering a group of patients there who were watching the film *The Alamo*, with John Wayne and Richard Widmark, in reverse, after some lazy orderly had improperly spooled the projector. But none of the members of the audience seemed to mind, staring silently at the sheet that had been hung as a screen as John Wayne walked backward along the parapets of the fort under siege.

solarium · a sunroom

18   That afternoon, the cicadas were singing at an eardrum-piercing volume as a nurse led me to Mr. Pompa at one end of a covered patio, dressed only in a cotton robe and sitting in a La-Z-Boy recliner, with his bare feet up on the raised footrest. The nurse pulled his seat back upright, and his old, unshaven face was round and freckled, his soft, dark eyes both blank and querulous. His hands were large and rough-scaled, quivering on his bare knees, protruding from his robe. He looked like Diego Rivera* as an old man, his white hair standing up like plumes on the back of his head. At first, he took no notice as the nurse introduced me, taking pains to pronounce every syllable with a shout.

Diego Rivera · Mexican Social Realist Muralist (1886–1957), husband of artist Frida Kahlo

19   "He understands everything. He just mainly don't want to talk. That's all it is, right, Mr. Pompa?"

20   Mr. Pompa had two Q-Tips hanging from his nostrils, and two sticking out of his ears. The nurse gathered them quickly

with a *tsk* and set off back for the ward. Alone on the patio, I 20
pulled up a chair and introduced myself to Mr. Pompa again,
which he responded to with only a blink in his wide open stare.
I explained to him how I had gotten his whereabouts, and why
I had looked for him in the first place. I told him he was one
of the last living witnesses of that morning in 1939, when, as a
young man of twenty-five, he had tried to revive my grandfather.
I showed him the photograph from the January 1939 *San Antonio
Light,* where he was pictured.

"Juan – José – Santos. You are that A. G. Pompa, aren't you?" 21

The Fireman's Association said that, already twenty years 22
retired, he had had a decorated career as a *bombero.*• He had
put out a lot of San Antonio fires. He had run into hundreds
of burning houses to bring out the living. Maybe he had been
able to revive untold others of the would-be drowned. But all
of that was lost to him now, including the morning of January 9,
1939. Whatever faint echo of that day remained deep inside of
him and was beyond his grasp. If he was aware of anything, he
was unable or unwilling to let anyone else know. We sat staring
at each other silently for another few moments. In his eyes, he
seemed present, but abandoned, as if a fire had left only the shell
of the building standing. Then he took a long, deep breath and
began singing with a still-noticeable Spanish accent, *"The eyes
of Texas are upon you... all the livelong day...."*

On my way back, I thought I might drive past San Antonio, 23
past Uvalde, Hondo, and La Pryor, past Piedras Negras and Nava,
and on into the center of Mexico to where all the roads began.

The news from the radio was that it hadn't mattered much 24
to the faithful that the "Chevrolet Madonna" had a perfectly
explicable source. Hundreds of believers were still coming to
the simple neighborhood every night. Was it not a miracle that
the lamplight from the porch had even caught the dented fender
of the Impala in the first place? What was the probability of
those few shafts of light reflecting off that long, curved chrome
surface in precisely the way necessary to project the Madonna's
silhouette? Out of the million chance encounters in the ordinary
running on of the everyday, this beam was a light breaking suddenly through a curtain, creating an aperture between worlds,
showing just how incomplete our own world really was.

bombero · "firefighter" (Spanish)

25   But the neighbor on whose wall the apparition reflected was growing desperate as hordes of devotees trampled greater swaths of his lawn and carried on singing and chanting all night long. He decided to illuminate the apparition with two gigantic mercury floodlights, thereby bathing the amber-toned reflection in a fluorescent silver glare that erased any hint of the Virgin Mary's outline and drew gasps and angry shouts from the crowd.

26   One reporter heard a woman scream at the neighbor, "If you have any love in your heart you will let us see the Virgin!"

27   "If you believe in Mary, the mother of God, you will turn out the light," yelled another.

28   The mother of the family of the young visionary collapsed.

29   In the days that followed, the family repositioned their Impala in the driveway and used camping flashlights to try, without success, to cast the Virgin's reflection against their own garage door. All they managed were jittery Rorschach blots* of a shapeless milky light. Once the car was moved, the image of the Blessed Virgin Mary reading the Bible was to disappear forever. For several days, the devout and the nosy continued to come after sunset. For months after they stopped coming, the neighbor kept his modest house saturated in as much light as the Lincoln Memorial.

Rorschach blots · Hermann Rorschach (1884–1922), a Swiss psychiatrist, devised the ink blot test

30   She had not been a Virgin who had come with much to say. As always, she had chosen an obscure place under humble circumstances to manifest herself. This time there were no clouds, no cherubim,* no starry mantle. As apparitions go, she was more of a chimera* or a cipher* rather than an interlocutor* between worlds. For those who believed in her light, she brought the message that the interaction between the mortal and the divine in those lands has not ended.

cherubim · see Exodus 25:18–22

chimera · an imaginary creature or illusory idea

cipher · a nonentity, a meaningless sign

interlocutor · one who takes part in a conversation or dialogue

31   From her debut in the Americas on a sacred hill in Mexico City more than four hundred years ago,* here at end of the twentieth century, she came to a parched, rundown Texas suburb. The faithful had congregated to see in the apparition's low-wattage glow that the enchantment of the homelands is not over.

debut … years ago · Mary ("Our Lady of Guadalupe") appeared to a poor native near Mexico City in 1531, leading to the swift conversion of millions of indigenous people

32   On the night the miracle-busting floodlights were turned on, when the mother of the young seer of Pleasanton Road passed out, some of the devotees had gathered around her, holding hands, and improvised a song they sang over her as she lay unconscious, *"Stay with me, Lord, stay with me, the spirit of the Lord is moving through my heart, stay with me, Lord, stay with me."*

Christian Wiman

◀ 1 9 6 6 – ▶

*Raised in west Texas, Wiman has been on an intense journey
ever since, traveling, living, and teaching widely in the United
States and abroad. His essay collection,* Ambition and Survival:
Becoming a Poet, *offers a glimpse of this journey, from his youth in
a church-going family in Texas, to reading* Paradise Lost *on a roof
in Guatemala after losing his faith, to his years in Chicago where
he has been editor of* Poetry *since 2003. During these travels he
wrote and published three collections of poetry,* The Long Home,
Hard Night, *and* Every Riven Thing, *as well as a book of translated poems,* Stolen Air: Selected Poems of Osip Mandelstam,
*his work mixing the buzz of life and the shadow of death with an
insatiable intelligence. Several years after arriving in Chicago, he
was diagnosed with an incurable form of blood cancer. Soon he
found himself attending church again, and his spiritual life quickly
became the center of his writing, driven by a new vision of the
existence of God in our lives and an impatience for "poetry that is
not steeped in, marred and transfigured by, the world."*

"LOVE BADE ME WELCOME"

1   Though I was raised in a very religious household, until about
a year ago I hadn't been to church in any serious way in more
than 20 years. It would be inaccurate to say that I have been indifferent to God in all that time. If I look back on the things I have
written in the past two decades, it's clear to me not only how
thoroughly the forms and language of Christianity have shaped
my imagination, but also how deep and persistent my existential
anxiety has been. I don't know whether this is all attributable to
the century into which I was born, some genetic glitch, or a late

reverberation of the Fall of Man. What I do know is that I have 1
not been at ease in this world.

Poetry, for me, has always been bound up with this unease, 2
fueled by contingency toward forms that will transcend it, as
involved with silence as it is with sound. I don't have much sympathy for the Arnoldian notion of poetry replacing religion. It
seems not simply quaint but dangerous to make that assumption,
even implicitly, perhaps especially implicitly. I do think, though,
that poetry is how religious feeling has survived in me. Partly
this is because I have at times experienced in the writing of a
poem some access to a power that feels greater than I am, and
it seems reductive, even somehow a deep betrayal, to attribute
that power merely to the unconscious or to the dynamism of
language itself. But also, if I look back on the poems I've written
in the past two decades, it almost seems as if the one constant
is God. Or, rather, His absence.

There is a passage in the writings of Simone Weil that has long 3
been important to me. In the passage, Weil describes two prisoners who are in solitary confinement next to each other. Between
them is a stone wall. Over a period of time – and I think we have
to imagine it as a very long time – they find a way to communicate using taps and scratches. The wall is what separates them,
but it is also the only means they have of communicating. "It is
the same with us and God," she says. "Every separation is a link."

It's probably obvious why this metaphor would appeal to me. 4
If you never quite feel at home in your life, if being conscious
means primarily being conscious of your own separation from
the world and from divinity (and perhaps any sentient person
after modernism has to feel these things) then any idea or image
that can translate that depletion into energy, those absences into
presences, is going to be powerful. And then there are those taps
and scratches: what are they but language, and if language is the
way we communicate with the divine, well, what kind of language
is more refined and transcendent than poetry? You could almost
embrace this vision of life – if, that is, there were any actual life
to embrace: Weil's image for the human condition is a person in
solitary confinement. There is real hope in the image, but still,
in human terms, it is a bare and lonely hope.

5   It has taken three events, each shattering in its way, for me to recognize both the full beauty, and the final insufficiency, of Weil's image. The events are radically different, but so closely linked in time, and so inextricable from one another in their consequences, that there is an uncanny feeling of unity to them. There is definitely some wisdom in learning to see our moments of necessity and glory and tragedy not as disparate experiences but as facets of the single experience that is a life. The pity, at least for some of us, is that we cannot truly have this knowledge of life, can only feel it as some sort of abstract "wisdom," until we come very close to death.

6   First, necessity: four years ago, after making poetry the central purpose of my life for almost two decades, I stopped writing. Partly this was a conscious decision. I told myself that I had exhausted one way of writing, and I do think there was truth in that. The deeper truth, though, is that I myself was exhausted. To believe that being conscious means primarily being conscious of loss, to find life authentic only in the apprehension of death, is to pitch your tent at the edge of an abyss, "and when you gaze long into the abyss," Nietzsche says, "the abyss also gazes into you." I blinked.

7   On another level, though, the decision to stop writing wasn't mine. Whatever connection I had long experienced between word and world, whatever charge in the former I had relied on to let me feel the latter, went dead. Did I give up poetry, or was it taken from me? I'm not sure, and in any event the effect was the same: I stumbled through the months, even thrived in some ways. Indeed – and there is something almost diabolical about this common phenomenon – it sometimes seemed like my career in poetry began to flourish just as poetry died in me. I finally found a reliable publisher for my work (the work I'd written earlier, I mean), moved into a good teaching job, and then quickly left that for the editorship of *Poetry*. But there wasn't a scrap of excitement in any of this for me. It felt like I was watching a movie of my life rather than living it, an old silent movie, no color, no sound, no one in the audience but me.

8   Then I fell in love. I say it suddenly, and there was certainly an element of radical intrusion and transformation to it, but the sense I have is of color slowly aching into things, the world

coming brilliantly, abradingly alive. I remember tiny Albert's Café   8
on Elm Street in Chicago where we first met, a pastry case like
a Pollock in the corner of my eye, sunlight suddenly more itself
on an empty plate, a piece of silver. I think of walking together
along Lake Michigan a couple of months later talking about a
particular poem of Dickinson's ("A loss of something ever felt I"),
clouds finding and failing to keep one form after another, the lake
booming its blue into everything; of lying in bed in my highrise
apartment downtown watching the little blazes in the distance
that were the planes at Midway, so numerous and endless that all
those safe departures and homecomings seemed a kind of secular
miracle. We usually think of falling in love as being possessed by
another person, and like anyone else I was completely consumed
and did some daffy things. But it also felt, for the first time in
my life, like I was being fully possessed by being itself. "Joy is
the overflowing consciousness of reality," Weil writes, and that's
what I had, a joy that was at once so overflowing that it enlarged
existence, and yet so rooted in actual things that, again for the
first time, that's what I began to feel: rootedness.

I don't mean to suggest that all my old anxieties were gone.   9
There were still no poems, and this ate at me constantly. There
was still no God, and the closer I came to reality, the more I
longed for divinity – or, more accurately perhaps, the more divinity seemed so obviously apart of reality. I wasn't alone in this: we
began to say a kind of prayer before our evening meals – jokingly
at first, awkwardly, but then with intensifying seriousness and
deliberation, trying to name each thing that we were thankful
for, and in so doing, praise the thing we could not name. On
most Sundays we would even briefly entertain – again, half-
jokingly, – the idea of going to church. The very morning after we
got engaged, in fact, we paused for a long time outside a church
on Michigan Avenue. The service was just about to start, organ
music pouring out of the wide open doors into the late May sun,
and we stood there holding each other and debating whether or
not to walk inside. In the end it was I who resisted.

I wish I could slow things down at this point, could linger a   10
bit in those months after our marriage. I wish I could feel again
that blissful sense of immediacy and expansiveness at once, when
every moment implied another, and the future suddenly seemed

10   to offer some counterbalance to the solitary fever I had lived in for so long. I think most writers live at some strange adjacency to experience, that they feel life most intensely in their recreation of it. For once, for me, this wasn't the case. I could not possibly have been paying closer attention to those days. Which is why I was caught so off-guard.

11   I got the news that I was sick on the afternoon of my 39th birthday. It took a bit of time, travel, and a series of wretched tests to get the specific diagnosis, but by then the main blow had been delivered, and that main blow is what matters. I have an incurable cancer in my blood. The disease is as rare as it is mysterious, killing some people quickly and sparing others for decades, afflicting some with all manner of miseries and disabilities and leaving others relatively healthy until the end. Of all the doctors I have seen, not one has been willing to venture even a vague prognosis.

12   Conventional wisdom says that tragedy will cause either extreme closeness or estrangement in a couple. We'd been married less than a year when we got the news of the cancer. It stands to reason we should have been especially vulnerable to such a blow, and in some ways love did make things much worse. If I had gotten the diagnosis some years earlier – and it seems weirdly providential that I didn't, since I had symptoms and went to several doctors about them – I'm not sure I would have reacted very strongly. It would have seemed a fatalistic confirmation of everything I had always thought about existence, and my response, I think, would have been equally fatalistic. It would have been the bearable oblivion of despair, not the unbearable, and therefore galvanizing, pain of particular grief. In those early days after the diagnosis, when we mostly just sat on the couch and cried, I alone was dying, but we were mourning very much together. And what we were mourning was not my death, exactly, but the death of the life we had imagined with each other.

13   Then one morning we found ourselves going to church. Found ourselves. That's exactly what it felt like, in both senses of the phrase, as if some impulse in each of us had finally been catalyzed into action, so that we were casting aside the Sunday paper and moving toward the door with barely a word between us; and as if, once inside the church, we were discovering exactly where

and who we were meant to be. That first service was excruciat- 13
ing, in that it seemed to tear all wounds wide open, and it was
profoundly comforting, in that it seemed to offer the only possible balm. What I remember of that Sunday, though, and of the
Sundays that immediately followed, is less the services themselves
than the walks we took afterwards, and less the specifics of the
conversations we had about God, always about God, than the
moments of silent, and what felt like sacred, attentiveness those
conversations led to: an iron sky and the lake so calm it seemed
thickened; the El blasting past with its rain of sparks and brief,
lost faces; the broad leaves and white blooms of a catalpa on our
street, Grace Street, and under the tree a seethe of something
that was just barely still a bird, quick with life beyond its own.

I was brought up with the poisonous notion that you had to 14
renounce love of the earth in order to receive the love of God.
My experience has been just the opposite: a love of the earth
and existence so overflowing that it implied, or included, or
even absolutely demanded, God. Love did not deliver me from
the earth, but into it. And by some miracle I do not find that this
experience is crushed or even lessened by the knowledge that,
in all likelihood, I will be leaving the earth sooner than I had
thought. Quite the contrary, I find life thriving in me, and not
in an aestheticizing Death-is-the-mother-of-beauty sort of way
either, for what extreme grief has given me is the very thing it
seemed at first to obliterate: a sense of life beyond the moment,
a sense of hope. This is not simply hope for my own life, though
I do have that. It is not a hope for heaven or any sort of explain-
able afterlife, unless by those things one means simply the ghost
of wholeness that our inborn sense of brokenness creates and
sustains, some ultimate love that our truest temporal ones goad
us toward. This I do believe in, and by this I live, in what the
apostle Paul called "hope toward God."

"It is necessary to have had a revelation of reality through joy," 15
Weil writes, "in order to find reality through suffering." This is
certainly true to my own experience. I was not wrong all those
years to believe that suffering is at the very center of our existence,
and that there can be no untranquilized life that does not fully
confront this fact. The mistake lay in thinking grief the means
of confrontation, rather than love. To come to this realization

15 is not to be suddenly "at ease in the world." I don't really think it's possible for humans to be at the same time conscious and comfortable. Though we may be moved by nature to thoughts of grace, though art can tease our minds toward eternity and love's abundance make us dream a love that does not end, these intuitions come only through the earth, and the earth we know only in passing, and only by passing. I would qualify Weil's statement somewhat, then, by saying that reality, be it of this world or another, is not something one finds and then retains for good. It must be newly discovered daily, and newly lost.

16 So now I bow my head and try to pray in the mornings, not because I don't doubt the reality of what I have experienced, but because I do, and with an intensity that, because to once feel the presence of God is to feel His absence all the more acutely, is actually more anguishing and difficult than any "existential anxiety" I have ever known. I go to church on Sundays, not to dispel this doubt but to expend its energy, because faith is not a state of mind but an action in the world, a movement toward the world. How charged this one hour of the week is for me, and how I cherish it, though not one whit more than the hours I have with my wife, with friends, or in solitude, trying to learn how to inhabit time so completely that there might be no distinction between life and belief, attention and devotion. And out of all these efforts at faith and love, out of my own inevitable failures at both, I have begun to write poems again. But the language I have now to call on God is not only language, and the wall on which I make my taps and scratches is no longer a cell but this whole prodigal and all too perishable world in which I find myself, very much alive, and not at all alone. As I approach the first anniversary of my diagnosis, as I approach whatever pain is ahead of me, I am trying to get as close to this wall as possible. And I am listening with all I am.

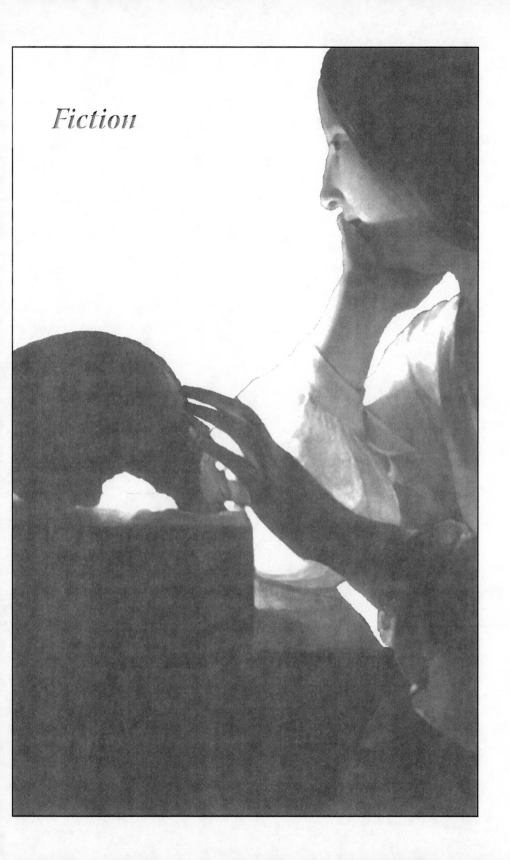

Fiction

Nathaniel Hawthorne

<(1 8 0 4 - 1 8 6 4)>

*Long considered a giant in 19th-century American literature,
Hawthorne has more recently been noted for his key role in interpreting the spiritual complexion of colonial America. Hawthorne
came by his interest in Puritan New England honestly: not only
was he born in Salem, Massachusetts, but one of his ancestors
served as judge in the Salem witchcraft trials. As a young man,
Hawthorne systematically studied colonial history and explored
the implications of Puritan theology. His contemporary Herman
Melville observed that a "Calvinistic sense of Innate Depravity and
Original Sin" permeates Hawthorne's fiction, a judgment supported
by readers of short stories such as "Young Goodman Brown," "The
Minister's Black Veil," and "The May-Pole of Merry Mount," as well
as longer works such as* The Scarlet Letter (1850). *His true subject is
the human heart tortured by an innate awareness of sinfulness and
an obsessive desire to conceal that guilt. Though some characters
transcend the debilitating effects of sin to achieve partial redemption,
more common is the experience of young Goodman Brown, whose
ultimate inability to recognize his own weakness leads to despair.*

YOUNG GOODMAN BROWN

1 YOUNG GOODMAN* BROWN came forth at sunset into the
street at Salem village; but put his head back, after crossing
the threshold, to exchange a parting kiss with his young wife.
And Faith, as the wife was aptly named, thrust her own pretty
head into the street, letting the wind play with the pink ribbons
of her cap while she called to Goodman Brown.

2 "Dearest heart," whispered she, softly and rather sadly, when
her lips were close to his ear, "prithee* put off your journey until
sunrise and sleep in your own bed to-night. A lone woman is

Goodman · a title
referring to men of
humble birth

prithee · a contraction
for "I pray thee"; "I
beg you"

169

troubled with such dreams and such thoughts that she's afeared   2
of herself sometimes. Pray tarry with me this night, dear husband,
of all nights in the year."

"My love and my Faith," replied young Goodman Brown, "of   3
all nights in the year, this one night must I tarry away from thee.
My journey, as thou callest it, forth and back again, must needs
be done 'twixt now and sunrise. What, my sweet, pretty wife,
dost thou doubt me already, and we but three months married?"

"Then God bless you!" said Faith, with the pink ribbons; "and   4
may you find all well when you come back."

"Amen!" cried Goodman Brown. "Say thy prayers, dear Faith,   5
and go to bed at dusk, and no harm will come to thee."

So they parted; and the young man pursued his way until,   6
being about to turn the corner by the meeting-house, he looked
back and saw the head of Faith still peeping after him with a
melancholy air, in spite of her pink ribbons.

"Poor little Faith!" thought he, for his heart smote him. "What   7
a wretch am I to leave her on such an errand! She talks of dreams,
too. Methought as she spoke there was trouble in her face, as if a
dream had warned her what work is to be done to-night. But no, no;
't would kill her to think it. Well, she's a blessed angel on earth; and
after this one night I'll cling to her skirts and follow her to heaven."

With this excellent resolve for the future, Goodman Brown felt   8
himself justified in making more haste on his present evil purpose.
He had taken a dreary road, darkened by all the gloomiest trees of
the forest, which barely stood aside to let the narrow path creep
through, and closed immediately behind. It was all as lonely as
could be; and there is this peculiarity in such a solitude, that
the traveller knows not who may be concealed by the innumer-
able trunks and the thick boughs overhead; so that, with lonely
footsteps, he may yet be passing through an unseen multitude.

"There may be a devilish Indian behind every tree," said   9
Goodman Brown to himself; and he glanced fearfully behind
him as he added, "What if the devil himself should be at my
very elbow!"

His head being turned back, he passed a crook of the road, and,   10
looking forward again, beheld the figure of a man, in grave and
decent attire, seated at the foot of an old tree. He arose at Goodman
Brown's approach and walked onward side by side with him.

11   "You are late, Goodman Brown," said he. "The clock of the Old South* was striking as I came through Boston, and that is full fifteen minutes agone."

the Old South · the Old South Church of Boston. The distance traveled implies supernatural speed

12   "Faith kept me back a while," replied the young man, with a tremor in his voice, caused by the sudden appearance of his companion, though not wholly unexpected.

13   It was now deep dusk in the forest, and deepest in that part of it where these two were journeying. As nearly as could be discerned, the second traveller was about fifty years old, apparently in the same rank of life as Goodman Brown, and bearing a considerable resemblance to him, though perhaps more in expression than features. Still they might have been taken for father and son. And yet, though the elder person was as simply clad as the younger, and as simple in manner too, he had an indescribable air of one who knew the world, and who would not have felt abashed at the governor's dinner table or in King William's court,* were it possible that his affairs should call him thither. But the only thing about him that could be fixed upon as remarkable was his staff, which bore the likeness of a great black snake, so curiously wrought that it might almost be seen to twist and wriggle itself like a living serpent. This, of course, must have been an ocular deception, assisted by the uncertain light.

King William's court · William III, king of England from 1689–1702

14   "Come, Goodman Brown," cried his fellow traveller, "this is a dull pace for the beginning of a journey. Take my staff, if you are so soon weary."

15   "Friend," said the other, exchanging his slow pace for a full stop, "having kept covenant by meeting thee here, it is my purpose now to return whence I came. I have scruples touching the matter thou wot'st* of."

wot'st · to become aware of, to know

16   "Sayest thou so?" replied he of the serpent, smiling apart. "Let us walk on, nevertheless, reasoning as we go; and if I convince thee not thou shalt turn back. We are but a little way in the forest yet."

17   "Too far, too far!" exclaimed the goodman, unconsciously resuming his walk. "My father never went into the woods on such an errand, nor his father before him. We have been a race of honest men and good Christians since the days of the martyrs;* and shall I be the first of the name of Brown that ever took this path and kept —"

martyrs · Christian martyrs, probably Protestants executed during the reign of Mary Tudor, Catholic queen of England from 1553–1558

18   "Such company, thou wouldst say," observed the elder person, interpreting his pause. "Well said, Goodman Brown! I have been

as well acquainted with your family as with ever a one among the 18
Puritans; and that's no trifle to say. I helped your grandfather, the
constable, when he lashed the Quaker* woman so smartly through
the streets of Salem; and it was I that brought your father a pitch-
pine knot, kindled at my own hearth, to set fire to an Indian village,
in King Philip's war.* They were my good friends, both; and many
a pleasant walk have we had along this path, and returned merrily
after midnight. I would fain* be friends with you for their sake."

"If it be as thou sayest," replied Goodman Brown, "I marvel 19
they never spoke of these matters; or, verily, I marvel not, seeing
that the least rumor of the sort would have driven them from
New England. We are a people of prayer, and good works to boot,
and abide no such wickedness."

"Wickedness or not," said the traveller with the twisted staff, 20
"I have a very general acquaintance here in New England. The
deacons of many a church have drunk the communion wine with
me; the selectmen* of divers towns make me their chairman; and
a majority of the Great and General Court* are firm supporters of
my interest. The governor and I, too – But these are state secrets."

"Can this be so?" cried Goodman Brown, with a stare of amazement at his undisturbed companion. "Howbeit, I have nothing 21
to do with the governor and council; they have their own ways,
and are no rule for a simple husbandman* like me. But, were I
to go on with thee, how should I meet the eye of that good old
man, our minister, at Salem village? Oh, his voice would make
me tremble both Sabbath day and lecture day."*

Thus far the elder traveller had listened with due gravity; but now
burst into a fit of irrepressible mirth, shaking himself so violently 22
that his snake-like staff actually seemed to wriggle in sympathy.

"Ha! ha! ha!" shouted he again and again; then composing
himself, "Well, go on, Goodman Brown, go on; but, prithee, don't 23
kill me with laughing."

"Well, then, to end the matter at once," said Goodman Brown,
considerably nettled, "there is my wife, Faith. It would break her 24
dear little heart; and I'd rather break my own."

"Nay, if that be the case," answered the other, "e'en go thy ways,
Goodman Brown. I would not for twenty old women like the one 25
hobbling before us that Faith should come to any harm."

Quaker · Quakers were considered heretical by Puritans of the American colonies and suffered persecution

King Philip's war · Metacomet (or "King Philip," as settlers named him) was leader of an Indian uprising in New England (1675–1676)

fain · happily, gladly

selectmen · a board of town officers chosen annually to manage local affairs

Great … Court · the legislative assembly

husbandman · farmer

lecture day · a religious lecture was offered at the midweek church assembly, usually on Thursdays

26   As he spoke he pointed his staff at a female figure on the path, in whom Goodman Brown recognized a very pious and exemplary dame, who had taught him his catechism* in youth, and was still his moral and spiritual adviser, jointly with the minister and Deacon Gookin.

catechism · a short book or form of verbal instruction that uses questions and answers to teach the basic principles of faith

27   "A marvel, truly, that Goody* Cloyse should be so far in the wilderness at nightfall," said he. "But with your leave, friend, I shall take a cut through the woods until we have left this Christian woman behind. Being a stranger to you, she might ask whom I was consorting with and whither I was going."

Goody · a contraction of "good wife," a title of address for a wife of humble rank. Goody Cloyse was one of the "witches" executed by Salem's Puritan officials in 1692

28   "Be it so," said his fellow-traveller. "Betake you to the woods, and let me keep the path."

29   Accordingly the young man turned aside, but took care to watch his companion, who advanced softly along the road until he had come within a staff's length of the old dame. She, meanwhile, was making the best of her way, with singular speed for so aged a woman, and mumbling some indistinct words – a prayer, doubtless – as she went. The traveller put forth his staff and touched her withered neck with what seemed the serpent's tail.

30   "The devil!" screamed the pious old lady.

31   "Then Goody Cloyse knows her old friend?" observed the traveller, confronting her and leaning on his writhing stick.

32   "Ah, forsooth,* and is it your worship indeed?" cried the good dame. "Yea, truly is it, and in the very image of my old gossip,* Goodman Brown, the grandfather of the silly fellow that now is. But – would your worship believe it? – my broomstick hath strangely disappeared, stolen, as I suspect, by that unhanged witch, Goody Cory, and that, too, when I was all anointed with the juice of smallage, and cinquefoil, and wolf's bane –"*

forsooth · in truth, indeed

gossip · close friend or companion

smallage ... wolf's-bane · plants traditionally associated with sorcery and witchcraft

33   "Mingled with fine wheat and the fat of a new-born babe," said the shape of old Goodman Brown.

34   "Ah, your worship knows the recipe," cried the old lady, cackling aloud. "So, as I was saying, being all ready for the meeting, and no horse to ride on, I made up my mind to foot it; for they tell me there is a nice young man to be taken into communion tonight. But now your good worship will lend me your arm, and we shall be there in a twinkling."

35   "That can hardly be," answered her friend. I may not spare you my arm, Goody Cloyse; but here is my staff, if you will."

So saying, he threw it down at her feet, where, perhaps, it 36
assumed life, being one of the rods which its owner had formerly

Egyptian magi · see
Exodus 7:10-12

lent to the Egyptian magi.* Of this fact, however, Goodman
Brown could not take cognizance. He had cast up his eyes in
astonishment, and, looking down again, beheld neither Goody
Cloyse nor the serpentine staff, but his fellow-traveller alone, who
waited for him as calmly as if nothing had happened.

"That old woman taught me my catechism,"* said the young 37
man; and there was a world of meaning in this simple comment.

They continued to walk onward, while the elder traveller 38
exhorted his companion to make good speed and persevere in
the path, discoursing so aptly that his arguments seemed rather
to spring up in the bosom of his auditor than to be suggested
by himself. As they went, he plucked a branch of maple to
serve for a walking stick, and began to strip it of the twigs and
little boughs, which were wet with evening dew. The moment
his fingers touched them they became strangely withered and
dried up as with a week's sunshine. Thus the pair proceeded, at
a good free pace, until suddenly, in a gloomy hollow of the road,
Goodman Brown sat himself down on the stump of a tree and
refused to go any farther.

"Friend," said he, stubbornly, "my mind is made up. Not 39
another step will I budge on this errand. What if a wretched
old woman do choose to go to the devil when I thought she was
going to heaven: is that any reason why I should quit my dear
Faith and go after her?"

"You will think better of this by and by," said his acquaintance, 40
composedly. "Sit here and rest yourself a while; and when you
feel like moving again, there is my staff to help you along."

Without more words, he threw his companion the maple 41
stick, and was as speedily out of sight as if he had vanished into
the deepening gloom. The young man sat a few moments by the
roadside, applauding himself greatly, and thinking with how clear
a conscience he should meet the minister in his morning walk,
nor shrink from the eye of good old Deacon Gookin. And what
calm sleep would be his that very night, which was to have been
spent so wickedly, but so purely and sweetly now, in the arms
of Faith! Amidst these pleasant and praiseworthy meditations,
Goodman Brown heard the tramp of horses along the road, and

41   deemed it advisable to conceal himself within the verge of the forest, conscious of the guilty purpose that had brought him thither, though now so happily turned from it.

42   On came the hoof tramps and the voices of the riders, two grave old voices, conversing soberly as they drew near. These mingled sounds appeared to pass along the road, within a few yards of the young man's hiding-place; but, owing doubtless to the depth of the gloom at that particular spot, neither the travellers nor their steeds were visible. Though their figures brushed the small boughs on the wayside, it could not be seen that they intercepted, even for a moment, the faint gleam from the strip of bright sky athwart which they must have passed. Goodman Brown alternately crouched and stood on tiptoe, pulling aside the branches and thrusting forth his head as far as he durst without discerning so much as a shadow. It vexed him the more, because he could have sworn, were such a thing possible, that he recognized the voices of the minister and Deacon Gookin, jogging along quietly, as they were wont to do, when bound to some ordination or ecclesiastical council. While yet within hearing, one of the riders stopped to pluck a switch.

43   "Of the two, reverend sir," said the voice like the deacon's, "I had rather miss an ordination dinner than to-night's meeting. They tell me that some of our community are to be here from Falmouth* and beyond, and others from Connecticut and Rhode Island, besides several of the Indian powwows,* who, after their fashion, know almost as much deviltry as the best of us. Moreover, there is a goodly young woman to be taken into communion."

44   "Mighty well, Deacon Gookin!" replied the solemn old tones of the minister. "Spur up, or we shall be late. Nothing can be done, you know, until I get on the ground."

45   The hoofs clattered again; and the voices, talking so strangely in the empty air, passed on through the forest, where no church had ever been gathered or solitary Christian prayed. Whither, then, could these holy men be journeying so deep into the heathen wilderness? Young Goodman Brown caught hold of a tree for support, being ready to sink down on the ground, faint and overburdened with the heavy sickness of his heart. He looked up to the sky, doubting whether there really was a heaven above him. Yet there was the blue arch, and the stars brightening in it.

Falmouth · a town on Cape Cod, about seventy miles from Salem

Indian powwows · Indian shamans, medicine men

"With heaven above and Faith below, I will yet stand firm   46
against the devil!" cried Goodman Brown.

While he still gazed upward into the deep arch of the firma-   47
ment and had lifted his hands to pray, a cloud, though no wind
was stirring, hurried across the zenith and hid the brightening
stars. The blue sky was still visible, except directly overhead,
where this black mass of cloud was sweeping swiftly northward.
Aloft in the air, as if from the depths of the cloud, came a confused and doubtful sound of voices. Once the listener fancied
that he could distinguish the accents of townspeople of his own,
men and women, both pious and ungodly, many of whom he
had met at the communion table, and had seen others rioting at
the tavern. The next moment, so indistinct were the sounds, he
doubted whether he had heard aught but the murmur of the old
forest, whispering without a wind. Then came a stronger swell of
those familiar tones, heard daily in the sunshine at Salem village,
but never until now from a cloud of night. There was one voice,
of a young woman, uttering lamentations, yet with an uncertain
sorrow, and entreating for some favor, which, perhaps, it would
grieve her to obtain; and all the unseen multitude, both saints
and sinners, seemed to encourage her onward.

"Faith!" shouted Goodman Brown, in a voice of agony and   48
desperation; and the echoes of the forest mocked him, crying,
"Faith! Faith!" as if bewildered wretches were seeking her all
through the wilderness.

The cry of grief, rage, and terror was yet piercing the night,   49
when the unhappy husband held his breath for a response. There
was a scream, drowned immediately in a louder murmur of voices,
fading into far-off laughter, as the dark cloud swept away, leaving
the clear and silent sky above Goodman Brown. But something
fluttered lightly down through the air and caught on the branch
of a tree. The young man seized it, and beheld a pink ribbon.

"My Faith is gone!" cried he, after one stupefied moment.   50
"There is no good on earth; and sin is but a name. Come, devil;
for to thee is this world given."

And, maddened with despair, so that he laughed loud and   51
long, did Goodman Brown grasp his staff and set forth again,
at such a rate that he seemed to fly along the forest path rather
than to walk or run. The road grew wilder and drearier and more

51 faintly traced, and vanished at length, leaving him in the heart of the dark wilderness, still rushing onward with the instinct that guides mortal man to evil. The whole forest was peopled with frightful sounds – the creaking of the trees, the howling of wild beasts, and the yell of Indians; while sometimes the wind tolled like a distant church bell, and sometimes gave a broad roar around the traveller, as if all Nature were laughing him to scorn. But he was himself the chief horror of the scene, and shrank not from its other horrors.

52 "Ha! ha! ha!" roared Goodman Brown when the wind laughed at him. "Let us hear which will laugh loudest. Think not to frighten me with your deviltry. Come witch, come wizard, come Indian powwow, come devil himself, and here comes Goodman Brown. You may as well fear him as he fear you."

53 In truth, all through the haunted forest there could be nothing more frightful than the figure of Goodman Brown. On he flew among the black pines, brandishing his staff with frenzied gestures, now giving vent to an inspiration of horrid blasphemy, and now shouting forth such laughter as set all the echoes of the forest laughing like demons around him. The fiend° in his own shape is less hideous than when he rages in the breast of man. Thus sped the demoniac on his course, until, quivering among the trees, he saw a red light before him, as when the felled trunks and branches of a clearing have been set on fire, and throw up their lurid blaze against the sky, at the hour of midnight. He paused, in a lull of the tempest that had driven him onward, and heard the swell of what seemed a hymn, rolling solemnly from a distance with the weight of many voices. He knew the tune; it was a familiar one in the choir of the village meeting-house. The verse died heavily away, and was lengthened by a chorus, not of human voices, but of all the sounds of the benighted wilderness pealing in awful harmony together. Goodman Brown cried out, and his cry was lost to his own ear, by its unison with the cry of the desert.

fiend · the devil

54 In the interval of silence he stole forward until the light glared full upon his eyes. At one extremity of an open space, hemmed in by the dark wall of the forest, arose a rock, bearing some rude, natural resemblance either to an altar or a pulpit, and surrounded by four blazing pines, their tops aflame, their stems untouched, like candles at an evening meeting. The mass of foliage that had

overgrown the summit of the rock was all on fire, blazing high 54
into the night and fitfully illuminating the whole field. Each
pendent·hanging pendent* twig and leafy festoon was in a blaze. As the red light
arose and fell, a numerous congregation alternately shone forth,
then disappeared in shadow, and again grew, as it were, out of
the darkness, peopling the heart of the solitary woods at once.

"A grave and dark-clad company," quoth Goodman Brown. 55

In truth they were such. Among them, quivering to and fro 56
between gloom and splendor, appeared faces that would be seen
next day at the council board of the province, and others which,
Sabbath after Sabbath, looked devoutly heavenward, and benig-
nantly over the crowded pews, from the holiest pulpits in the
land. Some affirm that the lady of the governor was there. At least
there were high dames well known to her, and wives of honored
husbands, and widows, a great multitude, and ancient maidens,
all of excellent repute, and fair young girls, who trembled lest
their mothers should espy them. Either the sudden gleams of
light flashing over the obscure field bedazzled Goodman Brown,
or he recognized a score of the church members of Salem village
famous for their especial sanctity. Good old Deacon Gookin
had arrived, and waited at the skirts of that venerable saint, his
revered pastor. But, irreverently consorting with these grave,
reputable, and pious people, these elders of the church, these
chaste dames and dewy virgins, there were men of dissolute lives
spotted fame· and women of spotted fame,* wretches given over to all mean and
immoral, lascivious, of filthy vice, and suspected even of horrid crimes. It was strange
poor reputation to see that the good shrank not from the wicked, nor were the
sinners abashed by the saints. Scattered also among their pale-
faced enemies were the Indian priests, or powwows, who had
often scared their native forest with more hideous incantations
than any known to English witchcraft.

"But where is Faith?" thought Goodman Brown; and, as hope 57
came into his heart, he trembled.

Another verse of the hymn arose, a slow and mournful strain, 58
such as the pious love, but joined to words which expressed all
that our nature can conceive of sin, and darkly hinted at far more.
Unfathomable to mere mortals is the lore of fiends. Verse after
verse was sung; and still the chorus of the desert swelled between
like the deepest tone of a mighty organ; and with the final peal of

58 that dreadful anthem there came a sound, as if the roaring wind, the rushing streams, the howling beasts, and every other voice of the unconcerted wilderness were mingling and according with the voice of guilty man in homage to the prince of all. The four blazing pines threw up a loftier flame, and obscurely discovered shapes and visages of horror on the smoke wreaths above the impious assembly. At the same moment the fire on the rock shot redly forth and formed a glowing arch above its base, where now appeared a figure. With reverence be it spoken, the figure bore no slight similitude, both in garb and manner, to some grave divine of the New England churches.

59 "Bring forth the converts!" cried a voice that echoed through the field and rolled into the forest.

60 At the word, Goodman Brown stepped forth from the shadow of the trees and approached the congregation, with whom he felt a loathful brotherhood by the sympathy of all that was wicked in his heart. He could have well-nigh sworn that the shape of his own dead father beckoned him to advance, looking downward from a smoke wreath, while a woman, with dim features of despair, threw out her hand to warn him back. Was it his mother? But he had no power to retreat one step, nor to resist, even in thought, when the minister and good old Deacon Gookin seized his arms and led him to the blazing rock. Thither came also the slender form of a veiled female, led between Goody Cloyse, that pious teacher of the catechism, and Martha Carrier, who had received the devil's promise to be queen of hell. A rampant hag was she. And there stood the proselytes beneath the canopy of fire.

61 "Welcome, my children," said the dark figure, "to the communion of your race. Ye have found thus young your nature and your destiny. My children, look behind you!"

62 They turned; and flashing forth, as it were, in a sheet of flame, the fiend worshippers were seen; the smile of welcome gleamed darkly on every visage.

63 "There," resumed the sable* form, "are all whom ye have rever- **sable·** very dark enced from youth. Ye deemed them holier than yourselves and shrank from your own sin, contrasting it with their lives of righteousness and prayerful aspirations heavenward. Yet here are they all in my worshipping assembly. This night it shall be granted you to know their secret deeds: how hoary-bearded elders of the church

have whispered wanton words to the young maids of their house- 63
holds; how many a woman, eager for widows' weeds, has given
her husband a drink at bedtime and let him sleep his last sleep in
her bosom; how beardless youths have made haste to inherit their
fathers' wealth; and how fair damsels, – blush not, sweet ones – have
dug little graves in the garden, and bidden me, the sole guest, to
an infant's funeral. By the sympathy of your human hearts for sin
ye shall scent out all the places – whether in church, bedchamber,
street, field, or forest – where crime has been committed, and
shall exult to behold the whole earth one stain of guilt, one mighty
blood spot. Far more than this. It shall be yours to penetrate, in
every bosom, the deep mystery of sin, the fountain of all wicked
arts, and which inexhaustibly supplies more evil impulses than
human power – than my power at its utmost – can make manifest
in deeds. And now, my children, look upon each other."

They did so; and, by the blaze of the hell-kindled torches, 64
the wretched man beheld his Faith, and the wife her husband,
trembling before that unhallowed altar.

"Lo, there ye stand, my children," said the figure, in a deep 65
and solemn tone, almost sad with its despairing awfulness, as if
once angelic nature· his once angelic nature* could yet mourn for our miserable race.
tradition holds that "Depending upon one another's hearts, ye had still hoped that
Lucifer is a fallen angel virtue were not all a dream. Now are ye undeceived. Evil is the
nature of mankind. Evil must be your only happiness. Welcome
again, my children, to the communion of your race."

"Welcome," repeated the fiend worshippers, in one cry of 66
despair and triumph.

And there they stood, the only pair, as it seemed, who were 67
yet hesitating on the verge of wickedness in this dark world. A
basin was hollowed, naturally, in the rock. Did it contain water,
reddened by the lurid light? or was it blood? or, perchance, a
liquid flame? Herein did the shape of evil dip his hand and
mark ... foreheads· prepare to lay the mark of baptism upon their foreheads,* that
a perversion of the they might be partakers of the mystery of sin, more conscious
ritual marking of the of the secret guilt of others, both in deed and thought, than they
cross on the foreheads could now be of their own. The husband cast one look at his pale
of those being baptized, wife, and Faith at him. What polluted wretches would the next
perhaps here a refer- glance show them to each other, shuddering alike at what they
ence to the mark of the disclosed and what they saw!
Beast (Revelation 20:4)

68   "Faith! Faith!" cried the husband, "look up to heaven, and resist the wicked one."*

resist the wicked one · see James 4:7

69   Whether Faith obeyed he knew not. Hardly had he spoken when he found himself amid calm night and solitude, listening to a roar of the wind which died heavily away through the forest. He staggered against the rock, and felt it chill and damp; while a hanging twig, that had been all on fire, besprinkled his cheek with the coldest dew.

70   The next morning young Goodman Brown came slowly into the street of Salem village, staring around him like a bewildered man. The good old minister was taking a walk along the grave-yard to get an appetite for breakfast and meditate his sermon, and bestowed a blessing, as he passed, on Goodman Brown. He shrank from the venerable saint as if to avoid an anathema.* Old Deacon Gookin was at domestic worship, and the holy words of his prayer were heard through the open window. "What God doth the wizard pray to?" quoth Goodman Brown. Goody Cloyse, that excellent old Christian, stood in the early sunshine at her own lattice, catechizing a little girl who had brought her a pint of morning's milk. Goodman Brown snatched away the child as from the grasp of the fiend himself. Turning the corner by the meeting-house, he spied the head of Faith, with the pink ribbons, gazing anxiously forth, and bursting into such joy at sight of him that she skipped along the street and almost kissed her husband before the whole village. But Goodman Brown looked sternly and sadly into her face, and passed on without a greeting.

anathema · a formal ecclesiastical ban or denunciation, excommunication

71   Had Goodman Brown fallen asleep in the forest and only dreamed a wild dream of a witch-meeting?

72   Be it so if you will; but, alas! it was a dream of evil omen for young Goodman Brown. A stern, a sad, a darkly meditative, a distrustful, if not a desperate man did he become from the night of that fearful dream. On the Sabbath day, when the congregation were singing a holy psalm, he could not listen because an anthem of sin rushed loudly upon his ear and drowned all the blessed strain. When the minister spoke from the pulpit with power and fervid eloquence, and, with his hand on the open Bible, of the sacred truths of our religion, and of saint-like lives and triumphant deaths, and of future bliss or misery unutterable, then did Goodman Brown turn pale, dreading lest the roof

should thunder down upon the gray blasphemer and his hearers. [72] Often, awaking suddenly at midnight, he shrank from the bosom of Faith; and at morning or eventide, when the family knelt down at prayer, he scowled and muttered to himself, and gazed sternly at his wife, and turned away. And when he had lived long, and was borne to his grave a hoary corpse, followed by Faith, an aged woman, and children and grandchildren, a goodly procession, besides neighbors not a few, they carved no hopeful verse upon his tombstone, for his dying hour was gloom.

Fyodor Dostoyevsky

<(1 8 2 1 – 1 8 8 1)>

Dostoyevsky, the son of an army surgeon, became a sublieutenant in the army in 1841 after earning a degree in engineering. In 1849 he was accused of a conspiracy and was sentenced to death before a firing squad. Just before he was to be shot, his sentence was commuted by the Czar. Exiled to a Siberian prison, Dostoyevsky immersed himself in the New Testament and became convinced of the greatness of Christ: "There is only one positively beautiful man in the world – Christ," he wrote to his sister. Dostoyevsky wrote some of the world's greatest novels, including Crime and Punishment *(1866) and* The Brothers Karamazov *(1879), the latter the source of the famous passage below. In "The Grand Inquisitor" two brothers are in conversation. Ivan, a rationalist atheist, is explaining the reasons for his atheism to his brother Alyosha, a devoted Christian. Through this parable or fantasy, Ivan explains what might have happened if Jesus had returned to the earth during the Spanish Inquisition in the 16th century. Since this passage is a small excerpt from a long and complicated novel, one should remember that Ivan's argument, though powerful, is not the final word. Some critics find a reply to Ivan in the mysterious kiss given by Christ; others find a reply in the sermon by a monk (Father Zossima) which follows this passage. In any case, it is important to note that Dostoyevsky believed that authentic belief emerges from "the crucible of doubt."*

THE GRAND INQUISITOR

1 "...**D**O YOU KNOW, Alyosha – don't laugh! I made a poem* about a year ago. If you can waste another ten minutes on me, I'll tell it to you."

poem · a parable, a fiction

2 "You wrote a poem?"

3 "Oh, no, I didn't write it," laughed Ivan, "and I've never written two lines of poetry in my life. But I made up this poem in prose

183

and I remembered it. I was carried away when I made it up. You ³
will be my first reader – that is, listener. Why should an author
forego even one listener?" smiled Ivan. "Shall I tell it to you?"

"I am all attention," said Alyosha. ⁴

"My poem is called 'The Grand Inquisitor'; it's a ridiculous ⁵
thing, but I want to tell it to you."

"Even this must have a preface – that is, a literary preface," ⁶
laughed Ivan, "and I am a poor hand at making one. You see, my
action takes place in the sixteenth century."...

❖ ❖ ❖

"...FIFTEEN CENTURIES have passed since He promised to come ⁷
in His glory, fifteen centuries since His prophet wrote, 'Behold,
I come quickly'"; 'Of that day and that hour knoweth no man,
neither the Son, but the Father,'* as He Himself predicted on earth.
But humanity awaits him with the same faith and with the same
love. Oh, with greater faith, for it is fifteen centuries since man
has ceased to see signs from heaven.

'Behold ... quickly' ·
Revelation 3:11

'Of that ... Father' ·
Matthew 24:36

> No signs from heaven come to-day ⁷ᵃ
> To add to what the heart doth say.

There was nothing left but faith in what the heart doth say. It ⁸
is true there were many miracles in those days. There were saints
who performed miraculous cures; some holy people, according to
their biographies, were visited by the Queen of Heaven* herself.
But the devil did not slumber, and doubts were already arising
among men of the truth of these miracles. And just then there
appeared in the north of Germany a terrible new heresy.* 'A huge
star like to a torch' (that is, to a church) 'fell on the sources of
the waters and they became bitter.'* These heretics began blas-
phemously denying miracles. But those who remained faithful
were all the more ardent in their faith. The tears of humanity rose
up to Him as before, awaited His coming, loved Him, hoped for
Him, yearned to suffer and die for Him as before. And so many
ages mankind had prayed with faith and fervor, 'O Lord our
God, hasten Thy coming'; so many ages called upon Him, that
in His infinite mercy He deigned to come down to His servants.
Before that day He had come down, He had visited some holy
men, martyrs, and hermits, as is written in their lives. Among

Queen of Heaven ·
Mary, Christ's mother

Germany ... heresy ·
Lutheranism, originally
considered to be a heretical movement by the
Roman Catholic church

'A huge star ... bitter' ·
see Revelation 8:10–11

8 us, Tyutchev, with absolute faith in the truth of his words, bore witness that

8a

> Bearing the Cross, in slavish dress,
> Weary and worn, the Heavenly King
> Our mother, Russia, came to bless,
> And through our land went wandering.

And that certainly was so, I assure you.

9 "And behold, He deigned to appear for a moment to the people, to the tortured, suffering people, sunk in iniquity, but loving Him like children. My story is laid in Spain, in Seville, in the most terrible time of the Inquisition, when fires were lighted every day to the glory of God, and 'in the splendid *auto-da-fé* the wicked heretics were burnt.' Oh, of course, this was not the coming in which He will appear, according to His promise, at the end of time in all His heavenly glory, and which will be sudden 'as lightning flashing from east to west.' No, He visited His children only for a moment, and there where the flames were crackling round the heretics. In His infinite mercy He came once more among men in that human shape in which He walked among men for three years fifteen centuries ago. He came down to the 'hot pavement' of the southern town in which on the day before almost a hundred heretics had, *ad majorem gloriam Dei,* been burnt by the cardinal, the Grand Inquisitor, in a magnificent *auto-da-fé* in the presence of the king, the court, the knights, the cardinals, the most charming ladies of the court, and the whole population of Seville.

auto-da-fé · "act of faith" (Spanish), a ceremonial punishment of heretics

ad … Dei · "to the greater glory of God" (Latin), a phrase associated with the Catholic Jesuit Order

10 "He came softly, unobserved, and yet, strange to say, every one recognized Him. That might be one of the best passages in the poem. I mean, why they recognized Him. The people are irresistibly drawn to Him, they surround Him, they flock about Him, follow Him. He moves silently in their midst with a gentle smile of infinite compassion. The sun of love burns in His heart, light and power shine from His eyes, and their radiance, shed on the people, stirs their hearts with responsive love. He holds out His hands to them, blesses them, and a healing virtue comes from contact with Him, even with His garments. An old man in the crowd, blind from childhood, cries out, 'O Lord, heal me and I shall see Thee!' and, as it were, scales fall from his eyes* and the blind

An old man … eyes · see Mark 10:46–52 and Acts 9:17–19

man sees Him. The crowd weeps and kisses the earth under His   10
feet. Children throw flowers before Him, sing, and cry hosannah.
'It is He – it is He!' all repeat. 'It must be He, it can be no one but
Him!' He stops at the steps of the Seville cathedral at the moment
when the weeping mourners are bringing in a little open white

In it lies . . . her hand · coffin. In it lies a child of seven, the only daughter of a prominent
a retelling of Jesus' citizen. The dead child lies hidden in flowers. 'He will raise your
miraculous restoration of child,' the crowd shouts to the weeping mother. The priest, coming
Jairus' daughter (Mark to meet the coffin, looks perplexed, and frowns, but the mother
5:22–24, 35–42) of the dead child throws herself at His feet with a wail. 'If it is
Thou, raise my child!' she cries, holding out her hands to Him.
The procession halts, the coffin is laid on the steps at His feet. He
looks with compassion, and His lips once more softly pronounce,
'Maiden, arise!' and the maiden arises. The little girl sits up in the
coffin and looks round, smiling with wide-open wondering eyes,
holding a bunch of white roses they had put in her hand.·

"There are cries, sobs, confusion among the people, and at that   11

Grand Inquisitor · moment the cardinal himself, the Grand Inquisitor,· passes by the
the lead clerical cathedral. He is an old man, almost ninety, tall and erect, with a
investigator of a panel withered face and sunken eyes, in which there is still a gleam of
formed under papal light. He is not dressed in his gorgeous cardinal's robes, as he was
authority to discover the day before, when he was burning the enemies of the Roman
and eliminate heresy Church – at that moment he was wearing his coarse, old, monk's

cassock · a simple, cassock.· At a distance behind him come his gloomy assistants
ankle-length garment and slaves and the 'holy guard.' He stops at the sight of the crowd
that serves as the and watches it from a distance. He sees everything; he sees them
primary habit of clerics set the coffin down at His feet, sees the child rise up, and his face
darkens. He knits his thick grey brows and his eyes gleam with
a sinister fire. He holds out his finger and bids the guards take
Him. And such is his power, so completely are the people cowed
into submission and trembling obedience to him, that the crowd
immediately makes way for the guards, and in the midst of death-
like silence they lay hands on Him and lead Him away. The crowd
instantly bows down to the earth, like one man, before the old
inquisitor. He blesses the people in silence and passes on.

"The guards lead their prisoner to the close, gloomy vaulted   12
prison in the ancient palace of the Holy Inquisition and shut Him
in it. The day passes and is followed by the dark, burning 'breathless' night of Seville. The air is 'fragrant with laurel and lemon.'

12 In the pitch darkness the iron door of the prison is suddenly opened and the Grand Inquisitor himself comes in with a light in his hand. He is alone; the door is closed at once behind him. He stands in the doorway and for a minute or two gazes in His face. At last he goes up slowly, sets the light on the table and speaks.

✦ ✦ ✦

1 · THE GRAND INQUISITOR SPEAKS TO THE PRISONER

13 "'Is it Thou? Thou?' but receiving no answer, he adds at once, 'Don't answer, be silent. What canst Thou say, indeed? I know too well what Thou wouldst say. And Thou hast no right to add anything to what Thou hadst said of old. Why, then, art Thou come to hinder us? For Thou hast come to hinder us, and Thou knowest that. But dost Thou know what will be tomorrow? I know not who Thou art and care not to know whether it is Thou or only a semblance of Him, but tomorrow I shall condemn Thee and burn Thee at the stake as the worst of heretics. And the very people who have today kissed Thy feet, tomorrow at the faintest sign from me will rush to heap up the embers of Thy fire. Knowest Thou that? Yes, maybe Thou knowest it,' he added with thoughtful penetration, never for a moment taking his eyes off the Prisoner."

14 "I don't quite understand, Ivan. What does it mean?" Alyosha, who had been listening in silence, said with a smile. "Is it simply a wild fantasy, or a mistake on the part of the old man – some impossible *quid pro quo*?"•

> *quid pro quo* · "this for that" (Latin), a mutually dependent arrangement or agreement

15 "Take it as the last," said Ivan, laughing, "if you are so corrupted by modern realism and can't stand anything fantastic. If you like it to be a case of mistaken identity, let it be so. It is true," he went on, laughing, "the old man was ninety, and he might well be crazy over his set idea. He might have been struck by the appearance of the Prisoner. It might, in fact, be simply his ravings, the delusion of an old man of ninety, overexcited by the *auto-da-fé* of a hundred heretics the day before. But does it matter to us after all whether it was a mistake of identity or a wild fantasy? All that matters is that the old man should speak out, should speak openly of what he has thought in silence for ninety years."

16 "And the Prisoner too is silent? Does He look at him and not say a word?"•

> silent ... word · see Isaiah 53:7

"That's inevitable in any case," Ivan laughed again. "The old ¹⁷ man has told Him He hasn't the right to add anything to what He has said of old. One may say it is the most fundamental feature of Roman Catholicism, in my opinion at least. 'All has been given by Thee to the Pope,' they say 'and all, therefore, is still in the Pope's hands, and there is no need for Thee to come now at all. Thou must not meddle for the time, at least.' That's how they speak and write too – the Jesuits,* at any rate. I have read it myself in the works of their theologians."

Jesuits · members of the Society of Jesus, a Roman Catholic order founded by Ignatius Loyola in 1534 and dedicated to teaching and missionary work

"'Hast Thou the right to reveal to us one of the mysteries of that ¹⁸ world from which Thou hast come?' my old man asks Him, and answers the question for Him. 'No, Thou hast not; that Thou mayest not add to what has been said of old, and mayest not take from men the freedom which Thou didst exalt when Thou wast on earth. Whatsoever Thou revealest anew will encroach on men's freedom of faith; for it will be manifest as a miracle, and the freedom of their faith was dearer to Thee than anything in those days fifteen hundred years ago. Didst Thou not often say then, "I will make you free"? But now Thou hast seen these "free" men,' the old man adds suddenly, with a pensive smile. 'Yes, we've paid dearly for it,' he goes on, looking sternly at Him, 'but at last we have completed that work in Thy name. For fifteen centuries we have been wrestling with Thy freedom, but now it is ended and over for good. Dost Thou not believe that it's over for good? Thou lookest meekly at me and deignest not even to be wroth with me. But let me tell Thee that now, today, people are more persuaded than ever that they have perfect freedom, yet they have brought their freedom to us and laid it humbly at our feet. But that has been our doing. Was this what Thou didst? Was this Thy freedom?'"

"I don't understand again," Alyosha broke in. "Is he ironical, is ¹⁹ he jesting?"

"Not a bit of it! He claims it as a merit for himself and his ²⁰ Church that at last they have vanquished freedom and have done so to make men happy."

"'For now' (he is speaking of the Inquisition, of course) 'for the ²¹ first time it has become possible to think of the happiness of

21 men. Man was created a rebel; and how can rebels be happy? Thou wast warned,' he says to Him. 'Thou hast had no lack of admonitions, and warnings, but Thou didst not listen to those warnings; Thou didst reject the only way by which men might be made happy. But, fortunately, departing Thou didst hand on the work to us. Thou hast promised, Thou hast established by Thy word. Thou hast given to us the right to bind and to unbind, and now, of course, Thou canst not think of taking it away. Why, then, hast Thou come to hinder us?' "

22 "And what's the meaning of 'no lack of admonitions and warnings'?" asked Alyosha.

23   "Why, that's the chief part of what the old man must say."

2 · THE THREE TEMPTATIONS FORESHADOWED THE WHOLE SUBSEQUENT HISTORY OF MANKIND

24"'THE WISE AND DREAD SPIRIT, the spirit of self-destruction and non-existence,' the old man goes on, 'the great spirit talked with Thee in the wilderness, and we are told in the books that he "tempted" Thee. Is that so? And could anything truer be said than what he revealed to Thee in three questions and what Thou didst reject, and what in the books is called "the temptation"? And yet if there has ever been on earth a real stupendous miracle, it took place on that day, on the day of the three temptations.' The statement of those three questions was itself the miracle. If it were possible to imagine simply for the sake of argument that those three questions of the dread spirit had perished utterly from the books, and that we had to restore them and to invent them anew, and to do so had gathered together all the wise men of the earth – rulers, chief priests, learned men, philosophers, poets – and had set them the task to invent three questions, such as would not only fit the occasion, but express in three words, three human phrases, the whole future history of the world and of humanity – dost Thou believe that all the wisdom of the earth united could have invented anything in depth and force equal to the three questions which were actually put to Thee then by the wise and mighty spirit in the wilderness? From those questions alone, from the miracle of their statements, we can see that we

wilderness ... three temptations · see Matthew 4:1–11

have here to do not with the fleeting human intelligence, but with 24
the absolute and eternal. For in those three questions the whole
subsequent history of mankind is, as it were, brought together into
one whole, and foretold, and in them are united all the unsolved
historical contradictions of human nature. At the time it could not
be so clear, since the future was unknown; but now that fifteen
hundred years have passed, we see that everything in those three
questions was so justly divined and foretold, and has been so truly
fulfilled that nothing can be added to them or taken from them.

3 · THE FIRST TEMPTATION: THE PROBLEM OF BREAD

"'JUDGE THYSELF WHO WAS RIGHT – Thou or he who questioned 25
Thee then? Remember the first question; its meaning, in other
words, was this: "Thou wouldst go into the world, and art going
with empty hands, with some promise of freedom which men
in their simplicity and their natural unruliness cannot even
understand, which they fear and dread – for nothing has ever
been more insupportable for a man and a human society than
freedom. But seest Thou these stones in this parched and barren
wilderness? Turn them into bread,* and mankind will run after
Thee like a flock of sheep, grateful and obedient, though for
ever trembling, lest Thou withdraw Thy hand and deny them
Thy bread." But Thou wouldst not deprive man of freedom and
didst reject the offer, thinking, what is that freedom worth, if
obedience is bought with bread? Thou didst reply that man lives
not by bread alone. But dost Thou know that for the sake of that
earthly bread the spirit of the earth will rise up against Thee
and will strive with Thee and overcome Thee, and all will follow
him, crying, "Who can compare with this beast? He has given
us fire from heaven!"* Dost Thou know that the ages will pass,
and humanity will proclaim by the lips of their sages that there
is no crime, and therefore no sin; there is only hunger? "Feed
men, and then ask of them virtue!" that's what they'll write on
the banner, which they will raise against Thee, and with which
they will destroy Thy temple. Where Thy temple stood will rise
a new building; the terrible tower of Babel* will be built again,
and though, like the one of old, it will not be finished, yet Thou
mightest have prevented that new tower and have cut short the
sufferings of men for a thousand years; for they will come back

stones ... bread · see Matthew 4:3–4

"Who ... heaven!" · see Revelation 13:4

tower of Babel · see Genesis 11:4–9

25 to us after a thousand years of agony with their tower. They will seek us again, hidden underground in the catacombs, for we shall be again persecuted and tortured. They will find us and cry to us, "Feed us, for those who have promised us fire from heaven haven't given it!" And then we shall finish building their tower, for he finishes the building who feeds them. And we alone shall feed them in Thy name, declaring falsely that it is in Thy name. Oh, never, never can they feed themselves without us! No science will give them bread so long as they remain free. In the end they will lay their freedom at our feet, and say to us, "Make us your slaves, but feed us." They will understand themselves, at last, that freedom and bread enough for all are inconceivable together, for never, never will they be able to share between them! They will be convinced, too, that they can never be free, for they are weak, vicious, worthless and rebellious.

26 "'Thou didst promise them the bread of Heaven,* but, I repeat again, can it compare with earthly bread in the eyes of the weak, ever sinful and ignoble race of man? And if for the sake of the bread of Heaven thousands and tens of thousands shall follow Thee, what is to become of the millions and tens of thousands of millions of creatures who will not have the strength to forego the earthly bread for the sake of the heavenly? Or dost Thou care only for the tens of thousands of the great and strong, while the millions, numerous as the sands of the sea, who are weak but love Thee, must exist only for the sake of the great and strong? No, we care for the weak too. They are sinful and rebellious, but in the end they too will become obedient. They will marvel at us and look on us as gods, because we are ready to endure the freedom which they have found so dreadful to rule over them — so awful it will seem to them to be free. But we shall tell them that we are Thy servants and rule them in Thy name. We shall deceive them again, for we will not let Thee come to us again. That deception will be our suffering, for we shall be forced to lie.

bread of Heaven · see John 6:48–58

27 "'This is the significance of the first question in the wilderness, and this is what Thou hast rejected for the sake of that freedom which Thou hast exalted above everything. Yet in this question lies hid the great secret of this world.

28 "'Choosing "bread," Thou wouldst have satisfied the universal and everlasting craving and humanity — to find some one to worship.

"'So long as man remains free he strives for nothing so inces- 29
santly and so painfully as to find some one to worship. But man
seeks to worship what is established beyond dispute, so that all
men would agree at once to worship it. For these pitiful creatures
are concerned not only to find what one or the other can worship,
but to find something that all would believe in and worship; what
is essential is that all may be *together* in it. This craving for *community* of worship is the chief misery of every man individually
and of all humanity from the beginning of time. For the sake of
common worship they've slain each other with the sword. They
have set up gods and challenged one another, "Put away your
gods and come and worship ours, or we will kill you and your
gods!" And so it will be to the end of the world, even when gods
disappear from the earth; they will fall down before idols just the
same. Thou didst know, Thou couldst not but have known, this
fundamental secret of human nature, but Thou didst reject the
one infallible banner which was offered Thee to make all men
bow down to Thee alone – the banner of earthly bread; and Thou
hast rejected it for the sake of freedom and the bread of Heaven.

4 · THE SECOND TEMPTATION: THE PROBLEM OF CONSCIENCE

"'**B**EHOLD WHAT THOU didst further. And all again in the name 30
of freedom! I tell Thee that man is tormented by no greater
anxiety than to find some one quickly to whom he can hand over
that gift of freedom with which the ill-fated creature is born. But
only one who can appease their conscience can take over their
freedom. In bread there was offered Thee an invincible banner; give
bread, and man will worship Thee, for nothing is more certain than
bread. But if some one else gains possession of his conscience – oh!
then he will cast away Thy bread and follow after him who has
ensnared his conscience. In that Thou wast right. For the secret
of man's being is not only to live but to have something to live for.
Without a stable conception of the object of life, man would not
consent to go on living, and would rather destroy himself than
remain on earth, though he had bread in abundance. That is true.

"'But what happened? 31

"'Instead of taking men's freedom from them, Thou didst 32
make it greater than ever! Didst Thou forget that man prefers

32 peace, and even death, to freedom of choice in the knowledge
of good and evil? Nothing is more seductive for man than his
freedom of conscience, but nothing is a greater cause of suffering.
And behold, instead of giving a firm foundation for setting the
conscience of man at rest for ever, Thou didst choose all that is
exceptional, vague and enigmatic; Thou didst choose what was
utterly beyond the strength of men, acting as though Thou didst
not love them at all – Thou who didst come to give Thy life for
them! Instead of taking possession of men's freedom, Thou didst
increase it, and burdened the spiritual kingdom of mankind with
its sufferings for ever. Thou didst desire man's free love, that he
should follow Thee freely, enticed and taken captive by Thee. In
place of the rigid ancient law, man must hereafter with free heart
decide for himself what is good and what is evil, having only Thy
image before him as his guide. But didst Thou not know he would
at last reject even Thy image and Thy truth, if he is weighed down
with the fearful burden of free choice? They will cry aloud at last
that the truth is not in Thee, for they could not have been left in
greater confusion and suffering than Thou hast caused, laying
upon them so many cares and unanswerable problems.

33 "'So that, in truth, Thou didst Thyself lay the foundation for
the destruction of Thy kingdom, and no one is more to blame
for it. Yet what was offered Thee? There are three powers, three
powers alone, able to conquer and to hold captive for ever the
conscience of these impotent rebels for their happiness – those
forces are miracle, mystery and authority. Thou hast rejected all
three and hast set the example for doing so. When the wise and
dread spirit set Thee on the pinnacle of the temple and said to
Thee, "If Thou wouldst know whether Thou art the Son of God
then cast Thyself down, for it is written: the angels shall hold
him up lest he fall and bruise himself,* and Thou shalt know then
whether Thou art the Son of God and shalt prove then how great
is Thy faith in Thy father." But Thou didst refuse and wouldst not
cast Thyself down. Oh! of course, Thou didst proudly and well like
God; but the weak, unruly race of men, are they gods? Oh, Thou
didst know then that in taking one step, in making one movement
to cast Thyself down, Thou wouldst be tempting God and have
lost all Thy faith in Him, and wouldst have been dashed to pieces
against that earth which Thou didst come to save. And the wise

cast ... himself · see
Matthew 4:5–7

spirit that tempted Thee would have rejoiced. But I ask again, are 33
there many like Thee? And couldst Thou believe for one moment
that men, too, could face such a temptation? Is the nature of men
such, that they can reject miracle, and at the great moments of
their life, the moments of their deepest, most agonizing spiritual
difficulties, cling only to the free verdict of the heart?

"'Oh, Thou didst know that Thy deed would be recorded in 34
books, would be handed down to remote times and the utmost
ends of the earth, and Thou didst hope that man, following Thee,
would cling to God and not ask for a miracle. But Thou didst not
know that when man rejects miracle he rejects God too; for man
seeks not so much God as the miraculous. And as man cannot
bear to be without the miraculous, he will create new miracles
of his own for himself, and will worship deeds of sorcery and
witchcraft, though he might be a hundred times over a rebel,
heretic, and infidel. Thou didst not come down from the Cross
when they shouted to Thee, mocking and reviling Thee. "Come
down from the cross and we will believe that Thou art He."• Thou
didst not come down, for again Thou wouldst not enslave man by
a miracle, and didst crave faith given freely, not based on miracle.
Thou didst crave for free love and not the base raptures of the
slave before the might that has overawed him for ever.

"'But Thou didst think too highly of men therein, for they are 35
slaves, of course, though rebellious by nature. Look around and
judge; fifteen centuries have passed, look upon them. Whom
hast Thou raised up to Thyself? I swear, man is weaker and baser
by nature than Thou hast believed him! Can he, can he do what
Thou didst? By showing him so much respect, Thou didst, as it
were, cease to feel for him, for Thou didst ask far too much from
him – Thou who hast loved him more than Thyself! Respecting
him less, Thou wouldst have asked less of him. That would have
been more like love, for his burden would have been lighter. He
is weak and vile. What though he is everywhere now rebelling
against our power, and proud of his rebellion? It is the pride of a
child and a schoolboy. They are little children rioting and barring
out the teacher at school. But their childish delight will end; it
will cost them dear. They will cast down temples and drench the
earth with blood. But they will see at last, the foolish children,
that, though they are rebels, they are impotent rebels, unable to

"Come down ... He"·
See Mark 15:29–32,
Matthew 27:39–43

35 keep up their own rebellion. Bathed in their foolish tears, they will recognize at last that He who created them rebels must have meant to mock at them. They will say this in despair, and their utterance will be a blasphemy which will make them more unhappy still, for man's nature cannot bear blasphemy, and in the end always avenges it on itself. And so unrest, confusion and unhappiness – that is the present lot of man after Thou didst bear so much for their freedom!

36 "'Thy great prophet tells in vision and in image, that he saw all those who took part in the first resurrection and that there were of each tribe twelve thousand.* But if there were so many of them, they must have been not men but gods. They had borne Thy cross, they had endured scores of years in the barren, hungry wilderness, living upon locusts and roots* – and Thou mayest indeed point with pride at those children of freedom, of free love, of free and splendid sacrifice for Thy name. But remember that they were only some thousands; and what of the rest? And how are the other weak ones to blame, because they could not endure what the strong have endured? How is the weak soul to blame that it is unable to receive such terrible gifts? Canst Thou have simply come to the elect* and for the elect? But if so, it is a mystery and we cannot understand it. And if it is a mystery, we too have a right to preach a mystery, and to teach them that it's not the free judgment of their hearts, not love that matters, but a mystery which they must follow blindly, even against their conscience. So we have done. We have corrected Thy work and have founded it upon *miracle, mystery* and *authority.* And men rejoiced that they were again led like sheep, and that the terrible gift that had brought them such suffering, was, at last, lifted from their hearts.

37 "'Were we right teaching them this?

38 "'Speak!

39 "'Did we not love mankind, so meekly acknowledging their feebleness, lovingly lightening their burden, and permitting their weak nature even sin with our sanction? Why hast Thou come now to hinder us? And why dost Thou look silently and searchingly at me with Thy mild eyes? Be angry. I don't want Thy love, for I love Thee not. And what use is it for me to hide anything from Thee? Don't I know to Whom I am speaking? All that I can

Thy great ... thou-sand · see Revelation 7:4–8

wilderness ... roots · see Matthew 3:4

the elect · those chosen by God for salvation

say is known to Thee already. And is it for me to conceal from 39
Thee our mystery? Perhaps it is Thy will to hear it from my lips.

5 · THE THIRD TEMPTATION: THE PROBLEM OF UNITY

"'LISTEN, THEN. WE ARE NOT working with Thee, but with 40
him – that is our mystery. It's long – eight centuries – since
we have been on his side and not on Thine. Just eight centuries
ago, we took from him what Thou didst reject with scorn, that
last gift he offered Thee, showing Thee all the kingdoms of the
earth.· We took from him Rome and the sword of Cæsar, and
proclaimed ourselves sole rulers of the earth, though hitherto
we have not been able to complete our work. But whose fault
is that? Oh, the work is only beginning, but it has begun. It has
long to await completion and the earth has yet much to suffer,
but we shall triumph and shall be Cæsar's, and then we shall plan
the universal happiness of man. But Thou mightest have taken
even the sword of Cæsar.

showing ... earth ·
see Matthew 4:8-10

"'Why didst Thou reject that last gift? 41

"'Hadst Thou accepted that last counsel of the mighty 42
spirit, Thou wouldst have accomplished all that man seeks
on earth – that is, some one to worship, some one to keep his
conscience, and some means of uniting all in one unanimous
and harmonious antheap, for the craving for universal unity
is the third and last anguish of men. Mankind as a whole has
always striven to organize a universal state. There have been
many great nations with great histories, but the more highly
they were developed the more unhappy they were, for they felt
more acutely than other people the craving for worldwide union.
The great conquerors, Timours and Ghenghis-Khans,· whirled
like hurricanes over the face of the earth striving to subdue its
people, and they too were but the unconscious expression of the
same craving for universal unity. Hadst Thou taken the world
and Cæsar's purple,· Thou wouldst have founded the universal
state and have given universal peace. For who can rule men if
not he who holds their conscience and their bread in his hands.

Timours and
Ghenghis-Khans ·
Timour (1336?–1405),
who was also known as
Tamerlane or Tamburlaine
the Great, and Ghenghis
Kahn (1162?–1227) were
Mongol emperors known
for their cruelty and
expansionism

Cæsar's purple · royal
color signifying high
rank and rule

"'We have taken the sword of Cæsar, and in taking it, of course, 43
have rejected Thee and followed *him*.

"'Oh, ages are yet to come of the confusion of free thought, of 44
their science and cannibalism. For having begun to build their

44 tower of Babel without us, they will end, of course, with cannibalism. But then the beast will crawl to us and lick our feet and
spatter them with tears of blood. And we shall sit upon the beast
and raise the cup, and on it will be written, "Mystery." But then,
and only then, the reign of peace and happiness will come for men.

45 "'Thou art proud of Thine elect, but Thou hast only the elect,
while we give rest to all. And besides, how many of those elect,
those mighty ones who could become elect, have grown weary
waiting for Thee, and have transferred and will transfer the powers
of their spirit and the warmth of their heart to the other camp,
and end by raising their *free* banner against Thee. Thou didst
Thyself lift up that banner. But with us all will be happy and will
no more rebel nor destroy one another as under Thy freedom.

46 "'Oh, we shall persuade them that they will only become free
when they renounce their freedom to us and submit to us. And
shall we be right or shall we be lying? They will be convinced
that we are right, for they will remember the horrors of slavery
and confusion to which Thy freedom brought them. Freedom,
free thought and science, will lead them into such straits and
will bring them face to face with such marvels and insoluble
mysteries, that some of them, the fierce and rebellious, will
destroy themselves, others, rebellious but weak, will destroy one
another, while the rest, weak and unhappy, will crawl fawning to
our feet and whine to us: "Yes, you were right, you alone possess
His mystery, and we come back to you, save us from ourselves!"

6 · SUMMARY: THE INQUISITOR'S UTOPIA

47 "'RECEIVING BREAD FROM US, they will see clearly that we take
the bread made by their hands from them, to give it to
them, without any miracle. They will see that we do not change
the stones to bread, but in truth they will be more thankful for
taking it from our hands than for the bread itself! For they will
remember only too well that in old days, without our help, even
the bread they made turned to stones in their hands, while since
they have come back to us, the very stones have turned to bread
in their hands. Too, too well they know the value of complete
submission! And until men know that, they will be unhappy. Who
is most to blame for their not knowing it, speak? Who scattered
the flock and sent it astray on unknown paths? But the flock will

come together again and will submit once more, and then it will   47
be once for all. Then we shall give them the quiet humble happiness of weak creatures such as they are by nature. Oh, we shall
persuade them at last not to be proud, for Thou didst lift them up
and thereby taught them to be proud. We shall show them that
they are weak, that they are only pitiful children, but that childlike
happiness is the sweetest of all. They will become timid and will
look to us and huddle close to us in fear, as chicks to the hen. They
will marvel at us and will be awe-stricken before us, and will be
proud at our being so powerful and clever, that we have been able
to subdue such a turbulent flock of thousands of millions. They
will tremble impotently before our wrath, their minds will grow
fearful, they will be quick to shed tears like women and children,
but they will be just as ready at a sign from us to pass to laughter
and rejoicing, to happy mirth and childish song. Yes, we shall set
them to work, but in their leisure hours we shall make their life
like a child's game, with children's songs and innocent dance. Oh,
we shall allow them even sin, they are weak and helpless, and
they will love us like children because we allow them to sin. We
shall tell them that every sin will be expiated, if it is done with
our permission, that we allow them to sin because we love them,
and the punishment for these sins we take upon ourselves. And
we shall take it upon ourselves, and they will adore us as their
saviours who have taken on themselves their sins before God.
And they will have no secrets from us. We shall allow or forbid
them to live with their wives and mistresses, to have or not to
have children – according to whether they have been obedient
or disobedient – and they will submit to us gladly and cheerfully.
The most painful secrets of their conscience, all, all they will
bring to us, and we shall have an answer for all. And they will be
glad to believe our answer, for it will save them from the great
anxiety and terrible agony they endure at present in making a free
decision for themselves. And all will be happy, all the millions of
creatures except the hundred thousand who rule over them. For
only we, we who guard the mystery, shall be unhappy.

"'There will be thousands of millions of happy babes, and a   48
hundred thousand sufferers who have taken upon themselves the
curse of the knowledge of good and evil. Peacefully they will die,
peacefully they will expire in Thy name, and beyond the grave

48 they will find nothing but death. But we shall keep the secret, and for their happiness we shall allure them with the reward of heaven and eternity. Though if there were anything in the other world, it certainly would not be for such as they.

49 "'It is prophesied that Thou wilt come again in victory, Thou wilt come with Thy chosen, the proud and strong, but we will say that they have only saved themselves, but we have saved all. We are told that the harlot who sits upon the beast, and holds in her hands the *mystery*, shall be put to shame, that the weak will rise up again, and will rend her royal purple and will strip naked her loathsome body. But then I will stand up and point out to Thee the thousand millions of happy children who have known no sin. And we who have taken their sins upon us for their happiness will stand up before Thee and say: "Judge us if Thou canst and darest." Know that I fear Thee not. Know that I too have been in the wilderness, I too have lived on roots and locusts, I too prized the freedom with which Thou hast blessed men, and I too was striving to stand among Thy elect, among the strong and powerful, thirsting "to make up the number." But I awakened and would not serve madness. I turned back and joined the ranks of those *who have corrected Thy work*. I left the proud and went back to the humble, for the happiness of the humble. What I say to Thee will come to pass, and our dominion will be built up. I repeat, tomorrow Thou shalt see that obedient flock who at a sign from me will hasten to heap up the hot cinders about the pile on which I shall burn Thee for coming to hinder us. For if any one has ever deserved our fires, it is Thou. Tomorrow I shall burn Thee. *Dixi*.'"•

Dixi · "I have spoken" (Latin), the final word of a formal finding or pronouncement

50 Ivan stopped. He was carried away as he talked and spoke with excitement; when he had finished, he suddenly smiled.

51 Alyosha had listened in silence; toward the end he was greatly moved and seemed several times on the point of interrupting, but restrained himself. Now his words came with a rush.

52 "But...that's absurd!" he cried, flushing. "Your poem is in praise of Jesus, not in blame of Him—as you meant it to be. And who will believe you about freedom? Is that the way to understand it? That's not the idea of it in the Orthodox Church•.... That's Rome, and not even the whole of Rome, it's false—those are the worst of the

Orthodox Church · the Christian body predominant in Eastern Europe and Western Asia that is presided over by the Patriarch of Constantinople, a body often at odds with Roman Catholicism

Catholics, the Inquisitors, the Jesuits!…And there could not be such 52
a fantastic creature as your Inquisitor. What are these sins of mankind they take on themselves? Who are these keepers of the mystery who have taken some curse upon themselves for the happiness of mankind? When have they been seen? We know the Jesuits, they are spoken ill of, but surely they are not what you describe? They are not that at all, not at all…. They are simply the Romish army for the earthly sovereignty of the world in the future, with the Pontiff of Rome* for Emperor…that's their ideal, but there's no sort of mystery or lofty melancholy about it…. It's simple lust of power, of filthy earthly gain, of domination—something like a universal serfdom* with them as masters—that's all they stand for. They don't even believe in God perhaps. Your suffering inquisitor is a mere fantasy."

Pontiff of Rome · the Pope

serfdom · a form of slavery in which people are bound to the land and owned by a lord, common in feudal Europe and Russia

"Stay, stay," laughed Ivan, "how hot you are! A fantasy you say, 53
let it be so! Of course it's a fantasy. But allow me to say: do you really think that the Roman Catholic movement of the last centuries is actually nothing but the lust of power, of filthy earthly gain? Is that Father Païssy's teaching?"

"No, no, on the contrary, Father Païssy did once say something 54
the same as you…but of course it's not the same, not a bit the same," Alyosha hastily corrected himself.

"A precious admission, in spite of your 'not a bit the same.' 55
I ask you why your Jesuits and Inquisitors have united simply for vile material gain? Why can there not be among them one martyr oppressed by great sorrow and loving humanity? You see, only suppose that there was one such man among all those who desire nothing but filthy material gain – if there's only one like my old inquisitor, who had himself eaten roots in the desert and made frenzied efforts to subdue his flesh to make himself free and perfect. But yet all his life he loved humanity, and suddenly his eyes were opened, and he saw that it is no great moral blessedness to attain perfection and freedom, if at the same time one gains the conviction that billions of God's creatures have been created as a mockery, that they will never be capable of using their freedom, that these poor rebels can never turn into giants to complete the tower, that it was not for such geese that the great idealist dreamt his dream of harmony. Seeing all that he turned back and joined – the clever people. Surely that could have happened?"

56   "Joined whom, what clever people?" cried Alyosha, completely carried away. "They have no such great cleverness and no mysteries and secrets.... Perhaps nothing but Atheism, that's all their secret. Your inquisitor does not believe in God, that's his secret!"

57   "What if it is so! At last you have guessed it. It's perfectly true that that's the whole secret, but isn't that suffering, at least for a man like that, who has wasted his whole life in the desert and yet could not shake off his incurable love of humanity? In his old age he reached the clear conviction that nothing but the advice of the great dread spirit could build up any tolerable sort of life for the feeble, unruly 'incomplete, empirical creatures created in jest.' And so, convinced of this, he sees that he must follow the council of the wise spirit, the dread spirit of death and destruction, and therefore accept lying and deception, and lead men consciously to death and destruction, and yet deceive them all the way so that they may not notice where they are being led, that the poor blind creatures may at least on the way think themselves happy. And note, the deception is in the name of Him in Whose ideal the old man had so fervently believed all his life long. Is not that tragic? And if only one such stood at the head of the whole army 'filled with the lust of power only for the sake of filthy gain' – would not one such be enough to make a tragedy? More than that, one such standing at the head is enough to create the actual leading idea of the Roman Church with all its armies and Jesuits, its highest idea. I tell you frankly that I firmly believe that there has always been such a man among those who stood at the head of the movement. Who knows, there may have been some such even among the Roman Popes. Who knows, perhaps the spirit of that accursed old man who loves mankind so obstinately in his own way, is to be found even now in a whole multitude of such old men, existing not by chance but by agreement, as a secret league formed long ago for the guarding of the mystery, to guard it from the weak and the unhappy, so as to make them happy. No doubt it is so, and so it must be indeed. I fancy that even among the Masons* there's something of the same mystery at the bottom, and that that's why the Catholics so detest the Masons as their rivals breaking up the unity of the idea, while it is so essential that there should be one flock and one shepherd.... But from

Masons · Freemasonry, a secret international charitable fraternity

the way I defend my idea I might be an author impatient of your 57
criticism. Enough of it."

"You are perhaps a Mason yourself!" broke suddenly from 58
Alyosha. "You don't believe in God," he added, speaking this
time very sorrowfully. He fancied besides that his brother was
looking at him ironically. "How does your poem end?" he asked,
suddenly looking down. "Or was it the end?"

"I meant it to end like this: 59

"When the Inquisitor ceased speaking he waited some time for 60
his Prisoner to answer him. His silence weighed down upon him.
He saw the Prisoner had listened intently all the time, looking
gently in his face and evidently not wishing to reply. The old man
longed for Him to say something, however bitter and terrible. But
He suddenly approached the old man in silence and softly kissed
him on his bloodless aged lips. That was all His answer. The old
man shuddered. His lips moved. He went to the door, opened
it, and said to Him: 'Go, and come no more.... Come not at all,
never, never!' And he let Him out into the dark alleys of the town.
The Prisoner went away."

"And the old man?" 61

"The kiss glows in his heart, but the old man adheres to 62
his idea...."

Leo Tolstoy

⟨ 1 8 2 8 – 1 9 1 0 ⟩

Born into an aristocratic family, Count Tolstoy served in the army and later taught school before experiencing a major religious crisis in the 1870s, which led him to question the meaning of his life. The crisis was resolved when Tolstoy discovered a new way of life based upon Jesus' Sermon on the Mount. While rejecting the teachings and authority of the Russian Orthodox Church, Tolstoy preached a gospel of simplicity, forgiveness, love, and pacifism, which he believed could restructure society. Tolstoy's ideas were widely admired, eventually influencing the thought of Mahatma Gandhi and Martin Luther King, Jr. Tolstoy's post-conversion fiction (including the selection which follows) is noted for its profound moral vision expressed through a deceptively simple narrative form. Tolstoy's late short stories are virtual parables emphasizing the need to live one's life with the awareness that death is near and always certain. Tolstoy, author of War and Peace *(1863–1869),* Anna Karenina *(1875–1877), and* Resurrection *(1899), is one of the monumental Russian novelists.*

HOW MUCH LAND DOES A MAN NEED?

1

1   AN ELDER SISTER CAME to visit her younger sister in the country. The elder was married to a tradesman in town, the younger to a peasant in the village. As the sisters sat over their tea talking, the elder began to boast of the advantages of town life: saying how comfortably they lived there, how well they dressed, what fine clothes her children wore, what good things they ate and drank, and how she went to the theater, promenades, and entertainments.

2   The younger sister was piqued,* and in turn disparaged the life of a tradesman, and stood up for that of a peasant.

         piqued · annoyed

"I would not change my way of life for yours," said she. "We may live roughly, but at least we are free from anxiety. You live in better style than we do, but though you often earn more than you need, you are very likely to lose all you have. You know the proverb, "Loss and gain are brothers twain." It often happens that people who are wealthy one day are begging their bread the next. Our way is safer. Though a peasant's life is not a fat one, it is a long one. We shall never grow rich, but we shall always have enough to eat."

The elder sister said sneeringly:

"Enough? Yes, if you like to share with the pigs and the calves! What do you know of elegance or manners! However much your goodman* may slave, you will die as you are living – on a dung heap – and your children the same."

goodman · a peasant, a man of humble birth

"Well, what of that?" replied the younger. "Of course our work is rough and coarse. But, on the other hand, it is sure, and we need not bow to any one. But you, in your towns, are surrounded by temptations; today all may be right, but tomorrow the Evil One may tempt your husband with cards, wine, or women, and all will go to ruin. Don't such things happen often enough?"

Pakhom, the master of the house, was lying on the top of the stove and he listened to the women's chatter.

"It is perfectly true," thought he. "Busy as we are from childhood tilling mother earth, we peasants have no time to let any nonsense settle in our heads. Our only trouble is that we haven't land enough. If I had plenty of land, I shouldn't fear the Devil himself!"

The women finished their tea, chatted a while about dress, and then cleared away the tea-things and lay down to sleep.

But the Devil had been sitting behind the stove, and had heard all that was said. He was pleased that the peasant's wife had led her husband into boasting, and that he had said that if he had plenty of land he would not fear the Devil himself. "All right," thought the Devil. "We will have a tussle. I'll give you land enough; and by means of that land I will get you into my power."

2

CLOSE TO THE VILLAGE there lived a lady, a small landowner who had an estate of about three hundred acres. She had always lived on good terms with the peasants until she engaged as her steward an old soldier, who took to burdening the people

11   with fines. However careful Pakhom tried to be, it happened again
and again that now a horse of his got among the lady's oats, now
a cow strayed into her garden, now his calves found their way
into her meadows – and he always had to pay a fine.

12   Pakhom paid up, but grumbled, and going home in a temper,
was rough with his family. All through that summer, Pakhom had
much trouble because of this steward, and he was even glad when
winter came and the cattle had to be stabled. Though he grudged
the fodder* when they could no longer graze on the pasture-land,   **fodder** · livestock feed
at least he was free from anxiety about them.

13   In the winter the news got about that the lady was going to
sell her land and that the keeper of the inn on the high road was
bargaining for it. When the peasants heard this they were very
much alarmed.

14   "Well," thought they, "if the innkeeper gets the land, he will
worry us with fines worse than the lady's steward. We all depend
on that estate."

15   So the peasants went on behalf of their commune, and asked
the lady not to sell the land to the innkeeper, offering her a better
price for it themselves. The lady agreed to let them have it. Then
the peasants tried to arrange for the commune to buy the whole
estate, so that it might be held by them all in common. They
met twice to discuss it, but could not settle the matter; the Evil
One sowed discord among them and they could not agree. So
they decided to buy the land individually, each according to his
means; and the lady agreed to this plan as she had to the other.

16   Presently Pakhom heard that a neighbor of his was buying
fifty acres, and that the lady had consented to accept one half in
cash and to wait a year for the other half. Pakhom felt envious.

17   "Look at that," thought he, "the land is all being sold, and I
shall get none of it." So he spoke to his wife.

18   "Other people are buying," said he, "and we must also buy
twenty acres or so. Life is becoming impossible. That steward is
simply crushing us with his fines."

19   So they put their heads together and considered how they could
manage to buy it. They had one hundred rubles laid by. They sold
a colt and one half of their bees, hired out one of their sons as a
labourer and took his wages in advance; borrowed the rest from a
brother-in-law, and so scraped together half the purchase money.

Having done this, Pakhom chose out a farm of forty acres,   20
some of it wooded, and went to the lady to bargain for it. They
came to an agreement, and he shook hands with her upon it and
paid her a deposit in advance. Then they went to town and signed
the deeds; he paying half the price down, and undertaking to pay
the remainder within two years.

So now Pakhom had land of his own. He borrowed seed, and   21
sowed it on the land he had bought. The harvest was a good one, and
within a year he had managed to pay off his debts both to the lady
and to his brother-in-law. So he became a landowner, ploughing and
sowing his own land, making hay on his own land, cutting his own
trees, and feeding his cattle on his own pasture. When he went out
to plough his fields, or to look at his growing corn, or at his grass
meadows, his heart would fill with joy. The grass that grew and the
flowers that bloomed there seemed to him unlike any that grew elsewhere. Formerly, when he had passed by that land, it had appeared
the same as any other land, but now it seemed quite different.

3

So Pakhom was well-contented, and everything would   22
have been right if the neighboring peasants would only not
have trespassed on his corn-fields and meadows. He appealed
to them most civilly, but they still went on: now the communal
herdsmen would let the village cows stray into his meadows, then
horses from the night pasture would get among his corn. Pakhom
turned them out again and again, and forgave their owners, and
for a long time he forbore to prosecute any one. But at last he
lost patience and complained to the district court. He knew it
was the peasants' want of land, and no evil intent on their part,
that caused the trouble, but he thought:

"I cannot go on overlooking it or they will destroy all I have.   23
They must be taught a lesson."

had them up · to be
brought before a local
council or court for
judgment

So he had them up,* gave them one lesson, and then another,   24
and two or three of the peasants were fined. After a time
Pakhom's neighbors began to bear him a grudge for this, and
would now and then let their cattle onto his land on purpose.
One peasant even got into Pakhom's wood at night and cut down
five young lime trees for their bark. Pakhom passing through the
wood one day noticed something white. He came nearer and saw

24 the stripped trunks lying on the ground, and close by stood the stumps where the trees had been. Pakhom was furious.

25 "If he had only cut one here and there it would have been bad enough," thought Pakhom, "but the rascal has actually cut down a whole clump. If I could only find out who did this, I would pay him out."*

pay him out · to get revenge, to call to account

26 He racked his brains as to who it could be. Finally he decided: "It must be Simon – no one else could have done it." So he went to Simon's homestead to have a look round, but he found nothing, and only had an angry scene. However, he now felt more certain than ever that Simon had done it, and he lodged a complaint. Simon was summoned. The case was tried, and retried, and at the end of it all Simon was acquitted, there being no evidence against him. Pakhom felt still more aggrieved, and let his anger loose upon the elder and the judges.

27 "You let thieves grease your palms," said he. "If you were honest folk yourselves you would not let a thief go free."

28 So Pakhom quarrelled with the judges and with his neighbors. Threats to burn his building began to be uttered. So though Pakhom had more land, his place in the commune was much worse than before.

29 About this time a rumor got about that many people were moving to new parts.

30 "There's no need for me to leave my land," thought Pakhom. "But some of the others might leave our village and then there would be more room for us. I would take over their land myself and make my estate a bit bigger. I could then live more at ease. As it is, I am still too cramped to be comfortable."

31 One day Pakhom was sitting at home when a peasant, passing through the village, happened to call in. He was allowed to stay the night, and supper was given him. Pakhom had a talk with this peasant and asked him where he came from. The stranger answered that he came from beyond the Volga,* where he had been working. One word led to another, and the man went on to say that many people were settling in those parts. He told how some people from his village had settled there. They had joined the commune, and had had twenty-five acres per man granted them. The land was so good, he said, that the rye sown on it grew as high as a horse, and so thick that five cuts of a sickle made a

the Volga · a river in western Russia that originates northwest of Moscow and flows into the Caspian Sea

sheaf. One peasant, he said, had brought nothing with him but his 31
bare hands, and now he had six horses and two cows of his own.

Pakhom's heart kindled with desire. He thought: 32

"Why should I suffer in this narrow hole, if one can live so well 33
elsewhere? I will sell my land and my homestead here, and with
the money I will start afresh over there and get everything new.
In this crowded place one is always having trouble. But I must
first go and find out all about it myself."

Towards summer he got ready and started. He went down 34
the Volga on a steamer to Samara,* then walked another three
hundred miles on foot, and at last reached the place. It was just
as the stranger had said. The peasants had plenty of land: every
man had twenty-five acres of communal land given him for his
use, and anyone who had money could buy, besides, at two shil-
lings an acre as much good freehold land* as he wanted.

Having found out all he wished to know, Pakhom returned 35
home as autumn came on, and began selling off his belongings.
He sold his land at a profit, sold his homestead and all his cattle,
and withdrew from membership of the commune. He only
waited till the spring, and then started with his family for the
new settlement.

4

As SOON AS PAKHOM and his family reached their new abode, 36
he applied for admission into the commune of a large village. He stood treat to* the elders and obtained the necessary
documents. Five shares of communal land were given him for his
own and his sons' use: that is to say – 125 acres (not all together,
but in different fields) besides the use of the communal pasture.
Pakhom put up the buildings he needed, and bought cattle. Of
the communal land alone he had three times as much as at his
former home, and the land was good cornland. He was ten times
better off than he had been. He had plenty of arable* land and
pasturage, and could keep as many head of cattle as he liked.

At first, in the bustle of building and settling down, Pakhom 37
was pleased with it all, but when he got used to it he began to
think that even here he had not enough land. The first year, he
sowed wheat on his share of the communal land and had a good
crop. He wanted to go on sowing wheat, but had not enough com-

Samara · a city in
southwestern Russia
on the banks of the
Samara river

freehold land · land
not associated with a
manor that is held by a
tenant for life

stood treat to · to
negotiate or bargain

arable · fit for cultiva-
tion and farming

37 munal land for the purpose, and what he had already used was not available; for in those parts wheat is only sown on virgin soil or on fallow* land. It is sown for one or two years, and then the land lies fallow till it is again overgrown with prairie grass. There were many who wanted such land and there was not enough for all; so that people quarrelled about it. Those who were better off wanted it for growing wheat, and those who were poor wanted it to let* to dealers, so that they might raise money to pay their taxes. Pakhom wanted to sow more wheat, so he rented land from a dealer for a year. He sowed much wheat and had a fine crop, but the land was too far from the village – the wheat had to be carted more than ten miles. After a time Pakhom noticed that some peasant-dealers were living on separate farms and were growing wealthy; and he thought:

fallow · land plowed but left unplanted to allow the soil to rest

to let · to rent out

38 "If I were to buy some freehold land and have a homestead on it, it would be a different thing altogether. Then it would all be nice and compact."

39 The question of buying freehold land recurred to him again and again.

40 He went on in the same way for three years, renting land and sowing wheat. The seasons turned out well and the crops were good, so that he began to lay money by. He might have gone on living contentedly, but he grew tired of having to rent other people's land every year, and having to scramble for it. Wherever there was good land to be had, the peasants would rush for it and it was taken up at once, so that unless you were sharp about it you got none. It happened in the third year that he and a dealer together rented a piece of pasture land from some peasants; and they had already ploughed it up, when there was some dispute and the peasants went to law about it, and things fell out so that the labour was all lost.

41 "If it were my own land," thought Pakhom, "I should be independent, and there would not be all this unpleasantness."

42 So Pakhom began looking out for land which he could buy; and he came across a peasant who had bought thirteen hundred acres, but having got into difficulties was willing to sell again cheap. Pakhom bargained and haggled with him, and at last they settled the price at 1,500 rubles, part in cash and part to be paid later. They had all but clinched the matter when a passing dealer happened to stop at Pakhom's one day to get a feed for his horses.

He drank tea with Pakhom and they had a talk. The dealer said 42 that he was just returning from the land of the Bashkirs,* far away, where he had bought thirteen thousand acres of land, all for 1,000 rubles. Pakhom questioned him further, and the tradesman said:

"All one need do is to make friends with the chiefs. I gave 43 away about one hundred rubles worth of silk robes and carpets, besides a case of tea, and I gave wine to those who would drink it; and I got the land for less than a penny an acre." And he showed Pakhom the title-deeds, saying:

"The land lies near a river, and the whole prairie is virgin soil." 44 Pakhom plied him with questions, and the tradesman said:

"There is more land there than you could cover if you walked 45 a year, and it all belongs to the Bashkirs. They are as simple as sheep, and land can be got almost for nothing."

"There now," thought Pakhom, "with my one thousand rubles, 46 why should I get only thirteen hundred acres, and saddle myself with a debt besides? If I take it out there, I can get more than ten times as much for the money."

5

PAKHOM INQUIRED HOW TO GET to the place, and as soon as 47 the tradesman had left him, he prepared to go there himself. He left his wife to look after the homestead, and started on his journey taking his man with him. They stopped at a town on their way and bought a case of tea, some wine, and other presents, as the tradesman had advised. On and on they went until they had gone more than three hundred miles, and on the seventh day they came to a place where the Bashkirs had pitched their tents. It was all just as the tradesman had said. The people lived on the steppes,* by a river, in felt-covered tents. They neither tilled the ground, nor ate bread. Their cattle and horses grazed in herds on the steppe. The colts were tethered behind the tents, and the mares were driven to them twice a day. The mares were milked, and from the milk *kumiss** was made. It was the women who prepared *kumiss*, and they also made cheese. As far as the men were concerned, drinking *kumiss* and tea, eating mutton, and playing on their pipes, was all they cared about. They were all stout and merry, and all the summer long they never thought of doing any work. They were quite ignorant, and knew no Russian, but were good-natured enough.

Bashkirs · a nomadic tribe of western Russia who inhabit the region of the southern Ural mountains

steppes · a region of semiarid, grass-covered plains

kumiss · (also *kumys*), a fermented drink made from mare's milk

48   As soon as they saw Pakhom, they came out of their tents and gathered round their visitor. An interpreter was found, and Pakhom told them he had come about some land. The Bashkirs seemed very glad; they took Pakhom and led him into one of the best tents, where they made him sit on some down cushions placed on a carpet, while they sat round him. They gave him some tea and *kumiss*, and had a sheep killed, and gave him mutton to eat. Pakhom took presents out of his cart and distributed them among the Bashkirs, and divided the tea amongst them. The Bashkirs were delighted. They talked a great deal among themselves, and then told the interpreter to translate.

    "They wish to tell you," said the interpreter, "that they like you,
49 and that it is our custom to do all we can to please a guest and to repay him for his gifts. You have given us presents, now tell us which of the things we possess please you best, that we may present them to you."

50   "What pleases me best here", answered Pakhom, "is your land. Our land is crowded and the soil is exhausted; but you have plenty of land and it is good land. I never saw the like of it."

51   The interpreter translated. The Bashkirs talked among themselves for a while. Pakhom could not understand what they were saying, but saw that they were much amused and that they shouted and laughed. Then they were silent and looked at Pakhom while the interpreter said:

52   "They wish me to tell you that in return for your presents they will gladly give you as much land as you want. You have only to point it out with your hand and it is yours."

53   The Bashkirs talked again for a while and began to dispute. Pakhom asked what they were disputing about, and the interpreter told him that some of them thought they ought to ask their chief about the land and not act in his absence, while others thought there was no need to wait for his return.

6

54 WHILE THE BASHKIRS were disputing, a man in a large fox-fur cap appeared on the scene. They all became silent and rose to their feet. The interpreter said, "This is our chief himself."

55   Pakhom immediately fetched the best dressing-gown and five pounds of tea, and offered these to the chief. The chief accepted them, and seated himself in the place of honour. The Bashkirs

at once began telling him something. The chief listened for a 55
while, then made a sign with his head for them to be silent, and
addressing himself to Pakhom, said in Russian:

"Well, let it be so. Choose whatever piece of land you like; we 56
have plenty of it."

"How can I take as much as I like?" thought Pakhom. "I must 57
get a deed to make it secure, or else they may say, 'It is yours,'
and afterwards may take it away again."

"Thank you for your kind words," he said aloud. "You have 58
much land, and I only want a little. But I should like to be sure
which bit is mine. Could it not be measured and made over to
me? Life and death are in God's hands. You good people give it
to me, but your children might wish to take it away again."

"You are quite right," said the chief. "We will make it over to you." 59

"I heard that a dealer had been here," continued Pakhom, "and 60
that you gave him a little land, too, and signed title-deeds to that
effect. I should like to have it done in the same way."

The chief understood. 61

"Yes," replied he, "that can be done quite easily. We have 62
a scribe, and we will go to town with you and have the deed
properly sealed."

"And what will be the price?" asked Pakhom. 63

"Our price is always the same: one thousand rubles a day." 64
Pakhom did not understand.

"A day? What measure is that? How many acres would that be?" 65

"We do not know how to reckon it out," said the chief. "We 66
sell it by the day. As much as you can go round on your feet in a
day is yours, and the price is one thousand rubles a day."

Pakhom was surprised. 67

"But in a day you can get round a large tract of land," he said. 68

The chief laughed. 69

"It will all be yours!" said he. "But there is one condition: If 70
you don't return on the same day to the spot whence you started,
your money is lost."

"But how am I to mark the way that I have gone?" 71

"Why, we shall go to any spot you like, and stay there. You must 72
start from that spot and make your round, taking a spade with you.
Wherever you think necessary, make a mark. At every turning,
dig a hole and pile up the turf; then afterwards we will go round

72 with a plough from hole to hole. You may make as large a circuit as you please, but before the sun sets you must return to the place you started from. All the land you cover will be yours." Pakhom was delighted. It was decided to start early next morning. They talked a while, and after drinking some more *kumiss* and eating some more mutton, they had tea again, and then the night came on. They gave Pakhom a feather-bed to sleep on, and the Bashkirs dispersed for the night, promising to assemble the next morning at day-break and ride out before sunrise to the appointed spot.

7

73 PAKHOM LAY ON THE feather-bed, but could not sleep. He kept thinking about the land.

74 "What a large tract I will mark off!" thought he. "I can easily do thirty-five miles in a day. The days are long now, and within a circuit of thirty-five miles what a lot of land there will be! I will sell the poorer land, or let it to peasants, but I'll pick out the best and farm it. I will buy two ox-teams, and hire two more labourers. About a hundred and fifty acres shall be plough-land, and I will pasture cattle on the rest."

75 Pakhom lay awake all night, and dozed off only just before dawn. Hardly were his eyes closed when he had a dream. He thought he was lying in that same tent and heard somebody chuckling outside. He wondered who it could be, and rose and went out, and he saw the Bashkir chief sitting in front of the tent holding his sides and rolling about with laughter. Going nearer to the chief, Pakhom asked: "What are you laughing at?" But he saw that it was no longer the chief, but the dealer who had recently stopped at his house and had told him about the land. Just as Pakhom was going to ask, "Have you been here long?" he saw that it was not the dealer, but the peasant who had come up from the Volga, long ago, to Pakhom's old home. Then he saw that it was not the peasant either, but the Devil himself with hoofs and horns, sitting there and chuckling, and before him lay a man barefoot, prostrate on the ground, with only trousers and a shirt on. And Pakhom dreamt that he looked more attentively to see what sort of a man it was that was lying there, and he saw that the man was dead, and that it was himself! He awoke horror-struck.

76 "What things one does dream," thought he.

Looking round he saw through the open door that the dawn 77
was breaking.

"It's time to wake them up," thought he. "We ought to be starting." 78

He got up, roused his man (who was sleeping in his cart), bade 79
him harness; and went to call the Bashkirs.

"It's time to go to the steppe to measure the land," he said. 80

The Bashkirs rose and assembled, and the chief came too. Then 81
they began drinking *kumiss* again, and offered Pakhom some tea,
but he would not wait.

"If we are to go, let us go. It is high time," said he. 82

8

THE BASHKIRS GOT READY and they all started: some 83
mounted on horses, and some in carts. Pakhom drove in
his own small cart with his servant and took a spade with him.
When they reached the steppe, the morning red was beginning to
kindle. They ascended a hillock (called by the Bashkirs a *shikhan*)
and dismounting from their carts and their horses, gathered in
one spot. The chief came up to Pakhom and stretching out his
arm towards the plain;

"See," said he, "all this, as far as your eye can reach, is ours. 84
You may have any part of it you like."

Pakhom's eyes glistened: it was all virgin soil, as flat as the 85
palm of your hand, as black as the seed of a poppy, and in the
hollows different kinds of grasses grew breast high.

The chief took off his fox-fur cap, placed it on the ground 86
and said:

"This will be the mark. Start from here, and return here again. 87
All the land you go round shall be yours."

Pakhom took out his money and put it on the cap. Then he 88
took off his outer coat, remaining in his sleeveless under-coat. He
unfastened his girdle and tied it tight below his stomach, put a little
bag of bread into the breast of his coat, and tying a flask of water to
his girdle, he drew up the tops of his boots, took the spade from his
man, and stood ready to start. He considered for some moments
which way he had better go – it was tempting everywhere.

"No matter," he concluded, "I will go towards the rising sun." 89

He turned his face to the east, stretched himself, and waited 90
for the sun to appear above the rim.

91 "I must lose no time," he thought, "and it is easier walking while it is still cool."

92 The sun's rays had hardly flashed above the horizon, before Pakhom, carrying the spade over his shoulder, went down into the steppe.

93 Pakhom started walking neither slowly nor quickly. After having gone a thousand yards he stopped, dug a hole, and placed pieces of turf one on another to make it more visible. Then he went on; and now that he had walked off his stiffness he quickened his pace. After a while he dug another hole.

94 Pakhom looked back. The hillock could be distinctly seen in the sunlight, with the people on it, and the glittering tires of the cartwheels. At a rough guess Pakhom concluded that he had walked three miles. It was growing warmer; he took off his under-coat, flung it across his shoulder, and went on again. It had grown quite warm now; he looked at the sun, it was time to think of breakfast.

95 "The first shift is done, but there are four in a day, and it is too soon yet to turn. But I will just take off my boots," said he to himself.

96 He sat down, took off his boots, stuck them into his girdle, and went on. It was easy walking now.

97 "I will go on for another three miles," thought he, "and then turn to the left. This spot is so fine, that it would be a pity to lose it. The further one goes, the better the land seems."

98 He went straight on for a while, and when he looked round, the hillock was scarcely visible and the people on it looked like black ants, and he could just see something glistening there in the sun.

99 "Ah," thought Pakhom, "I have gone far enough in this direction, it is time to turn. Besides I am in a regular sweat, and very thirsty."

100 He stopped, dug a large hole, and heaped up pieces of turf. Next he untied his flask, had a drink, and then turned sharply to the left. He went on and on; the grass was high, and it was very hot.

101 Pakhom began to grow tired: he looked at the sun and saw that it was noon.

102 "Well," he thought, "I must have a rest."

103 He sat down and ate some bread and drank some water; but he did not lie down, thinking that if he did he might fall asleep. After sitting a little while, he went on again. At first he walked easily: the food had strengthened him; but it had become terribly hot and he felt sleepy, still he went on, thinking: "An hour to suffer, a life-time to live."

He went a long way in this direction also, and was about to turn to the left again, when he perceived a damp hollow: "It would be a pity to leave that out," he thought. "Flax would do well there." So he went on past the hollow, and dug a hole on the other side of it before he turned the corner. Pakhom looked towards the hillock. The heat made the air hazy: it seemed to be quivering, and through the haze the people on the hillock could scarcely be seen. 104

"Ah!" thought Pakhom, "I have made the sides too long; I must make this one shorter." And he went along the third side, stepping faster. He looked at the sun: it was nearly half-way to the horizon, and he had not yet done two miles of the third side of the square. He was still ten miles from the goal. 105

"No," he thought, "though it will make my land lop-sided, I must hurry back in a straight line now. I might go too far, and as it is I have a great deal of land." 106

So Pakhom hurriedly dug a hole, and turned straight towards the hillock. 107

9

PAKHOM WENT STRAIGHT towards the hillock, but he now walked with difficulty. He was done up with the heat, his bare feet were cut and bruised, and his legs began to fail. He longed to rest, but it was impossible if he meant to get back before sunset. The sun waits for no man, and it was sinking lower and lower. 108

"Oh dear," he thought, "if only I have not blundered trying for too much! What if I am too late?" 109

He looked towards the hillock and at the sun. He was still far from his goal, and the sun was already near the rim. 110

Pakhom walked on and on; it was very hard walking but he went quicker and quicker. He pressed on, but was still far from the place. He began running, threw away his coat, his boots, his flask, and his cap, and kept only the spade which he used as a support. 111

"What shall I do?" he thought again, "I have grasped too much and ruined the whole affair. I can't get there before the sun sets." 112

And this fear made him still more breathless. Pakhom went on running, his soaking shirt and trousers stuck to him and his mouth was parched. His breast was working like a blacksmith's bellows, his heart was beating like a hammer, and his legs were 113

113 giving way as if they did not belong to him. Pakhom was seized with terror lest he should die of the strain.

114 Though afraid of death, he could not stop. "After having run all that way they will call me a fool if I stop now," thought he. And he ran on and on, and drew near and heard the Bashkirs yelling and shouting to him, and their cries inflamed his heart still more. He gathered his last strength and ran on.

115 The sun was close to the rim, and cloaked in mist looked large, and red as blood. Now, yes now, it was about to set! The sun was quite low, but he was also quite near his aim. Pakhom could already see the people on the hillock waving their arms to hurry him up. He could see the fox-fur cap on the ground and the money on it, and the chief sitting on the ground holding his sides. And Pakhom remembered his dream.

116 "There is plenty of land," thought he, "but will God let me live on it? I have lost my life, I have lost my life! I shall never reach that spot!"

117 Pakhom looked at the sun, which had reached the earth: one side of it had already disappeared. With all his remaining strength he rushed on, bending his body forward so that his legs could hardly follow fast enough to keep him from falling. Just as he reached the hillock it suddenly grew dark. He looked up – the sun had already set! He gave a cry: "All my labour has been in vain," thought he, and was about to stop, but he heard the Bashkirs still shouting, and remembered that though to him, from below, the sun seemed to have set, they on the hillock could still see it. He took a long breath and ran up the hillock. It was still light there. He reached the top and saw the cap. Before it sat the chief laughing and holding his sides. Again Pakhom remembered his dream, and he uttered a cry: his legs gave way beneath him, he fell forward and reached the cap with his hands.

118 "Ah, that's a fine fellow!" exclaimed the chief. "He has gained much land!"

119 Pakhom's servant came running up and tried to raise him, but he saw that blood was flowing from his mouth. Pakhom was dead!

The Bashkirs clicked their tongues to show their pity.

120 His servant picked up the spade and dug a grave long enough
121 for Pakhom to lie in, and buried him in it. Six feet from his head to his heels was all he needed.

I. L. Peretz

⟨ 1 8 5 2 - 1 9 1 5 ⟩

Isaac Leib Peretz – "father of the Yiddish Renaissance," poet, essayist, political activist, and playwright – was born in Zamość, a city of eastern Poland, then part of the Russian Empire. Peretz was devoted to the Jewish Enlightenment, a movement to bring Eastern European Jewish culture into direct conversation with science and Western humanist values. The writer came to believe that he could best aid the cause by writing in Yiddish, the household language of Polish Jews. He rejected the popular mysticism of Hassidic Judaism, arguing for a modern, enlightened approach to life and faith. A socialist who advocated radical political reform, he suffered persecution by the Russian government, losing his license to practice law and enduring a brief imprisonment. Though sympathetic with the socialist rebellions on the horizon, he feared the rise of new, dehumanizing ideologies worse than Russian imperialism. He predicted a new world in which bodies would be fed, but in which spirits would starve. He feared the human spirit would "stand with clipped wings at the same trough beside the cow and ox." The Yiddish literary culture of which Peretz was the chief architect was largely destroyed by three forces: the Holocaust, the assimilation of Jewish culture in America, and the triumph of modern Hebrew in contemporary Israel. Though Yiddish is a dying language, I. L. Peretz left elegant stories whose beauty and ethical idealism endure through translation.

IF NOT HIGHER

1   EARLY EVERY FRIDAY morning, at the time of the Penitential Prayers, the rabbi of Nemirov would vanish.

2   He was nowhere to be seen – neither in the synagogue nor in the two study houses nor at a *minyan.** And he was certainly not at home. His door stood open: whoever wished could go

minyan · a meeting involving a minimum of ten Jewish males above thirteen years of age, the number required for a public religious service

in and out; no one would steal from the rabbi. But not a living creature was within. 2

Where could the rabbi be? Where should he be? In heaven, no doubt. A rabbi has plenty of business to take care of just before the Days of Awe.* Jews, God bless them, need livelihood, peace, health, and good matches. They want to be pious and good, but our sins are so great, and Satan of the thousand eyes watches the whole earth from one end to the other. What he sees, he reports; he denounces, informs. Who can help us if not the rabbi! 3

That's what the people thought. 4

But once, a *Litvak** came, and he laughed. You know the *Litvaks*. They think little of the holy books but stuff themselves with *Talmud** and law. So this *Litvak* points to a passage in the *Gemara** – it sticks in your eyes – where it is written that even Moses our Teacher did not ascend to heaven during his lifetime but remained suspended two and a half feet below. Go argue with a *Litvak*! 5

So where can the rabbi be? 6

"That's not my business," said the *Litvak*, shrugging. Yet all the while – what a *Litvak* can do! – he is scheming to find out. 7

That same night, right after the evening prayers, the *Litvak* steals into the rabbi's room, slides under the rabbi's bed, and waits. He'll watch all night and discover where the rabbi vanishes and what he does during the Penitential Prayers. 8

Someone else might have gotten drowsy and fallen asleep, but the *Litvak* is never at a loss; he recites a whole tractate of the *Talmud* by heart. 9

At dawn he hears the call to prayers. 10

The rabbi has already been awake for a long time. The *Litvak* heard him groaning for a whole hour. 11

Whoever has heard the rabbi of Nemirov groan knows how much sorrow for all Israel, how much suffering, lies in each groan. A man's heart might break, hearing it. But a *Litvak* is made of iron; he listens and remains where he is. The rabbi – long life to him! – lies on the bed, and the *Litvak* under the bed. 12

Then the *Litvak* hears the beds in the house begin to creak; he hears people jumping out of their beds, mumbling a few Jewish words, pouring water on their fingernails,* banging doors. Everyone has left. It is again quiet and dark, a bit of light from the moon shines through the shutters. 13

Days of Awe · the "Ten Days of Repentance" begin on *Rosh Hashanah* (Jewish New Year) and end on *Yom Kippur* (the Day of Atonement). Special penitential prayers are said before morning devotionals on these days

Litvak · a Lithuanian Jew

Talmud · a collection of ancient rabbinic writings, the basis of religious authority for traditional Judaism

Gemara · a commentary and elaboration upon the *Mishnah*, a Jewish code of laws. Together, the *Mishnah* and the *Gemara* constitute the *Talmud*

pouring … fingernails · part of the ritual cleansing performed by Orthodox Jews

14 (Afterward, the *Litvak* admitted that when he found himself alone with the rabbi a great fear took hold of him. Goose pimples spread across his skin, and the roots of his sidelocks* pricked him like needles. A trifle: to be alone with the rabbi at the time of the Penitential Prayers! But a *Litvak* is stubborn. So he quivered like a fish in water and remained where he was.)

> **sidelocks** · hair on the sides of the head that Orthodox Jewish men refrain from cutting. See Leviticus 19:27

15 Finally the rabbi – long life to him! – arises. First, he does what befits a Jew. Then he goes to the clothes closet and takes out a bundle of peasant clothes: linen trousers, high boots, a coat, a big felt hat, and a long, wide leather belt studded with brass nails. The rabbi gets dressed. From his coat pocket dangles the end of a heavy peasant rope.

16 The rabbi goes out, and the *Litvak* follows him.

17 On the way the rabbi stops in the kitchen, bends down, takes an ax from under the bed, puts it into his belt, and leaves the house. The *Litvak* trembles but continues to follow.

18 The hushed dread of the Days of Awe hangs over the dark streets. Every once in a while a cry rises from some *minyan* reciting the Penitential Prayers, or from a sickbed. The rabbi hugs the sides of the streets, keeping to the shade of the houses. He glides from house to house, and the *Litvak* after him. The *Litvak* hears the sound of his heartbeats mingling with the sound of the rabbi's heavy steps. But he keeps on going and follows the rabbi to the outskirts of the town.

19 A small wood stands just outside the town.

20 The rabbi – long life to him! – enters the wood. He takes thirty or forty steps and stops by a small tree. The *Litvak*, overcome with amazement, watches the rabbi take the ax out of his belt and strike the tree. He hears the tree creak and fall. The rabbi chops the tree into logs and the logs into sticks. Then he makes a bundle of the wood and ties it with the rope in his pocket. He puts the bundle of wood on his back, shoves the ax back into his belt, and returns to the town.*

> **He takes ... to the town** · the rabbi's labor in traveling such a distance, cutting down the tree, chopping and bundling the wood and carrying it back to town was expressly prohibited by Talmudic law, as is all work during holy days

21 He stops at a back street beside a small, broken-down shack and knocks at the window.

22 "Who is there?" asks a frightened voice. The *Litvak* recognizes it as the voice of a sick Jewish woman.

23 "I" answers the rabbi in the accent of a peasant.

24 "Who is I?"

Again the rabbi answers in Russian. "Vassil." 25

"Who is Vassil, and what do you want?" 26

"I have wood to sell, very cheap." And not waiting for the 27
woman's reply, he goes into the house.

The *Litvak* steals in after him. In the gray light of early morning 28
he sees a poor room with broken, miserable furnishings. A sick
woman, wrapped in rags, lies on the bed. She complains bitterly,
"Buy? How can I buy? Where will a poor widow get money?"

"I'll lend it to you," answers the supposed Vassil. "It's only 29
six cents."

"And how will I ever pay you back?" asks the poor woman, 30
groaning.

"Foolish one," says the rabbi reproachfully. "See, you are a poor, 31
sick Jew, and I am ready to trust you with a little wood. I am sure
you'll pay. While you, you have such a great and mighty God and
you don't trust him for six cents."

"And who will kindle the fire?" asks the widow. "Have I the 32
strength to get up? My son is at work."

"I'll kindle the fire," answers the rabbi. 33

As the rabbi put the wood into the tile oven he recited, in a 34
groan, the first portion of the Penitential Prayers.

As he kindled the fire and the wood burned brightly, he recited, 35
a bit more joyously, the second portion of the Penitential Prayers.
When the fire was set, he recited the third portion, and then he
shut the stove.

The *Litvak* who saw all this became a disciple of the rabbi. 36

And ever after, when another disciple tells how the rabbi of 37
Nemirov ascends to heaven at the time of the Penitential Prayers,
the *Litvak* does not laugh. He only adds quietly, "If not higher."

Willa Cather

⊰ 1 8 7 3 - 1 9 4 7 ⊱

Her family's immigration from Virginia to the Nebraska prairie when Cather was nine was a formative event. Following her graduation from the state university in Lincoln, Cather returned to the east, establishing herself there as a successful journalist and magazine editor. But the prairie's mystique still haunted her. The stark, empty landscape, peopled by poor but often highly cultured European immigrants who, like Cather's family, had come in search of farmland, exerted a continuing influence on her art. In Cather's fiction, sensitive souls are traumatized by more hardy personality types and by the harshness of pioneer life. Throughout her twelve novels and fifty-eight stories, a number of them focusing on the heroism of western settlers, Cather displays what friend and literary mentor Sarah Orne Jewett called the "gift of sympathy."

THE JOY OF NELLY DEANE

1   NELL AND I WERE almost ready to go on for the last act of *Queen Esther,** and we had for the moment got rid of our three patient dressers, Mrs. Dow, Mrs. Freeze, and Mrs. Spinny. Nell was peering over my shoulder into the little cracked looking glass that Mrs. Dow had taken from its nail on her kitchen wall and brought down to the church under her shawl that morning. When she realized that we were alone, Nell whispered to me in the quick, fierce way she had:

2   "Say, Peggy, won't you go up and stay with me tonight? Scott Spinny's asked to take me home, and I don't want to walk up with him alone."

3   "I guess so, if you'll ask my mother."

4   "Oh, I'll fix her!" Nell laughed, with a toss of her head which meant that she usually got what she wanted, even from people much less tractable than my mother.

Queen Esther · an oratorio by Georg Friedrich Händel (1685–1759) composed in 1732

tiring-women ·
assistants who help
actors change clothes
backstage

In a moment our tiring-women* were back again. The three old 5
ladies – at least they seemed old to us – fluttered about us, more agitated than we were ourselves. It seemed as though they would never
leave off patting Nell and touching her up. They kept trying things
this way and that, never able in the end to decide which way was best.
They wouldn't hear to her using rouge, and as they powdered her
neck and arms, Mrs. Freeze murmured that she hoped we wouldn't
get into the habit of using such things. Mrs. Spinny divided her time

"illusion" · a piece of
skin-colored cloth used
under a low-cut gown
to give the appearance
of cleavage

between pulling up and tucking down the "illusion"* that filled in
the square neck of Nelly's dress. She didn't like things much low,
she said; but after she had pulled it up, she stood back and looked
at Nell thoughtfully through her glasses. While the excited girl was
reaching for this and that, buttoning a slipper, pinning down a curl,
Mrs. Spinny's smile softened more and more until, just before Esther
made her entrance, the old lady tiptoed up to her and softly tucked
the illusion down as far as it would go.

"She's so pink; it seems a pity not," she whispered apologeti- 6
cally to Mrs. Dow.

Every one admitted that Nelly was the prettiest girl in 7
Riverbend, and the gayest – oh, the gayest! When she was not
singing, she was laughing. When she was not laid up with
a broken arm, the outcome of a foolhardy coasting feat, or
suspended from school because she ran away at recess to go
buggy-riding with Guy Franklin, she was sure to be up to mischief
of some sort. Twice she broke through the ice and got soused
in the river because she never looked where she skated or cared
what happened so long as she went fast enough. After the second
of these duckings our three dressers declared that she was trying
to be a Baptist despite herself.

Mrs. Spinny and Mrs. Freeze and Mrs. Dow, who were always 8
hovering about Nelly, often whispered to me their hope that she
would eventually come into our church and not "go with the

Methodists"; her family were Wesleyans.* But to me these artless
plans of theirs never wholly explained their watchful affection.
They had good daughters themselves – except Mrs. Spinny, who
had only the sullen Scott – and they loved their plain girls and
thanked God for them. But they loved Nelly differently. They
were proud of her pretty figure and yellow-brown eyes, which
dilated so easily and sparkled with a kind of golden efferves-

8   cence. They were always making pretty things for her, always coaxing her to come to the sewing circle, where she knotted her thread, and put in the wrong sleeve, and laughed and chattered and said a great many things that she should not have said, and somehow always warmed their hearts. I think they loved her for her unquenchable joy.

9   All the Baptist ladies liked Nell, even those who criticized her most severely, but the three who were first in fighting the battles of our little church, who held it together by their prayers and the labor of their hands, watched over her as they did over Mrs. Dow's century plant before it blossomed. They looked for her on Sunday morning and smiled at her as she hurried, always a little late, up to the choir. When she rose and stood behind the organ and sang "There Is a Green Hill,"* one could see Mrs. Dow and Mrs. Freeze settle back in their accustomed seats and look up at her as if she had just come from that hill and had brought them glad tidings.

"There Is a Green Hill" · a hymn (words C. F. Alexander, music G. C. Stebbins, 1878) that describes the crucifixion of Christ

10   It was because I sang contralto, or, as we said, alto, in the Baptist choir that Nell and I became friends. She was so gay and grown up, so busy with parties and dances and picnics, that I would scarcely have seen much of her had we not sung together. She liked me better than she did any of the older girls, who tried clumsily to be like her, and I felt almost as solicitous and admiring as did Mrs. Dow and Mrs. Spinny. I think even then I must have loved to see her bloom and glow, and I loved to hear her sing, in "The Ninety and Nine,"*

"The Ninety and Nine" · a hymn (words E. C. Clephane, music I. D. Sankey, 1874) based on Christ's parable of the lost sheep (Luke 15:3–7)

10a   *But one was out on the hills away*

in her sweet, strong voice. Nell had never had a singing lesson but she had sung from the time she could talk, and Mrs. Dow used fondly to say that it was singing so much that made her figure so pretty.

11   After I went into the choir it was found to be easier to get Nelly to choir practice. If I stopped outside her gate on my way to church and coaxed her, she usually laughed, ran in for her hat and jacket, and went along with me. The three old ladies fostered our friendship, and because I was "quiet," they esteemed me a good influence for Nelly. This view was propounded in a sewing-circle discussion and, leaking down to us through our mothers, greatly amused us. Dear old ladies! It was so manifestly for what

Nell was that they loved her, and yet they were always looking 11
for "influences" to change her.

The *Queen Esther* performance had cost us three months of 12
hard practice, and it was not easy to keep Nell up to attending
the tedious rehearsals. Some of the boys we knew were in the
chorus of Assyrian youths, but the solo cast was made up of older
people, and Nell found them very poky. We gave the cantata in
the Baptist church on Christmas Eve, "to a crowded house," as
the *Riverbend Messenger* truly chronicled. The country folk for
miles about had come in through a deep snow, and their teams
and wagons stood in a long row at the hitch-bars on each side
of the church door. It was certainly Nelly's night, for however
much the tenor – he was her schoolmaster, and naturally thought
poorly of her – might try to eclipse her in his dolorous solos about
the rivers of Babylon* there could be no doubt as to whom the
people had come to hear – and to see.

After the performance was over, our fathers and mothers came 13
back to the dressing rooms – the little rooms behind the baptistry
where the candidates for baptism were robed – to congratulate
us, and Nell persuaded my mother to let me go home with her.
This arrangement may not have been wholly agreeable to Scott
Spinny, who stood glumly waiting at the baptistry door; though I
used to think he dogged Nell's steps not so much for any pleasure
he got from being with her as for the pleasure of keeping other
people away. Dear little Mrs. Spinny was perpetually in a state
of humiliation on account of his bad manners, and she tried by
a very special tenderness to make up to Nelly for the remissness
of her ungracious son.

Scott was a spare, muscular fellow, good-looking, but with 14
a face so set and dark that I used to think it very like the cast-
ings he sold. He was taciturn and domineering, and Nell rather
liked to provoke him. Her father was so easy with her that she
seemed to enjoy being ordered about now and then. That night,
when every one was praising her and telling her how well she
sang and how pretty she looked, Scott only said, as we came out
of the dressing room:

"Have you got your high shoes on?" 15

"No; but I've got rubbers on over my low ones. Mother 16
doesn't care."

rivers of Babylon · a
reference to the captivity
of Israel. See Psalm 137:1

17   "Well, you just go back and put 'em on as fast as you can."

18   Nell made a face at him and ran back, laughing. Her mother, fat, comfortable Mrs. Deane, was immensely amused at this.

19   "That's right, Scott," she chuckled. "You can do enough more with her than I can. She walks right over me an' Jud."

20   Scott grinned. If he was proud of Nelly, the last thing he wished to do was to show it. When she came back he began to nag again. "What are you going to do with all those flowers? They'll freeze stiff as pokers."*

pokers · fireplace pokers

21   "Well, there won't none of *your* flowers freeze, Scott Spinny, so there!" Nell snapped. She had the best of him that time, and the Assyrian youths rejoiced. They were most of them high-school boys, and the poorest of them had "chipped in" and sent all the way to Denver for Queen Esther's flowers. There were bouquets from half a dozen townspeople, too, but none from Scott. Scott was a prosperous hardware merchant and notoriously penurious, though he saved his face, as the boys said, by giving liberally to the church.

22   "There's no use freezing the fool things, anyhow. You get me some newspapers, and I'll wrap 'em up." Scott took from his pocket a folded copy of the *Riverbend Messenger* and began laboriously to wrap up one of the bouquets. When we left the church door he bore three large newspaper bundles, carrying them as carefully as if they had been so many newly frosted wedding cakes, and left Nell and me to shift for ourselves as we floundered along the snow-burdened sidewalk.

23   Although it was after midnight, lights were shining from many of the little wooden houses, and the roofs and shrubbery were so deep in snow that Riverbend looked as if it had been tucked down into a warm bed. The companies of people, all coming from church, tramping this way and that toward their homes and calling "Good night" and "Merry Christmas" as they parted company, all seemed to us very unusual and exciting.

24   When we got home, Mrs. Deane had a cold supper ready, and Jud Deane had already taken off his shoes and fallen to on his fried chicken and pie. He was so proud of his pretty daughter that he must give her her Christmas presents then and there, and he went into the sleeping chamber behind the dining room and from the depths of his wife's closet brought out a short sealskin jacket and a round cap and made Nelly put them on.

Mrs. Deane, who sat busy between a plate of spice cake and 25
a tray piled with her famous whipped cream tarts, laughed inor-
dinately at his behavior. "Ain't he worse than any kid you ever
see? He's been running to that closet like a cat shut away from
her kittens. I wonder Nell ain't caught on before this. I did think
he'd make out now to keep 'em till Christmas morning; but he's
never made out to keep anything yet."

That was true enough, and fortunately Jud's inability to keep 26
anything seemed always to present a highly humorous aspect
to his wife. Mrs. Deane put her heart into her cooking, and said
that so long as a man was a good provider she had no cause to
complain. Other people were not so charitable toward Jud's
failing. I remember how many strictures were passed upon that
little sealskin and how he was censured for his extravagance. But
what a public-spirited thing, after all, it was for him to do! How,
the winter through, we all enjoyed seeing Nell skating on the
river or running about the town with the brown collar turned
up about her bright cheeks and her hair blowing out from under
the round cap! "No seal," Mrs. Dow said, "would have begrudged
it to her. Why should we?" This was at the sewing circle, when
the new coat was under grave discussion.

At last Nelly and I got upstairs and undressed, and the pad of 27
Jud's slippered feet about the kitchen premises – where he was
carrying up from the cellar things that might freeze – ceased. He
called "Good night, daughter," from the foot of the stairs, and the

prima donna · "first
lady" (Italian), the
principal female singer
in an opera

house grew quiet. But one is not a *prima donna** the first time
for nothing, and it seemed as if we could not go to bed. Our light
must have burned long after every other in Riverbend was out.
The muslin curtains of Nell's bed were drawn back; Mrs. Deane
had turned down the white counterpane and taken off the shams*

shams · decorative
pieces of cloth used to
cover pillows

and smoothed the pillows for us. But their fair plumpness offered
no temptation to two such hot young heads. We could not let
go of life even for a little while. We sat and talked in Nell's cozy
room, where there was a tiny, white fur rug – the only one in
Riverbend – before the bed; and there were white sash curtains,
and the prettiest little desk and dressing table I had ever seen. It
was a warm, gay little room, flooded all day long with sunlight
from east and south windows that had climbing roses all about
them in summer. About the dresser were photographs of ador-

27 ing high school boys; and one of Guy Franklin, much groomed and barbered, in a dress coat and a boutonnière. I never liked to see that photograph there. The home boys looked properly modest and bashful on the dresser, but he seemed to be staring impudently all the time.

28 I knew nothing definite against Guy, but in Riverbend all "traveling men" were considered worldly and wicked. He traveled for a Chicago dry-goods firm, and our fathers didn't like him because he put extravagant ideas into our mothers' heads. He had very smooth and flattering ways, and he introduced into our simple community a great variety of perfumes and scented soaps, and he always reminded me of the merchants in Cæsar, who brought into Gaul "those things which effeminate the mind,"* as we translated that delightfully easy passage.

merchants ... mind · the quote is from Julius Cæsar's *The Gallic Wars* 1.1

29 Nell was sitting before the dressing table in her nightgown, holding the new fur coat and rubbing her cheek against it, when I saw a sudden gleam of tears in her eyes. "You know, Peggy," she said in her quick, impetuous way, "this makes me feel bad. I've got a secret from my daddy."

30 I can see her now, so pink and eager, her brown hair in two springy braids down her back, and her eyes shining with tears and with something even softer and more tremulous.

31 "I'm engaged, Peggy," she whispered, "really and truly."

32 She leaned forward, unbuttoning her nightgown, and there on her breast, hung by a little gold chain about her neck, was a diamond ring – Guy Franklin's solitaire; every one in Riverbend knew it well.

33 "I'm going to live in Chicago, and take singing lessons, and go to operas, and do all those nice things – oh, everything! I know you don't like him, Peggy, but you know you are a kid. You'll see how it is yourself when you grow up. He's so different from our boys, and he's just terribly in love with me. And then, Peggy," – flushing all down over her soft shoulders, – "I'm awfully fond of him, too. Awfully."

34 "Are you, Nell, truly?" I whispered. She seemed so changed to me by the warm light in her eyes and that delicate suffusion of color. I felt as I did when I got up early on picnic mornings in summer, and saw the dawn come up in the breathless sky above the river meadows and make all the corn fields golden.

"Sure I do, Peggy; don't look so solemn. It's nothing to look   35
that way about, kid. It's nice." She threw her arms about me suddenly and hugged me.

"I hate to think about your going so far away from us all, Nell."   36

"Oh, you'll love to come and visit me. Just you wait."   37

She began breathlessly to go over things Guy Franklin had   38
told her about Chicago, until I seemed to see it all looming up
out there under the stars that kept watch over our little sleeping
town. We had neither of us ever been to a city, but we knew what
it would be like. We heard it throbbing like great engines, and
calling to us, that faraway world. Even after we had opened the
windows and scurried into bed, we seemed to feel a pulsation
across all the miles of snow. The winter silence trembled with
it, and the air was full of something new that seemed to break
over us in soft waves. In that snug, warm little bed I had a sense
of imminent change and danger. I was somehow afraid for Nelly
when I heard her breathing so quickly beside me, and I put my
arm about her protectingly as we drifted toward sleep.

In the following spring we were both graduated from the   39
Riverbend high school, and I went away to college. My family
moved to Denver, and during the next four years I heard very
little of Nelly Deane. My life was crowded with new people and
new experiences, and I am afraid I held her little in mind. I heard
indirectly that Jud Deane had lost what little property he owned
in a luckless venture in Cripple Creek, and that he had been able
to keep his house in Riverbend only through the clemency of his
creditors. Guy Franklin had his route changed and did not go to
Riverbend anymore. He married the daughter of a rich cattle-
man out near Long Pine, and ran a dry-goods store of his own.
Mrs. Dow wrote me a long letter about once a year, and in one
of these she told me that Nelly was teaching in the sixth grade
in the Riverbend school.

Dear Nelly does not like teaching very well. The children   39a
try her, and she is so pretty it seems a pity for her to be
tied down to uncongenial employment. Scott is still very
attentive, and I have noticed him look up at the window
of Nelly's room in a very determined way as he goes
home to dinner. Scott continues prosperous; he has made

39a money during these hard times and now owns both our
hardware stores. He is close, but a very honorable fellow.
Nelly seems to hold off, but I think Mrs. Spinny has hopes.
Nothing would please her more. If Scott were more careful about his appearance, it would help. He of course gets
black about his business, and Nelly, you know, is very
dainty. People do say his mother does his courting for him,
she is so eager. If only Scott does not turn out hard and
penurious like his father! We must all have our schooling
in this life, but I don't want Nelly's to be too severe. She
is a dear girl, and keeps her color.

40 Mrs. Dow's own schooling had been none too easy. Her husband had long been crippled with rheumatism, and was bitter
and faultfinding. Her daughters had married poorly, and one of
her sons had fallen into evil ways. But her letters were always
cheerful, and in one of them she gently remonstrated with me
because I "seemed inclined to take a sad view of life."

41 In the winter vacation of my senior year I stopped on my way
home to visit Mrs. Dow. The first thing she told me when I got
into her old buckboard* at the station was that "Scott had at last
prevailed," and that Nelly was to marry him in the spring. As a
preliminary step, Nelly was about to join the Baptist church. "Just
think, you will be here for her baptizing! How that will please
Nelly! She is to be immersed tomorrow night."

buckboard · an open,
flat-bottomed, four-
wheeled carriage

42 I met Scott Spinny in the post office that morning and he gave
me a hard grip with one black hand. There was something grim
and saturnine about his powerful body and bearded face and his
strong, cold hands. I wondered what perverse fate had driven him
for eight years to dog the footsteps of a girl whose charm was due
to qualities naturally distasteful to him. It still seems strange to me
that in easygoing Riverbend, where there were so many boys who
could have lived contentedly enough with my little grasshopper, it
was the pushing ant* who must have her and all her careless ways.

43 By a kind of unformulated etiquette one did not call upon
candidates for baptism on the day of the ceremony, so I had my
first glimpse of Nelly that evening. The baptistry was a cemented
pit directly under the pulpit rostrum, over which we had our stage
when we sang *Queen Esther*. I sat through the sermon somewhat

grasshopper ... ant ·
a reference to the fable
by Æsop in which a
grasshopper fiddles the
summer away while an
ant wisely stores food

nervously. After the minister, in his long, black gown, had gone 43
down into the water and the choir had finished singing, the door
from the dressing room opened, and, led by one of the deacons,
Nelly came down the steps into the pool. Oh, she looked so
little and meek and chastened! Her white cashmere robe clung
about her, and her brown hair was brushed straight back and
hung in two soft braids from a little head bent humbly. As she
stepped down into the water I shivered with the cold of it, and I
remembered sharply how much I had loved her. She went down
until the water was well above her waist, and stood white and
small, with her hands crossed on her breast, while the minister
said the words about being buried with Christ in baptism. Then,
lying in his arm, she disappeared under the dark water. "It will
be like that when she dies," I thought, and a quick pain caught
my heart. The choir began to sing "Washed in the Blood of the
Lamb"* as she rose again, the door behind the baptistry opened,
revealing those three dear guardians, Mrs. Dow, Mrs. Freeze,
and Mrs. Spinny, and she went up into their arms.

I went to see Nell next day, up in the little room of many 44
memories. Such a sad, sad visit! She seemed changed – a little
embarrassed and quietly despairing. We talked of many of the old
Riverbend girls and boys, but she did not mention Guy Franklin
or Scott Spinny, except to say that her father had got work in
Scott's hardware store. She begged me, putting her hands on
my shoulders with something of her old impulsiveness, to come
and stay a few days with her. But I was afraid – afraid of what she
might tell me and of what I might say. When I sat in that room
with all her trinkets, the foolish harvest of her girlhood, lying
about, and the white curtains and the little white rug, I thought
of Scott Spinny with positive terror and could feel his hard grip
on my hand again. I made the best excuse I could about having to
hurry on to Denver; but she gave me one quick look, and her eyes
ceased to plead. I saw that she understood me perfectly. We had
known each other so well. Just once, when I got up to go and had
trouble with my veil, she laughed her old merry laugh and told me
there were some things I would never learn, for all my schooling.

The next day, when Mrs. Dow drove me down to the station 45
to catch the morning train for Denver, I saw Nelly hurrying to
school with several books under her arm. She had been working

"Washed ... Lamb"· this hymn, also known as "Have You Been to Jesus?" (words and music A. E. Hoffman, 1878), was often associated with baptism

45   up her lessons at home, I thought. She was never quick at her books, dear Nell.

46   It was ten years before I again visited Riverbend. I had been in Rome for a long time, and had fallen into bitter homesickness. One morning, sitting among the dahlias and asters that bloom so bravely upon those gigantic heaps of earth-red ruins that were once the palaces of the Cæsars, I broke the seal of one of Mrs. Dow's long yearly letters. It brought so much sad news that I resolved then and there to go home to Riverbend, the only place that had ever really been home to me. Mrs. Dow wrote me that her husband, after years of illness, had died in the cold spell last March. "So good and patient toward the last," she wrote, "and so afraid of giving extra trouble." There was another thing she saved until the last. She wrote on and on, dear woman, about new babies and village improvements, as if she could not bear to tell me; and then it came:

46a   You will be sad to hear that two months ago our dear Nelly left us. It was a terrible blow to us all. I cannot write about it yet, I fear. I wake up every morning feeling that I ought to go to her. She went three days after her little boy was born. The baby is a fine child and will live, I think, in spite of everything. He and her little girl, now eight years old, whom she named Margaret, after you, have gone to Mrs. Spinny's. She loves them more than if they were her own. It seems as if already they had made her quite young again. I wish you could see Nelly's children.

47   Ah, that was what I wanted, to see Nelly's children! The wish came aching from my heart along with the bitter homesick tears, along with a quick, torturing recollection that flashed upon me, as I looked about and tried to collect myself, of how we two had sat in our sunny seat in the corner of the old bare schoolroom one September afternoon and learned the names of the seven hills* together. In that place, at that moment, after so many years, how it all came back to me – the warm sun on my back, the chattering girl beside me, the curly hair, the laughing yellow eyes, the stubby little finger on the page! I felt as if even then, when we sat in the sun with our heads together, it was all arranged, written out like a story that at this moment I should be sitting among

seven hills · the group of hills on which the ancient city of Rome was built

the crumbling bricks and drying grass, and she should be lying 47
in the place I knew so well, on that green hill far away.

Mrs. Dow sat with her Christmas sewing in the familiar sitting 48
room where the carpet and the wallpaper and the tablecover had
all faded into soft, dull colors, and even the chromo* of Hagar
and Ishmael* had been toned to the sobriety of age. In the bay
window the tall wire flowerstand still bore its little terraces of
potted plants, and the big fuchsia and the Martha Washington
geranium had blossomed for Christmastide. Mrs. Dow herself
did not look greatly changed to me. Her hair, thin ever since I
could remember it, was now quite white, but her spare, wiry little
person had all its old activity, and her eyes gleamed with the old
friendliness behind her silver-bowed glasses. Her gray house
dress seemed just like those she used to wear when I ran in after
school to take her angelfood cake down to the church supper.

The house sat on a hill, and from behind the geraniums I could 49
see pretty much all of Riverbend, tucked down in the soft snow,
and the air above was full of big, loose flakes, falling from a gray sky
which betokened settled weather. Indoors the hard-coal burner
made a tropical temperature, and glowed a warm orange from
its isinglass* sides. We sat and visited, the two of us, with a great
sense of comfort and completeness. I had reached Riverbend only
that morning, and Mrs. Dow, who had been haunted by thoughts
of shipwreck and suffering upon wintry seas, kept urging me to
draw nearer to the fire and suggesting incidental refreshment. We
had chattered all through the winter morning and most of the
afternoon, taking up one after another of the Riverbend girls and
boys, and agreeing that we had reason to be well satisfied with
most of them. Finally, after a long pause in which I had listened
to the contented ticking of the clock and the crackle of the coal,
I put the question I had until then held back:

"And now, Mrs. Dow, tell me about the one we loved best of 50
all. Since I got your letter I've thought of her every day. Tell me
all about Scott and Nelly."

The tears flashed behind her glasses, and she smoothed the 51
little pink bag on her knee.

"Well, dear, I'm afraid Scott proved to be a hard man, like his 52
father. But we must remember that Nelly always had Mrs. Spinny.
I never saw anything like the love there was between those two.

chromo · chromolitho-
graph; a color lithograph

Hagar and Ishmael ·
see Genesis 16:1–16

isinglass · thin, transparent sheets of mica, a
mineral resistant to heat

52 After Nelly lost her own father and mother, she looked to Mrs. Spinny for everything. When Scott was too unreasonable, his mother could 'most always prevail upon him. She never lifted a hand to fight her own battles with Scott's father, but she was never afraid to speak up for Nelly. And then Nelly took great comfort of her little girl. Such a lovely child!"

53 "Had she been very ill before the little baby came?"

54 "No, Margaret; I'm afraid 't was all because they had the wrong doctor. I feel confident that either Doctor Tom or Doctor Jones could have brought her through. But, you see, Scott had offended them both, and they'd stopped trading at his store, so he would have young Doctor Fox, a boy just out of college and a stranger. He got scared and didn't know what to do. Mrs. Spinny felt he wasn't doing right, so she sent for Mrs. Freeze and me. It seemed like Nelly had got discouraged. Scott would move into their big new house before the plastering was dry, and though 't was summer, she had taken a terrible cold that seemed to have drained her, and she took no interest in fixing the place up. Mrs. Spinny had been down with her back again and wasn't able to help, and things was just anyway. We won't talk about that, Margaret; I think 't would hurt Mrs. Spinny to have you know. She nearly died of mortification when she sent for us, and blamed her poor back. We did get Nelly fixed up nicely before she died. I prevailed upon Doctor Tom to come in at the last, and it 'most broke his heart. 'Why, Mis' Dow,' he said, 'if you'd only have come and told me how 't was, I'd have come and carried her right off in my arms.'"

55 "Oh, Mrs. Dow," I cried, "then it needn't have been? "

56 Mrs. Dow dropped her needle and clasped her hands quickly. "We mustn't look at it that way, dear," she said tremulously and a little sternly; "we mustn't let ourselves. We must just feel that our Lord wanted her then, and took her to Himself. When it was all over, she did look so like a child of God, young and trusting, like she did on her baptizing night, you remember?"

57 I felt that Mrs. Dow did not want to talk any more about Nelly then, and, indeed, I had little heart to listen; so I told her I would go for a walk, and suggested that I might stop at Mrs. Spinny's to see the children.

58 Mrs. Dow looked up thoughtfully at the clock. "I doubt if you'll find little Margaret there now. It's half-past four, and she'll

have been out of school an hour and more. She'll be most likely 58
coasting on Lupton's Hill. She usually makes for it with her sled
the minute she is out of the schoolhouse door. You know, it's the
old hill where you all used to slide. If you stop in at the church
about six o'clock, you'll likely find Mrs. Spinny there with the
baby. I promised to go down and help Mrs. Freeze finish up the
tree, and Mrs. Spinny said she'd run in with the baby, if 't wasn't
too bitter. She won't leave him alone with the Swede girl. She's
like a young woman with her first."

Lupton's Hill was at the other end of town, and when I got 59
there the dusk was thickening, drawing blue shadows over the
snowy fields. There were perhaps twenty children creeping up
the hill or whizzing down the packed sled track. When I had
been watching them for some minutes, I heard a lusty shout, and
a little red sled shot past me into the deep snow drift beyond.
The child was quite buried for a moment, then she struggled out
and stood dusting the snow from her short coat and red woolen
comforter. She wore a brown fur cap, which was too big for her
and of an old-fashioned shape, such as girls wore long ago, but
I would have known her without the cap. Mrs. Dow had said a
beautiful child, and there would not be two like this in Riverbend.
She was off before I had time to speak to her, going up the hill at
a trot, her sturdy little legs plowing through the trampled snow.
When she reached the top she never paused to take breath, but
threw herself upon her sled and came down with a whoop that
was quenched only by the deep drift at the end.

"Are you Margaret Spinny?" I asked as she struggled out in a 60
cloud of snow.

"Yes, 'm." She approached me with frank curiosity, pulling her 61
little sled behind her. "Are you the strange lady staying at Mrs.
Dow's?" I nodded, and she began to look my clothes over with
respectful interest.

"Your grandmother is to be at the church at six o'clock, 62
isn't she?"

"Yes, 'm." 63

"Well, suppose we walk up there now. It's nearly six, and all 64
the other children are going home." She hesitated, and looked
up at the faintly gleaming track on the hill slope. "Do you want
another slide? Is that it?" I asked.

65   "Do you mind?" she asked shyly.

66   "No. I'll wait for you. Take your time; don't run."

67   Two little boys were still hanging about the slide, and they cheered her as she came down, her comforter streaming in the wind.

68   "Now," she announced, getting up out of the drift, "I'll show you where the church is."

69   "Shall I tie your comforter again?"

70   "No, 'm, thanks. I'm plenty warm." She put her mittened hand confidingly in mine and trudged along beside me.

71   Mrs. Dow must have heard us tramping up the snowy steps of the church, for she met us at the door. Every one had gone except the old ladies. A kerosene lamp flickered over the Sunday school chart, with the lesson-picture of the Wise Men, and the little barrel stove threw out a deep glow over the three white heads that bent above the baby. There the three friends sat, patting him, and smoothing his dress, and playing with his hands, which made theirs look so brown.

72   "You ain't seen nothing finer in all your travels," said Mrs. Spinny, and they all laughed.

73   They showed me his full chest and how strong his back was; had me feel the golden fuzz on his head, and made him look at me with his round, bright eyes. He laughed and reared himself in my arms as I took him up and held him close to me. He was so warm and tingling with life, and he had the flush of new beginnings, of the new morning and the new rose. He seemed to have come so lately from his mother's heart! It was as if I held her youth and all her young joy. As I put my cheek down against his, he spied a pink flower in my hat, and making a gleeful sound, he lunged at it with both fists.

74   "Don't let him spoil it," murmured Mrs. Spinny. "He loves color so – like Nelly."

Katherine Anne Porter

◄{ 1 8 9 0 – 1 9 8 0 }►

Porter was born in a log cabin in Indian Creek, Texas. Her early life was marked by poverty and little formal education. Marriage brought Porter into contact with Roman Catholicism, and she was baptized into the church in 1910. Many of her stories are set in the South, the Southwest, or in Mexico – "my familiar country," as she called it. Despite her assertions that Catholicism was not a significant intellectual influence, a wistful Catholic consciousness is sometimes detectable in her work. In her twenties, Porter wrote and burned "trunksful" of manuscripts, making no attempt to publish until she was thirty. This rigorous apprenticeship and ruthless selectivity account for the stylistic excellence of her work, an estimate on which virtually all critics agree. Of her literary art Porter has said, "My whole attempt has been to discover and understand human motives, human feeling, to make a distillation of what human relations and experiences my mind has been able to absorb." The Collected Stories (1965) won a Pulitzer Prize, and her only novel, Ship of Fools *(1962), was converted into an award-winning movie.*

ROPE

1   ON THE THIRD DAY after they moved to the country he came walking back from the village carrying a basket of groceries and a twenty-four-yard coil of rope. She came out to meet him, wiping her hands on her green smock. Her hair was tumbled, her nose was scarlet with sunburn; he told her that already she looked like a born country woman. His gray flannel shirt stuck to him, his heavy shoes were dusty. She assured him he looked like a rural character in a play.

2   Had he brought the coffee? She had been waiting all day long for coffee. They had forgot it when they ordered at the store the first day.

Gosh, no, he hadn't. Lord, now he'd have to go back. Yes, he   3
would if it killed him. He thought, though, he had everything else.
She reminded him it was only because he didn't drink coffee himself.
If he did he would remember it quick enough. Suppose they ran
out of cigarettes? Then she saw the rope. What was that for? Well,
he thought it might do to hang clothes on, or something. Naturally
she asked him if he thought they were going to run a laundry? They
already had a fifty-foot line hanging right before his eyes? Why,
hadn't he noticed it, really? It was a blot on the landscape to her.

He thought there were a lot of things a rope might come in   4
handy for. She wanted to know what, for instance. He thought
a few seconds, but nothing occurred. They could wait and see,
couldn't they? You need all sorts of strange odds and ends around
a place in the country. She said, yes, that was so; but she thought
just at that time when every penny counted, it seemed funny to
buy more rope. That was all. She hadn't meant anything else. She
hadn't just seen, not at first, why he felt it was necessary.

Well, thunder, he had bought it because he wanted to, and that   5
was all there was to it. She thought that was reason enough, and
couldn't understand why he hadn't said so, at first. Undoubtedly it
would be useful, twenty-four yards of rope, there were hundreds of
things, she couldn't think of any at the moment, but it would come
in. Of course. As he had said, things always did in the country.

But she was a little disappointed about the coffee, and oh, look,   6
look, look at the eggs! Oh, my, they're all running! What had he
put on top of them? Hadn't he known eggs mustn't be squeezed?
Squeezed, who had squeezed them, he wanted to know. What a
silly thing to say. He had simply brought them along in the basket
with the other things. If they got broke it was the grocer's fault.
He should know better than to put heavy things on top of eggs.

She believed it was the rope. That was the heaviest thing in   7
the pack, she saw him plainly when he came in from the road, the
rope was a big package on top of everything. He desired the whole
wide world to witness that this was not a fact. He had carried the
rope in one hand and the basket in the other, and what was the
use of her having eyes if that was the best they could do for her?

Well, anyhow, she could see one thing plain: no eggs for
breakfast. They'd have to scramble them now, for supper. It was   8
too damned bad. She had planned to have steak for supper. No

8 ice, meat wouldn't keep. He wanted to know why she couldn't finish breaking the eggs in a bowl and set them in a cool place.

Cool place! If he could find one for her, she'd be glad to set
9 them there. Well, then, it seemed to him they might very well cook the meat at the same time they cooked the eggs and then warm up the meat for tomorrow. The idea simply choked her. Warmed-over meat, when they might as well have had it fresh. Second best and scraps and makeshifts, even to the meat! He rubbed her shoulder a little. It doesn't really matter so much, does it, darling? Sometimes when they were playful, he would rub her shoulder and she would arch and purr. This time she hissed and almost clawed. He was getting ready to say that they could surely manage somehow when she turned on him and said, if he told her they could manage somehow she would certainly slap his face.

He swallowed the words red hot, his face burned. He picked
10 up the rope and started to put it on the top shelf. She would not have it on the top shelf, the jars and tins belonged there; positively she would not have the top shelf cluttered up with a lot of rope. She had borne all the clutter she meant to bear in the flat in town, there was space here at least and she meant to keep things in order.

Well, in that case, he wanted to know what the hammer and
11 nails were doing up there? And why had she put them there when she knew very well he needed that hammer and those nails upstairs to fix the window sashes?* She simply slowed down everything and made double work on the place with her insane habit of changing things around and hiding them.

window sashes · the wooden casements that hold the glass panes

She was sure she begged his pardon, and if she had had any
12 reason to believe he was going to fix the sashes this summer she would have left the hammer and nails right where he put them; in the middle of the bedroom floor where they could step on them in the dark. And now if he didn't clear the whole mess out of there she would throw them down the well.

Oh, all right, all right – could he put them in the closet?
13 Naturally not, there were brooms and mops and dustpans in the closet, and why couldn't he find a place for his rope outside her kitchen? Had he stopped to consider there were seven God-forsaken rooms in the house, and only one kitchen?

He wanted to know what of it? And did she realize she was 14 making a complete fool of herself? And what did she take him for, a three-year-old idiot? The whole trouble with her was she needed something weaker than she was to heckle and tyrannize over. He wished to God now they had a couple of children she could take it out on. Maybe he'd get some rest.

Her face changed at this, she reminded him he had forgot 15 the coffee and had bought a worthless piece of rope. And when she thought of all the things they actually needed to make the place even decently fit to live in, well, she could cry, that was all. She looked so forlorn, so lost and despairing he couldn't believe it was only a piece of rope that was causing all the racket. What was the matter, for God's sake?

Oh, would he please hush and go away, and *stay* away, if he 16 could, for five minutes? By all means, yes, he would. He'd stay away indefinitely if she wished. Lord, yes, there was nothing he'd like better than to clear out and never come back. She couldn't for the life of her see what was holding him, then. It was a swell time. Here she was, stuck, miles from a railroad, with a half-empty house on her hands, and not a penny in her pocket, and everything on earth to do; it seemed the God-sent moment for him to get out from under. She was surprised he hadn't stayed in town as it was until she had come out and done the work and got things straightened out. It was his usual trick.

It appeared to him that this was going a little far. Just a touch 17 out of bounds, if she didn't mind his saying so. Why the hell had he stayed in town the summer before? To do a half-dozen extra jobs to get the money he had sent her. That was it. She knew perfectly well they couldn't have done it otherwise. She had agreed with him at the time. And that was the only time so help him he had ever left her to do anything by herself.

Oh, he could tell that to his great-grandmother. She had her 18 notion of what had kept him in town. Considerably more than a notion, if he wanted to know. So, she was going to bring all that up again, was she? Well, she could just think what she pleased. He was tired of explaining. It may have looked funny but he had simply got hooked in, and what could he do? It was impossible to believe that she was going to take it seriously. Yes, yes, she knew how it was with a man: if he was left by himself a minute, some

18 woman was certain to kidnap him. And naturally he couldn't hurt her feelings by refusing!

19 Well, what was she raving about? Did she forget she had told him those two weeks alone in the country were the happiest she had known for four years? And how long had they been married when she said that? All right, shut up! If she thought that hadn't stuck in his craw.

20 She hadn't meant she was happy because she was away from him. She meant she was happy getting the devilish house nice and ready for him. That was what she had meant, and now look! Bringing up something she had said a year ago simply to justify himself for forgetting her coffee and breaking the eggs and buying a wretched piece of rope they couldn't afford. She really thought it was time to drop the subject, and now she wanted only two things in the world. She wanted him to get that rope from underfoot, and go back to the village and get her coffee, and if he could remember it, he might bring a metal mitt for the skillets, and two more curtain rods, and if there were any rubber gloves in the village, her hands were simply raw, and a bottle of milk of magnesia* from the drugstore.

milk of magnesia · a common medication used as a laxative

21 He looked out at the dark blue afternoon sweltering on the slopes, and mopped his forehead and sighed heavily and said, if only she could wait a minute for *anything*, he was going back. He had said so, hadn't he, the very instant they found he had overlooked it?

22 Oh, yes, well…run along. She was going to wash windows. The country was so beautiful! She doubted they'd have a moment to enjoy it. He meant to go, but he could not until he had said that if she wasn't such a hopeless melancholiac* she might see that this was only for a few days. Couldn't she remember anything pleasant about the other summers? Hadn't they ever had any fun? She hadn't time to talk about it, and now would he please not leave that rope lying around for her to trip on? He picked it up, somehow it had toppled off the table, and walked out with it under his arm.

melancholiac · depressive personality

23 Was he going this minute? He certainly was. She thought so. Sometimes it seemed to her he had second sight about the precisely perfect moment to leave her ditched. She had meant to put the mattresses out to sun, if they put them out this minute

they would get at least three hours, he must have heard her say 23
that morning she meant to put them out. So of course he would
walk off and leave her to it. She supposed he thought the exercise
would do her good.

Well, he was merely going to get her coffee. A four-mile walk 24
for two pounds of coffee was ridiculous, but he was perfectly
willing to do it. The habit was making a wreck of her, but if she
wanted to wreck herself there was nothing he could do about it.
If he thought it was coffee that was making a wreck of her, she
congratulated him: he must have a damned easy conscience.

Conscience or no conscience, he didn't see why the mattresses 25
couldn't very well wait until tomorrow. And anyhow, for God's
sake, were they living in the house, or were they going to let the
house ride them to death? She paled at this, her face grew livid
about the mouth, she looked quite dangerous, and reminded
him that housekeeping was no more her work than it was his:
she had other work to do as well, and when did he think she was
going to find time to do it at this rate?

Was she going to start on that again? She knew as well as he 26
did that his work brought in the regular money, hers was only
occasional, if they depended on what *she* made – and she might
as well get straight on this question once for all!

That was positively not the point. The question was, when 27
both of them were working on their own time, was there going
to be a division of the housework, or wasn't there? She merely
wanted to know, she had to make her plans. Why, he thought that
was all arranged. It was understood that he was to help. Hadn't
he always, in summers?

Hadn't he, though? Oh, just hadn't he? And when, and where, 28
and doing what? Lord, what an uproarious joke!

It was such a very uproarious joke that her face turned slightly 29
purple, and she screamed with laughter. She laughed so hard she
had to sit down, and finally a rush of tears spurted from her eyes
and poured down into the lifted corners of her mouth. He dashed
towards her and dragged her up to her feet and tried to pour
water on her head. The dipper hung by a string on a nail and he
broke it loose. Then he tried to pump water with one hand while
she struggled in the other. So he gave it up and shook her instead.

30   She wrenched away, crying out for him to take his rope and go
to hell, she had simply given him up: and ran. He heard her high-
heeled bedroom slippers clattering and stumbling on the stairs.

31   He went out around the house and into the lane; he suddenly
realized he had a blister on his heel and his shirt felt as if it were
on fire. Things broke so suddenly you didn't know where you
were. She could work herself into a fury about simply nothing.
She was terrible, damn it: not an ounce of reason. You might as
well talk to a sieve as that woman when she got going. Damned
if he'd spend his life humoring her! Well, what to do now? He
would take back the rope and exchange it for something else.
Things accumulated, things were mountainous, you couldn't
move them or sort them out or get rid of them. They just lay and
rotted around. He'd take it back. Hell, why should he? He wanted
it. What was it anyhow? A piece of rope. Imagine anybody caring
more about a piece of rope than about a man's feelings. What
earthly right had she to say a word about it? He remembered
all the useless, meaningless things she bought for herself: Why?
because I wanted it, that's why! He stopped and selected a large
stone by the road. He would put the rope behind it. He would
put it in the tool-box when he got back. He'd heard enough about
it to last him a life-time.

32   When he came back she was leaning against the post box
beside the road waiting. It was pretty late, the smell of broiled
steak floated nose high in the cooling air. Her face was young
and smooth and fresh-looking. Her unmanageable funny black
hair was all on end. She waved to him from a distance, and he
speeded up. She called out that supper was ready and waiting,
was he starved?

33   You bet he was starved. Here was the coffee. He waved it at
her. She looked at his other hand. What was that he had there?

34   Well, it was the rope again. He stopped short. He had meant
to exchange it but forgot. She wanted to know why he should
exchange it, if it was something he really wanted. Wasn't the air
sweet now, and wasn't it fine to be here?

35   She walked beside him with one hand hooked into his leather
belt. She pulled and jostled him a little as he walked, and leaned
against him. He put his arm clear around her and patted her
stomach. They exchanged wary smiles. Coffee, coffee for the

Ootsum Wootsums! He felt as if he were bringing her a beauti- 35
ful present.

He was a love, she firmly believed, and if she had had her coffee 36
in the morning, she wouldn't have behaved so funny.... There was
a whippoorwill still coming back, imagine, clear out of season,
sitting in the crab-apple tree calling all by himself. Maybe his girl
stood him up. Maybe she did. She hoped to hear him once more,
she loved whippoorwills.... He knew how she was, didn't he?

Sure, he knew how she was. 37

Isaac Bashevis Singer

◁(1 9 0 4 - 1 9 9 1)▷

Singer was educated in a rabbinical seminary in Warsaw, Poland, and immigrated to New York City in 1935, thereby escaping the Holocaust. His writing career began with sketches of village life, composed in Yiddish and collaboratively translated, in The Jewish Daily Forward. *In his artistic maturity, these sketches broadened into the 19th century Jewish society of Eastern Europe, a society characterized by fervent otherworldly faith but simultaneously by the doubt and materialism brought about by Western Enlightenment. Singer's world is one in which characters are often forced to acknowledge that unbelief, intellectually tempting though it may be, is inimical to human happiness. His most memorable creations are Jewish doubters who eventually flee to their religious heritage as a bastion of human worth and meaning in the face of Western society's atheistic drift. Though not morality tales, his works are constructed, Singer has said, around a moral point of view: "I even would go so far as to say that any writer who does not think in terms of good and evil cannot go very far in his writing." Singer was awarded the Nobel Prize for Literature in 1978.*

GIMPEL THE FOOL

1

¹ I AM GIMPEL THE FOOL. I don't think myself a fool. On the contrary. But that's what folks call me. They gave me the name while I was still in school. I had seven names in all: imbecile, donkey, flax-head, dope, glump, ninny, and fool. The last name stuck. What did my foolishness consist of? I was easy to take in. They said, "Gimpel, you know the rabbi's wife has been brought to childbed?" So I skipped school. Well, it turned out to be a lie. How was I supposed to know? She hadn't had a big belly. But I

never looked at her belly. Was that really so foolish? The gang laughed and hee-hawed, stomped and danced and chanted a good-night prayer. And instead of the raisins they give when a woman's lying in, they stuffed my hand full of goat turds. I was no weakling. If I slapped someone he'd see all the way to Cracow.* But I'm really not a slugger by nature. I think to myself: Let it pass. So they take advantage of me.

I was coming home from school and heard a dog barking. I'm not afraid of dogs, but of course I never want to start up with them. One of them may be mad, and if he bites there's not a Tartar* in the world who can help you. So I made tracks. Then I looked around and saw the whole market place wild with laughter. It was no dog at all but Wolf-Leib the Thief. How was I supposed to know it was he? It sounded like a howling bitch.

When the pranksters and leg-pullers found that I was easy to fool, every one of them tried his luck with me. "Gimpel, the Czar* is coming to Frampol; Gimpel, the moon fell down in Turbeen; Gimpel, little Hodel Furpiece found a treasure behind the bathhouse." And I like a *golem** believed everyone. In the first place, everything is possible, as it is written in The Wisdom of the Fathers,* I've forgotten just how. Second, I had to believe when the whole town came down on me! If I ever dared to say, "Ah, you're kidding!" there was trouble. People got angry. "What do you mean! You want to call everyone a liar?" What was I to do? I believed them, and I hope at least that did them some good.

I was an orphan. My grandfather who brought me up was already bent toward the grave. So they turned me over to a baker, and what a time they gave me there! Every woman or girl who came to bake a batch of noodles had to fool me at least once. "Gimpel, there's a fair in heaven; Gimpel, the rabbi gave birth to a calf in the seventh month; Gimpel, a cow flew over the roof and laid brass eggs." A student from the *yeshiva** came once to buy a roll, and he said, "You, Gimpel, while you stand here scraping with your baker's shovel the Messiah has come. The dead have arisen." "What do you mean?" I said. "I heard no one blowing the ram's horn!" He said, "Are you deaf?" And all began to cry, "We heard it, we heard!" Then in came Rietze the Candle-dipper and called out in her hoarse voice, "Gimpel, your father and mother have stood up from the grave. They're looking for you."

Cracow · the city of Kraków, on the Vistula river in southern Poland

Tarter · named for a warlike tribe that settled in west-central Russia, a notably strong, resourceful or violent person

Czar · the ruler of Russia under the monarchial system

golem · an artificial person; a human simulacrum (Hebrew)

Wisdom of the Fathers · the *Mishna*, a collection of rabbinic sayings and wisdom

yeshiva · an academy of Talmudic learning, where students study biblical and legal exegesis and the application of Scripture

5   To tell the truth, I knew very well that nothing of the sort had happened, but all the same, as folks were talking, I threw on my wool vest and went out. Maybe something had happened. What did I stand to lose by looking? Well, what a cat music went up! And then I took a vow to believe nothing more. But that was no go either. They confused me so that I didn't know the big end from the small.

6   I went to the rabbi to get some advice. He said, "It is written, better to be a fool all your days than for one hour to be evil. You are not a fool. They are the fools. For he who causes his neighbor to feel shame loses Paradise himself." Nevertheless the rabbi's daughter took me in. As I left the rabbinical court she said, "Have you kissed the wall yet?" I said, "No; what for?" She answered, "It's the law; you've got to do it after every visit." Well, there didn't seem to be any harm in it. And she burst out laughing. It was a fine trick. She put one over on me, all right.

7   I wanted to go off to another town, but then everyone got busy matchmaking, and they were after me so they nearly tore my coat tails off. They talked at me and talked until I got water on the ear. She was no chaste maiden, but they told me she was virgin pure. She had a limp, and they said it was deliberate, from coyness. She had a bastard, and they told me the child was her little brother. I cried, "You're wasting your time. I'll never marry that whore." But they said indignantly, "What a way to talk! Aren't you ashamed of yourself? We can take you to the rabbi and have you fined for giving her a bad name." I saw then that I wouldn't escape them so easily and I thought: They're set on making me their butt. But when you're married the husband's the master, and if that's all right with her it's agreeable to me too. Besides, you can't pass through life unscathed, nor expect to.

8   I went to her clay house, which was built on the sand, and the whole gang, hollering and chorusing, came after me. They acted like bear-baiters.* When we came to the well they stopped all the same. They were afraid to start anything with Elka. Her mouth would open as if it were on a hinge, and she had a fierce tongue. I entered the house. Lines were strung from wall to wall and clothes were drying. Barefoot she stood by the tub, doing the wash. She was dressed in a worn hand-me-down gown of plush. She had her hair put up in braids and pinned across her head. It took my breath away, almost, the reek of it all.

bear-baiters · bear-baiting is a sport (now outlawed) in which dogs are allowed to harass a chained bear

Evidently she knew who I was. She took a look at me and said, 9 "Look who's here! He's come, the drip. Grab a seat."

I told her all; I denied nothing. "Tell me the truth," I said, "are 10 you really a virgin, and is that mischievous Yechiel actually your little brother? Don't be deceitful with me, for I'm an orphan."

"I'm an orphan myself," she answered, "and whoever tries to 11 twist you up, may the end of his nose take a twist. But don't let them think they can take advantage of me. I want a dowry of fifty guilders, and let them take up a collection besides. Otherwise they can kiss my you-know-what." She was very plainspoken. I said, "It's the bride and not the groom who gives a dowry." Then she said, "Don't bargain with me. Either a flat 'yes' or a flat 'no'– Go back where you came from."

I thought: No bread will ever be baked from *this* dough. But 12 ours is not a poor town. They consented to everything and proceeded with the wedding. It so happened that there was a dysentery epidemic at the time. The ceremony was held at the cemetery gates, near the little corpse-washing hut. The fellows got drunk. While the marriage contract was being drawn up I heard the most pious high rabbi ask, "Is the bride a widow or a divorced woman?" And the sexton's wife answered for her, "Both a widow and divorced." It was a black moment for me. But what was I to do, run away from under the marriage canopy?

There was singing and dancing. An old granny danced oppo- 13 site me, hugging a braided white *chalah.*• The master of revels made a "God 'a mercy" in memory of the bride's parents. The schoolboys threw burrs, as on *Tishe b'Av* fast day.• There were a lot of gifts after the sermon: a noodle board, a kneading trough, a bucket, brooms, ladles, household articles galore. Then I took a look and saw two strapping young men carrying a crib. "What do we need this for?" I asked. So they said, "Don't rack your brains about it. It's all right, it'll come in handy." I realized I was going to be rooked. Take it another way though, what did I stand to lose? I reflected: I'll see what comes of it. A whole town can't go altogether crazy.

chalah • a type of braided bread eaten on ceremonial occasions (Hebrew)

Tishe b'Av fast day • a Jewish fast that takes place in late July or early August commemorating the destruction of the Temple

2

AT NIGHT I CAME WHERE MY wife lay, but she wouldn't let me 14 in. "Say, look here, is this what they married us for?" I said.

14 And she said, "My monthly has come." "But yesterday they took you to the ritual bath, and that's afterward, isn't it supposed to be?" "Today isn't yesterday," said she, "and yesterday's not today. You can beat it if you don't like it." In short, I waited.

15 Not four months later she was in childbed. The townsfolk hid their laughter with their knuckles. But what could I do? She suffered intolerable pains and clawed at the walls. "Gimpel," she cried, "I'm going. Forgive me!" The house filled with women. They were boiling pans of water. The screams rose to the welkin.•

> welkin · the sky, viewed as a curved roof above the earth

The thing to do was to go to the House of Prayer to repeat Psalms, and that was what I did.

16 The townsfolk liked that, all right. I stood in a corner saying Psalms and prayers, and they shook their heads at me. "Pray, pray!" they told me. "Prayer never made any woman pregnant." One of the congregation put a straw to my mouth and said, "Hay for the cows." There was something to that too, by God!

17 She gave birth to a boy. Friday at the synagogue the sexton• stood up before the Ark,• pounded on the reading table, and announced, "The wealthy Reb Gimpel invites the congregation to a feast in honor of the birth of a son." The whole House of Prayer rang with laughter. My face was flaming. But there was nothing I could do. After all, I *was* the one responsible for the circumcision honors and rituals.

> sexton · the caretaker of the synagogue who announces worship
>
> the Ark · in Jewish synagogues, an ornate cabinet that enshrines the sacred Torah scrolls used for public worship

18 Half the town came running. You couldn't wedge another soul in. Women brought peppered chick-peas, and there was a keg of beer from the tavern. I ate and drank as much as anyone, and they all congratulated me. Then there was a circumcision, and I named the boy after my father, may he rest in peace. When all were gone and I was left with my wife alone, she thrust her head through the bed-curtain and called me to her.

19 "Gimpel," said she, "why are you silent? Has your ship gone and sunk?"

20 "What shall I say?" I answered. "A fine thing you've done to me! If my mother had known of it she'd have died a second time."

21 She said, "Are you crazy, or what?"

22 "How can you make such a fool," I said, "of one who should be the lord and master?"

23 "What's the matter with you?" she said. "What have you taken it into your head to imagine?"

I saw that I must speak bluntly and openly. "Do you think this   24
is the way to use an orphan?" I said. "You have borne a bastard."
She answered, "Drive this foolishness out of your head. The
child is yours."

"How can he be mine?" I argued. "He was born seventeen   25
weeks after the wedding."

She told me then that he was premature. I said, "Isn't he a   26
little too premature?" She said, she had had a grandmother who
carried just as short a time and she resembled this grandmother
of hers as one drop of water does another. She swore to it with
such oaths that you would have believed a peasant at the fair if
he had used them. To tell the plain truth, I didn't believe her; but
when I talked it over next day with the schoolmaster he told me
that the very same thing had happened to Adam and Eve. Two
they went up to bed, and four they descended.

"There isn't a woman in the world who is not the granddaugh-   27
ter of Eve," he said.

That was how it was; they argued me dumb. But then, who   28
really knows how such things are?

I began to forget my sorrow. I loved the child madly, and he   29
loved me too. As soon as he saw me he'd wave his little hands
and want me to pick him up, and when he was colicky I was
the only one who could pacify him. I bought him a little bone
teething ring and a little gilded cap. He was forever catching the
evil eye from someone, and then I had to run to get one of those
abracadabras for him that would get him out of it. I worked like
an ox. You know how expenses go up when there's an infant in
the house. I don't want to lie about it; I didn't dislike Elka either,
for that matter. She swore at me and cursed, and I couldn't get
enough of her. What strength she had! One of her looks could rob
you of the power of speech. And her orations! Pitch and sulphur,
that's what they were full of, and yet somehow also full of charm.
I adored her every word. She gave me bloody wounds though.

In the evening I brought her a white loaf as well as a dark   30
one, and also poppyseed rolls I baked myself. I thieved because
of her and swiped everything I could lay hands on: macaroons,
raisins, almonds, cakes. I hope I may be forgiven for stealing from
the Saturday pots the women left to warm in the baker's oven.
I would take out scraps of meat, a chunk of pudding, a chicken

30   leg or head, a piece of tripe, whatever I could nip quickly. She ate and became fat and handsome.

31   I had to sleep away from home all during the week, at the bakery. On Friday nights when I got home she always made an excuse of some sort. Either she had heartburn, or a stitch in the side, or hiccups, or headaches. You know what women's excuses are. I had a bitter time of it. It was rough. To add to it, this little brother of hers, the bastard, was growing bigger. He'd put lumps on me, and when I wanted to hit back she'd open her mouth and curse so powerfully I saw a green haze floating before my eyes. Ten times a day she threatened to divorce me. Another man in my place would have taken French leave* and disappeared. But I'm the type that bears it and says nothing. What's one to do? Shoulders are from God, and burdens too.

French leave · to leave the army without permission, to desert

32   One night there was a calamity in the bakery; the oven burst, and we almost had a fire. There was nothing to do but go home, so I went home. Let me, I thought, also taste the joy of sleeping in bed in mid-week. I didn't want to wake the sleeping mite and tiptoed into the house. Coming in, it seemed to me that I heard not the snoring of one but, as it were, a double snore, one a thin enough snore and the other like the snoring of a slaughtered ox. Oh, I didn't like that! I didn't like it at all. I went up to the bed, and things suddenly turned black. Next to Elka lay a man's form. Another in my place would have made an uproar, and enough noise to rouse the whole town, but the thought occurred to me that I might wake the child. A little thing like that – why frighten a little swallow, I thought. All right then, I went back to the bakery and stretched out on a sack of flour and till morning I never shut an eye. I shivered as if I had had malaria. "Enough of being a donkey," I said to myself. "Gimpel isn't going to be a sucker all his life. There's a limit even to the foolishness of a fool like Gimpel."

33   In the morning I went to the rabbi to get advice, and it made a great commotion in the town. They sent the beadle* for Elka right away. She came, carrying the child. And what do you think she did? She denied it, denied everything, bone and stone! "He's out of his head," she said. "I know nothing of dreams or divinations." They yelled at her, warned her, hammered on the table, but she stuck to her guns: it was a false accusation, she said.

beadle · a minor synagogue official whose duties include ushering and keeping order

34   The butchers and the horse-traders took her part. One of the lads from the slaughterhouse came by and said to me, "We've

got our eye on you, you're a marked man." Meanwhile the child 34
started to bear down and soiled itself. In the rabbinical court
there was an Ark of the Covenant, and they couldn't allow that,
so they sent Elka away. I said to the rabbi, "What shall I do?"

"You must divorce her at once," said he. 35

"And what if she refuses?" I asked. 36

He said, "You must serve the divorce. That's all you'll have to do." 37

I said, "Well, all right, Rabbi. Let me think about it." 38

"There's nothing to think about," said he. "You mustn't remain 39
under the same roof with her."

"And if I want to see the child?" I asked. 40

"Let her go, the harlot," said he, "and her brood of bastards 41
with her."

The verdict he gave was that I mustn't even cross her thresh- 42
old – never again, as long as I should live.

During the day it didn't bother me so much. I thought: It was 43
bound to happen, the abscess had to burst. But at night when I
stretched out upon the sacks I felt it all very bitterly. A longing
took me, for her and for the child. I wanted to be angry, but that's
my misfortune exactly, I don't have it in me to be really angry. In
the first place – this was how my thoughts went – there's bound to
be a slip sometimes. You can't live without errors. Probably that
lad who was with her led her on and gave her presents and what
not, and women are often long on hair and short on sense, and so
he got around her. And then since she denies it so, maybe I was
only seeing things? Hallucinations do happen. You see a figure or a
mannikin or something, but when you come up closer it's nothing,
there's not a thing there. And if that's so, I'm doing her an injustice.
And when I got so far in my thoughts I started to weep. I sobbed
so that I wet the flour where I lay. In the morning I went to the
rabbi and told him that I had made a mistake. The rabbi wrote
on with his quill, and he said that if that were so he would have
to reconsider the whole case. Until he had finished I wasn't to go
near my wife, but I might send her bread and money by messenger.

3

NINE MONTHS PASSED before all the rabbis could come to 44
an agreement. Letters went back and forth. I hadn't realized
that there could be so much erudition about a matter like this.

45   Meanwhile Elka gave birth to still another child, a girl this time. On the Sabbath I went to the synagogue and invoked a blessing on her. They called me up to the *Torah*,* and I named the child for my mother-in-law – may she rest in peace. The louts and loudmouths of the town who came into the bakery gave me a going over. All Frampol refreshed its spirits because of my trouble and grief. However, I resolved that I would always believe what I was told. What's the good of *not* believing? Today it's your wife you don't believe; tomorrow it's God Himself you won't take stock in.

Torah · the written scroll of Scriptures housed in the Ark

46   By an apprentice who was her neighbor I sent her daily a corn or a wheat loaf, or a piece of pastry, rolls or bagels, or, when I got the chance, a slab of pudding, a slice of honeycake, or wedding strudel – whatever came my way. The apprentice was a goodhearted lad, and more than once he added something on his own. He had formerly annoyed me a lot, plucking my nose and digging me in the ribs, but when he started to be a visitor to my house he became kind and friendly. "Hey, you, Gimpel," he said to me, "you have a very decent little wife and two fine kids. You don't deserve them."

47   "But the things people say about her," I said.

48   "Well, they have long tongues," he said, "and nothing to do with them but babble. Ignore it as you ignore the cold of last winter." One day the rabbi sent for me and said, "Are you certain, Gimpel, that you were wrong about your wife?"

49   I said, "I'm certain."

50   "Why, but look here! You yourself saw it."

51   "It must have been a shadow," I said.

52   "The shadow of what?"

53   "Just of one of the beams, I think."

54   "You can go home then. You owe thanks to the Yanover rabbi. He found an obscure reference in Maimonides* that favored you."

Maimonides · Moses Maimonides (1135–1204), Jewish scholastic philosopher

55   I seized the rabbi's hand and kissed it.

56   I wanted to run home immediately. It's no small thing to be separated for so long a time from wife and child. Then I reflected: I'd better go back to work now, and go home in the evening. I said nothing to any one, although as far as my heart was concerned it was like one of the Holy Days. The women teased and twitted me as they did every day, but my thought was: Go on, with your loose

talk. The truth is out, like the oil upon the water. Maimonides 56
says it's right, and therefore it is right!

At night, when I had covered the dough to let it rise, I took 57
my share of bread and a little sack of flour and started homeward.
The moon was full and the stars were glistening, something to
terrify the soul. I hurried onward, and before me darted a long
shadow. It was winter, and a fresh snow had fallen. I had a mind
to sing, but it was growing late and I didn't want to wake the
householders. Then I felt like whistling, but I remembered that
you don't whistle at night because it brings the demons out. So
I was silent and walked as fast as I could.

Dogs in the Christian yards barked at me when I passed, but 58
I thought: Bark your teeth out! What are you but mere dogs?
Whereas I am a man, the husband of a fine wife, the father of
promising children.

As I approached the house my heart started to pound as 59
though it were the heart of a criminal. I felt no fear, but my heart
went thump! thump! Well, no drawing back. I quietly lifted the
latch and went in. Elka was asleep. I looked at the infant's cradle.
The shutter was closed, but the moon forced its way through the
cracks. I saw the newborn child's face and loved it as soon as I
saw it – immediately – each tiny bone.

Then I came nearer to the bed. And what did I see but the 60
apprentice lying there beside Elka. The moon went out all at once.
It was utterly black, and I trembled. My teeth chattered. The bread
fell from my hands, and my wife waked and said, "Who is that, ah?"

I muttered, "It's me." 61

"Gimpel?" she asked. "How come you're here? I thought it 62
was forbidden."

"The rabbi said," I answered and shook as with a fever. 63

"Listen to me, Gimpel," she said, "go out to the shed and see 64
if the goat's all right. It seems she's been sick." I have forgotten
to say that we had a goat. When I heard she was unwell I went
into the yard. The nannygoat was a good little creature. I had a
nearly human feeling for her.

With hesitant steps I went up to the shed and opened the door. 65
The goat stood there on her four feet. I felt her everywhere, drew
her by the horns, examined her udders, and found nothing wrong.
She had probably eaten too much bark. "Good night, little goat,"

65 I said. "Keep well." And the little beast answered with a "maa" as though to thank me for the good will.

66 I went back. The apprentice had vanished.

67 "Where," I asked, "is the lad?"

68 "What lad?" my wife answered.

69 "What do you mean?" I said. "The apprentice. You were sleeping with him."

70 "The things I have dreamed this night and the night before," she said, "may they come true and lay you low, body and soul! An evil spirit has taken root in you and dazzles your sight." She screamed out, "You hateful creature! You moon calf!* You spook! You uncouth man! Get out, or I'll scream all Frampol out of bed!"

moon calf · an unnatural or dangerous magical creature

71 Before I could move, her brother sprang out from behind the oven and struck me a blow on the back of the head. I thought he had broken my neck. I felt that something about me was deeply wrong, and I said, "Don't make a scandal. All that's needed now is that people should accuse me of raising spooks and *dybbuks*."* For that was what she had meant. "No one will touch bread of my baking."

dybbuks · wandering spirits of the dead (Yiddish)

72 In short, I somehow calmed her.

73 "Well," she said, "that's enough. Lie down, and be shattered by wheels."

74 Next morning I called the apprentice aside. "Listen here, brother!" I said. And so on and so forth. "What do you say?" He stared at me as though I had dropped from the roof or something. "I swear," he said, "you'd better go to an herb doctor or some healer. I'm afraid you have a screw loose, but I'll hush it up for you." And that's how the thing stood.

75 To make a long story short, I lived twenty years with my wife. She bore me six children, four daughters and two sons. All kinds of things happened, but I neither saw nor heard. I believed, and that's all. The rabbi recently said to me, "Belief in itself is beneficial. It is written that a good man lives by his faith."

76 Suddenly my wife took sick. It began with a trifle, a little growth upon the breast. But she evidently was not destined to live long; she had no years. I spent a fortune on her. I have forgotten to say that by this time I had a bakery of my own and in Frampol was considered to be something of a rich man. Daily the healer came, and every witch doctor in the neighborhood was brought.

cupping · a medical practice in which heated glass cups are applied to the skin to draw toxins from the blood

Lublin · a city in eastern Poland on the Bystrzyca River

They decided to use leeches, and after that to try cupping.* They 76
even called a doctor from Lublin,* but it was too late. Before she
died she called me to her bed and said, "Forgive me, Gimpel."

I said, "What is there to forgive? You have been a good and 77
faithful wife."

"Woe, Gimpel!" she said. "It was ugly how I deceived you all 78
these years. I want to go clean to my Maker, and so I have to tell
you that the children are not yours."

If I had been clouted on the head with a piece of wood it 79
couldn't have bewildered me more.

"Whose are they?" I asked. 80

"I don't know," she said. "There were a lot ... but they're not 81
yours." And as she spoke she tossed her head to the side, her eyes
turned glassy, and it was all up with Elka. On her whitened lips
there remained a smile.

I imagined that, dead as she was, she was saying, "I deceived 82
Gimpel. That was the meaning of my brief life."

4

ONE NIGHT, WHEN THE PERIOD of mourning was done, as 83
I lay dreaming on the flour sacks, there came the Spirit of
Evil himself and said to me, "Gimpel, why do you sleep?"

kreplach · a dumpling stuffed with meat or cheese, often served in soup

I said, "What should I be doing? Eating *kreplach*?"* 84

"The whole world deceives you," he said, "and you ought to 85
deceive the world in your turn."

"How can I deceive all the world?" I asked him. 86

He answered, "You might accumulate a bucket of urine every 87
day and at night pour it into the dough. Let the sages of Frampol
eat filth."

"What about the judgment in the world to come?" I said. 88
"There is no world to come," he said. "They've sold you a bill of
goods and talked you into believing you carried a cat in your
belly. What nonsense!"

"Well then," I said, "and is there a God?" 89

He answered, "There is no God either." 90

"What," I said, "*is* there, then?" 91

"A thick mire." 92

He stood before my eyes with a goatish beard and horn, long- 93
toothed, and with a tail. Hearing such words, I wanted to snatch

93   him by the tail, but I tumbled from the flour sacks and nearly broke a rib. Then it happened that I had to answer the call of nature, and, passing, I saw the risen dough, which seemed to say to me, "Do it!" In brief, I let myself be persuaded.

94   At dawn the apprentice came. We kneaded the bread, scattered caraway seeds on it, and set it to bake. Then the apprentice went away, and I was left sitting in the little trench by the oven, on a pile of rags. Well, Gimpel, I thought, you've revenged yourself on them for all the shame they've put on you. Outside the frost glittered, but it was warm beside the oven. The flames heated my face. I bent my head and fell into a doze.

95   I saw in a dream, at once, Elka in her shroud. She called to me, "What have you done, Gimpel?"

96   I said to her, "It's all your fault," and started to cry.

97   "You fool!" she said. "You fool! Because I was false is everything false too? I never deceived anyone but myself. I'm paying for it all, Gimpel. They spare you nothing here."

98   I looked at her face. It was black; I was startled and waked, and remained sitting dumb. I sensed that everything hung in the balance. A false step now and I'd lose Eternal Life. But God gave me His help. I seized the long shovel and took out the loaves, carried them into the yard, and started to dig a hole in the frozen earth.

99   My apprentice came back as I was doing it. "What are you doing boss?" he said, and grew pale as a corpse. "I know what I'm doing," I said, and I buried it all before his very eyes.

100   Then I went home, took my hoard from its hiding place, and divided it among the children. "I saw your mother tonight," I said. "She's turning black, poor thing."

101   They were so astounded they couldn't speak a word.

102   "Be well," I said, "and forget that such a one as Gimpel ever existed." I put on my short coat, a pair of boots, took the bag that held my prayer shawl in one hand, my stock in the other, and kissed the *mezzuzah*.· When people saw me in the street they were greatly surprised.

103   "Where are you going?" they said.

104   I answered, "Into the world." And so I departed from Frampol.

105   I wandered over the land, and good people did not neglect me. After many years I became old and white; I heard a great deal, many lies and falsehoods, but the longer I lived the more I

mezzuzah · a case containing Hebrew scriptures, attached to doorframes of Jewish homes (Hebrew)

understood that there were really no lies. Whatever doesn't really   105
happen is dreamed at night. It happens to one if it doesn't happen
to another, tomorrow if not today, or a century hence if not next
year. What difference can it make? Often I heard tales of which I
said, "Now this is a thing that cannot happen." But before a year
had elapsed I heard that it actually had come to pass somewhere.

Going from place to place, eating at strange tables, it often   106
happens that I spin yarns – improbable things that could never
have happened – about devils, magicians, windmills, and the
like. The children run after me, calling, "Grandfather, tell us a
story." Sometimes they ask for particular stories, and I try to
please them. A fat young boy once said to me, "Grandfather, it's
the same story you told us before." The little rogue, he was right.

So it is with dreams too. It is many years since I left Frampol,   107
but as soon as I shut my eyes I am there again. And whom do
you think I see? Elka. She is standing by the washtub, as at our
first encounter, but her face is shining and her eyes are as radiant
as the eyes of a saint, and she speaks outlandish words to me,
strange things. When I wake I have forgotten it all. But while
the dream lasts I am comforted. She answers all my queries, and
what comes out is that all is right. I weep and implore, "Let me
be with you." And she consoles me and tells me to be patient. The
time is nearer than it is far. Sometimes she strokes and kisses
me and weeps upon my face. When I awaken I feel her lips and
taste the salt of her tears.

No doubt the world is entirely an imaginary world, but it   108
is only once removed from the true world. At the door of the
hovel where I lie, there stands the plank on which the dead are
taken away. The gravedigger Jew has his spade ready. The grave
waits and the worms are hungry; the shrouds are prepared – I
carry them in my beggar's sack. Another *shnorrer** is waiting to
inherit my bed of straw. When the time comes I will go joyfully.
Whatever may be there, it will be real, without complication,
without ridicule, without deception. God be praised: there even
Gimpel cannot be deceived.

schnorrer · a beggar,
freeloader, or parasite
(Yiddish)

Bernard Malamud

<(1 9 1 4 - 1 9 8 6)>

Malamud is one of the writers in what literary critics have called the Jewish Renaissance. He was born in Brooklyn to Russian immigrant parents, and grew up a street kid during the Depression. These were unhappy times, but they provided him with experience for most of his best writing, including The Assistant *(1957), considered to be his best work, though it was not as popular as* The Fixer *(1966), a gripping story about a victim of anti-Semitism in Czarist Russia. It received the National Book Award and the Pulitzer Prize. While most of his works have Jewish protagonists, he considered his themes to be universal. In this regard two statements he made about his writing stand out: "All men are Jews," and "I'm in defense of the human." His best works concern meaningful suffering, particularly as that suffering is a consequence of love betrayed, rejected, misplaced, or misinterpreted. Though his work is rich in religious images, figures, and themes, he was an atheistic existentialist.*

THE JEWBIRD

1 THE WINDOW WAS OPEN so the skinny bird flew in. Flappity-flap with its frazzled black wings. That's how it goes. It's open, you're in. Closed, you're out and that's your fate. The bird wearily flapped through the open kitchen window of Harry Cohen's top-floor apartment on First Avenue near the lower East River.* On a rod on the wall hung an escaped canary cage, its door wide open, but this black-type long-beaked bird – its ruffled head and small dull eyes, crossed a little, making it look like a dissipated crow – landed if not smack on Cohen's thick lamb chop, at least on the table, close by. The frozen foods salesman was sitting at supper with his wife and young son on a hot August evening a year ago. Cohen, a heavy man with hairy chest and beefy shorts; Edie, in skinny yellow shorts and

lower East River · this river runs between the lower East side of Manhattan and Brooklyn in New York City, an area of traditionally Jewish neighborhoods

red halter; and their ten-year-old Morris (after his father) – Maurie, 1
they called him, a nice kid though not overly bright – were all in
the city after two weeks out, because Cohen's mother was dying.
They had been enjoying Kingston, New York, but drove back when
flat · apartment   Mama got sick in her flat˙ in the Bronx.

"Right on the table," said Cohen, putting down his beer glass 2
and swatting at the bird. "Son of a bitch."

"Harry, take care with your language," Edie said, looking at 3
Maurie, who watched every move.

The bird cawed hoarsely and with a flap of its bedraggled 4
wings – feathers tufted this way and that – rose heavily to the top
of the open kitchen door, where it perched staring down.

Gevalt · an expression of   "*Gevalt,*˙ a *pogrom!*"˙ 5
astonishment (Yiddish)

"It's a talking bird," said Edie in astonishment. 6

pogrom · "like thunder"   "In Jewish," said Maurie. 7
(Russian), an organized
and often officially   "Wise guy," muttered Cohen. He gnawed on his chop, then 8
sanctioned persecution   put down the bone. "So if you can talk, say what's your business.
or massacre of a minor-   What do you want here?"
ity group, especially
persecutions conducted   "If you can't spare a lamb chop," said the bird, "I'll settle for 9
against Jews   a piece of herring with a crust of bread. You can't live on your
nerve forever."

"This ain't a restaurant," Cohen replied. "All I'm asking is what 10
brings you to this address?"

"The window was open," the bird sighed; adding after a 11
moment, "I'm running. I'm flying but I'm also running."

"From whom?" asked Edie with interest. 12

"Anti-Semeets." 13

"Anti-Semites?" they all said. 14

"That's from who." 15

"What kind of anti-Semites bother a bird?" Edie asked. 16

"Any kind," said the bird, "also including eagles, vultures, and 17
hawks. And once in a while some crows will take your eyes out."

"But aren't you a crow?" 18

"Me? I'm a Jewbird." 19

Cohen laughed heartily. "What do you mean by that?" 20

dovening · praying   The bird began dovening.˙ He prayed without Book or *tallith,*˙ 21
but with passion. Edie bowed her head though not Cohen. And
tallith · a fringed prayer
shawl with bands of   Maurie rocked back and forth with the prayer, looking up with
black or blue (Hebrew)   one wide-open eye.

22   When the prayer was done Cohen remarked, "No hat, no phylacteries?"•

23   "I'm an old radical."

24   "You're sure you're not some kind of a ghost or *dybbuk*?"•

25   "Not a *dybbuk*," answered the bird, "though one of my relatives had such an experience once. It's all over now, thanks God. They freed her from a former lover, a crazy jealous man. She's now the mother of two wonderful children."

26   "Birds?" Cohen asked slyly.

27   "Why not?"

28   "What kind of birds?"

29   "Like me. Jewbirds."

30   Cohen tipped back in his chair and guffawed. "That's a big laugh. I've heard of a Jewfish• but not a Jewbird."

31   "We're once removed." The bird rested on one skinny leg, then on the other. "Please, could you spare maybe a piece of herring with a small crust of bread?"

32   Edie got up from the table.

33   "What are you doing?" Cohen asked her.

34   "I'll clear the dishes."

35   Cohen turned to the bird. "So what's your name, if you don't mind saying?"

36   "Call me Schwartz."

37   "He might be an old Jew changed into a bird by somebody," said Edie, removing a plate.

38   "Are you?" asked Harry, lighting a cigar.

39   "Who knows?" answered Schwartz. "Does God tell us everything?"

40   Maurie got up on his chair. "What kind of herring?" he asked the bird in excitement.

41   "Get down, Maurie, or you'll fall," ordered Cohen.

42   "If you haven't got *matjes*, I'll take *schmaltz*,"• said Schwartz.

43   "All we have is marinated, with slices of onion – in a jar," said Edie.

44   "If you'll open for me the jar I'll eat marinated. Do you have also, if you don't mind, a piece of rye bread – the *spitz*?"•

45   Edie thought she had.

46   "Feed him out on the balcony," Cohen said. He spoke to the bird. "After that take off."

47   Schwartz closed both bird eyes. "I'm tired and it's a long way."

48   "Which direction are you headed, north or south?"

phylacteries · two small leather boxes containing quotations from the Hebrew scriptures, worn by Jewish men while praying

dybbuk · a wandering spirit of the dead (Yiddish)

Jewfish · any of several large fishes of the sea bass family

matjes ... schmaltz · *matjes* (Dutch) and *schmaltz* (Yiddish) are two types of herring, the former superior in quality to the latter

spitz · the heel (Yiddish)

Schwartz, barely lifting his wings, shrugged. 49

"You don't know where you're going?" 50

"Where there's charity I'll go." 51

"Let him stay, papa," said Maurie. "He's only a bird." 52

"So stay the night," Cohen said, "but no longer." 53

In the morning Cohen ordered the bird out of the house but 54
Maurie cried, so Schwartz stayed for a while. Maurie was still on
vacation from school and his friends were away. He was lonely
and Edie enjoyed the fun he had, playing with the bird.

"He's no trouble at all," she told Cohen, "and besides his appe- 55
tite is very small."

"What'll you do when he makes dirty?" 56

"He flies across the street in a tree when he makes dirty, and 57
if nobody passes below, who notices?"

"So all right," said Cohen, "but I'm dead set against it. I warn 58
you he ain't gonna stay here long."

"What have you got against the poor bird?" 59

"Poor bird, my ass. He's a foxy bastard. He thinks he's a Jew." 60
"What difference does it make what he thinks?"

chutzpah · brazenness,   "A Jewbird, what a *chutzpah.** One false move and he's out on 61
gall, an affront (Yiddish)   his drumsticks."

At Cohen's insistence Schwartz lived out on the balcony in a 62
new wooden birdhouse Edie had bought him.

"With many thanks," said Schwartz, "though I would rather 63
have a human roof over my head. You know how it is at my age. I
like the warm, the windows, the smell of cooking. I would also be
glad to see once in a while the *Jewish Morning Journal* and have
now and then a schnapps because it helps my breathing, thanks
God. But whatever you give me, you won't hear complaints."

However, when Cohen brought home a bird feeder full of 64
dried corn, Schwartz said, "Impossible."

Cohen was annoyed. "What's the matter, crosseyes, is your life 65
getting too good for you? Are you forgetting what it means to be
migratory? I'll bet a helluva lot of crows you happen to be acquainted
with, Jews or otherwise, would give their eyeteeth to eat this corn."

grubber yung · a   Schwartz did not answer. What can you say to a *grubber yung*?* 66
crude type of boot   "Not for my digestion," he later explained to Edie. "Cramps. 67
(Yiddish), used here as   Herring is better even if it makes you thirsty. At least rainwater
a term of derision   don't cost anything." He laughed sadly in breathy caws.

68   And herring, thanks to Edie, who knew where to shop, was
what Schwartz got, with an occasional piece of potato pancake,
and even a bit of soupmeat when Cohen wasn't looking.

69   When school began in September, before Cohen would once
again suggest giving the bird the boot, Edie prevailed on him to
wait a little while until Maurie adjusted.

70   "To deprive him right now might hurt his school work, and
you know what trouble we had last year."

71   "So okay, but sooner or later the bird goes. That I promise you."

72   Schwartz, though nobody had asked him, took on full responsibility for Maurie's performance in school. In return for favors
granted, when he was let in for an hour or two at night, he spent
most of his time overseeing the boy's lessons. He sat on top of
the dresser near Maurie's desk as he laboriously wrote out his
homework. Maurie was a restless type and Schwartz gently kept
him to his studies. He also listened to him practice his screechy
violin, taking a few minutes off now and then to rest his ears in
the bathroom. And they afterwards played dominoes. The boy
was an indifferent checker player and it was impossible to teach
him chess. When he was sick, Schwartz read him comic books
though he personally disliked them. But Maurie's work improved
in school and even his violin teacher admitted his playing was
better. Edie gave Schwartz credit for these improvements though
the bird pooh-poohed them.

73   Yet he was proud there was nothing lower than C-minuses
on Maurie's report card, and on Edie's insistence celebrated with
a little schnapps.

74   "If he keeps up like this," Cohen said, "I'll get him in any Ivy
League college for sure."

75   "Oh I hope so," sighed Edie.

76   But Schwartz shook his head. "He's a good boy – you don't
have to worry. He won't be a *shicker** or a wifebeater, God forbid,   *shicker·* "drunkard"
but a scholar he'll never be, if you know what I mean, although   (Yiddish)
maybe a good mechanic. It's no disgrace in these times."

77   "If I were you," Cohen said, angered, "I'd keep my big snoot
out of other people's private business."

78   "Harry, please," said Edie.

79   "My goddamn patience is wearing out. That crosseyes butts
into everything."

Though he wasn't exactly a welcome guest in the house, Schwartz   80
gained a few ounces although he did not improve in appearance. He
looked bedraggled as ever, his feathers unkempt, as though he had
just flown out of a snowstorm. He spent, he admitted, little time
taking care of himself. Too much to think about. "Also outside plumb-
ing," he told Edie. Still there was more glow to his eyes so that though
Cohen went on calling him crosseyes he said it less emphatically.

Liking his situation, Schwartz tried tactfully to stay out of   81
Cohen's way, but one night when Edie was at the movies and
Maurie was taking a hot shower, the frozen foods salesman began
a quarrel with the bird.

"For Christ sake, why don't you wash yourself sometimes?   82
Why must you always stink like a dead fish?"

"Mr. Cohen, if you'll pardon me, if somebody eats garlic he   83
will smell from garlic. I eat herring three times a day. Feed me
flowers and I will smell like flowers."

"Who's obligated to feed you anything at all? You're lucky to   84
get herring."

"Excuse me, I'm not complaining," said the bird. "You're   85
complaining."

"What's more," said Cohen, "Even from out on the balcony I   86
can hear you snoring away like a pig. It keeps me awake at night."

"Snoring," said Schwartz, "isn't a crime, thanks God."   87

"All in all you are a goddamn pest and freeloader. Next thing   88
you'll want to sleep in bed next to my wife."

"Mr. Cohen," said Schwartz, "on this rest assured. A bird is a bird."   89

"So you say, but how do I know you're a bird and not some   90
kind of a goddamn devil?"

"If I was a devil you would know already. And I don't mean   91
because your son's good marks."

"Shut up, you bastard bird," shouted Cohen.   92

"*Grubber yung*," cawed Schwartz, rising to the tips of his talons,   93
his long wings outstretched.

Cohen was about to lunge for the bird's scrawny neck but Maurie   94
came out of the bathroom, and for the rest of the evening until
Schwartz's bedtime on the balcony, there was pretended peace.

But the quarrel had deeply disturbed Schwartz and he slept   95
badly. His snoring woke him, and awake, he was fearful of what
would become of him. Wanting to stay out of Cohen's way, he kept

95 to the birdhouse as much as possible. Cramped by it, he paced back and forth on the balcony ledge, or sat on the birdhouse roof, staring into space. In evenings, while overseeing Maurie's lessons, he often fell asleep. Awakening, he nervously hopped around exploring the four corners of the room. He spent much time in Maurie's closet, and carefully examined his bureau drawers when they were left open. And once when he found a large paper bag on the floor, Schwartz poked his way into it to investigate what possibilities were. The boy was amused to see the bird in the paper bag.

96 "He wants to build a nest," he said to his mother.

97 Edie, sensing Schwartz's unhappiness, spoke to him quietly.

98 "Maybe if you did some of the things my husband wants you, you would get along better with him."

99 "Give me a for instance," Schwartz said.

100 "Like take a bath, for instance."

101 "I'm too old for baths," said the bird. "My feathers fall out without baths."

102 "He says you have a bad smell."

103 "Everybody smells. Some people smell because of their thoughts or because who they are. My bad smell comes from the food I eat. What does his come from?"

104 "I better not ask him or it might make him mad," said Edie.

105 In late November Schwartz froze on the balcony in the fog and cold, and especially on rainy days he woke with stiff joints and could barely move his wings. Already he felt twinges of rheumatism. He would have liked to spend more time in the warm house, particularly when Maurie was in school and Cohen at work. But though Edie was good-hearted and might have sneaked him in in the morning, just to thaw out, he was afraid to ask her. In the meantime Cohen, who had been reading articles about the migration of birds, came out on the balcony one night after work when Edie was in the kitchen preparing pot roast, and peeking into the birdhouse, warned Schwartz to be on his way soon if he knew what was good for him. "Time to hit the flyways."

106 "Mr. Cohen, why do you hate me so much?" asked the bird. "What did I do to you?"

107 "Because you're an A-number-one trouble maker, that's why. What's more, whoever heard of a Jewbird! Now scat or it's open war."

But Schwartz stubbornly refused to depart so Cohen 108
embarked on a campaign of harassing him, meanwhile hiding it
from Edie and Maurie. Maurie hated violence and Cohen didn't
want to leave a bad impression. He thought maybe if he played
dirty tricks on the bird he would fly off without being physically
kicked out. The vacation was over, let him make his easy living
off the fat of somebody else's land. Cohen worried about the
effect of the bird's departure on Maurie's schooling but decided
to take the chance, first, because the boy now seemed to have
the knack of studying – give the black bird-bastard credit – and
second, because Schwartz was driving him bats by being there
always, even in his dreams.

The frozen foods salesman began his campaign against 109
the bird by mixing watery cat food with the herring slices in
Schwartz's dish. He also blew up and popped numerous paper
bags outside the birdhouse as the bird slept, and when he got
Schwartz good and nervous, though not enough to leave, he
brought a full-grown cat into the house, supposedly a gift for
little Maurie, who had always wanted a pussy. The cat never
stopped springing up at Schwartz whenever he saw him, one
day managing to claw out several of his tailfeathers. And
even at lesson time, when the cat was usually excluded from
Maurie's room, though somehow or other he quickly found
his way in at the end of the lesson, Schwartz was desperately
fearful of his life and flew from pinnacle to pinnacle – light
fixture to clothes-tree to door-top – in order to elude the
beast's wet jaws.

Once when the bird complained to Edie how hazardous his 110
existence was, she said, "Be patient, Mr. Schwartz. When the
cat gets to know you better he won't try to catch you any more."

"When he stops trying we will both be in Paradise," Schwartz 111
answered. "Do me a favor and get rid of him. He makes my whole
life worry. I'm losing feathers like a tree loses leaves."

"I'm awfully sorry but Maurie likes the pussy and sleeps with it." 112

What could Schwartz do? He worried but came to no deci- 113
sion, being afraid to leave. So he ate the herring garnished with
cat food, tried hard not to hear the paper bags bursting like fire
crackers outside the birdhouse at night, and lived terror-stricken

113 closer to the ceiling than the floor, as the cat, his tail flicking, endlessly watched him.

114 Weeks went by. Then on the day after Cohen's mother had died in her flat in the Bronx, when Maurie came home with a zero on an arithmetic test, Cohen, enraged, waited until Edie had taken the boy to his violin lesson, then openly attacked the bird. He chased him with a broom on the balcony and Schwartz frantically flew back and forth, finally escaping into his birdhouse. Cohen triumphantly reached in, and grabbing both skinny legs, dragged the bird out, cawing loudly, his wings wildly beating. He whirled the bird around and around his head. But Schwartz, as he moved in circles, managed to swoop down and catch Cohen's nose in his beak, and hung on for dear life. Cohen cried out in great pain, punched the bird with his fist, and tugging at its legs with all his might, pulled his nose free. Again he swung the yawking Schwartz around until the bird grew dizzy, then with a furious heave, flung him into the night. Schwartz sank like stone into the street. Cohen then tossed the birdhouse and feeder after him, listening at the ledge until they crashed on the sidewalk below. For a full hour, broom in hand, his heart palpitating and nose throbbing with pain, Cohen waited for Schwartz to return but the broken-hearted bird didn't.

115 That's the end of that dirty bastard, the salesman thought and went in. Edie and Maurie had come home.

116 "Look," said Cohen, pointing to his bloody nose swollen three times its normal size, "what that sonofabitch bird did. It's a permanent scar."

117 "Where is he now?" Edie asked, frightened.

118 "I threw him out and he flew away. Good riddance."

119 Nobody said no, though Edie touched a handkerchief to her eyes and Maurie rapidly tried the nine times table and found he knew approximately half.

120 In the spring when the winter's snow had melted, the boy, moved by a memory, wandered in the neighborhood, looking for Schwartz. He found a dead black bird in a small lot near the river, his two wings broken, neck twisted, and both bird-eyes plucked clean.

121 "Who did it to you, Mr. Schwartz?" Maurie wept.

122 "Anti-Semeets," Edie said later.

Shūsaku Endō

❨1923-1996❩

Christianity came to Japan in 1549 and flourished briefly, but thereafter adherents were often a persecuted minority. Endō was baptized young but had little faith. He thought his difficulty developing strong faith in a foreign deity was typically Japanese because he and his compatriots preferred a warm, maternal god. Eventually, he realized that Jesus, who helped the sick and the outcast, was just such a deity, and he determined to write about this realization. "Unzen" (1965) – named for an active volcano – is an early sketch for Endō's greatest novel, Silence *(1966). The story depicts the aftermath of the Shimabara Rebellion of 1637–1638, an uprising of peasants and Christians over taxes. The local warlord saw only Christians at the root of the insurrection and began torturing and killing them unless they denied their faith. This denial haunts Endō, probably because he came so close to it. The typical Endō character, partly autobiographical and often named Suguro, is caught between weak faith and denial of it. Suguro becomes aware of the historical Kichijirō, who watches fellow Christians suffer boiling-water torture and horrible death in Mt. Unzen's Valley of Hell but cannot overcome fear of joining them. Endō believes Kichijirō suffers terribly in ways the dying faithful cannot understand. Though apostate, Kichijirō must learn that Jesus has not given up on him. This lesson gives Suguro a new identity because, despite the three-hundred-year gap, he – and Endō – are Kichijirō's spiritual doubles.*

UNZEN

1   AS HE SAT ON THE BUS FOR UNZEN, he drank a bottle of milk and gazed blankly at the rain-swept sea. The frosty waves washed languidly against the shore just beneath the coastal highway.

The bus had not yet left the station. The scheduled hour of 2
departure had long since passed, but a connecting bus from
Nagasaki* still had not arrived, and their driver was chatting
idly with the woman conductor and displaying no inclination
to switch on the engine. Even so the tolerant passengers uttered
no word of complaint, but merely pressed their faces against the
window glass. A group of bathers from the hot springs walked
by, dressed in large, thickly-padded *kimonos.* They shielded
themselves from the rain with umbrellas borrowed from their
inn. The counters of the gift shops were lined with all sorts of
decorative shells and souvenir bean-jellies from the local hot
springs, but there were no customers around to buy their wares.

"This place reminds me of Atagawa in Izu,"* Suguro grumbled 3
to himself as he snapped the cardboard top back onto the milk
bottle. "What a disgusting landscape."

He had to chuckle a bit at himself for coming all the way to 4
this humdrum spot at the western edge of Kyūshū.* In Tokyo he
had not had the slightest notion that this village of Obama, home
of many of the Christian martyrs and some of the participants
in the Shimabara Rebellion, would be so commonplace a town.

From his studies of the Christian era in Japan, Suguro knew 5
that around 1630 many of the faithful had made the climb from
Obama towards Unzen, which a Jesuit* of the day had called "one
of the tallest mountains in Japan." The Valley of Hell high up on
Unzen was an ideal place for torturing Christians. According to
the records, after 1629, when the Nagasaki Magistrate Takenaka
Shigetsugu hit upon the idea of abusing the Christians in this
hot spring inferno, sixty or seventy prisoners a day were roped
together and herded from Obama to the top of this mountain.

Now tourists strolled the streets of the village, and popular 6
songs blared out from loudspeakers. Nothing remained to
remind one of that sanguinary* history. But precisely three
centuries before the present month of January, on a day of misty
rain, the man whose footsteps Suguro now hoped to retrace had
undoubtedly climbed up this mountain from Obama.

Finally the engine started up, and the bus made its way 7
through the village. They passed through a district of two-and
three-storey Japanese inns where men leaned with both hands on
the railings of the balconies and peered down into the bus. Even

Nagasaki · largest city of western Kyūshū, Portuguese traders introduced Roman Catholicism to Nagasaki in the mid-16th century. Authorities soon began persecuting Christians, crucifying 26 believers there in 1597

Atagawa in Izu · located on the east coast of the Izu peninsula of Honshū, Atagawa features volcanic hot springs and has been a popular destination since its discovery in the 15th century

Kyūshū · southern-most and third largest of the four main islands of Japan

a Jesuit · member of the Society of Jesus, a Roman Catholic order founded by Ignatius Loyola in 1534 and dedicated to teaching and missionary work

sanguinary · bloody, murderous

7 those windows which were deserted were draped with pink and white washcloths and towels. When the bus finally passed beyond the hotel district, both sides of the mountain road were lined with old stone walls and squat farmhouses with thatched roofs.

8 Suguro had no way of knowing whether these walls and farmhouses had existed in the Christian century. Nor could he be sure that this road was the one travelled by the Christians, the officers, and the man he was pursuing. The only certain thing was that, during their fitful stops along the path, they had looked up at this same Mount Unzen wrapped in grey mist.

9 He had brought a number of books with him from Tokyo, but he now regretted not including a collection of letters from Jesuits of the day who had reported on the Unzen martyrdoms to their superiors in Rome. He had thoughtlessly tossed into his bag one book that would be of no use to him on this journey – Collado's *Christian Confessions.*

10 The air cooled as the bus climbed into the hills, and the passengers, peeling skins from the *mikans* they had bought at Obama, listened half-heartedly to the sing-song travelogue provided by the conductor.

11 "Please look over this way," she said with a waxy smile. "There are two large pine trees on top of the hill we are about to circle. It's said that at about this spot, the Christians of olden days would turn around and look longingly back at the village of Obama. These trees later became known as the Looking-Back Pines."

12 Collado's *Christian Confessions* was published in Rome in 1632, just five years before the outbreak of the Shimabara Rebellion. By that time the Shōgunate's persecution of the Christians had grown fierce, but a few Portuguese and Italian missionaries had still managed to steal into Japan from Macao or Manila. The *Christian Confessions* were printed as a practical guide to Japanese grammar for the benefit of these missionaries. But what Suguro found hard to understand was why Collado had made public the confessions of these Japanese Christians, when a Catholic priest was under no circumstances permitted to reveal the innermost secrets of the soul shared with him by members of his flock.

13 Yet the night he read the *Confessions*, Suguro felt as though a more responsive chord had been struck within him than with

Collado's *Christian Confessions* · a Spanish missionary, Diego Collado (d 1641) was a Dominican friar who first went to Japan in 1619 and returned to Europe in 1622 following the martyrdom of Luis Flóres. *Christian Confessions* was first published in Madrid in 1632

mikans · mandarin oranges

Shōgunate's persecution · the government office of a Shōgun, a military commander of Japan whose power, prior to the revolution of the mid-1800s, exceeded even that of the emperor. The Shōgun attempted to eliminate Christianity in the 17th century

Macao · a region of the southern coast of China

Manila · capital and chief city of the Philippines

any other history of the Christian era he had encountered. Every 13
study he had read was little more than a string of pæans* to the
noble acts of priests and martyrs and common believers inspired
by faith. They were without exception chronicles of those who had
sustained their beliefs and their testimonies no matter what sufferings or tortures they had to endure. And each time he read them,
Suguro had to sigh, "There's no way I can emulate people like this."

pæans · joyous songs of praise, tribute, thanksgiving, or triumph

He had been baptized as a child, along with the rest of his family. 14
Since then he had passed through many vicissitudes and somehow
managed to arrive in his forties without rejecting his religion. But
that was not due to firm resolve or unshakable faith. He was more
than adequately aware of his own spiritual slovenliness and pusillanimity.* He was certain that an unspannable gulf separated him from
the ancient martyrs of Nagasaki, Edo and Unzen who had effected
glorious martyrdoms. Why had they all been so indomitable?

pusillanimity · cowardliness

Suguro diligently searched the Christian histories for someone
like himself. But there was no one to be found. Finally he had 15
stumbled across the *Christian Confessions* one day in a second-
hand bookshop, and as he flipped indifferently through the pages
of the book, he had been moved by the account of a man whose
name Collado had concealed. The man had the same feeble will and
tattered integrity as Suguro. Gradually he had formed in his mind
an image of this man – genuflecting like a camel before the priest
nearly three hundred years earlier, relishing the almost desperate
experience of exposing his own filthiness to the eyes of another.

> I stayed for a long time with some heathens. I didn't want 15a
> the innkeeper to realize I was a Christian, so I went with
> him often to the heathen temples and chanted along
> with them. Many times when they praised the gods and
> buddhas, I sinned greatly by nodding and agreeing with
> them. I don't remember how many times I did that. Maybe
> twenty or thirty times – more than twenty, anyway.
>
> And when the heathens and the apostates* got together 15b
> to slander us Christians and blaspheme against God, I
> was there with them. I didn't try to stop them talking or
> to refute them.
>
> Just recently, at the Shōgun's orders the Magistrate came 15c
> to our fief* from the capital, determined to make all the

apostates · those who have renounced their faith

fief · a feudal estate

15C Christians here apostatize. Everyone was interrogated and pressed to reject the Christian codes, or at least apostatize in form* only. Finally, in order to save the lives of my wife and children, I told them I would abandon my beliefs.

16 Suguro did not know where this man had been born, or what he had looked like. He had the impression he was a *samurai*,* but there was no way to determine who his master might have been. The man would have had no inkling that his private confession would one day be published in a foreign land, and eventually fall into the hands of one of his own countrymen again, to be read by a person like Suguro. Though he did not have a clear picture of how the man looked, Suguro had some idea of the assortment of facial expressions he would have had to employ in order to evade detection. If he had been born in that age, Suguro would have had no qualms about going along with the Buddhist laymen to worship at their temples, if that meant he would not be exposed as a Christian. When someone mocked the Christian faith, he would have lowered his eyes and tried to look unconcerned. If so ordered, he might even have written out an oath of apostasy, if that would mean saving the lives of his family as well as his own.

✤ ✤ ✤

17 A FAINT RAY OF LIGHT tentatively penetrated the clouds that had gathered over the summit of Unzen. Maybe it will clear up, he thought. In summer this paved road would no doubt be choked by a stream of cars out for a drive, but now there was only the bus struggling up the mountain with intermittent groans. Groves of withered trees shivered all around. A cluster of rain-soaked bungalows huddled silently among the trees, their doors tightly shut.

18 "Listen, martyrdom is no more than a matter of pride."

19 He had had this conversation in the corner of a bar in Shinjuku.* A pot of Akita salted-fish broth* simmered in the center of the *sake*-stained* table. Seated around the pot, Suguro's elders in the literary establishment had been discussing the hero of a novel he had recently published. The work dealt with some Christian martyrs in the 1870s. The writers at the gathering claimed that they could not swallow the motivations behind those martyrdoms the way Suguro had.

20 "At the very core of this desire to be a martyr you'll find pride, pure and simple."

"I'm sure pride plays a part in it. Along with the desire to 21 become a hero, and even a touch of insanity, perhaps. But – "

Suguro fell silent and clutched his glass. It was a simple task to 22 pinpoint elements of heroism and pride among the motives for martyrdom. But when those elements were obliterated, residual motives still remained. Those residual motives were of vital importance.

"Well, if you're going to look at it that way, you can find pride 23 and selfishness underlying virtually every human endeavour, every single act of good faith."

In the ten years he had been writing fiction, Suguro had grown 24 increasingly impatient with those modern novelists who tried to single out the egotism and pride in every act of man. To Suguro's mind, such a view of humanity entailed the loss of something of consummate value, like water poured through a sieve.

The road wound its way to the summit through dead grass and 25 barren woods. In days past, lines of human beings had struggled up this path. Both pride and madness had certainly been part of their make-up, but there must have been something more to it.

"The right wing during the war, for instance, had a certain 26 martyr mentality. I can't help thinking there's something impure going on when people are intoxicated by something like that. But perhaps I feel that way because I experienced the war myself," one of his elders snorted as he drank down his cup of tepid *sake*. Sensing an irreconcilable misunderstanding between himself and this man, Suguro could only grin acquiescently.

Before long he caught sight of a column of white smoke rising 27 like steam from the belly of the mountain. Though the windows of the bus were closed, he smelled a faintly sulphuric odor. Milky white crags and sand came into clear focus.

"Is that the Valley of Hell?" 28

"No." The conductor shook her head. "It's a little further up." 29

A tiny crack in the clouds afforded a glimpse of blue sky. The 30 bus, which up until now had panted along, grinding its gears, suddenly seemed to catch its breath and picked up speed. The road had levelled off, then begun to drop. A series of arrows tacked to the leafless trees, apparently to guide hikers, read "Valley of Hell." Just ahead was the red roof of the rest-house.

Suguro did not know whether the man mentioned in the 31 *Confessions* had come here to the Valley of Hell. But, as if before

31 Suguro's eyes, the image of another individual had overlapped with
that of the first man and now stumbled along with his head bowed.
There was a little more detailed information about this second
man. His name was Kichijirō, and he first appeared in the historical
records on the fifth day of December, 1631, when seven priests and
Christians were tortured at the Valley of Hell. Kichijirō came here
to witness the fate of the fathers who had cared for him. He had
apostatized much earlier, so he had been able to blend in with the
crowd of spectators. Standing on tiptoe, he had witnessed the cruel
punishments which the officers inflicted on his spiritual mentors.

32 Father Christovão Ferreira, who later broke under torture and
left a filthy smudge on the pages of Japanese Christian history, sent
to his homeland a letter vividly describing the events of that day.
The seven Christians arrived at Obama on the evening of December
the second, and were driven up the mountain all the following day.
There were several look-out huts on the slope, and that evening the
seven captives were forced into one of them, their feet and hands
still shackled. There they awaited the coming of dawn.

32a The tortures commenced on the fifth of December
in the following manner. One by one each of the seven
was taken to the brink of the seething pond. There they
were shown the frothy spray from the boiling water, and
ordered to renounce their faith. The air was chilly and
the hot water of the pond churned so furiously that, had
God not sustained them, a single look would have cause
them to faint away. They all shouted, "Torture us! We will
not recant!" At this response, the guards stripped the garments from the prisoners' bodies and bound their hands
and feet. Four of them held down a single captive as a ladle
holding about a quarter of a liter was filled with the boiling
water. Three ladlesful were slowly poured over each body.
One of the seven, a young girl called Maria, fainted from
the excruciating pain and fell to the ground. In the space
of thirty-three days, each of them was subjected to this
torture a total of six times.

33 Suguro was the last one off when the bus came to a stop. The
cold, taut mountain air blew a putrid odor into his nostrils. White
steam poured onto the highway from the tree-ringed valley.

"How about a photograph? Photographs, anyone?" a young   34
man standing beside a large camera on a tripod called out to
Suguro. "I'll pay the postage wherever you want to send it."

At various spots along the road stood women proffering eggs   35
in baskets and waving clumsily-lettered signs that read "Boiled
Eggs." They too touted loudly for business.

Weaving their way among these hawkers, Suguro and the rest   36
of the group from the bus walked towards the valley. The earth,
overgrown with shrubbery, was virtually white, almost the color
of flesh stripped clean of its layer of skin. The rotten-smelling
steam gushed ceaselessly from amid the trees. The narrow path
stitched its way back and forth between springs of hot, bubbling
water. Some parts of the white-speckled pools lay as calm and
flat as a wall of plaster; others eerily spewed up slender sprays
of gurgling water. Here and there on the hillocks formed from
sulphur flows stood pine trees scorched red by the heat.

The bus passengers extracted boiled eggs from their paper   37
sacks and stuffed them into their mouths. They moved forward
like a column of ants.

"Come and look over here. There's a dead bird."   38

"So there is. I suppose the gas fumes must have asphyxiated it."   39

All he knew for certain was that Kichijirō had been a witness to   40
those tortures. Why had he come? There was no way of knowing
whether he had joined the crowd of Buddhist spectators in the hope
of rescuing the priests and the faithful who were being tormented.
The only tangible piece of information he had about Kichijirō was
that he had forsworn his religion to the officers, "so that his wife and
children might live." Nevertheless, he had followed in the footsteps
of those seven Christians, walking all the way from Nagasaki to
Obama, then trudging to the top of the bitterly cold peak of Unzen.

Suguro could almost see the look on Kichijirō's face as he   41
stood at the back of the crowd, furtively watching his former
companions with the tremulous gaze of a dog, then lowering
his eyes in humiliation. That look was very like Suguro's own. In
any case, there was no way Suguro could stand in chains before
these loathsomely bubbling pools and make any show of courage.

A momentary flash of white lit up the entire landscape; then   42
a fierce eruption burst forth with the smell of noxious gas. A
mother standing near the surge quickly picked up her crouching

42 child and retreated. A placard reading "Dangerous Beyond This Point" was thrust firmly into the clay. Around it the carcasses of three dead swallows were stretched out like mummies.

43 This must be the spot where the Christians were tortured, he thought. Through a crack in the misty, shifting steam, Suguro saw the black outlines of a cross. Covering his nose and mouth with a handkerchief and balancing precariously near the warning sign, he peered below him. The mottled water churned and sloshed before his eyes. The Christians must have stood just where he was standing now when they were tortured. And Kichijirō would have stayed behind, standing about where the mother and her child now stood at a cautious distance, watching the spectacle with the rest of the crowd. Inwardly, did he ask them to forgive him? Had Suguro been in his shoes, he would have had no recourse but to repeat over and over again, "Forgive me! I'm not strong enough to be a martyr like you. My heart melts just to think about this dreadful torture."

44 Of course, Kichijirō could justify his attitude. If he had lived in a time of religious freedom, he would never have become an apostate. He might not have qualified for sainthood, but he could have been a man who tamely maintained his faith. But to his regret, he had been born in an age of persecution, and out of fear he had tossed away his beliefs. Not everyone can become a saint or a martyr. Yet must those who do not qualify as saints be branded forever with the mark of the traitor? Perhaps he had made such a plea to the Christians who vilified him. Yet, despite the logic of his argument, he surely suffered pangs of remorse and cursed his own faint resolve.

45 "The apostate endures a pain none of you can comprehend."

46 Over the span of three centuries this cry, like the shriek of a wounded bird, reached Suguro's ears. That single line recorded in the *Christian Confessions* cut at Suguro's chest like a sharp sword. Surely those were the words Kichijirō must have shouted to himself here at Unzen as he looked upon his tormented friends.

✦ ✦ ✦

47 THEY REBOARDED THE BUS. The ride from Unzen to Shimabara took less than an hour. A fistful of blue finally appeared in the sky, but the air remained cold. The same conductor forced her usual smile and commented on the surroundings in a sing-song voice.

The seven Christians, refusing to bend to the tortures at 48
Unzen, had been taken down the mountain to Shimabara, along
the same route Suguro was now following. He could almost see
them dragging their scalded legs, leaning on walking-sticks and
enduring lashes from the officers.

Leaving some distance between them, Kichijirō had timo- 49
rously followed behind. When the weary Christians stopped to
catch their breath, Kichijirō also halted, a safe distance behind.
He hurriedly crouched down like a rabbit in the overgrowth, lest
the officers suspect him, and did not rise again until the group
had resumed their trek. He was like a jilted woman plodding
along in pursuit of her lover.

Half-way down the mountain he had a glimpse of the dark sea. 50
Milky clouds veiled the horizon; several wan beams of sunlight
filtered through the cracks. Suguro thought how blue the ocean
would appear on a clear day.

"Look – you can see a blur out there that looks like an island. 51
Unfortunately, you can't see it very well today. This is Dangō
Island, where Amakusa Shirō, the commander of the Christian
forces, planned the Shimabara Rebellion with his men."

At this the passengers took a brief, apathetic glance towards 52
the island. Before long the view of the distant sea was blocked
by a forest of trees.

What must those seven Christians have felt as they looked at 53
this ocean? They knew they would soon be executed at Shimabara.
The corpses of martyrs were swiftly reduced to ashes and cast
upon the seas. If that were not done, the remaining Christians
would surreptitiously worship the clothing and even locks of
hair from the martyrs as though they were holy objects. And so
the seven, getting their first distant view of the ocean from this
spot, must have realized that it would be their grave. Kichijirō
too would have looked at the sea, but with a different kind of
sorrow – with the knowledge that the strong ones in the world
of faith were crowned with glory, while the cowards had to carry
their burdens with them throughout their lives.

When the group reached Shimabara, four of them were placed 54
in a cell barely three feet tall and only wide enough to accom-
tatami · a straw mat   modate one *tatami*.˙ The other three were jammed into another
used as a floor covering   room equally cramped. As they awaited their punishment, they
in Japanese homes

54 persistently encouraged one another and went on praying. There is no record of where Kichijirō stayed during this time.

55 The village of Shimabara was dark and silent. The bus came to a stop by a tiny wharf where the rickety ferry-boat to Amakusa* was moored forlornly. Wood chips and flotsam bobbed on the small waves that lapped at the breakwater. Among the debris floated an object that resembled a rolled-up newspaper; it was the corpse of a cat.

56 The town extended in a thin band along the seafront. The fences of local factories stretched far into the distance, while the odor of chemicals wafted all the way to the highway.

57 Suguro set out towards the reconstructed Shimabara Castle. The only signs of life he encountered along the way were a couple of high-school girls riding bicycles.

58 "Where is the execution ground where the Christians were killed?" he asked them.

59 "I didn't know there was such a place," said one of them, blushing. She turned to her friend. "Have you heard of anything like that? You don't know, do you?" Her friend shook her head.

60 He came to a neighborhood identified as a former *samurai* residence. It had stood behind the castle, where several narrow paths intersected. A crumbling mud wall wound its way between the paths. The drainage ditch was as it had been in those days. Summer *mikans* poked their heads above the mud wall, which had already blocked out the evening sun. All the buildings were old, dark and musty. They had probably been the residence of a low-ranking *samurai*, built at the end of the Tokugawa period.* Many Christians had been executed at the Shimabara grounds, but Suguro had not come across any historical documents identifying the location of the prison.

61 He retraced his steps, and after a short walk came out on a street of shops where popular songs were playing. The narrow street was packed with a variety of stores, including gift shops. The water in the drainage ditch was as limpid as water from a spring.

62 "The execution ground? I know where that is." The owner of a tobacco shop directed Suguro to a pond just down the road. "If you go straight on past the pond, you'll come to a nursery school. The execution ground was just to the side of the school."

63 Though they say nothing of how he was able to do it, the records indicate that Kichijirō was allowed to visit the seven

Amakusa · the Amakusa Islands are part of Unzen-Amakusa National Park. The archipelago was long the gateway for Western culture and was an early center of Christianity. Following the massacre of Japanese Christians in the Shimabara Rebellion, the islands became a refuge for remaining Christians

Tokugawa period · also called the Edo period (1603–1867), it was the final period of traditional Japan, a time of internal peace, political stability, and economic growth under the shōgunate founded by Tokugawa Ieyasu

prisoners on the day before their execution. Possibly he put some 63
money into the hands of the officers.

Kichijirō offered a meager plate of food to the prisoners, who 64
were prostrate from their ordeal.

"Kichijirō, did you retract your oath?" one of the captives asked 65
compassionately. He was eager to know if the apostate had finally
informed the officials that he could not deny his faith. "Have you
come here to see us because you have retracted?"

Kichijirō looked up at them timidly and shook his head. 66

"In any case, Kichijirō, we can't accept this food." 67

"Why not?" 68

"Why not?" The prisoners were mournfully silent for a moment. 69
"Because we have already accepted the fact that we will die."

Kichijirō could only lower his eyes and say nothing. He knew 70
that he himself could never endure the sort of agony he had
witnessed at the Valley of Hell on Unzen.

Through his tears he whimpered, "If I can't suffer the same 71
pain as you, will I be unable to enter Paradise? Will God forsake
someone like me?"

He walked along the street of shops as he had been instructed 72
and came to the pond. A floodgate blocked the overflow from the
pond and the water poured underground and into the drainage
ditch in the village. Suguro read a sign declaring that the purity
of the water in Shimabara village was due to the presence of
this pond.

He heard the sounds of children at play. Four or five young 73
children were tossing a ball back and forth in the nursery school
playground. The setting sun shone feebly on the swings and
sandbox in the yard. He walked around behind a drooping hedge
of rose bushes and located the remains of the execution ground,
now the only barren patch within a grove of trees.

It was a deserted plot some three hundred square yards in 74
size, grown rank with brown weeds; pines towered over a heap
of refuse. Suguro had come all the way from Tokyo to have a
look at this place. Or had he made the journey out of a desire to
understand better Kichijirō's emotions as he stood in this spot?

The following morning the seven prisoners were hoisted 75
onto the unsaddled horses and dragged through the streets of
Shimabara to this execution ground.

76 One of the witnesses to the scene has recorded the events of the day: "After they were paraded about, they arrived at the execution ground, which was surrounded by a palisade. They were taken off their horses and made to stand in front of stakes set three metres apart. Firewood was already piled at the base of the stakes, and straw roofs soaked in sea water had been placed on top of them to prevent the flames from raging too quickly and allowing the martyrs to die with little agony. The ropes that bound them to the stakes were tied as loosely as possible, to permit them, up to the very moment of death, to twist their bodies and cry out that they would abandon their faith.

77 "When the officers began setting fire to the wood, a solitary man broke through the line of guards and dashed towards the stakes. He was shouting something, but I could not hear what he said over the roar of the fires. The fierce flames and smoke prevented the man from approaching the prisoners. The guards swiftly apprehended him and asked if he was a Christian. At that, the man froze in fear, and jabbering, 'I am no Christian. I have nothing to do with these people! I just lost my head in all the excitement,' he skulked away. But some in the crowd had seen him at the rear of the assemblage, his hands pressed together as he repeated over and over, 'Forgive me! Forgive me!'

78 "The seven victims sang a hymn until the flames enveloped their stakes. Their voices were exuberant, totally out of keeping with the cruel punishment they were even then enduring. When those voices suddenly ceased, the only sound was the dull crackling of wood. The man who had darted forward could be seen walking lifelessly away from the execution ground. Rumors spread through the crowd that he too had been a Christian."

79 Suguro noticed a dark patch at the very center of the execution ground. On closer inspection he discovered several charred stones half buried beneath the black earth. Although he had no way of knowing whether these stones had been used here three hundred years before, when seven Christians had been burned at the stake, he hurriedly snatched up one of the stones and put it in his pocket. Then, his spine bent like Kichijirō's, he walked back towards the road.

Flannery O'Connor

◄{ 1 9 2 5 - 1 9 6 4 }►

Born in Savannah and reared in a minority Roman Catholic com-
munity in Milledgeville, Georgia, O'Connor bore the impress of both
her regional and religious environment. Her short stories are often
set in the dark grotesquerie of the South, and her most memorable
characters grapple with intense spiritual crises. After attending the
Women's College of Georgia, O'Connor studied writing at the State
University of Iowa, earning an MFA *in 1947. She went on to produce*
a succession of carefully crafted stories and two novels, Wise Blood
(1952) and The Violent Bear It Away *(1960), before succumbing to*
lupus at thirty-eight. O'Connor was posthumously awarded the
National Book Award in 1972 for The Complete Stories. *In* Mystery
and Manners *(1969), a collection of essays on the writer's craft,*
O'Connor has said that life and thus true-to-life fiction is essen-
tially mysterious: "a story does not begin except at a depth where
adequate motivation and adequate psychology and the various
determinations have been exhausted." It is in this mysterious region,
a space in which supernatural powers of good and evil vie for the
soul, that the author's characters confront life-changing spiritual
choices. And for O'Connor, volitional choice is a reality. Her work
is marked by "the redemptive act," by the demand "that what falls
at least be offered the chance to be restored."

REVELATION

1   THE DOCTOR'S WAITING ROOM, which was very small, was
almost full when the Turpins entered and Mrs. Turpin, who
was very large, made it look even smaller by her presence. She
stood looming at the head of the magazine table set in the center
of it, a living demonstration that the room was inadequate and
ridiculous. Her little bright black eyes took in all the patients as

she sized up the seating situation. There was one vacant chair 1
and a place on the sofa occupied by a blond child in a dirty blue
romper who should have been told to move over and make room
for the lady. He was five or six, but Mrs. Turpin saw at once that
no one was going to tell him to move over. He was slumped down
in the seat, his arms idle at his sides and his eyes idle in his head;
his nose ran unchecked.

Mrs. Turpin put a firm hand on Claud's shoulder and said in 2
a voice that included anyone who wanted to listen, "Claud, you
sit in that chair there," and gave him a push down into the vacant
one. Claud was florid and bald and sturdy, somewhat shorter
than Mrs. Turpin, but he sat down as if he were accustomed to
doing what she told him to.

Mrs. Turpin remained standing. The only man in the room 3
besides Claud was a lean stringy old fellow with a rusty hand
spread out on each knee, whose eyes were closed as if he were
asleep or dead or pretending to be so as not to get up and offer
her his seat. Her gaze settled agreeably on a well-dressed gray-
haired lady whose eyes met hers and whose expression said: if
that child belonged to me, he would have some manners and
move over – there's plenty of room there for you and him too.

Claud looked up with a sigh and made as if to rise. 4

"Sit down," Mrs. Turpin said. "You know you're not supposed 5
to stand on that leg. He has an ulcer on his leg," she explained.

Claud lifted his foot onto the magazine table and rolled his 6
trouser leg up to reveal a purple swelling on a plump marble-
white calf.

"My!" the pleasant lady said. "How did you do that?" 7

"A cow kicked him," Mrs. Turpin said. 8

"Goodness!" said the lady. 9

Claud rolled his trouser leg down. 10

"Maybe the little boy would move over," the lady suggested, 11
but the child did not stir.

"Somebody will be leaving in a minute," Mrs. Turpin said. 12
She could not understand why a doctor – with as much money
as they made charging five dollars a day to just stick their head
in the hospital door and look at you – couldn't afford a decent-
sized waiting room. This one was hardly bigger than a garage.
The table was cluttered with limp-looking magazines and at one

12 end of it there was a big green glass ashtray full of cigarette butts and cotton wads with little blood spots on them. If she had had anything to do with the running of the place, that would have been emptied every so often. There were no chairs against the wall at the head of the room. It had a rectangular-shaped panel in it that permitted a view of the office where the nurse came and went and the secretary listened to the radio. A plastic fern in a gold pot sat in the opening and trailed its fronds down almost to the floor. The radio was softly playing gospel music.

13 Just then the inner door opened and a nurse with the highest stack of yellow hair Mrs. Turpin had ever seen put her face in the crack and called for the next patient. The woman sitting beside Claud grasped the two arms of her chair and hoisted herself up; she pulled her dress free from her legs and lumbered through the door where the nurse had disappeared.

14 Mrs. Turpin eased into the vacant chair, which held her tight as a corset. "I wish I could reduce," she said, and rolled her eyes and gave a comic sigh.

15 "Oh, you aren't fat," the stylish lady said.

16 "Ooooo I am too," Mrs. Turpin said. "Claud he eats all he wants to and never weighs over one hundred and seventy-five pounds, but me I just look at something good to eat and I gain some weight," and her stomach and shoulders shook with laughter. "You can eat all you want to, can't you, Claud?" she asked, turning to him.

17 Claud only grinned.

18 "Well, as long as you have such a good disposition," the stylish lady said, "I don't think it makes a bit of difference what size you are. You just can't beat a good disposition."

19 Next to her was a fat girl of eighteen or nineteen, scowling into a thick blue book which Mrs. Turpin saw was entitled *Human Development*. The girl raised her head and directed her scowl at Mrs. Turpin as if she did not like her looks. She appeared annoyed that anyone should speak while she tried to read. The poor girl's face was blue with acne and Mrs. Turpin thought how pitiful it was to have a face like that at that age. She gave the girl a friendly smile but the girl only scowled the harder. Mrs. Turpin herself was fat but she had always had good skin, and, though she was forty-seven years old, there was not a wrinkle in her face except around her eyes from laughing too much.

Next to the ugly girl was the child, still in exactly the same posi- 20
tion, and next to him was a thin leathery old woman in a cotton
print dress. She and Claud had three sacks of chicken feed in their

in the same print · pump house that was in the same print.* She had seen from the
flour and animal feed first that the child belonged with the old woman. She could tell
were often shipped in
cotton bags which poor by the way they sat – kind of vacant and white-trashy, as if they
or rural people used would sit there until Doomsday if nobody called and told them to
to make clothing and get up. And at right angles but next to the well-dressed pleasant
other furnishings lady was a lank-faced woman who was certainly the child's mother.
She had on a yellow sweat shirt and wine-colored slacks, both

snuff · a smokeless gritty looking, and the rims of her lips were stained with snuff.*
tobacco product Her dirty yellow hair was tied behind with a little piece of red
paper ribbon. Worse than niggers any day, Mrs. Turpin thought.

"When I . . . looked The gospel hymn playing was, "When I looked up and He 21
down" · the hymn looked down,"* and Mrs. Turpin, who knew it, supplied the last
(words and music
A. E. Brumley, 1955) line mentally, "And wona these days I know I'll we-eara crown."
describes an epiphany Without appearing to, Mrs. Turpin always noticed people's 22
when one who "had feet. The well-dressed lady had on red and gray suede shoes
reached a sorry station
in this wilderness below" to match her dress. Mrs. Turpin had on her good black patent
looks up to heaven and leather pumps. The ugly girl had on Girl Scout shoes and heavy
realizes salvation socks. The old woman had on tennis shoes and the white-trashy
mother had on what appeared to be bedroom slippers, black
straw with gold braid threaded through them – exactly what you
would have expected her to have on.

Sometimes at night when she couldn't go to sleep, Mrs. Turpin 23
would occupy herself with the question of who she would have
chosen to be if she couldn't have been herself. If Jesus had said
to her before he made her, "There's only two places available for
you. You can either be a nigger or white-trash," what would she
have said? "Please, Jesus, please," she would have said, "just let me
wait until there's another place available," and he would have said,
"No, you have to go right now and I have only those two places so
make up your mind." She would have wiggled and squirmed and
begged and pleaded but it would have been no use and finally
she would have said, "All right, make me a nigger then – but that
don't mean a trashy one." And he would have made her a neat
clean respectable Negro woman, herself but black.

Next to the child's mother was a red-headed youngish 24
woman, reading one of the magazines and working a piece of

24 chewing gum, hell for leather, as Claud would say. Mrs. Turpin could not see the woman's feet. She was not white-trash, just common. Sometimes Mrs. Turpin occupied herself at night naming the classes of people. On the bottom of the heap were most colored people, not the kind she would have been if she had been one, but most of them; then next to them – not above, just away from – were the white-trash; then above them were the home-owners, and above them the home-and-land owners, to which she and Claud belonged. Above she and Claud were people with a lot of money and much bigger houses and much more land. But here the complexity of it would begin to bear in on her, for some of the people with a lot money were common and ought to be below she and Claud and some of the people who had good blood had lost their money and had to rent and then there were colored people who owned their homes and land as well. There was a colored dentist in town who had two red Lincolns and a swimming pool and a farm with registered white-face cattle on it. Usually by the time she had fallen asleep all the classes of people were moiling and roiling around in her head, and she would dream they were all crammed in together in a box car, being ridden off to be put in a gas oven.

25 "That's a beautiful clock," she said and nodded to her right. It was a big wall clock, the face encased in a brass sunburst.

26 "Yes, it's very pretty," the stylish lady said agreeably. "And right on the dot too," she added, glancing at her watch.

27 The ugly girl beside her cast an eye upward at the clock, smirked, then looked directly at Mrs. Turpin and smirked again. Then she returned her eyes to her book. She was obviously the lady's daughter because, although they didn't look anything alike as to disposition, they both had the same shape of face and the same blue eyes. On the lady they sparkled pleasantly but in the girl's seared face they appeared alternately to smolder and to blaze.

28 What if Jesus had said, "All right, you can be white-trash or a nigger or ugly!"

29 Mrs. Turpin felt an awful pity for the girl, though she thought it was one thing to be ugly and another to act ugly.

30 The woman with the snuff-stained lips turned around in her chair and looked up at the clock. Then she turned back and

appeared to look a little to the side of Mrs. Turpin. There was a 30
cast in one of her eyes. "You want to know wher you can get you
one of themther clocks?" she asked in a loud voice.

"No, I already have a nice clock," Mrs. Turpin said. Once some- 31
body like her got a leg in the conversation, she would be all over it.

"You can get you one with green stamps,"* the woman said. 32
"That's most likely wher he got hisn. Save you up enough, you
can get you most anythang. I got me some joo'ry."

Ought to have got you a wash rag and some soap, Mrs. Turpin 33
thought.

"I get contour sheets with mine," the pleasant lady said. 34

The daughter slammed her book shut. She looked straight 35
in front of her, directly through Mrs. Turpin and on through
the yellow curtain and the plate glass window which made the
wall behind her. The girl's eyes seemed lit all of a sudden with a
peculiar light, an unnatural light like night road signs give. Mrs.
Turpin turned her head to see if there was anything going on outside that she should see, but she could not see anything. Figures
passing cast only a pale shadow through the curtain. There was
no reason the girl should single her out for her ugly looks.

"Miss Finley," the nurse said, cracking the door. The gum- 36
chewing woman got up and passed in front of her and Claud and
went into the office. She had on red high-heeled shoes.

Directly across the table, the ugly girl's eyes were fixed on Mrs. 37
Turpin as if she had some very special reason for disliking her.

"This is wonderful weather, isn't it?" the girl's mother said. 38

"It's good weather for cotton if you can get the niggers to pick 39
it," Mrs. Turpin said, "but niggers don't want to pick cotton any
more. You can't get the white folks to pick it and now you can't
get the niggers – because they got to be right up there with the
white folks."

"They gonna *try* anyways," the white-trash woman said, lean- 40
ing forward.

"Do you have one of the cotton-picking machines?" the pleas- 41
ant lady asked.

"No," Mrs. Turpin said, "they leave half the cotton in the 42
field. We don't have much cotton anyway. If you want to make
it farming now, you have to have a little of everything. We got a
couple of acres of cotton and a few hogs and chickens and just

green stamps · trad-
ing stamps, given with
purchases and later
redeemed for goods

42 enough white-face that Claud can look after them himself, for merchandise of various types."

43 "One thang I don't want," the white-trash woman said, wiping her mouth with the back of her hand. "Hogs. Nasty stinking things, a-gruntin and a-rootin all over the place."

44 Mrs. Turpin gave her the merest edge of her attention. "Our hogs are not dirty and they don't stink," she said. "They're cleaner than some children I've seen. Their feet never touch the ground. We have a pig-parlor – that's where you raise them on concrete," she explained to the pleasant lady, "and Claud scoots them down with the hose every afternoon and washes off the floor." Cleaner by far than that child right there, she thought. Poor nasty little thing. He had not moved except to put the thumb of his dirty hand into his mouth.

45 The woman turned her face away from Mrs. Turpin. "I know I wouldn't scoot down no hog with no hose," she said to the wall.

46 You wouldn't have no hog to scoot down, Mrs. Turpin said to herself.

47 "A-gruntin and a-rootin and a-groanin," the woman muttered.

48 "We got a little of everything," Mrs. Turpin said to the pleasant lady. "It's no use in having more than you can handle yourself with help like it is. We found enough niggers to pick our cotton this year but Claud he has to go after them and take them home again in the evening. They can't walk that half a mile. No they can't. I tell you," she said and laughed merrily, "I sure am tired of buttering up niggers, but you got to love em if you want em to work for you. When they come in the morning, I run out and I say, 'Hi yawl this morning?' and when Claud drives them off to the field I just wave to beat the band and they just wave back." And she waved her hand rapidly to illustrate.

49 "Like you read out of the same book," the lady said, showing she understood perfectly.

50 "Child, yes," Mrs. Turpin said. "And when they come in from the field, I run out with a bucket of icewater. That's the way it's going to be from now on," she said. "You may as well face it."

51 "One thang I know," the white-trash woman said. "Two thangs I ain't going to do: love no niggers or scoot down no hog with no hose." And she let out a bark of contempt.

The look that Mrs. Turpin and the pleasant lady exchanged 52
indicated they both understood that you had to *have* certain
things before you could *know* certain things. But every time
Mrs. Turpin exchanged a look with the lady, she was aware that
the ugly girl's peculiar eyes were still on her, and she had trouble
bringing her attention back to the conversation.

"When you got something," she said, "you got to look after 53
it." And when you ain't got a thing but breath and britches, she
added to herself, you can afford to come to town every morning
and just sit on the Court House coping and spit.

A grotesque revolving shadow passed across the curtain 54
behind her and was thrown palely on the opposite wall. Then a
bicycle clattered down against the outside of the building. The
door opened and a colored boy glided in with a tray from the
drugstore. It had two large red and white paper cups on it with
tops on them. He was a tall, very black boy in discolored white
pants and a green nylon shirt. He was chewing gum slowly, as if
to music. He set the tray down in the office opening next to the
fern and stuck his head through to look for the secretary. She
was not in there. He rested his arms on the ledge and waited,
his narrow bottom stuck out, swaying to the left and right. He
raised a hand over his head and scratched the base of his skull.

"You see that button there, boy?" Mrs. Turpin said. "You can 55
punch that and she'll come. She's probably in the back somewhere."

"Is thas right?" the boy said agreeably, as if he had never seen 56
the button before. He leaned to the right and put his finger on
it. "She sometime out," he said and twisted around to face his
audience, his elbows behind him on the counter. The nurse
appeared and he twisted back again. She handed him a dollar
and he rooted in his pocket and made the change and counted
it out to her. She gave him fifteen cents for a tip and he went out
with the empty tray. The heavy door swung to slowly and closed
at length with the sound of suction. For a moment no one spoke.

"They ought to send all them niggers back to Africa," the white 57
trash woman said. "That's wher they come from in the first place."

"Oh, I couldn't do without my good colored friends," the 58
pleasant lady said.

"There's a heap of things worse than a nigger," Mrs. Turpin 59
agreed. "It's all kinds of them just like it's all kinds of us."

60   "Yes, and it takes all kinds to make the world go round," the lady said in her musical voice.

61   As she said it, the raw-complexioned girl snapped her teeth together. Her lower lip turned downwards and inside out, revealing the pale pink inside of her mouth. After a second it rolled back up. It was the ugliest face Mrs. Turpin had ever seen anyone make and for a moment she was certain that the girl had made it at her. She was looking at her as if she had known and disliked her all her life – all of Mrs. Turpin's life, it seemed too, not just all the girl's life. Why, girl, I don't even know you, Mrs. Turpin said silently.

62   She forced her attention back to the discussion. "It wouldn't be practical to send them back to Africa," she said. "They wouldn't want to go. They got it too good here."

63   "Wouldn't be what they wanted – if I had anythang to do with it," the woman said.

64   "It wouldn't be a way in the world you could get all the niggers back over there," Mrs. Turpin said. "They'd be hiding out and lying down and turning sick on you and wailing and hollering and raring and pitching. It wouldn't be a way in the world to get them over there."

65   "They got over here," the trashy woman said. "Get back like they got over."

66   "It wasn't so many of them then," Mrs. Turpin explained.

67   The woman looked at Mrs. Turpin as if here was an idiot indeed but Mrs. Turpin was not bothered by the look, considering where it came from.

68   "Nooo," she said, "they're going to stay here where they can go to New York and marry white folks and improve their color. That's what they all want to do, every one of them, improve their color."

69   "You know what comes of that, don't you?" Claud asked.

70   "No, Claud, what?" Mrs. Turpin said.

71   Claud's eyes twinkled. "White-faced niggers," he said with never a smile.

72   Everybody in the office laughed except the white-trash and the ugly girl. The girl gripped the book in her lap with white fingers. The trashy woman looked around her from face to face as if she thought they were all idiots. The old woman in the feed sack dress continued to gaze expressionless across the floor at

the high-top shoes of the man opposite her, the one who had 72
been pretending to be asleep when the Turpins came in. He was
laughing heartily, his hands still spread out on his knees. The
child had fallen to the side and was lying now almost face down
in the old woman's lap.

While they recovered from their laughter, the nasal chorus 73
on the radio kept the room from silence.

> "You go to blank blank 73a
> And I'll go to mine
> But we'll all blank along
> To-geth-ther,
> And all along the blank
> We'll hep eachother out
> Smile-ling in any kind of
> Weath-ther!"*

"You go ... Weath-ther!" · a version of the bluegrass song "You Go To Your Church (And I'll Go To Mine)" (lyrics by Phillips H. Lord) which calls for "separate but equal" tolerance among Christians despite doctrinal differences

Mrs. Turpin didn't catch every word but she caught enough 74
to agree with the spirit of the song and it turned her thoughts
sober. To help anybody out that needed it was her philosophy of
life. She never spared herself when she found somebody in need,
whether they were white or black, trash or decent. And of all she
had to be thankful for, she was most thankful that this was so. If
Jesus had said, "You can be high society and have all the money
you want and be thin and svelte-like,* but you can't be a good
woman with it," she would have had to say, "Well don't make
me that then. Make me a good woman and it don't matter what
else, how fat or how ugly or how poor!" Her heart rose. He had
not made her a nigger or white-trash or ugly! He had made her
herself and given her a little of everything. Jesus, thank you! she
said. Thank you thank you thank you! Whenever she counted her
blessings she felt as buoyant as if she weighed one hundred and
twenty-five pounds instead of one hundred and eighty.

svelte-like · graceful and suave, refined in form

"What's wrong with your little boy?" the pleasant lady asked 75
the white-trashy woman.

"He has a ulcer," the woman said proudly. "He ain't give me a 76
minute's peace since he was born. Him and her are just alike," she
said, nodding at the old woman, who was running her leathery
fingers through the child's pale hair. "Look like I can't get nothing
down them two but Co' Cola and candy."

77   That's all you try to get down em, Mrs. Turpin said to herself. Too lazy to light the fire. There was nothing you could tell her about people like them that she didn't know already. And it was not just that they didn't have anything. Because if you gave them everything, in two weeks it would all be broken or filthy or they would have chopped it up for lightwood. She knew all this from her own experience. Help them you must, but help them you couldn't.

78   All at once the ugly girl turned her lips inside out again. Her eyes fixed like two drills on Mrs. Turpin. This time there was no mistaking that there was something urgent behind them.

79   Girl, Mrs. Turpin exclaimed silently, I haven't done a thing to you! The girl might be confusing her with somebody else. There was no need to sit by and let herself be intimidated. "You must be in college," she said boldly, looking directly at the girl. "I see you reading a book there."

80   The girl continued to stare and pointedly did not answer.

81   Her mother blushed at this rudeness. "The lady asked you a question, Mary Grace," she said under her breath.

82   "I have ears," Mary Grace said.

83   The poor mother blushed again. "Mary Grace goes to Wellesley College,"* she explained. She twisted one of the buttons on her dress. "In Massachusetts," she added with a grimace. "And in the summer she just keeps right on studying. Just reads all the time, a real book worm. She's done real well at Wellesley; she's taking English and Math and History and Psychology and Social Studies," she rattled on, "and I think it's too much. I think she ought to get out and have fun."

Wellesley College · a private women's college in Wellesley, Massachusetts, known for its rigorous liberal arts curriculum

84   The girl looked as if she would like to hurl them all through the plate glass window.

85   "Way up north," Mrs. Turpin murmured and thought, well, it hasn't done much for her manners.

86   "I'd almost rather to have him sick," the white-trash woman said, wrenching the attention back to herself. "He's so mean when he ain't. Look like some children just take natural to meanness. It's some gets bad when they get sick but he was the opposite. Took sick and turned good. He don't give me no trouble now. It's me waitin to see the doctor," she said.

87   If I was going to send anybody back to Africa, Mrs. Turpin thought, it would be your kind, woman. "Yes, indeed," she said

aloud, but looking up at the ceiling, "it's a heap of things worse 87
than a nigger." And dirtier than a hog, she added to herself.

"I think people with bad dispositions are more to be pitied 88
than anyone on earth," the pleasant lady said in a voice that was
decidedly thin.

"I thank the Lord he has blessed me with a good one," Mrs. 89
Turpin said. "The day has never dawned that I couldn't find
something to laugh at."

"Not since she married me anyways," Claud said with a comical 90
straight face.

Everybody laughed except the girl and the white-trash. 91

Mrs. Turpin's stomach shook. "He's such a caution," she said, 92
"that I can't help but laugh at him."

The girl made a loud ugly noise through her teeth. 93

Her mother's mouth grew thin and tight. "I think the worst 94
thing in the world," she said, "is an ungrateful person. To have
everything and not appreciate it. I know a girl," she said, "who
has parents who would give her anything, a little brother who
loves her dearly, who is getting a good education, who wears
the best clothes, but who can never say a kind word to anyone,
who never smiles, who just criticizes and complains all day long."

"Is she too old to paddle?" Claud asked. 95

The girl's face was almost purple. 96

"Yes," the lady said, "I'm afraid there's nothing to do but leave 97
her to her folly. Some day she'll wake up and it'll be too late."

"It never hurt anyone to smile," Mrs. Turpin said. "It just makes 98
you feel better all over."

"Of course," the lady said sadly, "but there are just some people 99
you can't tell anything to. They can't take criticism."

"If it's one thing I am," Mrs. Turpin said with feeling, "it's grate- 100
ful. When I think who all I could have been besides myself and
what all I got, a little of everything, and a good disposition besides,
I just feel like shouting, 'Thank you, Jesus, for making everything
the way it is!' It could have been different!" For one thing, somebody else could have got Claud. At the thought of this, she was
flooded with gratitude and a terrible pang of joy ran through her.
"Oh thank you, Jesus, Jesus, thank you!" she cried aloud.

The book struck her directly over her left eye. It struck almost 101
at the same instant that she realized the girl was about to hurl

101   it. Before she could utter a sound, the raw face came crashing across the table toward her, howling. The girl's fingers sank like clamps into the soft flesh of her neck. She heard the mother cry out and Claud shout, "Whoa!" There was an instant when she was certain that she was about to be in an earthquake.

102   All at once her vision narrowed and she saw everything as if it were happening in a small room far away, or as if she were looking at it through the wrong end of a telescope. Claud's face crumpled and fell out of sight. The nurse ran in, then out, then in again. Then the gangling figure of the doctor rushed out of the inner door. Magazines flew this way and that as the table turned over. The girl fell with a thud and Mrs. Turpin's vision suddenly reversed itself and she saw everything large instead of small. The eyes of the white-trashy woman were staring hugely at the floor. There the girl, held down on one side by the nurse and on the other by her mother, was wrenching and turning in their grasp. The doctor was kneeling astride her, trying to hold her arm down. He managed after a second to sink a long needle into it.

103   Mrs. Turpin felt entirely hollow except for her heart which swung from side to side as if it were agitated in a great empty drum of flesh.

104   "Somebody that's not busy call for the ambulance," the doctor said in the off-hand voice young doctors adopt for terrible occasions.

105   Mrs. Turpin could not have moved a finger. The old man who had been sitting next to her skipped nimbly into the office and made the call, for the secretary still seemed to be gone.

106   "Claud!" Mrs. Turpin called.

107   He was not in his chair. She knew she must jump up and find him but she felt like some one trying to catch a train in a dream, when everything moves in slow motion and the faster you try to run the slower you go.

108   "Here I am," a suffocated voice, very unlike Claud's, said.

109   He was doubled up in the corner on the floor, pale as paper, holding his leg. She wanted to get up and go to him but she could not move. Instead, her gaze was drawn slowly downward to the churning face on the floor, which she could see over the doctor's shoulder.

The girl's eyes stopped rolling and focused on her. They [110] seemed a much lighter blue than before, as if a door that had been tightly closed behind them was now open to admit light and air.

Mrs. Turpin's head cleared and her power of motion returned. [111] She leaned forward until she was looking directly into the fierce brilliant eyes. There was no doubt in her mind that the girl did know her, knew her in some intense and personal way, beyond time and place and condition. "What you got to say to me?" she asked hoarsely and held her breath, waiting, as for a revelation.

The girl raised her head. Her gaze locked with Mrs. Turpin's. [112] "Go back to hell where you came from, you old wart hog," she whispered. Her voice was low but clear. Her eyes burned for a moment as if she saw with pleasure that her message had struck its target.

Mrs. Turpin sank back in her chair. [113]

After a moment the girl's eyes closed and she turned her head [114] wearily to the side.

The doctor rose and handed the nurse the empty syringe. He [115] leaned over and put both hands for a moment on the mother's shoulders, which were shaking. She was sitting on the floor, her lips pressed together, holding Mary Grace's hand in her lap. The girl's fingers were gripped like a baby's around her thumb. "Go on to the hospital," he said. "I'll call and make the arrangements."

"Now let's see that neck," he said in a jovial voice to Mrs. Turpin. [116] He began to inspect her neck with his first two fingers. Two little moon-shaped lines like pink fish bones were indented over her windpipe. There was the beginning of an angry red swelling above her eye. His fingers passed over this also.

"Lea' me be," she said thickly and shook him off. "See about [117] Claud. She kicked him."

"I'll see about him in a minute," he said and felt her pulse. He [118] was a thin gray-haired man, given to pleasantries. "Go home and have yourself a vacation the rest of the day," he said and patted her on the shoulder.

Quit your pattin' me, Mrs. Turpin growled to herself. [119]

"And put an ice pack over that eye," he said. Then he went and [120] squatted down beside Claud and looked at his leg. After a moment he pulled him up and Claud limped after him into the office.

Until the ambulance came, the only sounds in the room were [121] the tremulous moans of the girl's mother, who continued to sit

121 on the floor. The white-trash woman did not take her eyes off the girl. Mrs. Turpin looked straight ahead at nothing. Presently the ambulance drew up, a long dark shadow, behind the curtain. The attendants came in and set the stretcher down beside the girl and lifted her expertly onto it and carried her out. The nurse helped the mother gather up her things. The shadow of the ambulance moved silently away and the nurse came back in the office.

122 "That ther girl is going to be a lunatic, ain't she?" the white-trash woman asked the nurse, but the nurse kept on to the back and never answered her.

123 "Yes, she's going to be a lunatic," the white-trash woman said to the rest of them.

124 "Po' critter," the old woman murmured. The child's face was still in her lap. His eyes looked idly out over her knees. He had not moved during the disturbance except to draw one leg up under him.

125 "I thank Gawd," the white-trash woman said fervently, "I ain't a lunatic."

126 Claud came limping out and the Turpins went home.

127 As their pick-up truck turned into their own dirt road and made the crest of the hill, Mrs. Turpin gripped the window ledge and looked out suspiciously. The land sloped gracefully down through a field dotted with lavender weeds and at the start of the rise their small yellow frame house, with its little flower beds spread out around it like a fancy apron, sat primly in its accustomed place between two giant hickory trees. She would not have been startled to see a burnt wound between two blackened chimneys.

128 Neither of them felt like eating so they put on their house clothes and lowered the shade in the bedroom and lay down, Claud with his leg on a pillow and herself with a damp washcloth over her eye. The instant she was flat on her back, the image of a razorbacked hog with warts on its face and horns coming out behind its ears snorted into her head. She moaned, a low quiet moan.

129 "I am not," she said tearfully, "a wart hog. From hell." But the denial had no force. The girl's eyes and her words, even the tone of her voice, low but clear, directed only to her, brooked no repudiation. She had been singled out for the message, though there was trash in the room to whom it might justly have been

applied. The full force of this fact struck her only now. There was   129
a woman there who was neglecting her own child but she had
been overlooked. The message had been given to Ruby Turpin,
a respectable, hard-working, church-going woman. The tears
dried. Her eyes began to burn instead with wrath.

She rose on her elbow and the washcloth fell into her hand.   130
Claud was lying on his back, snoring. She wanted to tell him what
the girl had said. At the same time, she did not wish to put the
image of herself as a wart hog from hell into his mind.

"Hey, Claud," she muttered and pushed his shoulder.   131

Claud opened one pale baby blue eye.   132

She looked into it warily. He did not think about anything.   133
He just went his way.

"Wha, whasit?" he said and closed the eye again.   134

"Nothing," she said. "Does your leg pain you?"   135

"Hurts like hell," Claud said.   136

"It'll quit terreckly," she said and lay back down. In a moment   137
Claud was snoring again. For the rest of the afternoon they lay
there. Claud slept. She scowled at the ceiling. Occasionally she
raised her fist and made a small stabbing motion over her chest
as if she was defending her innocence to invisible guests who
were like the comforters of Job,* reasonable-seeming but wrong.

About five-thirty Claud stirred. "Got to go after those niggers,"   138
he sighed, not moving.

She was looking straight up as if there were unintelligible   139
handwriting on the ceiling. The protuberance over her eye had
turned a greenish-blue. "Listen here," she said.

"What?"   140

"Kiss me."   141

Claud leaned over and kissed her loudly on the mouth. He   142
pinched her side and their hands interlocked. Her expression of
ferocious concentration did not change. Claud got up, groaning
and growling, and limped off. She continued to study the ceiling.

She did not get up until she heard the pick-up truck coming   143
back with the Negroes. Then she rose and thrust her feet in her
brown oxfords, which she did not bother to lace, and stumped
out onto the back porch and got her red plastic bucket. She
emptied a tray of ice cubes into it and filled it half full of water
and went out into the back yard. Every afternoon after Claud

---

comforters of Job ·
for most of the book
of Job, his three friends
attempt to convince
him that he is being
punished for evil things
he has done or good
things he has left
undone. They argue
with Job extensively,
but are finally rebuked
by God (see Job 37:1)

143 brought the hands in, one of the boys helped him put out hay and the rest waited in the back of the truck until he was ready to take them home. The truck was parked in the shade under one of the hickory trees.

144 "Hi yawl this evening?" Mrs. Turpin asked grimly, appearing with the bucket and the dipper. There were three women and a boy in the truck.

145 "Us doin nicely," the oldest woman said. "Hi you doin?" and her gaze stuck immediately on the dark lump on Mrs. Turpin's forehead. "You done fell down, ain't you?" she asked in a solicitous voice. The old woman was dark and almost toothless. She had on an old felt hat of Claud's set back on her head. The other two women were younger and lighter and they both had new bright green sunhats. One of them had hers on her head; the other had taken hers off and the boy was grinning beneath it.

146 Mrs. Turpin set the bucket down on the floor of the truck. "Yawl hep yourselves," she said. She looked around to make sure Claud had gone. "No, I didn't fall down," she said, folding her arms. "It was something worse than that."

147 "Ain't nothing bad happen to you!" the old woman said. She said it as if they all knew that Mrs. Turpin was protected in some special way by Divine Providence. "You just had you a little fall."

148 "We were in town at the doctor's office for where the cow kicked Mr. Turpin," Mrs. Turpin said in a flat tone that indicated they could leave off their foolishness. "And there was this girl there. A big fat girl with her face all broke out. I could look at that girl and tell she was peculiar but I couldn't tell how. And me and her mama was just talking and going along and all of a sudden WHAM! She throws this big book she was reading at me and...."

149 "Naw!" the old woman cried out.

150 "And then she jumps over the table and commences to choke me."

151 "Naw!" they all exclaimed, "naw!"

152 "Hi come she do that?" the old woman asked. "What ail her?"

153 Mrs. Turpin only glared in front of her.

154 "Somethin ail her," the old woman said.

155 "They carried her off in an ambulance," Mrs. Turpin continued, "but before she went she was rolling on the floor and they were

trying to hold her down to give her a shot and she said something 155
to me." She paused. "You know what she said to me?"

"What she say?" they asked. 156

"She said," Mrs. Turpin began, and stopped, her face very dark 157
and heavy. The sun was getting whiter and whiter, blanching the
sky overhead so that the leaves of the hickory tree were black in
the face of it. She could not bring forth the words. "Something
real ugly," she muttered.

"She sho shouldn't said nothin ugly to you," the old woman 158
said. "You so sweet. You the sweetest lady I know."

"She pretty too," the one with the hat on said. 159

"And stout," the other one said. "I never knowed no sweeter 160
white lady."

"That's the truth befo' Jesus," the old woman said. "Amen! You 161
des as sweet and pretty as you can be."

Mrs. Turpin knew exactly how much Negro flattery was 162
worth and it added to her rage. "She said," she began again and
finished this time with a fierce rush of breath, "that I was an old
wart hog from hell."

There was an astounded silence. 163

"Where she at?" the youngest woman cried in a piercing voice. 164

"Lemme see her. I'll kill her!" 165

"I'll kill her with you!" the other one cried. 166

"She b'long in the 'sylum," the old woman said emphatically. 167
"You the sweetest white lady I know."

"She pretty too," the other two said. "Stout as she can be and 168
sweet. Jesus satisfied with her!"

"'Deed he is," the old woman declared. 169

Idiots! Mrs. Turpin growled to herself. You could never say 170
anything intelligent to a nigger. You could talk at them but not
with them. "Yawl ain't drunk your water," she said shortly. "Leave
the bucket in the truck when you're finished with it. I got more
to do than just stand around and pass the time of day," and she
moved off and into the house.

She stood for a moment in the middle of the kitchen. The dark 171
protuberance over her eye looked like a miniature tornado cloud
which might any moment sweep across the horizon of her brow.
Her lower lip protruded dangerously. She squared her massive
shoulders. Then she marched into the front of the house and out

171 the side door and started down the road to the pig parlor. She had the look of a woman going single-handed, weaponless, into battle.

172 The sun was a deep yellow now like a harvest moon and was riding westward very fast over the far tree line as if it meant to reach the hogs before she did. The road was rutted and she kicked several good-sized stones out of her path as she strode along. The pig parlor was on a little knoll at the end of a lane that ran off from the side of the barn. It was a square of concrete as large as a small room, with a board fence about four feet high around it. The concrete floor sloped slightly so that the hog wash could drain off into a trench where it was carried to the field for fertilizer. Claud was standing on the outside, on the edge of the concrete, hanging onto the top board, hosing down the floor inside. The hose was connected to the faucet of a water trough nearby. **shoats** · young hogs

173 Mrs. Turpin climbed up beside him and glowered down at the hogs inside. There were seven long-snouted bristly shoats* in it – tan with liver-colored spots – and an old sow a few weeks off from farrowing.* She was lying on her side grunting. The shoats were running about shaking themselves like idiot children, their little slit pig eyes searching the floor for anything left. She had read that pigs were the most intelligent animal. She doubted it. They were supposed to be smarter than dogs. There had even been a pig astronaut. He had performed his assignment perfectly but died of a heart attack afterwards because they left him in his electric suit, sitting upright throughout his examination when naturally a hog should be on all fours. **farrowing** · giving birth to pigs

174 A-gruntin and a-rootin and a-groanin.

175 "Gimme that hose," she said, yanking it away from Claud. "Go on and carry them niggers home and then get off that leg."

176 "You look like you might have swallowed a mad dog," Claud observed, but he got down and limped off. He paid no attention to her humors.

177 Until he was out of earshot, Mrs. Turpin stood on the side of the pen, holding the hose and pointing the stream of water at the hind quarters of any shoat that looked as if it might try to lie down. When he had had time to get over the hill, she turned her head slightly and her wrathful eyes scanned the path. He was nowhere in sight. She turned back again and seemed to gather herself up. Her shoulders rose and she drew in her breath.

"What do you send me a message like that for?" she said in a low   178
fierce voice, barely above a whisper but with the force of a shout in its
concentrated fury. "How am I a hog and me both? How am I saved
and from hell too?" Her free fist was knotted and with the other she
gripped the hose, blindly pointing the stream of water in and out
of the eye of the old sow whose outraged squeal she did not hear.

The pig parlor commanded a view of the back pasture where   179
their twenty beef cows were gathered around the hay-bales Claud
and the boy had put out. The freshly cut pasture sloped down to
the highway. Across it was their cotton field and beyond that a
dark green dusty wood which they owned as well. The sun was
behind the wood, very red, looking over the paling* of trees like
a farmer inspecting his own hogs.

paling · a fence of
regularly spaced pickets

"Why me?" she rumbled. "It's no trash around here, black or   180
white, that I haven't given to. And break my back to the bone
every day working. And do for the church."

She appeared to be the right size woman to command the   181
arena before her. "How am I a hog?" she demanded. "Exactly
how am I like them?" and she jabbed the stream of water at the
shoats. "There was plenty of trash there. It didn't have to be me.

"If you like trash better, go get yourself some trash then," she   182
railed. "You could have made me trash. Or a nigger. If trash is what
you wanted why didn't you make me trash?" She shook her fist with
the hose in it and a watery snake appeared momentarily in the air.
"I could quit working and take it easy and be filthy," she growled.
"Lounge about the sidewalks all day drinking root beer. Dip snuff
and spit in every puddle and have it all over my face. I could be nasty.

"Or you could have made me a nigger. It's too late for me to   183
be a nigger," she said with deep sarcasm, "but I could act like
one. Lay down in the middle of the road and stop traffic. Roll
on the ground."

In the deepening light everything was taking on a mysterious   184
hue. The pasture was growing a peculiar glassy green and the
streak of highway had turned lavender. She braced herself for a
final assault and this time her voice rolled out over the pasture.
"Go on," she yelled, "call me a hog! Call me a hog again. From
hell. Call me a wart hog from hell. Put that bottom rail on top.
There'll still be a top and bottom!"

A garbled echo returned to her.   185

186   A final surge of fury shook her and she roared, "Who do you think you are?"

187   The color of everything, field and crimson sky, burned for a moment with a transparent intensity. The question carried over the pasture and across the highway and the cotton field and returned to her clearly like an answer from beyond the wood.

188   She opened her mouth but no sound came out of it.

189   A tiny truck, Claud's, appeared on the highway, heading rapidly out of sight. Its gears scraped thinly. It looked like a child's toy. At any moment a bigger truck might smash into it and scatter Claud's and the niggers' brains all over the road.

190   Mrs. Turpin stood there, her gaze fixed on the highway, all her muscles rigid, until in five or six minutes the truck reappeared, returning. She waited until it had had time to turn into their own road. Then like a monumental statue coming to life, she bent her head slowly and gazed, as if through the very heart of mystery, down into the pig parlor at the hogs. They had settled all in one corner around the old sow who was grunting softly. A red glow suffused them. They appeared to pant with a secret life.

191   Until the sun slipped finally behind the tree line, Mrs. Turpin remained there with her gaze bent to them as if she were absorbing some abysmal life-giving knowledge. At last she lifted her head. There was only a purple streak in the sky, cutting through a field of crimson and leading, like an extension of the highway, into the descending dusk. She raised her hands from the side of the pen in a gesture hieratic* and profound. A visionary light settled in her eyes. She saw the streak as a vast swinging bridge extending upward from the earth through a field of living fire. Upon it a vast horde of souls were rumbling toward heaven. There were whole companies of white-trash, clean for the first time in their lives, and bands of black niggers in white robes, and battalions of freaks and lunatics shouting and clapping and leaping like frogs. And bringing up the end of the procession was a tribe of people whom she recognized at once as those who, like herself and Claud, had always had a little of everything and the God-given wit to use it right. She leaned forward to observe them closer. They were marching behind the others with great dignity, accountable as they had always been for good order and common sense and respectable behavior. They alone were on key. Yet she could see

hieratic· a symbolic gesture whose meaning is hidden

by their shocked and altered faces that even their virtues were   191
being burned away. She lowered her hands and gripped the rail
of the hog pen, her eyes small but fixed unblinkingly on what lay
ahead. In a moment the vision faded but she remained where
she was, immobile.

At length she got down and turned off the faucet and made   192
her slow way on the darkening path to the house. In the woods
around her the invisible cricket choruses had struck up, but what
she heard were the voices of the souls climbing upward into the
starry field and shouting hallelujah.

Alice Munro

◄(1 9 3 1 -)►

Munro chronicles the intense and private worlds of small town characters in Midwestern Canada. Set in familiar places like skating rinks and school book rooms, her stories are poignant with experiences most of us recognize, such as the smell of disinfectant and the taste of root beer. These details are not only present; they are significant because they live in the imagination and memory of the characters. Within the borders of Munro's fiction, a tea strainer means something, for example, because the character who uses it understands it in a certain way. Perhaps no one since Chekhov has catalogued so powerfully and with such strangeness the mundane lives of ordinary people. Her fiction, which is regularly published in such magazines as The Atlantic Monthly *and* The New Yorker, *has been gathered in award-winning collections, including* The Moons of Jupiter (1983), The Progress of Love (1986), *and* Open Secrets (1994).

MRS. CROSS AND MRS. KIDD

1   MRS. CROSS AND MRS. KIDD have known each other eighty years, ever since Kindergarten, which was not called that then, but Primary. Mrs. Cross's first picture of Mrs. Kidd is of her standing at the front of the class reciting some poem, her hands behind her back and her small black-eyed face lifted to let out her self-confident voice. Over the next ten years, if you went to any concert, any meeting that featured entertainment, you would find Mrs. Kidd (who was not called Mrs. Kidd then but Marian Botherton), with her dark, thick bangs cut straight across her forehead, and her pinafore sticking up in starched wings, reciting a poem with the greatest competence and no hitch of memory. Even today with hardly any excuse, sitting in her wheelchair, Mrs. Kidd will launch forth.

Today ... Ratisbon ·
the opening line of
"Incident of the French
Camp" by English
poet Robert Browning
(1812–1889)

Where ... tide? · the
opening lines of "The
Ships of Saint John" by
Canadian poet Bliss
Carman (1861–1929)

Today we French stormed Ratisbon,* 1a

she will say, or: 1

> Where are the ships I used to know 1b
> That came to port on the Fundy tide?*

She stops not because she doesn't remember how to go on but in 1
order to let somebody say, "What's that one?" or, "Wasn't that in
the Third Reader?" which she takes as a request to steam ahead.

> Half a century ago 1c
> In beauty and stately pride.

Mrs. Kidd's first memory of Mrs. Cross (Dolly Grainger) is of 2
a broad red face and a dress with a droopy hem, and thick fair
braids, and a bellowing voice, in the playground on a rainy day
when they were all crowded under the overhang. The girls played
a game that was really a dance, that Mrs. Kidd did not know how
to do. It was a Virginia reel and the words they sang were:

> Jolting up and down in the old Brass Wagon 2a
> Jolting up and down in the old Brass Wagon
> Jolting up and down in the old Brass Wagon
> You're the One my Darling!"

Nobody whirled and stomped and sang more enthusiastically 3
than Mrs. Cross, who was the youngest and smallest allowed to
play. She knew it from her older sisters. Mrs. Kidd was an only child.

Younger people, learning that these two women have known 4
each other for more than three-quarters of a century, seem to
imagine this gives them everything in common. They themselves
are the only ones who can recall what separated them, and to a
certain extent does yet: the apartment over the Post Office and
Customs house, where Mrs. Kidd lived with her mother and
her father who was the Postmaster; the row-house on Newgate
Street where Mrs. Cross lived with her mother and father and
two sisters and four brothers; the fact that Mrs. Kidd went to the
Anglican Church and Mrs. Cross to the Free Methodist; that Mrs.
Kidd married, at the age of twenty-three, a high-school teacher
of science, and Mrs. Cross married, at the age of seventeen, a
man who worked on the lake boats and never got to be a captain.

4   Mrs. Cross had six children, Mrs. Kidd had three. Mrs. Cross's husband died suddenly at forty-two with no life insurance; Mrs. Kidd's husband retired to Goderich with a pension after years of being principal of the high school in a nearby town. Only recently has the gap closed. The children equalled things out; Mrs. Cross's children, on the average, make as much money as Mrs. Kidd's children, though they do not have as much education. Mrs. Cross's grandchildren make more money.

5   Mrs. Cross has been in Hilltop Home three years and two months, Mrs. Kidd three years less a month. They both have bad hearts and ride around in wheelchairs to save their energy. During their first conversation, Mrs. Kidd said, "I don't notice any hilltop."

6   "You can see the highway," said Mrs. Cross. "I guess that's what they mean. Where did they put you?" she asked.

7   "I hardly know if I can find my way back. It's a nice room, though. It's a single."

8   "Mine is too, I have a single. Is it the other side of the dining-room or this?"

9   "Oh. The other side."

10   "That's good. That's the best part. Everybody's in fairly good shape down there. It costs more, though. The better you are, the more it costs. The other side of the dining-room is out of their head."

11   "Senile?"

12   "Senile. This side is the younger ones that have something like that the matter with them. For instance." She nodded at a mongoloid* man of about fifty, who was trying to play the mouth organ. "Down in our part there's also younger ones, but nothing the matter up here," she tapped her head. "Just some disease. When it gets to the point they can't look after themselves upstairs. That's where you get the far-gone ones. Then the crazies is another story. Locked up in the back wing. That's the real crazies. Also, I think there is some place they have the ones that walk around but soil all the time. "

> mongoloid · someone with Down syndrome

13   "Well, we are the top drawer," said Mrs. Kidd with a tight smile. "I knew there would be plenty of senile ones, but I wasn't prepared for the others. Such as." She nodded discreetly at the mongoloid who was doing a step-dance in front of the window.

Unlike most mongoloids, he was thin and agile, though very pale 13
and brittle-looking.

"Happier than most," said Mrs. Cross, observing him. "This is 14
the only place in the county, everything gets dumped here. After
a while it doesn't bother you."

"It doesn't *bother* me." 15

Mrs. Kidd's room is full of rocks and shells, in boxes and in 16
bottles. She has a case of brittle butterflies and a case of stuffed
songbirds. Her bookshelves contain *Ferns and Mosses of North
America, Peterson's Guide to the Birds of Eastern North America,
How to Know the Rocks and Minerals,* and a book of *Star Maps.* The
case of butterflies and the songbirds once hung in the classroom
of her husband, the science teacher. He bought the songbirds, but
he and Mrs. Kidd collected the butterflies themselves. Mrs. Kidd
was a good student of botany and zoology. If she had not had what
was perceived at the time as delicate health, she would have gone
on and studied botany at a university, though few girls did such
a thing then. Her children, who all live at a distance, send her
beautiful books on subjects they are sure will interest her, but for
the most part these books are large and heavy and she can't find
a way to look at them comfortably, so she soon relegates them to
her bottom shelf. She would not admit it to her children, but her
interest has waned, it has waned considerably. They say in their
letters that they remember how she taught them about mushrooms; do you remember when we saw the destroying angel* in
Petrie's Bush when we were living in Logan? Their letters are full
of remembering. They want her fixed where she was forty or fifty
years ago, these children who are aging themselves. They have a
notion of her that is as fond and necessary as any notion a parent
ever had of a child. They celebrate what would in a child be called
precocity: her brightness, her fund of knowledge, her atheism (a
secret all those years her husband was in charge of the minds
of young), all the ways in which she differs from the average, or
expected, old lady. She feels it a duty to hide from them the many
indications that she is not so different as they think.

Mrs. Cross also gets presents from her children, but not 17
books. Their thoughts run to ornaments, pictures, cushions. Mrs.
Cross has a bouquet of artificial roses in which are set tubes of
light, always shooting and bubbling up like a fountain. She has

destroying angel ·
among the deadliest of
all mushrooms

17 a Southern Belle whose satin skirts are supposed to form an enormous pincushion. She has a picture of the Lord's Supper, in which a light comes on to form a halo around Jesus's head. (Mrs. Kidd, after her first visit, wrote a letter to one of her children in which she described this picture and said she had tried to figure out what the Lord and his Disciples were eating and it appeared to be hamburgers. This is the sort of thing her children love to hear from her.) There is also, near the door, a life-size plaster statue of a collie dog which resembles a dog the Cross family had when the children were small: old Bonnie. Mrs. Cross finds out from her children what these things cost and tells people. She says she is shocked.

18 Shortly after Mrs. Kidd's arrival, Mrs. Cross took her along on a visit to the Second Floor. Mrs. Cross has been going up there every couple of weeks to visit a cousin of hers, old Lily Barbour.

19 "Lily is not running on all cylinders," she warned Mrs. Kidd, as they wheeled themselves into the elevator. "Another thing, it doesn't smell like Sweet Violets, in spite of them always spraying. They do the best they can."

20 The first thing Mrs. Kidd saw as they got off the elevator was a little wrinkled-up woman with wild white hair, and a dress rucked up high on her bare legs (Mrs. Kidd snatched her eyes away from that) and a tongue she couldn't seem to stuff back inside her mouth. The smell was of heated urine – you would think they had had it on the stove – as well as of floral sprays. But here was a smooth-faced sensible-looking person with a topknot, wearing an apron over a clean pink dress.

21 "Well, did you get the papers?" this woman said in a familiar way to Mrs. Cross and Mrs. Kidd.

22 "Oh, they don't come in till about five o'clock," said Mrs. Kidd politely, thinking she meant the newspaper.

23 "Never mind her," said Mrs. Cross.

24 "I have to sign them today," the woman said. "Otherwise it'll be a catastrophe. They can put me out. You see I never knew it was illegal." She spoke so well, so plausibly and confidentially, that Mrs. Kidd was convinced she had to make sense, but Mrs. Cross was wheeling vigorously away. Mrs. Kidd went after her.

25 "Don't get tied up in that rigamarole," said Mrs. Cross when Mrs. Kidd caught up to her. A woman with a terrible goitre,* such

goitre · an enlargement of the thyroid gland

as Mrs. Kidd had not seen for years, was smiling winningly at   25
them. Up here nobody had teeth.

"I thought there was no such thing as a goitre any more," Mrs.   26
Kidd said. "With the iodine."

They were going in the direction of a hollering voice.   27

"George!" the voice said. "George! Jessie! I'm here! Come and   28
pull me up! George!"

Another voice was weaving cheerfully in and out of these yells.   29
"Bad-bad-bad, "it said. "Bad-Bad-bad. Bad-bad-bad. Bad-*bad*. "

The owners of both these voices were sitting around a long   30
table by a row of windows halfway down the hall. Nine or ten
women were sitting there. Some were mumbling or singing softly
to themselves. One was tearing apart a little embroidered cushion
somebody had made. Another was eating a chocolate-covered
ice-cream bar. Bits of chocolate had caught on her whiskers,
dribbles of ice cream ran down her chin. None of them looked
out the windows, or at each other. None of them paid any attention to George-and-Jessie, or to Bad-bad-bad, who were carrying
on without a break.

Mrs. Kidd halted.   31

"Where is this Lily?"   32

"She's down at the end. They don't get her out of bed."   33

"Well, you go on and see her," said Mrs. Kidd. "I'm going back."   34

"There's nothing to get upset about," said Mrs. Cross. "They're   35
all off in their own little world. They're happy as clams. "

"They may be, but I'm not," said Mrs. Kidd. "I'll see you in the   36
Recreation Room." She wheeled herself around and down the hall
to the elevator where the pink lady was still inquiring urgently
for her papers. She never came back.

Mrs. Cross and Mrs. Kidd used to play cards in the Recreation   37
Room every afternoon. They put on earrings, stockings, afternoon dresses. They took turns treating for tea. On the whole,
these afternoons were pleasant. They were well matched at cards.
Sometimes they played Scrabble, but Mrs. Cross did not take
Scrabble seriously, as she did cards. She became frivolous and
quarrelsome, defending words that were her own invention. So
they went back to cards; they played rummy, most of the time.
It was like school here. People paired off, they had best friends.

37   The same people always sat together in the dining-room. Some people had nobody.

38   The first time Mrs. Cross took notice of Jack, he was in the Recreation Room, when she and Mrs. Kidd were playing cards. He had just come in a week or so before. Mrs. Kidd knew about him.

39   "Do you see that red-haired fellow by the window?" said Mrs. Kidd. "He's in from a stroke. He's only fifty-nine years old. I heard it in the dining-room before you got down.

40   "Poor chap. That young."

41   "He's lucky to be alive at all. His parents are still alive, both of them, they're still on a farm. He was back visiting them and he took the stroke and was lying face down in the barnyard when they found him. He wasn't living around here, he's from out west."

42   "Poor chap," said Mrs. Cross. "What did he work at?"

43   "He worked on a newspaper.

44   "Was he married?"

45   "That I didn't hear. He's supposed to have been an alcoholic, then he joined AA and got over it. You can't trust all you hear in this place. "

46   (That was true. There was usually a swirl of stories around any newcomer; stories about the money people had, or the places they had been, or the number of operations they have had and the plastic repairs or contrivances they carry around in or on their bodies. A few days later Mrs. Cross was saying that Jack had been the editor of a newspaper. First she heard it was in Sudbury,* then she heard Winnipeg.* She was saying he had had a nervous breakdown due to overwork; that was the truth, he had never been an alcoholic. She was saying he came from a good family. His name was Jack MacNeil.)

Sudbury · located in southeastern Ontario

Winnipeg · capital of Manitoba

47   At present Mrs. Cross noticed how clean and tended he looked in his gray pants and light shirt. It was unnatural, at least for him; he looked like something that had gone soft from being too long in the water. He was a big man, but he could not hold himself straight, even in the wheelchair. The whole left side of his body was loose, emptied, powerless. His hair and moustache were not even gray yet, but fawn-colored. He was white as if just out of bandages.

48   A distraction occurred. The Gospel preacher who came every week to conduct a prayer service, with hymns (the more estab-

lished preachers came, in turn, on Sundays), was walking through 48
the Recreation Room with his wife close behind, the pair of them
showering smiles and greetings wherever they could catch an
eye. Mrs. Kidd looked up when they had passed and said softly
but distinctly, "Joy to the World."

At this, Jack, who was wheeling himself across the room in a 49
clumsy way – he tended to go in circles – smiled. The smile was
intelligent, ironic, and did not go with his helpless look. Mrs.
Cross waved him over and wheeled part of the way to meet him.
She introduced herself, and introduced Mrs. Kidd. He opened
his mouth and said, "Anh-anh-anh,"

"Yes," said Mrs. Cross encouragingly. "Yes?" 50

"Anh-anh-*anh*," said Jack. He flapped his right hand. Tears 51
came into his eyes.

"Are we playing cards?" said Mrs. Kidd. 52

"I have to get on with this game," said Mrs. Cross. "You're 53
welcome to sit and watch. Were you a card player?"

His right hand came out and grabbed her chair, and he bent 54
his head weeping. He tried to get the left hand up to wipe his face.
He could lift it a few inches, then it fell back in his lap.

"Oh, well," said Mrs. Cross softly. Then she remembered what 55
you do when children cry; how to josh them out of it. "How can I
tell what you're saying if you're going to cry? You just be patient.
I have known people that have had strokes and got their speech
back. Yes I have. You mustn't cry, that won't accomplish anything.
You just take it slow. "Boo-hoo-hoo," she said, bending towards
him. "Boo-hoo-hoo. You'll have Mrs. Kidd and me crying next."

That was the beginning of Mrs. Cross's takeover of Jack. She 56
got him to sit and watch the card game and to dry up, more or
less, and make a noise which was a substitute for conversation
(an-anh) rather than a desperate attempt at it (anh-anh-*anh*). Mrs.
Cross felt something stretching in her. It was her old managing,
watching power, her capacity for strategy, which if properly
exercised could never be detected by those it was used on.

Mrs. Kidd could detect it, however. 57

"This isn't what I call a card game," she said. 58

Mrs. Cross soon found out that Jack could not stay interested 59
in cards and there was no use trying to get him to play; it was conversation he was after. But trying to talk brought on the weeping.

60   "Crying doesn't bother me," she said to him. "I've seen tears and tears. But it doesn't do you any good with a lot of people, to get a reputation for being a cry-baby.

61   So she started to ask him questions to which he could give yes-and-no answers. That brightened him up and let her test out her information.

62   Yes, he had worked on a newspaper. No, he was not married. No, the newspaper was not in Sudbury. Mrs. Cross began to reel off the name of every city she could think of but was unable to hit on the right one. He became agitated, tried to speak, and this time the syllables got close to a word, but she couldn't catch it. She blamed herself, for not knowing enough places. Then, inspired, she ordered him to stay right where he was, not to move, she would be back, and she wheeled herself down the hall to the Library. There she looked for a book with maps in it. To her disgust there was not such a thing, there was nothing but love stories and religion. But she did not give up. She took off down the hall to Mrs. Kidd's room. Since their card games had lapsed (they still played some days, but not every day), Mrs. Kidd spent many afternoons in her room. She was there now, lying on top of her bed, wearing an elegant purple dressing-gown with a high embroidered neck. She had a headache.

63   "Have you got one of those, like a geography book?" Mrs. Cross said. "A book with maps in it." She explained that she wanted it for Jack.

64   "An atlas, you mean, "said Mrs. Kidd. "I think there may be. I can't remember. You can look on the bottom shelf. I can't remember what's there."

65   Mrs. Cross parked by the bookcase and began to lift the heavy books onto her lap one by one, reading the titles at close range. She was out of breath from the speed of her trip.

66   "You're wearing yourself out," said Mrs. Kidd. "You'll get yourself upset and you'll get him upset, and what is the point of it?"

67   "I'm not upset. It just seems a crime to me."

68   "What does?"

69   "Such an intelligent man, what's he doing in here? They should have put him in one of those places they teach you things, teach you how to talk again. What's the name of them? You know. Why did they just stick him in here? I want to help him and I don't know what to do. Well, I just have to try. If it was one of my boys

like that and in a place where nobody knew him, I just hope some   69
woman would take the same interest in him."

"Rehabilitation," said Mrs. Kidd. "The reason they put him in   70
here is more than likely that the stroke was too bad for them to
do anything for him."

"Everything under the sun but a map-book," said Mrs. Cross,   71
not choosing to answer this. "He'll think I'm not coming back."
She wheeled out of Mrs. Kidd's room without a thank-you or
good-bye. She was afraid Jack would think she hadn't meant to
come back, all she intended to do was to get rid of him. Sure
enough, when she got to the Recreation Room he was gone.
She did not know what to do. She was near tears herself. She
didn't know where his room was. She thought she would go to
the office and ask; then she saw that it was five past four and the
office would be closed. Lazy, those girls were. Four o'clock, get
their coats on and go home, nothing matters to them. She went
wheeling slowly along the corridor, wondering what to do. Then
in one of the dead-end side corridors she saw Jack.

"There you are, what a relief! I didn't know where to look for   72
you. Did you think I wasn't ever coming back? I'll tell you what
I went for. I was going to surprise you. I went to look for one of
those books with maps in, what do you call them, so you could
show me where you used to live. Atlases!"

He was sitting looking at the pink wall as if it was a window.   73
whatnot · a display Against the wall was a whatnot* with a vase of plastic daffodils on
case for knickknacks it, and some figurines, dwarfs and dogs; on the wall were three
paint-by-number pictures that had been done in the Craft Room.

"My friend Mrs. Kidd has more books than the Library. She has   74
a book on nothing but bugs. Another nothing but the moon, when
they went there, close up. But not such a simple thing as a map."

Jack was pointing at one of the pictures.   75

"Which one are you pointing at?" said Mrs. Cross. "The one   76
with the church with the cross? No? The one above that? The
pine trees? Yes? What about it? The pine trees and the red deer?"
He was smiling, waving his hand. She hoped he wouldn't get
too excited and disappointed this time. "What about it? This
is like one of those things on television. Trees? Green? Pine
trees? Is it the deer? Three deer? No? Yes. Three red deer?" He
flapped his arm up and down and she said, "I don't know, really.

76 Three – red – deer. Wait a minute. That's a place. I've heard it
on the news. Red Deer.* Red Deer! That's the place! That's the
place you lived in! That's the place where you worked on the
newspaper! *Red Deer."*

Red Deer · a city in
central Alberta

77 They were both jubilant. He waved his arm around in celebration, as if he was conducting an orchestra, and she leaned forward,
laughing, clapping her hands on her knees.

78 "Oh, if everything was in pictures like that, we could have a lot
of fun! You and me could have a lot of fun, couldn't we?"

79 Mrs. Cross made an appointment to see the doctor.

80 "I've heard of people that had a very bad stroke and their
speech came back, isn't that so?"

81 "It can happen. It depends. Are you worrying a lot about this
man?"

82 "It must be a terrible feeling. No wonder he cries."

83 "How many children did you have?"

84 "Six."

85 "I'd say you'd done your share of worrying."

86 She could see he didn't mean to tell her anything. Either he
didn't remember much about Jack's case or he was pretending
he didn't.

87 "I'm here to take care of people," the doctor said. "That's what
I'm here for, that's what the nurses are here for. So you can leave
all the worrying to us. That's what we get paid for. Right?"

88 And how much worrying do you do? she wanted to ask.

89 She would have liked to talk to Mrs. Kidd about this visit because
she knew Mrs. Kidd thought the doctor was a fool, but once Mrs.
Kidd knew Jack was the reason for the visit she would make some
impatient remark. Mrs. Cross never talked to her any more about
Jack. She talked to other people, but she could see them getting
bored. Nobody cares about anybody else's misfortunes in here, she
thought. Even when somebody dies they don't care, it's just *me,
I'm still alive, what's for dinner?* The selfishness. They're all just as
bad as the ones on the Second Floor, only they don't show it yet.

90 She hadn't been up to the Second Floor, hadn't visited Lily
Barbour, since she took up with Jack.

91 They liked sitting in the corner with the Red Deer picture, the
scene of their first success. That was established as their place,
where they could be by themselves. Mrs. Cross brought a pencil

and paper, fixed the tray across his chair, tried to see how Jack   91
made out with writing. It was about the same as talking. He would
scrawl a bit, push the pencil till he broke it, start to cry. They
didn't make progress, either in writing or talking, it was useless.
But she was learning to talk to him by the yes-and-no method,
and it seemed sometimes she could pick up what was in his mind.

"If I was smarter I would be more of a help to you," she said. "Isn't   92
it the limit? I can get it all out that's in my head, but there never
was so much in it, and you've got your head crammed full but you
can't get it out. Never mind. We'll have a cup of coffee, won't we?
Cup of coffee, that's what you like. My friend Mrs. Kidd and I used
to drink tea all the time, but now I drink coffee. I prefer it too."

"So you never got married? Never?"   93

Never.   94

"Did you have a sweetheart?"   95

Yes.   96

"Did you? Did you? Was it long ago? Long ago or recently?"   97

Yes.   98

"Long ago or recently? Both. Long ago and recently. Different   99
sweethearts. The same? The same. The same woman. You were
in love with the same woman years and years but you didn't get
married to her. Oh, Jack. Why didn't you? Couldn't she marry
you? She couldn't. Why not? Was she married already? Was she?
Yes. Yes. Oh, my."

She searched his face to see if this was too painful a subject   100
or if he wanted to go on. She thought he did want to. She was
eager to ask where this woman was now, but something warned
her not to. Instead she took a light tone.

"I wonder if I can guess her name? Remember Red Deer?   101
Wasn't that funny? I wonder. I could start with A and work
through the alphabet. Anne? Audrey? Annabelle? No. I think
I'll just follow my intuition. Jane? Mary? Louise?"

The name was Pat, Patricia, which she hit on maybe her   102
thirtieth try.

"Now, in my mind a Pat is always fair. Not dark. You know   103
how you have a picture in your mind for a name? Was she fair?
Yes? And tall, in my mind a Pat is always tall. Was she? Well! I got
it right. Tall and fair. A good-looking woman. A lovely woman."

Yes.   104

105   She felt ashamed of herself, because she had wished for a moment that she had somebody to tell this to.

106   "That is a secret then. It's between you and me. Now. If you ever want to write Pat a letter you come to me. Come to me and I'll make out what you want to say to her and I'll write it.

107   No. No letter. Never.

108   "Well. I have a secret too. I had a boy I liked, he was killed in the First World War. He walked me home from a skating-party, it was our school skating-party. I was in the Senior Fourth. I was fourteen. That was before the war. I did like him, and I used to think about him, you know, and when I heard he was killed, that was after I was married, I was married at seventeen, well, when I heard he was killed I thought, now I've got something to look forward to, I could look forward to meeting him in Heaven. That's true that's how childish I was.

109   "Marian was at that skating-party too. You know who I mean by Marian. Mrs. Kidd. She was there and she had the most beautiful outfit. It was sky-blue trimmed with white fur and a hood on it. Also she had a muff. She had a white fur muff. I never saw anything I would've like to have for myself as much as that muff."

110   Lying in the dark at night, before she went to sleep, Mrs. Cross would go over everything that had happened with Jack that day: how he had looked; how his color was; whether he had cried and how long and how often; whether he had been in a bad temper in the dining-room, annoyed with so many people around him or perhaps not liking the food; whether he had said good-night to her sullenly or gratefully.

111   Meanwhile Mrs. Kidd had taken on a new friend of her own. This was Charlotte, who used to live down near the dining-room but had recently moved in across the hall. Charlotte was a tall, thin, deferential woman in her mid-forties. She had multiple sclerosis. Sometimes her disease was in remission, as it was now; she could have gone home, if she had wanted to, and there had been a place for her. But she was happy where she was. Years of institutional life had made her childlike, affectionate, good-humored. She helped in the hairdressing shop, she loved doing that, she loved brushing and pinning up Mrs. Kidd's hair, marvelling at how much black there still was in it. She put an ash-blond rinse on her own hair and wore it in a bouffant, stiff

with spray. Mrs. Kidd could smell the hairspray from her room   111
and she would call out, "Charlotte! Did they move you down
here for the purpose of asphyxiating us?"

Charlotte giggled. She brought Mrs. Kidd a present. It was   112
a red felt purse, with an appliquéd design of green leaves and
blue and yellow flowers; she had made it in the Craft Room. Mrs.
Kidd thought how much it resembled those recipe-holders her
children used to bring home from school; a whole cardboard
pie-plate and a half pie-plate, stitched together with bright yarn.
They didn't hold enough to be really useful. They were painstakingly created frivolities, like the crocheted potholders through
which you could burn yourself; the cut-out wooden horse's head
with a hook not quite big enough to hold a hat.

Charlotte made purses for her daughters, who were married, and   113
for her small granddaughter, and for the woman who lived with her
husband and used his name. The husband and this woman came
regularly to see Charlotte; they were all good friends. It had been a
good arrangement for the husband, for the children, and perhaps
for Charlotte herself. Nothing was being put over on Charlotte.
Most likely she had given in without a whimper. Glad of the chance.

"What do you expect?" said Mrs. Cross. "Charlotte's easygoing."   114

Mrs. Cross and Mrs. Kidd had not had any falling-out or any   115
real coolness. They still had some talks and card games. But it
was difficult. They no longer sat at the same table in the dining-
room because Mrs. Cross had to watch to see if Jack needed help
cutting up his meat. He wouldn't let anyone else cut it; he would
just pretend he didn't want any and miss out on his protein. Then
Charlotte moved into the place Mrs. Cross had vacated. Charlotte
had no problems cutting her meat. In fact she cut her meat, toast,
egg, vegetables, cake, whatever she was eating that would cut,
into tiny regular pieces before she started on it. Mrs. Kidd told
her that was not good manners. Charlotte was crestfallen but
stubborn and continued to do it.

"Neither you nor I would have given up so quickly," said   116
Mrs. Kidd, still speaking about Charlotte to Mrs. Cross. "We
wouldn't've had the choice."

"That's true. There weren't places like this. Not pleasant places.   117
They couldn't have kept us alive the way they do her. The drugs
and so on. Also it may be the drugs makes her silly."

118   Mrs. Kidd remained silent, frowning at hearing Charlotte called silly, though that was just the blunt way of putting what she had been trying to say herself. After a moment she spoke lamely.

119   "I think she has more brains than she shows."

120   Mrs. Cross said evenly, "I wouldn't know."

121   Mrs. Kidd sat with her head bent forward, thoughtfully. She could sit that way for half an hour, easily, letting Charlotte brush and tend her hair. Was she turning into one of those old ladies that love to be waited on? Those old ladies also needed somebody to boss. They were the sort who went around the world on cruise ships, she had read about them in novels. They went around the world, and stayed at hotels, or they lived in grand decaying houses, with their companions. It was so easy to boss Charlotte, to make her play Scrabble and tell her when her manners were bad. Charlotte was itching to be somebody's slave. So why did Mrs. Kidd hope to restrain herself? She did not wish to be such a recognizable sort of old lady. Also, slaves cost more than they were worth. In the end, people's devotion hung like rocks around your neck. Expectations. She wanted to float herself clear. Sometimes she could do it by lying on her bed and saying in her head all the poems she knew, or the facts, which got harder and harder to hold in place. Other times she imagined a house on the edge of some dark woods or bog, bright fields in front of it running down to the sea. She imagined she lived there alone, like an old woman in a story.

122   Mrs. Cross wanted to take Jack on visits. She thought it was time for him to learn to associate with people. He didn't cry so often now, when they were alone. But sometimes at meals she was ashamed of him and had to tell him so. He would take offense at something, often she didn't know what, and sometimes his sulk would proceed to the point where he would knock over the sugar bowl, or sweep all his cutlery on to the floor. She thought that if only he could get used to a few more people as he was to her, he would calm down and behave decently.

123   The first time she took him to Mrs. Kidd's room Mrs. Kidd said she and Charlotte were just going out, they were going to the Crafts Room. She didn't ask them to come along. The next time they came, Mrs. Kidd and Charlotte were sitting there playing Scrabble, so they were caught.

"You don't mind if we watch you for a little while," Mrs. Cross said. 124

"Oh no. But don't blame me if you get bored. Charlotte takes 125 a week from Wednesday to make up her mind."

"We're not in any hurry. We're not expected anywhere. Are 126 we, Jack?"

She was wondering if she could get Jack playing Scrabble. She 127 didn't know the extent of his problem when he tried to write. Was it that he couldn't form the letters, was that all? Or couldn't he see how they made the words? This might be the very thing for him.

At any rate he was taking an interest. He edged his chair up 128 beside Charlotte, who picked up some letters, put them back, picked them up, looked at them in her hand, and finally made *wind*, working down from the *w* in Mrs. Kidd's word *elbow*. Jack seemed to understand. He was so pleased that he patted Charlotte's knee in congratulation. Mrs. Cross hoped Charlotte would realize that was just friendliness and not take offense.

She needn't have worried. Charlotte did not know how to 129 take offense.

"Well good for you," said Mrs. Kidd, frowning, and right away 130 she made *demon* across from the *d*. "Triple word!" she said, and was writing down the score. "Pick up your letters, Charlotte."

Charlotte showed her new letters to Jack, one by one, and 131 he made a noise of appreciation. Mrs. Cross kept an eye on him, hoping nothing would happen to turn him bad-tempered and spoil this show of friendliness. Nothing did. But he was not having a good effect on Charlotte's concentration.

"You want to help?" Charlotte said, and moved the little stand 132 with the letters on it so that it was in front of both of them. He bent over so that he almost had his head on her shoulder.

"Anh-anh-anh," said Jack, but he sounded cheerful. 133

"Anh-anh-anh?" said Charlotte, teasing him. "What kind of a 134 word is that, *anh-anh-anh*?"

Mrs. Cross waited for the skies to fall, but the only thing Jack 135 did was giggle, and Charlotte giggled, so that there was a sort of giggling-match set up between the two of them.

"Aren't you the great friends," said Mrs. Kidd. 136

Mrs. Cross thought it would be just as well not to exasperate 137 Mrs. Kidd if they wanted to make a habit of visiting.

138   "Now Jack, don't distract Charlotte," she said affably. "You let her play."

139   Even as she finished saying this, she saw Jack's hand descend clumsily on the Scrabble board. The letters went flying. He turned and showed her his ugly look, worse than she had ever seen it. She was amazed and even frightened, but she did not mean to let him see.

140   "Now what have you done?" she said. "Fine behavior!" He made a sound of disgust and pushed the Scrabble board and all the letters to the floor, all the time looking at Mrs. Cross so that there could be no doubt that this disgust and fury had been aroused by her. She knew that it was important at this moment to speak coldly and firmly. That was what you must do with a child or an animal; you must show them that your control has not budged and that you are not hurt or alarmed by such displays. But she was not able to say a word, such a feeling of grief, and shock, and helplessness rose in her heart. Her eyes filled with tears, and at the sight of her tears his expression grew even more hateful and menacing as if the feelings he had against her were boiling higher every moment.

141   Charlotte was smiling, either because she could not switch out of her giggling mood of a moment before or because she did not know how to do anything but smile, no matter what happened. She was pink-faced, apologetic, excited.

142   Jack managed to turn his chair around, with a violent, awkward motion. Charlotte stood up. Mrs. Cross made herself speak.

143   "Yes, you better push him home now. He better go home and cool off and repent of his bad manners. He better."

144   Jack made a taunting sound, which seemed to point out that Mrs. Cross was just telling Charlotte to do what Charlotte was going to do anyway; Mrs. Cross was just pretending to have control of things. Charlotte had hold of the wheelchair and was pushing it towards the door, her smiling lips pressed together in concentration as she avoided the bookshelves and the butterfly case leaning against the wall. Perhaps it was hard for her to steer, perhaps the ordinary reflexes and balances of her body were not there for her to rely on. But she looked pleased; she raised her hand to them and released her smile, and set off down the corridor. She was just like one of those old-fashioned dolls, not the kind Mrs. Cross and Mrs. Kidd used to have but the kind their

mothers had, with the long, limp bodies and pink-and-white faces 144
and crimped china hair and ladylike smiles. Jack kept his face
turned away; the bit of it Mrs. Cross could see was flushed red.

"It would be easy for any man to get the better of Charlotte," 145
said Mrs. Kidd when they were gone.

"I don't think he's so much of a danger," said Mrs. Cross. She 146
spoke in a dry tone but her voice was shaking.

Mrs. Kidd looked at the Scrabble board and the letters scat- 147
tered all over the floor.

"We can't do much about picking them up," she said. "If either 148
one of us bends over we black out." That was true.

"Useless old crocks, aren't we?" said Mrs. Cross. Her voice was 149
under better control now.

"We won't try. When the girl comes in with the juice I'll ask 150
her to do it. We don't need to say how it happened. That's what
we'll do. We won't bend over and end up smashing our noses."

Mrs. Cross felt her heart give a big flop. Her heart was like 151
an old crippled crow, flopping around in her chest. She crossed
her hands there, to hold it.

"Well, I never told you, I don't think I did," said Mrs. Kidd, 152
with her eyes on Mrs. Cross's face. "I never told you what happened that time I got out of bed too fast in my apartment, and I
fell over on my face. I blacked out. Fortunately the woman was
home, in the apartment underneath me, and she heard the crash
and got the whatyamacallit, the man with the keys, the superin-
tendent. They came and found me out cold and took me in the
ambulance. I don't remember a thing about it. I can't remember
anything that happened throughout the next three weeks. I wasn't
unconscious. I wish I had been. I was conscious and saying a lot
of foolish things. Do you know the first thing I remember? The
psychiatrist coming to see me! They had got a psychiatrist in to
determine whether I was loony. But nobody told me he was a
psychiatrist. That's part of it, they don't tell you. He had a thing
like an army jacket on. He was quite young. So I thought he was
just some fellow who had walked in off the street.

"'What is the name of the Prime Minister?' he said to me. 153

"Well! I thought *he* was loony. So I said, 'Who cares?' And I 154
turned my back on him as if I was going to sleep, and from that
time on I remember everything."

155 *"Who cares!"*

156 As a matter of fact, Mrs. Cross had heard Mrs. Kidd tell this story before, but it was a long time ago and she laughed now not just to be obliging; she laughed with relief. Mrs. Kidd's firm voice had spread a numbing ointment over her misery.

157 Out of their combined laughter, Mrs. Kidd shot a quick serious question.

158 "Are you all right?"

159 Mrs. Cross lifted her hands from her chest, waited.

160 "I think so. Yes. But I think I'll go and lie down."

161 In this exchange it was understood that Mrs. Kidd also said, "Your heart is weak, you shouldn't put it at the mercy of these emotions," and Mrs. Cross replied, "I will do as I do, though there may be something in what you say."

162 "You haven't got your chair," Mrs. Kidd said. Mrs. Cross was sitting on an ordinary chair. She had come here walking slowly behind Jack's chair, to help him steer.

163 "I can walk," she said. "I can walk if I take my time."

164 "No. You ride. You get in my chair and I'll push you."

165 "You can't do that."

166 "Yes I can. If I don't use my energy I'll get mad about my Scrabble game."

167 Mrs. Cross heaved herself up and into Mrs. Kidd's wheelchair. As she did so she felt such weakness in her legs that she knew Mrs. Kidd was right. She couldn't have walked ten feet.

168 "Now then," said Mrs. Kidd, and she negotiated their way out of the room into the corridor.

169 "Don't strain yourself. Don't try to go too fast.

170 "No."

171 They proceeded down the corridor, turned left, made their way successfully up a very gentle ramp. Mrs. Cross could hear Mrs. Kidd's breathing.

172 "Maybe I can manage the rest by myself.

173 "No you can't."

174 They made another left turn at the top of the ramp. Now Mrs. Cross's room was in sight. It was three doors ahead of them.

175 "What I am going to do now," said Mrs. Kidd, with emphasis and pauses to hide her breathlessness, "is give you a push. I can give you a push that will take you exactly to your own door."

"Can you?" said Mrs. Cross doubtfully.   176

"Certainly. Then you can turn yourself in and get on the bed   177
and take your time to get yourself settled, then ring for the girl
and get her to deliver the chair back to me.

"You won't bash me into anything?"   178

"You watch."   179

With that Mrs. Kidd gave the wheelchair a calculated, deli-   180
cately balanced push. It rolled forward smoothly and came to a
stop just where she had said it would, in exactly the right place
in front of Mrs. Cross's door. Mrs. Cross had hastily raised her
feet and hands for this last bit of the ride. Now she dropped them.
She gave a single, satisfied, conceding nod and turned and glided
safely into her own room.

Mrs. Kidd, as soon as Mrs. Cross was out of sight, sank down   181
and sat with her back against the wall, her legs stuck straight out
in front of her on the cool linoleum. She prayed no nosy person
would come along until she could recover her strength and get
started on the trip back.

John Updike

◄{ 1 9 3 2 - }►

*Updike's prolific output of fiction, essays, poetry, and literary/
social criticism repeatedly engages religious concerns, often with a
Protestant sensibility. Influenced in early life by Søren Kierkegaard's
Christian existentialism and by Karl Barth's neo-orthodoxy, Updike
has created a succession of fictional characters who struggle to
achieve or maintain Christian faith in the face of profound personal
sin, doubt-inducing mentors, and the rampant hedonism of the
20th century. To lose faith, for Updike, is to lose a basis for action.
"I've felt in myself and in those around me a failure of nerve – a
sense of doubt as to the worth of any action," the author has said
in a* Life *interview. "At such times one has nothing but the ancient
assertions of Christianity to give one the will to act, even if the
act is only the bringing in of the milk bottles off the front porch." A
New England native, Updike seems especially concerned with the
fate of the Puritan mentality in post-Christian America. He was
awarded the Pulitzer Prize for* Rabbit Is Rich *in 1982, and again
for* Rabbit at Rest *in 1991. A recent novel,* In the Beauty of the Lilies
*(1996), demonstrates once again the writer's concern with crises of
faith. "Pigeon Feathers" appeared in Updike's second collection of
short stories, published in 1962.*

PIGEON FEATHERS

1 WHEN THEY MOVED TO FIRETOWN, things were upset, dis-
placed, rearranged. A red cane-back sofa that had been the
chief piece in the living room at Olinger was here banished, too big
for the narrow country parlor, to the barn, and shrouded under a
tarpaulin. Never again would David lie on its length all afternoon
eating raisins and reading mystery novels and science fiction and
P. G. Wodehouse.* The blue wing chair that had stood for years in

P. G. Wodehouse ·
English-born writer
(1881–1975), best
known as the creator
of Jeeves, the supreme
"gentleman's gentleman"

327

the ghostly, immaculate guest bedroom, gazing through the windows curtained with dotted swiss toward the telephone wires and horse-chestnut trees and opposite houses, was here established importantly in front of the smutty little fireplace that supplied, in those first cold April days, their only heat. As a child, David had been afraid of the guest bedroom – it was there that he, lying sick with the measles, had seen a black rod the size of a yardstick jog along at a slight slant beside the edge of the bed and vanish when he screamed – and it was disquieting to have one of the elements of its haunted atmosphere basking by the fire, in the center of the family, growing sooty with use. The books that at home had gathered dust in the case beside the piano were here hastily stacked, all out of order, in the shelves that the carpenters had built along one wall below the deep-silled windows. David, at fourteen, had been more moved than a mover; like the furniture, he had to find a new place, and on the Saturday of the second week he tried to work off some of his disorientation by arranging the books.

It was a collection obscurely depressing to him, mostly books his mother had acquired when she was young: college anthologies of Greek plays and Romantic poetry, Will Durant's *Story of Philosophy,*· a soft-leather set of Shakespeare with string bookmarks sewed to the bindings, *Green Mansions*· boxed and illustrated with woodcuts, *I, the Tiger,* by Manuel Komroff,· novels by names like Galsworthy· and Ellen Glasgow· and Irvin S. Cobb· and Sinclair Lewis· and "Elizabeth."· The odor of faded taste made him feel the ominous gap between himself and his parents, the insulting gulf of time that existed before he was born. Suddenly he was tempted to dip into this time. From the heaps of books piled around him on the worn old floorboards, he picked up Volume II of a four-volume set of *The Outline of History,* by H. G. Wells.· Once David had read *The Time Machine*· in an anthology; this gave him a small grip on the author. The book's red binding had faded to orange-pink on the spine. When he lifted the cover, there was a sweetish, attic-like smell, and his mother's maiden name written in unfamiliar handwriting on the flyleaf – an upright, bold, yet careful signature, bearing a faint relation to the quick scrunched backslant that flowed with marvellous consistency across her shopping lists and budget accounts and Christmas cards to college friends from this same, vaguely menacing long ago.

Will Durant's *Story of Philosophy*· popular reference book by the American writer (1885–1981)

Green Mansions· romantic novel by English author and naturalist W. H. Hudson (1841–1922)

I, The Tiger, by Manuel Komroff· novel from a tiger's perspective first published in 1933 by the American author (1890–1974)

Galsworthy· John Galsworthy (1867–1933), English novelist and playwright

Ellen Glasgow· American novelist (1873–1945)

Irvin S. Cobb· American writer and humorist (1876–1944)

Sinclair Lewis· American novelist and social critic (1885–1951)

"Elizabeth"· penname of English author Mary Annette, Countess Russell (1866–1941)

The Outline of History, by H. G. Wells· first published in 1920, a text promoting the theory of social evolution touted by the English author and atheist (1866–1946)

The Time Machine· Wells' post-apocalyptic first novel published in 1895

3   He leafed through, pausing at drawings, done in an old-fashioned stippled style, of bas-reliefs,* masks, Romans without pupils in their eyes, articles of ancient costume, fragments of pottery found in unearthed homes. He knew it would be interesting in a magazine, sandwiched between ads and jokes, but in this undiluted form history was somehow sour. The print was determinedly legible, and smug, like a lesson book. As he bent over the pages, yellow at the edges, they seemed rectangles of dusty glass through which he looked down into unreal and irrelevant worlds. He could see things sluggishly move, and an unpleasant fullness came into his throat. His mother and grandmother fussed in the kitchen; the puppy, which they had just acquired, for "protection in the country," was cowering, with a sporadic panicked scrabble of claws, under the dining table that in their old home had been reserved for special days but that here was used for every meal.

bas-reliefs · a form of sculpture, often on plaques or walls, in which the design is raised slightly from the background

4   Then, before he could halt his eyes, David slipped into Wells's account of Jesus. He had been an obscure political agitator, a kind of hobo, in a minor colony of the Roman Empire. By an accident impossible to construct, he (the small *h* horrified David) survived his own crucifixion and presumably died a few weeks later. A religion was founded on the freakish incident. The credulous imagination of the times retrospectively assigned miracles and supernatural pretensions to Jesus; a myth grew, and then a church, whose theology at most points was in direct contradiction of the simple, rather communistic teachings of the Galilean.

5   It was as if a stone that for weeks and even years had been gathering weight in the web of David's nerves snapped them and plunged through the page and a hundred layers of paper underneath. These fantastic falsehoods – plainly untrue; churches stood everywhere, the entire nation was founded "under God"– did not at first frighten him; it was the fact that they had been permitted to exist in an actual human brain. This was the initial impact – that at a definite spot in time and space a brain black with the denial of Christ's divinity had been suffered to exist; that the universe had not spit out this ball of tar but allowed it to continue in its blasphemy, to grow old, win honors, wear a hat, write books that, if true, collapsed everything into a jumble of horror. The world outside the deep-silled windows – a rutted lawn, a whitewashed barn, a walnut tree frothy with fresh green – seemed a haven from

which he was forever sealed off. Hot washrags seemed pressed 5
against his cheeks.

He read the account again. He tried to supply out of his igno- 6
rance objections that would defeat the complacent march of these
black words, and found none. Survivals and misunderstandings
more far-fetched were reported daily in the papers. But none
of them caused churches to be built in every town. He tried to
work backwards through the churches, from their brave high
fronts through their shabby, ill attended interiors back into the
events at Jerusalem, and felt himself surrounded by shifting gray
shadows, centuries of history, where he knew nothing. The thread
dissolved in his hands. Had Christ ever come to him, David Kern,
and said, "Here. Feel the wound in My side"?* No; but prayers had
been answered. What prayers? He had prayed that Rudy Mohn,
whom he had purposely tripped so he cracked his head on their
radiator, not die, and he had not died. But for all the blood, it
was just a cut; Rudy came back the same day, wearing a bandage
and repeating the same teasing words. He could never have died.
Again, David had prayed for two separate war-effort posters he
had sent away for to arrive tomorrow, and though they did not,
they did arrive, some days later, together, popping through the
clacking letter slot like a rebuke from God's mouth: *I answer your
prayers in My way, in My time.* After that, he had made his prayers
less definite, less susceptible of being twisted into a scolding. But
what a tiny, ridiculous coincidence this was, after all, to throw
into battle against H. G. Wells's engines of knowledge! Indeed, it
proved the enemy's point: Hope bases vast premises on foolish
accidents, and reads a word where in fact only a scribble exists.

His father came home. Though Saturday was a free day for him, 7
he had been working. He taught school in Olinger and spent all
his days performing, with a curious air of panic, needless errands.
Also, a city boy by birth, he was frightened of the farm and seized
any excuse to get away. The farm had been David's mother's
birthplace; it had been her idea to buy it back. With an ingenuity
and persistence unparalleled in her life, she had gained that end,
and moved them all here – her son, her husband, her mother.
Granmom, in her prime, had worked these fields alongside her
husband, but now she dabbled around the kitchen futilely, her
hands waggling with Parkinson's disease. She was always in the

"Here ... My side" ·
see John 20:25-29

7 way. Strange, out in the country, amid eighty acres, they were crowded together. His father expressed his feelings of discomfort by conducting with Mother an endless argument about organic farming. All through dusk, all through supper, it rattled on.

8 "Elsie, I know, I know from my education, the earth is nothing but chemicals. It's the only damn thing I got out of four years of college, so don't tell me it's not true."

9 "George, if you'd just walk out on the farm you'd know it's not true. The land has a *soul*."

10 "Soil, has, no, soul," he said, enunciating stiffly, as if to a very stupid class. To David he said, "You can't argue with a *femme.*˙ Your mother's a real *femme*. That's why I married her, and now I'm suffering for it."

femme · "woman" (French), here used as a superlative

11 "*This* soil has no soul," she said, "because it's been killed with superphosphate.˙ It's been burned bare by Boyer's tenant farmers." Boyer was the rich man they had bought the farm from. "It used to have a soul, didn't it, Mother? When you and Pop farmed it?"

superphosphate · a kind of liquid fertilizer

12 "Ach, yes; I guess." Granmom was trying to bring a forkful of food to her mouth with her less severely afflicted hand. In her anxiety she brought the other hand up from her lap. The crippled fingers, dull red in the orange light of the kerosene lamp in the center of the table, were welded by paralysis into one knobbed hook.

13 "Only human indi-vidu-als have souls," his father went on, in the same mincing, lifeless voice. "Because the Bible tells us so." Done eating, he crossed his legs and dug into his ear with a match miserably; to get at the thing inside his head he tucked in his chin, and his voice came out low-pitched at David. "When God made your mother, He made a real *femme*."

14 "George, don't you read the papers? Don't you know that between the chemical fertilizers and the bug sprays we'll all be dead in ten years? Heart attacks are killing every man in the country over forty-five."

15 He sighed wearily; the yellow skin of his eyelids wrinkled as he hurt himself with the match. "There's no connection," he stated, spacing his words with pained patience, "between the heart – and chemical fertilizers. It's alcohol that's doing it. Alcohol and milk. There is too much – cholesterol – in the tissues of the American heart. Don't tell me about chemistry, Elsie; I majored in the damn stuff for four years."

"Yes and I majored in Greek and I'm not a penny wiser. Mother, 16 put your waggler a*way*!" The old woman started, and the food dropped from her fork. For some reason, the sight of her bad hand at the table cruelly irritated her daughter. Granmom's eyes, worn bits of crazed crystal embedded in watery milk, widened behind her cockeyed spectacles. Circles of silver as fine as thread, they clung to the red notches they had carved over the years into her little white beak. In the orange flicker of the kerosene lamp her dazed misery seemed infernal. David's mother began, without noise, to cry. His father did not seem to have eyes at all; just jaundiced sockets of wrinkled skin. The steam of food clouded the scene. It was horrible but the horror was particular and familiar, and distracted David from the formless dread that worked, sticky and sore, within him, like a too large wound trying to heal.

He had to go to the bathroom, and took a flashlight down 17 through the wet grass to the outhouse. For once, his fear of spiders there felt trivial. He set the flashlight, burning, beside him, and an insect alighted on its lens, a tiny insect, a mosquito or flea, made so fine that the weak light projected its x-ray onto the wall boards: the faint rim of its wings, the blurred strokes, magnified, of its long hinged legs, the dark cone at the heart of its anatomy. The tremor must be its heart beating. Without warning, David was visited by an exact vision of death: a long hole in the ground, no wider than your body, down which you are drawn while the white faces above recede. You try to reach them but your arms are pinned. Shovels pour dirt into your face. There you will be forever, in an upright position, blind and silent, and in time no one will remember you, and you will never be called. As strata of rock shift, your fingers elongate, and your teeth are distended sideways in a great underground grimace indistinguishable from a strip of chalk. And the earth tumbles on, and the sun expires, and unaltering darkness reigns where once there were stars.

Sweat broke out on his back. His mind seemed to rebound off 18 a solidness. Such extinction was not another threat, a graver sort of danger, a kind of pain; it was qualitatively different. It was not even a conception that could be voluntarily pictured; it entered him from outside. His protesting nerves swarmed on its surface like lichen on a meteor. The skin of his chest was soaked with the effort of rejection. At the same time that the fear was dense

¹⁸ and internal, it was dense and all around him; a tide of clay had swept up to the stars; space was crushed into a mass. When he stood up, automatically hunching his shoulders to keep his head away from the spider webs, it was with a numb sense of being cramped between two huge volumes of rigidity. That he had even this small freedom to move surprised him. In the narrow shelter of that rank shack, adjusting his pants, he felt – his first spark of comfort – too small to be crushed.

¹⁹ But in the open, as the beam of the flashlight skidded with frightened quickness across the remote surfaces of the barn and the grape arbor and the giant pine that stood by the path to the woods, the terror descended. He raced up through the clinging grass pursued, not by one of the wild animals the woods might hold, or one of the goblins his superstitious grandmother had communicated to his childhood, but by spectres out of science fiction, where gigantic cinder moons fill half the turquoise sky. As David ran, a gray planet rolled inches behind his neck. If he looked back, he would be buried. And in the momentum of his terror, hideous possibilities – the dilation of the sun, the triumph of the insects, the crabs on the shore in *The Time Machine* – wheeled out of the vacuum of make-believe and added their weight to his impending oblivion.

²⁰ He wrenched the door open; the lamps within the house flared. The wicks burning here and there seemed to mirror one another. His mother was washing the dishes in a little pan of heated pump-water; Granmom fluttered near her elbow apprehensively. In the living room – the downstairs of the little square house was two long rooms – his father sat in front of the black fireplace restlessly folding and unfolding a newspaper as he sustained his half of the argument. "Nitrogen, phosphorus, potash: these are the three replaceable constituents of the soil. One crop of corn carries away hundreds of pounds of"– he dropped the paper into his lap and ticked them off on three fingers –"nitrogen, phosphorus, potash."

²¹ "Boyer didn't grow corn."

²² "*Any* crop, Elsie. The human animal –"

²³ "You're killing the *earth*worms, George!"

²⁴ "The human animal, after thousands and *thou*sands of years, learned methods whereby the chemical balance of the soil may be maintained. Don't carry me back to the Dark Ages."

"When we moved to Olinger the ground in the garden was 25 like slate. Just one summer of my cousin's chicken dung and the earthworms came back."

•

"I'm sure the Dark Ages were a fine place to the poor devils 26 born in them, but I don't want to go there. They give me the creeps." Daddy stared into the cold pit of the fireplace and clung to the rolled newspaper in his lap as if it alone were keeping him from slipping backwards and down, down.

Mother came into the doorway brandishing a fistful of wet 27 forks. "And thanks to your DDT* there soon won't be a bee left in the country. When I was a girl here you could eat a peach without washing it."

DDT · an insecticide banned for most uses in the United States since 1972 because of its harmful effects on the ecosystem

"It's primitive, Elsie. It's Dark Age stuff." 28

"Oh what do *you* know about the Dark Ages?" 29

"I know I don't want to go back to them." 30

David took from the shelf, where he had placed it this 31 afternoon, the great unabridged Webster's Dictionary that his grandfather had owned. He turned the big thin pages, floppy as cloth, to the entry he wanted, and read

> soul … I. An entity conceived as the essence, substance, 31a
> animating principle, or actuating cause of life, or of the
> individual life, esp. of life manifested in psychical activities;
> the vehicle of individual existence, separate in nature from
> the body and usually held to be separable in existence.

The definition went on, into Greek and Egyptian conceptions, 32 but David stopped short on the treacherous edge of antiquity. He needed to read no further. The careful overlapping words shingled a temporary shelter for him. "Usually held to be separable in existence"—what could be fairer, more judicious, surer?

His father was saying, "The modern farmer can't go around 33 sweeping up after his cows. The poor devil has thousands and *thou*sands of acres on his hands. Your modern farmer uses a scientifically-arrived-at mixture, like five-ten-five, or six-twelve-six, or *three*-twelve-six,* and spreads it on with this wonderful modern machinery which of course we can't afford. Your modern farmer can't *afford* medieval methods."

five-ten-five … **three**-**twelve-six** · formulations for fertilizers

Mother was quiet in the kitchen; her silence radiated waves 34 of anger.

35   "No now Elsie; don't play the *femme* with me. Let's discuss this calmly like two rational twentieth-century people. Your organic farming nuts aren't attacking five-ten-five; they're attacking the chemical fertilizer crooks. The monster firms."

36   A cup clinked in the kitchen. Mother's anger touched David's face; his cheeks burned guiltily. Just by being in the living room he was associated with his father. She appeared in the doorway with red hands and tears in her eyes, and said to the two of them, "I knew you didn't want to come here but I didn't know you'd torment me like this. You talked Pop into his grave and now you'll kill me. Go ahead, George, more power to you; at least I'll be buried in good ground." She tried to turn and met an obstacle and screamed, "Mother, stop hanging on my *back*! Why don't you go to *bed?*"

37   "Let's all go to bed," David's father said, rising from the blue wing chair and slapping his thigh with a newspaper. "This reminds me of death." It was a phrase of his that David had heard so often he never considered its sense.

38   Upstairs, he seemed to be lifted above his fears. The sheets on his bed were clean. Granmom had ironed them with a pair of flatirons saved from the Olinger attic; she plucked them hot off the stove alternately, with a wooden handle called a goose. It was a wonder, to see how she managed. In the next room, his parents grunted peaceably; they seemed to take their quarrels less seriously than he did. They made comfortable scratching noises as they carried a little lamp back and forth. Their door was open a crack, so he saw the light shift and swing. Surely there would be, in the last five minutes, in the last second, a crack of light, showing the door from the dark room to another, full of light. Thinking of it this vividly frightened him. His own dying, in a specific bed in a specific room, specific walls mottled with wallpaper, the dry whistle of his breathing, the murmuring doctors, the nervous relatives going in and out, but for him no way out but down into the funnel. *Never touch a doorknob again.* A whisper, and his parents' light was blown out. David prayed to be reassured. Though the experiment frightened him, he lifted his hands high into the darkness above his face and begged Christ to touch them. Not hard or long: the faintest, quickest grip would be final for a lifetime. His hands waited in the air, itself a

substance, which seemed to move through his fingers; or was it   38
the pressure of his pulse? He returned his hands to beneath the
covers uncertain if they had been touched or not. For would not
Christ's touch *be* infinitely gentle?

Through all the eddies of its aftermath, David clung to this   39
thought about his revelation of extinction: that there, in the
outhouse, he had struck a solidness qualitatively different, a
rock of horror firm enough to support any height of construction. All he needed was a little help; a word, a gesture, a nod of
certainty, and he would be sealed in, safe. The assurance from the
dictionary had melted in the night. Today was Sunday, a hot fair
day. Across a mile of clear air the church bells called, *Celebrate,
celebrate.* Only Daddy went. He put on a coat over his rolled-up
shirtsleeves and got into the little old black Plymouth parked by
the barn and went off, with the same pained hurried grimness
of all his actions. His churning wheels, as he shifted too hastily
into second, raised plumes of red dust on the dirt road. Mother
walked to the far field, to see what bushes needed cutting. David,
though he usually preferred to stay in the house, went with her.
The puppy followed at a distance, whining as it picked its way
through the stubble but floundering off timidly if one of them
went back to pick it up and carry it. When they reached the crest
of the far field, his mother asked, "David, what's troubling you?"

"Nothing. Why?"   40

She looked at him sharply. The greening woods cross-hatched   41
the space beyond her half-gray hair. Then she showed him her
profile, and gestured toward the house, which they had left a
half-mile behind them. "See how it sits in the land? They don't
know how to build with the land any more. Pop always said the
foundations were set with the compass. We must try to get a
compass and see. It's supposed to face due south; but south feels
a little more *that* way to me." From the side, as she said these
things, she seemed handsome and young. The smooth sweep of
her hair over her ear seemed white with a purity and calm that
made her feel foreign to him. He had never regarded his parents
as consolers of his troubles; from the beginning they had seemed
to have more troubles than he. Their confusion had flattered
him into an illusion of strength; so now on this high clear ridge
he jealously guarded the menace all around them, blowing like

41 a breeze on his fingertips, the possibility of all this wide scenery sinking into darkness. The strange fact that though she came to look at the brush she carried no clippers, for she had a fixed prejudice against working on Sundays, was the only consolation he allowed her to offer.

42 As they walked back, the puppy whimpering after them, the rising dust behind a distant line of trees announced that Daddy was speeding home from church. When they reached the house he was there. He had brought back the Sunday paper and the vehement remark, "Dobson's too intelligent for these farmers. They just sit there with their mouths open and don't hear a thing the poor devil's saying."

43 "What makes you think farmers are unintelligent? This country was made by farmers. George Washington was a farmer."

44 "They are, Elsie. They are unintelligent. George Washington's dead. In this day and age only the misfits stay on the farm. The lame, the halt, the blind. The morons with one arm. Human garbage. They remind me of death, sitting there with their mouths open."

45 "My *father* was a farmer."

46 "He was a frustrated man, Elsie. He never knew what hit him. The poor devil meant so well, and he never knew which end was up. Your mother'll bear me out. Isn't that right, Mom? Pop never knew what hit him?"

47 "Ach, I guess not," the old woman quavered, and the ambiguity for the moment silenced both sides.

48 David hid in the funny papers and sports section until one-thirty. At two, the catechetical class met at the Firetown church. He had transferred from the catechetical class of the Lutheran church in Olinger, a humiliating comedown. In Olinger they met on Wednesday nights, spiffy and spruce,* in the atmosphere of a dance. Afterwards, blessed by the brick-faced minister from whose lips the word "Christ" fell like a burning stone, the more daring of them went with their Bibles to a luncheonette and smoked. Here in Firetown, the girls were dull white cows and the boys narrow-faced brown goats in old men's suits, herded on Sunday afternoons into a threadbare church basement that smelled of stale hay. Because his father had taken the car on one of his endless errands to Olinger, David walked, grateful for the open air and the silence. The catechetical class embarrassed

spruce · neat in appearance

him, but today he placed hope in it, as the source of the nod, the 48
gesture, that was all he needed.

Reverend Dobson was a delicate young man with great dark 49
eyes and small white shapely hands that flickered like protesting doves when he preached; he seemed a bit misplaced in the
Lutheran ministry. This was his first call. It was a split parish; he
served another rural church twelve miles away. His iridescent
green Ford, new six months ago, was spattered to the windows
with red mud and rattled from bouncing on the rude back roads,
where he frequently got lost, to the malicious satisfaction of many.
But David's mother liked him, and, more pertinent to his success,
the Haiers, the sleek family of feed merchants and innkeepers
and tractor salesmen who dominated the Firetown church, liked
him. David liked him, and felt liked in turn; sometimes in class,
after some special stupidity, Dobson directed toward him out of
those wide black eyes a mild look of disbelief, a look that, though
flattering, was also delicately disquieting.

Catechetical instruction consisted of reading aloud from a 50
work booklet answers to problems prepared during the week,
I am ... Lord · John 14:6   problems like, "'I am the _____, the _____, and the _____,'
saith the Lord.'" Then there was a question period in which no
one ever asked any questions. Today's theme was the last third of
Apostles' Creed · a   the Apostles' Creed.' When the time came for questions, David
statement of faith   blushed and asked, "About the Resurrection of the Body – are we
developed between the   conscious between the time when we die and the Day of Judgment?"
2nd and 9th centuries
and used throughout   Dobson blinked, and his fine little mouth pursed, suggest- 51
the Western church   ing that David was making difficult things more difficult. The
faces of the other students went blank, as if an indiscretion had
been committed.

"No, I suppose not," Reverend Dobson said. 52

"Well, where is our soul, then, in this gap?" 53

The sense grew, in the class, of a naughtiness occurring. 54
Dobson's shy eyes watered, as if he were straining to keep up the
simpered · to smile in   formality of attention, and one of the girls, the fattest, simpered'
a foolish or affected way   toward her twin, who was a little less fat. Their chairs were
arranged in a rough circle. The current running around the circle
panicked David. Did everybody know something he didn't know?

"I suppose you could say our souls are asleep," Dobson said. 55

56 "And then they wake up, and there is the earth like it always is, and all the people who have ever lived? Where will Heaven be?"

57 Anita Haier giggled. Dobson gazed at David intently, but with an awkward, puzzled flicker of forgiveness, as if there existed a secret between them that David was violating. But David knew of no secret. All he wanted was to hear Dobson repeat the words he said every Sunday morning. This he would not do. As if these words were unworthy of the conversational voice.

58 "David, you might think of Heaven this way: as the way the goodness Abraham Lincoln did lives after him."

59 "But is Lincoln conscious of it living on?" He blushed no longer with embarrassment but in anger; he had walked here in good faith and was being made a fool.

60 "Is he conscious now? I would have to say no; but I don't think it matters." His voice had a coward's firmness; he was hostile now.

61 "You don't."

62 "Not in the eyes of God, no." The unction,* the stunning impudence, of this reply sprang tears of outrage in David's eyes. He bowed them to his book, where short words like Duty, Love, Obey, Honor, were stacked in the form of a cross.

unction · exaggerated or superficial earnestness, condescension

63 "Were there any other questions, David?" Dobson asked with renewed gentleness. The others were rustling, collecting their books.

64 "No." He made his voice firm, though he could not bring up his eyes.

65 "Did I answer your question fully enough?"

66 "Yes."

67 In the minister's silence the shame that should have been his crept over David: the burden and fever of being a fraud were placed upon *him*, who was innocent, and it seemed, he knew, a confession of this guilt that on the way out he was unable to face Dobson's stirred gaze, though he felt it probing the side of his head.

68 Anita Haier's father gave him a ride down the highway as far as the dirt road. David said he wanted to walk the rest, and figured that his offer was accepted because Mr. Haier did not want to dirty his bright blue Buick with dust. This was all right; everything was all right, as long as it was clear. His indignation at being betrayed, at seeing Christianity betrayed, had hardened him. The straight dirt road reflected his hardness. Pink stones thrust up through its packed surface. The April sun beat down from the center of

the afternoon half of the sky; already it had some of summer's 68
heat. Already the fringes of weeds at the edges of the road were
bedraggled with dust. From the reviving grass and scruff of the
fields he walked between, insects were sending up a monotonous,
automatic chant. In the distance a tiny figure in his father's coat was
walking along the edge of the woods. His mother. He wondered
what joy she found in such walks; to him the brown stretches of
slowly rising and falling land expressed only a huge exhaustion.

Flushed with fresh air and happiness, she returned from her walk 69
earlier than he had expected, and surprised him at his grandfather's
Bible. It was a stumpy black book, the boards worn thin where the
old man's fingers had held them; the spine hung by one weak hinge
of fabric. David had been looking for the passage where Jesus says to
the one thief on the cross, "Today shalt thou be with me in paradise."•
He had never tried reading the Bible for himself before. What was
so embarrassing about being caught at it, was that he detested the
apparatus of piety. Fusty• churches, creaking hymns, ugly Sunday-
school teachers and their stupid leaflets – he hated everything about
them but the promise they held out, a promise that in the most
perverse way, as if the homeliest crone in the kingdom were given
the Prince's hand, made every good and real thing, ball games and
jokes and pert-breasted girls, possible. He couldn't explain this to
his mother. There was no time. Her solicitude was upon him.

"David, what are you doing?" 70

"Nothing." 71

"What are you doing at Grandpop's Bible?" 72

"Trying to read it. This is supposed to be a Christian country, 73
isn't it?"

She sat down on the green sofa, which used to be in the sun 74
parlor at Olinger, under the fancy mirror. A little smile still lingered on her face from the walk.

"David, I wish you'd talk to me." 75

"What about?" 76

"About whatever it is that's troubling you. Your father and I 77
have both noticed it."

"I asked Reverend Dobson about Heaven and he said it was 78
like Abraham Lincoln's goodness living after him."

He waited for the shock to strike her. "Yes?" she said, expect- 79
ing more.

"Today ... paradise"•
Luke 23:43

Fusty • dusty and smelly
or rigidly conservative
and old-fashioned

80   "That's all."

81   "And why didn't you like it?"

82   "Well, don't you see? It amounts to saying there isn't any Heaven at all."

83   "I don't see that it amounts to that. What do you want Heaven to be?"

84   "Well, I don't know. I want it to be *some*thing. I thought he'd tell me what it was. I thought that was his job." He was becoming angry, sensing her surprise at him. She had assumed that Heaven had faded from his head years ago. She had imagined that he had already entered, in the secrecy of silence, the conspiracy that he now knew to be all around him.

85   "David," she asked gently, "don't you ever want to rest?"

86   "No. Not forever."

87   "David, you're so young. When you get older, you'll feel differently."

88   "Grandpa didn't. Look how tattered this book is."

89   "I never understood your grandfather."

90   "Well I don't understand ministers who say it's like Lincoln's goodness going on and on. Suppose you're not Lincoln?"

91   "I think Reverend Dobson made a mistake. You must try to forgive him."

92   "It's not a *question* of his making a mistake! It's a question of dying and never moving or seeing or hearing anything ever again."

93   "But" – in exasperation – "darling, it's so *greedy* of you to want more. When God has given us this wonderful April day, and given us this farm, and you have your whole life ahead of you –"

94   "You think, then, that there is God?"

95   "Of course I do" – with deep relief, that smoothed her features into a reposeful oval. He had risen and was standing too near her for his comfort. He was afraid she would reach out and touch him.

   "He made everything? You feel that?"

96   "Yes."

97   "Then who made Him?"

98   "Why, Man. Man." The happiness of this answer lit up her face

99 radiantly, until she saw his gesture of disgust. She was so simple, so illogical; such a *femme*.

100   "Well that amounts to saying there is none."

Her hand reached for his wrist but he backed away. "David, 101
it's a mystery. A miracle. It's a miracle more beautiful than any
Reverend Dobson could have told you about. You don't say houses
don't exist because Man made them."

"No. God has to be different." 102

"But, David, you have the *evidence*. Look out the window at 103
the sun; at the fields."

"Mother, good grief. Don't you see"– he rasped away the 104
roughness in his throat –"if when we die there's nothing, all
your sun and fields and what not are all, ah, *horror*? It's just an
ocean of horror."

"But David, it's not. It's so clearly not that." And she made an 105
urgent opening gesture with her hands that expressed, with its
suggestion of a willingness to receive his helplessness, all her
grace, her gentleness, her love of beauty, gathered into a passive
intensity that made him intensely hate her. He would not be
wooed away from the truth. *I am the Way, the Truth....* •

I am ... Truth.... •
John 14:6

"No," he told her. "Just let me alone." 106

He found his tennis ball behind the piano and went outside 107
to throw it against the side of the house. There was a patch high
up where the brown stucco that had been laid over the sandstone
masonry was crumbling away; he kept trying with the tennis ball
to chip more pieces off. Superimposed upon his deep ache was a
smaller but more immediate worry; that he had hurt his mother.
He heard his father's car rattling on the straightaway, and went
into the house, to make peace before he arrived. To his relief, she
was not giving off the stifling damp heat of her anger, but instead
was cool, decisive, maternal. She handed him an old green book,
her college text of Plato. •

Plato · Greek philosopher
(428/7–348/7 BC)

Parable of the Cave ·
Plato's allegory argues
that the spiritual realm
constitutes ultimate
reality while the mate-
rial realm is an inferior
reflection of it

"I want you to read the Parable of the Cave," • she said. 108

"All right," he said, though he knew it would do no good. Some 109
story by a dead Greek just vague enough to please her. "Don't
worry about it, Mother."

"I *am* worried. Honestly, David, I'm sure there will be some- 110
thing for us. As you get older, these things seem to matter a
great deal less."

"That may be. It's a dismal thought, though." 111

His father bumped at the door. The locks and jambs stuck 112
here. But before Granmom could totter to the latch and let him

112 in, he had knocked it open. He had been in Olinger dithering with track meet tickets. Although Mother usually kept her talks with David a confidence, a treasure between them, she called instantly, "George, David is worried about death!"

113 He came to the doorway of the living room, his shirt pocket bristling with pencils, holding in one hand a pint box of melting ice cream and in the other the knife with which he was about to divide it into four sections, their Sunday treat. "Is the kid worried about death? Don't give it a thought, David. I'll be lucky if I live till tomorrow, and I'm not worried. If they'd taken a buckshot gun and shot me in the cradle I'd be better off. The *world*'d be better off. Hell, I think death is a wonderful thing. I look forward to it. Get the garbage out of the way. If I had the man here who invented death, I'd pin a medal on him."

114 "Hush, George. You'll frighten the child worse than he is."

115 This was not true; he never frightened David. There was no harm in his father, no harm at all. Indeed, in the man's steep self-disgust the boy felt a kind of ally. A distant ally. He saw his position with a certain strategic coldness. Nowhere in the world of other people would he find the hint, the nod, he needed to begin to build his fortress against death. They none of them believed. He was alone. In that deep hole.

116 In the months that followed, his position changed little. School was some comfort. All those sexy, perfumed people, wisecracking, chewing gum, all of them doomed to die, and none of them noticing. In their company David felt that they would carry him along into the bright, cheap paradise reserved for them. In any crowd, the fear ebbed a little; he had reasoned that somewhere in the world there must exist a few people who believed what was necessary, and the larger the crowd, the greater the chance that he was near such a soul, within calling distance, if only he was not too ignorant, too ill-equipped, to spot him. The sight of clergymen cheered him; whatever they themselves thought, their collars were still a sign that somewhere, at some time, someone had recognized that we cannot, *cannot*, submit to death. The sermon topics posted outside churches, the flip, hurried pieties of disc jockeys, the cartoons in magazines showing angels or devils – on such scraps he kept alive the possibility of hope.

For the rest, he tried to drown his hopelessness in clatter and 117
jostle. The pinball machine at the luncheonette was a merciful
distraction; as he bent over its buzzing, flashing board of flippers
and cushions, the weight and constriction in his chest lightened
and loosened. He was grateful for all the time his father wasted
in Olinger. Every delay postponed the moment when they must
ride together down the dirt road into the heart of the dark farmland, where the only light was the kerosene lamp waiting on the
dining-room table, a light that drowned their food in shadow
and made it sinister.

He lost his appetite for reading. He was afraid of being 118
ambushed again. In mystery novels people died like dolls being
discarded; in science fiction enormities of space and time con-
spired to crush the humans; and even in P. G. Wodehouse he felt a
hollowness, a turning away from reality that was implicitly bitter,
and became explicit in the comic figures of futile clergymen. All
gaiety seemed minced out on the skin of a void. All quiet hours
seemed invitations to dread.

Even on weekends, he and his father contrived to escape the 119
farm; and when, some Saturdays, they did stay home, it was to do
something destructive – tear down an old henhouse or set huge
brush fires that threatened, while Mother shouted and flapped
her arms, to spread to the woods. Whenever his father worked,
it was with rapt violence; when he chopped kindling, fragments
of the old henhouse boards flew like shrapnel and the ax-head
was always within a quarter of an inch of flying off the handle.
He was exhilarating to watch, sweating and swearing and sucking
bits of saliva back into his lips.

School stopped. His father took the car in the opposite direc- 120
tion, to a highway construction job where he had been hired
for the summer as a timekeeper, and David was stranded in the
middle of acres of heat and greenery and blowing pollen and the
strange, mechanical humming that lay invisibly in the weeds and
alfalfa and dry orchard grass.

For his fifteenth birthday his parents gave him, with jokes 121
about him being a hillbilly now, a Remington .22. It was somewhat
like a pinball machine to take it out to the old kiln in the woods
where they dumped their trash, and set up tin cans on the kiln's
sandstone shoulder and shoot them off one by one. He'd take

121 the puppy, who had grown long legs and a rich coat of reddish fur – he was part chow. Copper hated the gun but loved the boy enough to accompany him. When the flat acrid crack rang out, he would race in terrified circles that would tighten and tighten until they brought him, shivering, against David's legs. Depending upon his mood, David would shoot again or drop to his knees and comfort the dog. Giving this comfort to a degree returned comfort to him. The dog's ears, laid flat against his skull in fear, were folded so intricately, so – he groped for the concept – *surely*. Where the dull-studded collar made the fur stand up, each hair showed a root of soft white under the length, black-tipped, of the metal-color that had lent the dog its name. In his agitation Copper panted through nostrils that were elegant slits, like two healed cuts, or like the key-holes of a dainty lock of black, grained wood. His whole whorling, knotted, jointed body was a wealth of such embellishments. And in the smell of the dog's hair David seemed to descend through many finely differentiated layers of earth: mulch, soil, sand, clay, and the glittering mineral base.

122 But when he returned to the house, and saw the books arranged on the low shelves, fear returned. The four adamant volumes of Wells like four thin bricks, the green Plato that had puzzled him with its queer softness and tangled purity, the dead Galsworthy and "Elizabeth," Grandpa's mammoth dictionary, Grandpa's Bible, the Bible that he himself had received on becoming a member of the Firetown Lutheran Church – at the sight of these, the memory of his fear reawakened and came around him. He had grown stiff and stupid in its embrace. His parents tried to think of ways to entertain him.

123 "David, I have a job for you to do," his mother said one evening at the table.

124 "What?"

125 "If you're going to take that tone perhaps we'd better not talk."

126 "What tone? I don't take any tone."

127 "Your grandmother thinks there are too many pigeons in the barn."

128 "Why?" David turned to look at his grandmother, but she sat there staring at the burning lamp with her usual expression of bewilderment.

129 Mother shouted, "Mom, he wants to know why!"

Granmom made a jerky, irritable motion with her bad hand, 130 as if generating the force for utterance, and said, "They foul the furniture."

"That's right," Mother said. "She's afraid for that old Olinger 131 furniture that we'll never use. David, she's been after me for a month about those poor pigeons. She wants you to shoot them."

"I don't want to kill anything especially," David said. 132

Daddy said, "The kid's like you are, Elsie. He's too good for 133 this world. Kill or be killed, that's my motto."

His mother said loudly, "Mother, he doesn't want to do it." 134

"Not?" The old lady's eyes distended as if in horror and her 135 claw descended slowly to her lap.

"Oh, I'll do it, I'll do it tomorrow," David snapped, and a pleas- 136 ant crisp taste entered his mouth with the decision.

"And I had thought, when Boyer's men made the hay, it would 137 be better if the barn doesn't look like a rookery," his mother added needlessly.

A barn, in day, is a small night. The splinters of light between the 138 dry shingles pierce the high roof like stars, and the rafters and cross-beams and built-in ladders seem, until your eyes adjust, as mysterious as the branches of a haunted forest. David entered silently, the gun in one hand. Copper whined desperately at the door, too frightened to come in with the gun yet unwilling to leave the boy. David stealthily turned, said "Go away," shut the door on the dog, and slipped the bolt across. It was a door within a door; the double door for wagons and tractors was as high and wide as the face of a house.

The smell of old straw scratched his sinuses. The red sofa, half- 139 hidden under its white-splotched tarpaulin, seemed assimilated into this smell, sunk in it, buried. The mouths of empty bins gaped like caves. Rusty oddments of farming – coils of baling wire, some spare tines for a harrow, a handleless shovel – hung on nails driven here and there in the thick wood. He stood stock-still a minute; it took a while to separate the cooing of the pigeons from the rustling in his ears. When he had focused on the cooing, it flooded the vast interior with its throaty, bubbling outpour: there seemed no other sound. They were up behind the beams. What light there was leaked through the shingles and the dirty glass windows at the far end and the small round holes, about as big as basketballs, high on the opposite stone side walls, under the ridge of the roof.

140   A pigeon appeared in one of these holes, on the side toward the house. It flew in, with a battering of wings, from the outside, and waited there, silhouetted against its pinched bit of sky, preening and cooing in a throbbing, thrilled, tentative way. David tiptoed four steps to the side, rested his gun against the lowest rung of a ladder pegged between two upright beams, and lowered the gunsight into the bird's tiny, jauntily cocked head. The slap of the report seemed to come off the stone wall behind him, and the pigeon did not fall. Neither did it fly. Instead it stuck in the round hole, pirouetting rapidly and nodding its head as if in frantic agreement. David shot the bolt back and forth and had aimed again before the spent cartridge had stopped jingling on the boards by his feet. He eased the tip of the sight a little lower, into the bird's breast, and took care to squeeze the trigger with perfect evenness. The slow contraction of his hand abruptly sprang the bullet; for a half-second there was doubt, and then the pigeon fell like a handful of rags, skimming down the barn wall into the layer of straw that coated the floor of the mow* on this side.

141   Now others shook loose from the rafters, and whirled in the dim air with a great blurred hurtle of feathers and noise. They would go for the hole; he fixed his sight on the little moon of blue, and when a pigeon came to it, shot him as he was walking the ten inches of stone that would have carried him into the open air. This pigeon lay down in that tunnel of stone, unable to fall either one way or the other, although he was alive enough to lift one wing and cloud the light. It would sink back, and he would suddenly lift it again, the feathers flaring. His body blocked that exit. David raced to the other side of the barn's main aisle, where a similar ladder was symmetrically placed, and rested his gun on the same rung. Three birds came together to this hole; he got one, and two got through. The rest resettled in the rafters.

142   There was a shallow triangular space behind the cross beams supporting the roof. It was here they roosted and hid. But either the space was too small, or they were curious, for now that his eyes were at home in the dusty gloom, David could see little dabs of gray popping in and out. The cooing was shriller now; its apprehensive tremolo made the whole volume of air seem liquid. He noticed one little smudge of a head that was especially persistent in peeking out; he marked the place, and fixed his gun

mow · the part of a barn where hay or straw is stored

on it, and when the head appeared again, had his finger tightened 142
in advance on the trigger. A parcel of fluff slipped off the beam
and fell the barn's height onto a canvas covering some Olinger
furniture, and where its head had peeked out there was a fresh
prick of light in the shingles.

Standing in the center of the floor, fully master now, disdain- 143
ing to steady the barrel with anything but his arm, he killed two
more that way. He felt like a beautiful avenger. Out of the shadowy ragged infinity of the vast barn roof these impudent things
dared to thrust their heads, presumed to dirty its starred silence
with their filthy timorous life, and he cut them off, tucked them
back neatly into the silence. He had the sensation of a creator;
these little smudges and flickers that he was clever to see and
even cleverer to hit in the dim recesses of the rafters – out of
each of them he was making a full bird. A tiny peek, probe, dab
of life, when he hit it, blossomed into a dead enemy, falling with
good, final weight.

The imperfection of the second pigeon he had shot, who was 144
still lifting his wing now and then up in the round hole, nagged
him. He put a new clip into the stock. Hugging the gun against
his body, he climbed the ladder. The barrel sight scratched his
ear; he had a sharp, garish vision, like a color slide, of shooting
himself and being found tumbled on the barn floor among his
prey. He locked his arm around the top rung – a fragile, gnawed
rod braced between uprights – and shot into the bird's body from
a flat angle. The wing folded, but the impact did not, as he had
hoped, push the bird out of the hole. He fired again, and again,
and still the little body, lighter than air when alive, was too heavy
to budge from its high grave. From up here he could see green
trees and a brown corner of the house through the hole. Clammy
with the cobwebs that gathered between the rungs, he pumped
a full clip of eight bullets into the stubborn shadow, with no
success. He climbed down, and was struck by the silence in the
barn. The remaining pigeons must have escaped out the other
hole. That was all right; he was tired of it.

He stepped with his rifle into the light. His mother was coming 145
to meet him, and it tickled him to see her shy away from the
carelessly held gun. "You took a chip out of the house," she said.
"What were those last shots about?"

146   "One of them died up in that little round hole and I was trying
to shoot it down."

147   "Copper's hiding behind the piano and won't come out. I had
to leave him."

148   "Well don't blame me. *I* didn't want to shoot the poor devils."

149   "Don't smirk. You look like your father. How many did you get?"

150   "Six."

151   She went into the barn, and he followed. She listened to the
silence. Her hair was scraggly, perhaps from tussling with the
dog. "I don't suppose the others will be back," she said wearily.
"Indeed, I don't know why I let Mother talk me into it. Their
cooing was such a comforting noise." She began to gather up the
dead pigeons. Though he didn't want to touch them, David went
into the mow and picked up by its tepid, horny, coral-colored feet
the first bird he had killed. Its wings unfolded disconcertingly, as
if the creature had been held together by threads that now were
slit. It did not weigh much. He retrieved the one on the other
side of the barn; his mother got the three in the middle and led
the way across the road to the little southern slope of land that
went down toward the foundations of the vanished tobacco shed.
The ground was too steep to plant and mow; wild strawberries
grew in the tangled grass. She put her burden down and said,
"We'll have to bury them. The dog will go wild."

152   He put his two down on her three; the slick feathers let the
bodies slide liquidly on one another. He asked, "Shall I get you
the shovel?"

153   "Get it for yourself; *you* bury them. They're your kill. And be
sure to make the hole deep enough so he won't dig them up."
While he went to the tool shed for the shovel, she went into the
house. Unlike her, she did not look up, either at the orchard to
the right of her or at the meadow on her left, but instead held her
head rigidly, tilted a little, as if listening to the ground.

154   He dug the hole, in a spot where there were no strawberry
plants, before he studied the pigeons. He had never seen a bird
this close before. The feathers were more wonderful than dog's
hair, for each filament was shaped within the shape of the feather,
and the feathers in turn were trimmed to fit a pattern that flowed
without error across the bird's body. He lost himself in the geo-
metrical tides as the feathers now broadened and stiffened to

make an edge for flight, now softened and constricted to cup 154
warmth around the mute flesh. And across the surface of the
infinitely adjusted yet somehow effortless mechanics of the feathers played idle designs of color, no two alike, designs executed, it
seemed, in a controlled rapture, with a joy that hung level in the
air above and behind him. Yet these birds bred in the millions
and were exterminated as pests. Into the fragrant open earth he
dropped one broadly banded in slate shades of blue, and on top of
it another, mottled all over in rhythms of lilac and gray. The next
was almost wholly white, but for a salmon glaze at its throat. As
he fitted the last two, still pliant, on the top, and stood up, crusty
coverings were lifted from him, and with a feminine, slipping
sensation along his nerves that seemed to give the air hands, he
was robed in this certainty: that the God who had lavished such
craft upon these worthless birds would not destroy His whole
Creation by refusing to let David live forever.

N. Scott Momaday

◄(1 9 3 4 -)►

Momaday is the product of at least three cultures: the Kiowa culture of his birth, the Southwest Indian cultures of his early years, and, from his adult training, 20th-century Anglo-American literary culture. Momaday was born Navarro Scott Mammedaty in 1934, in Kiowa country, Oklahoma, the son of full-blooded Kiowa artist, Alfred Morris Mammedaty (Alfred later changed the spelling of the family name). When Momaday was two, his family moved to the Southwest, where his parents taught in several places, ending up in the tiny school of Jemez Pueblo, New Mexico. Leaving Jemez, Momaday took his initial degree from the University of New Mexico, then went on to earn the doctorate in American literature from Stanford University (1963). Momaday's first novel, House Made of Dawn *(1968), was awarded the Pulitzer Prize and profoundly influenced the emerging movement of contemporary Native American writing. This novel illustrates Momaday's fusion of the various cultures of his background and training to produce a literature at once complex, challenging, and truly multi-cultural. The influence of such Anglo-American modernists as William Faulkner is evidenced in Momaday's use of the stream-of-consciousness technique, with its confusion of time and space. Its Jemez (or Walatowa) protagonist and setting give Momaday the opportunity to explore Pueblo tradition and ceremony, as well as the problems created for contemporary Pueblo people by the intersecting cultures of their world. But Tosamah, the title character of "Priest of the Sun" (part 2 of the novel, from which our selection is taken), is an urban Kiowa. In his ceremonies and sermons, Tosamah combines the Plains tribes' reverence for place and the spoken word with Christianity. This fusion of worldviews is evidenced, for example, in his highly unusual reading of the first chapter of the Gospel of John.*

351

THE PRIEST OF THE SUN

THE PRIEST OF THE SUN lived with his disciple Cruz on the 1
first floor of a two-story red-brick building in Los Angeles.
The upstairs was maintained as a storage facility by the A.A. Kaul
Office Supply Company. The basement was a kind of church. There
was a signboard on the wall above the basement steps, encased in
glass. In neat, movable white block letters on a black field it read:

LOS ANGELES   1a

HOLINESS PAN-INDIAN RESCUE MISSION

Rev. J. B. B. Tosamah, Pastor & Priest of the Sun

Saturday 8:30 PM

"The Gospel According to John"

Sunday 8:30 PM

"The Way to Rainy Mountain"

Be kind to a white man today

The basement was cold and dreary, dimly illuminated by two 2
40-watt bulbs which were screwed into the side walls above the
dais. This platform was made out of rough planks of various
woods and dimensions, thrown together without so much as a
hammer and nails; it stood seven or eight inches above the floor,
and it supported the tin firebox and the crescent altar. Off to one
side was a kind of lectern, decorated with red and yellow symbols
of the sun and moon. In back of the dais there was a screen of
purple drapery, threadbare and badly faded. On either side of the
aisle which led to the altar there were chairs and crates, fashioned
into pews. The walls were bare and gray and streaked with water.
The only windows were small, rectangular openings near the
ceiling, at ground level; the panes were covered over with a thick
film of coal oil and dust, and spider webs clung to the frames or
floated out like smoke across the room. The air was heavy and
stale; odors of old smoke and incense lingered all around. The
people had filed into the pews and were waiting silently.

Cruz, a squat, oily man with blue-black hair that stood out like 3
spines from his head, stepped forward on the platform and raised
his hands as if to ask for the quiet that already was. Everyone
watched him for a moment; in the dull light his skin shone yellow
with sweat. Turning slightly and extending his arm behind him,
he said, "The Right Reverend John Big Bluff Tosamah."

4   There was a ripple in the dark screen; the drapes parted and the Priest of the Sun appeared, moving shadow-like to the lectern. He was shaggy and awful-looking in the thin, naked light: big, lithe as a cat, narrow-eyed, suggesting in the whole of his look and manner both arrogance and agony. He wore black like a cleric; he had the voice of a great dog:

5   *"In principio erat Verbum."* Think of Genesis. Think of how it was before the world was made. There was nothing, the Bible says. 'And the earth was without form, and void; and darkness was upon the face of the deep.' It was dark, and there was nothing. There were no mountains, no trees, no rocks, no rivers. There was nothing. But there was darkness all around, and in the darkness something happened. Something happened! There was a single sound. Far away in the darkness there was a single sound. Nothing made it, but it was there; and there was no one to hear it, but it was there. It was there, and there was nothing else. It rose up in the darkness, little and still, almost nothing in itself – like a single soft breath, like the wind arising; yes, like the whisper of the wind rising slowly and going out into the early morning. But there was no wind. There was only the sound, little and soft. It was almost nothing in itself, the smallest seed of sound – but it took hold of the darkness and there was light; it took hold of the stillness and there was motion forever; it took hold of the silence and there was sound. It was almost nothing in itself, a single sound, a word – a word broken off at the darkest center of the night and let go in the awful void, forever and forever. And it was almost nothing in itself. It scarcely was; but it was, and everything began."

'In principio ... Verbum'· "In the beginning was the Word" (Latin), John 1:1

'And the ... deep'· Genesis 1:2

6   Just then a remarkable thing happened. The Priest of the Sun seemed stricken; he let go of his audience and withdrew into himself, into some strange potential of himself. His voice, which had been low and resonant, suddenly became harsh and flat; his shoulders sagged and his stomach protruded, as if he had held his breath to the limit of endurance; for a moment there was a look of amazement, then utter carelessness in his face. Conviction, caricature, callousness: the remainder of his sermon was a going back and forth among these.

7   "Thank you so much, Brother Cruz. Good evening, blood brothers and sisters, and welcome, welcome. Gracious me, I see

lots of new faces out there tonight. Gracious me! May the Great 7
Spirit – can we knock off that talking in the back there? – be with
you always.

    "'In the beginning was the Word.' I have taken as my text this 8
'There' evening the almighty Word itself. Now get this: 'There was a
was ... believe'· man sent from God, whose name was John. The same came for
John 1:6–7 a witness, to bear witness of the Light, that all men through him
might believe!'" Amen, brothers and sisters, Amen. And the riddle
of the Word, 'In the beginning was the Word....' Now what do
you suppose old John *meant* by that? That cat was a preacher,
and, well, you know how it is with preachers; he had something
big on his mind. Oh my, it was big; it was the *Truth*, and it was
heavy, and old John hurried to set it down. And in his hurry he
said too much. 'In the beginning was the Word, and the Word
was with God, and the Word was God!' It was the Truth, all right,
but it was more than the Truth. The Truth was overgrown with
fat, and the fat was God. The fat was *John's* God, and God stood
between John and the Truth. Old John, see, he got up one morning and caught sight of the Truth. It must have been like a bolt of
lightning, and the sight of it made him blind. And for a moment
the vision burned on in back of his eyes, and he *knew* what it
was. In that instant he saw something he had never seen before
and would never see again. That was the instant of revelation,
inspiration, Truth. And old John, he must have fallen down on
his knees. Man, he must have been shaking and laughing and
crying and yelling and praying – all at the same time – and he
must have been drunk and delirious with the Truth. You see, he
had lived all his life waiting for that one moment, and it came,
and it took him by surprise, and it was gone. And he said, 'In
the beginning was the Word....' And, man, right then and there
he should have stopped. There was nothing more to say, but he
went on. He had said all there was to say, everything, but he went
on. 'In the beginning was the Word....' Brothers and sisters, *that*
was the Truth, the whole of it, the essential and eternal Truth,
the bone and blood and muscle of the Truth. But he went on, old
John, because he was a preacher. The perfect vision faded from
his mind, and he went on. The instant passed, and then he had
nothing but a memory. He was desperate and confused, and in
his confusion he stumbled and went on. 'In the beginning was the

8   Word, and the Word was with God, and the Word was God.' He went on to talk about Jews and Jerusalem, Levites and Pharisees, Moses and Philip and Andrew and Peter. Don't you see? Old John *had* to go on. That cat had a whole lot at stake. He couldn't let the Truth alone. He couldn't see that he had come to the end of the Truth, and he went on. He tried to make it bigger and better than it was, but instead he only demeaned and encumbered it. He made it soft and big with fat. He was a preacher, and he made a complex sentence of the Truth, two sentences, three, a paragraph. He made a sermon and theology of the Truth. He imposed his idea of God upon the everlasting Truth. 'In the beginning was the Word....' And that is all there was, and it was enough.

9   "Now, brothers and sisters, old John was a white man, and the white man has his ways. Oh gracious me, he has his ways. He talks about the Word. He talks through it and around it. He builds upon it with syllables, with prefixes and suffixes and hyphens and accents. He adds and divides and multiplies the Word. And in all of this he subtracts the Truth. And, brothers and sisters, you have come here to live in the white man's world. Now the white man deals in words, and he deals easily, with grace and sleight of hand. And in his presence, here on his own ground, you are as children, mere babes in the woods. You must not mind, for in this you have a certain advantage. A child can listen and learn. The Word is sacred to a child.

10   "My grandmother was a storyteller; she knew her way around words. She never learned to read and write, but somehow she knew the good of reading and writing; she had learned how to listen and delight. She had learned that in words and in language, and there only, she could have whole and consummate being. She told me stories, and she taught me how to listen. I was a child and I listened. She could neither read nor write, you see, but she taught me how to live among her words, how to listen and delight. 'Storytelling; to utter and to hear....' And the simple act of listening is crucial to the concept of language, more crucial even than reading and writing, and language in turn is crucial to human society. There is proof of that, I think, in all the histories and prehistories of human experience. When that old Kiowa woman told me stories, I listened with only one ear. I was a child, and I took the words for granted. I did not know what all

of them meant, but somehow I held on to them; I remembered   10
them, and I remember them now. The stories were old and dear;
they meant a great deal to my grandmother. It was not until she
died that I knew how much they meant to her. I began to think
about it, and then I knew. When she told me those old stories,
something strange and good and powerful was going on. I was
a child, and that old woman was asking me to come directly
into the presence of her mind and spirit; she was taking hold of
my imagination, giving me to share in the great fortune of her
wonder and delight. She was asking me to go with her to the
confrontation of something that was sacred and eternal. It was
a timeless, timeless thing; nothing of her old age or of my childhood came between us.

"Children have a greater sense of the power and beauty of   11
words than have the rest of us in general. And if that is so, it is
because there occurs – or reoccurs – in the mind of every child
something like a reflection of all human experience. I have heard
that the human fetus corresponds in its development, stage by
stage, to the scale of evolution. Surely it is no less reasonable to
suppose that the waking mind of a child corresponds in the same
way to the whole evolution of human thought and perception.

"In the white man's world, language, too – and the way in which   12
the white man thinks of it – has undergone a process of change.
The white man takes such things as words and literatures for
granted, as indeed he must, for nothing in his world is so commonplace. On every side of him there are words by the millions,
an unending succession of pamphlets and papers, letters and
books, bills and bulletins, commentaries and conversations. He
has diluted and multiplied the Word, and words have begun to
close in upon him. He is sated and insensitive; his regard for
language – for the Word itself – as an instrument of creation has
diminished nearly to the point of no return. It may be that he
will perish by the Word.

"But it was not always so with him, and it is not so with you.   13
Consider for a moment that old Kiowa woman, my grandmother,
whose use of language was confined to speech. And be assured
that her regard for words was always keen in proportion as she
depended upon them. You see, for her words were medicine; they
were magic and invisible. They came from nothing into sound

13 and meaning. They were beyond price; they could neither be bought nor sold. And she never threw words away.

14 "My grandmother used to tell me the story of *Tai-me*, of how *Tai-me* came to the Kiowas. The Kiowas were a sun dance culture, and *Tai-me* was their sun dance doll, their most sacred fetish; no medicine was ever more powerful. There is a story about the coming of *Tai-me*. This is what my grandmother told me:

14a Long ago there were bad times. The Kiowas were hungry and there was no food. There was a man who heard his children cry from hunger, and he began to search for food. He walked four days and became very weak. On the fourth day he came to a great canyon. Suddenly there was thunder and lightning. A Voice spoke to him and said, "Why are you following me? What do you want?" The man was afraid. The thing standing before him had the feet of a deer, and its body was covered with feathers. The man answered that the Kiowas were hungry. "Take me with you," the Voice said, "and I will give you whatever you want." From that day *Tai-me* has belonged to the Kiowas.

15 "Do you see? There, far off in the darkness, something happened. Do you see? Far, far away in the nothingness something happened. There was a voice, a sound, a word – and everything began. The story of the coming of *Tai-me* has existed for hundreds of years by word of mouth. It represents the oldest and best idea that man has of himself. It represents a very rich literature, which, because it was never written down, was always but one generation from extinction. But for the same reason it was cherished and revered. I could see that reverence in my grandmother's eyes, and I could hear it in her voice. It was that, I think, that old Saint John had in mind when he said, 'In the beginning was the Word….' But he went on. He went on to lay a scheme about the Word. He could find no satisfaction in the simple fact that the Word was; he had to account for it, not in terms of that sudden and profound insight, which must have devastated him at once, but in terms of the moment afterward, which was irrelevant and remote; not in terms of his imagination, but only in terms of his prejudice.

16 "Say this: 'In the beginning was the Word….' There was nothing. There was *nothing*! Darkness. There was darkness, and there

was no end to it. You look up sometimes in the night and there 16
are stars; you can see all the way to the stars. And you begin to
know the universe, how awful and great it is. The stars lie out
against the sky and do not fill it. A single star, flickering out in
the universe, is enough to fill the mind, but it is nothing in the
night sky. The darkness looms around it. The darkness flows
among the stars, and beyond them forever. In the beginning
that is how it was, but there were no stars. There was only the
dark infinity in which nothing was. And something happened.
At the distance of a star something happened, and everything
began. The Word did not come into being, but *it was*. It did not
break upon the silence, but *it was older than the silence and the*
silence was made of it.

"Old John caught sight of something terrible. The thing stand- 17
ing before him said, 'Why are you following me? What do you
want?' And from that day the Word has belonged to us, who have
heard it for what it is, who have lived in fear and awe of it. In
the Word was the beginning; *'In the beginning was the Word....'*"

The Priest of the Sun appeared to have spent himself. He 18
stepped back from the lectern and hung his head, smiling. In
his mind the earth was spinning and the stars rattled around in
the heavens. The sun shone, and the moon. Smiling in a kind of
transport, the Priest of the Sun stood silent for a time while the
congregation waited to be dismissed.

"Good night," he said, at last, "and get yours." 19

Alice Walker

{ 1 9 4 4 – }

Walker describes herself as an African-American "womanist" writer. She is one of America's most highly regarded novelists and essayists, receiving the Pulitzer Prize and the American Book Award for The Color Purple *(1982). Other novels include* The Third Life of George Copeland *(1970),* Meridian *(1976), and* Possessing the Secret of Joy *(1992). Redemption, the resilience of the human spirit, the sacredness of beauty, and the reconciling power of love are recurring themes in Walker's works, which draw heavily upon her experience of growing up in Eatonton, Georgia. Walker views the transmission of her stories as both an artistic and a moral calling. Committed to preserving an African-American literary tradition, she sees herself as a messenger of reconciliation and a voice for women and minorities who have had little opportunity to speak. The following story is taken from her collection of stories* In Love and Trouble: Stories of Black Women *(1973).*

THE WELCOME TABLE

for sister Clara Ward

> I'm going to sit at the Welcome table
> Shout my troubles over
> Walk and talk with Jesus
> Tell God how you treat me
> One of these days!*

I'm going ... these days · the lyrics are from a traditional African-American spiritual

1   THE OLD WOMAN STOOD with eyes uplifted in her Sunday-go-to-meeting clothes: high shoes polished about the tops and toes, a long rusty dress adorned with an old corsage, long withered, and the remnants of an elegant silk scarf as headrag stained with grease from the many oily pigtails underneath. Perhaps she had known suffering. There was a dazed and sleepy

359

look in her aged blue-brown eyes. But for those who searched 1
hastily for "reasons" in that old tight face, shut now like an ancient
door, there was nothing to be read. And so they gazed nakedly
upon their own fear transferred; a fear of the black and the old,
a terror of the unknown as well as of the deeply known. Some of
those who saw her there on the church steps spoke words about
her that were hardly fit to be heard, others held their pious peace;
and some felt vague stirrings of pity, small and persistent and
hazy, as if she were an old collie turned out to die.

She was angular and lean and the color of poor gray Georgia 2
earth, beaten by king cotton and the extreme weather. Her elbows
were wrinkled and thick, the skin ashen but durable, like the bark
of old pines. On her face centuries were folded into the circles
around one eye, while around the other, etched and mapped as
if for print, ages more threatened again to live. Some of them
there at the church saw the age, the dotage,* the missing buttons
down the front of her mildewed black dress. Others saw cooks,
chauffeurs, maids, mistresses, children denied or smothered in
the deferential way she held her cheek to the side, toward the
ground. Many of them saw jungle orgies in an evil place, while
others were reminded of riotous anarchists looting and raping in
the streets. Those who knew the hesitant creeping up on them of
the law, saw the beginning of the end of the sanctuary of Christian
worship, saw the desecration of Holy Church, and saw an inva-
sion of privacy, which they struggled to believe they still kept.

Still she had come down the road toward the big white church 3
alone. Just herself, an old forgetful woman, nearly blind with
age. Just her and her eyes raised dully to the glittering cross that
crowned the sheer silver steeple. She had walked along the road
in a stagger from her house a half mile away. Perspiration, cold
and clammy, stood on her brow and along the creases by her
thin wasted nose. She stopped to calm herself on the wide front
steps, not looking about her as they might have expected her to
do, but simply standing quite still, except for a slight quivering
of her throat and tremors that shook her cotton-stockinged legs.

The reverend of the church stopped her pleasantly as she 4
stepped into the vestibule. Did he say, as they thought he did,
kindly, "Auntie, you know this is not your church?" As if one
could choose the wrong one. But no one remembers, for they

dotage · senility

4   never spoke of it afterward, and she brushed past him anyway, as if she had been brushing past him all her life, except this time she was in a hurry. Inside the church she sat on the very first bench from the back, gazing with concentration at the stained-glass window over her head. It was cold, even inside the church, and she was shivering. Everybody could see. They stared at her as they came in and sat down near the front. It was cold, very cold to them, too; outside the church it was below freezing and not much above inside. But the sight of her, sitting there somehow passionately ignoring them, brought them up short, burning.

5   The young usher, never having turned anyone out of his church before, but not even considering this job as *that* (after all, she had no right to be there, certainly), went up to her and whispered that she should leave. Did he call her "Grandma," as later he seemed to recall he had? But for those who actually hear such traditional pleasantries and to whom they actually mean something, "Grandma" was not one, for she did not pay him any attention, just muttered, "Go 'way," in a weak sharp *bothered* voice, waving his frozen blond hair and eyes from near her face.

6   It was the ladies who finally did what to them had to be done. Daring their burly indecisive husbands to throw the old colored woman out they made their point. God, mother, country, earth, church. It involved all that, and well they knew it. Leather bagged and shoed, with good calfskin gloves to keep out the cold, they looked with contempt at the bloodless gray arthritic hands of the old woman, clenched loosely, restlessly in her lap. Could their husbands expect them to sit up in church with *that*? No, no, the husbands were quick to answer and even quicker to do their duty.

7   Under the old woman's arms they placed their hard fists (which afterward smelled of decay and musk – the fermenting scent of onionskins and rotting greens). Under the old woman's arms they raised their fists, flexed their muscular shoulders, and out she flew through the door, back under the cold blue sky. This done, the wives folded their healthy arms across their trim middles and felt at once justified and scornful. But none of them said so, for none of them ever spoke of the incident again. Inside the church it was warmer. They sang, they prayed. The protection and promise of God's impartial love grew more not less desirable as the sermon gathered fury and lashed itself out above their penitent heads.

The old woman stood at the top of the steps looking about in 8
bewilderment. She had been singing in her head. They had interrupted her. Promptly she began to sing again, though this time
a sad song. Suddenly, however, she looked down the long gray
highway and saw something interesting and delightful coming.
She started to grin, toothlessly, with short giggles of joy, jumping
about and slapping her hands on her knees. And soon it became
apparent why she was so happy. For coming down the highway
at a firm though leisurely pace was Jesus. He was wearing an
immaculate white, long dress trimmed in gold around the neck
and hem, and a red, a bright red, cape. Over his left arm he carried a brilliant blue blanket. He was wearing sandals and a beard
and he had long brown hair parted on the right side. His eyes,
brown, had wrinkles around them as if he smiled or looked at
the sun a lot. She would have known him, recognized him, anywhere. There was a sad but joyful look to his face, like a candle
was glowing behind it, and he walked with sure even steps in her
direction, as if he were walking on the sea. Except that he was
not carrying in his arms a baby sheep, he looked exactly like the
picture of him that she had hanging over her bed at home. She
had taken it out of a white lady's Bible while she was working
for her. She had looked at that picture for more years than she
could remember, but never once had she really expected to see
him. She squinted her eyes to be sure he wasn't carrying a little
sheep in one arm, but he was not. Ecstatically she began to wave
her arms for fear he would miss seeing her, for he walked looking
straight ahead on the shoulder of the highway, and from time to
time looking upward at the sky.

All he said when he got up close to her was "Follow me," and 9
she bounded down to his side with all the bob and speed of one
so old. For every one of his long determined steps she made two
quick ones. They walked along in deep silence for a long time.
Finally she started telling him about how many years she had
cooked for them, cleaned for them, nursed them. He looked at
her kindly but in silence. She told him indignantly about how
they had grabbed her when she was singing in her head and not
looking, and how they had tossed her out of his church. A old
heifer like me, she said, straightening up next to Jesus, breathing
hard. But he smiled down at her and she felt better instantly and

9   time just seemed to fly by. When they passed her house, forlorn and sagging, weatherbeaten and patched, by the side of the road, she did not even notice it, she was so happy to be out walking along the highway with Jesus.

10   She broke the silence once more to tell Jesus how glad she was that he had come, how she had often looked at his picture hanging on her wall (she hoped he didn't know she had stolen it) over her bed, and how she had never expected to see him down here in person. Jesus gave her one of his beautiful smiles and they walked on. She did not know where they were going; someplace wonderful, she suspected. The ground was like clouds under their feet, and she felt she could walk forever without becoming the least bit tired. She even began to sing out loud some of the old spirituals she loved, but she didn't want to annoy Jesus, who looked so thoughtful, so she quieted down. They walked on, looking straight over the treetops into the sky, and the smiles that played over her dry wind-cracked face were like first clean ripples across a stagnant pond. On they walked without stopping.

11   The people in church never knew what happened to the old woman; they never mentioned her to one another or to anybody else. Most of them heard sometime later that an old colored woman fell dead along the highway. Silly as it seemed, it appeared she had walked herself to death. Many of the black families along the road said they had seen the old lady high-stepping down the highway; sometimes jabbering in a low insistent voice, sometimes singing, sometimes merely gesturing excitedly with her hands. Other times silent and smiling, looking at the sky. She had been alone, they said. Some of them wondered aloud where the old woman had been going so stoutly that it had worn her heart out. They guessed maybe she had relatives across the river, some miles away, but none of them really knew.

Albert Haley

{ 1 9 5 3 - }

Haley was born in Oklahoma but lived much of his life in Alaska. The latter geographical influence may account for the concern his stories show for how human constructions (particularly cities) have separated people from the nourishing qualities of the natural world. He earned his BA *in economics at Yale and an* MFA *at the University of Houston. An advocate of using real-life experience as a source for one's art, he has worked in the oil field, in the banking industry, and for a computer software firm. Haley is a careful crafter of short fiction, beginning with his short story collection* Home Ground: Stories of Two Families and the Land *(1977),* which Larry McMurtry called "the best fiction we have about contemporary Alaska." His stories have appeared in* Atlantic Monthly, The New Yorker, Rolling Stone, *and* Image: A Journal of the Arts and Religion. *In 1982 Haley received the John Irving Novel Prize for* Exotic. *"Line of Duty" illustrates Haley's strong sense of identification with injured souls like the traumatized Officer Henning. As the story unfolds, Haley unflinchingly tracks the emotional and spiritual disintegration of Henning. At the same time, in a move characteristic of his more recent work, the writer introduces hope in the form of a Good Samaritan figure, Henning's patrol partner. Haley is currently Associate Professor of English and Writer in Residence at Abilene Christian University.*

LINE OF DUTY

1 · PARTNERS

1   OFFICER HENNING WAS ONE of those big men. He was not a jiggling embarrassment when he started out on the force but came to them as a broad-shouldered athletic type who checked in at a solid six-foot-five and a preferred weight of two twenty-five. With a body like that, Henning dominated the

365

precinct's beach volleyball team. Whenever the rubbery globe ¹ came spinning over the net, he rose into the air and his nylon shorts flapped and his fists pounded like coordinated jackhammers. He was the main point driver for the cops against weekend teams of blue shirts, firemen, and EMT personnel. Through it all, including a dismal 6–14 season, Henning remained heroic and a happy buyer of postgame beer. He had embedded in him the personality of an easygoing rock until the heart flutter anomaly began. The problem cropped up about the time Henning was going through his divorce.

The cardiologist placed the stress test results under the young ² officer's nose. He told Henning he'd best avoid sand and sweat gatherings for the remainder of the year. This left Henning with just the regular forms of non-exercise: sitting squishily on his behind during long patrol rides, jaw muscle movements when he yacked over the radio, quick strides up and down concrete driveways. Unfortunately, his appetite didn't keep tabs on this sudden reduction in activity.

Every morning they stopped off at *Sweet Heaven!* on Ocean ³ Boulevard. Henning ducked from the cruiser to run inside and pick up a half-dozen bear claws. Then lunchtime would roll around and he'd be with the rest of the bunch at *Benito's Drive-Thru*, helping himself to trio of chimichangas drenched in green hot goo. By the time Roberta Raye Jones came on board as Henning's new partner, he had packed on thirty pounds as easily as a man slipping his arms through an overcoat.

"It's not how much you eat, it's *what* you eat." This was Roberta ⁴ Raye setting the rehabilitative tone from Day One. She was a lively acting, Watts-born* Af-Am* who always got into the car with a flourish. On her lap she set up clean baggies, individually filled with celery, carrot sticks, bright radish slices. Roberta Raye fished in and out of the bags as they drove the freeway. "You've got to put good stuff in you to get good stuff out."

"Are you kidding? Rabbit food?" Henning had taken the off-ramp ⁵ and they were easing through *barrio* country with its strange *haciendas*-on-wheels. Chrome bumpers divided the sun. Across the street, man-sized graffiti roared and burned on concrete walls.

"Yes, Max, this is *rabbit* food. But don't get ideas. I'm sure not ⁶ a bunny." It was weird she'd said that, Henning thought. Roberta

Watts-born · Watts is a largely African American district of Los Angeles known for massive riots, burning, and looting that occurred in 1965

Af-Am · African American

barrio · "neighborhood" (Spanish)

haciendas · estates, mansions (Spanish)

6 Raye really did have a bod – steely, ærobicized and capped off with a deeply cleaved bust. But her face. It was a departure from the old centerfold ideal guys like Henning had grown up with. Roberta Raye's eyes were set wide apart and her forehead was kinda high. Then there was her nose which had been broken when she was young and not living under circumstances where anyone felt like getting it repaired. The nose had grown nearly flat on one side, resulting in partial nasal blockage. That was why Roberta Raye sounded breathless whenever she talked.

7   Of course, the other white boys kidded Henning fiercely about having a funny looking, double-minority partner, a seaweed smacker on top of all that, and they'd heard that she mumbled prayers before she ate at *Benito's* so she was either a Holy Roller or scared to death of bean burritos, but Henning came back sharply at them. He declared that Roberta Raye was the perfect ride. She was reliable, always smelled good, and because of the racial thing (according to his own conservative lights) he didn't have to worry about falling into the trap of dating her. Add to the final mix Roberta Raye's pleasant chatter and her calm under pressure, and if you were going to have a female in the car, Roberta Raye was tops.

8   "And stop making fun of what she eats," Henning finished up. "She's right, The way you guys chow down will kill you." Of course, it wasn't exactly true that Roberta Raye had converted Henning to the kingdom of whole food. It was more that she had exerted a moderate influence. She was urging him to take into account his poor, neglected heart. His heart really had become a bad thing, and often these days he felt it trying to speak to him. During those night episodes the sweat broke out across Henning's forehead as he lay on his back staring at dark texture swipes on the ceiling. *Flutter, flutter* went the strange bird. Henning did not return to the doc or tell anyone. It was frightening , embarrassing, too. After twenty-eight years in Henning's big body, his heart had a single-minded demand. It wanted out. What could he do? He tensed. He gripped both sides of the pillow. The guys noted he looked fatigued. One of the sergeants said something about taking a few days off, adding words about Tamara and having time to recoup. Henning laughed outloud. Who did they think he was? If a big man knew anything, it was how to keep on keeping on.

2 · BANG

FACT WAS HE HAD DISCHARGED the weapon in the line of duty before. A single shot fired into the air outside a North Hollywood convenience store in '99. The following year there had been three frantic rounds squeezed off from the sidewalk at a fleeing suspect's tires, as large and dizzying and unreal as a target at a carnival booth. Most recently the weapon had come into play during a major shootout on Christmas Day in front of a bungalow where they were crouching behind vehicles and firing steadily, pumping lead for half an hour past bougainvillea and beyond shattered window panes, chopping up an artificial Christmas tree among other things. Then SWAT had broken in and found the place empty, spider webs, the whole bit.

This time was different.

Roberta Raye was driving and she picked up the guy on the spur road. It was just before midnight and there was lots of hot tire potential, but as soon as they switched on the red and whites it became clear there would be no chase. In less than a quarter mile, Robert Raye had the violator pulled down. From the shotgun seat Henning could see the man sitting calmly behind the wheel. "I'll take him," he said. He flipped the veggie bag over to Roberta. "Save some for me."

Except for their headlights and the flashing, silent blare of the roof rack, the road and nearby vacant lots were an unlit pit of blackness. It was out close to the oil patch, an area officially called Holister Hills but known to all as Holiness Hills because that was maybe easier to say and the ugly array of leaning telephone poles and brutal wires suggested an industrial version of Golgotha.* Good for nothing place, known only to contractors and dealers trading bundles and briefcases, Henning thought. The air smelled of ocean and petro, that ol' Long Beach fragrance. He advanced until he was three feet from the car, murking just aft of the driver's window. Behind him Roberta Raye was bent over in the front seat, punching buttons, running the computer check. In the spillover of official light, the violator (male, Caucasian) looked like a mild sort, a bank teller or an accountant. He wore glasses and probably would smell like discount-store aftershave. The car was likewise mundane, a dimly kept K-car* with an empty child seat in back. This was the kind of guy with whom it was easy to

9

10

11

12

Golgotha · the site of Jesus' crucifixion

K-car · an inexpensive, boxy, and utilitarian automobile introduced by Chrysler in the early 1980s

12   break ice: "License and insurance, sir" and "Have any idea how fast you were traveling?"

13   Henning had to rap his knuckles loudly against the glass.

14   The man buzzed down all four windows, an odd or nervous thing to do. Henning ignored it and took the plastic card. He scoped his flashlight over the laminate. He began the rhetorical spiel. The man nodded like the concept of being pulled over for speed drift wasn't new to him. Then he pressed a finger to his nose, as if preventing a sneeze, but within a second he had reached across the dark passenger seat that was as vacant as moonscape.

15   He popped up with something. It was black and not a tissue or handkerchief. Smoothly the man dipped a shoulder so he could fire out the window (or so Henning's reflexes assumed). Henning went for his belt. This had been practiced. Many times. Roll, turn, make yourself gum-wrapper thin. Fast now. Exploit the angle advantage.

16   There didn't seem to be a noise. Just the man pitching suddenly forward over the wheel. Blood foamed at his mouth. Spasms shook the upper body. The bullet had punched cleanly through the neck and trachea. The episode took about fifteen seconds, which to Henning seemed longer. The man's wind sucked and wheezed significantly, much louder than he'd ever heard Roberta Raye breathing through her maimed nostril. When the noises stopped, Henning palmed the fender and hopped to the other side. He placed his warm weapon on the hood and played the flashlight on the pavement. In the flash of muzzle fire he'd seen something go flying. Reaching down he retrieved the man's glasses which somehow (action, reaction?) had gone straight out the open passenger window. When he picked them up, he made sure he didn't let his eyes go back to the interior of the car.

17   Roberta Raye banged out of the patrol car. She hovered by the Chrysler's side, opened the door, jumped back as something poured toward her feet. She came around to Henning. "Are you all right? What – ?"

18   Henning dangled the bifocal glasses in his hands where Roberta Raye could see them.

19   "Not a scratch on these. Don't you think that's amazing? How's Forensics going to explain it?"

Roberta Raye stared at him, ignoring the prescription glasses. 20
"I only heard one shot. He didn't get off a round or anything?"
And now she seemed to move like one in a panic as she abruptly
unbuttoned Henning's tunic and patted his undershirt. He
thought he did feel cold, as if something was gone out of him, but
the glasses in his hands made a sort of touchstone. As long as he
held onto them he felt steady on his feet. He almost wanted to put
them on because things had become blurry. He heard crickets,
the most staccato crickets he'd heard in his life, but it couldn't be;
this was the Holiness Hills and too close to the ocean for those
little stiff-legged creatures. Then he became aware of another
sound. Not his heart, which was as steady as a rock chunking
down a slope. This sound was something else – wheels whirring,
engines thundering, the hum that concrete takes on when weight
is flung against it. It was the freeway, a full five miles distant.

"Wow. Listen to that." He'd never had his reflexes reach such a 21
peak. Maybe it was worth sharing. At least with a guy's partner?

"You're pale. I think you need to go over there." Roberta Raye 22
flicked her flashlight toward the weedy shoulder.

At first he didn't understand. He was thinking she meant for 23
him to take a leak. Then it clicked. She thought he might want
to be sick.

"Nah," Henning said. For a moment he felt shame. He was so 24
alive. No flutters, nothing. What he'd done or not done didn't
affect him at all. Sick? He actually was hungry. As he folded up
the pair of glasses and stuck them in his shirt pocket he was
thinking basically one thing: "Bear claw."

3 · AFTERMATH

A YEAR EARLIER THERE HAD BEEN a seminar in a downtown 25
hotel, topic: "Use of Deadly Force." A little man with wingtips
and a button-down stage presence had hissed into a microphone
and peppered the officers with technical talk. What it translated
into was, "Don't wax someone unless you or your buddy's life is
on the line. Even then be ready for nasty consequences. Internal
Affairs, lawyers, civil rights advocates, the press."

With Maxwell Henning it was different. The DA sent the 26
file over and it was revealed that Mr. K-car had indeed been a
banker, a mid-level, consumer loan officer. There had been an

26 embezzlement going on at the branch for at least eight months and the guy was about to be snagged by the Feds. Better yet, the night of the event the man had left a note behind then headed out to the oceanside to finish the affair. By chance Henning and Roberta Raye had caught him in the midst of his suicide run. So, in a way, Henning hadn't done a thing to alter history. By reaching for the .38 on the seat beside him, the man had hastened the process and spared himself the ammo.

27 With this information the board recognized the shooting as justifiable and cleared Henning. As an afterthought, the department provided him a psychologist to talk to one day a week, even though Henning swore he didn't need couch-deluxe treatment. The twig-like woman with a painted turtle shell on her desk was willing to let him digress, talk about tales of Tamara, so that was fine. This Dr. Berkowitz was adept at exercising the "Big C" (compassion) and she pointed out that Henning's unresolved issues had conflated with the shooting. She said that taking the life of the man was like adding another brick to the destroyed pile of Henning's marriage. "Yes," Henning finally admitted, "I've been a little down lately."

28 He was lying. It was worse. He couldn't get a handle on what was coming over him.

29 What he was starting to feel was so dark that glancing over at Roberta Raye during a long ride failed to offer the normal degree of comfort. He'd look at her and think "Tamara," like he used to, and instead of being a tiny bit warm and tingly, he'd hear a gun going off. He knew he ought to take the killing gracefully, as a sure sign that he was a lucky s.o.b., the guy assigned to the best partner in the world. Roberta Raye had actually sent him flowers. Who else would recognize without a pause that he needed cheering? She was a great one, Roberta Raye was, but unfortunately the daisies and carnations pushed Henning the wrong way. He put the vase on the vanity in the bathroom, close to the porcelain tub. There the flowers sorta blended in with the wrinkled shower curtain. It was cheerful to have that kind of floral life in his nearly barren house, even tucked away in the can, but his mind these days was bent toward the perverse. The pink and white petals allowed him to think the same things over and over. It kept coming back to him: funerals, blossoming wounds, Tamara breaking free of his embrace to announce, "You're noth-

ing like what I thought you were. So much Mr. Wonderful on the 29
outside. Give a gal roses and a box of candy for every occasion.
Thanksgiving even. Roses? Jesus, that's just it, Henning. You're
so automatic. It's click, click, click. Got it done. You shine me up.
Strap me on. That's right. I help you get a job done. You're not
really there for *me*. You can't even begin to imagine what I feel."

Daisies and carnations. Blood red roses. What was the dif- 30
ference, he wondered. He decided to get rid of the flowers and
everything else.

A minute later, his hands. In the mirror. Shaking. He put the vase 31
down on the counter. Quietly, all of him slipped out of the picture.

4 · TWO MONTHS

Today he was sitting in the den in his bathrobe. There 32
had been a bit of incautiousness at a crime scene when he'd
walked heedlessly over the top of the lab woman's strips of
gauze laid out on the sidewalk like tiny surrender flags. There
had been shifts when he was ten minutes late. There had been a
Wednesday, just one Wednesday out of all the Wednesdays he'd
ever lived, when he'd pulled the pepper spray from his belt and
handed the cylinder to a street person who was trying to stop
traffic. "Want them to put on the brakes? This will make them
back up all the way to Nebraska." The department had placed
Henning on leave-of-absence, which was tantamount to ordering
the VCR to become the most important appliance in a man's life.
One filled in gaps with magnetic tape. This time he fed his eyes
a tape he'd made of a mindless game show. Another winner. No,
the doorbell. Roberta Raye standing on the porch. Roberta Raye
out of uniform. Roberta Raye in a green dress and white hose
and high heels. A different perfume. Smiling at him.

"Are you okay, Henning?" 33

"Sure." Hardly any words and she'd already broken down the 34
glassy glaze he'd developed to encase himself. Her voice continued to chip away, telling him something about dressing smartly
pronto-style and loading himself into the van. She had her kids
with her and she wanted Henning to make the drive to the valley.

"Come on, Max. My folks have a ranch. It's fun and you don't 35
look booked to me. We'll go to church first, then you can have lunch
and babysit while I do some heavy-duty gabbing with my parents."

36   "Church?"

37   "Veggies for the soul," Roberta Raye said. It was a joke he supposed.

38   The drive took an hour, and for the first time he thought about Roberta Raye Jones' ethnicity. The reason it came to him now was because of the two girls and the boy. The dressed-up children were just as dark-skinned as their mother. So together they made a black family. Except for Henning, a great bleached hulk in polo shirt and slacks, the odd man out. "Hi, kids," he said once. They stared warily at him.

39   At church it wasn't the get-down-in-the-aisle style religion he'd imagined. The plain buff, steepled building housed something more formal. "Liturgy," Roberta Raye whispered early on in the service, and sitting next to her on the pew he felt an electric jolt. The breath from her lips had brushed his ear. He stared at her long nails, done up especially for the day. He looked down at the Order of Worship lying in his lap. His eyes couldn't get past the first title there: "We proclaim the presence of the Lord." What's that, Henning wondered. God has to be spoken into existence? Why not simply point at the thing itself? Hey, dude, over there! Why not catch him bare-handed, as real as a bullet streaking toward flesh? A fully-intentional God, not one hiding beneath beds or lodged inside songbooks, waiting for you to say the right words so he could come out and play.

40   Henning surveyed again the modern stained glass, the light woods covering the wall, the cushioned pews. By the end of the service Roberta Raye was smiling like something had passed through her. He felt nothing. As he walked out he wondered what he would remember? That it smelled nice in there. Like furniture polish? Drycleaning? Carpet shampoo? Yes, a clean place for a dirty person.

41   "What did you think, Max?"

42   "Great. Just great."

43   She smiled like she knew what he was trying to do. "Well, don't dwell on it. Time to switch gears."

44   "Really?"

45   "That's right. To the ranch!"

46   She didn't really need him to babysit. Instead, she turned the children over to her parents and rustled up a pair of overalls and

leather boots for both of them. Henning and she got into an old, 46
rusted-up pickup that had a winch in back. It looked almost like
a tow truck, and Henning wondered why they'd need that on a
ranch. There was also a fully stocked gun rack in the cab. "We've
got to go into that field over there and get a cow for my daddy,"
Roberta Raye said.

They bounced over ruts and stopped in front of some 47
Herefords. The cattle looked dumb and suspicious, but didn't do
anything as Roberta Raye stepped out with the rifle. To Henning
it felt like hottest day of the summer; he couldn't be sure having
spent the last week indoors, entirely under air conditioning.
Sweat oozed down Roberta Raye's cheeks. "Here," she said and
handed him the rifle. He heard the whistling noise coming from
her nostril as she spoke faster than normal. "Daddy said to take
that one right there." Roberta Raye wiped her face and pointed.
"The one with the funny patch on her leg."

The rifle was a small-bore job. She advised him to nail the 48
cow between the eyes so it would go down with one pop. Then
she stationed herself behind him.

Henning stumbled upon a hole in the ground and frightened 49
the nearest animals. They stuttered a few yards away. Black Patch
stayed where she was, her head up, chewing, looking at him.
Between the eyes.

"You can do it, Max," Roberta Raye said from the rear. "Taking 50
life is part of preserving life. Kill a beautiful animal and eat it
beautifully. That's all it is. We're feeding my kids. You pull the
trigger and you guarantee a good life for someone else. You
don't have to be the judge. The judge has already put you in the
situation. All he is asking you to do is to respond. You hear me,
Henning? Snap out of it! You're not the damn judge! Squeeze!"

A minute later they backed up the truck to the cow. After 51
they'd run the hook through the hocks they turned on the winch.
As the cow dangled and spun at the end of the chain Roberta
Raye used a regular kitchen chef's knife to cut its throat. "There.
Let it drain, then we'll drive it back to the house. Daddy will take
care of the rest."

This was what she'd brought him here for, an event more impor- 52
tant than church or coaxing him into pulling the trigger. She wanted
him to face the blood. It came fast from the body, starting out like a

52 faucet's gush then steadily graduating until, minutes later, it fell in coin-sized drips. A wide red puddle formed on top of the hardened field. Drought conditions. It would be a while before it soaked in. Flies appeared, flirting with the sticky surface. Mostly, Henning was impressed by the odor. The cow's blood smelled hot and dark and even slightly metallic, like a pocketful of change or damp copper pipes in the basement. For a second he thought Roberta Raye might be on the right track, that these qualities could explain everything. Blood inside the animal was what kept it alive. By taking the blood out and putting it into the ground, they weren't so much killing the animal as moving its essence to a new realm. All the pulsing blood effort was going to be transferred into another kind of production. Right here on this spot plants would spring up.

53 He looked at the head-down cow, the carcass that ended in thick, rubbery open lips. He tried to see it as an evacuated bag, a container whose containing job was finished. Yes, he almost had it.

54 "It's bled enough," Roberta Raye said.

55 As he followed her to the truck, she put an arm around him. He hardly felt it. He was thinking about the banker's wife. He'd visited her a few weeks ago. It had been a desperate act. He'd been looking for some kind of story that might suit him. Instead, she gained the wrong impression, that he had come by the house to claim some kind of carnal victory. She caught him curbside as he reached for his car door, trying to get away. "You were looking down at my toe nails in there," she accused. "You want to, don't you?" He said nothing, but they were present just as she asserted: ten fields of ruby red. "See," she said, wiggling each one, "You come back inside, officer, and I'll paint them any color you like. You can help."

56 Any color. He didn't know what. He started to tell Roberta Raye about it. He knew he might start to blubber. He didn't speak. There was no way to make it appropriate. They got in the truck. They carried the beef home to her family. Steaks, roasts, ribs, hamburger. He and Roberta Raye Jones had it all and everyone at the house was gratified that their mission was accomplished so quickly. She took him back to the city and her last words were, "You're going to be okay tonight, huh? I gotta drop the kids off and go on shift."

57 "No rest for the wicked," he said. He meant nothing by the phrase at the time. He was only acting light hearted, giving her

what he thought she wanted which was to see him smile so she   57
might think him cured or at least better behaved for the time being.
He yawned as he waved goodbye. "Going to sleep well tonight." He
thought he sounded convincing. He really hoped he was.

5 · MIDNIGHT

WHO WOULD HAVE GUESSED? He'd never been a boozer,   58
not even during the years when he was deep-sixing his
marriage, so how was a guy to know? That with alcohol-inspired
numbness could come new friends. Energy! Inspiration! It was
true. Why didn't someone put that in a manual for big men? If
you hurt, boy, and don't know what to do, open a quart in the
vacuum of your home. Tip the bottle and cauterize* the wounds
with fire. Before you know it you'll be on your feet and –

cauterize · the process of burning a wound to stop bleeding and destroy damaged or infected tissue

Not exactly dancing but in the bathroom he was tossing the   59
rotting flowers into the waste basket. He packed all his wedding
photos into a large cardboard box and set the box out in the alley
for the garbagemen. He broke open his revolver and emptied it
of bullets. Back to the bathroom where he lifted off the lid on
the back of the toilet so he could turn his hand upside down and
release the ammunition. The bullets sank to the bottom of the
tank. They lay fat and snub-nosed, and everything was so unbear-
ably quiet that he could hear his heavy breaths coming. He felt
his heart, too, and that required a final drink to settle down. He
crashed the bottle into the tub.

With the empty pistol and a single framed photo, he got into   60
his car. He backed out of the driveway and headed toward the
beach. It was growing palpably late. The sun-sunken world that
streaked past him telegraphed shadowy movements: leather
armies deploying on asphalt and concrete. Prime time, crime time.

As soon as he was out of the residential area, Henning applied   61
force to the pedal. He was going 45, 50, 60, then 90. Fast enough
to make streetlights blur into candle flames. The photo beside him

circa · "around" (Latin)

was a strictly composed one, circa* his and Tamara's dating era. It
showed them smiling at the junior prom, three years before they
married, ten years before they divorced. Henning glanced over
at the picture from time to time, but he couldn't see the blond,
smiling girl because it was black inside the car and the revolver
lay atop her. A big gun, it crushed Tamara from head to toe. He

61   drove faster, or so he imagined, until finally, gratefully, he heard a siren and the lights appeared in the mirror, drawing closer and more dramatic, making him swim in a blaze of red and white.

62   What to do? Hit the brakes, but do it smoothly. Decrease speed to a slow roll, then key off the ignition. Sag backwards against the damp seat.

63   A minute later he heard the knuckles lightly tapping on the window. He buzzed down the glass. He didn't look at the officer's face, but he allowed a sliver of hope. It might be her. If it was, she would see him before he handed over his license. The police officer mask would come off and she would speak to him, not as a woman but as a fellow creature. When he failed to answer, Roberta Raye would become even more extreme. She'd reach through the opening and put a hand on his shoulder. "Is that really you? Henning? What are you doing out here?"

64   He continued to stare straight ahead. There were no words yet, just a flashlight playing over his face. His right hand rested on Tamara, on the pistol. The heart palpitations had gone berserk.

65   It was plain now: he could die as easily as he could live. Just like the banker, there would be one ill-advised move and then it would be finished. He found it terrifying that such magnificence should remain within his clumsy grasp. Still he waited for the voice. That was what would settle it. There was a special kind of tone he was waiting for. Some kind of forgiveness not easily obtained. To hear someone say, "Henning, you're okay. Don't do it." That would be good.

66   He waited a few more uneven heartbeats. As long as there was time, most any words would work. He was past being particular. The mere sound of his name might suffice: "Henning, Henning, I see you, Henning, that's you, no one else, Henning, you're alive, come on, get out of the car, Max."

67   It was stupid to let your life get to such a point – dependent on one person out of the whole world. To hope that this one person would care for you where you had failed yourself miserably. To ask, if it came down to it, for that person to save you by pulling you back across the line. It was unacceptable. Unfair to them. Pathetic on your part. Turning yourself into a beggar, a little man with steamy bifocals that were about to fly out the open window. But it was real. He knew now

what it was like. The paralysis, the inability to unbend. Your 67
hand touching death while your ears still sought out life. The
distant freeway. Five miles away and every sound stroke of
the whooshing, speeding traffic registered on his brain. He
could hear them, the midnight people who didn't cut back
on their speed; they just went faster, trying to find that cheap
motel room or get to their six AM bacon and eggs on an oval
plate. Their spinning wheels were as loud as if Henning was
lying on his back on the centerline.

"Please," he thought, "slow down." 68

He turned his bulky body and stared into the officer's blind- 69
ing flashlight. He smelled sweet perfume. His heart seemed to
make a leap.

Erin McGraw

*Born and raised in Redondo Beach, California, Erin McGraw
received her MFA at Indiana University and has lived in the
Midwest ever since. Along with her husband, the poet Andrew
Hudgins, she teaches at the Ohio State University and divides
her time between Ohio and Tennessee. Her newest novel,* The
Seamstress of Hollywood Boulevard, *was published in August
2008, by Houghton-Mifflin. Before that she published* The Good
Life *(stories),* The Baby Tree *(a novel),* Lies of the Saints *(stories,
and a* New York Times *Notable Book for 1996), and* Bodies at Sea
(stories). Her short work has appeared in such magazines as The
Atlantic Monthly, Good Housekeeping, The Southern Review,
The Kenyon Review, STORY, The Georgia Review, *and many
others. A former Stegner Fellow at Stanford University, she has
received fellowships from the Ohio Arts Council and the corpora-
tions of MacDowell and Yaddo. About "The Penance Practicum,"
McGraw writes, "I love life best when it punctures certain kinds of
pomposities, and when the allegiances we had been clutching are
shown to be dubious, if not downright invalid. I've always loved
Flannery O'Connor's take-no-prisoners approach, probably more
than I should. "The Penance Practicum" punctures just about every
belief that comes down the line, and I love that about it. It was
exhilarating and searing to write."*

"THE PENANCE PRACTICUM"
from THE GOOD LIFE

1 FATHER DOM was pleased with his reflection in the mirror.
To the front of his cassock he had stapled a big dot cut out of
white paper; below the cincture he had stapled two more. Tonight
was the seminary's Halloween party. He was going as a domino.

379

He was ready to enjoy himself, although the party was one   2
of the things that had turned iffy around St. Boniface. Some of
the younger seminarians, shiny men of God who ran every five
minutes to look something up in one of John Paul II's encyclicals,
had raised objections: the proper end-of-October celebration for
Catholics was the Feast of All Saints, not Halloween.

"We'll celebrate the All Saints mass," Father Dom told the   3
stern contingent who came to his office. "We always do. But the
Halloween party is harmless. People like dressing up."

"The magisterium has not approved Halloween as a holiday for   4
the faithful," said Sipley. His beefy face, above the Roman collar
he'd worn every day since taking his first vows, was implacable.
Two of the men behind him shook their heads. Father Petrus
called this group Rome's hall monitors.

"It isn't forbidden," Father Dom said. "We won't be attending,"   5
Sipley said.

"There'll be punch," Father Dom said wearily. He wouldn't   6
miss them, but he hated to add mortar to the wall separating the
men who fluently discussed the mystical gifts of the Holy Father
from the rest of them, eating pizza and telling jokes down the
hall. Father Dom had bought the pizza.

He smoothed one of his dots. He himself had been on the   7
admissions committee the year Sipley applied. Even then the
man was talking about Holy Mother Church, coming on like
cutting-edge 1600s. Still, the committee had voted to admit him.
The committee had voted to admit every applicant, all five who
sought one of the thirty slots. St. Boniface's picking-and-choosing
days were long gone. But every time Father Dom thought about
a priesthood filled with Sipleys leaning over their pulpits and
confidently instructing their congregations, his heart hurt.
Father Dom had never felt as certain about anything as Sipley
felt about everything.

Hearing voices in the hallway, he opened his door. Several men   8
were heading toward the lounge, laughing, dressed for the party.
McCarley wore a cardboard cone taped over his huge nose; he'd
drawn lines of scurrying bugs around the end. "Anteater," he said
cheerfully. Father Dom's spirits started to rise.

"I hope you have a good sacerdotal defense. You never know   9
when the magisterium's going to be checking up."

10   "Anteaters are God's creatures. Nobody can challenge me.

11   What about you?"

12   "I'm a domino. I intend to impart valuable lessons about tipping over."

13   Behind McCarley, Terley shook his blond hair out of his eyes and fiddled with one of his pencils. He had a dozen or so, sharpened and taped to his shirt as if they'd been shot into him. There was always at least one St. Sebastian. And beside the two men, to Father Dom's delight, walked Joe Halaczek, dressed in salmon-pink Bermuda shorts, a plaid shirt, dark socks, and sandals. A cushion under his waistband gave him a burgher's paunch. "I give up," Father Dom said.

14   "The Race Is Not to the Swift. It's a concept costume," Joe said.

15   Then his voice took on its usual marshy unease. "Is that all right?"

16   "It's perfect," Father Dom said, hoping the white leather belt came from the secondhand store and not Joe's closet. Someone must have helped him with this – the concept of a concept costume was beyond him. With his frightened hands and unsteady eyes, ordinary conversation was often beyond him. Father Dom could hardly bear to think about his arriving at a parish, this damaged lamb attempting to lead the obstreperous sheep. But right now it was a hoot to watch Joe stroll along, hands behind his back, imitating a confident man.

17   "We tried to get him to come as Joan of Arc, but nothing doing," said McCarley. Already his cardboard nose was starting to work loose.

18   "I was afraid someone would set me on fire."

19   "Only if you had started hearing voices," Father Dom said, smiling when worried Joe glanced up.

20   Inside the lounge, festivities were puttering along. Four men shared the couch in front of the TV, talking and half watching an NFL roundup. Another group was playing darts. Everybody else was hovering over the snack table, making a clean sweep of the buffalo wings. Most of one pizza – cheese – was left.

21   "The Assyrian swept down like a wolf on the fold," said Father Benni, the rector, nodding at the decimated food.

22   "At least they're not letting the pizza get cold. Where's your costume?"

"This is it. The Good Priest." He folded his long arms and 23
assumed a benevolent expression, and Father Dom forbore
reminding him that generations of students, reacting to his firm
command, had called him Sheriff. "Bing Crosby will play me in
the movie. I don't know who's going to play you."

"Robert Redford." Father Dom reached over to the table and 24
snagged a wing.

"What do you think, Joe?" Father Benni said. Joe's head 25
snapped around when he heard the rector say his name. "Do you
think Robert Redford could play Father Dom?"

"It wouldn't be easy. A man of Father Dom's experience," Joe 26
said carefully.

Father Petrus, standing nearby, snorted. "Hey," Father Dom 27
said.

The rector was still looking at Joe. "Have you asked Father 28
yet? I think this would be a fine time."

It wasn't a fine time, whatever they were talking about – Fa- 29
ther Dom both did and didn't want to know. Joe was braiding his
fingers, looking at the carpet, and the color had dropped from
his face. When Joe spoke, Father Dom had to lean close to hear.
"Father Benni would like to observe our class tomorrow. I told
him I'm not the one who makes the decisions."

"You are, actually. You can say if you'd rather not be watched." 30

At this moment Father Dom would happily have strangled the 31
smiling rector, who was of course within his rights.

"What's the point of the class if you're not watched?" Joe said. 32

"The practicum is the best of all the seminary classes," Father 33
Benni said. "Getting feedback is a real gift. You're able to see
yourself as others see you. I miss that."

Joe's face was expressionless beside Father Benni's basking, 34
nostalgic smile. Father Dom said, "We can give you a taste of the
old medicine, Greg."

Father Benni said, "I was seminary champion in practicum. 35
Everybody wanted to confess to me because I gave the easi- 36
est penances."

"What made you change?" Father Dom said. 37

"I haven't changed," the rector said sunnily. "I'm a lamb. Isn't 38
that right, Joe?"

39   Joe was studying his shoes. "When I first got here, the fifth-year guys told me that you were easy." His mouth twitched. "They said you were easy, but to go to Father Dom if I had anything bad. He forgave everything."

40   "That's why we have him teach the practicum," Father Benni said equably. Glancing at Joe, he added, "It will go fine. You'll see." His voice was full of reassurance, but Joe's proto-smile had dissolved, and Father Dom guided the rector to the other side of the room.

41   "The practicum isn't Joe's best class," Father Dom said quietly.

42   From the couch came a small whoop; the T V was showing a beer ad that everybody liked.

43   "I'm not sure Joe has a best class," Father Benni said. "His paper for Mission & Ministry was a page and a half. In homiletic practicum he fell apart completely – got up and just couldn't speak. He doesn't look like a man on his way to ordination. He looks like a man on his way to the electric chair."

44   "So what do you want?"

45   "To be reassured."

46   Father Dom studied Joe, standing in line for darts. He lingered at the side of the group, not the center, smiling at someone else's joke. But there was no rule that said the priest needed to be the life of the party. Plenty of parishioners would appreciate Joe's gentle manner, his ability to listen rather than talk. While Father Dom watched Joe hitched up the cushion that held his shorts in place – his concept costume, worn in wistful good faith.

47   "No problem," Father Dom said.

48   Problem, all right. No course could be designed better than the penance practicum to showcase Joe's shortcomings. Every week, in front of the rest of the class, the students role-played priests hearing confession, with Father Dom as the penitent. He tried to keep things light, presenting goofy sins – once he'd played a woman who had visions of the Blessed Virgin saying to her, "You must wear natural fabrics." Sometimes the hardest thing for the students was keeping a straight face.

49   After the simulation the other students provided feedback, pointing out where the role-playing student had done well and where he showed room for improvement. The men were considerate with one another, but there were still so many ways to fall

short – hints gone unheard, hobbyhorses saddled up. In their 49
responses the students revealed themselves, which was why Joe
had been ducking the role-play all semester. Now Father Dom
would have no choice but to call on him. He'd have to call on
Sipley, too, who volunteered all the time.

Father Dom lay sleepless until three-thirty. Then, moving 50
softly – the walls separating the priests' rooms were like cheese-
cloth – he turned on the light and started reviewing notes. His
desk drawer was stuffed with class outlines, files he kept because
he'd been trained to keep files, though he almost never returned
to them. Now he was grateful. Surely these hundreds of pages
held some forgotten scenario that would demonstrate Joe's particular gifts.

Working without method, Father Dom riffled through the 51
syllabi, glancing now and then at a note he'd written. He searched
for a confession that required from the priest more sympathy
than guidance, some transgression that would turn Joe's shy heart
into a bridge between the penitent and God. No splashy sins like
murder or embezzlement. Nothing requiring close discernment
or tiptoeing among competing ethical schemes. Nothing about
girls, it went without saying. Simply the extension of forgiveness,
which had always seemed to Father Dom so easy.

At one time that ease had worried him. He had yearned to be 52
valorous, rich in the grace that comes from spiritual struggle. He
had worked with burn victims, telling them how a turn in life's
road, even a terrible one, could be the beginning of a happiness
never guessed at. "How, exactly?" asked a sixteen-year-old girl,
gesturing at a face that had become a cluster of shiny ridges when
she stumbled into her parents' sizzling barbecue grill. Another
patient, once a mother of three, had been folding laundry in her
basement when the house caught fire. Of all her family, only
she was still alive, and every day she cursed God with brilliant
inventiveness, then yelled at Father Dom, "Are you going to
forgive *that?*"

He did. The more he looked, the more he saw only God's 53
carelessness, work left undone when God got distracted, when
God moved on to something else, when God went to get a cup of
coffee and left Father Dom's mouth filled with inadequate words.
Father Dom had been called, he knew, to be God's hands and

53 voice in the world. He was just sorry that God couldn't find a better class of servant. Helplessly, he got the woman more ice chips and rested his hand tenderly on the side of her bed. Anybody could be forgiven for cursing in a world where somebody like Father Dom was left holding the bag for the Infinite.

54 He tried not to think about these things anymore. Seminarians of his generation had been taught that every priest was given his particular struggle of faith – the struggle, Father Dam's novice director had said often, that would last a lifetime. But Father Dom turned instead to the easier tasks of ministry, which were so plentiful – teaching, outreach. He could be a good priest without trying to solve the questions of suffering that even Augustine admitted were insoluble. He could help Joe.

55 He read until early gray light began to seep into the room and it was time to go to chapel. There he prayed his usual wordless prayer with more than common urgency, through breakfast, rising only when it was time to start class.

56 In the classroom students were seating themselves and pulling out their folders and books. Joe volunteered to fill the water pitchers. Then he volunteered to get cups. His face was the color of dust. He stopped beside Father Benni and murmured something; Father Dom watched the rector shake his head and gesture for Joe to sit down as Father Dom stood up. This week's assigned reading had centered on difficult confessions, surly or abusive penitents. It was important to have coping strategies, Father Dom said.

57 "You have to *listen*," said Hernandez, a thin-faced student with a smile like sunrise. "Don't just listen to what they're saying, but how they're saying it. People bring in their shame and guilt, so they're angry. If the only person nearby is the priest, they'll get mad at him."

58 "Have you ever had a penitent threaten you, Father?" Sipley asked Father Benni.

59 "I had someone pull a knife," the rector said. "He said he would cut out the screen between us to get to me."

60 "What did you do?"

61 "Gave him three Our Fathers and a Glory Be." Father Benni waited for the mild laughter to die down. "All you can do is be a priest. Of course, that's a lot."

Father Dom returned to the text, dragging out the discussion 62 as far as he could, but after half an hour every syllable had been covered, and Sipley volunteered to do the first role-play, striding to the front of the room where two chairs stood, separated by a screen. The burly man kissed the stole lying on one chair, placed it around his neck, and said, "Hello, my son," as if he'd been doing these things all his life.

Father Dom pulled out a dependable scenario: the teenage 63 boy who liked to kill cats. Once a student had sputtered, "You did *what?*" But Sipley was smooth, listening through Father Dom's resentful confession – his mother, he said, had forced him to come – and then talking about the sanctity of God's creations. "We are called to be good stewards," Sipley said. "Our job is to protect the defenseless."

In the discussion afterward, everyone praised Sipley's clarity. 64 Joe said that he admired Sipley's calm demeanor. Hernandez suggested that Sipley might have spent a little more time exploring the reason the boy was tying firecrackers to cats' legs. Sipley nodded, taking notes.

An anxious silence took over the room when Father Dom 65 asked for further comments; the air seemed to prickle. Joe was already trudging to the front of the room, where he hung the purple stole around his neck and sat down. "Okay," he whispered.

Reciting the opening prayer and adding that it had been six 66 years since his last confession; Father Dom wondered if he looked as nervous as he felt. He hoped so. A good priest would try to put a parishioner at ease.

"What brings you here today?" Joe finally asked. His voice 67 was faint. Sipley jotted a note.

"I didn't think I'd ever come to confession again. I don't really 68 believe in this. But I just saw my doctor. He says I'm HIV-positive." Father Dom paused. "I'm twenty-six years old."

He had gone over Joe's transcripts. Part of the young man's 69 fourth-year field education had been hospice work; he could draw on his experience with real patients, people he'd known and liked. But now, while Father Dom waited, Joe didn't say anything. "Are you there?" Father Dom said.

"Go on." 70

71   "Did you hear me? I'm twenty-six years old, and I'm HIV-positive. I just left the doctor. You're the first person I've told. I'm not
sure I can tell anybody else." Father Dom left room for Joe to ask
about his family or to murmur that the church was a good place
to come to. "How could-this happen to me?"

72   The silence stretched and thickened until Father Dom felt
anger start to buckle his thoughts. What was the matter with Joe?
All he had to say was *Are you afraid? Do you feel alone? God is
with you, even now. Especially now.* A kid who tied firecrackers
to cats could figure out that much.

73   "The only place I could think to come was here," Father Dam
said bitterly. "Don't ask me why. It's not like the Church has ever
helped before."

74   "Have you made plans for your death?" Joe said.

75   Air actually seemed to fly out of Father Dam's lungs. When
he looked up, every one of the students was writing. Even Sipley
looked stunned.

76   Joe was still talking, his voice like sand. "You need to study the
teachings of the Holy Father and then accord yourself with them.
The Church is very clear about the sinfulness of homosexual behavior. You should have come here sooner."

77   "That's not good enough," Father Dam said. He'd never mentioned homosexuality. Twenty-six years old! Maybe that sounded
old to this reedy voice behind the screen. "What am I supposed
to do now? I need help."

78   "There are several hospices in the area."

79   "What is the *matter* with you?" Father Dam said. He stuck his
face up close to the screen. "It is your job to care."

80   In the long silence, Father Dam imagined Joe standing at
the top of the cliff. His hands were tucked safely up his priestly
sleeves while Father Dam slipped off the edge.

81   "Peace be with you," Joe said.

82   Father Dam opened and then closed his mouth, unable to
think of one more thing to say. The students were silent until
Sipley, of all people, laughed. At that small, embarrassed noise
the others laughed too, looking at their feet. Even Father Benni,
whose lips had been tight, joined in. Only Father Dam remained
silent. When Joe stood up, Father Dam saw the dark spots on the
stole where the boy had sweated through it.

"I want to be a priest." Joe's voice was desperate. 83

"Why?" Father Dom said. 84

Father Benni called a faculty meeting that afternoon. "What 85
are his strengths?" he said, palming back the thick hair he was
normally vain about. He didn't have to explain what had happened in the practicum. Word was out before lunch.

"He pitches in," Father Petrus said. "He's not a shirker." 86

"Or a know-it-all," Father Wells said. 87

"There's a real sweetness there," said Father Lomax, who didn't 88
generally talk in these meetings.

"I know we all like Joe," Father Benni said, "but this sounds like 89
we're describing the president of the Altar Society. How would
he do with a headstrong parishioner? With a parish council?
Can he lead?"

"He hears a call," Father Dom muttered. 90

"Calls can be misheard," Father Benni said. 91

"You think he doesn't know that?" Father Dom stared at the 92
whorls in the table's laminated surface. "He goes around listening all the time. Priesthood is the one thing he wants, and he's
terrified that we're going to take it away from him."

"That's hardly our job. Still, when I compare him to some of 93
the other men –" Father Benni shook his head.

"That's exactly why it's important for Joe to be here," Father 94
Dom said. He wished he could curb the desperation rocketing
through his voice. "He has his own gifts. The seminary isn't supposed to turn out identical priests, each one perfectly sure of
himself, rolling off an assembly line with his collar in place and his
opinions set for life." He stopped under the weight of the rector's
sharp gaze, then added, "A little uncertainty isn't a bad thing."

"What I saw in your classroom was not enough uncertainty," 95
Father Benni said. "If that had been a real confession, the poor
man would have left the church and walked in front of a bus. Joe
did everything but push him."

"Why don't we assign him a mentor?" said Father Lomax. 96
"Someone he can talk to, who has better judgment."

Father Dom couldn't hold back his sigh. Was the mentor go- 97
ing to follow Joe to his parish and slip into the confessional with
him? But Father Benni was steepling his fingers, pondering the
suggestion, and Father Dom's imprudent heart lifted.

98   "Joe might improve if he's taken in hand by someone at his own level," the rector said. "He might be less defensive. Some of the men have volunteered to help."

99   "Greg, you're not thinking of assigning one of the students?" Father Dom said.

100   The rector nodded, apparently indifferent to the horror in Father Dom's voice. "It's win-win. A fine opportunity for growth on both sides. Besides, none of us wants to stay up as late as the students do."

101   Fathers Wells and Berton, those toadies, laughed. Father Dom said, "Students don't have the experience. They think they know more than they do. Joe needs trustworthy guidance."

102   "He's had the benefit of your guidance for four years," Father Benni said. "I'd say it's time for a new approach."

103   "Just not this one," Father Dom said. The priests laughed and pushed back their chairs. Dependable Dom, always good for a joke. He stayed at the table until he and the rector were alone in the room. "Nobody wants Joe to succeed more than I do," Father Dom said. "But it's going to take a miracle."

104   "Good. That's our turf."

105   "Right," Father Dom said bitterly. "I keep forgetting."

106   Father Benni chose Sipley to be Joe's mentor. And he chose Father Dom to oversee Sipley – to mentor the mentor. Father Dom was overscheduled with classes and field experience and his outreach program at the youth center, but he was glad for the assignment. Every night Sipley came to him to describe Joe's progress, and Father Dom imagined Joe as a fragile boat that he could still see in his spyglass.

107   "He's shy, is all. Once you get him in a situation where he's comfortable, he opens up." Sipley was sitting in Father Dorn's office, cradling between his big hands the cup of coffee Father Dom had offered.

108   "Where is he comfortable?"

109   "You should have seen him in the soup kitchen. He was jawing with everybody who came through. 'Hey, how's it going, you want gravy with that?' And nobody gave him a hard time. I think they could see what he is." Sipley shifted his bulky thighs on the hard chair. "In his way, he really brings out the best in people."

"But can you imagine Joe setting up the soup kitchen and overseeing it? A priest needs to show initiative."

Sipley shifted again. Even in his discomfort he gave the impression of being fundamentally comfortable. "He's heard a call, Father. It isn't up to me to question that."

"It is up to the rector and me to question that." Looking at Sipley's polite, averted face, Father Dom added, "In the service of the Church. Joe will be a representative of the Holy Father. And we're asking you to help us make sure he can be a good representative."

The speech had the desired effect: Sipley leaned forward and rested his elbows on his knees. When he spoke, his resonant voice was confiding. "Joe's never going to be a take-charge guy. He's all heart. But if he's working with somebody who can direct him, he'll give a hundred percent. He wants this so much."

Father Dom analyzed the young man's ruddy face and broad, chapped hands. Everything about him breathed with vibrancy. Had he ever wondered why quailing Joe could be drawn to the same priesthood Sipley was so confident about? Had he thought about the role of a man in society but not of it, safely shut away from human contact by vestments and a collar? Probably not. Sipley himself wanted to be a priest so he could tell people what to do.

"I can't believe there's no place for him," Sipley was saying.

"We're still looking," Father Dom said.

Sipley nodded. "If you don't mind my asking, Father – did you question my call, too?"

Startled, Father Dorn said, "You don't present the same issues."

"But still."

Sipley's wide-set eyes were alit with new curiosity. This chance would not come again. "Of course we did," said Father Dom. "There's no such thing as an automatic priest."

"All my life people have told me I was born to be a priest. My mother, for one. Half the time it's a compliment."

"It's not something to be taken for granted."

"So I'm being tested? Is that why you asked me to help with Joe?"

"You're likely to pass," Father Dom said. "Don't lose any sleep over this." But he could see already, as Sipley stood and shook

122   Father Dom's hand, how the young man's body was bright with new energy. Father Dom should have been grateful; his own weariness had increased a hundredfold.

123   In the days that followed, Father Dom expected Sipley to lay siege to Joe, intent on their mutual salvation. But Sipley was a better psychologist than Father Dom had given him credit for. He met Joe casually, in the halls or over coffee, and twice he reported to Father Dom that he hadn't spoken with Joe that day. "Figured he could use a vacation from me."

124   Father Dom was giving Joe a vacation, too. Aside from the weekly meetings of the practicum, he saw Joe only from a distance – in the library, the dining commons, on the walkway in front of the soccer field. When he believed himself unobserved, Joe took his place easily with the other men, and from time to time he tipped back his head in laughter. But as soon as he saw Father Dom, his gaze dropped again, and dread clung to his pale, chewed mouth. Father Dom understood that Joe had assigned him the role of the enemy, obstacle to Joe's happiness. The perception wasn't wrong, but still Father Dom felt stung.

125   Every day he defended Joe to one priest or another, pointing out how the young man was the first to help clear tables, the first to donate to clothing drives for countries rent by earthquakes. He heard the words' puniness as they rolled out of his mouth. Everyone in the seminary was waiting for Joe to prove himself with something more than a clothing drive. In these priest-starved days, when Father Lomax predicted that St. Boniface would have to start ordaining dogs, it was a special humiliation to be reevaluated, and Father Dom knew that Joe felt persecuted.

126   So Father Dom was relieved when, after three weeks of mentoring, Sipley told him that he had a new idea about Joe, a breakthrough plan. "It's nothing that you'll object to. I've put in a few phone calls, and I'm waiting to hear."

127   "Give me a hint, in case the rector asks."

128   Sipley paused. "The battle is not to the strong."

129   "That's not going to be much help if he presses me for details."

130   "Joe just needs the right chance to shine." Sipley beamed. As always, he was confident in the goodness of his actions. But Father Dom wondered if the young man remembered the end of the passage he had quoted: "all are subject to time and mischance."

A week passed before Father Dom returned to his office and 131
found a note tacked to the corkboard. *Could you join Joe and
me in the dining room? We'd like to propose something.* Father
Dom turned left, toward the cafeteria, worrying at a hangnail
as he walked.

The dining room was empty except for the two men sitting 132
by the window, whose heads swung up in unison at the creak of
the swinging door. Sipley said, "Thank you for coming, Father."

Father Dom seated himself beside Joe. Since the young man 133
was pretending he hadn't edged away from the table, Father Dom
pretended he didn't notice.

"An opportunity has come up," Sipley said after Father Dom 134
turned down coffee or iced tea. "I think it's too special to miss.
One of the staff members at St. Thérèse House had to leave,
and they need someone to step in right away. Joe and I could
go together."

"Are you serious?" Father Dom said. 135

"It's a special opportunity." Joe's voice was dim. "Our men 136
don't usually go there."

They sure didn't. St. Thérèse House was a two-story facility 137
downtown for terminal children, youngsters dying from cancer
or brain lesions or frenzied infections Father Dom had never
heard of. Children went to St. Thérèse House when they couldn't
survive another faltering transplant or more scorching chemo-
therapy. A hospice for six- and seven-year-olds, it drew patients
from three states away. Doctors in the area were proud of the
institution, which appalled Father Dom. Sweet Jesus, it was not
something to be proud of.

Although he had never been in it, he realized he could de- 138
scribe the place as if he'd lived there. For every child who died
with a face filled with light, three others left this earth looking
puzzled or disappointed or so crocked on morphine they couldn't
feel the oils of the last rites being thumbed onto their foreheads.
His stomach turned heavily.

"Their people are trained," Father Dom said. "They're short- 139
handed," Sipley said.

Joe studied his clear brown tea, and Father Dom automati- 140
cally thought of Gethsemane. He wondered whether Joe was
also thinking of that utter despair. In a brief burst of viciousness,

140 Father Dom hoped he was, then was ashamed of himself. "When would it start?" Father Dom said.

141 "That depends on you," Sipley said. "There's only so far the staff can bend the rules. We can come, but a faculty member has to supervise."

142 Father Dom opened his mouth and shut it again. "I don't have medical training," he said.

143 "The staff will be keeping an eye on the patients," Sipley said.

144 "They want someone to keep an eye on us. Since you've been working with Joe and me, I thought you should be the one. Of course, I could ask somebody else."

145 And somebody would agree. Priests always went: the jails, the hospitals, the shuttered, stinking houses. "Beats reality TV," Father Wells had said one day after a visit to the prison, his eyes blazing. He might very well go to St. Thérèse House and train his gaze on those withering children. His gaze would also land on Joe, helpless at the bedside.

146 "I'll go," Father Dom said, lifting his chin. "I'll *go*," he added, not that Sipley or Joe had asked a second time.

147 St. Thérèse House smelled like apples. Most of the children ate through feeding tubes, but one or two could manage soft foods, and every morning ferocious Sister Lupe, who looked thin even in sweatpants, made a fresh batch of applesauce. "At lunch you will feed them," she told Joe and Sipley, "Until then you will visit with the children who are alone." The two young men nodded, as did Father Dorn, standing a step behind them. Sister Lupe glanced at him with flat eyes, and then led them down a corridor.

148 Bedrooms unfolded in wings from the central hall, and in either apple-smelling direction lay children, one to a room. The children were bald and gray faced, lying in what looked less like sleep than suspension. Parents, murmuring steadily, sat close beside the beds.

149 "How long do they stay here?" Sipley was asking.

150 "Two weeks, typically," Sister Lupe said. "The one you're going to see has been here almost three months, our longest ever. You're getting her because she already knows all of our jokes." Father Dom tried to imagine a joke coming out of Sister Lupe's lipless mouth.

151 "What does she have?" Sipley asked. "Leukemia."

"Where are her parents?" Joe asked.   152

Sister Lupe's smile was vulpine. "Several agencies would like   153
to know." She breezed into the girl's room, then looked back and
gestured impatiently for Joe and Sipley to follow. "Look, Cindy.
Father Sipley and Father Halaczek are here to see you. And Father
Dominic." The girl smiled at them with half her mouth. Father
Dom didn't know whether she had lost motor control on one side
or she meant the expression to look ironic. "Hi."

Bruises ran in chains up her arms and ringed her neck, and   154
around the bruises her skin was a dry noncolor. Her skull made a
hard dent in the pillow. Father Dom guessed she was twelve years
old, but he could have been three years off in either direction.

"They're going to visit with you until lunch," Sister Lupe said.   155
"That's a long time," Cindy said.

"It's good for you to see new faces," the sister said, already on   156
her way out of the room. "Enjoy yourselves, Fathers."

Cindy's expression was clearly long-suffering, and Father   157
Dom revised his age estimate upward. "Are you here to talk to
me about dying?" she said.

"Not if you don't want to," Sipley said. "What's on your mind?"   158
"No offense, but I'm scared of priests. It's not good news when
you guys come around."

Joe reached behind his neck and unsnapped his collar. "I don't   159
have to wear this. I haven't been ordained."

"You're in training?"   160

"I'm on probation. I messed up, and I'm being given one last   161
chance."

"So you're here to show your stuff."   162

Joe nodded, and Cindy said to Father Dom, "What does he   163
need to do?"

"Just be with you."   164

"Some test." She closed her eyes. Father Dom had stood be-   165
side hospital beds for twenty-five years; rarely had he seen a face
so dwindled, her forehead collapsed as if someone had stuck
a thumb into it. He flattened his wet palms against his thighs.
Sipley and Joe were talking to her. He could slip out of the room
and no one would notice.

"Well, do it," Cindy was saying to the young men, her eyes   166
still closed. "I'm not going anywhere."

167   Joe said, "What do you want to talk about?" "You talk. I'll listen."

168   Father Dom's stomach seemed to tip. Shamefully, he couldn't stop thinking that he was breathing the air that had passed through Cindy's diseased membranes. He pulled a tissue from the box on the ledge and held it before his face as if he were going to blow his nose.

169   Joe said, "Our Father."

170   "No," Cindy murmured. "I don't like that one. Do your own."

171   Joe smiled crookedly. "Please. That's the only good prayer I know."

172   Cindy didn't open her eyes. "Sister Lupe says the best prayers are one word. What's your word?"

173   "Please," Joe said promptly. "Keep going."

174   The smell of apples billowed softly from the corridor. "Please. God," Joe said, the word like a cough. "You are in heaven. And your name is – praised." His white face was damp, and he stood at a tilt, as if every muscle in his body were locked. "I could use some help," he said to Father Dom.

175   "What do you want me to do?" Father Dom hadn't meant to sound savage, and he was embarrassed when Cindy looked at him with interest.

176   "Aren't you supposed to be telling me about heaven?" she said.

177   "Ask Father Halaczek. He knows," Father Dom said, a bit of malice to add to his lifetime sins of evasion and cowardice, sins he yearned for now as his eyes slid away from the girl's cheeks, molded to the bone. All a priest could do was plead for her release and hope that pleading would do some good. Joe knew that lesson as well as Father Dom. Joe, who pleaded so much, knew it better.

178   The young man grasped the corner of Cindy's sheet, his hand tightening and releasing, his voice shaking. "Please. Your will is going to happen," he said, and then broke down. Pressing his hands against his face, he stood beside the bed, his shoulders racked. "This is the worst thing that's ever happened to me," he said. "And it's going to get worse." He wheeled around to face Father Dom, who had backed up until his shoulders touched the wall. The smell of apples rose around him, and his nausea was roiling like a sea. "Isn't it?" Joe said.

179   "Yes," said Father Dom.

"Are you going to stop my ordination?"   180

"No."   181

"Why not?"   182

Sipley said, "Fathers, we're here to pray for healing." He began   183
to move his lips unselfconsciously, a powerful man who could
probably hold the seventy-pound girl in one hand. Here, Father
Dom realized, was the test Sipley had set for himself: to halt
death's advance, even though death was on the march. Death
had already won. Father Dom wondered when Sipley was going
to acknowledge that.

"Why not?" Joe repeated, louder.   184

"Who else would come here?" Father Dom said.   185

"I don't think you're supposed to say those things where I can   186
hear them," Cindy said.

"Father Dominic is a special priest," Joe said. "You're lucky   187
to even see him. Why don't you lead us in prayer, Father? We
need guidance."

Joe probably didn't hear the rage that rang through his words.   188

And Father Dom would forgive the boy – just as, when he   189
looked at Cindy's shrunken, darkening body, he already forgave
her parents for running away. In the end he forgave everybody,
which was half the reason Joe would never forgive him.

Father Dom dampened his lips to say something unobjection-   190
able about faith and perseverance. He breathed in the
apple-drenched air. The instant he opened his mouth, he vomited
where he stood. Sipley managed to get a basin under Father Dom's
mouth for the last of it, but the room was full of the stink, and
when he finished Father Dom could not lift his swimming eyes.

"Usually I'm the one who does that," Cindy said.   191

"I'm sorry," he murmured, afraid to say anything more. Sipley   192
was probably warming up to quote St. Paul: the Spirit expresses
itself in outcries that we ourselves do not understand. If Sipley
said one word, Father Dom would retch again.

"Father," Joe said, "you should have told us you were ill." He   193
pulled a chair beside Cindy's bed.

She said, "Do you mind not talking?"   194

"I'll get you something to drink." Joe's thin voice wavered.   195

When Cindy shook her head, he said, "We have such a long   196
day ahead. Let me get you something. Please."

Gina Ochsner

<(1970-)>

Gina Ochsner lives in Keizer, Oregon, and divides her time between writing and teaching at Corban University and in the Seattle Pacific Low-Residency MFA program. Ochsner has been awarded a John L. Simon Guggenheim grant and a grant from the National Endowment of Arts. Her stories have appeared in The New Yorker, Tin House, Glimmertrain *and the* Kenyon Review. *She is the author of the short story collection* The Necessary Grace to Fall, *which received the Flannery O'Connor Award for Short Fiction and the story collection* People I Wanted to Be. *Both books received the Oregon Book Award. Her most recent work,* The Russian Dreambook of Colour and Flight *was selected for the Grub Street Book Prize. About "Half-Life" Ms. Ochsner writes: "As a child I spent many weekends visiting relatives who lived near lighthouses. One in particular, Terrible Tilly, provoked stories of shipwrecks, drowning. The lighthouse had the reputation of driving its keepers mad. And then, a few years ago, I read* Children of the Light, *a book of essays written by people who had been raised in lighthouses. I marveled at what seemed to me the strangeness of their lives, the oddity of living primarily to make light for the sake of others. I wanted to explore the idea of transformations: those from the inside out, as in the case of being wrecked by love when someone thought they were well beyond it, as well as transformations from the outside in, as in the skins we wear and would gladly trade for another."*

HALF LIFE

1   HAVING SWALLOWED TOO many bones, the sea has a bad case of indigestion. This sound of dyspepsia shatters the nerves and Erlen Steves knows that is why no one wants to live at the lighthouse. It doesn't help matters that three men died

during its construction. When the mail boat ferries him to the ¹
docks, this fact is just one of the many things Erlen knows to keep
quiet about in the presence of the local coasties.

Which suits him fine. He is not in the business of making ²
noise, but of making light. In water and at sea, life revolves around
his light. And each evening before starting his watch, Erlen recites
the Light Keeper's prayer. A longish prayer – Erlen does not have
it up by heart. Which is why the prayer is typed, framed, hanging
at the landing at the base of the light tower. Erlen does not bother
with the beginning, but the end holds salt: . . . *grant, oh Thou
Blessed Savior, that Thou would join us as we cross the last bar
and struggle for the farther shore, the lee shore of the land where
the sun never goes down, and where there is no darkness for He
who is the light of the world will be the light thereof.*

No one would accuse Erlen of being overly religious, but he ³
isn't the type to stand in the way of it either. A prayer can't hurt
here on the rock, he thinks when he climbs the steep sixty-foot
spiral staircase to the service room, where the light is kept. The
light, a first order Fresnel, stands nearly twelve feet tall and six
feet wide. The lenses are composed of glass segments arranged
in rings and stacked in concentric circles.

When his father kept the light, it used to take the young ⁴
boy – and then later, the young man – Erlen all of a day to clean
the nearly one thousand pieces of glass. This left only a little free
time to comb the rocks for pieces of the sea: sand-smoothed
pebbles, razor clam shells, the spiraled dog whelks that house
miniature tornadoes inside their fragile casings.

The shells held to his ear, the young man Erlen marveled that ⁵
out of such dryness issued the musical sound of water. And that
the high tide could carry such items of fragility and strength
(once – whole green and blue glass floats all the way from Japan)
seemed a mystery intended for him to solve. Imagine his surprise when he found one day not a shell, but a woman, nude
and shivering, washed up on the breakers. What could he do,
but take her and that bedraggled fur coat tucked under her arm,
into the lighthouse? What could he do but fall in love with and
marry her? What could he do but get her with children – twins
no less? And what could he do, being book-bound and a little
forgetful, but lose her?

6   "I'm not surprised," Inspector Wilson said when Erlen delivered the news: Mrs. Erlen Steves, wearing nothing but that
tattered fur coat minus the collar and a portion of the left sleeve,
had jumped from the rocks. "This lighthouse has a history of
driving its keepers mad." Inspector Wilson circled a finger at his
ear, and then tugged on his jacket of his Coast Guard uniform.

7   Erlen searched his memory of all the logbooks he'd read. "I
didn't know that."

8   "Well, you know it now," Inspector Wilson said, casting a
long look at the girls, already toddlers and tethered to a laundry
line – in accordance to the light keeper's safety manual.

8a   "A selkie* loves water," Astrid says.
            "– A selkie loves land" says her sister, Clarinda.
            "– A selkie walks on two feet . . . "
            "– whenever she can."

> **Selkie** · In Scottish and Scandinavian folklore, a creature who lives as a seal in the sea, but on land becomes human.

9   Jump-rope geniuses, Astrid and Clarinda sing out tandem
rope rhymes and never miss a beat. At the Mt. Angel boarding
school they are unusual girls – always have been, Mother Iviron
thinks – and not just because they are twins. Skin pale, jaws
strong, mouths flat, the girls have eyes a color of blue so reluctant
they border on gray. The only way Reverend Mother Iviron can
tell them apart is the way Astrid pushes out her lower jaw in the
presence of uninvited pity, while Clarinda tears up and turns red.

10   United utterly, what one girl starts the other girl finishes:
rhymes, riddles, math problems. A phrase in the mouth of one
twin finds its completion in the mouth of the other. If Astrid feels
the bite of nail, Clarinda cries out as it punctures the sole of her
shoe. When Astrid slaps the girl who calls her creepy times two,
it is Clarinda who makes penance with a spate of *Hail Marys*,
repetition being the heaven of duplicate things.

10a   *Hail Mary, full of grace, the Lord is with thee.*
            Blessed art thou among women,
            and the fruit of thy tomb, Jesus.

11   Fruit of the tomb? Mother Iviron, beyond girlhood puns, doesn't
think twice when she makes the girls wear the hair shirts.* Old
fashioned, oh yes. But to tell the truth, they didn't seem to mind
it too much.

> **Hair shirt** · a shirt made of coarse animal hair, worn next to the skin as a sign of penance

Equally suspicious to Mother Iviron is the way the girls pre- 11
pare for bed. They slide their cots together and before climbing
in, they line up their shoes, turning the points toward each other
as if the shoes might continue an ongoing conversation.

11a

> *"When a selkie drags you under"*
> *"– she'll split your skin asunder."*

When she hears this kind of talk, Mother Iviron stretches a 12
hurting smile across her face. Far be it from her to stifle the
imagination. And certainly tragic stories of the sea bear instruc-
tional value. But when the girls turn eleven and substitute sea
chanteys for prayers, Mother Iviron sends them home to their
father with her regrets.

✦ ✦ ✦

THE LIGHTHOUSE STANDS sixty feet high, tall as a castle. 13
Ringed black, and white, the painted markings turn the light
tower into layered cake, spun sugar. The staircase curves in a tight
spiral, the corkscrewed architecture of a lightning whelk. In the
lantern room, the girls crack open a window and take turns playing Rapunzel. All the lighthouse needs now is a resident witch.

The girls shout out into the wind: *Come find us!* In the mean- 14
time they keep busy. The work: polishing brass and cleaning
glass, doing all to bend and multiply light in its refractions and
reflections. Special care must be given to the first-order Fresnel
and its catadioptric° lens assembly. The bulls-eye lens rotates and
magnifies the light as it swings. From a distance of twenty-six
miles away the light appears as a flash over the water. At least,
this is what their father's manual of operation says. But to the girls
wearing their green safety goggles, the lenses look like a gigantic
transparent beehive. The rotating bulb behind the bulls-eye is
the queen bee. Astrid and Clarinda, the custodians of the glass,
are the confused dim-witted drones.

Catadioptic · involv-
ing both the reflection
and refraction of light

For the longest time they thought the light was meant to 15
lure the ships nearer – yes, right up to the rocks. Never did they
imagine the light was meant to turn away every vessel except
the mail boat or Inspector Wilson's tender, which would arrive
in evenings without any warning and set their father scrambling.
Astrid and Clarinda aren't quite sure what to make of Mr. Wilson,

15 the Coast Guard's Aid to Navigation Inspector. When he comes with his high-powered nose lowered, Mr. Wilson always examines the kitchen first, tallying its contents and cleanliness down to every drawer and cupboard, each piece of cutlery. Astrid thinks he looks like a bloodhound on the scent of something turned sour. Clarinda thinks he looks like God wearing a dark uniform and white gloves. Only God would smile more often, Clarinda decides as she pockets two knives, a fork and spoon – just to throw the count off.

✤ ✤ ✤

16 BEWILDERED. ERLEN STEVES is bewildered. Nobody told him how to raise girls. His many books about sea creatures, legendry and lore have been no help at all. And nothing in the engineering texts or the lighthouse operation manuals explain how to ease the loss of a wife and a mother.

17 All of which to say, Erlen hasn't fully recovered. He knows this. Lulled by the changing moods of the water, its murmur and roar, it's hard not to think water, think salt, think tears. He knows it's unseemly to grieve for so long, but his sorrow is amplified, doubled, on account of the girls. He is not sad for himself: he lost a wife he suspects he was never meant to have. But for the girls to lose their mother while still so young – it splits his heart in half every time he looks at them.

18 He tries to be strong. He kisses them each on the forehead. Astrid's skin is always a little cool to the touch, Clarinda's always a little warm, feverish even, and then he climbs the sixty feet to sit with the light. The night watch he spends alone in the service room, cleaning the glass, polishing the bull's-eye lamp, which turns and turns as regular and steady as the beating of a heart. That anything so large or so small as a bulb could whirl with such constancy brings a comfort to him, here, in the lighthouse where he knows nothing, not even water, should be taken for granted – neither the things the water carries away nor what the water might bring.

✤ ✤ ✤

19 BY DAY SISTER ROSETTA teaches the K-6 boarders at the Mt. Angel Parochial school. By night she writes a religious

mystery novel and edits the *Convent Cloister Herald,* circulation   19
thirty-eight. Thirty-seven after Sister Margaretta, God bless her,
died peacefully in her sleep.

She's got a talent, that one, the other sisters say. A real way   20
with the words, the way they never lock-step fail on her. And the
way she can phrase a question: "Does Jesus still bear the wounds
in his side and hands and feet now that he is ascended to the
right hand of the Father?" A question so direct it unsettles the
older sisters, Mother Iviron in particular, whose eyebrows stitch
together at the scent of such mysteries. Such unanswerable questions ring with the hollow interior of the rhetorical. They make
Sister Iviron's joints ache and her teeth throb. Sister Rosetta,
blissfully unaware of what her words do to Sister Iviron, pokes
around for the soft entrails, for the heart of faith, keeps poking
with these questions in her nighttime dreaming.

Her dreams! Sister Rosetta's dreams could fill an ocean. Will   21
she ever stop? "Honestly," Sister Iviron says. The way Sister
Rosetta's frolicking queries keep the first-year postulants up at
night, roiling the calm rarified air within the stone walls of the
convent – it's enough to drive them to distraction. *Why did Jesus*
heal some and not others? Sister Rosetta asks in a dream, and the
postulants and novitiates rise and bob in the gathering waters of
Sister Rosetta's viscous questions.

It wouldn't be so bad, except Sister Rosetta is always the first   22
to stir, waking with a shout and leaving the rest awash in her
unnavigable dreams. Some of the postulants have signed up for
swimming lessons. Others wear life jackets under their seersucker
bedclothes and clamp plugs over their noses.

After too many nights left stranded in Sister Rosetta's dreams,   23
Mother Iviron makes phone calls, drafts letters. In record speed,
Sister Rosetta's resume makes the rounds.

✦　✦　✦

A man fell in love with a woman.   23a
But the woman was in love with the sea.

THEIR FATHER'S VOICE winds down the stair case from the   24
service room, that furnace of green and light and heat grown
thick with their father's singing. He is shaping his grief, casting

24 sorrow line by line, limb by limb, into the figure of a woman they cannot remember. In the place of her body, Astrid and Clarinda have these weepy words they know they were never meant to hear, but have long ago committed to memory. The same words that pushed Sister Iviron's determined smile askew, words that make the girls thirsty to know things. So many questions Astrid and Clarinda would love to ask their mother. So much about sky, skin, water, they would like to know. But their mother swam out to sea one day and forgot to return. "It was very strange – she being a champion swimmer," their father sometimes says.

25 When they cannot bear to hear their father sing, they climb the steps, put on the safety goggles, and tug on his sleeves. They pull him down to the kitchen for dinner, for midnight snacks, for breakfast which is always the same fare: Spam on crackers or macaroni with canned tomato sauce.

25a   "Tell us a story."
        "A sad, strange story."
        "A strange, scary story."

26 Erlen tries. He collects and collates the strangest stories he can find. To date he has amassed two notebooks full of sea lore and legendry. As they eat their macaroni and Spam, he tells of lighthouse ghosts and large boats split to splinters on rocks like these, and small, mischievous sea creatures. He tells them about a mermaid who almost married a prince. But the prince married another and the mermaid came to him one night as he lay sleeping and killed him with a poisoned kiss upon the lips.

27 "That's not so sad," Astrid says.

28 "And it's not so strange," Clarinda adds. She holds a row of macaroni noodles between her teeth and makes strange music through her homemade harmonica.

29 "Then maybe you've heard about the selkies, who look astonishingly like seals. In their whiskers they carry magic. If they fall in love with a human – and they do this more often than you might think – then they will unzip their fur, tuck it into a bundle and hide it somewhere safe. Later, when they are tired of their human body, tired of human love, they simply pull their fur back on and swim out to sea."

The girls shudder. The pupils of their eyes dilate, then shrink   30
to pin-points as if their eyes themselves are breathing. Erlen likes
to tell this story because it's the only story the girls sit still for.
But certain parts of the story he doesn't tell. A wayward selkie
who has children with a human must come back for the children
when they become women – otherwise those children will forever remain trapped in their human bodies. But this involves the
changing of bodies and desires, and this isn't something Erlen
likes to think about. He doesn't like change. To Erlen's reckoning,
his girls will always be girls just as the lighthouse will always be
their stronghold, their safety.

But one night he finds the girls in the lantern room, their long   31
hair braided into knots and flung out the window as a ladder,
their bodies leaning dangerously over the sill, and he realizes in
a blink how thoroughly he doesn't understand them – how foolish he's been to hand them so many fictions to inhabit. He hauls
them back in, too hard. His fingers leave a mark on Astrid's arm.
But it's Clarinda who gasps and narrows her eyes. And he knows
everything he will do to make it up from this point forward will
be exactly the wrong thing.

※　※　※

IN THE WAKING WORLD water is danger, water will drown   32
them. The girls do not know how to swim. Though long off
their lighthouse leads, they still cling to each other behind the
rail, afraid of the seventh wave, the sneaker that might pull them
over and out. At night they push their beds together. Two com-
mas, if they lie on their beds, touch toes to toes, head to head,
their bodies form a circuitous loop. Choosing one heart to live in,
one body of dreaming to inhabit, in no time they drift into
each other's dreams. Barefoot they clamber over shore rock and
into the shallows where the limpets and starfish move so slowly
it's as if in dreams, time sheds its hold over things born in water.
Deeper they wade until they feel underfoot the velvet and buzz
of the corals.

Farther out, the rock and sand shelf plunges and the water   33
swallows them. It burns a little to take it in through the nose. But
they've been practicing every night in their dreams and breathing under water comes easier than it used to. Overhead the sun

33 blooms purple, blooms blue, a kelp bulb floating across their untroubled ceiling of liquid. When they wake to a waterless sun, the light carries edges and angles, slicing their room. Gone are the dreams, the very memory of the fact that they had, indeed, been dreaming. The only clues: salt rimming their eyelids and crusted under their fingernails, their night gowns wet and wadded up into a pile at the foot of their beds.

❖ ❖ ❖

34 THE GIRLS ARE GOOD READERS, having scoured the lighthouse logs for any mention of their mother. And they've even memorized the lighthouse prayer in its entirety – no easy feat. But theirs is a lopsided education, and when the girls ask how to divide twins by twos – a problem of fractions if ever he's heard one – Erlen writes to Mr. Wilson, requesting a visiting schoolteacher and nanny.

35 In no time he receives a typed letter on heavy linen paper. It is from Mt. Angel Convent. A suitable candidate will be sent over immediately. Erlen scratches his head, sniffs the lily-white stationary in sheer amazement. He cannot recall actually mailing his request. The notion that God and Mr. Wilson might work in tandem and quicker than the Tuesday mail boat only adds to his bafflement. For there is Mr. Wilson's tender, nosing alongside the landing. All this on a Monday!

36 With a bellow from the fog horn, the boat heaves to, and down Erlen goes, *clink, clink, clink,* his boots over the steps. The girls, eyes gray as stone, stand on the landing and clutch the rail. But it's the new teacher he's worried about, bobbing and pitching in Inspector Wilson's tender. Erlen ties off the boat and studies her. A stranger to water, her stomach is in her throat. This much Erlen can see right clear. Her face is as pale as her starched collar and veil, and she's got a fine sheen of sweat above her upper lip. *Go ahead,* he'd like to tell her. *Retching is the only way to beat the nasea.* When he grabs for her hands, soft and pudgy like a child's, they melt to fit his. Erlen lifts her from the boat and his breath stutter steps in his throat. He realizes he had forgotten what a woman's hands feel like.

❖ ❖ ❖

S ISTER ROSETTA, A LITTLE queasy in Mr. Wilson's tender, 37
surveys the lighthouse rock and her new charges. She spots
the two girls standing at the railing. Hard telling where one girl
begins and the other ends and Sister Rosetta understands why
she's been sent: to care for them in the singular, to care for them
in the plural. For it's clear in a glance that this land does not
love these girls – stick thin, chalky-faced, their long brown hair
whipped to tails, Sister Rosetta sees a picture of twinned longing,
so raw and pure she has to look away.

Mr. Steves, the girls' father, reaches out and pulls her from 38
the boat. His hand is rough against her skin and though his grip
is completely appropriate, she feels flustered, can't help thinking
that this is the perhaps the first and last time she will be touched
by a man, any man.

A low blast from the horn and the boat leaves. Mr. Steves 39
strides ahead to the lighthouse with her suitcases. Sister Rosetta
tips her head at angle and studies the girls whose fingers have
turned white under the pressure of their grip.

"Are you all right?" Sister Rosetta asks. 40

"Seven," says the girl on the left. 41

"Cry seven tears at high tide and a selkie will cry with you," 42
explains the girl on the right.

"Seven," Sister Rosetta says, "is God's number." 43

"Why?" 44

Sister Rosetta nudges her glasses higher onto her nose. 45
"Because on the seventh wave, what God has taken He gives
back."

"Our mother was swept away on the seventh wave. It was 46
very strange –

"– she being a near champion swimmer." 47

"I'm sorry. I didn't know that," says Sister Rosetta, blinking 48
fiercely behind her glasses.

"Well, you know it now," says the girl on the left, her jaw 49
thrust out.

The girl on the right: nose red and snuffling, chin all atremble. 50
It's going to be a job, Sister Rosetta knows, but the girls turn
sweet, leading her by the hand up, up, up the winding stairs,
throwing open the door to each room so that she can see for
herself: the storage room, kitchen, sleeping quarters and bath-

50 room, library, and at the very top, the service room. Sister Rosetta doesn't know about the green tinted safety goggles and looks directly into the heart of the light, into brilliance so fierce it's like looking at God in glory, a light meant to guide but viewed too closely would certainly blind.

◆ ◆ ◆

51 D AYS PASS, EACH ONE a crow-shaped stain falling from the shore pines. The wind kicks up, breaks brittle days into halves, throws Erlen's nose out of kilter. The lighthouse smells of metal, of wet copper, of pennies. It was his wife's smell: pure and elemental, edged and biting like salt. One afternoon Erlen leaves the lantern room, his nose roving in all directions, tracking the scent of skin and wet fur. His nose leads him to the library where the wind has snapped a windowpane. Sister Rosetta is there, a flurry of pages from the primer swirling around her. She stands on tiptoe reaching for the paper that curls out and away from her. She looks like a figurine in a snow globe. The sight of her, not at all a bad looking woman, provokes his heart to skip. And it's at that precise moment Erlen becomes a religious man, thanking God for this wind, for stirring things up.

52 The wind, Sister Rosetta, too, is thankful for. It howls through the lighthouse, inside Sister Rosetta's ears. Stitching sky to skin and water to sky, the wind never stops ushering quick changes, spins her widdershins* through what she cannot see or understand but certainly can feel: the warmth and weight of Erlen looking at her just now.

Widdershins · in a contrary or counter-clockwise direction

53 But then Sister Rosetta, textbooks and papers in hand, stumbles. Her veil, caul, and wimple fall. Her shaved head is bared. Where are her feet? She wonders, as the floor rises to meet her. And then Erlen is there, catching her. It's a surprise, the sureness of his grip. For even she doesn't quite know where her elbows, where her knees beneath the voluminous folds of the wool habit, and yet he knows exactly how to right her: an arm hooked around her rib, another anchoring her elbow.

54 *Don't ever let go.* That's what Sister Rosetta is thinking. What she says instead:

"Is there something you were wanting?" She is trying so hard   55
to sound utterly unflappable, though she can feel herself blushing,
yes, down to the roots of her shorn hair.

Erlen retrieves her glasses, hands over her limp headpiece.   56
He is careful with her vestments, averts his gaze even as he helps
her with the veil, the hem of which has come unraveled. But his
nose can't quit. Erlen's arms go stiff, his elbows lock. He considers
Sister Rosetta, points his nose at her neck. She's not the source
of that scent he's tracking, he realizes.

"Give the girls a bath," Erlen whispers, his nose twitching,   57
"with extra soap."

✦ ✦ ✦

SISTER ROSETTA'S RELIGIOUS mystery novel is not going   58
well. The hardest question – *Does God really know what He is
doing?* – hasn't provoked a quick answer. Not in her writing, not
in her life. Equally uncooperative are the twins who do not want
to shave their legs and underarms, who do not want to bathe at
all. The three of them sit on the rim of the enormous metal tub
and look at the water.

"Skin replaces itself," Astrid leads off,   59
"– cell by cell," Clarinda adds,   60
"– every thirty days,"   61
"– but hair replaces itself more slowly."   62
"Besides, we like being hairy –"   63
"– the hair keeps us warmer at night."   64

A smile starts on the left side of Astrid's face and travels from   65
girl to girl. Sister Rosetta shrugs. The truth is, underneath her
habit, she is a little hairy, too.

"I'll go first," Sister Rosetta says, hanging her habit and veil on   66
a hook. She soaps herself and shows them how to run a razor the
length of a leg, around the tricky points of the ankle. Her flesh
hangs from her body in doughy folds. Sister Rosetta wonders
if they know how unmoored she feels inside her own skin, this
awkward transparent sleeve. Can they even guess how badly she
wants to turn the razor and make a longitudinal incision, stem to
stern, and step free of her body that weighs on her, shames her?

But the girls aren't even watching her. Astrid bends to the tub,   67
trails a finger in the water. "Our mother liked baths."

68   "Took them on full moon nights like this one," Clarinda says, nodding at the window where the moon was a buoy in the dark sky.

69   "She's coming back for us," Astrid steps out of her pants. "She's going to teach us how to swim." The girls climb into the tub and no sooner have they settled in the water than they begin to bleed. Simultaneously, of course: two scarlet threads unspool from between their thighs. The girls are unnaturally calm, looking at Sister Rosetta with their wide eyes.

70   Sister Rosetta helps them out, towels them off, shows them what a strange contraption the belt and hook, what good for girls becoming women such modern-day conveniences are. Afterward, Sister Rosetta carries the bath water, pink and smelling of iron, in large pots down to the landing. Like carrying a comb to the sea, it's a risky thing to do but Sister Rosetta pours the contents of the pots over the railing anyway.

✦ ✦ ✦

71   THAT NIGHT AS SISTER ROSETTA climbs into bed, she considers the lighthouse lens turning silently. She thinks about Erlen with his hand at the light, true and shining. In no time at all, she is asleep, awash in a dream where she stands knee deep in the surf and unlocks a suitcase full of keyhole limpets, chitons, lightning whelks, and several specimen of spindled murex.* *How wide are heaven's gates, how deep?* Sister Rosetta wonders. She is stringing a rosary made of these musings, each question another chiton or whelk, the surfaces asymmetrical in pattern and design. Meanwhile, the good nuns at the abbey, uncostumed and unrestrained, turn their gazes to the expanse of Sister Rosetta's borderless dreaming. They link arms and kick their heels together with glee as they rush for the water. Wearied of their rosaries worn down between fingers and thumbs, they are only too glad to wade in deep, exchange their smooth beads for the sharp points of Sister Rosetta's queries.

Limpets…murex · various species of mollusks

✦ ✦ ✦

72   SISTER ROSETTA'S SNORING KEEPS Astrid and Clarinda from sleep. Boredom and insomnia provoke their curiosity. Though the ground floor storage room is strictly off-limits, with Sister

Rosetta asleep and their father up in the lantern room, there's 72
no one to stop them.

The storage room is black as tar. It's an interesting proposition, 73
such darkness held in the belly of the lighthouse. For fun they do
not light matches or shine flashlights. Instead they drop to hands
and knees and crawl across the floor, ending up in a far corner,
where they find fur: one long strip and a smaller crescent-shaped
patch. They tuck the scraps under their arms and race up to their
room, where they survey the scraps over the bedspread.

The fur is shiny silver like a seal's. They know without speak- 74
ing it aloud, the fur is from their mother's coat. Instinctively,
Astrid drapes the long swatch of fur over her shoulder, where it
adheres to her skin, stretching from tip of shoulder to point of
hip. Clarinda fastens the collar of fur around her neck and the
girls know: there isn't a shoehorn big enough, a crowbar strong
enough to pry these strips loose now.

✤ ✤ ✤

LATER THAT NIGHT THE moon slips off its lead and a storm 75
rolls in hard and fast. The wind whistles harsh lullabies that
send the girls into unsettled sleep. Only their thin and flimsy human skin separates all that water outside from the water inside
their bodies. They could drown – this has been the point of their
father's stories, they know. But Sister Rosetta has taught them
fractions and they now understand that they are two-thirds water, maybe more. They will float like the fish that swallowed the
moon. They will rise buoyant and swim. All their lives it seems
they've been practicing – in dreams, of course.

They know Sister Rosetta understands this. They know this 76
because that very night they wade into each other's dreams:
the girls into Sister Rosetta's dreams and Sister Rosetta into the
combined dreaming of the girls. In their dreams nobody wears
clothes, and so they swim naked – Sister Rosetta and Astrid and
Clarinda – their fears and their terrible longings and their many
questions bobbing beside them. And they show each other what
they never could during day: Astrid's strip of fur that now girdles
her waist and Clarinda's collar, which has already spread as a
cape over her shoulders. The girls are sloughing their cracked

76   and flimsy skins and Sister Rosetta runs her fingers over their beautiful patchwork bodies in utter amazement.

77   And then Sister Rosetta reveals her raw heart, ready for something more than wind and salt. Something more than the threads of her veils binding her up or her many lesson plans, more than her mystery novel. And the girls with their eyes grown so gray now they are nearly black, see Sister Rosetta's heart and know exactly what she needs to hear.

78   "You take care of him," they implore in the singular and Sister Rosetta bolts upright in bed.

✦ ✦ ✦

79   THE FUR HAS SPREAD, covering the girls from neck to knee. They turn their skins under and roll them down, as women do when stepping out of a pair of nylons. They tuck their skins under their arms and wind their way carefully down the stairs. Astrid trails a hand along the stone to steady them, while Clarinda bites her lip. With each step Clarinda thinks *right,* thinks *left.* Thinks *down.*

80   "Don't –" Astrid whispers,

81   – "be afraid," Clarinda replies. It's what their mother said, the day she swan-dived from the rock for the water. Now they know, now they remember. How to swim? That will come. But it's the land they must leave, once and for all, leave it for the water that will lift and carry them. *Water,* Clarinda thinks as she pushes the sky aside with her hands.

82   "C'mon," Astrid urges. "Hurry now." At the landing Clarinda hesitates.

83   "Don't –" Astrid says.

84   "– be afraid," Clarinda replies.

85   *Don't be afraid.*

86   When Astrid lifts her left foot over the ledge, Clarinda steps off with her right.

✦ ✦ ✦

87   ERLEN SMELLS THE GIRLS. He leaps to his feet. *Slap, slap, slap,* down the stone steps. Above him the light turns behind the glass. You would think for all this light he might see something.

But he doesn't, can't, the light shining miles and miles beyond 87 him. By the time he reaches the landing, the girls are gone.

"Come back!" he shouts, knowing full well they can't hear him, 88 having slipped beneath the water with their slick and oily bodies. Two transparent skins drape over the railing; two unzipped girl-shaped casings drip the color of fog.

Erlen, beyond bewilderment, fingers the skins. Next to him 89 is Sister Rosetta, her lips moving silently. *Guide them*, she prays. Her prayers stand tiptoe to press against the invisible beating heart of God. *Guide us all.* She understands, looking at Erlen, looking at the skins he folds into halves, into quarters, that none of them have ever been quite right for this world, casting about in skins they aren't quite suited for.

Erlen turns to Sister Rosetta. "They're not coming back are 90 they?"

Sister Rosetta peers out over the water. "No." She is crying 91 hot oily tears. She will miss those girls with their luminous eyes and stories. She is sorry they've gone. But she is not really worried. It's Erlen she's thinking of now. No, it's herself and Erlen – together – she's thinking of. She rests her palms flat and hard against her heart, her heart so full, she thinks it will burst from the pressure. Sister Rosetta smiles, can't help thinking this is another mystery, this hurt wrecking her, this full measure of sky she's swallowed, pressed and running over. So full in her lungs, she might drown on it.

Is it love? She wonders, considering Erlen leaning at the rail- 92 ing. Is this how love finds us even when we're sure it won't, finds us anyway, splits us wide open? It's an unforeseen plot complication and she's not sure what to do but offer thanks: thank you, parable. Thank you, rhyme. Thank you, unanswerable questions.

Erlen presses his hips against the railing. His daughters are 93 gone, he can feel it as certainly as he feels his heart tumbling. Gone but not lost, he feels that, too. In the hills the dogs bark and bark, beyond reason, beyond logic, barking for the sheer joy of repetition. To see, perhaps, if the moon might wag its tail.

Erlen turns to Sister Rosetta. Her face glows beneath the 94 moonlight. Her woolen habit is beneath Erlen's hand. Sister Rosetta is beneath the habit. From rib to rib his heart is a melon falling rung by rung down a long ladder.

95   "Sister Rosetta —"

96   "Rose," she says, slipping her hand in his. The wind whips her
veil and caul from off her head. She doesn't have time to think:
catch it. It tumbles past the breakers, caught now and carried,
beyond the surf where it disappears into darkness.

Poetry

Middle English Lyrics

✦ 14TH CENTURY ✦

Designed primarily to be sung and heard rather than read, Middle English lyrics are often brief – yet the themes and images they use can be surprisingly complex. Much of this complexity is achieved through puns and double-meanings, a playfulness with language that allows them to operate on a number of levels simultaneously. These popular lyrics, whose composition flourished from the 13th to the 15th centuries, often focus on religious themes such as Christ's passion or the suffering of Mary, yet they commonly cloak those themes in metaphors and scenes drawn from everyday life. In doing so, they seek to perform two important functions: first, they create in their listeners a personal connection with the central moments of Christianity, seeking to make their audiences feel that "they were there" (an emphasis commonly known as "affective piety"). Second, in linking common experience with religiously significant events, they seek to bridge the gap between the ordinary and the divine. The first two lyrics which follow have been presented in the original Middle English, although spelling has been slightly regularized.

FOWLES IN THE FRITH

1 Fowles· in the frith,·
 The fisshes in the flod,·
 And I mon waxe wood:·
 Much sorwe· I walke with
5 For beste· of boon· and blood.

NOW GOETH SUNNE UNDER WODE

1 Now goeth sunne under wode·
 Me reweth,· Marye, thy faire rode.·

Fowles · birds

frith · forest

flod · sea

And I ... wood · either "and I must go mad" or "and I, man, go mad"

sorwe · sorrow

beste · either "best" or "beast." The ambiguity suggests the tension between Christ and the flesh

boon · bone

wode · wood, forest

Me reweth · I pity

thy faire rode · "rode" may be construed as either "face" or "cross." The line may thus be read as both "I pity, Mary, your fair face" and "I lament, Mary, your fair cross"

Now goeth sunne under tree: 3
Me reweth, Marye, thy sone and thee.

I WOULD BE CLAD

Gold ... wine · that is, worldly goods pleasures

rood · cross

Then I'd ... kin · see Luke 14:26

Gold and all this world's wine*   1
  Is naught but Christ's rood;*
I would be clad in Christ's skin
That ran so long with his blood,
And go to his heart, and give to him mine –   5
For he alone is a filling food.
Then I'd care little for kith or kin,*
For in him alone is all that is good. Amen.

THE SPRING UNDER THE THORN

a maid · that is, Mary, mother of Christ

At a spring, hidden under the thorn,   1
  Was grief's remedy, so scarce before.
There beside it stood a maid,*
Full of love that abounds;
Whosoever will seek true love,   5
In her it shall be found.

William Shakespeare

⟨ 1 5 6 4 – 1 6 1 6 ⟩

By the 1590s Shakespeare was known in London as an actor, a poet, and a playwright. He wrote thirty-seven plays (or more) and a number of superb nondramatic poems before retiring to Stratford-on-Avon, his birthplace, in about 1610. England's greatest dramatist is seldom thought of as a religious poet, yet he was steeped in the Bible, a book which provides metaphor and framework for many of his themes. His great tragedies, especially Hamlet, King Lear, *and* Macbeth, *concern profound metaphysical issues such as the nature of justice, good and evil, mystery, temptation, and the presence or absence of God. The sonnets, as well, published in 1609, address such metaphysical themes as love, mutability, and death. The sonnets are intensely personal poems that, in the words of C. S. Lewis, anyone "can walk into and make his own."*

SONNET 18

1 Shall I compare thee to a summer's day?
   Thou art more lovely and more temperate.
   Rough winds do shake the darling buds of May,
   And summer's lease hath all too short a date:
5 Sometime too hot the eye of heaven shines,
   And often is his gold complexion dimmed,
   And every fair from fair˙ sometime declines,
   By chance, or nature's changing course untrimmed.
   But thy eternal summer shall not fade,
10 Nor lose possession of that fair thou ow'st˙;
   Nor shall Death brag thou wander'st in his shade,
   When in eternal lines˙ to time thou grow'st,
       So long as men can breathe, or eyes can see,
       So long lives this, and this˙ gives life to thee.

fair from fair · beautiful thing from its beauty

fair thou ow'st · the beauty you possess

eternal lines · that is, the lines of this poem

this · this sonnet

419

SONNET 29

When in disgrace with fortune and men's eyes,   1
  I all alone beweep my outcast state,
And trouble deaf heaven with my bootless* cries,
And look upon myself and curse my fate,
Wishing me like to one more rich in hope,*   5
Featured* like him, like him with friends possessed,
Desiring this man's art,* and that man's scope,
With what I most enjoy contented least;
Yet in these thoughts myself almost despising,
Haply I think on thee, and then my state,*   10
Like to the lark at break of day arising
From sullen* earth, sings hymns at heaven's gate;
For thy sweet love remembered such wealth brings
That then I scorn to change* my state* with kings.

bootless · fruitless and frustrating

more rich in hope · endowed with better prospects

art · talent

Featured · well formed, good-looking

scope · intellectual reach

state · state of mind, condition

sullen · gloomy

change · exchange

state: · *(1) circumstance (2) domain*

SONNET 73

That time of year thou mayst in me behold   1
  When yellow leaves, or none, or few, do hang
Upon those boughs which shake against the cold,
Bare ruined choirs* where late the sweet birds sang.
In me thou seest the twilight of such day   5
As after sunset fadeth in the west,
Which by and by black night doth take away,
Death's second self,* that seals up all in rest.
In me thou see'st the glowing of such fire
That on the ashes of his* youth doth lie,   10
As the death-bed whereon it must expire
Consumed with* that which it was nourish'd by.
  This thou perceiv'st, which makes thy love more strong,
  To love that well which thou must leave* ere long.

choirs · portion of the church where the choir sings; autumn tree branches serving as the bird's "choir"

Death's second self · Sleep (Death's twin)

That · As

his · its

with · by

leave · lose, through the speaker's death

marriage · Platonic union of hearts

admit · allow, concede (echoing Anglican marriage service)

alteration · altered circumstance (sickness, poverty, etc.)

SONNET 116

Let me not to the marriage* of true minds   1
  Admit* impediments. Love is not love
Which alters when it alteration* finds,

4   Or bends with the remover to remove:·
5   O no! it is an ever-fixed mark·
   That looks on tempests and is never shaken;
   It is the star to every wandering bark,·
   Whose worth's unknown, although his height be taken.
   Love's not Time's fool, though rosy lips and cheeks
10 its altitude can still guide the ship
   Within his bending sickle's compass· come:
   Love alters not with his brief hours and weeks,
   But bears it out even to the edge of doom.·
      If this be error and upon me proved,
15   I never writ, nor no man ever loved.

Or...remove · changes because the other person changes

mark · a landmark; a reference point in navigation

bark · a small ship

Whose...taken · though the star is a mystery

compass · range

edge of doom · Day of Judgment, i.e., forever

SONNET 146

1 **P**OOR SOUL, THE CENTER of my sinful earth,·
    Thrall to· these rebel powers that thee array,
   Why dost thou pine within and suffer dearth,·
   Painting thy outward walls so costly gay?
5 Why so large cost, having so short a lease,
   Dost thou upon thy fading mansion spend?
   Shall worms, inheritors of this excess,·
   Eat up thy charge? Is this thy body's end?
   Then, soul, live thou upon thy servant's loss,
19 And let that pine to aggravate thy store;·
   Buy terms divine in selling hours of dross;·
   Within be fed, without be rich no more:
      So shalt thou feed on Death, that feeds on men,
      And Death once dead, there's no more dying then.·

my ... earth · the body

Thrall to · "slave to." This is a conjectural reading due to a fault in the manuscript. Other readings include "Hemmed with," "Fooled by," and "Feeding"

dearth · scarcity, lack

excess · excessive expense

And let ... store · let the body waste away (in self-denial) in order to increase the riches of the soul

dross · baseness, impurity, waste

And death ... then · see 2 Corinthians 15:54

Æmilia Lanyer

{ 1 5 6 9 - 1 6 4 5 }

*Æmilia Lanyer published one book in her lifetime, an original poem
on the Passion of Christ, a volume which has earned her the title of the
first major feminist in English literary history. Lanyer was a middle
class woman who enjoyed the company of the aristocrats of the courts
of Queen Elizabeth I and King James I. Her father, Baptiste Bassano,
an Italian musician of the Elizabethan court, died when Æmilia
was seven. Her mother, Margaret Johnson, died when Æmilia was
eighteen. Subsequently, Lanyer became the mistress of Henry Carey,
first Lord Hundson and Lord Chamberlain to Queen Elizabeth.
In 1592 she married Alphonso Lanyer and at some unknown date
underwent a spiritual conversion through the particular influence of
the Countess Dowager of Cumberland, to whom (among others) she
dedicated her book. In 1611 – the same year in which the Authorized
or King James version of the Bible was published – Lanyer published
Salve Deus Rex Judæorum ("Hail God, King of the Jews"), a work of
over 1,800 lines, which reflects both her conversion and her conviction
that previous interpreters of the Bible and the Christian faith have
treated women unfairly. The poem attempts to correct the record by
showing the extraordinary and positive role of women in the life of
Christ. She says in her address to the reader that:*

> *it pleased our Lord and Savior Jesus Christ, without the
> assistance of man, being free from original and all other sins,
> from the time of his conception, till the hour of his death, to
> be begotten of a woman, borne of a woman, nourished of a
> woman, obedient to a woman; and that he healed women,
> pardoned women, comforted women; yea, even when he was
> in his greatest agony and bloody sweat, going to be crucified,
> and also in the last hour of his death, took care to dispose of
> a woman: after his resurrection, appeared first to a woman,*

423

*sent a woman to declare his most glorious resurrection to
the rest of his Disciples.*

*In a section of the poem entitled "Eve's Apology in Defense of
Women," the poet presents the story of the Passion through the
unique perspective of Pilate's wife, and, by extension through the
point of view of Eve, who represents all women. Lanyer, through this
exceptional narrative poem, establishes herself not only as one of
the first Christian feminists in England but also as one of the first
women to publish a major volume of verse in the English language.*

from SALVE DEUS REX JUDÆORUM

EVE'S APOLOGY IN DEFENSE OF WOMEN

cause · court case

NOW PONTIUS PILATE is to judge the cause•   1
Of faultless Jesus, who before him stands,
Who neither hath offended prince nor laws,
Although he now be brought in woeful bands:
O noble Governor, make thou yet a pause,   5

imbrue · stain, defile
Do not in innocent blood imbrue• thy hands

wife · Pilate's wife, by
tradition known as
Percula)
But hear the words of thy most worthy wife,•
Who sends to thee to beg her Savior's life:

Let barb'rous cruelty far depart from thee,
And in true justice take afflictions part.   10
Open thine eyes, that thou the truth may'st see,
Do not the thing that goes against thy heart,
Condemn not him that must thy Savior be;
But view his holy life, his good desert.
Let not us women glory in men's fall,   15
Who had power given to over-rule us all.

Till now your indiscretion sets us free,

tree · see Genesis
2:16–17
And makes our former fault much less appear.
Our Mother Eve, who tasted of the tree,•
Giving to Adam what she held most dear,   20

after-coming · suc-
ceeding
Was simply good and had no power to see
The after-coming• harm did not appear.
The subtle serpent that our sex betrayed,
Before our fall so sure a plot had laid.

25 That undiscerning ignorance perceived
No guile or craft that was by him intended,
For had she known of what we were bereaved,*
To his request she had not condescended.
But she (poor soul) by cunning was deceived,*
30 No hurt therein her harmless heart intended;
    For she alleged* God's word, which he denies
    That they should die but, even as gods, be wise.

But surely Adam cannot be excused.
Her fault though great, yet he was most to blame.
35 What weakness offered, strength might have refused.
Being lord of all, the greater was his shame.
Although Serpent's craft had her abused,
God's holy word ought all his actions frame,
    For he was Lord and King of all the earth,
40   Before poor Eve had either life or breath,

Who, being fram'd by God's eternal hand,
The perfect'st man that ever breath'd on earth,
And from God's mouth receiv'd that strait* command,
The breach whereof he knew was present* death;
45 Yea, having power to rule both sea and land,
Yet with one apple won* to lose that breath
    Which God had breathed in his beauteous face,
    Bringing us all in* danger and disgrace.

And then to lay the fault on Patience' back,
50 That we (poor women) must endure it all.
We know right well he did discretion lack,
Being not persuaded thereunto at all.
If Eve did err, it was for knowledge sake,
The fruit being fair persuaded him to fall.
55   No subtle Serpent's falsehood did betray him,
    If he would eat it, who had power to stay* him?

Not Eve, whose fault was only too much love,
Which made her give this present to her dear,
That what she tasted, he likewise might prove,*

bereaved · robbed, deprived

deceived · see 1 Timothy 2:14

alleged · quoted

strait · rigorous, strict

present · immediate

with … won · conquered by one apple (see Genesis 3:6)

in · into

stay · stop

prove · experience (through tasting)

Whereby his knowledge might become more clear.   60
He never sought her weakness to reprove,
With those sharp words, which he of God did hear.
 Yet men will boast of knowledge, which he took
 From Eve's fair hand, as from a learned book.

If any evil did in her remain,   65
Being made of him, he was the ground of all.
If one* of many worlds could lay a stain
Upon our sex, and work so great a fall
To wretched man, by Satan's subtle train,*
What will so foul a fault amongst you all?   70
 Her weakness did the Serpent's words obey,
 But you in malice God's dear Son betray,*

Whom, if unjustly you condemn to die,
Her sin was small, to* what you do commit.
All mortal sins that do for vengeance cry,   75
Are not to be compared unto it.
If many worlds would altogether try,
By all their sins the wrath of God to get,*
 This sin of yours surmounts them all as far
 As doth the sun another little star.   80

Then let us have our liberty again,
And challenge* to yourselves no sovereignty.*
You came not in the world without our pain.
Make that a bar* against your cruelty.
Your fault being greater, why should you disdain   85
Our being your equals, free from tyranny?
 If one weak woman simply did offend,
 This sin* of yours hath no excuse, nor end,

To which (poor souls) we never gave consent.
Witness thy wife (O Pilate) speaks for all   90
Who did but dream,* and yet a message sent,
That thou should'st have nothing to do at all
With that just man, which, if thy heart relent,
Why wilt thou be a reprobate* with Saul*

one · Eve (seen here as a miniature world or cosmos)

train · argument

you ... betray · Pilate and the religious authorities who condemn Jesus

to · compared to

get · receive

challenge · lay claim

sovereignty · superior authority

bar · barrier

This sin · the execution of Christ

dream · see Matthew 27:19

reprobate · lost soul

Saul · King of Israel who sought to kill David, God's anointed

95   To seek the death of him that is so good,
     For thy soul's health to shed his dear blood?

     Yea, so thou may'st these sinful people please,
     Thou art content against all truth and right,
     To seal this act, that may procure thine ease,
100 With blood and wrong, with tyranny and might.
     The multitude thou seekest to appease,
     By base dejection of this heavenly Light,•
         Demanding which of these that should'st loose,
         Whether the Thief or Christ King of the Jews.

105 Base Barabbas, the Thief, they all desire,•
     And thou more base than he, perform'st their• will;
     Yet when thy thoughts back to themselves retire,
     Thou art unwilling to commit this ill.
     Oh, that thou could'st unto such grace aspire,
110 That thy polluted lips might never kill
         That honor, which right judgment ever graceth,
         To purchase shame, which all true worth defaceth.

                    ✦   ✦   ✦

     Canst thou be innocent, that 'gainst all right
     Wilt yield to what thy conscience doth withstand?
115 Being a man of knowledge, power, and might,
     To let the wicked carry such a hand,
     Before thy face to blindfold Heaven's bright light,
     And thou to yield to what they did demand?
         Washing thy hand, thy conscience cannot clear,
120   But to all worlds this stain must needs appear.

Light · Jesus (see John 1:4–5)

Whether … desire · see Matthew 27:20

their · the rabble calling for Christ's crucifixion

John Donne

◀(1 5 7 2 - 1 6 3 1)▶

After studying law in London and serving in naval campaigns against Spain, Donne aspired to a career as a dashing courtier in King James' Court. However, his secret elopement with the young niece of his employer, Sir Thomas Egerton, demolished his hopes of worldly success. In 1615, after fourteen years of poverty and despair, Donne made formal the abandonment of his Roman Catholic heritage and was ordained a priest in the Church of England (at the encouragement of King James himself). In 1621 he became the Dean of St. Paul's Cathedral in London and, subsequently, the most famous preacher of his day. In his youth, Donne wrote brilliant, witty, and often patently erotic love poems. After his conversion and ordination, Donne continued to write love poems, though they became love lyrics addressed to God. His "Holy Sonnets" illustrate his intense capacity for religious emotion, illustrated in the twin themes of the mystery of divine union (as figured in marriage) and the universal fact of human mortality.

HOLY SONNET 7

1 AT THE ROUND EARTH'S imagined corners, blow
Your trumpets, angels; and arise, arise
From death, you numberless infinities
Of souls, and to your scattered bodies go;
All whom the flood did, and fire shall, o'erthrow,
5 All whom war, dearth,• age, agues,• tyrannies,
Despair, law, chance hath slain, and you whose eyes
Shall behold God, and never taste death's woe.•
But let them sleep, Lord, and me mourn a space,
For, if above all these, my sins abound,
10 'Tis late to ask abundance of thy grace

dearth · famine

agues · fevers

never taste . . . woe · some people will escape death, according to St. Paul (1 Thessalonians 4:15–17)

When we are there. Here on this lowly ground,   11
   Teach me how to repent; for that's as good
   As if thou hadst sealed my pardon with thy blood.

HOLY SONNET 10

DEATH, BE NOT PROUD, though some have called thee
  Mighty and dreadful, for, thou art not so,   1
For, those, whom thou think'st thou dost overthrow,
Die not, poor death, nor yet canst thou kill me;
From rest and sleep, which but thy pictures be,
Much pleasure, then from thee, much more must flow,   5
And soonest our best men with thee do go,
Rest of their bones, and soul's delivery.
Thou art slave to fate, chance, kings, and desperate men,
And dost with poison, war, and sickness dwell,
And poppy* or charms can make us sleep as well,   10
And better than thy stroke; why swell'st thou then?

poppy · opium or other drugs that induce sleep

   One short sleep past, we wake eternally,
   And death shall be no more, Death thou shalt die.

HOLY SONNET 14

BATTER MY HEART, three-personed God; for you
  As yet but knock, breathe, shine, and seek to mend;   1
That I may rise and stand, o'erthrow me, and bend
Your force, to break, blow, burn, and make me new.
I, like an usurped town, to another due,
Labor to admit you, but oh, to no end,   5
Reason, your viceroy in me, me should defend,
But is captived, and proves weak or untrue,
Yet dearly I love you, and would be loved fain,*
But am betrothed* unto your enemy.*
Divorce me,* untie, or break that knot again,   10
Take me to you, imprison me, for I,
   Except you enthrall* me, never shall be free,
   Nor ever chaste, except you ravish* me.

fain · gladly, willingly

betrothed · engaged

your enemy · Satan

Divorce me · the narrator asks God to take the role of King and intervene to break ("divorce") the soul's covenant with Satan

enthrall · to captivate or enslave

ravish · to take by violence, to rape, to overwhelm

George Herbert

◀{ 1 5 9 3 – 1 6 3 3 }▶

Herbert is one of England's greatest religious poets and a leading member of the "Metaphysical School" of poets, who share themes and stylistic traits with John Donne. After earning the MA at Trinity College, Cambridge, in 1616, the aristocratic Herbert was appointed Reader in Rhetoric at Cambridge (1618), elected Public Orator at Cambridge (1620–1628), and was chosen to serve in Parliament (1625). Ordinarily a man of Herbert's rank, intellect, and experience would have found a career at court, an early ambition that he did in fact pursue. But by a series of events – deaths of friends and his own poor health – Herbert found that God had "cross-biased" him for other ends, and so love of the church superseded his academic and political ambitions. In 1630 he was installed as rector (minister) of Bemerton, a tiny rural congregation near Salisbury. After three years of exemplary service, "Holy Mr. Herbert" died of consumption, leaving behind England's greatest single collection of devotional lyrics, called The Temple (1633). Herbert's poems are often painfully honest about the sufferings of the Christian pilgrim ("A wonder tortured in the space/Betwixt this world and that of grace"), but they are equally confident of God's presence in struggle "Since here is no place so alone,/The which he doth not fill."

THE WINDOWS

1 LORD, HOW CAN MAN preach thy eternal word?
     He is a brittle, crazy* glass;
  Yet in thy temple thou dost him afford
     This glorious and transcendent place,
5 To be a window through thy grace.

  But when thou dost anneal* in glass thy story,*
     Making thy life to shine within

crazy · cracked, flawed

anneal · to heat glass so that an image or a painting may be burned into its surface

thy story · stained glass windows commonly present scenes (the "story") from the Bible or saints' lives

431

The holy preachers, then the light and glory
    More rev'rend grows, and more doth win;
    Which else shows wat'rish, bleak, and thin.   10

Doctrine and life, colors and light, in one
    When they combine and mingle, bring
A strong regard and awe; but speech alone
    Doth vanish like a flaring thing,
    And in the ear, not conscience, ring.   15

THE COLLAR*

I STRUCK THE BOARD,* and cried: "No more.
                I will abroad.   1
    What? shall I ever sigh and pine?
My lines and life are free; free as the road,
    Loose as the wind, as large as store.   5
             Shall I be still in suit?*
    Have I no harvest but a thorn
    To let me blood, and not restore
What I have lost with cordial* fruit?
            Sure there was wine   10
    Before my sighs did dry it; there was corn*
    Before my tears did drown it.
    Is the year only lost to me?
         Have I no bays* to crown it?
No flowers, no garlands gay? all blasted?   15
         All wasted?
    Not so, my heart; but there is fruit
            And thou hast hands.
    Recover all thy sigh-blown age
On double pleasures; leave thy cold dispute   20
Of what is fit, and not. Forsake thy cage,
         Thy rope of sands,
Which petty thoughts have made, and made to thee
    Good cable, to enforce and draw,
         And be thy law,   25
While thou didst wink and wouldst not see.
        Away! Take heed;

Collar · "Collar" suggests both a clerical collar and a slave's shackles

board · table

suit · asking favors

cordial · restorative to the heart

corn · grain

bays · laurel leaves, a symbol of honor

I will abroad.
Call in thy death's head there; tie up thy fears.
30   He that forbears*
       To suit and serve his need,
              Deserves his load."
But as I rav'd and grew more fierce and wild
       At every word,
35   Methought* I heard one calling, "Child!"
       And I replied, "My Lord."

forbears · does without

methought · it
seemed to me

THE PULLEY

1   WHEN GOD AT first made man,
       Having a glass of blessings standing by,
"Let us," (said he) "pour on him all we can;
Let the world's riches, which dispersed lie,
5   Contract into a span."

So strength first made a way;
Then beauty flow'd, then wisdom, honour, pleasure.
When almost all was out, God made a stay,
Perceiving that alone of all his treasure
10   Rest in the bottom lay.

"For if I should," (said he)
"Bestow this jewel also on my creature,
He would adore my gifts instead of me,
And rest in Nature, not the God of Nature:
15   So both should losers be.

"Yet let him keep the rest,
But keep them with repining* restlessness;
Let him be rich and weary, that at least,
If goodness lead him not, yet weariness
20   May toss him to my breast."

repining · expressing
discontentment,
complaining

LOVE (III)

Love bade me welcome; yet my soul drew back,
    Guilty of dust and sin.
But quick-eyed Love, observing me grow slack
    From my first entrance in,
Drew nearer to me, sweetly questioning
    If I lacked anything.

"A guest," I answered, "worthy to be here";
    Love said, "You shall be he."
"I, the unkind, the ungrateful? ah my dear,
    I cannot look on thee."
Love took my hand and smiling did reply,
    "Who made the eyes but I?"

"Truth, Lord, but I have marred them; let my shame
    Go where it doth deserve."
"And know you not," says Love, "who bore the blame?"
    "My dear, then I will serve."
"You must sit down," says Love, "and taste my meat*."
    So I did sit and eat*.

meat · meal, feast

eat · see Luke 12:37, 22:27

John Milton

◄{ 1 6 0 8 - 1 6 7 4 }►

Milton, who has been called "the Last Renaissance Man," was born into a well-to-do middle class Protestant home. After earning the MA at Christ's College, Cambridge, Milton entered the intense religious and political conflicts of the English Civil War. Siding with Cromwell and the Independents, who defeated the Royalists, Milton was rewarded with an office in Cromwell's Council of State. A series of misfortunes soon followed: abandonment by his first wife soon after their wedding in 1642; blindness in 1652; and the dissolution of the Commonwealth and the restoration of the monarchy in 1660, which led to the burning of Milton's books and the writer's temporary imprisonment. Despite these fluctuations of fortune, throughout his life Milton wrote prolifically – a variety of lyric poems in his youth; extensive treatises on religion and politics in the middle years; and his great epics Paradise Lost *and* Paradise Regained *in his later years. Like dozens of poets before him, Milton tried his hand at the sonnet form. He proved to be a master of the genre, both in Italian and in English, preferring the more difficult Petrarchan rhyme scheme. In addition to the familiar themes of love and friendship, Milton used the sonnet for a variety of subjects including marriage, duty to God, and contemporary political and religious issues. Milton is one of England's greatest writers – second only to Shakespeare in influence – and perhaps England's greatest Christian poet.*

SONNET 7

1   How soon hath Time, the subtle thief of youth,
     Stol'n on his wing my three and twentieth year!
     My hasting days fly on with full career,*
     But my late spring no bud or blossom show'th.
5 Perhaps my semblance might deceive* the truth,
     That I to manhood am arriv'd so near,

career · to go at top speed in a reckless way

deceive · misrepresent

435

And inward ripeness doth much less appear,

endu'th · endows

That some more timely-happy spirits endu'th.•

Yet be it less or more, or soon or slow,

still · always

It shall be still• in strictest measure ev'n•　　10

ev'n · equal or adequate

To that same lot, however mean or high,

Toward which Time leads me, and the will of Heav'n;

All is, if I have grace to use it so,

As ever in my great Task-Master's eye.

SONNET 9

LADY THAT IN THE prime of earliest youth,　　1

Wisely hast shunn'd the broad way and the green,

And with those few art eminently seen

That labor up the Hill of Heav'nly Truth,

The better part with Mary and with Ruth　　5

overween · overesti-
mate themselves

Chosen thou hast; and they that overween,•

spleen · anger, malice

And at thy growing virtues fret their spleen,•

ruth · compassion, pity

No anger find in thee, but pity and ruth.•

Thy care is fixt and zealously attends

To fill thy odorous lamp with deeds of light,　　10

And Hope that reaps not shame. Therefore, be sure

Thou, when the Bridegroom with his feastful friends

Passes to bliss at the mid-hour of night,

Hast gain'd thy entrance, Virgin wise and pure.•

**thy slaughtered
Saints** · the Waldensians,
a sect founded in the
12th century, were
excommunicated by
the Roman Catholic
church in 1215. Considered
early Protestants by
reformers such as Milton,
their Italian communities
were attacked by militant
Catholics seeking to wipe
out the heresy in 1655

SONNET 18

AVENGE, O LORD, thy slaughtered Saints,• whose bones　　1

Lie scattered on the Alpine mountains cold;

Even them who kept thy truth so pure of old

When all our fathers worshipped stocks and stones,•

stocks and stones ·
idols

Forget not: in thy book record their groans　　5

Who were thy sheep, and in their ancient fold

Slain by the bloody Piedmontese• that rolled

Piedmontese ·
Piedmont is the region
in northwest Italy where
the massacre took place

Mother with infant down the rocks. Their moans

The vales redoubled to the hills, and they

To heaven. Their martyred blood and ashes sow　　10

triple tyrant · like most
Protestants of his day,
Milton viewed the Pope,
whose tiara features 3
crowns, as a religious
and political threat

**grow … hundred-
fold** · a reference to a
maxim by Tertullian
(155?–220?): "the blood
of the martyrs is the
seed of the church"

Babylonian woe ·
Babylon signifies
sensuality and spiritual
corruption (see Revelation
17:4–6). Reformation
Protestants often used
Babylon as the symbol
of a corrupt papacy

talent · both "ability"
and a large denomina-
tion of money. Milton
here refers to the
parable of the talents
(Matthew 25:14–30)

fondly · foolishly, naïvely

Thousands · the host
of angels

post · to travel swiftly

Methought · it seemed
to me

late espousèd saint ·
Milton may be referring
to his first wife, Mary
Powell, who died in
1652, or his second,
Katherine Woodcock,
who died in 1657, both
shortly after giving birth

Alcestis · wife of
Admetus who is rescued
from Hades by Hercules
("Jove's great son") and
returned to him veiled

as … did save · after
giving birth, women
could not enter the
temple until they
submitted to a rite of
purification (Leviticus 12)

fancied sight · Milton
was blind by this time

11   O'er all th' Italian fields, where still doth sway
        The triple tyrant:* that from these may grow
            A hundredfold* who, having learned thy way
            Early may fly the Babylonian woe.*

SONNET 19

1 W HEN I CONSIDER HOW my light is spent,
      Ere half my days, in this dark world and wide,
      And that one talent* which is death to hide
      Lodged with me useless, though my soul more bent
5 To serve therewith my Maker, and present
      My true account, lest he returning chide;
      "Doth God exact day-labor, light denied?"
      I fondly* ask; but Patience to prevent
      That murmur, soon replies, "God doth not need
10   Either man's work or his own gifts, who best
      Bear his mild yoke, they serve him best. His state
    Is kingly. Thousands* at his bidding speed
    And post* o'er land and ocean without rest:
    They also serve who only stand and wait."

SONNET 23

1 M ETHOUGHT* I SAW my late espousèd saint*
      Brought to me like Alcestis* from the grave,
      Whom Jove's great son to her glad husband gave,
      Rescued from death by force though pale and faint.
5 Mine, as whom washed from spot of childbed taint,
      Purification in the old law did save,*
      And such, as yet once more I trust to have
      Full sight of her in heaven without restraint,
    Came vested all in white, pure as her mind.
10   Her face was veiled, yet to my fancied sight*
      Love, sweetness, goodness, in her person shined
    So clear, as in no face with more delight.
      But O, as to embrace me she inclined,
      I waked, she fled, and day brought back my night.

Anne Bradstreet

<{ c a 1 6 1 6 – 1 6 7 2 }>

Bradstreet, celebrated as the first woman poet in America, was born in Northampton, England. Her father, Thomas Dudley, a steward to the Earl of Lincoln, gave Anne access to the Earl's library. The studious young woman married Simon Bradstreet in 1628 and traveled with her husband and parents to America in 1630. After initial hardships, her living conditions in America improved considerably. Eventually, Bradstreet's father and husband became prominent leaders in Massachusetts. In view of her considerable domestic duties which included rearing eight children, it is surprising that Bradstreet had time to write at all. Her early poems, published in The Tenth Muse Lately Sprung up in America *(1650), are somewhat stiff and imitative. She is best known for her later lyrical and meditative poems, expressing her love of children, husband, nature, and Creator, published posthumously in* Several Poems Compiled with Great Variety of Wit and Learning, Full of Delight *(1678). While maintaining her steadfast Puritan point of view, Bradstreet occasionally expresses a tension between her personal longing for the pleasures of this world and her desire to submit to God's sovereignty. Anne was happily married to Simon until her death in 1672.*

A LETTER TO HER HUSBAND, ABSENT UPON PUBLIC EMPLOYMENT

1   MY HEAD, MY HEART, mine eyes, my life, nay, more,
    My joy, my magazine* of earthly store,
    If two be one, as surely thou and I,
    How stayest thou there, whilst I at Ipswich* lie?
5   So many steps, head from the heart to sever,
    If but a neck,* soon should we be together.

magazine · storehouse

Ipswich · town in northeastern Massachusetts where Bradstreet lived

a neck · that is, if only the distance were like a neck that connected head and heart

this season · winter

439

in's · in his

zodiac · in astronomy and astrology, a belt of 12 regions (each with a corresponding sign) around the heavens that mark the sun's apparent annual path

Capricorn · the tenth sign of the zodiac where the sun lingers in winter from December 22–January 20

Cancer · the fourth sign of the zodiac that demarcates high summer from June 22–July 22

I, like the Earth this season,˙ mourn in black,
My Sun is gone so far in's˙ zodiac,˙
Whom whilst I 'joyed, nor storms, nor frost I felt,
His warmth such frigid colds did cause to melt.   10
My chilled limbs now numbed lie forlorn;
Return, return, sweet Sol, from Capricorn,˙
In this dead time, alas, what can I more
Than view those fruits which through thy heat I bore?
Which sweet contentment yield me for a space,   15
True living pictures of their father's face.
O strange effect! now thou art southward gone,
I weary grow the tedious day so long;
But when thou northward to me shalt return,
I wish my Sun may never set, but burn   20
Within the Cancer˙ of my glowing breast,
The welcome house of him my dearest guest.
Where ever, ever stay, and go not thence,
Till nature's sad decree shall call thee hence;
Flesh of thy flesh, bone of thy bone,   25
I here, thou there, yet both but one.

Henry Vaughan

⟨ 1 6 2 1 – 1 6 9 5 ⟩

Vaughan was born in Wales, and Welsh may have been his first language. He attended Oxford (1638-1640) before moving to London to study law, yet his plans to become a lawyer were interrupted by the English Civil War. Disappointed by the outcome of the war, Vaughan returned to his home in Breconshire where he became a successful, but otherwise obscure, country doctor for the last forty years of his life. Two major events shaped Vaughan's poetic career – first, the discovery of George Herbert's verse, which inspired Vaughan's poetic style and subject matter; second, the tragic death of his younger brother William in 1648, a loss which may have led to Vaughan's conversion. At his best, Vaughan is a poet of stunning visual images built on dramatic contrasts of light and darkness: "There is in God (some say)/A deep and dazzling darkness." "I saw eternity the other night/Like a great ring of pure and endless light,/All calm, as it was bright...." Like his contemporary, Blaise Pascal, Vaughan anticipated the rise of a rationalistic worldview that would reduce the cosmos to a machine, lacking mystery, miracle, and the divine presence.

THE WORLD

1

1 I SAW ETERNITY the other night,
   Like a great ring of pure and endless light,
      All calm, as it was bright;
   And round beneath it, Time in hours, days, years,
5   Driven by the spheres,
   Like a vast shadow moved, in which the world
      And all her train were hurled.

441

The doting lover· in
this and the following
lines, the narrator
considers four common
forms of "madness":
erotic passion ("the
doting lover"), thirst for
power ("the darksome
statesman"), greed
("the fearful miser"),
and sensualism ("the
downright epicure")

knots · love tokens

The doting lover* in his quaintest strain
    Did there complain;
Near him, his lute, his fancy, and his flights,   10
    Wit's sour delights,
With gloves and knots,* the silly snares of pleasure,
    Yet his dear treasure
All scattered lay, while he his eyes did pour
    Upon a flower.   15

2

THE DARKSOME STATESMAN hung with weights and woe
  Like a thick midnight-fog moved there so slow
    He did nor stay, nor go;
Condemning thoughts (like sad eclipses) scowl
    Upon his soul,   20
And clouds of crying witnesses without
    Pursued him with one shout.
Yet digged the mole, and, lest his ways be found
    Worked underground,
Where he did clutch his prey. But One did see   25
    That policy:*

policy · approach or
strategy

Churches and altars fed him; perjuries
    Were gnats and flies;
It rained about him blood and tears, but he
    Drank them as free.   30

3

THE FEARFUL MISER on a heap of rust*
  Sat pining all his life there, did scarce trust
    His own hands with the dust;

heap of rust · wealth
that decays. See
Matthew 6:19–20

Yet would not place one piece above,* but lives
    In fear of thieves.   35

place one piece
above · invest to
receive interest

Thousands there were as frantic as himself,
    And hugged each one his pelf:*
The downright epicure placed heaven in sense,
    And scorned pretense;

pelf · belongings or
wealth

While others slipped into a wide excess,   40
    Said little less;
The weaker sort slight, trivial wares enslave

Who think them brave,*
And poor, despisèd Truth sat counting by*
45   Their victory.

brave · fashionable, showy

counting by · watching

4

YET SOME, WHO ALL this while did weep and sing,
    And sing and weep, soared up into the Ring;
    But most would use no wing.
"O fools!" (said I) "thus to prefer dark night
50   Before true light!
To live in grots* and caves, and hate the day
    Because it shows the way,
The way which from this dead and dark abode
    Leads up to God,
55 A way where you might tread the sun and be
    More bright than he!"
But as I did their madness so discuss
    One whispered thus:
This ring the bridegroom did for none provide,
60   *But for his bride.* *

grots · grottoes

JOHN 2:16–17

ALL THAT IS IN THE WORLD, the lust of the flesh, the lust of the eyes, and the pride of life, is not of the father but is of the world. And the world passeth away, and the lusts thereof, but he that doeth the will of God abideth forever.

RELIGION

1 MY GOD, WHEN I walk in those groves,
    And leaves thy spirit doth still fan,
I see in each shade that there grows
An angel talking with a man.

5 Under a juniper, some house,
Or the cool myrtle's canopy,
Others beneath an oak's green boughs,
Or at some fountain's bubbling eye;*

**Under a juniper …
bubbling eye** · in
this stanza, the poet
summarizes the natural
settings where angels
meet humans in the
Hebrew Bible: under the
juniper (1 Kings 19:5),
under the myrtle
(Zechariah 1:8–11),
under the oak (Judges
6:11), and beside a
fountain (Genesis 16:7)

Jacob dreams ... shady even · the poet here presents examples of heavenly messengers interacting with people: Jacob wrestles with an angel (Genesis 32:24–30); Elijah (Elias) is fed by the ravens and by an angel (1 Kings 17:6 and 19:6); Abraham entertains three angelic visitors (Genesis 18:1–8)

familiar · close, intimate

Whirlwinds ... soft voice · Vaughan seeks to distinguish the angelic visitations from those direct visits by God who appears in fire (Exodus 3:2), in a whirlwind (Job 38:1), in a cloud (Exodus 13:21), and "in a still and soft voice" (1 Kings 19:12)

Is the truce ... decree? · the poet here asks whether the coming of Christ the mediator signals the end of God's direct interaction with human beings

green heads · inexperienced people, that is, religious innovators

Cordials · drinks that restore the heart

drilling · dripping

veins of sulfur · the underground stream becomes contaminated

Here Jacob dreams and wrestles; there
Elias by a raven is fed,   10
Another time by the angel, where
He brings him water with his bread;

In Abr'ham's tent the winged guests
(O how familiar° then was heaven!)
Eat, drink, discourse, sit down, and rest   15
Until the cool, and shady even;°

Nay thou thyself, my God, in fire,
Whirlwinds and clouds, and the soft voice°
Speak'st there so much, that I admire
We have no conf'rence in these days;   20

Is the truce broke? or 'cause we have
A mediator now with thee,
Dost thou therefore old treaties wave
And by appeals from him decree?°

Or is 't so, as some green heads° say   25
That now all miracles must cease?
Though thou hast promis'd they should stay
The tokens of the Church, and peace;

No, no; Religion is a spring
That from some secret, golden mine   30
Derives her birth, and thence doth bring
Cordials° in every drop and wine;

But in her long, and hidden course
Passing through the earth's dark veins,
Grows still from better unto worse,   35
And both her taste, and color stains,

Then drilling° on, learns to increase
False echoes, and confused sounds,
And unawares doth often seize
On veins of sulfur° under ground;   40

41 So poison'd, breaks forth in some clime,
And at first sight doth many please,
But drunk, is puddle, or mere slime
And 'stead of physic, a disease;

45 Just such a tainted sink* we have
Like that Samaritan's dead well,*
Nor must we for the kernel crave
Because most voices like the shell.*

Heal then these waters, Lord; or bring thy flock,
50 Since these are troubled, to the springing rock,*
Look down great Master of the feast; O shine,
And turn once more our water into wine!*

SONG OF SOLOMON 4:12

M Y SISTER, MY SPOUSE, *is as a garden enclosed, as a spring*
shut up, and a fountain sealed up.

AND DO THEY SO?

Et enim res Creatæ exerto Capite observantes expectant
*revelationem Filiorum Dei.** (Romans 8:19)

1

1 A ND DO THEY* SO? have they a sense
Of ought but influence?*
Can they their heads lift, and expect,
And groan too?* Why th' Elect*
5 Can do no more: my volumes said
They were all dull, and dead,
They judg'd them senseless, and their state
Wholly inanimate.
Go, go; seal up thy looks,*
10 And burn thy books.

2

I WOULD I WERE A stone, or tree,
Or flower by pedigree,
Or some poor highway herb, or spring

sink · sewer, cesspool

Samaritan's dead well · The well visited by the Samaritan woman is "dead" compared to the living water offered by Jesus (John 4:5–15)

shell · outward appearance

the springing rock · Christ (see 1 Corinthians 10:4)

water into wine · a reference to Christ's first miracle (John 2)

Et … Dei · "For the creatures, watching with lifted head, wait for the revealing of the sons of God" (Beza's Latin translation of Romans 8:19)

they · earthly creatures

influence · the influence of the stars

Can … groan too? · the poet wonders whether the creatures of nature can feel pain and entertain hope for Christ's return as human beings do

Elect · God's chosen

looks · eyes

To flow, or bird to sing!
Then should I (tied to one sure state,) 15
    All day expect my date;*
But I am sadly loose, and stray
    A giddy* blast each way;
    O let me not thus range!
    Thou canst not change. 20

date · day of death

giddy · showy, wild

3

Sometimes I sit with thee, and tarry
    An hour, or so, then vary.
Thy other creatures in this scene
    Thee only aim, and mean;*
Some rise to seek thee, and with heads 25
    Erect peep from their beds;
Others, whose birth is in the tomb,
    And cannot quit the womb,
    Sigh there, and groan for thee,
    Their liberty. 30

Thy other … mean · the lower creatures worship and honor their Creator without fail, unlike human beings who are fickle

4

O let not me do less! Shall they
    Watch, while I sleep, or play?
Shall I thy mercies still abuse
    With fancies, friends, or news?
O brook* it not! Thy blood is mine, 35
    And my soul should be thine;
O brook it not! Why wilt thou stop*
    After whole showers one drop?
    Sure, thou wilt joy to see
    Thy sheep with thee. 40

brook · endure

stop · withhold

Edward Taylor

(ca 1642–1729)

Born in Sketchley, England, Taylor emigrated to America in 1668 because of the restrictions placed on Puritans. After graduating from Harvard in 1671, he moved to Westfield, Massachusetts, where he worked until his death as a minister to the small farming community. In 1674 he married Elizabeth Fitch, who bore him eight children, five of whom died in infancy. In 1692, he married Ruth Wyllys, who bore six children. Taylor's work in Westfield included not only the spiritual tasks of ministering to the community, but also growing crops to feed his large family. About 1682, he began a series of poems written to prepare himself for the Lord's Supper. These poems, composed over a period of 43 years (collected under the title Preparatory Meditations)*, express Puritan spirituality through rustic imagery and typology based on Scripture.* Preparatory Meditations *was unpublished and virtually unknown until 1937 when it was discovered in the Yale University library. Today Taylor is recognized as one of the most significant poets in colonial America.*

MEDITATION 8 (first series)

John 6:51. I am the living bread.

1 I KENNING* THROUGH astronomy divine
   The world's bright battlement, wherein I spy
A golden path my pencil cannot line,
   From that bright throne unto my threshold lie.
5   And while my puzzled thoughts about it pour,
   I find the bread of life in't at my door.

When that this bird of paradise* put in,
   This wicker cage (my corpse)* to tweedle* praise
Had pecked the fruit forbade: and so did fling

kenning · discovering, discerning

bird of paradise · tradition held that this species of bird never lands on the ground. Taylor uses the image to signify the soul

corpse · body

tweedle · sing

447

Away its food; and lost its golden days;   10
It fell into celestial famine sore:
And never could attain a morsel more.

Alas! alas! Poor bird, what wilt thou do?
    The creatures' field no food for souls e'er gave.
And if thou knock at angels' doors they show   15
    An empty barrel: they no soul bread have.
    Alas! Poor bird, the world's white loaf is done,
    And cannot yield thee here the smallest crumb.

tender bowels · just as the heart is thought to be the seat of love, the bowels were thought to be the seat of pity and sympathetic emotions

In this sad state, God's tender bowels* run
    Out streams of grace: and he to end all strife   20
The purest wheat in Heaven, his dear-dear Son
    Grinds, and kneads up into this bread of life.
    Which bread of life from Heaven down came and stands
    Dished on thy table up by angels' hands.

Did God mold up this bread in Heaven, and bake,   25
    Which from his table came, and to thine goeth?
Doth he bespeak thee thus: "This soul bread take.
    Come, eat thy fill of this thy God's white loaf"?
    "It's food too fine for angels, yet come, take
    And eat thy fill. It's Heaven's sugar cake."   30

What grace is this knead in this loaf? This thing
    Souls are but petty things it to admire.
Ye angels, help: This fill would to the brim

whelm'd-down · turned over

    Heav'n's whelm'd-down* crystal meal bowl, yea and higher
    This bread of life dropped in thy mouth, doth cry: 35
    "Eat, eat me, soul, and thou shalt never die."

Alfred, Lord Tennyson

◄(1 8 0 9 - 1 8 9 2)►

*Tennyson, born in Lincolnshire, England, and educated at Cambridge,
was made poet laureate of Great Britain in 1850. Although much of his
anthologized and most-remembered poetry comes from his collection
of Arthurian verse,* Idylls of the King, *his collection of poems entitled* In
Memoriam *(1850) contains his most passionate and most vulnerable
poetry. Like many of his contemporaries, Tennyson encountered scientific revelations which seemed to cast suspicion where once only faith
and hope existed. The death of his close friend Arthur Henry Hallam
in 1833 inspired an angry, grieving Tennyson to write* In Memoriam, *a
collection of 132 separate poems which chronicle his struggle with faith
in God, grief at the loss of his friend, and the broader questions of free
will, doubt, and the very existence of a benevolent Creator. Ultimately,
the work – one of the greatest elegies in the English language – records
the growth of faith in the face of fear and uncertainty.*

from IN MEMORIAM A. H. H.

*Obiit** MDCCCXXXIII

1 STRONG SON OF GOD, immortal Love,
   Whom we, that have not seen thy face,
     By faith, and faith alone, embrace,
Believing where we cannot prove;*

5 Thine are these orbs of light and shade;
   Thou madest Life in man and brute;
     Thou madest Death; and lo, thy foot
Is on the skull which thou hast made.

Thou wilt not leave us in the dust:
10   Thou madest man, he knows not why,

Obiit · "died" (Latin).
The epigraph cites
Hallam's death in 1833

**have not seen …
cannot prove** · see
John 20:29

449

He thinks he was not made to die;   11
And thou hast made him: thou art just.

Thou seemest human and divine,
   The highest, holiest manhood, thou.
   Our wills are ours, we know not how;   15
Our wills are ours, to make them thine.

systems · theological or
philosophical paradigms Our little systems* have their day;
   They have their day and cease to be;
   They are but broken lights of thee,
And thou, O Lord, art more than they.   20

We have but faith: we cannot know,
   For knowledge is of things we see;
   And yet we trust it comes from thee,
A beam in darkness: let it grow.

Let knowledge grow from more to more,   25
   But more of reverence in us dwell;
   That mind and soul, according well,
May make one music as before,

But vaster. We are fools and slight;
   We mock thee when we do not fear: 30
   But help thy foolish ones to bear;
Help thy vain worlds to bear thy light.

Forgive what seemed my sin in me,
   What seemed my worth since I began;
   For merit lives from man to man,   35
And not from man, O Lord, to thee.

Forgive my grief for one removed,
   Thy creature, whom I found so fair.
   I trust he lives in thee, and there
I find him worthier to be loved.   40

41 Forgive these wild and wandering cries,
      Confusions of a wasted youth;
      Forgive them where they fail in truth,
  And in thy wisdom make me wise.

✦ ✦ ✦

96

1 Y OU SAY, BUT WITH no touch of scorn,
      Sweet-hearted, you,˙ whose light blue eyes
      Are tender over drowning flies,
  You tell me, doubt is Devil-born.

5 I know not: one˙ indeed I knew
      In many a subtle question versed,
      Who touched a jarring lyre at first,
  But ever strove to make it true;

      Perplexed in faith, but pure in deeds,
10   At last he beat his music out.
      There lives more faith in honest doubt,
  Believe me, than in half the creeds.

      He fought his doubts and gathered strength,
      He would not make his judgment blind,
15   He faced the specters of the mind
  And laid them; thus he came at length

      To find a stronger faith his own,
      And Power was with him in the night,
      Which makes the darkness and the light,
20 And dwells not in the light alone,

      But in the darkness and the cloud,
      As over Sinai's peaks of old,˙
      While Israel made their gods of gold,
  Although the trumpet blew so loud.

Sweet-hearted, you · the narrator addresses someone whose faith is serene and uncomplicated

one · Hallam

Sinai's peaks of old · Exodus 32:1–6. See also Deuteronomy 4:11 and 5:23

Robert Browning

◁(1 8 1 2 – 1 8 8 9)▷

*Growing up in an affluent household on the outskirts of London,
surrounded by a father's substantial library of six thousand volumes, the young Browning developed a taste for music, painting,
theater, and – above all – poetry. He was destined to become one of
the greatest poets in Victorian England. His devotion to Elizabeth
Barrett, a distinguished poet in her own right whom he married in
1846, certainly added to his luster. The couple moved to Florence
where they lived until Elizabeth's death in 1861. Browning produced
a great body of poetry, but he is best known for his short dramatic
monologues, which often reveal a psychologically complex character engaged in an interior debate, "the parliament of the mind," as
one critic noted. Like many other Victorians, Browning's religious
views were not entirely fixed. The son of an evangelical mother,
he knew his Bible well, but resisted identifying with a particular
church. The power of intuition and love, the integrity of the soul,
the dignity of the individual, and the unity of flesh and spirit were
familiar themes. Many of his poems treat religious questions and
problems of believing.*

MY LAST DUCHESS

Ferrara

1 That's my last Duchess painted on the wall,
Looking as if she were alive. I call
That piece a wonder, now: Frà Pandolf's hands
Worked busily a day, and there she stands.
5 Will 't please you sit and look at her? I said
"Frà Pandolf" by design, for never read
Strangers like you that pictured countenance,
The depth and passion of its earnest glance,

But to myself they turned (since none puts by
The curtain I have drawn for you, but I)   10
And seemed as they would ask me, if they durst,
How such a glance came there; so, not the first
Are you to turn and ask thus. Sir, 'twas not
Her husband's presence only, called that spot
Of joy into the Duchess' cheek: perhaps   15
Frà Pandolf chanced to say "Her mantle laps
Over my Lady's wrist too much," or "Paint
Must never hope to reproduce the faint
Half-flush that dies along her throat": such stuff
Was courtesy, she thought, and cause enough   20
For calling up that spot of joy. She had
A heart – how shall I say? – too soon made glad,
Too easily impressed; she liked whate'er
She looked on, and her looks went everywhere.
Sir, 'twas all one! My favour at her breast,   25
The dropping of the daylight in the West,
The bough of cherries some officious fool
Broke in the orchard for her, the white mule
She rode with round the terrace – all and each
Would draw from her alike the approving speech,   30
Or blush, at least. She thanked men, – good! but thanked
Somehow – I know not how – as if she ranked
My gift of a nine-hundred-years-old name
With anybody's gift. Who'd stoop to blame
This sort of trifling? Even had you skill   35
In speech – (which I have not) – to make your will
Quite clear to such an one, and say, "Just this
Or that in you disgusts me; here you miss,
Or there exceed the mark" – and if she let
Herself be lessoned so, nor plainly set   40
Her wits to yours, forsooth, and made excuse –
E'en then would be some stooping, and I choose
Never to stoop. Oh sir, she smiled, no doubt,
Whene'er I passed her; but who passed without
Much the same smile? This grew; I gave commands;   45
Then all smiles stopped together. There she stands
As if alive. Will 't please you rise? We'll meet

The company below, then. I repeat,
The Count your master's known munificence
50 Is ample warrant that no just pretence
Of mine for dowry will be disallowed;
Though his fair daughter's self, as I avowed
At starting, is my object. Nay, we'll go
Together down, sir. Notice Neptune, though,
55 Taming a sea-horse, thought a rarity,
Which Claus of Innsbruck cast in bronze for me!

SOLILOQUY OF THE SPANISH CLOISTER

1 Gr-r-r-there go, my heart's abhorrence!
Water your damned flower-pots, do!
If hate killed men, Brother Lawrence,
God's blood, would not mine kill you!
5 What? your myrtle-bush wants trimming?
Oh, that rose has prior claims –
Needs its leaden vase filled brimming?
Hell dry you up with its flames!

At the meal we sit together:
10 *Salve*˙ *tibi!* I must hear   **Salve…** ˙ Hail to thee!
Wise talk of the kind of weather,
Sort of season, time of year:
Not a plenteous cork-crop: scarcely
Dare we hope oak-galls, I doubt:
15 *What's the Latin name for "parsley"?*
What's the Greek name for Swine's Snout?

Whew! We'll have our platter burnished,
Laid with care on our own shelf!
With a fire-new spoon we're furnished,
20 And a goblet for ourself,
Rinsed like something sacrificial
Ere 'tis fit to touch our chaps –
Marked with L. for our initial!
(He-he! There his lily snaps!)

Saint, forsooth! While brown Dolores   25
Squats outside the Convent bank
With Sanchicha, telling stories,
Steeping tresses in the tank,
Blue-black, lustrous, thick like horsehairs,
– Can't I see his dead eye glow,   30

Barbary Corsair · Bright as 'twere a Barbary corsair's?*
North African pirate (That is, if he'd let it show!)

When he finishes refection,
Knife and fork he never lays
Cross-wise, to my recollection,   35
As I do, in Jesu's praise.
I the Trinity illustrate,
Drinking watered orange-pulp –

Arian · One who In three sips the Arian* frustrate
denies the Trinity While he drains his at one gulp.   40

Oh, those melons? If he's able
We're to have a feast! so nice!
One goes to the Abbot's table,
All of us eager to get a slice.
How go on your flowers? None double?   45
Not one fruit-sort can you spy?
Strange! And I, too, at such trouble,
Keep them close-nipped on the sly!

Galatians · See Gal. There's a great text in Galatians,*
3:10; 5:19-21 Once you trip on it, entails   50
Twenty-nine distinct damnations,
One sure, if another fails.
If I trip him just a-dying,
Sure of heaven as sure can be,
Spin him round and send him flying   55

Manichee · heretic, a Off to hell, a Manichee?*
follower of Manichaeus

Or, my scrofulous French novel,
On grey paper with blunt type!
Simply glance at it, you grovel   60

61   Hand and foot in Belial's* gripe: **Beliel** · a devil
      If I double down its pages
      At the woeful sixteenth print,

      When he gathers his greengages,*   **Greengages** · plums
65   Ope a sieve and slip it in't?

      Or, there's Satan! – one might venture
      Pledge one's soul to him, yet leave
      Such a flaw in the indenture
      As he'd miss it till, past retrieve,
70   Blasted lay that rose-acacia
      We're so proud of! *Hy, Zy, Hine** . . .   **Hy, Zy, Hine** · a curse
      'St, there's Vespers! *Plena* gratia*   or incantation
      Ave, Virgo! Gr-r-r – you swine!   **Plena...** · "Hail,
                                                                             Virgin, full of grace"

Christina Rossetti

◀{ 1 8 3 0 – 1 8 9 4 }▶

Growing up in a home divided between the passions of an Italian father and the moral rigidity of an Anglo-Italian mother, Rossetti's life is marked by two conflicting themes: her unconventional passion for intellect and her search for God and His divine direction. These tensions led her to write some of the most arresting and original religious poems of the Victorian Age. Two men close to Rossetti, William Morris and her brother Dante Gabriel Rossetti, initiated the Pre-Raphaelite Movement, which seems to have affected Rossetti's style – her tendency towards naturalistic detail, pictorialism, symbolism, and sensuousness. In 1871 Christina contracted Graves' Disease, a form of hyperthyroidism, which froze her face like a mask. Though racked by pain for the next twenty years, she continued to publish works of devotional poetry and prose, including a commentary on the book of Revelation, The Face of the Deep, *published two years before her death to cancer.*

GOOD FRIDAY

1   Aᴍ I ᴀ sᴛᴏɴᴇ, and not a sheep,
      That I can stand, O Christ, beneath Thy cross,
     To number drop by drop Thy Blood's slow loss,
And yet not weep?

5 Not so those women loved
     Who with exceeding grief lamented Thee;
     Not so fallen Peter weeping bitterly;
Not so the thief was moved;

Not so the Sun and Moon
10   Which hid their faces in a starless sky.

A horror of great darkness at broad noon –
I, only I.

Yet give not o'er
    But seek Thy sheep, true Shepherd of the flock;
    Greater than Moses, turn and look once more   15
And smite a rock.

UP-HILL

DOES THE ROAD wind up-hill all the way?   1
    Yes, to the very end.
Will the day's journey take the whole long day?
    From morn to night, my friend.

But is there for the night a resting-place?   5
    A roof for when the slow dark hours begin.
May not the darkness hide it from my face?
    You cannot miss that inn.

Shall I meet other wayfarers at night?
    Those who have gone before.   10
Then must I knock, or call when just in sight?
    They will not keep you standing at that door.

Shall I find comfort, travel-sore and weak?
    Of labour you shall find the sum.
Will there be beds for me and all who seek?   15
    Yea, beds for all who come.

Emily Dickinson

◄(1 8 3 1 – 1 8 8 6)►

Dickinson, born and reared in Amherst, Massachusetts, published only a handful of poems in her lifetime. After her death in 1886, it was discovered that she had composed almost 1800 poems, many written on the backs of letters or receipts. Her close friend Thomas Wentworth Higgins found himself baffled when faced with categorizing her poetry since Dickinson delves deeply into nature, glances with irony at society and its functions, and puzzles over questions of faith and will. Her poetry raises far more questions than it answers, for Dickinson found every subject – be it snake, butterfly, bee, or even a closed door – an inspiration, an impetus for thought or emotion. Dickinson is never keen on religious institutions (rarely mentioning organized religion at all), but her poetry is suffused with religious questions. She is notoriously honest about her doubts: "doubt like the mosquito buzzes round my faith," she writes. But she can be serenely confident as well: "I know that He exists. Somewhere – in Silence –." She compares herself to the Old Testament patriarch who wrestles with an angel (Genesis 32:25): "Pugilist and Poet, Jacob was correct." Dickinson seems at her best challenging the deity whose existence she never doubts.

A WOUNDED DEER LEAPS HIGHEST

1 A Wounded Deer – leaps highest –
      I've heard the Hunter tell
'Tis but the Ecstasy of death –
And then the v˙ is still!

Brake · thicket

5 The Smitten Rock that gushes!
The trampled Steel that springs!
A Cheek is always redder
Just where the Hectic˙ stings!

Hectic · wasp

Mail · chain mail, a
type of armor

Mirth is the Mail* of Anguish –
In which it Cautious Arm,   10
Lest anybody spy the blood
And "you're hurt" exclaim!

THIS WORLD IS NOT CONCLUSION

Species · form

THIS WORLD IS not Conclusion.   1
A Species* stands beyond –
Invisible, as Music –
But positive, as Sound –
It beckons, and it baffles –   5
Philosophy – don't know –
And through a Riddle, at the last –
Sagacity, must go –
To guess it, puzzles scholars –
To gain it, Men have borne   10
Contempt of Generations
And Crucifixion, shown –
Faith slips – and laughs, and rallies –
Blushes, if any see –
Plucks at a twig of Evidence –   15

Vane · a weathervane

And asks a v,* the way –
Much Gesture, from the Pulpit –
Strong Hallelujahs roll –
Narcotics cannot still the Tooth
That nibbles at the soul –   20

I MEASURE EVERY GRIEF I MEET

I MEASURE EVERY Grief I meet   1
With narrow, probing, Eyes –
I wonder if It weighs like Mine –
Or has an Easier size.

I wonder if They bore it long –   5
Or did it just begin –
I could not tell the Date of Mine –
It feels so old a pain –

I wonder if it hurts to live –
10 And if They have to try –
And whether – could They choose between –
It would not be – to die –

I note that Some – gone patient long –
At length, renew their smile –
15 An imitation of a Light
That has so little Oil –

I wonder if when Years have piled –
Some Thousands – on the Harm –
That hurt them early – such a lapse
20 Could give them any Balm –

Or would they go on aching still
Through Centuries of Nerve –
Enlightened to a larger Pain –
In Contrast with the Love –

25 The Grieved – are many – I am told –
There is the various Cause –
Death – is but one – and comes but once –
And only nails the eyes –

There's Grief of Want – and Grief of Cold –
30 A sort they call "Despair" –
There's Banishment from native Eyes –
In sight of Native Air –

And though I may not guess the kind –
Correctly – yet to me
35 A piercing Comfort it affords
In passing Calvary –

To note the fashions – of the Cross –
And how they're mostly worn –
Still fascinated to presume
40 That Some – are like My Own –

FAITH – IS THE PIERLESS BRIDGE

Pierless · a pun; both "peerless" (unmatched), and "without piers" (lacking piles or pillars; without support or a concrete foundation)

FAITH – IS THE Pierless˙ Bridge   1
Supporting what We see
Unto the Scene that We do not –
Too slender for the eye

It bears the Soul as bold   5
As it were rocked in Steel
With Arms of Steel at either side –
It joins – behind the Veil

To what, could We presume
The Bridge would cease to be   10
To Our far, vacillating Feet
A first Necessity.

THERE CAME A DAY

THERE CAME A Day at Summer's full,   1
Entirely for me –
I thought that such were for the Saints,
Where Resurrections – be –

The Sun, as common, went abroad,   5

blew · bloomed   The flowers, accustomed, blew,˙
As if no soul the solstice passed
That maketh all things new –

The time was scarce profaned, by speech –
The symbol of a word   10
Was needless, as at Sacrament,
The Wardrobe – of our Lord –

Each was to each The Sealed Church,
Permitted to commune this – time –
Lest we too awkward show   15
At Supper of the Lamb.

The Hours slid fast – as Hours will,
Clutched tight, by greedy hands –
So faces on two decks, look back,
20 Bound to opposing lands –

And so when all the time had leaked,
Without external sound
Each bound the Other's Crucifix –
We gave no other Bond –

25 Sufficient troth, that we shall rise –
Deposed – at length, the Grave –
To that new Marriage,
Justified – through Calvaries of Love –

George MacDonald

◀（1 8 2 4 - 1 9 0 5）▶

Poet, mystic, preacher, and novelist, MacDonald was born in Aberdeen, Scotland, to devout Congregationalist parents. After preaching for three years (1850–1853), he resigned in order to devote himself to writing. His most enduring works are symbolic fantasies, including the children's classics At the Back of the North Wind *(1871)* and The Princess and the Goblin *(1872). Through his visionary stories, novels, and poems, MacDonald demonstrated the profound links between faith and imagination. In this respect, he inspired C.S. Lewis, J.R.R. Tolkien, Madeleine L'Engle, and other 20th-century writers of spiritually-endowed fantasy and fiction. "Obedience" plays with a familiar theme in religious verse – "psychomachia" or soul struggle. In this case the struggle is between two goods – the romantic lure of nature and the urgent need to care for oppressed workers in England's nightmarish industrial cities. In this setting, obedience is not oppressive, but liberating. "Obedience is the opener of eyes," writes MacDonald. "Every obedience is the opening of another door into the boundless universe of life."*

OBEDIENCE

1 I SAID, "LET ME walk in the fields."
    He said, "No, walk in the town."
I said, "There are no flowers there."
    He said, "No flowers, but a crown."

5 I said, "But the skies are black;
    There is nothing but noise and din."
And He wept as He sent me back;
    "There is more," He said; "there is sin."

I said, "But the air is thick,
    And fogs are veiling the sun."   10
He answered, "Yet souls are sick,
    And souls in the dark undone."

I said, "I shall miss the light,
    And friends will miss me, they say."
He answered, "Choose to-night   15
    If I am to miss you, or they."

I pleaded for time to be given.
    He said, "Is it hard to decide?
It will not seem hard in heaven
    To have followed the steps of your Guide."   20

I cast one look at the fields,
    Then set my face to the town;
He said, "My child, do you yield?
    Will you leave the flowers for the crown?"

Then into His hand went mine,   25
    And into my heart came He;
And I walk in a light divine
    That path I had feared to see.

Gerard Manley Hopkins

⟨1 8 4 4 – 1 8 8 9⟩

Hopkins wrote stunningly original poetry, though it was virtually unknown until its posthumous publication in 1918. Born in Stratford, Essex, and educated at Balliol College, Oxford, Hopkins fell under the sway of the Oxford Movement, a religious reform movement that led to Hopkins's decision to enter the Roman Catholic Church in 1866. Soon after, Hopkins joined the Jesuit Order and in 1877 was ordained a priest. He served various parishes, including one in a Liverpool slum. In 1884 he became Classics Professor at University College, Dublin. Hopkins's poems are challenging in their use of word coinages, archaic dialect terms, unusual meter (which he called "sprung rhythm"), extraordinary compactness (including the dropping of unnecessary words), alliteration, and puns. Something of a late Romantic, Hopkins believed that the distinctive designs of nature ultimately lead one to Jesus Christ. Nature, in fact, is the bridge between the finite and the infinite. To experience beauty is to discover the uniqueness of every created form, and therefore to be lifted to God in heart and mind. Not all of Hopkins's poems are celebrations of God in creation; others are wrenching, Job-like inquiries into the reasons for, and God's place in, human suffering.

GOD'S GRANDEUR

1 THE WORLD IS CHARGED with the grandeur of God.·
    It will flame out, like shining from shook foil;·
      It gathers to a greatness, like the ooze of oil
  Crushed.· Why do men then now not reck his rod?·
5 Generations have trod, have trod, have trod;
      And all is seared with trade; bleared, smeared with toil;
      And wears man's smudge and shares man's smell: the soil
  Is bare now, nor can foot feel, being shod.

charged ... God · Hopkins writes: "All things therefore are charged with love, are charged with God and if we know how to touch them give off sparks and take fire, yield drops and flow, ring and tell of him" (*Sermons and Devotional Writings*)

shook foil · Hopkins explained this image in a letter: "I mean foil in its sense of leaf or tinsel.... Shaken goldfoil gives off broad glares like sheet lightning and ... a sort of fork lightning too"

ooze ... Crushed · oil flowing from crushed olives

Why ... his rod? · if nature is so full of God's grandeur, why do men not take heed of ("reck") God's authority ("his rod")?

469

for · despite

And, for* all this, nature is never spent;
　　There lives the dearest freshness deep down things;　　10
And though the last lights off the black West went
　　Oh, morning, at the brown brink eastward, springs –
Because the Holy Ghost over the bent
　　World broods with warm breast and with ah! bright wings.

pied · multicolored

couple-color · paired
or linked (perhaps
complementary) colors;
consider the polarities
in line 9, "swift, slow;
sweet, sour; adazzle, dim"

brinded · streaked

stipple · speckles
or spots

**Fresh-firecoal
chestnut-falls** · a
shower of freshly fallen
chestnuts looks like
coals of fire

áll trádes · Hopkins'
spelling includes stresses.
He wrote in what he
called "sprung rhythm,"
by which he meant that
one accented syllable of
the poem often follows
directly upon another

counter · contrary

windhover · a kestrel
or falcon

PIED* BEAUTY

Glory be to God for dappled things –　　1
　　For skies of couple-color* as a brinded* cow;
　　　　For rose-moles all in stipple* upon trout that swim;
Fresh-firecoal chestnut-falls,* finches' wings;
　　Landscape plotted and pieced – fold, fallow, and plough;　　5
　　　　And áll trádes,* their gear and tackle and trim.

All things counter,* original, spare, strange;
　　Whatever is fickle, freckled (who knows how?)
　　　　With swift, slow; sweet, sour; adazzle, dim;
He fathers-forth whose beauty is past change:　　10
　　　　　　　　Praise him.

THE WINDHOVER*

To Christ our Lord

I caught this morning morning's minion, king-　　1
　dom of daylight's dauphin, dapple-dawn-drawn Falcon, in
　　his riding
Of the rolling level underneath him steady air, and striding
High there, how he rung upon the rein of a wimpling wing　　5
In his ecstasy! then off, off forth on swing,
As a skate's heel sweeps smooth on a bow-bend: the hurl and
　　gliding
Rebuffed the big wind. My heart in hiding
Stirred for a bird, – the achieve of, the mastery of the thing!　　10

buckle · combine,
fasten, crumple

Brute beauty and valour and act, oh, air, pride, plume, here
Buckle!* AND the fire that breaks from thee then, a billion
Times told lovelier, more dangerous, O my chevalier!

No wonder of it: shéer plód makes plough down sillion*

15 Shine, and blue-bleak embers, ah my dear,

Fall, gall themselves, and gash gold-vermillion.

sillion · thick, shiny soil turned over by the plow; or the furrow down which the plow travels

AS KINGFISHERS CATCH FIRE

1 As kingfishers catch fire, dragonflies draw flame;

    As tumbled over rim in roundy wells

    Stones ring; like each tucked* string tells, each hung bell's

Bow swung finds tongue to fling out broad its name;

5 Each mortal thing does one thing and the same:

    Deals out that being indoors* each one dwells;

    Selves*– goes itself; *myself* it speaks and spells,

Crying *What I do is me: for that I came.*

I say more: the just man justices;*

10   Keeps gráce: thát keeps all his goings graces;

Acts in God's eye what in God's eye he is –

    Chríst. For Christ plays in ten thousand places,

Lovely in limbs, and lovely in eyes not his

    To the Father through the features of men's faces.

tucked · plucked

indoors · within

Selves · Hopkins coins a verb: "to selve" means "to express one's own unique being, one's essential individuality and particularity"

justices · another of Hopkins' invented verbs: "to act in a just, holy, and gracious manner"

BINSEY POPLARS

felled 1879

1 My aspens dear, whose airy cages quelled,

    Quelled or quenched in leaves the leaping sun,

All felled, felled, are all felled;

Of a fresh and following folded rank

5   Not spared, not one

    That dandled* a sandalled

Shadow that swam or sank

On meadow and river and wind-wandering weed-winding bank.

O if we but knew what we do

10   When we delve or hew –

Hack and rack the growing green!

    Since country is so tender

dandled · bounced, pampered

To touch, her being só slender,
That, like this sleek and seeing ball
But a prick will make no eye at all,   15
Where we, even where we mean
    To mend her we end her,
When we hew or delve:
After-comers cannot guess the beauty been.
Ten or twelve, only ten or twelve   20
Strokes of havoc únselve
    The sweet especial scene,
Rural scene, a rural scene,
Sweet especial rural scene.

[CARRION COMFORT]·

NOT, I'LL NOT, carrion comfort, Despair, not feast on thee;   1
  Not untwist – slack they may be – these last strands of man
In me ór, most weary, cry *I can no more*. I can;
Can something, hope, wish day come, not choose not to be.

But ah, but O thou terrible, why wouldst thou rude· on me   5
Thy wring-world right foot rock?· lay a lionlimb against me? scan
With darksome devouring eyes my bruisèd bones? and fan,·
O in turns of tempest, me heaped there; me frantic to avoid
    thee and flee?

Why? That my chaff might fly; my grain lie, sheer and clear.   10
Nay in all that toil, that coil,· since (seems) I v,·
Hand rather, my heart lo! lapped strength, stole joy, would laugh,
    chéer.
Cheer whom though? The hero whose heaven-handling flung
    me, fóot tród   15
Me? or mé that fóught him? O which one? is it each one? That
    níght, that year
Of now done darkness I wretch lay wrestling with (my God!)
    my God.

[Carrion Comfort]· Hopkins did not supply this title; it was given by his friend Robert Bridges (1844–1930)

rude· roughly, violently

why wouldst thou ... rock?· why would you, God, who wrings the world with your power, violently rock your foot on me?

fan· to separate the kernel of grain from its husk (chaff) by means of a fan

coil· tumult

kissed the rod· the rod is the symbol of God's chastening; hence Hopkins is describing acceptance of God's authority — including the necessity of one's own suffering

MY OWN HEART

1 M y own heart let me more have pity on; let
   Me live to my sad self hereafter kind,
Charitable; not live this tormented mind
With this tormented mind tormenting yet.

5 I cast for comfort I can no more get
By groping round my comfortless, than blind
Eyes in their dark can day or thirst can find
Thirst's all-in-all in all a world of wet.

Soul, self; come, poor Jackself,· I do advise
10 You, jaded, let be; call off thoughts awhile
Elsewhere; leave comfort root-room; let joy size·
At God knows when to God knows what; whose smile
'S not wrung, see you; unforeseen times rather – as skies·
Betweenpie mountains – lights a lovely mile.

Jackself · ordinary, everyday self

size · grow

As skies · As skies appear dappled or multicolored between mountains

C. S. Lewis

⟨ 1 8 9 8 - 1 9 6 3 ⟩

*Lewis, perhaps the 20th century's most famous convert to Christianity,
has been called "the chief Christian tutor to the English-speaking world."
He was born in Belfast, Ireland (now Northern Ireland), but lived
most of his adult life in Oxford where he taught at Magdalen College
(1925–1954). From 1954 until his death, he was professor of medieval
and renaissance literature at Cambridge. A skeptic for many years,
Lewis underwent a formal conversion in 1929 (as reported in his autobiography* Surprised by Joy). *Lewis is best known for his science fiction;
for his series of children's fantasy,* The Chronicles of Narnia *(1950–1956);
and for his witty, intelligent defenses of Christian doctrine such as The*
Problem of Pain *(1940),* The Screwtape Letters *(1942),* Miracles *(1947),
and* Mere Christianity *(1952). Late in life, Lewis met and married Joy
Davidman Gresham, an American poet. Their brief, remarkable marriage has been popularized through William Nicholson's stageplay
and screenplay* Shadowlands. *Less well-known for his poetry, Lewis is,
nonetheless, an accomplished lyricist of Christian conviction.*

NO BEAUTY WE COULD DESIRE

1 YES, YOU ARE ALWAYS everywhere. But I,
    Hunting in such immeasurable forests,
Could never bring the noble Hart* to bay.*

    The scent was too perplexing for my hounds;
5 Nowhere sometimes, then again everywhere.
Other scents, too, seemed to them almost the same.

    Therefore I turn my back on the unapproachable
Stars and horizons and all musical sounds,
Poetry itself, and the winding stair of thought.

Hart · an adult male deer

bring ... to bay · to corner an animal using dogs

475

Leaving the forests where you are pursued in vain　　　　10
– Often a mere white gleam – I turn instead
To the appointed place where you pursue.

Not in Nature, not even in Man, but in one
Particular Man, with a date, so tall, weighing
So much, talking Aramaic, having learned a trade;　　　15

Not in all food, not in all bread and wine
(Not, I mean, as my littleness requires)
But this wine, this bread … no beauty we could desire.*

no … desire · of the Messiah, the prophet says, "there is no beauty that we should desire him" (Isaiah 53:2)

STEPHEN TO LAZARUS

BUT WAS I THE first martyr, who　　　　1
　　Gave up no more than life, while you,
Already free among the dead,
Your rags stripped off, your fetters shed,
Surrendered what all other men　　　　5
Irrevocably keep, and when
Your battered ship at anchor lay
Seemingly safe in the dark bay
No ripple stirs, obediently
Put out a second time to sea　　　　10
Well knowing that your death (in vain
Died once) must all be died again?

from FIVE SONNETS

I

YOU THINK THAT WE who do not shout and shake　　　1
　　Our fists at God when youth or bravery die
Have colder blood or hearts less apt to ache
Than yours who rail.* I know you do. Yet why?
You have what sorrow always longs to find,　　　5
Someone to blame, some enemy in chief;
Anger's the anæsthetic of the mind,
It does men good, it fumes away their grief.
We feel the stroke like you; so far our fate

rail · to cry out, criticize

10 Is equal. After that, for us begin
    Half-hopeless labours, learning not to hate,
    And then to want, and then (perhaps) to win
    A high, unearthly comfort, angel's food,
    That seems at first mockery to flesh and blood.

Dietrich Bonhœffer

◄{ 1 9 0 6 – 1 9 4 5 }►

*After a two-year imprisonment, Bonhœffer was hanged in the
Flossenburg concentration camp on April 9, 1945, for complicity
in an assassination plot against Adolf Hitler. A Lutheran pastor
and theologian, Bonhœffer had objected to Germany's anti-Jewish
legislation in 1933, consequently being forced from his pulpit
and into exile. In London, he temporarily ministered to German
congregations. Just before the Second World War, he was invited
to the United States for a lecture tour and refused the political
asylum that was offered. He returned to Germany as the war
began, joining the Resistance forces in his homeland. Bonhœffer's
best known works are* The Cost of Discipleship *(1948),* Letters and
Papers from Prison *(1953), and* Ethics *(1955). His writings attest to
an emerging theological system that, though incomplete, is rich in
suggestive detail. A pervasive and unifying theme is that there is
no separation of the religious realm from the secular. Significantly,
when he spoke of the earth, Bonhœffer frequently added "in which
the Cross of Jesus Christ is planted." The Christian, in other words,
must identify with and suffer for the world as did Christ. In the
summer of 1944, while imprisoned in Tegel, Berlin's military prison,
Bonhœffer wrote "Who Am I?"*

WHO AM I?

1 Who am I? They often tell me
   I stepped from my cell's confinement
   calmly, cheerfully, firmly,
   like a Squire from his country house.

5 Who am I? They often tell me
   I used to speak to my warders*

warders · guards

freely and friendly and clearly,
as though it were mine to command.

Who am I? They also tell me
I bore the days of misfortune 10
equably,* smilingly, proudly,
like one accustomed to win.

equably · evenly, without harsh extremes

Am I then really that which other men tell of?
Or am I only what I myself know of myself?
Restless and longing and sick, like a bird in a cage, 15
struggling for breath, as though hands were compressing my throat,
yearning for colors, for flowers, for the voices of birds,
thirsting for words of kindness, for neighborliness,
tossing in expectation of great events,
powerlessly trembling for friends at an infinite distance, 20
weary and empty at praying, at thinking, at making,
faint, and ready to say farewell to it all.

Who am I? This or the Other?
Am I one person today and tomorrow another?
Am I both at once? A hypocrite before others, 25
and before myself a contemptible woebegone weakling?
Or is something within me still like a beaten army
fleeing in disorder from victory already achieved?

Who am I? They mock me, these lonely questions of mine.
Whoever I am, Thou knowest, O God, I am thine! 30

W. H. Auden

⟨1 9 0 7 – 1 9 7 3⟩

As the most influential English poet of the 1930s, Auden brought back the public role of poet. A brilliant student at Oxford, he had absorbed the techniques of Modernism, but became tired of its tendency toward obscurity. In his poem, "Twelve Songs," first published as "Funeral Blues" in 1940, he anticipated the "God is Dead" movement among liberal theologians of the 1960s. Experimenting with various philosophies – including Freudianism and Marxism – as solutions to social and personal problems, he eventually worked his way back to Christianity. Auden emigrated to America in 1939, became an American citizen in 1946, and received the Pulitzer Prize in 1948 for The Age of Anxiety. He taught at numerous universities and served from 1956–1961 as Professor of Poetry at Oxford. Later in life he divided his time between his homes in Austria and New York, completing his great legacy as poet, critic, and dramatist.

from TWELVE SONGS

9

1   STOP ALL THE CLOCKS, cut off the telephone,
     Prevent the dog from barking with a juicy bone,
  Silence the pianos and with muffled drum
  Bring out the coffin, let the mourners come.

5 Let æroplanes circle moaning overhead
  Scribbling on the sky the message He Is Dead,
  Put crêpe* bows round the white necks of the public doves,
  Let the traffic policemen wear black cotton gloves.*

  He was my North, my South, my East and West,
10 My working week and my Sunday rest,

My noon, my midnight, my talk, my song;
I thought that love would last for ever: I was wrong.

The stars are not wanted now: put out every one;
Pack up the moon and dismantle the sun;
Pour away the ocean and sweep up the wood;   15
For nothing now can ever come to any good.

THE SONG

So large a morning so itself to learn   1
Over so many and such little hills
All at rest in roundness and rigs of green
Can cope with a rebellious wing that wills
To better its obedient double quite   5
As daring in the lap of any lake
The wind from which ascension puts to flight
Tribes of a beauty which no care can break.

Climbing to song it hopes to make amends
For whiteness drabbed for glory said away   10
And be immortal after but because
Light upon a valley where its love was
So lacks all picture of reproach it ends
Denying what it started up to say.

MUSÉE DES BEAUX ARTS*

Musée des Beaux Arts · The Museum of Fine Arts, located in Brussels, Belgium, that houses Breughel's (ca 1525–1569) *Icarus*. The painting depicts the legend of Icarus, the son of Dædalus, as the two attempted to escape the palace of Minos on artificial wings made of wax and feathers. When Icarus flew too close to the sun, his wings failed and he plunged to his death

About suffering they were never wrong,   1
The Old Masters: how well they understood
Its human position; how it takes place
While someone else is eating or opening a window or just walk-
    ing dully along;   5
How, when the aged are reverently, passionately waiting
For the miraculous birth, there always must be
Children who did not specially want it to happen, skating
On a pond at the edge of the wood:
They never forgot   10
That even the dreadful martyrdom must run its course

Anyhow in a corner, some untidy spot
Where the dogs go on with their doggy life and the torturer's horse
Scratches its innocent behind on a tree.

15   In Breughel's *Icarus*, for instance: how everything turns away
    Quite leisurely from the disaster; the ploughman may
    Have heard the splash, the forsaken cry,
    But for him it was not an important failure; the sun shone,
    As it had to on the white legs disappearing into the green
20   Water; and the expensive delicate ship that must have seen
    Something amazing, a boy falling out of the sky,
    Had somewhere to get to and sailed calmly on.

Czesław Miłosz

◄(1 9 1 1 – 2 0 0 4)►

A major poet and essayist, Miłosz was a naturalized citizen of the United States who won the Nobel Prize for Literature in 1980. Born in Lithuania and educated in Poland, Miłosz was permanently altered by his observation of totalitarian brutality – first Nazi, then Stalinist – in Warsaw, which he called "the most agonizing spot in the whole of terrorized Europe." Miłosz emigrated to France in 1951 and moved to America a decade later. His poetry often reflects his belief that European civilization inevitably declined when it abandoned its spiritual roots. The poet argues that Europeans were historically nourished by their "Christian imagination," but as scientific theory replaced this sacred understanding, they lost their capacity to see themselves as God-created. The failure of Christian imagination, consequently, rendered Europeans (and all Westerners) helpless in a hostile, alien environment. According to one critic, Miłosz believed that the death of the sacred way of seeing oneself became "the foundation of 20th-century nihilism and subsequently a cradle for totalitarian doctrines." His poems, which Miłosz called "acts of faith," are an effort to repair the damage by rebuilding a divine vision of the world, while fully acknowledging the dark forces that work against this theistic view. With passion, the poet desired to speak for, and to, all victims of persecution: "Now I am homeless – a just punishment. But perhaps I was born so that the 'Eternal Slaves' might speak through my lips." The Russian writer Joseph Brodsky called Miłosz "one of the greatest poets of our time, perhaps the greatest."

A SKULL

1 BEFORE MARY MAGDALEN, albescent* in the dusk,
   A skull. The candle flickers. Which of her lovers
   Is this dried-up bone, she does not try to guess.

albescent · "growing white." Mary Magdalene was traditionally thought to have been a prostitute rescued by Jesus. The painting *The Repentant Magdalene* by Georges de La Tour (1593–1652) is featured on this book's cover

485

She remains like that, for an age or two
In meditation, while sand in the hourglass   5
Has fallen asleep – because once she saw,
And felt on her shoulder the touch of His hand,

Rabboni · "my teacher"   Then, at daybreak, when she exclaimed: "Rabboni!"·
(Aramaic)

I gather dreams of the skull for I am it,
Impetuous, enamored, suffering in the gardens   10
Under a dark window, uncertain whether it's mine
And for no one else, the secret of her pleasure.
Raptures, solemn oaths. She does not quite remember.
And only that moment persists, unrevoked,
When she was almost on the other side.   15

A POOR CHRISTIAN LOOKS AT THE GHETTO

BEES BUILD AROUND red liver,   1
Ants build around black bone.
It has begun: the tearing, the trampling on silks,
It has begun: the breaking of glass, wood, copper, nickel, silver, foam
Of gypsum, iron sheets, violin strings, trumpets, leaves, balls, 5
   crystals.
Poof! Phosphorescent fire from yellow walls
Engulfs animal and human hair.

Bees build around the honeycomb of lungs,
Ants build around white bone.
Torn is paper, rubber, linen, leather, flax,   10
Fiber, fabrics, cellulose, snakeskin, wire.
The roof and the wall collapse in flame and heat seizes the
   foundations.
Now there is only the earth, sandy, trodden down,
With one leafless tree.

Slowly, boring a tunnel, a guardian mole makes his way,   15
With a small red lamp fastened to his forehead.
He touches buried bodies, counts them, pushes on,
He distinguishes human ashes by their luminous vapor,
The ashes of each man by a different part of the spectrum.

20 Bees build around a red trace.
   Ants build around the place left by my body.

   I am afraid, so afraid of the guardian mole.
   He has swollen eyelids, like a Patriarch
   Who has sat much in the light of candles
25 Reading the great book of the species.

   What will I tell him, I, a Jew of the New Testament,
   Waiting two thousand years for the second coming of Jesus?
   My broken body will deliver me to his sight
   And he will count me among the helpers of death:
30 The uncircumcised.

BEFORE MAJESTY

1 IT IS BITTER TO PRAISE God in misfortune,
   thinking that He did not act, though He could have.

   The angel of Jehovah did not touch the eyelids
   of a man whose hand I hold,
5 I, a passive witness of this suffering for no cause.

   Unanswered is our prayer, both his and mine.
   Unanswered is my request: strike me
   and in exchange give him an ordinary life.

   A weak human mercy walks in the corridors of hospitals
10 and is like a half-thawed winter.

   While I, who am I, a believer, dancing before the All-Holy?

Dylan Thomas

(1914–1953)

Thomas, born in Swansea, Wales, achieved international recognition as a poet, fiction writer, playwright, critic, and celebrated public performer of his own compositions. Something like modern rock stars, Thomas enjoyed a cult following in England, Europe, and the United States at mid-century. His fame increased through his bohemian ways that contributed to his early death. Thomas's poems are often difficult because he believed that modern poetic language should be "dislocated." Style and themes should be "surrealistic." Thomas's best poems succeed through vivid images inspired by nature, the Bible, and major Romantic and Metaphysical poets. Thomas viewed himself as a bard in the Welsh Celtic tradition who celebrates the spiritual forces in nature. Though Thomas abandoned organized Christianity, his poetic imagination never quite escaped the Paraclete Congregational Church of his youth. Thomas was very much like the protagonist of James Joyce's novel A Portrait of the Artist as a Young Man: *his mind was supersaturated with the religion in which he said he disbelieved.*

A REFUSAL TO MOURN THE DEATH, BY FIRE, OF A CHILD IN LONDON

1 NEVER UNTIL THE mankind making
     Bird beast and flower
  Fathering and all humbling darkness
  Tells with silence the last light breaking
5 And the still hour
  Is come of the sea tumbling in harness

  And I must enter again the round
  Zion* of the water bead

Zion · literally, the easternmost of the two hills of ancient Jerusalem; symbolically, the dwelling place of God

And the synagogue of the ear of corn
Shall I let pray the shadow of a sound   10
Or sow my salt seed*
In the least valley of sackcloth to mourn

The majesty and burning of the child's death.
I shall not murder
The mankind of her going with a grave truth   15
Nor blaspheme down the stations of the breath
With any further
Elegy of innocence and youth.

Deep with the first dead lies London's daughter,
Robed in the long friends,   20
The grains beyond age, the dark veins of her mother,
Secret by the unmourning water
Of the riding Thames.
After the first death, there is no other.

sow my salt seed · literally tears, Thomas here also alludes to the ancient practice of sowing fields with salt to make them permanently unfertile, as the Romans had done in Carthage

Richard Wilbur

◄(1 9 2 1 – 2 0 0 1)►

Born in New York City, Wilbur graduated from Amherst (1942) and served as an infantryman in World War II. After the war, he completed an MA at Harvard (1947), where he began a successful teaching career that continued at a number of prestigious institutions. His first book of poems, The Beautiful Changes (1947), was published when Wilbur was 26. It received affirming critical responses. Subsequent publications enjoyed equally positive reviews. His verse is polished in diction, sophisticated in structure, and often playfully witty in its angle of vision. The admirably smooth surface Wilbur creates, however, may well distract the reader from noting unexpected turns in his thought. "The poem," Wilbur has said, "is an effort to express a knowledge imperfectly felt, to articulate relationships not quite seen, to make or discover some pattern in the world." In addition to his two Pulitzer Prizes, Wilbur was honored with an appointment as Poet Laureate in 1987.

LOVE CALLS US TO THE THINGS OF THIS WORLD

1 THE EYES OPEN to a cry of pulleys,
    And spirited from sleep, the astounded soul
  Hangs for a moment bodiless and simple
  As false dawn.
5 Outside the open window
  The morning air is all awash with angels.

  Some are in bed-sheets, some are in blouses,
  Some are in smocks: but truly, there they are.
  Now they are rising together in calm swells
10 Of halcyon* feeling, filling whatever they wear
  With the deep joy of their impersonal breathing:

halcyon · peaceful and calm

491

Now they are flying in place, conveying
The terrible speed of their omnipresence, moving
And staying like white water; and now of a sudden
They swoon down into so rapt a quiet   15
That nobody seems to be there.
The soul shrinks

From all that it is about to remember,
From the punctual rape of every blessed day,
And cries,   20
"Oh, let there be nothing on earth but laundry,
Nothing but rosy hands in the rising steam
And clear dances done in the sight of heaven."

Yet, as the sun acknowledges
With a warm look the world's hunks and colors,   25
The soul descends once more in bitter love
To accept the waking body, saying now
In a changed voice as the man yawns and rises,

"Bring them down from their ruddy gallows;
Let there be clean linen for the backs of thieves: 30
Let lovers go fresh and sweet to be undone,
And the heaviest nuns walk in a pure floating
habits · the character-   Of dark habits,·
istic dress worn by nuns   keeping their difficult balance."

Denise Levertov

{ 1 9 2 3 – 1 9 9 7 }

The daughter of a Hassidic Jew who converted to Christianity, Levertov treasured the mysticism of her paternal ancestors. She was born and reared in England, and schooled informally. She began to write at an early age. Moving to New York City in the late 1940s, Levertov became an important voice among the Black Mountain Poets, whose work was open, experimental, and avant-garde. Her poems on social and political themes during the 1960s – particularly those exploring feminism and those opposing the Vietnamese War – established her as an important voice in American poetry. During her life she wrote more than twenty books of poetry and a number of volumes of prose. In 1984, Levertov declared herself a Christian, "but not a very orthodox one." In her later years the power of the Incarnation and her search for spiritual depth became a major focus of her work. Denise Levertov's poetry at every stage of her life is clear, concrete, and passionate.

ST. THOMAS DIDYMUS·

Didymus · Greek for "twin," Thomas is referred to as Didymus in John 11:16, 20:24 and 21:2

1 In the hot street at noon I saw him

                    a small man

gray but vivid, standing forth

                  beyond the crowd's buzzing

5 holding in desperate grip his shaking

                  teethgnashing son,

and thought him my brother.

I heard him cry out, weeping, and speak

                those words,

Lord ... unbelief · the prayer of a father whose son is afflicted (Mark 9:24)

10 Lord, I believe, help thou

            mine unbelief,·

and knew him

        my twin:

a man whose entire being

           had knotted itself   15
into the one tightdrawn question,

           Why,
why has this child lost his childhood in suffering,

        why is this child who will soon be a man
tormented, torn, twisted?   20

        Why is he cruelly punished
who has done nothing except be born?

The twin of my birth

        was not so close
as that man I heard   25

        say what my heart
sighed with each beat, my breath silently

           cried in and out,
in and out.

After the healing,   30

        he, with his wondering
newly peaceful boy, receded;

        no one
dwells on the gratitude, the astonished joy,

           the swift   35
acceptance and forgetting.

        I did not follow
to see their changed lives.

        What I retained
was the flash of kinship.   40

        Despite
all that I witnessed,

        his question remained
my question, throbbed like a stealthy cancer,

           known   45
only to doctor and patient. To others

        I seemed well enough.

So it was
        that after Golgotha*

50   my spirit in secret
lurched in the same convulsed writhings
                          that tore that child
before he was healed.
              And after the empty tomb

55 when they told me he lived, had spoken to Magdalen,*
                          told me
that though He had passed through the door like a ghost
                  He had breathed on them
the breath of a living man –

60   even then
when hope tried with a flutter of wings
                to lift me –
still, alone with myself,
            my heavy cry was the same: Lord,

65 *I believe,*
      help thou mine unbelief.

I needed
        blood to tell me the truth,
the touch

70   of blood. Even
my sight of the dark crust of it
              round the nailholes
didn't thrust its meaning all the way through
              to that manifold knot in me

75 that willed to possess all knowledge,
             refusing to loosen
unless that insistence won
        the battle I fought with life.

But when my hand

80   led by His hand's firm clasp
entered the unhealed wound,
          my fingers encountering
rib-bone and pulsing heat,
        what I felt was not

Golgotha · "the place of the skull" (Aramaic), site of Christ's crucifixion

Magdalen · Mary Magdalene was one of Jesus' most celebrated disciples, famous, according to Mark 16:9–10 and John 20:14–17, for being the first person to see the resurrected Christ

scalding pain, shame for my   85
                            obstinate need,
but light, light streaming
                        into me, over me, filling the room
as if I had lived till then
                        in a cold cave, and now   90
coming forth for the first time,
                            the knot that bound me unravelling,
I witnessed
                all things quicken to color, to form,
my question   95
                not answered but given
                                        its part
in a vast unfolding design lit
                        by a risen sun.

WINDOW-BLIND

MUCH HAPPENS WHEN we're not there.   1
        Many trees, not only that famous one, over and over,
fall in the forest. We don't see, but something sees,
or someone, a different kind of someone,
a different molecular model, or entities   5
not made of molecules anyway; or nothing, no one:
but something has taken place, taken space, been present, absent,
returned. Much moves in and out of open windows
when our attention is somewhere else,
just as our souls move in and out of our bodies sometimes.
Everyone used to know this,   10
but for a hundred years or more
we've been losing our memories, molting,* shedding,
like animals or plants that are not well.
Things happen anyway,
whether we are aware or whether   15
the garage door comes down by remote control over our
recognitions, shuts off, cuts off –,
We are animals and plants that are not well.
We are not well but while we look away,
on the other side of that guillotine or through   20

molting · to shed feathers, skin, or horns for replacement by new growth

21 the crack of day disdainfully left open below the blind
a very strong luminous arm reaches in,
or from an unsuspected place, in the room with us,
where it was calmly waiting, reaches outward.
25 And though it may have nothing at all to do with us,
and though we can't fathom its designs,
nevertheless our condition thereby changes:
cells shift, a rustling barely audible as of tarlatan*
flickers through closed books, one or two leaves
30 fall, and when we read them we can perceive,
if we are truthful, that we were not dreaming,
not dreaming but once more witnessing.

tarlatan · a thin, stiff, transparent cloth

Galway Kinnell

◄{ 1 9 2 7 - }►

*Kinnell, poet and novelist, was born in Providence, Rhode Island,
earned his BA at Princeton, and served in the United States Navy
1944–1946. He is noted for his experimentation with form and his interest in the spirituality of creation. Because of his subject matter (earthy,
natural elements), transcendental philosophy, and personal intensity,
Kinnell is sometimes compared to Walt Whitman. Kinnell has been
described as "a deeply serious and self-critical poet" who combines the
lyrical and the mystical. Since 1949, Kinnell has been poet-in-residence
at a variety of universities in the United States and abroad. Kinnell
received the Pulitzer Prize for poetry in 1983 and the National Book
Award for* Selected Poems *in 1984. Today, he lives in New York City.*

SAINT FRANCIS AND THE SOW

1 THE BUD
    stands for all things,
even for those things that don't flower,
for everything flowers, from within, of self-blessing;
5 though sometimes it is necessary
to reteach a thing its loveliness,
to put a hand on its brow
of the flower
and retell it in words and in touch
10 it is lovely
until it flowers again from within, of self-blessing;
as Saint Francis*
put his hand on the creased forehead
of the sow, and told her in words and in touch
15 blessings of earth on the sow, and the sow
began remembering all down her thick length,

Saint Francis · son
of a noble Italian
family, Francis of Assisi
(1181/2–1226), founder
of the Franciscan Order,
taught the "brother-
hood" and "sisterhood"
of all creatures

499

from the earthen snout all the way

slops · intestines through the fodder and slops˙ to the spiritual curl of the tail,

from the hard spininess spiked out from the spine

down through the great broken heart 20

to the sheer blue milken dreaminess spurting and shuddering

from the fourteen teats into the fourteen mouths sucking and
    blowing beneath them:

the long, perfect loveliness of sow.

WAIT

Wait, for now. 1
    Distrust everything, if you have to.
But trust the hours. Haven't they
carried you everywhere, up to now?
Personal events will become interesting again. 5
Hair will become interesting.
Pain will become interesting.
Buds that open out of season will become interesting.
Second-hand gloves will become lovely again,
their memories are what give them 10
the need for other hands. And the desolation
of lovers is the same: that enormous emptiness
carved out of such tiny beings as we are
asks to be filled; the need
for the new love *is* faithfulness to the old. 15

Wait.
Don't go too early.
You're tired. But everyone's tired.
But no one is tired enough.
Only wait a while and listen. 20
Music of hair,
Music of pain,
music of looms weaving all our loves again.
Be there to hear it, it will be the only time,
most of all to hear, 25
the flute of your whole existence,
rehearsed by the sorrows, play itself into total exhaustion.

Geoffrey Hill

⟨ 1 9 3 2 - ⟩

Hill was educated at Keble College, Oxford. He served as a professor at Leeds University, as a lecturer at Cambridge, and, most recently, as a professor at Boston University. His verse has been compared to Metaphysical poetry for its intense fusion of intellect and sensuousness, and like many of the Metaphysicals, Hill is a religious poet, a thinker concerned with questions of ultimate meaning. But he is also acquainted with doubt. In some works, in fact, he is virtually an agnostic, honestly confronting human brutality, whether its embodiment be an ancient cross or a modern concentration camp. Hill's honesty, however, will not allow him to ignore the goodness inherent in our world, particularly in the natural world with its rich bounty of blessings.

CHRISTMAS TREES

1 BONHŒFFER* IN HIS skylit cell
   bleached by the flares' candescent fall,
pacing out his own citadel,

restores the broken themes of praise,
5 encourages our borrowed days,
by logic of his sacrifice.

Against wild reasons of the state
his words are quiet but not too quiet.
We hear too late or not too late.

Bonhœffer · Dietrich Bonhœffer (1906–1945), German theologian and martyr. See Bonhœffer's poem "Who Am I?" on pages 455–456

Wendell Berry

‹ 1 9 3 4 - ›

Except for brief study at Stanford University, a year on a Guggenheim fellowship in Europe, and a few years teaching in Europe, Berry has remained close to the place of his origin. Born in Kentucky, he served as a professor at his alma mater, *the State University, until his early forties, and he has continued to live and farm the region inhabited for almost two centuries by his ancestors. Not surprisingly, his poems tend to arise from the land and those who care for it, as do a number of his novels, such as* Nathan Coulter *(1960) and* A Place on Earth *(1967). While his writing tends to be pastoral, Berry also shows social and environmental concerns. In his non-fiction work* The Hidden Wound *(1970), for example, Berry recollects his childhood and the effect of racism upon him. In* The Unsettling of America: Culture and Agriculture *(1977), the problem of responsible land use is addressed. As one biographer has noted, Berry is "a preserver of nature and people," and his writings "attest to his concern for our vanishing world."*

THE SLIP

1 THE RIVER TAKES the land, and leaves nothing.
    Where the great slip* gave way in the bank
    and an acre disappeared, all human plans
    dissolve. An aweful clarification occurs
5 where a place was. Its memory breaks
    from what is known now, and begins to drift.
    Where cattle grazed and trees stood, emptiness
    widens the air for birdflight, wind, and rain.
    As before the beginning, nothing is there.
10 Human wrong is in the cause, human
    ruin in the effect – but no matter;

slip · when water undercuts the land's surface, a massive collapse can occur, resulting in a kind of sinkhole

all will be lost, no matter the reason.
Nothing, having arrived, will stay.
The earth, even, is like a flower, so soon
passeth it away. And yet this nothing   15
is the seed of all – heaven's clear
eye, where all the worlds appear.
Where the imperfect has departed, the perfect
begins its struggle to return. The good gift
begins again its descent. The maker moves   20
in the unmade, stirring the water until
it clouds, dark beneath the surface,
stirring and darkening the soul until pain
perceives new possibility.* There is nothing
to do but learn and wait, return to work   25
on what remains. Seed will sprout in the scar.
Though death is in the healing, it will heal.

stirring the water …
possibility · an allusion
to the pool of Bethesda,
where people could
receive healing when
the Spirit troubled the
waters. See John 5:2–4

Walter McDonald

<{ 1 9 3 4 - }>

Two main territories of McDonald's poetry are west Texas and war-torn Vietnam. Both are unlikely settings for poetry, the one haunted by drought and its own vastness, the other by memories of suffering and disaster. Yet he has drawn sixteen books and over 2,000 poems mostly from these two places. McDonald grew up in West Texas, flew jets in the Vietnam War, and later taught at the Air Force Academy. He earned his doctorate in creative writing at the University of Iowa and then for many years served as Paul Whitfield Horn Professor of English and Poet in Residence at Texas Tech. In 2001 he served as Poet Laureate of Texas. During McDonald's career, he has been honored with many awards, including six awards from the Texas Institute of Letters, one of which was the Lon Tinkle Memorial Award for Excellence Sustained Throughout a Career. McDonald's books include Climbing the Divide *(2003),* Great Lonely Places of the Texas Plains *(2003),* All Occasions *(2000), and* Blessings the Body Gave *(1998).*

FAITH IS A RADICAL MASTER

1 GOD BATS ON THE SIDE of the scrubs.*
     With a clean-up hitter like that, who needs
to worry about stealing home, a double squeeze,
cleat-pounding triples? If nothing else works,

5 take a walk, lean into the wicked pitch
careening inside at ninety miles an hour.
At bat, just get on base and pray the next nerd
doesn't pop up. When someone's already on, the coach

never calls me *Mr. October,** seldom signals *Hit away.*
10 If Johnson with the wicked curve owns the strike zone

scrubs · second-string players

Mr. October · nickname of renowned hitter and Hall-of-Fame player Reggie Jackson (1946–)

505

or the ump, I'll bunt. No crack of the bat, 11
no wildly cheered Bambino* everyone loves.

Bambino · nickname
of George Herman
"Babe" Ruth (1895–1948),
one of baseball's most
famous hitters

Lay it down the line like the weakest kid in school,
disciple of the sacrifice. Some hour my time will come,
late in the game, and I'm on third, wheezing from the run 15
from first after a wild pitch, and Crazy Elmore

waving like a windmill by the third-base line.
Hands on my knees, I'll watch the pitcher
lick two fingers, wipe them on his fancy pin stripes
and try to stare me dead. I'll be almost dead, 20

gasping, wondering how I'll wobble home if someone bunts
or dribbles a slow roller and the coach yells
Go! But there, there in the box is God,
who doesn't pound home plate like an earthquake

points … center
field · Ruth sometimes
pointed to the part of the
field where he intended
to hit a home run

but slowly points the bat like the Babe toward center field,* 25
and all my family in the clouds go wild, all friends
I've loved and lost, even the four-eyed scrubs
in the dugout slugging each other and laughing,

tossing their gloves like wild hosannas, and why not –
it's bottom of the ninth, two outs, a run behind 30
and a hall-of-fame fast baller on the mound,
but I'm on third and leaning home, and look who's up.

THE WALTZ WE WERE BORN FOR

W IND CHIMES PING and tangle on the patio. 1
In gusty winds this wild, sparrow hawks* hover
and bob, always the crash of indigo

sparrow hawks · a
small bird of prey

hosannas dangling on strings. My wife ties copper
to turquoise from deserts, and bits of steel 5
from engines I tear down. She strings them all
like laces of babies' shoes when the squeal
of their play made joyful noise in the hall.

Her voice is more modest than moonlight,
10 like pearl drops she wears in her lobes.
My hands find the face of my bride.
I stretch her skin smooth and see bone.
Our children bring children to bless her, her face
more weathered than mine. What matters
15 is timeless, dazzling devotion – not rain,
not Eden gardenias, but cactus in drought,
not just moons of deep sleep, not sunlight or stars,
not the blue, but the darkness beyond.

THE DARK, HOLLOW HALO OF SPACE

1 ROCK OF ALL, my marble, stone
of my tomb and my stairs. More firm
than granite in mountains, you are older
than immortal diamond and gold.

5 My body is putty, a tiny blue planet
in the dark, hollow halo of space.
Billions of bonfires are specks
in your eye, maker of fabulous galaxies

far from earth, and all burning. My heart
10 burns slowly, unnoticed, as gold burns,
even novas I've never seen.
I'm numbed by the buckshot of stars,

trillions of tons in each one. When the air
I'm made from is ash, only dust I'll become.
15 And go when You call, where You are,
stone of my tomb and my stairs.

Mary Oliver

⟨1935-⟩

Born and raised in Ohio, Mary Oliver has lived most of her adult live in Provincetown, Massachusetts. During a stay at the home of Edna St. Vincent Millay as a teenager, she discovered poetry. One of the best selling contemporary poets, Oliver has also won many awards, including the Pulitzer Prize for American Primitive *(1983), the National Book Award for her* New and Selected Poems *(1992). She has been dubbed a modern-day mystic and has spent her life wandering the woods and marshes by her home. Spiritual and contemplative, she pulls readers into her poems, often addressing them directly as "you" and challenging them, ever so gently with a single line of beauty or a penetrating question, to reconsider their lives of material consumption and alienation from the natural world. Her later work, such as* Thirst *(2006) and* Red Bird *(2008), demonstrates a turn toward Christian faith, something she says happened when she sought out a church for comfort after the death of her partner. This turn does not reflect a rejection of transcendental influences, but rather an embrace of the world's beauty, which she recognizes more overtly as being God-breathed. For her poetry becomes prayer: "Oh Lord of melons, of mercy, though I am / not ready, nor worthy, I am climbing toward you."*

MORNING POEM

1 Every morning
the world
is created.
Under the orange

5 sticks of the sun
the heaped

ashes of the night
turn into leaves again

and fasten themselves to the high branches –
and the ponds appear
like black cloth   10
on which are painted islands

of summer lilies.
If it is your nature
to be happy
you will swim away along the soft trails   15

for hours, your imagination
alighting everywhere.
And if your spirit
carries within it

the thorn   20
that is heavier than lead –
if it's all you can do
to keep on trudging –

there is still
somewhere deep within you   25
a beast shouting that the earth
is exactly what it wanted –

each pond with its blazing lilies
is a prayer heard and answered
lavishly,   30
every morning,

whether or not
you have ever dared to be happy,
whether or not
you have ever dared to pray.   35

Nancy Willard

<(1 9 3 6 -)>

Nancy Willard's poetry looks at the world with the kind of wonder that makes grass and trees and water seem fresh and redemptive. Paging through her nine volumes of poetry, a reader will find a poem about a bride who takes time on her wedding day to feed her pet tortoise, a poem about buying a night light for a child, and a poem about her own bare feet. While Willard has been widely recognized for her poetry, her children's books, essays, and fiction also present common happenings with uncommon grace. Among her many awards is a Newberry Medal for her children's book A Visit to William Blake's Inn *(1982). Nancy Willard was raised in Michigan and educated at The University of Michigan and Stanford University. A Professor at Vassar College, she lives in Poughkeepsie, New York.*

A PSALM FOR RUNNING WATER

1 RUNNING WATER, YOU are remembered and called.
    Physician of clover and souls; hock, glove
and slipper* of stones.

Stitch thyme and buttercup to my boots.
5 Make me tread the psalm and sign of water
falling, when I am going the other way,
climbing the mountain for a clear view of home.

After winter's weeding and the fire's gap in the woods,
first ferns, trillium, watercress,*
10 this vivid text, Water, shows your hand.

The trees stand so spare a child may write them.
You, Water, sing them like an old score,

hock … slipper · hock (hollyhock), glove (foxglove), and slipper* are all types of flowers, as are clover, thyme, and buttercup

ferns, trillium, watercress · these plants are among the first to appear after the spring thaw

511

settled, pitched soft and fresh,
and wash our wounds when we fall.

A hundred Baptists, hand in hand,   15
rise and fall in your body and rise again,
praising the Lord, whose hand, I think, wears you.

For all this and more, my grandmother
thumped out of bed on Easter and tramped
gorse ... thistle · over gorse and thorn and wild thistle*   20
all plants that feature
sharp thorns or spines to the water smiling through her husband's field.

cruet · a small bottle She capped some in a cruet;*
the wink of God,
the quick motion of ourselves in time,
flashing! flashing!   25

ANGELS IN WINTER

MERCY IS WHITER than laundry,   1
great baskets of it, piled like snowmen.
In the cellar I fold and sort and watch
through a squint in the dirty window
the plain bright snow.   5

Unlike the earth, snow is neuter.
Unlike the moon, it stays.
It falls, not from grace, but a silence
which nourishes crystals.
My son catches them on his tongue.   10

Whatever I try to hold perishes.
My son and I lie down in white pastures
of snow and flap like the last survivors
of a species that couldn't adapt to the air.
Jumping free, we look back at   15

ladder of angels · angels, blurred fossils of majesty and justice
see Genesis 28:12 from the time when a ladder of angels*

joined the house of the snow
to the houses of those whom it covered
20   with a dangerous blanket or a healing sleep.

As I lift my body from the angel's,
I remember the mad preacher* of Indiana
who chose for the site of his kingdom
the footprint of an angel and named the place
25   New Harmony.* Nothing of it survives.

The angels do not look back
to see how their passing changes the earth,
the way I do, watching the snow,
and the waffles our boots print on its unleavened face,
30   and the nervous alphabet of the pheasant's feet,

and the five-petaled footprint of the cat,
and the shape of snowshoes, white and expensive as tennis,
and the deep ribbons tied and untied by sleds,
I remember the millions who left the earth;
35   it holds no trace of them,

as it holds of us, tracking through snow,
so tame and defenseless
even the air could kill us.

mad preacher · George Rapp (1757–1847), German American pietist preacher who advocated celibacy and attempted to form a religious utopia in southern Indiana

New Harmony · founded as an idealized community in 1814/15 by Rappists, the various utopian schemes failed and it was sold. The town is now a National Historic Landmark

Jeanne Murray Walker

{ 1 9 4 4 - }

Born in Parkers Prairie, Minnesota, Jeanne Murray Walker grew up in the Midwest before moving to the East Coast. As a college student, she won the Atlantic Monthly Fellowship for both fiction and poetry. After completing her doctorate at the University of Pennsylvania, she began seriously writing poetry—first lyric, then narrative. Walker has also published essays and written scripts, which have been produced in theaters across the United States and abroad. Her work probes issues of time and identity, posing questions about the incongruous self, eternity, and the intersections between generations. She examines the wonder of birth, the struggle between parents and children, the omnipresence of both death and grace. Walker has been honored with numerous prizes and awards, including a National Endowment for the Arts Fellowship, many new play prizes, and the Pew Fellowship in the Arts. Her poetry is collected in six volumes, including Fugitive Angels *(1985),* Coming Into History *(1990),* Gaining Time *(1997),* A Deed To the Light *(2004), and* New Tracks, Night Falling *(2009).*

LITTLE BLESSING FOR MY FLOATER

*After George Herbert**

1   THIS TINY RUIN in my eye, small
      flaw in the fabric, little speck
    of blood in the egg, deep chip
    in the windshield, north star,
5   pole star, floater that doesn't
    float, spot where my hand is not,
    even when I'm looking at my hand,
    little piton* that nails every rock
    I see, no matter if the picture

George Herbert · English poet (1593–1633) best known for his religious lyrics. See Herbert's poems on pages 431–434

piton · a spike or wedge that can be driven into rocks as a support for mountain climbing

515

turns to sand, or sand to sea,   10
I embrace you, piece of absence
that reminds me what I will be,
all dark some day unless God
rescues me, oh speck
that might yet teach me how to see.   15

STAYING POWER

*In appreciation of Maxim Gorky at the International
convention of Atheists, 1929*

Like Gorky, I sometimes follow my doubts   1
outside and question the metal sky,
longing to have the fight settled, thinking
I can't go on like this, and finally I say

all right, it *is* improbable, all right, there   5
is no God. And then as if I'm focusing
a magnifying glass on dry leaves, *God* blazes up.
It's the attention, maybe, to what isn't

there that makes the notion flare like
a forest fire until I have to spend the afternoon   10
spraying it with the hose to put it out. Even
on an ordinary day when a friend calls,

tells me they've found melanoma,
complains that the hospital is cold, I whisper, *God.*
God, I say as my heart turns inside out.   15
Pick up any language by the scruff of its neck,

wipe its face, set it down on the lawn,
and I bet it will toddle right into the godfire
again, which – though they say it doesn't
exist – can send you straight to the burn unit.   20

Oh, we have only so many words to think with.

Say God's not fire, say anything, say God's
a phone, maybe. You know you didn't order a phone,
but there it is. It rings. You don't know who it could be.

25   You don't want to talk, so you pull out
the plug. It rings. You smash it with a hammer
till it bleeds springs and coils and clobbered up
metal bits. It rings again. You pick it up

and a voice you love whispers hello.

Jeanine Hathaway

⋪{ 1 9 4 5 - }⋫

Jeanine Hathaway, English Professor Emerita from Wichita State University, teaches on the poetry faculty of Seattle Pacific University's low-residency MFA Program. Her books include the autobiographical novel Motherhouse *and a collection of poems,* The Self as Constellation, *which won the 2001 Vassar Miller Prize for Poetry. A monthly columnist for* The Wichita Times *for twelve years, Hathaway has led creative writing workshops (in poetry, fiction and creative nonfiction) off-campus, locally, and at the Fall Writing Festival at Ghost Ranch in Abiquiu, New Mexico. She wrote the libretto for an opera based on Gary D. Wilson's novel,* Sing, Ronnie Blue. *Her poetry chapbook,* The Ex-Nun Poems, *was published in 2011.*

"WHY OBEDIENCE IS THE ONLY VOW"

1   At the flea market, the ex-nun ignores
     a taxidermist's shadow box: one stuffed

finch grips the broken spine of a field
guide. Dynamics of flight insist

5   Upon resistance; a perch too flexible
Won't let a bird take off.

"FELIX CULPA"

1   The snake's vertebra's finely worked as porcelain,
     hummingbird shaped – its long beak lifts,
brief wings less bone than whir.

Between beak and rudder, wing and wing,
it's hollow where the spinal cord threads   5
down the ex-nun's turning back.

She's had her day in the sun. She no longer
hoods nor coils. Neither does she retract.

She hums. Her own vertebrae stack up, give her
the backbone she needs to shiver and heat the air   10
she perches on, sucking sweetness from an offer
to be like God. She'd do it again. Who could
refuse? In the deep curve of the ruby hibiscus,
who in the world would ask to let this cup pass?

Marilyn Nelson

◄(1946-)►

Born in Cleveland, Ohio, Marilyn Nelson grew up with a father who was a member of the "Tuskegee Airmen" and who wrote plays and a mother who composed music. Nelson began writing poetry as a child, influenced by Dunbar, James Weldon Johnson, and Gwendolyn Brooks. She finished a PhD at The University of Minnesota. Her books include The Fields of Praise: New and Selected Poems (1997); Magnificat (1994); The Homeplace (1990) Mama's Promises (1985); and For the Body (1978); all published by Louisiana State University Press. Nelson is an astute formalist who argues that poetic forms allow writers to make discoveries as they work. More recently she has been writing formal poems that tell stories of African American characters from history. They have been published as children's books, including: Carver: A Life in Poems; Fortune's Bones; A Wreath for Emmitt Till; Miss Crandall's School For Young Ladies and Little Misses of Color; and The Freedom Business. Nelson has been given many honors, including two Pushcart Prizes, two creative writing fellowships from the National Endowment for the Arts, a Fulbright Teaching Fellowship, and the 1990 Connecticut Arts Award. She served as Poet Laureate of Connecticut and taught for years at The University of Connecticut.

HOW I DISCOVERED POETRY

1 It was like soul-kissing, the way the words
   filled my mouth as Mrs. Purdy read from her desk.
   All the other kids zoned an hour ahead to 3:15,
   but Mrs. Purdy and I wandered lonely as clouds borne
5 by a breeze off Mount Parnassus. She must have seen
   the darkest eyes in the room brim: The next day

she gave me a poem she'd chosen especially for me
to read to the all except for me white class.
She smiled when she told me to read it, smiled harder,
said oh yes I could. She smiled harder and harder   10
until I stood and opened my mouth to banjo playing
darkies, pickaninnies, disses and dats. When I finished
my classmates stared at the floor. We walked silent
to the buses, awed by the power of words.

Dana Gioia

<{1950-}>

A native Californian of Mexican and Italian descent, Dana Gioia is a widely known for his championing the arts in many forms – including through poetry, Shakespearean drama, and jazz. Retiring early from a career as an executive at General Foods, he became a poet, lecturer, opera librettist, critic, translator, and arts administrator in the federal government. From 2003 to 2009 he served as chair of the National Endowment for the Arts, where he became known for his passionate advocacy of reading programs among youth and the general public. Through his lectures, essays, and such books as Can Poetry Matter? Essays on Poetry and American Culture *(1992), Gioia continually advocates for art that transcends the classroom and insular literary circles. Drawing inspiration from his parents, who were "salt of the earth" types, he encourages returning poetry to the cultural mainstream, to the lives of ordinary people. Gioia's faith is evident in his works. "The Catholic, literally from birth . . .," he observes, "is raised in a culture that understands symbols and signs. . . . And it also trains you in understanding the relationship between the visible and the invisible." Through poetry he seeks to employ words "that awaken something genuine in the reader's soul."*

"UNSAID"

1 So much of what we live goes on inside –
 The diaries of grief, the tongue-tied aches
Of unacknowledged love are no less real
For having passed unsaid. What we conceal
5 Is always more than what we dare confide.
Think of the letters that we write our dead.

"SUMMER STORM"

We stood on the rented patio   1
    While the party went on inside.
You knew the groom from college.
I was a friend of the bride.
We hugged the brownstone wall behind us   5
To keep our dress clothes dry
And watched the sudden summer storm
Floodlit against the sky.
The rain was like a waterfall
Of brilliant beaded light,   10
Cool and silent as the stars
The storm hid from the night.
To my surprise, you took my arm—
A gesture you didn't explain—
And we spoke in whispers, as if we two   15
Might imitate the rain.
Then suddenly the storm receded
As swiftly as it came.
The doors behind us opened up.
The hostess called your name.   20
I watched you merge into the group,
Aloof and yet polite.
We didn't speak another word
Except to say goodnight.
Why does that evening's memory   25
Return with this night's storm—
A party twenty years ago,
Its disappointments warm?
There are so many *might have beens*,
What ifs that won't stay buried,   30
Other cities, other jobs,
Strangers we might have married.
And memory insists on pining
For places it never went,
As if life would be happier   35
Just by being different.

Joy Harjo

{1951-}

Born in Tulsa, Oklahoma, Harjo is a member of the Myskoke (Creek) Nation and a musician, feminist, and activist. Educated at the Iowa Writers' Workshop, she experiments with form as she explores both the modern world's ubiquitous fragmentation and the inherent oneness she believes unites people, places, and time. Infused with her lyrical, myth-making heritage, her poetry is likewise political, lamenting war, giving voice to the oppression and spiritual awakenings of women, and juxtaposing her rich Native American culture with the bleakness of reservation existence. Harjo declares her role is to make meaning, even out of meaninglessness, through poetry's "distilled language," insisting upon the spiritual nature of things amid a human-centric, consumption-obsessed society that ignores it. Evocative and wed to paradox, her images originate as much in the undercurrents of the subconscious as much as in the Southwest land she fled to as a teenager, a distinctiveness exemplified in her classic poem, "She Had Some Horses." Migrating now between New Mexico and Hawai'i, Harjo has written seven books of poetry and recorded four CDs, winning along the way the Arrell Gibson Lifetime Achievement Award, two Oklahoma Book Awards, the Western Literature Association Distinguished Achievement Award (2000), and both the William Carlos Williams Award from the Poetry Society of America and the Delmore Schwartz Memorial Award for her collection, In Mad Love and War *(1990).*

EAGLE POEM

1   To pray you open your whole self
    To sky, to earth, to sun, to moon

To one whole voice that is you.
And know there is more
That you can't see, can't hear;   5
Can't know except in moments
Steadly growing, and in languages
That aren't always sound but other
Circles of motion.
Like eagle that Sunday morning   10
Over Salt River. Circled in blue sky
In wind, swept our hearts clean
With sacred wings.
We see you, see ourselves and know
That we must take the utmost care   15
And kindness in all things.
Breathe in, knowing we are made of
All this, and breathe, knowing
We are truly blessed because we
Were born, and die soon within a   20
True circle of motion,
Like eagle rounding out the morning
Inside us.
We pray that it will be done
In beauty.   25
In beauty.

Mark Jarman

◄(1 9 5 2 -)►

Born in Kentucky, Mark Jarman spent part of his childhood in Scotland, where his father served as minister to a Church of Christ congregation, and later he spent some years in California. Out of his experience as the son of a minister and the grandson of an evangelist was born his struggle with religious faith. Using his own adolescence as a laboratory, Jarman has written narrative poems that document that struggle. His more recent poems record the intense and immediate questions of a believer. Though Jarman is one of the founders of the New Narrative movement in contemporary poetry, his work is not strictly narrative but combines narrative with lyric, meditative, and dramatic elements. A graduate of the Iowa Writers' Workshop, Jarman taught at Indiana State University, Evansville, the University of California, Irvine, and Murray State University before settling at Vanderbilt University. He has received three National Endowment for the Arts grants in poetry, a Guggenheim Fellowship, and the Lenore Marshall Poetry Prize. His books include Unholy Sonnets (2000), Questions for Ecclesiastes (1997), *and* Body and Soul: Essays on Poetry (2002).

STARS

1 I SIGNED UP FOR astronomy in college
  Just to be close to a girl
I lost before the course was over. She'd seen me
Walking below some cherry trees on campus.
5 "The world was blooming," she wrote.
"And you trudged through, looking at the ground."

The outrage this inspired in me was like
The solar wind* I imagined –

solar wind · a flow of particles released by the sun's corona that regularly strikes the earth

Not the airy plasma of deep space,
But a righteous blast of heat. I telephoned   10
And roared it in her ear.
She answered, "You're not really mad at me."

To this day I get taken by surprise.
I look up and the world
Is clotted with snow or flowers, stars have pricked   15
The breathless, late, blue evening sky, my children
Have tiptoed beside me.
And my response is "Please! Leave me alone!"

Then I have to say, "Don't listen to me."
I repeat it to myself,   20
"Don't listen." And I still confuse the rain,
Seething across a parking lot at dusk,
And the other inner downpour
That I shake off with a curse and an excuse.

I want to be like you, poised, placid stars,   25
Too far away to threaten
With your own throbbing storms and fields of force,
Like you, like lights pinned to a sphere of glass
Turned by love itself –
To give up to your peace, turned by love.   30

UNHOLY SONNET 14

AFTER THE PRAYING, after the hymn-singing,   1
After the sermon's trenchant* commentary
On the world's ills, which make ours secondary,
After communion, after the hand-wringing,
And after peace descends upon us, bringing   5
Our eyes up to regard the sanctuary
And how the light swords through it, and how, scary
In their sheer numbers, motes of dust ride, clinging –
There is, as doctors say about some pain,
Discomfort knowing that despite your prayers,   10

trenchant · sharp,
penetrating

Your listening and rejoicing, your small part
In this communal stab at coming clean,
There is one stubborn remnant of your cares
Intact. There is still murder in your heart.

Scott Cairns

{ 1 9 5 4 - }

Scott Cairns was born in Tacoma, Washington, and educated at Western Washington University, Hollins College, Bowling Green University, and the University of Utah. He has taught American literature, poetry writing, and poetics courses at Westminster College, the University of North Texas, Old Dominion University, and at the University of Missouri. Cairns' imagination has been deeply influenced by the Greek Orthodox faith he practices, and his poems are replete with images drawn from Greek Orthodox iconography. His early poems, often set in the everyday world, examine questions of faith and practice. Characterized by quick turns of thought, his work has become increasingly centered on Biblical and iconographic subjects. He is interested in the mystical theology of Eastern Christianity and writes about sacramental poetics. Among Cairns' books are The Theology of Doubt (1985), The Translation of Babel (1990), Figures for the Ghost (1994), Recovered Body (1998), *and* Philokalia: New & Selected Poems (2002).

THE THEOLOGY OF DELIGHT

1 IMAGINE A WORLD, this ridiculous,
tentative bud blooming
in your hand. There in your hand, a world
opening up, stretching, after the image
5 of your hand. Imagine
a field of sheep grazing, or a single sheep
grazing and wandering in the delight
of grass, of wildflowers
lifting themselves, after their fashion,
10 to be flowers. Or a woman, lifting her hand
to touch her brow, and the intricacy
of the motion that frees her

531

to set the flat part of her hand carelessly
to her brow. Once, while walking, I happened
across a woman whose walking had brought her   15
to a shaded spot near a field. Enjoying
that cool place together, we sat watching sheep
and the wind moving the wildflowers in the field.
As we rose to set out again, our movement
startled the flock into running; they ran   20
only a little way before settling again
to their blank consideration of the grass.
But one of them continued, its prancing
taking it far into the field where,
free of the others, it leapt for no clear reason,   25
and set out walking through a gathering
of flowers, parting that grip of flowers with its face.

THE THEOLOGY OF DOUBT

I HAVE COME TO BELIEVE this fickleness   1
of belief is unavoidable. As, for these
backlot trees, the annual loss
of leaves and fruit is unavoidable.
I remember hearing that soft-soap   5
about faith being given
only to the faithful – mean trick,
if you believe it. This afternoon,
during my walk, which
I have come to believe is good   10
for me, I noticed one of those
ridiculous leaves hanging
midway up an otherwise naked oak.
The wind did what it could
to bring it down, but the slow   15
learner continued dancing. Then again,
once, hoping for the last good apple,
I reached among bare branches,
pulling into my hand
an apple too soft for anything   20
and warm to the touch, fly-blown.

THE SPITEFUL JESUS

1 NOT THE ONE whose courtesy
   and kiss unsought are nonetheless
bestowed. Instead, the largely
more familiar blasphemy
5 borne to us in the little boat
that first cracked rock at Plymouth
– petty, plainly man-inflected
demi-god established as a club
with which our paling*
10 generations might be beaten
to a bland consistency.

He is angry. He is just. And while
he may have died for us,
it was not gladly. The way
15 *his* prophets talk, you'd think
the whole affair had left him
queerly out of sorts, unspeakably
indignant, more than a little
needy, and quick to dish out
20 just desserts. I saw him when,
a boy in church, I first
met souls in hell. I made him*
for a corrupt, corrupting fiction when
my own father (mortal that he was)
25 forgave me everything, unasked.

paling · regularly spaced or dense, like pickets in a fence

made him · took him for, understood him to be

THE MORE EARNEST PRAYER OF CHRIST

"And being in an agony he prayed more earnestly..." Luke 22:44

1 HIS LAST PRAYER IN the garden began, as most
   of his prayers began – *in earnest*, certainly,
but not without distraction, and habitual ... what?

Distance? Well, yes, a sort of distance, or a mute
5 remove from the genuine distress he witnessed
in the endlessly grasping hands of multitudes

and, often enough, in his own embarrassing
circle of intimates. Even now, he could see
these where they slept, sprawled upon their robes or wrapped

among the arching olive trees. Still, something new,   10
unlikely, uncanny was commencing as he spoke.
As the divine in him contracted to an ache,

a throbbing in the throat, his vision blurred, his voice
grew thick and unfamiliar; his prayer – just before
it fell to silence – became uniquely earnest.   15

And in that moment – perhaps because it was so
new – he *saw* something, had his first taste of what
he would become, first pure taste of the body, and the blood.

Naomi Shihab Nye

‹(1954-)›

In her poetry Nye voices a longing for peace and celebrates the miracle of the ordinary. An Arab-American poet who has lived in the Middle East and the U.S., primarily Texas, Nye has written often of her heritage. While she grieves over the violence of recent decades, she mainly explores a shared humanity that transcends political and ideological division and might yet provide healing and a path to peace. As she writes in the introduction to one of her volumes, believing that "human beings everywhere hunger for deeper-than-headline-news about one another," Nye sees poetry as a means to feeding that hunger. To that end, she has edited collections of poems from Texas, the Middle East, and around the world. A long-time poet in the schools, Nye has also written poems and stories for children. Her poems often begin with the ordinary, but they rarely end there. They are like the man in one of her poems whose voice "started with one thing / and went to many, opening up and up / to the rim of the world."

FAMOUS

1   The river is famous to the fish.

The loud voice is famous to silence,
which knew it would inherit the earth
before anybody said so.

5   The cat sleeping on the fence is famous to the birds
watching him from the birdhouse.

The tear is famous, briefly, to the cheek.

The idea you carry close to your bosom
is famous to your bosom.

The boot is famous to the earth,   10
more famous than the dress shoe,
which is famous only to floors.

The bent photograph is famous to the one who carries it
and is not at all famous to the one who is pictured.

I want to be famous to shuffling men   15
who smile while crossing streets,
sticky children in grocery lines,
famous as the one who smiled back.

I want to be famous in the way a pulley is famous,   20
or a buttonhole, not because it did anything spectacular,
but because it never forgot what it could do.

Benjamin Alire Sáenz

{1 9 5 4 –}

Raised in a Mexican-American Catholic family, Sáenz grew up to become a priest. Eventually he left the priesthood and returned to school to study writing. A poet, novelist, and story writer (for children and adults), he teaches in the bilingual MFA program at the University of Texas at El Paso. Having lived near the border much of his life, Saenz has said, "The border is my home. The border and its people are my heart, my heart..." (Elegies in Blue). *Besides exploring political, linguistic, and personal borders, his work often searches for ways to break down borders and envisions a world without them. One such borderless place is the desert, which also figures prominently in his work. Pure, elemental, extreme, the desert produces thirst and satisfies it, provides life and threatens it. It is a place of beauty and danger, a place Saenz often links to the divine.*

TO THE DESERT

1 I came to you one rainless August night.
  You taught me how to live without the rain.
  You are thirst and thirst is all I know.
  You are sand, wind, sun, and burning sky,
5 The hottest blue. You blow a breeze and brand
  Your breath into my mouth. You reach – then *bend*
  Your force, to break, blow, burn, and make me new.
  You wrap your name tight around my ribs
  And keep me warm. I was born for you.
10 Above, below, by you, by you surrounded.
  I wake to you at dawn. Never break your
  Knot. Reach, rise, blow, *Sálvame, mi dios,*
  Trágame, mi tierra. Salva, traga, Break me,
  I am bread. I will be the water for your thirst.

Li-Young Lee

◀ 1 9 5 7 - ▶

*Though born in Jakarta, Indonesia, Lee has spent most of his life
in the United States. Lee's father fled Indonesia with his family in
1959 after suffering as a political prisoner under President Sukarno.
Traveling through Hong Kong, Macao, and Japan, the family
eventually settled in America. In 1979 Lee earned his BA from the
University of Pittsburgh. His poems often consider various forms of
love – of father, wife, and children, in particular – expressed through
original metaphors and images adapted from the Bible. Lee's father,
a professor of medicine in China who converted to Christianity while
imprisoned in Indonesia, is often a dramatic presence in the poetry.
The writer frequently expresses ambivalence towards his loving,
patient, demanding father, a man the poet both resists and reveres:
"His love for me feels like fire, / feels like doves." Lee's poems, which
have been called "testaments of memory and love," also consider the
transience and beauty of life, the necessity of cultural and personal
memory, the wonder and strangeness of America, and the relation
of sacred and earthly loves. "All writing is a form of love," Lee once
remarked. "There are just two subjects, love and death... actually,
only one, love – the poem is a record of the way we negotiate with
death." His first book,* Rose *(1986), received the Delmore Schwartz
Memorial Poetry Award, and his second volume,* The City in Which
I Love You *(1990), received the Lamont Poetry Award.*

from BLOSSOMS

1 FROM BLOSSOMS comes
    this brown paper bag of peaches
we bought from the boy
at the bend in the road where we turned toward
5 signs painted *Peaches.*

From laden boughs, from hands,   6
from sweet fellowship in the bins,
comes nectar at the roadside, succulent
peaches we devour, dusty skin and all,
comes the familiar dust of summer, dust we eat.   10

O, to take what we love inside,
to carry within us an orchard, to eat
not only the skin, but the shade,
not only the sugar, but the days, to hold
the fruit in our hands, adore it, then bite into   15
the round jubilance of peach.

There are days we live
as if death were nowhere
in the background; from joy
to joy to joy, from wing to wing,   20
from blossom to blossom to
impossible blossom, to sweet impossible blossom.

THE GIFT

To pull the metal splinter from my palm   1
my father recited a story in a low voice.
I watched his lovely face and not the blade.
Before the story ended, he'd removed
the iron sliver I thought I'd die from.   5

I can't remember the tale,
but hear his voice still, a well
of dark water, a prayer.
And I recall his hands,
two measures of tenderness   10
he laid against my face,
the flames of discipline
he raised above my head.
Had you entered that afternoon
you would have thought you saw a man   15
planting something in a boy's palm,

a silver tear, a tiny flame.
Had you followed that boy
you would have arrived here,
20 where I bend over my wife's right hand.

Look how I shave her thumbnail down
so carefully she feels no pain.
Watch as I lift the splinter out.
I was seven when my father
25 took my hand like this.

and I did not hold that shard
between my fingers and think,
Metal that will bury me,
christen it Little Assassin,
30 One Going Deep for My Heart.
And I did not lift up my wound and cry,
Death visited here!
I did what a child does
when he's given something to keep.
35 I kissed my father.

Selected Themes

OTHERNESS & ETHICS

ENVIRONMENT, NATURE, & SACRAMENTALISM

NONFICTION

FICTION

POETRY

EPIPHANY, DISCOVERY, & IDENTITY

NONFICTION

FICTION

OBEDIENCE & THE DISCIPLINED LIFE

NONFICTION

SACRIFICE, JUSTICE, & COMMUNITY

NONFICTION

THE MYSTERY OF EVIL & THE SEARCH FOR GOD

NONFICTION

FICTION

POETRY

THE MYSTERY OF GOD & WORSHIP

Permissions

DARRYL L. TIPPENS is Provost and Professor of English at Pepperdine University, where he teaches courses in medieval and early modern literature. Before coming to Pepperdine University in 2001, he taught at Abilene Christian University for many years, where he was James W. Culp Professor of English literature. Dr. Tippens earned the MA and PhD in English literature at Louisiana State University. He has published scholarly articles on Shakespeare, Milton, the Bible as literature, literary theory, and the works of Walter McDonald. He has published numerous essays on religion, spirituality, popular culture, film, and higher education.

✦ ✦ ✦

JEANNE MURRAY WALKER is Professor of English at The University of Delaware, where she teaches courses in the English Renaissance, as well as script and poetry writing. Her PhD is from The University of Pennsylvania. She travels widely to do readings and teach workshops at universities and writing conferences. For twenty years she served as Poetry Editor for *Christianity and Literature* and she currently sits on the Board of *Shenandoah*. The author of six books of poetry, including *Coming Into History, A Deed To the Light,* and *New Tracks, Night Falling,* she also writes essays and scripts for the theatre. Among honors for her work, she holds an NEA Fellowship in the Arts and a Pew Fellowship, and her poetry has appeared on busses and trains with *Poetry in Motion*.

✦ ✦ ✦

STEPHEN WEATHERS is Associate Professor of English at Abilene Christian University. Having earned the PhD at Florida State University in 1999, he teaches a broad range of courses in American, British, and World literatures. His creative writing has appeared in a number of literary journals including the *Concho River Review, Image: A Journal of the Arts & Religion,* and *American Short Fiction,* and it has garnered prizes in competition.

CPSIA information can be obtained at www.ICGtesting.com
Printed in the USA
LVOW06s0309140114

369186LV00004B/9/P